Broken Eagles

Volume 1:
**THE CONTINGENTS OF
SAXONY AND BAVARIA**

Der gesprengte Theil der Dresdner Elb-Brücke den 19. März 1813 früh gegen 9 Uhr — einige Momente nach der Explosion treu aufgenommen.

Broken Eagles

Napoleon's German Allies
and the
Campaigns of 1813

Volume 1:
**THE CONTINGENTS OF
SAXONY AND BAVARIA**

John H. Gill

Greenhill Books

Broken Eagles
First published in 2025 by
Greenhill Books,
c/o Pen & Sword Books Ltd,
George House, Unit 12 & 13,
Beevor Street, Off Pontefract Road,
Barnsley, South Yorkshire S71 1HN

www.greenhillbooks.com
contact@greenhillbooks.com

ISBN: 978–1–80500–173–7
ePub ISBN 978–1–80500–174–4
PDF ISBN 978–1–80500–175–1

All rights reserved. No part of this book may be reproduced, transmitted, downloaded, decompiled or reverse engineered in any form or by any means, electronic or mechanical including photocopying, recording or by any information storage and retrieval system, without permission from the Publisher in writing. No part of this book may be used or reproduced in any manner for the purpose of training artificial intelligence technologies or systems.

© John H. Gill, 2025

The right of John H. Gill to be identified as author of this work has been asserted in accordance with Section 77 of the Copyrights, Designs and Patents Act 1988.

CIP data records for this title are available from the British Library

The Publisher's authorised representative in the EU for product safety is Authorised Rep Compliance Ltd., Ground Floor, 71 Lower Baggot Street, Dublin D02 P593, Ireland.
www.arccompliance.com

Edited and designed by Donald Sommerville
Typeset in 11/14 pt. Arno Pro Small Text

Printed and bound in the UK by CPI Group (UK) Ltd,
Croydon, CR0 4YY

Frontispiece: This sketch, drawn shortly after the explosion, shows the damage done to the iconic stone bridge over the Elbe at Dresden on 19 March 1813.

These volumes are dedicated to
Gregory James Gill
(1956–2022)
Best of Brothers.

Contents

Lists of Maps, Charts and Schematics	ix
List of Illustrations and Credits	xiii
Authorial Conventions	xv
Ranks and Titles	xvii
Preface	xix
Acknowledgements	xxv
Prologue	3

CHAPTER 1 **A War to the Death** 26
Spring of Disappointment 26; Autumn of Blood 76;
The Battle of Nations: Leipzig, 16–19 October 1813 109

CHAPTER 2 **Saxony: The Price of Loyalty** 123
From Kurprinz to König: This Nestor of
Monarchs 124; Retreat from Russia: The Battle
of Kalisch 130; Flight to Neutrality 149;
Are You Friends or Enemies? 160; Once More
with Eagles 172; The Autumn Campaign:
From Defeat to Defection 188

CHAPTER 3 **Bavaria: The First to Fall** 255
The Monarch in Munich: I Am a Bavarian 256;
January–April: The Long Road from Russia 266;
Between Hammer and Anvil: Bavarian Politics,
March–May 292; A Thrown-Together Division:
Bavaria's Army in March and April 301;
To Bautzen and Beyond: Military Operations
in May and June 311; Armistice Anxieties 321;
Last Actions as an Ally 329; The Wine Is Poured,
It Must Be Drunk 351

	Intermission	367
	Notes	369
APPENDIX	Synoptic Tables of Battles and Sieges/Blockades	455
	Index	458
	Gazetteer	466

In the second volume of this study:

Broken Eagles
Volume 2:
WÜRTTEMBERG, BADEN, HESSE-DARMSTADT, WESTPHALIA AND THE SMALLER STATES

CHAPTER 4	Württemberg: Unconditional Obedience
CHAPTER 5	Baden and Hesse-Darmstadt: Fighting to the Last
CHAPTER 6	Westphalia: Kingdom's End
CHAPTER 7	The Miniature Monarchies: A Spectrum of Soldiers
CHAPTER 8	Fortress Warfare: The Iron Yoke of Fate

Maps, Charts and Schematics

Maps

All maps © John H. Gill 2025. All rights reserved.

1.	Western and Central Europe in January 1813	page 15
2.	The Confederation of the Rhine (Rheinbund) in January 1813	20
3.	Theatre of War Overview	29
4.	Operations: February–April 1813	37
5.	Operations: May–June 1813	53
6.	The Battle of Lützen, 2 May 1813	57
7.	The Battle of Bautzen, 20–21 May 1813	61
8.	16 August 1813: Situation at the End of the Armistice	73
9.	Major Engagements in the Autumn Phase, August–October 1813	79
10.	The Battle of Dresden, 26–27 August 1813	83
11.	Operational Area for the Großbeeren and Dennewitz Offensives	86
12.	Oudinot's Advance to Großbeeren, 19–23 August 1813	88
13.	The Battle of Großbeeren, 23 August 1813	91
14.	The Battle of Dennewitz, 6 September 1813	96
15.	Operational Area Around Leipzig, Evening, 13 October 1813	105
16.	The Battle of Leipzig, 16–19 October 1813	114–115
17.	The City of Leipzig, Assaulted on 19 October 1813	119
18.	The 7th Corps March to Kalisch: 1–12 February 1813	132
19.	Battle of Kalisch: 13 February 1813	137
20.	Combat at Lüneburg: 2 April 1813	174
21.	Pursuit after Bautzen: Saxons and 7th Corps, 22–23 May 1813	185
22.	Saxon Cavalry at Dresden, 27 August 1813	191
23.	7th Corps Deployment at Großbeeren, 23 August 1813	195
24.	The Battle of Dennewitz: Rheinbund Detail, 6 September 1813	204
25.	German Defections at Leipzig, 18 October 1813	228
26.	Bavarian and Westphalian Retreat to Danzig, 1–17 January 1813	272
27.	The Fortress of Thorn, Winter 1813	275

28. Back to Bavaria, February to June 1813 — 287
29. Raglovich's Division, April to October 1813 — 306
30. The Bavarians at Bautzen, 20–21 May 1813 — 314
31. Surprise near Baruth, Night of 16/17 August 1813 — 330
32. Engagement at Zahna, 5 September 1813 — 335

Schematic

1. Raglovich at Dennewitz — 338

Key to Map Symbols

Countries are plain text: Bavaria
Regions/provinces are italics: *Silesia*
International border: ----------
Internal border: ············
Primary road: ——————
Secondary road: ------
Forests/large gardens: [symbol]
Marsh/water meadows: [symbol]
Windmills: [symbol]

Outlines for towns/villages include gardens as well as structures as these contributed to the defensive value of the buildings.

Fortresses or forts: ★
Battles and engagements: ✸

Units types are indicated by the following symbols with nationality shown by colour: white for Allied, black for French and grey for Napoleon's Rheinbund allies.

	Allied:	French:	Rheinbund:
Cavalry units:	[white]	[black]	[grey]
Infantry and mixed units:	[white]	[black]	[grey]

Artillery (all sides): [symbol]
Cavalry outposts: [symbols]

Examples:
Bavarian 29th Division = [29]
Allied III Corps = [III]

Allied movements (advance and retreat) are shown with dashed lines, while those of the French and Rheinbund troops are solid.

Allied movement = ------▶
French/Rheinbund movement = ——▶

Date format: day/month so that 19/6 = 19 June

Maps, Charts and Schematics   xi

Charts

1.	Rheinbund States and Contingents, April 1813	page 22
2A.	French Corps and Rheinbund Elements Overview	24
2B.	Rheinbund Fortress Garrisons	25
3.	Sample Allied Raiding Detachments, March–April 1813	46
4.	French Forces at the time of Lützen, 2 May 1813	54
5.	Allied Forces at the time of Lützen, 2 May 1813	55
6A.	French Forces at Bautzen, 20–21 May 1813	62
6B.	Allied Forces at Bautzen, 20–21 May 1813	63
7.	The Reorganised Grande Armée, August 1813	75
8.	The Allied Armies, August 1813	76–7
9.	The Allied Armies at Leipzig, 16–19 October 1813	110–111
10.	The Grande Armée at Leipzig, 16–19 October 1813	112
11.	Saxon Units 1812–1813	129
12.	7th Corps at Kalisch, 13 February 1813	134–135
13.	Russian Forces at Kalisch, 13 February 1813	138–139
14.	Saxon Reserve Forces, late February 1813	149
15.	Saxon Troops at Torgau, 29 March 1813	167
16.	Forces at Lüneburg, 2 April 1813	176
17.	Saxon Field Forces, mid-May 1813	180–181
18.	Reorganised 7th Corps, 17 August 1813	188–189
19.	Saxon Troops in 7th Corps, 10 September 1813	213
20.	Saxon Troops in 7th Corps, 21 September 1813	217
21.	The Saxon Division at Leipzig, 17–18 October 1813	226–227
22.	Bavarian Units in 1813	265
23.	The Thorn Garrison, 20 January–18 April 1813	276
24.	Rechberg's Division	289
25.	Raglovich's Division	304
26.	Bavarian Reorganisations, September–October 1813	344–345

Notes on Charts

Unless otherwise specified, all strength figures are for those officers and men (combined) 'present under arms' (*présens sous les armes, rücken aus*, etc.), that is, those who were available for combat at any particular moment. These figures also include some (such as drummers) who were not always considered 'combatants'. In French and in most German strength reports, 'present under arms' was *not* the same as 'effectives'. The total of 'effectives' would usually be much larger as it included those detached, sick, prisoners of war or otherwise absent in addition to those immediately at hand. Note that the number detached could be half or more of a unit's strength, especially in the case of light cavalry, which were favoured as scouts, escorts for senior officers and staff orderlies; furthermore, all cavalry units often had large numbers of dismounted men 'detached' in depots along the line of communications awaiting fresh horses.

Where multiple battalions of a regiment are present, an entry such as 'Würzburg Regiment (II, III)' indicates that the 2nd and 3rd Battalions of the Würzburg Infantry Regiment are present. If only one battalion is present, the entry will read 'V/Würzburg' (5th Battalion of the Würzburg Infantry Regiment).

Illustrations and Credits

Frontispiece

The destroyed bridge at Dresden, 19 March 1813 (*Author*).

Plates

1. The Baden Brigade covering the crossing of the Berezina (*Wikimedia*); Christian Martens's impression of Cossacks (*LABWHStA*).
2. Saxon uniforms: a) line infantry; b) light infantry; c) Guard Grenadier; d) hussar; e) Uhlan; f) *Zastrow* Cuirassier (*all Napoleonic Uniforms, vol. III*).
3. Saxon artillery at Bautzen, 21 May (*MHM*); Bavarian uniforms: a) line infantry; b) artillery; c) chevauleger; (*all Napoleonic Uniforms, vol. III*).
4. GL Carl Christian Erdmann Edler von LeCoq (*MHM*); GL Heinrich Wilhelm von Zeschau (*MHM*); Dresden bridge, mid-March (*ASKB*).
5. Plundering Cossacks (*Leipzig, GR017146*); Dresden bridge, mid-May (*ASKB*).
6. Battle of Großbeeren, 23 August: Saxon artillery (*Bautzen*); Napoleon and Friedrich August (*Dresden, 1977/k 463*).
7. Saxon trooper's helmet (*Poser*); Napoleon and the Saxon Guard (*Leipzig, V900074*).
8. The Leipzig Roßplatz (*Leipzig, S0022270*); Battle of Hanau (*ASKB*).
9. König Friedrich August; König Max I. Joseph; 'French Troops plundering and firing a village' (*all Author*).
10. GL Johann Adolf Freiherr von Thielmann; Montgelas; Kronprinz Ludwig; GM Joseph von Rechberg; GL Clemens von Raglovich; GdK Karl Philipp Graf von Wrede (*all Author*).
11. Burning brige at Meissen; Hellwig's raid on Langensalza (*both Author*).
12. Bavarian infantry at Bautzen (*Alamy*); Colomb's raiders (*Author*).

13. Saxon heavy cavalry at Dresden (*MHM*); Saxon trooper's cuirass (*Poser*).
14. Battle of Großbeeren, Saxon infantry; Reynier; Oudinot (*all Author*).
15. Bavarian infantry on the march; Napoleon's last crossing of the Elbe (*both Author*).
16. 'Heiterer Blick' farmstead near Leipzig (*Leipzig, MU001730*); Saxon soldiers rioting in Liege (*ASKB*).

Illustration Acknowledgements and Abbreviations

ASKB = Anne S. K. Brown Collection where the former curator, Mr Peter Harrington, repeatedly earned my special appreciation for his courtesy, knowledge and helpfulness.

Bautzen = Museum Bautzen with thanks to Diplom-Museolog Hagen Schulz.

Dresden = Städtische Galerie Dresden.

LABWHStA = Landesarchiv Baden-Württemberg, Hauptstaatsarchiv, Stuttgart.

Leipzig = Stadtgeschichtliches Museum Leipzig.

MHM = Militärhistorisches Museum der Bundeswehr, Dresden.

Napoleonic Uniforms, vol. III = John R. Elting, *Napoleonic Uniforms*, vol. III, Rosemont: Emperor's Press, 2000 (with special thanks to Mr Todd Fisher).

Poser = Dr Stefan Poser, Curator of the Völkerschlachtdenkmal, Leipzig (who also supplied helpful suggestions).

The curators and staffs at the following museums and archives have all been remarkably prompt and helpful in providing images and valuable suggestions: Hessisches Staatsarchiv, Landesarchiv Baden-Württemberg Hauptstaatsarchiv, Museum Bautzen, Militärhistorisches Museum der Bundeswehr, Städtische Galerie Dresden, Stadtgeschichtliches Museum Leipzig.

Authorial Conventions

Orthography

PERSONAL NAMES. There are no simple, easy answers when it comes to presenting names and titles from a variety of languages. Except for the most prominent individuals, therefore, I have used spellings and titles from their original languages or those most often encountered in contemporary sources. I have endeavoured thereby to retain the flavour of the age and remind us of the variety of nations involved in this war, while keeping things familiar for an English-language readership. Similarly, the titles 'tsar', 'Kaiser' and 'emperor' have been employed to make it easier to distinguish among Alexander I of Russia, Franz I of Austria and Napoleon when these monarchs are not named. As for spellings of names, I have generally taken these from Würzbach for Austrians, from Prussian official histories for the Prussians, and from Six, Pigeard and Quinlin on the French side. For Russian personal names, I have used the transliterations in Alexander Mikaberidze's invaluable volume on Russian generals of the era.

GEOGRAPHICAL NAMES. I have generally retained contemporaneous German and Austrian spellings of place names for populated places and geographic features. See the Gazetteer for modern Polish and Czech names.

MAPS. I have prepared all the maps specifically for this study. Basic geographical features and troop deployments are largely derived from the maps in the Prussian and Austrian official histories (such as Friederich, Glaise von Horstenau, Hoen, etc.) as well as Aster's works, supplemented by a host of inputs from other contemporary and modern sources. As this is a book about the Rheinbund troops in 1813, the maps here are designed to highlight the battles in which Rheinbund soldiers participated and the specific roles they played in those battles.

Other Conventions

French, German and Austrian ranks and noble titles are preserved insofar as this is feasible (a table relates these to current US and British ranks and lists rank abbreviations).

'Rheinbund' refers to the Confederation of the Rhine.

'German' generally refers to the host of small states between the Rhine and the Prussian border (i.e., not to Prussia or Austria).

'Allied', 'Allies' and 'Coalition', when capitalised, refer to the members of the 'Sixth Coalition' (Russia, Prussia, Austria, Sweden, Great Britain, Spain, Portugal, Sicily and Sardinia) opposed to Napoleon and his German and Danish confederates.

'Ligne' and 'Léger' refer respectively to French line and light infantry.

Units known by the names of their *Inhaber* ('patrons' or 'proprietors') or their commanders are presented in *italics* (Saxon *Zastrow* Cuirassiers).

Battalions or squadrons of a regiment are designated by Roman numerals (II/*Rechten* indicates the 2nd Battalion of the Saxon *Rechten* Infantry Regiment).

Coalition regimental references: Austrian regiments are designated by the titles derived from their *Inhaber* in *italics* rather than their numbers (*Koburg* Infantry Regiment); Prussian regimental titles are Anglicised (1st Silesian, not 1. *schleschiches*); Russian regimental names are Anglicised according to the standards employed by Alexander Mikaberidze in his works on 1812.

Arabic numerals indicate French *corps d'armée* (Vandamme's 1st Corps) and Roman numerals are used for the Coalition (Yorck's Prussian I Corps).

Orders of battle: despite this author's personal passion for painstakingly precise orders of battle, space constraints prohibit presentation of the enormous French and Allied armies through their many transmutations over a period of ten months. I endeavour here to provide the greatest possible detail on the Rheinbund units, but refer readers to the works by Fabry, Juhel, Nafziger and the great Prussian and Austrian official histories for specifics on the Grande Armée and its Coalition adversaries (see Bibliography, in Vol. 2 of the present work).

All dates are according to the Gregorian calendar (rather than Julian).

Ranks and Titles

Comparative Military Ranks and Abbreviations

German and Austrian ranks (Abbreviation)	French ranks (Abbreviation)	Modern British or US equivalents
Feldmarschall (FM)	(no equivalent rank)	Field Marshal or General
General der Kavallerie (GdK), der Infanterie or Feldzeugmeister (FZM)	(no equivalent rank)	Lieutenant General
General-Leutnant (GL) or Feldmarschall-Leutnant (FML)	Général de Division (GD)	Major General
General-Major (GM)	Général de Brigade (GB)	Brigadier General
[staff] Oberst	Adjutant-Commandant	[staff] Colonel
Oberst	Colonel	Colonel
Oberstleutnant	Major	Lieutenant Colonel
Major	Chef de Bataillon or Chef d'Escadron	Major
Stabs-Hauptmann	Adjoint	[staff] Captain
Hauptmann, Kapitän, or Rittmeister (cavalry)	Capitaine	Captain
Oberleutnant or Premierleutnant	Lieutenant	Lieutenant, First Lieutenant
Unterleutnant/Leutnant	Sous-Lieutenant	Second Lieutenant

Notes:
1. All comparisons are approximate; protocol and functions could vary widely.
2. Contemporary German-language sources frequently use '*Lieutenant*' in place of '*Leutnant*' and '*Obrist*' was often used in place of '*Oberst*' (thus '*Obrist-Lieutenant*').
3. In the French Army, the title '*Major Général*' indicated a function rather than a rank and was unique to Marshal Alexander Berthier, Napoleon's Chief of Staff.
4. Westphalians referred to themselves by both French and German rank titles; I have used the French versions in this work.

German and Austrian Noble Titles

German	English
Erbprinz	hereditary prince
Erzherzog	archduke
Freiherr	baron
Fürst	prince
Fürstin	princess
Graf	count
Großherzog	grand duke
Großherzogin	grand duchess
Herzog	duke
Herzogin	duchess
Kaiser	emperor
Kaiserin	empress
König	king
Königin	queen
Kronprinz	crown prince
Prinz	prince
Kurfürst	prince-elector

Note:
'Kurfürst' was a title specific to the Holy Roman Empire denoting a person who was entitled to vote for the emperor, hence 'prince-elector'.

Preface

THE CONFEDERATION OF THE RHINE, or Rheinbund, provides a puzzling lacuna in the history of the Napoleonic epoch. A curious political institution, the Rheinbund was a central element in Napoleon's foreign and military policy, presented a fundamental irritant to his opponents, and arguably exercised considerable influence on Germany's future development. This significance notwithstanding, there are few works – particularly in English – investigating its creation, evolution and demise.[1]

This study is an attempt to address at least one aspect of the Rheinbund's history: the military activities of its combat forces during the campaigns of April–October 1813, the final year of its ephemeral existence and the last time its contingents would fight alongside the imperial eagles that crowned the standards of their French allies. Like its predecessor, *With Eagles to Glory: Napoleon and His German Allies in the 1809 Campaign*, this work will cover the organisations, marches, sieges and combat operations of the numerous German contingents that augmented Napoleon's Grande Armée in this crucial year. Where the former book examined the Rheinbund troops during 1809, a year of ascendancy, this pair of volumes finds the alliance on the verge of dissolution.

Indeed, the year 1813 is a particularly rich period to explore as far as the Rheinbund is concerned. In the first place, the various German armies, like the French, had to be re-created, almost entirely anew, in the wake of the calamitous Russian campaign of 1812. The effort involved, in a time of great political turmoil, was little less, on a relative scale, than the phenomenal exertions of France itself. Second, this uncertain political atmosphere, especially the evident faltering of Napoleon's star, left a deep imprint on these apprentice armies. Some deserted, others wavered, yet many fought on with grim tenacity and often with remarkable loyalty. Third, the German troops were scattered about an immense theatre of operations, often as isolated battalions or as remnants of regiments; the detail and nuance of their participation in the shifting campaigns of 1813 can thus be lost in broader narratives, especially because the French and their Coalition opponents frequently gave little attention to the actions, or even the identities, of the variegated German contingents. Finally, the valour and dedication of many contingents notwithstanding, the war would end with the dissolution of the Rheinbund so that 1813 became the break with eagles that inspired the title of this study.

It is my hope that these volumes will draw some order out of this confusion and present the reader with a comprehensive picture of each Rheinbund unit's participation, howsoever brief, across the vast canvas of combat in 1813. Note, however, that this is a military history of combat forces, not an account of the intricate diplomatic machinations as the Rheinbund monarchs and their ministers attempted to craft strategies for survival in a challenging, unpredictable environment. Nor is this an attempt to present a detailed topography of the contested terrain of German nationalism.[2] Likewise, this study does not address the debates over the nature of the war of 1813 or 1813–14 as simply a 'war of princes' to throw Napoleon across the Rhine and reaffirm absolutist monarchical power in Germany or a 'war of peoples' whose outcome would see the various German states united in some fashion under a new political dispensation characterised by constitutions and a degree of representation (at least for the bourgeoisie).[3] Political manoeuvres and 'national' sentiments of different sorts (Prusso-German, pan-German, or local) certainly informed the activities of the different armies and will be incorporated as appropriate into the analysis that follows, but the focus here is on the troops and their commanders, not on the princes and diplomats caught between Napoleon and his multitudinous foes or on the convoluted evolution of German national identity.

The historiography of German nationalism and the associated identification of France as Germany's hereditary 'archenemy' (*Erbfeind*), however, is an important consideration in examining the Rheinbund troops during 1813. This is because of challenges embedded within much of the available source material. For more than a century, indeed as late as 1945, the wars of 1813–15 were commonly portrayed as the founding period of modern Germany, the decisive step on the path to its inevitable establishment as a unified political entity under Prussian leadership.[4] Without denying the importance of this era, such an approach ignored contingency and often meant that 'German' history became a mere 'appendage' to Prussian history with little space for anything other than neglect or scorn concerning those in central and southern German lands who had allied themselves for a time with the reviled French foe.[5] Indeed, the Rheinbund was specifically condemned in many influential histories as an institution of 'miserable impotence and servitude', its member states 'Germans against Germany'.[6]

Preface xxi

Sifting through post-Napoleonic German histories can thus be particularly problematic as many are suffused with assumptions of this Prusso-German nationalist discourse, projecting later attitudes back into the past to invent or exaggerate the degree of pro-'German' and anti-French sentiment in 1813. Others might distort their depictions of events by endeavouring to demonstrate that *their* homelands were the 'first' to detach themselves from the French emperor's grasp even as they distrust and disparage Prussia. Writing in the 1850s, for instance, a Saxon historian opens one paragraph by casting doubt on the ennobled 'German cause' as a vague concept and excoriating the Prussians and Russians for greed and mendacity: 'Thus the war that one wanted to characterise as a war for the "German cause" was opened with a speculation on the expansion of Prussia at the expense of its German neighbours!' He begins the very next paragraph, by averring that *his* country's monarch proved 'his true German spirit' in that 'he, despite many factors that seemed to tie him to the French alliance, nonetheless seriously thought about and acted on separating himself from the French alliance earlier than any other middle- or south-German Rheinbund prince'.[7] In contrast, Bavarian veteran and historian Hauptmann Eduard von Völderndorff und Waradein proudly noted that *his* fatherland had defected from the Rheinbund in early October at a time when Napoleon's power was still unbroken and the Battle of Leipzig not yet fought: 'Bavaria's accession to the great Coalition would be decisive in this moment and fill the French emperor with concern for his rear and for his communications with France.'[8]

The memoir literature presents similar challenges. Combined with all the cautions routinely associated with the various types of 'ego-documents' (self-justificatory, 'remembering with advantages', embellishments, inventions, and so on), many were composed decades after 1813 or published by descendants who believed it was necessary to emphasise virulent 'hatred' of 'the French yoke' or similar sentiments.[9] Such sentiments certainly existed in 1813 and earlier, but they might receive undo accentuation or even be inserted anachronistically in some memoirs.[10]

The unpublished *Tagebuch* (diary) of a Bavarian artillery *Unterleutnant* named Ferdinand Sigmund von Praun provides a curious example. The *Tagebuch* was transcribed by one of his relatives into handwritten German in 1843 (from the original French oddly enough) and offers numerous useful insights into the experience of the war from the point of view of a very junior officer on his first campaign. In the midst of relating battles and marches, however, the text suddenly lurches sideways and launches into a spate of venom against 'Buonaparte' and all things French. It then returns to its lively but matter-of-fact narrative of Praun's wartime activities. Whether Praun himself or his scribe relative inserted this bizarre intrusion is unknown, but the voice is entirely different from the rest of the manuscript, and it clearly was not written in 1813 (in all other cases, for instance, Praun refers to the French emperor as 'Napoleon' or the 'Kaiser', not by the intentionally demeaning name 'Buonaparte').[11] Württemberg Leutnant Christian von Martens provides a different example, shifting his tone from his manuscript to his published memoirs: he mocks or disdains his Prussian adversaries at several points in his original *Tagebuch*, but these instances are omitted or diluted in the version published in 1862–3.

Given the problems associated with memoirs, I have taken a very source-critical approach, but there is no cause to doubt the general 'trajectory' of these materials.[12] They remain invaluable and, in some cases, provide the only apertures we have to view certain situations. Moreover, memoirs and similar materials offer a means to allow the Rheinbund soldiers to tell the story themselves. I endeavour to do so in the following pages but offer this caveat at the start to help explain why some pieces were included and some excluded and so the reader can determine which are the most reliable and valuable.

A note on the use of the term 'German' is perhaps in order here. While acknowledging the existence of what Dennis Showalter termed a 'developing sense of common identity' among German-speaking populations,[13] the term 'German' as used in this work generally refers to the states and armies that were outside the borders of the Prussian and Austrian monarchies. This is especially important with regard to Prussia, because the common image has long tended to privilege the Prusso-German (or Borussian) version of 'German nationalism' and the consequent version of Germany's ineluctable historical development.[14] This has been particularly the case with German military history. Fortunately, more recent scholarship has illuminated many of the previously hidden facets of the German identity question, especially respecting the states of the southwest that were such key elements of the Rheinbund. Ute Planert's contributions are especially noteworthy in this regard and Peter Wilson's comprehensive new study places developments in a broad temporal as well as geographical context.[15] I endeavour here to be as careful as possible in using the designations Prussian, Austrian and German (Bavarian, Hessian, Baden, and others), but some imprecision is unavoidable, and I ask in advance for the reader's indulgence when such cases arise.

Beyond these persistent peculiarities of terminology, these two volumes follow the same structure as *With Eagles to Glory* with a chapter devoted to each Rheinbund contingent. It is my hope that this format presents this complicated history with the greatest clarity, allowing the reader to trace the activities of each army as it recovers its shattered survivors from the Russian frontier, cobbles together a new force, and engages in the bitter battles, great and small, that splattered the map of Germany with blood during this pivotal year. Each chapter, however, is also subdivided into chronological sections that correspond with the principal phases of the war's various campaigns. The reader may thus read each chapter on its own to gain an appreciation of the role each country's force played or may proceed from phase to phase through the chapters to paint a picture of all the Rheinbund armies at any particular stage of the war. Additionally, matrices at the end of both volumes provide a synoptic overview of the operations, sieges and battle participation of each contingent. As with the earlier *Eagles*, readers may choose the study method that best meets their requirements or inclinations.

Readers will also observe that some actions or events have received what might seem at first glance disproportionate attention. Some of this meticulous focus results from the availability of source material, but in most instances, I have chosen intentionally to spend more time and words on situations that are less well known in English-language histories. The Engagement at Kalisch on 13 February, for example, was critical for the Saxon contingent and affords useful insights into the attitudes and abilities of the Saxon formations, but is seldom described in any detail in English sources. The little-known siege of Thorn, a major piece of the Bavarian involvement, is another example. I hope that exploring such incidents in greater depth will broaden knowledge of the basic military facts associated with 1813 while simultaneously enhancing understanding of German participation in the year's several campaigns.

Finally, readers should note that the Confederation in April 1813 was lacking several states that had been members at the height of its existence: Arenberg, Salm-Kyrburg, Salm-Salm, Oldenburg, Mecklenburg-Schwerin and Mecklenburg-Strelitz. Arenberg and the two Salm principalities, all three of them original members, were eradicated in 1810 when Napoleon annexed them to France along with the Hanseatic cities and the Kingdom of Holland in an effort to tighten his economic embargo of British goods (the 'Continental Blockade').[16] Oldenburg, which had only joined with great reluctance in the autumn of 1808, likewise fell victim to Napoleon's 1810 annexation policy and disappeared. The two Mecklenburg duchies, also grudging allies of France starting in 1808, used the French defeat in Russia and Prussia's subsequent defection to dissolve their ties to the Rheinbund in March 1813. As they had joined Napoleon's enemies before the initial campaigns of 1813 truly opened, their forces are not discussed in these volumes. Likewise, the Hanseatic cities and the north German coastal regions are beyond the scope of this study. Although anti-French protests occurred in these areas and volunteers were recruited to fight as part of the Coalition, they were technically departments of France in 1813 and not part of the Rheinbund.

Acknowledgements

'Those friends thou hast, and their adoption tried, grapple them to thy soul with hoops of steel.'

Hamlet, I. 3.

AS ALWAYS, THERE ARE MANY PEOPLE TO THANK for bringing a work such as this to fruition. First and foremost, as in every other project I have ever undertaken, I must express my gratitude to my family: my wife Anne L. Rieman and our sons Grant and Hunter. They have tolerated absences, underwritten expenses, and endured endless discussions of obscure details and puzzling quandaries associated with the Rheinbund and its final year. Furthermore, Anne remains a thoughtful and diligent editor whose initial readings are invaluable to me. Words fail in trying to thank them adequately, so these few sentences will have to suffice in expressing my appreciation.

Remaining within the borders of the United States for a moment, I can also thank my friends Michael V. Leggiere, Alexander Mikaberidze, Sam A. Mustafa and Frederick C. Schneid (who also scanned material in Vincennes on my behalf). Their works continue to inform and inspire me. Steve Smith was generous with research as always (especially in helping locate Reboul's invaluable work), Bob Burnham kindly supplied many useful suggestions, and I benefited (again) from Westphalian materials supplied by Michael F. Pavković many years ago. Peter Harrington, another long-time friend and former curator of the Anne S. K. Brown Collection, once more helped find illustrations – he has been a boon to the military history community for decades and we wish him joy as he embarks on a new path in life. Anna Maria Boss and her colleagues at the German Historical Institute in Washington, DC, were also very generous with their assistance. For translations from Russian, I am happy to thank Michelle Hanssen, a Georgetown graduate student studying under my friend and colleague Dr Roger Kangas.

Journeying across the Atlantic, I may start with Dr Marcin Baranowski in Poland who courteously provided materials from his research into the Battle of Kalisch and other developments in Polish lands during 1813. In *la belle France*, Pierre Juhel was another friendly source for information and advice. Dr Bruno Colson in Namur, Belgium, was likewise very generous with archival items relating to Leipzig – his book on the Battle of the Nations remains the best single-volume history of that colossal struggle and he has recently co-edited *The Cambridge History of the Napoleonic Wars* with Alex Mikaberidze . In France, Claire Khelfaoui's assistance has been invaluable as she has located reams of material from the archives in Paris and Vincennes. Christophe Pénichon has been helpful helpful with cavalry details, and Leighton S. James of Swansea University, a collegial correspondent.

Given the subject of this study, it is hardly surprising that I owe debts of gratitude to the many Germans who have been helpful over many years. The staffs of the archives in Darmstadt, Dresden, Erfurt, Karlsruhe, Munich and Stuttgart have been superb, not only during personal visits but in fulfilling requests from the other side of the great grey Atlantic by email. Dr Klaus-Dieter Rack and Nasser Amini (both in Darmstadt), Frau Kremser (Stuttgart), Franziska Schumacher (Halberstadt), Ingo Möckel (Schleiz) and Carmen Böhm (Bayerisches Armeemuseum, Ingolstadt) deserve particular mention. The long list of friendly Germans includes Dr Martin Rink (during a delightful afternoon in Berlin some years ago), Uwe Baumbach, Uwe Ehmke, Dr Martin Klöffler, Oliver Schmidt, Alfred Umhey, Markus Stein, Dr Melanie Güttler, and Markus Gärtner. In Saxony specifically, I found gracious assistance from Ingo Busse, Dr Rudolf Jenak, Dr Judith Matzke, Dr Frank Metasch, Martin Munke, Dr Steffen Poser, Dr Ira Spieker and Jörg Titze (whose publications from the Saxon Archives have been singularly helpful). Above all, however, my thanks go to my friend, Dr Thomas Hemmann, who consistently went 'above and beyond the call of duty' in answering questions and locating recondite sources. *Vielen Dank!*

My gratitude to Greenhill goes back many years: to Lionel Leventhal as the first to guide me on this path and to Michael who is helping me continue the journey. I also wish to thank Donald Sommerville, who improved my book on Znaim and has again offered his superb editorial skills to these volumes.

All errors of interpretation or translation, of course, are my own, but all these kind people have been enormously helpful. So, my thanks to all, may Shakespeare's words in my epigraph here be companions to you as they have ever been to me.

It is my hope that this work will spark other research into various facets of the Confederation of the Rhine and, as always, I hope that you, the reader, will derive as much enjoyment in reading it as I have had in writing it.

Broken Eagles

Volume 1:
**THE CONTINGENTS OF
SAXONY AND BAVARIA**

Prologue

'But, when I do everything for the confederate sovereigns, I must hope that they will not abandon themselves and will not betray their own cause. They would betray it, if they do not cooperate with me with all their means.'

Napoleon to Rheinbund monarchs, 18 January 1813[1]

IN THE RAW, CHILL DAYS of November 1813, the Emperor Napoleon crossed the Rhine for the last time. He left behind, on the eastern side of the great river, the ruins of two enormous armies. One, vast and magnificent, had crossed the Niemen River into Russia in June 1812 only to dissolve in a scorching summer and pitiless winter on the endless expanses of the tsar's domains. The other, also massive but hastily assembled and therefore fragile, had crumbled away under the pressures of combat and privation in the gruelling campaigns that swept across Prussia and Saxony during 1813 in the War of the Sixth Coalition.[2] Amongst the wreckage of these two grand armies were thousands upon thousands of German soldiers, Napoleon's allies of the Confederation of the Rhine who had marched, fought, suffered and died alongside their French comrades in arms from the Vistula to the Rhine in what became Napoleon's last campaigns in Germany. Representing twenty-six monarchies[3] and numbering more than 70,000 present under arms at their height, these German troops were found in every corner of the theatre of war and played significant, often central, roles in the outcomes of the grand battles and grinding sieges that ended in the French emperor's retreat across the Rhine.[4] As important as they sometimes were, their involvement is often overlooked, simplified or subsumed into the larger narrative of this gargantuan struggle. This work is an effort to shed some comprehensive light on this obscure dimension of the Napoleonic epoch, hoping thereby to provide a deeper understanding of the sprawling canvas of conflict in 1813.

The Confederation of the Rhine, 1806–1812

The Confederation of the Rhine, or Rheinbund, was a mechanism for exerting French influence in the lands roughly between the Rhine and Elbe Rivers, a region often called the 'Third Germany' as it was neither Prussian nor Austrian. When Napoleon came to power in 1800, this 'Third Germany' consisted of a congeries of more than 300 secular and ecclesiastical territories ranging in extent from moderately sized duchies and electorates to microstates and individual abbeys within the broad embrace of the Holy Roman Empire ('*das heilige römische Reich deutscher Nationen*' or simply the '*Reich*'). Racked by the social and political upheavals of the era, however, the *Reich* was already showing signs of its imminent disintegration, especially after its Diet adopted the 'Report of the Imperial Delegation' or 'Imperial Recess' in March 1803. This act drastically reordered much of the old empire, eliminating dozens of previously separate political entities, enlarging others, curtailing Austrian influence and opening the way for a greater French role across the Rhine.[5] Emblematic of its coming demise was the fact that three of its member states – Bavaria, Baden and Württemberg – allied themselves with France against Austria in the autumn of 1805 even though the *Reich* was still in existence and the Habsburg Kaiser Franz II was still its titular emperor. These three monarchies thereby became participants, albeit peripherally, in Austria's great defeat and beneficiaries of French success that year.

In the wake of the French triumph at Austerlitz in December 1805 and the ensuing Treaty of Preßburg, frictions inherent in the old empire became intolerable to many of its German members (Austria, after all, had invaded fellow *Reich* member Bavaria in 1805). At the same time, Napoleon's interests and those of the key south German monarchs converged. For his part, the French emperor sought to consolidate his dominance of central and southern Germany. He thus established an alternative institution, the Confederation of the Rhine, on 12 July 1806 and announced that he would no longer recognise the old *Reich* or its Diet. On the German side, sixteen princes, acknowledging the obvious shift in power towards France and hoping to preserve their domains, perhaps even to expand their realms and authorities, signed the founding treaty and formally withdrew from the *Reich* on 1 August that year. The Habsburg emperor, Franz II, renounced all claims to the *Reich's* crown five days later (to retain an imperial title, he had had himself declared 'Franz I of Austria' in 1804 in anticipation of the *Reich's* dissolution). The Holy Roman Empire of the German Nations disappeared therewith after nearly one thousand years of existence at the heart of Europe. Napoleon and the Rheinbund would endeavour to take its place.

The Rheinbund served Napoleon's interests in several ways.[6] In the first place, it provided a buffer zone on France's western frontiers and deprived its enemies of the region's military and economic resources. Conversely, of course, the new institution granted France relatively unfettered access to German manpower and wealth. Napoleon would find this state of affairs useful in everything from providing endowments for his imperial nobility to prosecuting his economic war with Great Britain. He also saw the established German ruling houses as sources of legitimacy for his own new regime and contrived to bolster the status of his nascent dynasty by allying his relatives to some of Europe's oldest noble families in carefully selected marriages. In the most prominent examples, he arranged the wedding of his stepson, Eugène de Beauharnais, to Princess Augusta Amelia of Bavaria's ancient Wittelsbach family, married his youngest brother, Jérôme, to the king of Württemberg's daughter Katharine and forced Erbprinz (Hereditary Prince) Karl of Baden into an unwelcome alliance with his adopted niece Stéphanie de Beauharnais. These marriages, of course, also served the political purpose of binding the German states closer to France and to the emperor's own interests. Most significant for Napoleon, however, were the military forces that resulted from the Confederation. These amounted to more than 65,000 men from the original member states, and subsequent additions would almost double the total by the autumn of 1808 when the final state, the Duchy of Oldenburg, joined. Technically, France was not a member state, but Napoleon, as 'Protector' of the Confederation, obligated France to provide 200,000 soldiers for the 'common defence'.[7]

The alliance also served Napoleon's interests in Poland, albeit indirectly. Their country having been partitioned out of existence by Russia, Prussia and Austria during the 1790s, Polish elites eagerly sought the restoration of Poland as an independent state and looked to Revolutionary and Napoleonic France for support in this aspiration.[8] Their hopes for such an outcome soared when Napoleon defeated Prussia and Russia in 1806–7. The French emperor had ended that war by concluding an alliance with the tsar (the Treaties of Tilsit, July 1807), however, and he was keenly aware of Russia's adamantine opposition to the reestablishment of a Polish kingdom (unless, of course, the crown was placed on the tsar's head). To avoid directly threatening Russian national security interests while simultaneously satisfying at least some of the desires harboured by his ardent Polish adherents, Napoleon created the 'Duchy of Warsaw' from the Polish lands carved away from Prussia and placed this new entity under the sceptre of the Saxon king.[9] That monarch, Friedrich August, had been raised from prince-elector (*Kurfürst*) to king just months earlier when he agreed to join the Rheinbund in December 1806. Russian apprehensions were by no means erased, but this solution avoided both the title 'Poland' and its former status as a kingdom while leaving it at least nominally independent under a German ruler allied to France. Despite heavy interference from Paris and Poland's distance from the Saxon capital in Dresden (Prussian Silesia divided Saxony from the new duchy), Friedrich August and his cabinet took the arrangement seriously and sought to exploit the king's new status for the long-term benefit of the monarchy. Napoleon thus partially placated the Russians and the Poles, satisfied the Saxons with enhanced prestige and an enormous expansion in territory and population (in an instant, some 2.6 million Poles were added to the Saxon population of not quite 2 million), while acquiring near unimpeded access to Polish manpower and other resources for his own purposes. The duchy's population would nearly double to 4.3 million when much of Austrian Galicia was added after Austria's defeat in 1809, thus making Friedrich August at least technically responsible for a state twice the size of his own kingdom.

Although this new alliance was decidedly biased in favour of France, several points are worth highlighting when examining the Rheinbund's creation and brief history. First, Napoleon was neither the only beneficiary from the alliance nor the only actor in the system. Independent neutrality was impossible for small to middle-sized German monarchies wedged between Austria, Prussia and France (with Russia looming in the distance) and joining the Rheinbund was their only viable option as French power expanded. At the same time, these states, though certainly not wholly independent, were not simply 'an aggregation of robots'.[10] They all had their own interests and could often evade or mitigate French demands. Napoleon had intended, for instance, that the Confederation's remit include a diet, courts of arbitration and other structures, but these institutions were never established largely because of determined opposition from Bavaria and Württemberg, who feared infringement on their internal sovereignty. Likewise, Napoleon's desire to introduce the Code Napoléon as the common legal system across the Rhine was fulfilled in only a few cases and these were always adjusted to suit the preferences of the ruling regimes.[11] Presumably, Napoleon could have forced imposition of these aspects as urged by Karl Theodor von Dalberg, the Confederation's Prince Primate (*Fürstprimas*). The emperor, however, saw no reason to burden his relations with Rheinbund members as long as his military requirements were met. He thus desisted from attempts to persuade the southwest German states into adopting the Code after 1808 and he eventually came to prefer dealing with each state on a bilateral basis.[12] He imposed a constitution (Germany's first) on the 'model state' of Westphalia but made no effort at all to alter the antiquated traditions of internal governance in Saxony or the Mecklenburg duchies. Though often derided as helpless vassal states, the members, therefore, were not without a degree of agency.

Self-preservation and fear of French reprisals were key motivations for the German princes (and one princess), but they all had reasons of their own to join this new alliance and each endeavoured to exploit the situation to his or her own advantage. Most of the member monarchs, for example, acquired extensive new territories and commensurate, or exaggerated, new titles. Former electors of the *Reich* thus became kings, former dukes became grand dukes and counts became princes as a consequence of signing the alliance treaty. Baden's ruler, for example, was elevated from prince-elector to grand duke with the prestige of being addressed as 'his royal majesty', while his territory quadrupled in size and the number of subjects under his sceptre grew from 173,868 in 1771 to 1,001,520 by 1811.[13] In most cases, the new lands were also geographically contiguous, allowing for more cohesive polities and facilitating the promotion of centralised systems of governance. At the very least, the member rulers retained the lands and privileges they already had and did not swell the ranks of disgruntled, dispossessed princes and former imperial knights seeking succour across non-French Europe. Like Napoleon, some German monarchs sought to exploit marriage politics to their advantage, tying their established houses to the new French dynasty in the hopes of garnering future gains while preserving their status vis-à-vis their Rheinbund rivals. Württemberg's König (king) Friedrich, for instance, accepted the union between his daughter Katharine and Napoleon's brother Jérôme, the King of Westphalia, in part because he worried that his neighbours Bavaria and Baden already had marital links to the Bonaparte family.[14]

Moreover, while committing the majority of their soldiers to Napoleon and subordinating their foreign policies to those of France, they largely retained internal sovereignty, a crucial consideration for rulers who had chafed under the old *Reich*'s restrictions. The Rheinbund era thus became one of great reform as many German rulers, keen to consolidate their newly expanded realms and transform their state bureaucracies, took advantage of the latitude granted by the Confederation to modernise, strengthen and expand the power and authority of their increasingly centralised states. These sweeping reforms were often guided by a 'central personality' in the state bureaucracy such as Maximilian Graf von Montgelas in Bavaria or Sigismund Freiherr von Reitzenstein in Baden, and they often coincided with French concepts but were seldom dictated by Napoleon.[15] That is, the impulse to reform originated largely from within, not solely as a result of external pressure from Paris. Now largely free to ignore or marginalise domestic political opposition, they could exploit the opportunity under the Rheinbund to deepen their control over internal affairs as long as they satisfied Napoleon on the international front. Moreover, territorial expansion under Napoleon meant that many of the Rheinbund governments had to integrate large populations with diverse political, religious, cultural, judicial and commercial traditions into unified, centralised states. Instituting an array of administrative reforms provided these states with a tool to ease this often-dramatic transition. As historian William O. Shanahan remarked concerning Bavaria, the political measures enacted during this period 'began the process of transforming the Wittelsbach dynasty's rule over a miscellaneous aggregate of private possessions into an enlarged and consolidated public realm'.[16] Governance reform, however, was another area of differentiation among the Rheinbund's members. Thus the dramatic changes that became a common feature in the southwest Rheinbund monarchies were absent in states such as Saxony and the Mecklenburg duchies that acquired little or no new territory and remained encased in their outdated, almost arbitrary, styles of governance.[17] Even in states that introduced drastic changes, the gap between aspiration and achievement was often large. Nonetheless, the reforms instituted during the Rheinbund period laid important foundation stones for the future.[18]

Napoleon seldom intervened in these internal processes in well-governed states such as Bavaria, Württemberg or Hesse-Darmstadt. Several monarchies, on the other hand, experienced considerable imperial interference. Baden, for instance, was indifferently ruled from Napoleon's perspective, especially as far as turning out effective troops was concerned, and he felt no compunction in pressuring his new ally on its internal administration, particularly its military affairs. Westphalia and Berg, intended as 'model states' for the rest of the Confederation and ruled by members of the Bonaparte family, were likewise subjected to direct meddling from Paris. With the exception of these 'model states', however, the reforms introduced by the Rheinbund monarchs and their ministers under their conceptions of 'enlightened bureaucratic absolutism' were not mere copies of French procedures. In cases such as Bavaria, reforms were adopted to preempt French intrusion and maintain Bavarian control over internal affairs, and even in Baden the changes were adapted to local conditions.[19] Curiously, Napoleon refrained from interfering in Saxony and the Mecklenburg Duchies that eschewed all reform. Saxony – with the notable exception of its army – retained its antiquated administrative apparatus, and the Mecklenburgs were likewise uninterested in and unaffected by the reform trends washing over Europe from the late eighteenth century.

The second point relating to the Confederation states and their peoples is connected to the question of nationalism. Coming from the loose framework of the old *Reich* and motivated in large part by a desire to assert their own independence, the Rheinbund monarchs and their subjects, soldiers included, exhibited little in the way of pan-German nationalism. Indeed, many saw themselves, the smaller German states, as the 'true Germany' in contrast to the 'conglomerate states' of Austria and Prussia with their large non-German populations and their significant non-German interests.[20] Rather than nebulous notions of some pan-German unity that would leave them permanently subordinate to one of these two powers, the rulers, soldiers and bureaucrats of the 'Third Germany' were largely particularist, focused on their own states, their own parochial interests, and often at odds with or fearful of their Rheinbund neighbours. 'The small [states] in Germany want to be protected from the big', according to a perhaps embellished account from Metternich, 'The big want to rule according to their own fancies.'[21] In early 1806, for example, disputes over the location of the border between Bavaria and Württemberg led to brief exchanges of musketry as the two contested the lands Napoleon had allocated to them through the Treaty of Preßburg after Austerlitz.[22] Similarly, when pro-Austrian rebellion broke out in Bavaria's Vorarlberg region during the 1809 war, Württemberg's König Friedrich resented having to send his troops to fight insurgents in his fellow king's lands. At the same time, authorities in Baden feared that the domineering Friedrich would use this opportunity to occupy parts of their territory under the guise of military necessity and would then present a case to Napoleon for retaining the occupied areas after the war. Likewise, they squabbled over the spoils following the war of 1809, there being only so much territory for Napoleon to distribute.[23] Furthermore, most officers and men had no special sympathy for Austria or Prussia, the two large German powers that had repeatedly exploited, abused or neglected the 'Third Germany' for decades or longer. There were certainly prominent exceptions to this generalisation. Bavaria's young Crown Prince Ludwig was a passionate pan-Germanist and vociferously anti-French, for example, and his immediate neighbour, Crown Prince Friedrich Wilhelm of Württemberg, detested Napoleon. For slightly different reasons, Oldenburg and the Mecklenburg duchies, with familial and political–cultural ties to Prussia and Russia, were very reluctant members of the alliance.

On the whole, however, the common sense of belonging to a larger German cultural world did not translate into a desire by the Rheinbund princes or populations to submerge their own identities or to embrace some larger pan-German political union. Nor did these vague sentiments of Germanic identity suggest an automatic reluctance or refusal by Rheinbund troops to fight for Napoleon (even against fellow Germans or German-speakers) if their own sovereigns so ordered. Most Rheinbund soldiers had no affection for Prussia or Austria, but most also fought rebels in their own lands dutifully if sometimes regretfully. The small uprisings that broke out in Westphalia during 1809 were quashed by Westphalian soldiers fighting on behalf of their newly baked kingdom, for example, and when the Tyrol rose up against Bavarian rule that year, the bitter viciousness of the combat derived in part from the anger Bavarian soldiers felt towards insurgents whom they viewed as ungrateful and rebellious subjects unlawfully taking up arms against their rightful sovereign.[24] Anti-French complaints would grow after 1809, but opposition to or even hatred of Napoleon did not signify a corresponding embrace of Berlin or Vienna in most cases.

Third, the requirements of the Rheinbund resulted in sweeping changes for the armies of the German states, both in size and in what may be loosely labelled modernisation or reform.[25] As far as size was concerned, the various German princes had to expand their armies swiftly and suddenly as war with Prussia erupted less than three months after the pact had been signed in 1806. Drawing on their newly increased populations and utilising newly enacted conscription laws, the fledgling bureaucracies in these states often struggled to meet their treaty obligations (*see* Chart 1, page 22). Baden, for instance, hastily endeavoured to increase the size of its army from its pre-Confederation strength of barely 2,000 in 1803 to more than 8,000 by 1807. Over time, however, these processes became routine, often as part of larger bureaucratic reforms initiated by monarchs and officials eager to enhance and centralise the powers of their regimes. Reforms within these expanded armies, if sometimes painfully achieved, were also extensive. Some states had already begun to modernise their armed forces in the wake of the wars against Revolutionary France of 1792–1800, but alliance with Napoleon dramatically accelerated the pace of transformation. Among these reforms were changes – often major – in everything from the position of the soldier in society to recruitment, conscription, officer promotions, training, organisation, tactics and uniforms. Even hairstyles altered as officers discarded eighteenth-century wigs and soldiers cut off their outmoded queues. As their experience under the Rheinbund grew, therefore, most of the German contingents steadily improved, adapting to the exigencies of Napoleonic warfare.

On a personal level, the Rheinbund also brought advantages for military professionals in Germany. Conscription was widely hated, but for many, especially officers, the army meant secure employment, respected positions in society and the prospects of adventure and advancement. This was certainly the case with the numerous former Prussian officers who took positions in Rheinbund armies when Prussia's army was drastically reduced after the kingdom's defeat in 1806–7. Systems of reward and punishment, of course, reinforced loyalty to one's sovereign and incentivised dutiful obedience within the Rheinbund, but up to the retreat from Russia in late 1812, many men, perhaps most, also found themselves caught up in the excitement of serving alongside their French allies and under the great French emperor. 'We forgot that we fought under the conqueror of Germany,' wrote a soldier of the Westphalian Jäger-Carabiniers, 'we saw in Napoleon the mighty hero of the century.' Most regarded the French way of war as the model of modernity and could thus see themselves as being on the cutting edge of their profession. Such sentiments were naturally reinforced by participation in the history of victories garnered under Napoleon, 'the greatest commander of the age' as a Württemberg artillery officer described him in 1812.[26]

The memoir literature abounds with such recollections. 'As if touched by an electrical charge, the entire army was suddenly filled with joy and hope', remembered a Bavarian artillery corporal when Napoleon arrived at Abensberg on 20 April 1809.[27] Fighting 'under the eyes of the emperor' was thus professionally fulfilling as well as exciting. Even a somewhat sceptical and cynical Saxon hussar officer, watching Napoleon from close range at Wagram, remarked, 'Only now, in this eternally memorable hour, could I say that I have seen a battle!'[28] Similarly, a Saxon cuirassier officer, listening to Napoleon's proclamation on the morning of the Battle of Borodino in 1812 recalled that 'a more sincere and enthusiastic cheer had probably never been raised for Napoleon as in that moment from us'.[29] This enthusiasm was not feigned and it remained surprisingly strong even under the most trying circumstances.[30] Although the impact of the emperor's charisma faded after the Russian disaster as the composition of armies changed and Napoleon's overall situation deteriorated, it never entirely vanished and the 'electrical charge' of his presence – if now more fleeting – and the pride of serving under him would persist through 1813.

As noted above, the first three sovereigns to ally themselves with France were Bavaria, Baden and Württemberg. Under heavy French diplomatic pressure on the one side and threatened by Austria on the other, they chose Napoleon over the Habsburgs in the autumn of 1805, before the creation of the Confederation. They thus had their first taste of Napoleon's expectations and his style of warfare that year, albeit largely in rear-area security duties. All three monarchies were among the Rheinbund's founding membership and contingents from all three, joined by those from most of the other new partners, participated in the 1806–7 war with Prussia and Russia. A few battalions and squadrons fought at the great battles of Jena and Friedland, but most of the German troops spent the war protecting lines of communication or prosecuting sieges far from the main theatre of operations. These early forays into the Napoleonic battlefield were frequently disappointing both to the French and to their new allies. The contingents employed in the 1807 siege of Danzig (Gdańsk), for instance, occasioned peevish complaints from Marshal François Lefebvre, the commander charged with capturing the city. Nonetheless, the German contingents showed considerable promise, and, by 1809, most of the Confederation armies had improved dramatically. Indeed, the Franco-Austrian War of 1809 became a 'year of emergence' for the Rheinbund armies as they moved from line of communications duties to the front ranks in some of the greatest battles of the age directly under the eye of the emperor. Although the French continued to deprecate some contingents that year (notably the Saxons and Westphalians), others proved valuable assets to their French commanders and experienced French officers such as Davout, Lasalle and Vandamme were sincere in their praise of their German troops.[31]

This evolution into reliable French allies, however, was also dogged by nagging frictions. Napoleon, for instance, insisted on placing French generals in command of all his allied formations and his demands on the Rheinbund monarchs often exceeded their treaty commitments. Other routine French exactions, such as requisitions for horses, food, cloth, wine, leather and other goods or services, rankled as well. For the populations of the German states, however, the most odious aspect of the alliance was conscription. Although most conscription laws were drafted and enforced by local authorities and served the purposes of the Rheinbund rulers, the requirement for such laws in the first place was widely regarded as a French imposition driven by French dictates – a belief local authorities were content to accept. Whether this perception was strictly accurate or not, it was widespread and acquired an even more burdensome aspect from what seemed a rapid succession of French requests for German troops.

Objections to conscription grew after 1808 as the French emperor required many of his allies to contribute forces for the new war in Spain. Soldiers and civilians could understand the exertions and sacrifices resulting from swift and decisive wars against overbearing Prussia and Austria. Victories were celebrated and soldiers honoured after such campaigns, but the war in Spain was distant and seemed to have no relevance to the interests of the small German states or their people. Even those officers and men who initially marched for the Pyrenees with professional hopes of glory and advancement, quickly lost any such ardour in the realities of the grim and apparently interminable Iberian insurgency. As Oberst Heinrich von Porbeck, the commander of the Baden contingent in Spain, wrote in an April 1809 message to his sovereign: 'We have only one hope to sustain us in the turmoil here, namely that of an early return from this dreadful land.' He and the other commanders, he reported, 'will all gladly serve our fatherland in a coming war with Austria with double the enthusiasm we have for serving in Spain'.[32]

Regardless of where they served, however, the factor that caused perhaps the greatest resentment among the German troops was the routine disrespect and denigration they believed they received from many of their French comrades in arms.[33] Although tempered by favourable interactions and professional respect, the personal, concrete nature of these alleged aggravations was often more deeply felt and more enduringly remembered than issues of alienation at the national level. Problems such as these were manageable in times of battlefield triumph, but perceived French arrogance, the cruel war in Spain, and the seemingly endless demands on their various homelands created a swelling sense of discontent that would sap the alliance when it faced severe adversity.

Increasing difficulties with their French allies in the military sphere were echoed among the civilian populations of the Rheinbund states after 1810. Although the details are beyond the scope of this study, it is important to note that popular disenchantment with Napoleon and France was not uniform and arose from several different causes. In part, it was the direct result of French policies, most significantly in the economic dislocation stemming from Napoleon's Continental Blockade. Though some businesses thrived, many were ruined or deeply hurt, bringing joblessness, impoverishment and other hardships to elites and commoners alike in large sections of the Rheinbund economies. The enormous French armies that transited Germany were another factor as they brought civilian populations into direct contact with the men of the Grande Armée. As with soldiers, civilian attitudes were influenced favourably or unfavourably by personal, concrete experiences: the quartered soldier who politely helped the host family or the arrogant ruffians who were no better than uniformed brigands. Unfortunately for Napoleon's interests, the latter image predominated.[34]

Other causes could be found in the modernising reforms undertaken by many of the Rheinbund governments that brought unprecedented state intrusion into the daily lives of ordinary people. Conscription, seemingly endless quartering of troops and heavier taxation were the most detested and the most easily linked to French demands (even if these burdens at times served the interests of the various Confederation states to some degree), but other changes in law, governance and traditional practices were 'a devastatingly new experience for every subject'.[35] Furthermore, from the perspective of the citizen or subject in the Rheinbund, these latest changes were heaped atop a 'cascade of transformative events' since the 1790s: multiple wars, political upheavals, economic fluctuations, and social disruptions that left many Germans feeling deeply insecure.[36] It is hardly surprising that most people yearned for peace, stability and predictability. Nor is it especially surprising that many Germans associated their various worries and woes with France and its emperor. Disgruntlement was especially acute in Westphalia where the French presence was most intrusive, but it was growing across the Confederation even before Napoleon's invasion of Russia and would pose serious challenges to French and Rheinbund authorities when war came to the German lands in 1813.

Ruin in Russia

Despite its latent problems, the alliance remained strong in 1812 as its armies headed for the Russian border. Indeed, many men seem to have regarded the coming war with Russia as another opportunity to display their professional skills in a truly grand army under Napoleon's personal command. Many were awestruck at being part of such a vast and unprecedented military enterprise. 'The astonished world had never seen a finer, more battle-ready, more battle-hardened army,' wrote a Württemberg staff officer, 'an army for which history finds no comparison in terms of military fame, of experience and of boundless faith in its thus far ever-victorious commander'. There were exceptions (such as the Mecklenburg troops), but the Rheinbund armies were generally good to excellent in quality as they crossed the Niemen that fateful June. When Napoleon summoned the Bavarians to participate in the Russian invasion, for example, the contingent's French commander, Général de Division (GD) Laurent Gouvion Saint-Cyr, confidently stated that his corps 'was splendid, composed of experienced soldiers, well equipped, disciplined, and in good spirits'.[37] The officers and men agreed, one battalion commander recalling that the Bavarian troops were 'imbued with the best spirits, with confident trust in Napoleon's luck and skill as a commander – mentally and physically most perfectly equipped'.[38] A Württemberg army doctor proudly noted that his regiment was 'in superb and energetic condition' and composed of 'toughened and courageous men with an average age of 22 to 30 years'.[39]

Even forces that had performed poorly in 1809 had improved. The Saxon army had been completely remade in the intervening years and the

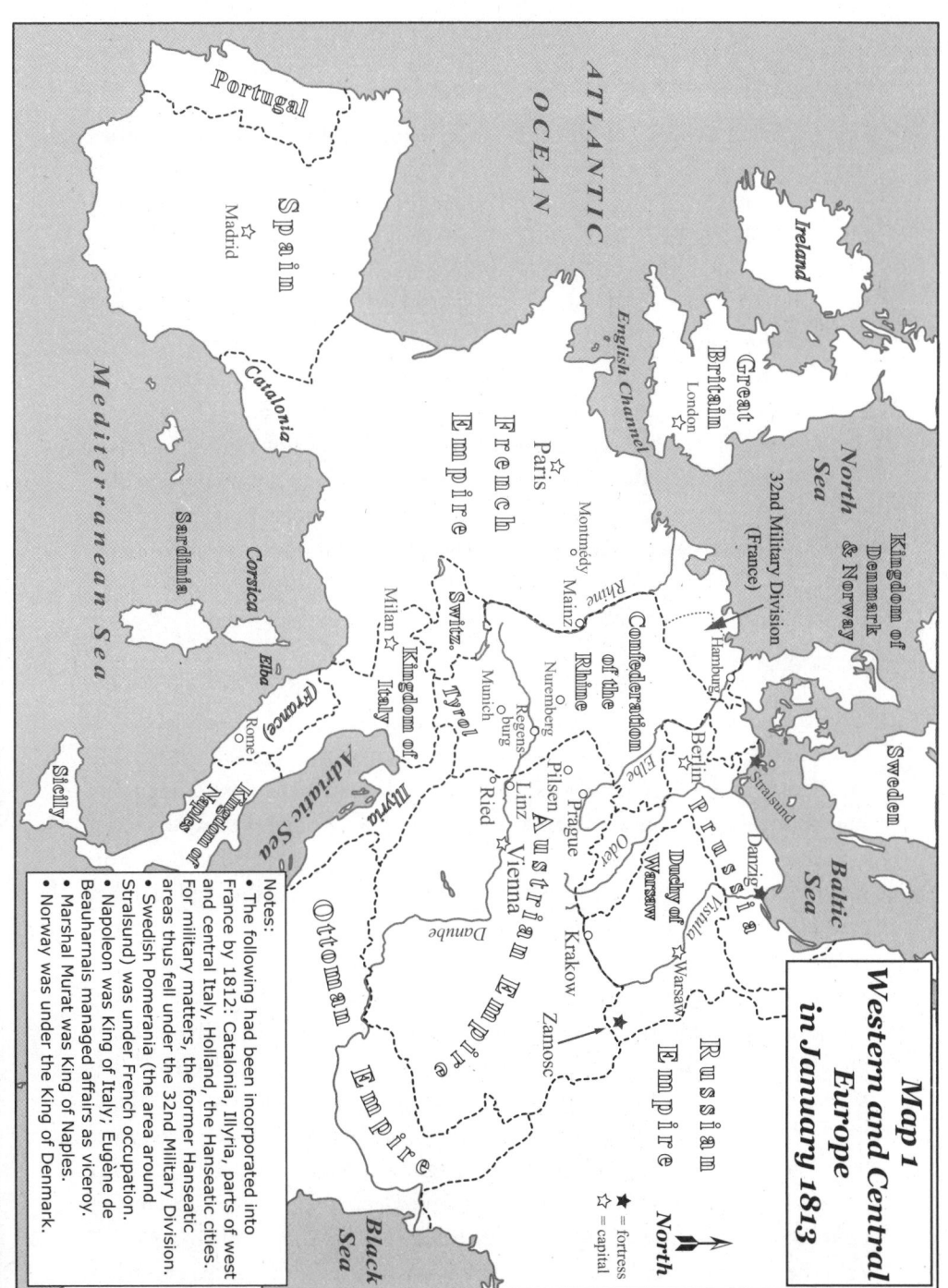

Map 1 Western and Central Europe in January 1813

Westphalians were well equipped, trained and disciplined when they headed east. 'One could rightly expect something great from them,' recorded a lieutenant of the 5th Westphalian Line that spring and Capitaine Heinrich Friedrich von Meibom of the 1st Infantry wrote that his regiment remained unhappily behind and twice asked its colonel to request permission to participate in the coming campaign. Once informed that they were assigned to the invasion, Major Johann Philip Bauer thus wrote to his brother that, 'The entire regiment, officers as well as soldiers, was in complete joy on this news that we would not be left behind.' This sentiment, of course, was by no means universal among the Westphalians or any other contingent. Ludwig Wilhelm von Conrady, commanding I/6th Infantry, was one: 'I had never entered upon a campaign with so little enthusiasm and indeed with no hope.'[40] Especially uneasy were those who had experienced the rigours of campaigning in Poland in 1806–7; they knew that Russia would be worse and felt 'a premonition of an unfortunate future' as they passed their homeland's border posts.[41] If some expressed doubts and entered the campaign with foreboding, however, many, likely most, were confident and even enthusiastic such as the Baden officers who imagined winter balls in Moscow or St Petersburg while they awaited orders to march east.[42]

The debacle that followed the ardour, anxiety, preparations and expectations associated with the invasion of Russia had dire repercussions for the Rheinbund. While it did not destroy the alliance, the Russian catastrophe undermined faith in Napoleon as a military leader and fuelled underlying anti-French sentiments among Germans from the Rhine to the Oder. Moreover, the tide of combat, hunger, cold and vast misery that engulfed the entire Grande Armée also devastated the fine Rheinbund armies that had marched across the Niemen in June 1812. 'We were nothing more than spectres', recalled a Württemberg lieutenant as, in the words of an artillery officer from the same contingent, 'the army dragged itself ahead, strewing the road with its dead, its dying and its mad'.[43] To take a typical example, the Baden Brigade, numbering more than 7,600 that summer, was reduced to 425 effectives when it collected itself in Prussia on 30 December. The Hessians took justifiable pride in having saved six of their guns, but of 4,700 infantry and artillerymen who had entered the campaign, their brigade could only muster 316 when Marshal Joachim Murat reviewed it in mid-December; of the 452 Hessian light horsemen, a mere 88 answered the roll call in Prussia on 4 January 1813.[44] And these were contingents that only became involved in serious combat at the end of the campaign in the nightmarish crossing of the Berezina River. In contrast, the Württemberg division that had marched all the way to Moscow with the main army and had fought at Smolensk and Borodino was 'in complete dissolution'. 'Each individual could only be concerned with his own self-preservation,' reported the contingent's distraught commander.[45] Even the Saxon 7th Corps, assigned a flanking mission and thus spared some of the main army's agonies, suffered heavily. On departing Warsaw in February 1813, the contingent counted only some 8,550 fit for duty from the 23,000 that had comprised the corps at the start of the war, and many of these would perish in bitter combats and endless, wretched marches before the survivors reached home.[46] Even though several thousand sick and wounded had already been sent back to Saxony, these losses were still staggering.

'I cannot tell you in words what the army has suffered,' wrote a lieutenant of the Berg contingent to his brother on 21 December 1812, 'I have lost everything, everything: horses, clothes, equipment, health, all is lost.'[47] His pitiful missive reminds us of the material costs that accompanied the appalling price in human lives. Equine and equipment losses in the 'splendid' Bavarian corps, for instance, were overwhelming: 5,800 horses, 22 standards, 38 guns, 260 caissons, 300 other vehicles and all the armaments and accoutrements for 30,000 men had vanished in the dreadful maelstrom across the Niemen.[48] In the words of a Württemberg officer, 'Never, in the entire reach of history, has the world seen an event that can match in ghastliness the destruction of the French army in the fields of Russia and Poland.'[49]

It would be otiose to review the human misery and stupefying losses attendant upon the horrors of the retreat in any further detail.[50] Suffice it to say that the Russian campaign shattered the Rheinbund armies and, as the war continued into Germany in the spring of 1813, the Russian experience would have deleterious material and psychological effects on Napoleon's German allies when he called upon them to raise new contingents. As far as manpower was concerned, the Rheinbund monarchs suddenly found themselves with almost no veteran soldiers. As a Baden general would observe: 'as is well known, the recent Russian campaign largely wiped out the experienced troops'.[51] The recruits who would fill the new contingents were thus not only young and inexperienced, in the great majority of cases they were completely untrained, unfamiliar with military life and unprepared for the hardships of campaigning. Additionally, the various German states struggled to equip their soldiers and to provide the thousands of horses required for cavalry squadrons, artillery batteries and supply trains. Beyond these daunting material problems, there were signs of serious psychological weaknesses in the resurrected contingents. Napoleon's defeat in Russia made the unpopular conscription systems in most states even more detested, so simply raising new battalions became more difficult and the men in the ranks were increasingly unwilling. Moreover, there were few veterans in place to provide continuity, experience and toughness to the units being re-created. The ragged core of veterans who were on hand were often suffering from combat stress themselves. Physically and mentally exhausted, many appeared lethargic, indifferent or numb. They were more difficult to motivate and had lost much of the drive and initiative that had characterised most Rheinbund officers and soldiers in earlier years when they had striven to emulate their French allies. The dearth of veterans, of course, also meant that many, often most, officer and NCO positions were filled by promoting either raw, inexperienced youths or weary, jaded survivors of the Russian catastrophe. Under such stresses, it is hardly surprising that the previously high standard of leadership in many German units declined precipitously.

Finally, the Russian experience altered the relationship between the new German troops and the French, including Napoleon, in several ways. In the first place, being largely composed of new recruits, the Rheinbund regiments that took the field in 1813 lacked the immanent tradition of victory and battlefield dominance that had animated France's German allies in earlier campaigns. This was compounded by the obvious diminishment of Napoleon's assumed nimbus of success. It is important not to overemphasise this point, but also important to recognise that German soldiers, fighting for what many now perceived as a possibly losing cause, would be less resilient to setbacks, less willing to take risks and more inclined to seek escape in desertion or evasion than they had been during the emperor's years of glory. This did not mean that they were insensitive to Napoleon's personal charisma or that they would not respond when called upon – particularly if the campaign trend was clearly in Napoleon's favour – but it did mean that German units would be less durable on the march and more fragile on the battlefield as compared to the 1806–12 period.

Second, the campaign in Russia had tarnished the image of the French army and worn away much of the tolerance for perceived French arrogance and imposition. The behaviour of the French troops in Russia and the war's conclusion in defeat and indescribable wretchedness made the French seem barely worthy of admiration, a sentiment that entrenched itself among soldiers and civilians alike when Germans witnessed the indiscipline, confusion and logistical deficiencies of the raw, young army Napoleon somehow hammered together in the spring of 1813. Alleged indignities inflicted on individual German officers and men by the French added a personal dimension to the general disaffection.[52]

Third, the seeming ubiquity of Coalition raiding parties throughout the French rear areas that year contributed in no small way to the prevailing sense of insecurity and doubt about the cause in which the Rheinbund contingents were now enlisted. Napoleon's strategy for security in his rear areas had always relied on clever deception, large numbers of second-line troops and the aura of victory surrounding his army and his person. This strategy had succeeded in both quelling unrest and containing enemy raiding detachments during the wars of 1805, 1806–7 and 1809, but it failed under the conditions prevalent in 1813. Allied raiders now seemed everywhere, threatening to ambush unwary replacement columns, supply trains and individuals all across central Germany and thus generating a widespread sense of insecurity that compounded doubts about the quality of the French army and its leadership. Cossacks, barbaric, elusive and riding on a cloud of terror from the steppes, were an especial source of dread. The Russian experience and the weaknesses of 1813's Grande Armée thus shaved away much of the insulation that had buffered Franco-German military relations in earlier years. With the French continuing to exhibit what many Germans saw as the presumptions of the past and the ill-used Germans less inclined to endure these presumptions, resentments arose, interactions became testy, collegiality declined and effectiveness suffered.

Into 1813: A New Year and a Broader War

The debilities of the new German contingents and the Franco-German frictions lurking just off-stage did not manifest themselves immediately and everywhere as the war moved west from the Russian frontier in the first months of 1813. The French emperor, his commanders and his Confederation allies were absorbed with the imperative business of gauging the scale of the Russian calamity and attempting to formulate appropriate responses, both political and military. On the domestic political front, the governments, elites and common people of the Rheinbund states were appalled by the scope of the defeat, the inexpressible wretchedness of the retreat and the horrifying loss of life. Furthermore, most were overcome by shock as neither monarchs, nor ministers nor subjects had heard much of anything from their armies since the summer. The extent of the disaster was revealed with terrifying suddenness late in the year when the Grande Armée's 29th Bulletin of 3 December 1812 appeared in the press to validate the fearful rumours that had been drifting west from across the Niemen (Neman) for some weeks.[53] At the same time, the ragged remnants of the Rheinbund armies were beginning to return home. Many, of course, never returned, prompting König Friedrich of Württemberg to write that 'every family in the kingdom has been plunged into

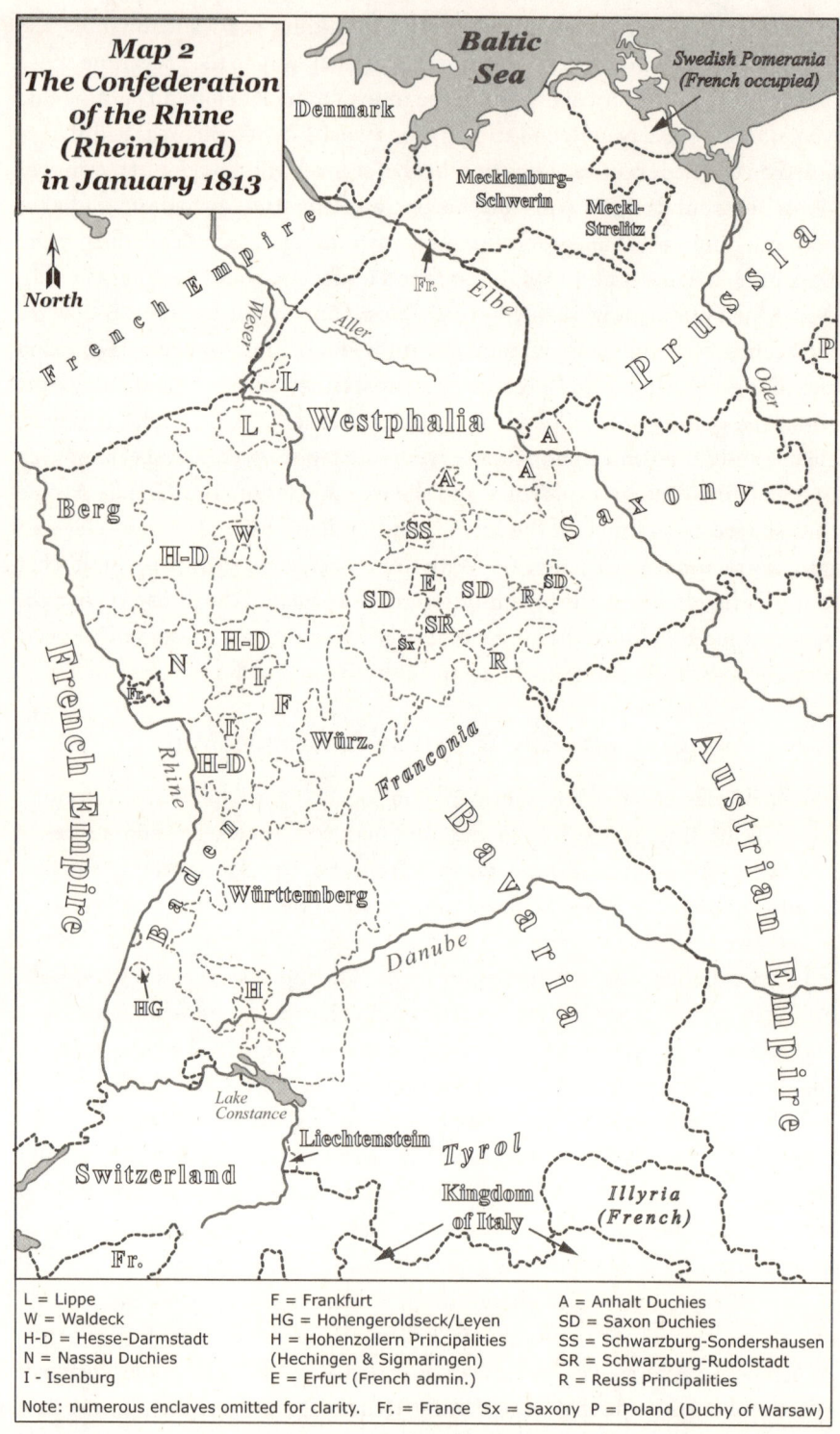

such deep grief and sorrow through the loss of fathers, sons and brothers'.[54] On the international front, Rheinbund regimes thus began to contemplate the possibility of Napoleon's overthrow and to consider hedging strategies to preserve themselves should he fall. As 1813 opened, however, they were still allied to the French emperor and still obligated to provide troops. On the military side, therefore, the dire strategic situation meant that many of the Rheinbund contingents were sent to the theatre of war in bits and pieces almost as fast as they could be assembled. This phenomenon will appear repeatedly in the ensuing pages.

Meanwhile, the shifting political context compounded the challenges faced by the German states. In the early months of the year, Prussia renounced its forced alliance with France, Sweden declared against Napoleon, and Tsar Alexander, rejecting the advice of the ailing Marshal Mikhail Illarionovich Kutuzov, decided to carry the war west beyond the Vistula. Along with Great Britain, these three states thus became the core of the anti-French alliance known as the Sixth Coalition. As Sweden was still mobilising, however, Russia and Prussia would be Napoleon's principal opponents during the spring campaign from April until an armistice was agreed in early June, with Britain providing essential financial and material support. Austria, which held itself aloof during the spring through a policy of cagey neutrality, joined the Coalition as summer and the armistice came to an end. When hostilities resumed in mid-August, therefore, all of Europe's major powers and many of the minor ones were arrayed against Napoleonic France from the Baltic to the Adriatic.

In these circumstances, the Rheinbund states faced urgent, indeed existential, policy decisions. On one side, they were tied to Napoleon by bonds of treaty alliance and national interest; his star had visibly faltered, but France remained the single most powerful nation on the continent and Napoleon remained one of history's greatest generals. On the other side, the Coalition was growing in strength and the new Allies were threatening to eradicate any state that did not desert its alliance with Napoleon. For reluctant Rheinbund members such as Mecklenburg-Schwerin and Mecklenburg-Strelitz, this was a great opportunity, and both quickly transferred their allegiance to the new Coalition. For others, especially Saxony and Bavaria that shared borders with Prussia and/or Austria, the policy path to preserving their dynasties and territories while retaining as much independence as possible was far less clear. Furthermore, their choices were not simple binary ones between France on the one side and the Coalition on the other. They also had to navigate among the sometimes contradictory and competing coercions and coaxings of the key

Chart 1: Rheinbund States and Contingents, April 1813

State	Joined Rheinbund	Troop Contingent
French Empire	July 1806	200,000
Kingdom of Bavaria	July 1806	30,000
Kingdom of Württemberg	July 1806	12,000
Grand Duchy of Baden	July 1806	8,000
Grand Duchy of Berg	July 1806	5,000
Grand Duchy of Hesse-Darmstadt	July 1806	4,000
Grand Duchy of Frankfurt	July 1806	2,800
Duchy of Nassau (Usingen and Weilburg)	July 1806	1,550
Principality of Hohenzollern-Hechingen	July 1806	93*
Principality of Hohenzollern-Sigmaringen	July 1806	197*
Principality of Isenburg-Birstein	July 1806	350*
Principality of Leyen (Hohengeroldseck)	July 1806	29*
Principality of Liechtenstein	July 1806	40*
Grand Duchy of Würzburg	Sept. 1806	2,000
Kingdom of Saxony	December 1806	20,000
Duchy of Sachsen-Weimar-Eisenach	December 1806	800
Duchy of Sachsen-Gotha-Altenburg	December 1806	1,100
Duchy of Sachsen-Meiningen	December 1806	300
Duchy of Sachsen-Hildburghausen	December 1806	200
Duchy of Sachsen-Coburg-Saalfeld	December 1806	400
Duchy of Anhalt-Bernburg	April 1807	240
Duchy of Anhalt-Dessau	April 1807	350
Duchy of Anhalt-Köthen	April 1807	210
Principality of Schwarzburg-Rudolstadt	April 1807	325
Principality of Schwarzburg-Sondershausen	April 1807	325
Principality of Waldeck	April 1807	400
Principality of Lippe-Detmold	April 1807	500
Principality of Schaumburg-Lippe	April 1807	150
Principality of Reuß-Greiz (senior line)	April 1807	450
Junior Princes of Reuß: Ebersdorf, Lobenstein, Schleiz	April 1807	
Kingdom of Westphalia	November 1807	25,000

* Troops provided by Nassau.

Note: The Duchies of Arenberg and Oldenburg as well as the Principalities of Salm-Salm and Salm-Kyrburg were absorbed into greater France in 1810. The two Mecklenburg duchies broke with the Rheinbund in March 1813.

Coalition governments. They had no desire to exchange French domination for some perhaps slightly less onerous hegemony exercised by Austria, Prussia or even distant Russia.

The potential for domestic unrest presented the German monarchs with an additional concern. Stoked by Napoleon's disaster in Russia and Allied propaganda, anti-French sentiment simmered across the states of the Rheinbund, occasionally erupting into outbreaks of violence. Though many perceived French hegemony as 'suffocating' and were disillusioned with the Rheinbund project, their resentments were aimed at France and its emperor and did not represent some form of 'newly awakened nationalism'.[55] Being anti-French did not mean being in favour of some vague pan-German vision. Most people remained 'impervious to the nationalist agitation' and the fuzzy romantic dreams of a future united Germany remained confined to 'small groups of zealots'.[56] Nonetheless, while the monarchs were still allied with Napoleon, this popular anti-French ferment threatened to place the Rheinbund rulers in opposition to many of their own subjects. With the chaos of the French Revolution as recent history, however, these rulers also feared that agitation against the alliance with France would evolve into broader anti-monarchical radicalism (often loosely termed 'Jacobinism') that would endanger the very foundations of their states and dynasties.[57] Furthermore, they worried (with good reason) that Prussia and Austria would foment anti-regime movements within their borders as a means of expanding influence, undermining the local rulers and perhaps retaking lands lost to Napoleonic conquest since 1805. The 'aggressive fantasies' of revolutionary pan-Germanism promoted by some prominent voices in the Coalition camp, most notably Baron Heinrich Friedrich Karl von und zum Stein, only accentuated these anxieties.[58]

Fearful of, but in many cases still personally loyal to Napoleon, plied with menaces and promises by the Allies and haunted by the spectre of domestic upheaval, the various kings, grand dukes, dukes, princes and one princess of the Rheinbund once more sent their soldiers to fight under French eagles in 1813. As a Württemberg veteran of both 1812 and 1813 would later write:

> Bit by bit, all the great, small and miniature contingents of the great ruler's numberless allies, newly organised and equipped at the burdensome expense of their respective lands, headed for the country where the overture of the campaign now beginning was expected, to poor, unfortunate Saxony which was already partly occupied by the enemy.[59]

This work will track the marches, battles and sieges of the diverse contingents during the spring and autumn campaigns, reviewing successes and

Chart 2A: French Corps and their Rheinbund Elements

Corps	Commander	Spring	Autumn
Guard Infantry	(varied)	Hesse	Hesse, Saxony, Westphalia
Guard Cavalry	(varied)	Berg	Berg
Guard Artillery	Dulauloy	–	Berg, Westphalia
1st	Vandamme > Mouton	–	Anhalt
2nd	Victor	–	Westphalia
3rd	Ney/Souham	Baden, Hesse, Frankfurt	Baden, Hesse*
4th	Bertrand	Württemberg	Württemberg
5th	Lauriston	–	–
6th	Marmont	–	Württemberg
7th	Reynier	Saxony, Würzburg	Saxony, Würzburg
8th	Poniatowski	(not yet organised)	–
9th	Augereau	(not yet organised)	–
10th	Rapp (Danzig)	Bavaria, Westphalia, & others	Bavaria, Westphalia, & others
11th	MacDonald/Gérard	Würzburg	Westphalia, Würzburg
12th	Oudinot	Bavaria	Bavaria, Westphalia, Hesse-Darmstadt†
13th	Davout	(not yet organised)	–
14th	Gouvion Saint-Cyr	(not yet organised)	–
1st Cavalry	Latour-Maubourg	Saxony	Saxony, Westphalia
2nd Cavalry	Sébastiani	–	–
3rd Cavalry	Arrighi	(not yet organised)	–
4th Cavalry	Kellermann/Sokolnicki	(not yet organised)	–
5th Cavalry	Lhéritier	(not yet organised)	–

Note: Temporary attachments and rear-area security troops not shown.

* The Baden and Hessian 39th Division was transferred to 11th Corps in August; the Baden Light Dragoons remained with 3rd Corps.

† The Rheinbund light cavalry brigade was assigned to 4th Corps after 12th Corps was disbanded in September.

Chart 2B: Rheinbund Fortress Garrisons

Corps	Commander	Spring	Autumn
Danzig		See 10th Corps *opposite*	
Dresden	Durosnel	Saxony, Westphalia	Saxony, Westphalia, Bavaria
Glogau	Laplane	Baden, Saxony	Frankfurt, Saxony
Küstrin	Fornier d'Albe	Westphalia, Württemberg	Westphalia, Württemberg
Magdeburg	Haxo > Le Marois	Westphalia	Westphalia, Rheinbund
Modlin	Daendels	Saxony, Würzburg	Saxony, Würzburg
Spandau	Bruny	–	(capitulated in April)
Stettin	Grandeau/Dufresse	6th Rheinbund?	6th Rheinbund?
Thorn	Maureillan	Bavaria	(capitulated in April)
Torgau	Narbonne > Dutaillis	Saxony*	Saxony, Würzburg, Hesse-Darmstadt
Wittenberg	Lapoype	–	–
Zamosc	Hauke	–	–

* The Saxons initially maintained Torgau as a 'neutral' fortress; it remained an important depot for the Saxon army after the kingdom returned to alliance with Napoleon.

disasters to assess their performance under these stressful and painfully confusing circumstances. In addition to the basic historical narrative, I will discuss the key differences in how these contingents responded to their situations. For each of these Germans states and each of their armies is a study in itself and a great deal of analytical clarity is lost if they are evaluated as a single, undifferentiated mass or if the changes that took place over time are overlooked. Indeed, in some cases, it is important to note how the various regiments of a single contingent might differ from one another. This history, however, will also highlight the many commonalities among the German contingents, large and small, that took the field one last time as French allies. It is hoped, thereby, to expand our understanding of these final great Napoleonic campaigns in Germany, to illuminate a relatively unexplored facet of Germany's relationship with Napoleon and to provide some background for new research into this endlessly fascinating era.

Chapter 1
A War to the Death

'One of the more distant consequences could be that the war will approach Germany.'

Napoleon to his brother Jérôme, King of Westphalia, 18 January 1813[1]

THE WAR OF 1813 was exceedingly complex, consisting of manifold, often overlapping campaigns, and divided into two grand phases with an extended armistice midway in its course. Moreover, convoluted political considerations compounded the multifarious military actions. These included not only interactions between Napoleon and his allies and adversaries, but also deep fissures among the Coalition members themselves over the aims of the war, its scope and its prosecution as well as serious frictions within the councils of the individual states opposing Napoleon. Added to these political factors among the major Coalition powers were their relations with the different members of the Rheinbund and the 'German' populace writ large, initiatives and connections that were seldom coordinated and indeed often at odds with those pursued by their putative allies. All of these political frictions, of course, affected the progress of operations, just as military developments shaped political deliberations. It is not the purpose of this work to present a detailed narrative and analysis of the war's many intricacies, but a general outline is essential to place the activities of the Rheinbund contingents in the requisite political–military context.

Spring of Disappointment

In broad terms, the war falls into a spring phase and an autumn phase, with an armistice spanning the period from early June through mid-August in between. The spring phase can be further divided into two stages: a set of preliminary operations from January until the end of April and the first major campaign beginning in May. During the first stage, French forces and their German allies, scattered and exhausted, fell back from Poland into central Germany as their commander, Napoleon's stepson, Eugène de Beauharnais, attempted to cope with pressure from the Allied armies and his imperial stepfather's often unrealistic expectations. Meanwhile, Napoleon was exerting himself to the uttermost to create a new Grande Armée, using the power of the centralised French state to stamp battalions out of the dust and demanding similar exertions from the members of the Rheinbund. The Coalition had problems of its own. The exhausted Russians were still recovering from the 1812 war, while the Prussians were endeavouring to break their bonds with Napoleon and raise a new army to liberate their homeland. Owing to these limitations on both sides, this preliminary stage was largely comprised of cautious manoeuvring. Though enlivened by the bold actions of aggressive Allied raiding parties, there were few major engagements. Napoleon's arrival in late April at the head of his newly minted army immediately changed the character of the war. Combat, vicious and bloody, exploded across Saxony and the French gained two hard-won victories at Lützen and Bautzen (Budyšin), but neither of these successes was sufficiently decisive to end the war on Napoleon's terms. With both sides near collapse, Napoleon agreed to an armistice in early June to allow for military recuperation and all manner of political intrigue. The spring of 1813 was thus a season of disappointment for both parties, neither of them able to secure the battlefield triumphs it needed to achieve its political objectives.

After Russia: *From the Niemen to the Elbe, January–March 1813*

As December 1812 dragged to a close, the last ragged survivors of Napoleon's once grand army stumbled across Russia's borders into Prussia and Poland. The appalling condition of the former Grande Armée's soldiers left an indelible impression on German populations, boosting anti-French sentiments and inducing no small degree of *Schadenfreude* among many, as the rector of a school in Küstrin recorded in his diary:

> The clothing of most of the soldiers had almost nothing military about it. They wrapped themselves in sheepskins, women's skirts, horse blankets and linen wall hangings, and carried their poor belongings tied up in bundles on sticks. It was a squalid sight that gave satirists plenty of material for their works. People publicly compared the past, so proud for the French, with the wretched present. The soldiery, usually so arrogant, so full of pretensions, had become immensely patient, well-behaved, and modest in Russia.[2]

Beyond these scenes of misery, the strategic situation for the French and their allies was grim indeed. In the centre, the bulk of the enormous force that had invaded Russia in June 1812 had been virtually destroyed, its sad remnants limping west, frostbitten and disorganised, towards assembly points along the Vistula. Marshal Joachim Murat, the King of Naples, appointed overall commander when Napoleon left the army on 5 December, was headed for Königsberg (Kaliningrad) with the weary headquarters. Circumstances to the north and south, on the other hand, seemed to offer some hope as the flanking forces, having been spared the giant battles and the hideous retreat of the central columns, were relatively intact. Withdrawing towards the Niemen in the north was Marshal Étienne Jacques MacDonald with his 10th Corps composed of the division Prussia had been forced to contribute (27th Division) and a mixed division of Polish, Bavarian and Westphalian troops (7th Division). In the south were the Austrian Auxiliary Corps commanded by Feldmarschall Carl Phillip Fürst zu Schwarzenberg and GD Jean Reynier with the 7th Corps consisting of the Saxon contingent and a French division. These two corps were arrayed in defensive positions north and east of Warsaw. Additionally, GD Prince Joseph Poniatowski was in Warsaw, urgently engaged in reconstructing the Polish army from the survivors of the 5th Corps after its decimation in Russia. Counting on these forces and reserves being hurried forward from garrisons in Germany, Napoleon initially hoped to hold advanced positions in the east, at best no further west than the Vistula. There he would put the army into winter quarters, rebuild his strength and resume operations in the spring. Unfortunately for his prospects, events on both flanks soon scotched these optimistic plans.

The first blow fell in the north. Here General-Leutnant (GL) Hans David Ludwig von Yorck, commander of the Prussian contingent in 10th Corps, concluded the Convention of Tauroggen (Tauragė) with the pursuing Russians and deserted the alliance with France by declaring his troops 'neutral' on 30 December 1812.[3] At a stroke, MacDonald lost half of his corps' total strength and all of his cavalry. 'He has thus left us to be taken by the enemy and without a single cavalryman,' wrote the marshal in reporting Yorck's defection to Murat.[4] Already in danger of being cut off by advancing Russian columns, MacDonald had no option but a rapid withdrawal west towards Königsberg with his lone remaining division. This division, the 7th under GD Charles Louis Dieudonné Grandjean, included the 1st Westphalian and 13th Bavarian Infantry Regiments as well as three Polish regiments for a total of perhaps 6,000 combatants. Grandjean's men fended off Russian cavalry on 2 January and fought a stiff rear-guard action at Labiau (Polessk) on the 3rd to reach Königsberg, but the city could not be held. Although MacDonald had been reinforced by some second-line troops from garrisons

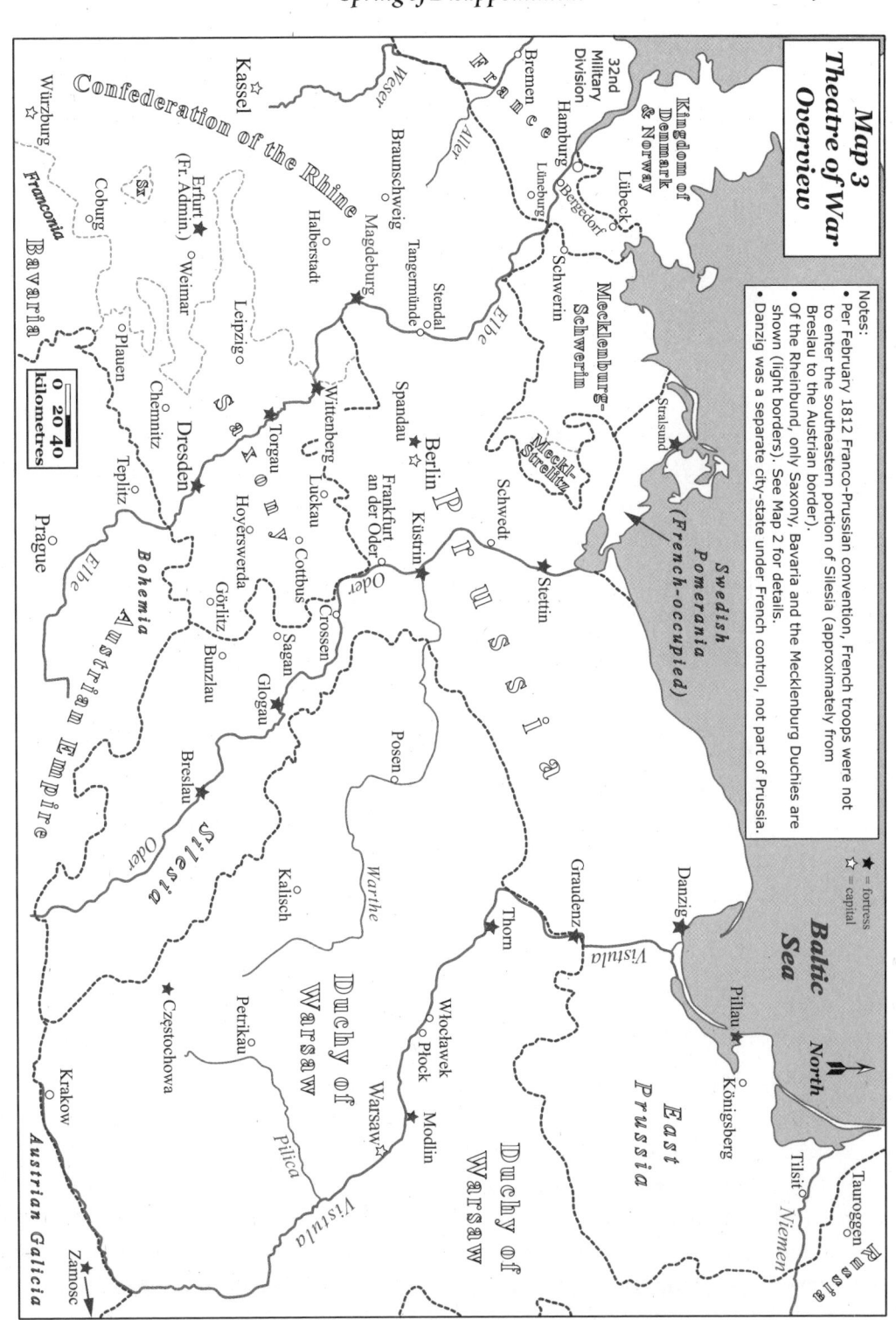

Map 3
Theatre of War Overview

in Germany, the Russians were threatening to encircle his weak corps and 'clouds of Cossacks' seemed to be everywhere. Prussia's attitude contributed to the pervasive sense of insecurity among the French. Prussia was nominally still an ally, but the kingdom's officials were brusquely uncooperative, the army's hostility was manifest in every meeting and the 'very unfavourable' sentiments of the local population made MacDonald fear 'an insurrection or at least an uprising'.[5] He thus continued his retreat to reach Danzig (Gdańsk) in mid-January where his 10th Corps was ordered to garrison the great fortress and new orders recalled him to France for reassignment. He will return to the story shortly at the head of a new corps and subsequent chapters will address events near Danzig and the experiences of the Rheinbund troops.

For the moment, it suffices to note Napoleon's assessment of Yorck's defection. In a lengthy missive to the Rheinbund monarchs on 18 January, the emperor wrote that his previous plans had been overthrown 'by the treason of General Yorck, who . . . has sided with the enemy'.

> The immediate consequences of this treason are that the King of Naples [Murat] will have to retire behind the Vistula and that my losses will mount owing to those who are in the hospitals in old Prussia. One of the more distant consequences could be that the war will approach Germany. I will take all necessary measures to protect the frontiers of the Confederation; but all the states of the Confederation must recognise, for their part, the necessity of taking actions proportionate to the existing circumstances. It is not only against the exterior enemy that they must protect themselves; there is an additional danger to fear: the spirit of revolt and anarchy.[6]

The emperor was in Paris, working tirelessly with all his remarkable energy to create a new Grande Armée and his references to Yorck and the potential threats facing the Rheinbund were only the prelude to his clever appeal to the German princes to do likewise. The tsar had named Stein a minister of state and Napoleon warned that the Confederation would face 'woes without number' should these people 'who aspire to change the face of Germany' succeed. Hope for socio-political stability and regime security thus lay with France. 'I have guaranteed the existence of these princes [of the Rheinbund], I have guaranteed it against their external enemies and against those who, inside, would want to attack their authority,' he adjured his allies in the 18 January letter, 'I will fulfil my commitments; the great sacrifices that I impose on my peoples, the great measures that I have just adopted, have no other purpose than to fulfil them.' Building on this exposition of French activity, he continued by mixing his expectations with dangers he knew would resonate in Rheinbund capitals:

> But, when I do everything for the confederate sovereigns, I must hope that they will not abandon themselves and will not betray their own cause. They would betray it, if they do not cooperate with me with all their means, if they do not take the most effective measures to put in the best state their infantry, their artillery, [and] especially their cavalry, if they do not do all that depends on them so that the war is moved away from Germany and that all the projects of the enemy are thwarted. They would still betray it, by not rendering the agitators of all sorts powerless to cause harm, by letting the public papers mislead opinion through false news, or corrupt it by pernicious doctrines, by not supervising, with a strict vigilance, both the preaching and the teaching, and all that can exert some influence on public tranquillity.
>
> I therefore ask Your Majesty not to neglect any of these measures, and to do everything possible to re-establish his contingent on the same footing as before the war [meaning 1812]. The result of our common efforts will be, in a second campaign, the triumph of the common cause, or, if the enemy desires to prevent this campaign by negotiations, we shall have, in the magnitude of our preparations, the certain pledge of an honourable and secure peace, the first condition of which will be to maintain all that exists, and to in no way touch the laws constituting the Confederation, nor the interests of its sovereigns.[7]

France's preparations and those of its German allies, however, would take time to produce even the rawest of new armies. In the operational theatre meanwhile, Yorck's defection weakened Napoleon's forces on the northern flank and undid his plans to defend east of the Vistula; and subtler, but equally deleterious, actions by his allies in the south were also undermining the French position. The three forces in this sector, as noted above, were the Austrian Auxiliary Corps, Reynier's 7th Corps and a substantial but ill-equipped and almost entirely untrained collection of new Polish troops.[8]

Austria, like Prussia, was a reluctant participant in the invasion of Russia and its principal military interest in the wake of the catastrophe was to preserve its Auxiliary Corps while its foreign minister, Clemens von Metternich, endeavoured to move the monarchy out of its alliance with France and towards an independent role on the European stage. In modern parlance, it was a 'hedging strategy' to win time by tacking carefully between the belligerent parties, doing the minimum necessary to maintain relations with both without committing itself fully in either direction. That is, Vienna wanted to avoid antagonising Napoleon while both limiting frictions with the tsar and keeping a wary eye on Russian behaviour.[9]

Schwarzenberg, the Austrian commander, understood this strategy very well. Although small engagements remained possible, the Russians and Austrians exerted themselves to avoid encounters and Schwarzenberg arranged with the Russians for his positions northeast of Warsaw to be outflanked so he would have an excuse to retire behind the Vistula.[10] This was just the prologue to further retreats. In accordance with orders he had received from Vienna and after several face-to-face exchanges with Russian officers and officials, Schwarzenberg concluded a temporary ceasefire agreement with the Russians, arranged for the transfer of Warsaw to Russian control and withdrew behind the Pilica River well to the south. The last Austrian troops evacuated Warsaw on 7 February, and, by the end of the month, the Auxiliary Corps was ensconced in a semicircle of cantonments north and northeast of Krakow (Kraków).

The French initially welcomed Schwarzenberg's efforts to secure a ceasefire as a means to gain time and curtail the Russian pursuit. The Saxons in particular benefited as Reynier was able to retire behind a screen of more or less neutral Austrian outposts. This brought a temporary respite from the constant alarms and skirmishes the 7th Corps had been experiencing, but the Saxons expressed astonishment and suspicion at reports that Austrians and Russians were lodging quite amicably within the same villages. 'The outpost duty was less burdensome for the Austrians', recorded the Saxon contingent's march journal, 'as they lived in the best understanding with the Russians and all hostilities were prohibited.'[11] The direction and extent of Schwarzenberg's retreat, however, could only have negative consequences for any hope of holding along the Vistula or retaining Polish territory. Napoleon had intended, if withdrawal became unavoidable, that all three of the corps around Warsaw should retire in a general westerly direction towards Kalisch (Kalisz).[12] He was infuriated when he learned that the Austrians had turned south for Krakow. 'It is the first step towards defection,' he told the Austrian envoy who delivered this unwelcome news in Paris on 3 February, 'You want to take your Auxiliary Corps out of play.'[13] Luckily for the Austrian commander, his move came while the French were shifting their headquarters to Posen (Poznań) and Murat was handing over command to Eugène, these developments thus providing a convenient cover for the Austrian withdrawal and the peaceful delivery of Warsaw to the approaching Russians.[14]

The movements undertaken by the Poles exacerbated the dangers to the French position between the Oder and the Vistula. Fearing that Napoleon's debacle in Russia would mean their country would once more be extinguished through absorption by Russia and Prussia, some Polish leaders made overtures to the tsar to install him on a Polish throne and thereby retain some degree of national existence. These efforts came to naught, but the tense and uncertain circumstances had an impact on military operations in that Poniatowski marched his corps of recruits to the little citadel of Częstochowa 200 kilometres southwest of Warsaw on what became the left flank of the Austrian line. Poniatowski's motives are obscure. As historian Jarosław Czubaty observes, he may have been simply playing for time, placing the army out of harm's way in the hopes that either Alexander or Napoleon would make a clear declaration of support for Poland's independent future.[15] Whatever the case, his actions took the bulk of the Polish contingent out of the operational picture for the next several months. Given the Saxon king's at least nominal suzerainty over the Duchy of Warsaw, the fate of these troops, and a small Saxon detachment that would escape with them in mid-February, was of great concern in Dresden and they would become the object of intense Austro-Saxon negotiations in the coming months.

In the near term, the operational consequences of these Austrian and Polish moves in late January and early February were substantial. They not only undid any French plans to hold the line of the Vistula they also placed most of Poland under Russian occupation, thereby eliminating the possibility of the duchy supplying Napoleon with recruits and resources. Furthermore, and more directly germane to the focus here, the fact that these two allied corps marched southwest towards Krakow rather than west towards Kalisch left Reynier on his own in a broad, flat, impoverished land swarming with Cossacks. His 7th Corps, composed of two Saxon divisions and a French one (including three Würzburg battalions) under GD Pierre Durutte, numbered some 15,000 men and was thus a respectable force, especially in the circumstances prevailing in early 1813. Unsupported, however, his command would be vulnerable as it detached several battalions to garrison Modlin (French, Saxon and Würzburg) and set out from Warsaw on 3 February to make its freezing way to Kalisch.

Meanwhile, the Prussian defection and Russian pressure had panicked Murat into ordering a hasty retreat. While he, the army's headquarters and whatever could be collected as relatively combat-capable units headed for Posen, the survivors of the old corps of the Grande Armée were shifted from the Vistula to new assembly points in the fortresses along the Oder

River. These troops, including various Rheinbund remnants and formations, reached their assigned destinations in late January and early February where they would form foundations for the garrisons that held these fortresses during the spring campaign. Murat, however, was no longer in command. A poor choice to lead a broken army in desperate circumstances, the King of Naples was overwhelmed by his responsibilities and anxious about the security of his throne. On arrival in Posen, therefore, he hurriedly turned command over to Eugène and departed for Italy on 17 January behind a cloud of excuses.[16]

Eugène was shepherding the remains of his 4th Corps towards Glogau (Glogow) when an urgent message called him to Posen. Murat, eager to flee, had to be persuaded to await Eugène's arrival before beginning his journey, but the transfer of command could hardly have been more peremptory and Eugène, utterly unprepared, thus suddenly found himself leading a scattered and shattered army in some of the most difficult circumstances imaginable. 'All the affairs here have been left in a grand confusion,' he told his wife, 'I shall have a terrible task; I dare not hope to emerge with glory.'[17] Napoleon was incandescent when Eugène's letter informed him of Murat's departure, but he could do little at distance other than dictate a scathing letter to his brother-in-law Murat and approve his stepson Eugène as the army's interim commander. 'My son, take command of the Grande Armée,' he wrote, 'I am sorry that I did not give it to you on my departure.'[18] For the next three months, that is until Napoleon's arrival in person, the dutiful Eugène would therefore be responsible for the imperial forces in Germany.[19]

The mobile forces available to Viceroy Eugène when he assumed command on 17 January were few. These consisted principally of a 'corps d'obsérvation' of 15,000 that he organised into four small 'divisions' posted in and around Posen east of the Warthe (Warta) River: one each of French, Poles, Bavarians and the remnants of the Imperial Guard along with a brigade of Westphalian replacements. Nonetheless, considerable numbers of fresh troops were gathering west of the Oder around Berlin, especially a fine pair of divisions that had marched up from Italy under GD Paul Grenier (29,000) and another division slowly assembling from various fortress garrisons (7,300). There was also a small 'division' of some 2,550 mostly Saxon troops under GD Joseph Morand in Stralsund, but this seems have been largely forgotten by French headquarters.[20] Eugène could no longer count on the Prussians, but he hoped that Schwarzenberg, Reynier and Poniatowski would soon arrive on the southern banks of the Warthe east of Kalisch on his right. In this he was to be disappointed, as described above, and only Reynier's 7th Corps was destined to join him. All of these organisations, however, even Grenier's divisions from Italy, were woefully deficient in cavalry. That arm had suffered more than any other in Russia and its much-diminished regiments were attempting to reconstitute west of the Elbe. Beyond these relatively mobile formations, Eugène also had the troops assigned to the numerous fortresses along the Oder and to the east. The largest of these was the force in Danzig (the future 10th Corps of some 30,000) but smaller garrisons were being collected in Stettin (Szczecin), Küstrin (Kostrzyn) and Glogau from the remnants of the Grande Armée. Additionally, a large Bavarian brigade occupied Thorn (Toruń) on the Vistula, Reynier had left a mixed garrison of French, Germans and Poles in Modlin north of Warsaw and a small force of Poles held Zamosc in the distant southeast.[21]

Eugène, thirty-one years old in early 1813, was an experienced and competent officer. His military talents are often underrated, but he had performed well in 1809 after initial setbacks and had capably led his 4th Corps during the Russian campaign. The circumstances he faced on assuming command that January, however, would have taxed the most skilful general and Eugène would often be found wanting in the coming weeks. His first misstep was the relatively early abandonment of the Posen position when only under modest pressure from Russian probes. Overestimation of enemy strength, the pervasive fear of Cossacks and other raiding detachments, the increasing hostility of his supposed Prussian allies and the weak state of his own forces were all understandable factors contributing to his decision, but more firmness and aggressive behaviour might have caused the enemy to hesitate. The 1812 campaign had left the Russians almost as exhausted as the French and, although Eugène could not know it, there were strong voices in the tsar's camp arguing for a halt to further advances into Germany (*see below*). Instead of a more pugnacious response, Eugène chose to withdraw, thereby confirming the Russian and Prussian (and Austrian) conviction that the French were demoralised and incapable of resistance. Worried by reports of enemy detachments edging around his left flank and alarmed at the destruction of a half-formed Lithuanian cavalry regiment by an audacious band of Cossacks, he succumbed to the general gloom in his headquarters and ordered a withdrawal. Whether he was justified in retreating from Posen or not, he compounded his strategic problem by spreading his small *corps d'observation* along the left (western) bank of the Oder in a cordon defence that dispersed his command and earned Napoleon's ire. The last unit to clear Posen (the Bavarian 'division') thus marched off on 13 February headed for Crossen (Krosno Odrzańskie) while other elements made for Frankfurt-an-der-Oder, Küstrin and Schwedt, leaving his little command spread in a thin screen across a front of 150 kilometres in separated detachments.

More bad news followed. To the south, Reynier suffered a sharp defeat when he was caught unprepared at Kalisch on 13 February, the same day that the Bavarians were leaving Posen. His corps maintained itself in good order, but the losses incurred left no option but retreat to Glogau. On Eugène's northern flank, aggressive Russian raiding detachments composed of Cossacks supported by small numbers of regulars and a few guns, made their way across the Oder north of Küstrin between 15 and 21 February. Some of these appeared unexpectedly outside Berlin on the 20th, generating anxious messages from Marshal Pierre Augereau, the city's commandant. In his nervousness, Augereau heightened the sense of imminent calamity with reports that the Prussian capital was about to erupt in bloody rebellion. Miniature disasters inflicted on a Westphalian replacement battalion and an Italian cavalry regiment by these Allied raiders only compounded the sense of defeat and discouragement in French headquarters. Eugène, who had already come to believe that he would have to retire behind the Elbe, thus saw his worst fears confirmed.[22] Rather than halting east of Berlin and showing a defiant countenance to gain time as the emperor desired, the viceroy left a garrison in the Spandau fortress and evacuated Berlin on the night of 3/4 March heading for Magdeburg and Wittenberg. The tiny Bavarian division commanded by General-Major (GM) Joseph Graf von Rechberg und Rothenlöwen was directed to Torgau and placed under Reynier's orders while Reynier himself marched for Dresden.[23]

By 9 March, Eugène had established his headquarters in Leipzig with the small Imperial Guard division and, other than fortress garrisons, almost all French and Rheinbund formations had crossed to the western bank of the Elbe. From right to left, these consisted of Reynier's 7th Corps, Rechberg's Bavarians and parts of the French 1st and 31st Divisions between Dresden and Meissen under the overall command of Marshal Louis Nicolas Davout. Torgau was occupied by Saxon GL Johann Adolf Freiherr von Thielmann with a variety of depot soldiers and new recruits numbering 6,000–8,000. A French garrison held Wittenberg with two divisions of a revived 11th Corps under Marshal MacDonald, while the new 1st Cavalry Corps was painfully trying to form itself west thereof. The new 5th Corps, 2nd Corps and 2nd Cavalry Corps were being constructed between Magdeburg and Stendahl under their respective commanders: GD Jacques Alexander Bernard Law Lauriston, Marshal Claude Victor and GD Horace François Bastien Sébastiani de la Porta. Finally, GD Joseph Morand was marching from Stralsund towards

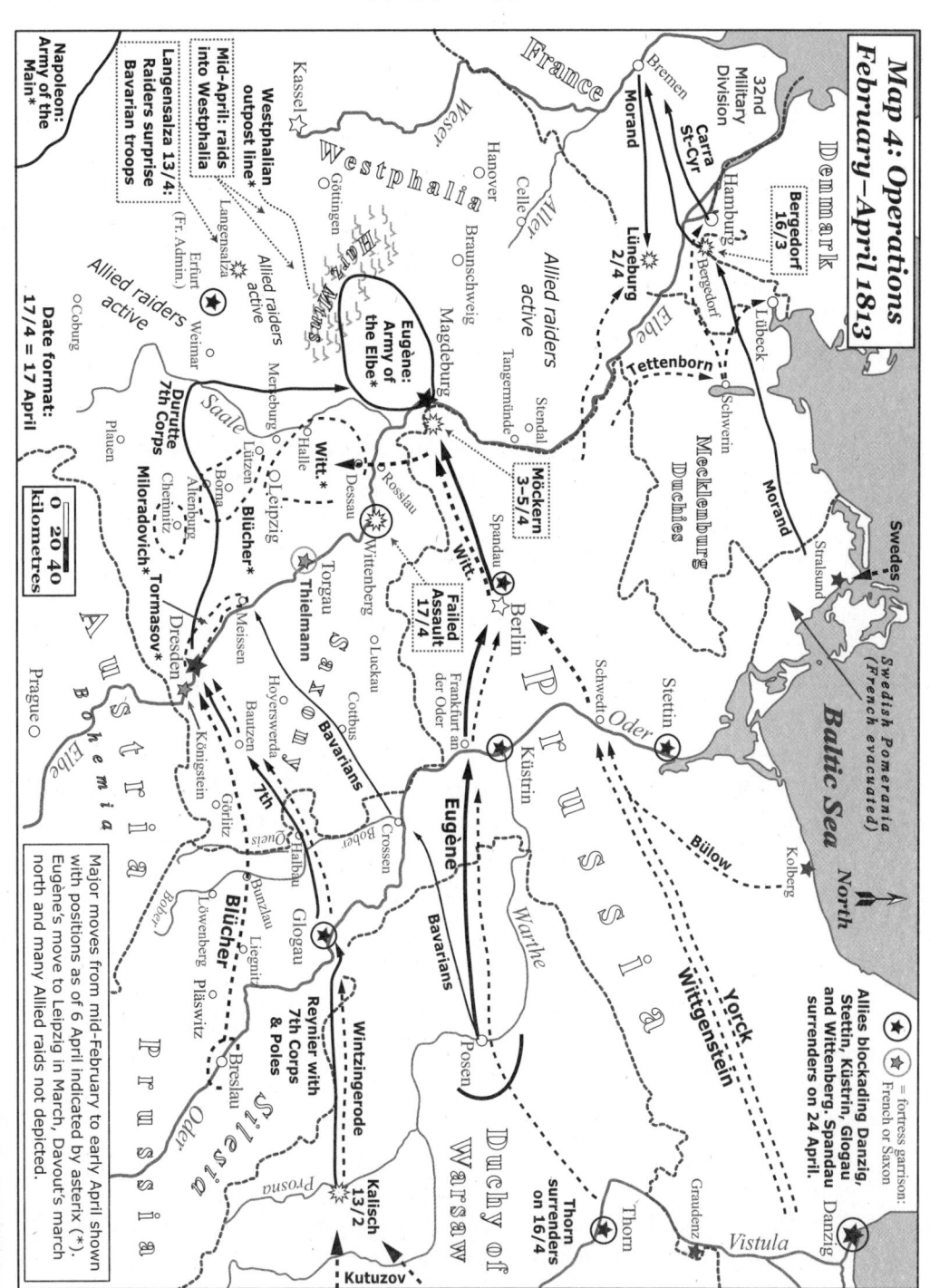

Hamburg with his small command of Saxons and French, while GD Claude Carra Saint-Cyr and the tiny Hamburg garrison were anxiously observing the rapid spread of anti-French sentiment within the population. Although Eugène's command, now entitled the 'Army of the Elbe', was growing in numbers as it gathered itself west of the great river, many of these units were hardly ready for active combat operations. The cavalry, such few squadrons as had been assembled, was in a particularly sad state. The viceroy's bleak outlook is thus hardly surprising. 'I hope that we will have a few weeks of tranquillity behind the Elbe,' he wrote to his wife on 8 March, 'and I hope the emperor will come soon, for all of this will be too much for me.'[24]

As Eugène was attempting to create a coherent defence behind the Elbe, disconcerting signs were appearing in the structure of the Rheinbund. Disturbances had flared in Berg, Frankfurt and Westphalia already and there were fears of wider popular unrest, but the most urgent problem was the increasingly ambiguous status of Saxony. The kingdom was not only one of the largest states in the Confederation and a major troop contributor, it was also clearly going to be the arena within which much of the coming campaign would occur. Napoleon would want to rely on the Saxon king, army, bureaucracy and people for soldiers, supplies, intelligence and political support during the fighting, while denying all these resources to the Coalition. The Allies, of course, sought to cajole or force Saxony to switch sides and repudiate the Rheinbund. The Saxon king, Friedrich August, had fled from Dresden to Plauen on 23 February as war neared his eastern frontier. Now on the western edge of his domain, he and his advisors endeavoured to craft a policy that would promote retention of the kingdom's territory and sovereignty (including the Duchy of Warsaw), ensure the safe return of the Polish and Saxon troops near Krakow and spare the country the ravages of war. While these deliberations were taking place, Thielmann in Torgau was to maintain a proper and strict but undeclared neutrality, permitting neither the French nor the Allies access to the fortress and curtailing Saxon contributions to French operations. This peculiar situation is discussed in some detail in Chapter 2, but at this point the main implication to note is that Saxony's behaviour meant the Elbe crossing at Torgau was not available to either belligerent and that the Saxon army was, for the time being, a passive observer rather than an active participant in the war.

Eugène's withdrawal behind the Elbe thus had multiple negative consequences for Napoleon's prospects in Germany, frustrating the emperor at the time and leading to harsh judgements by subsequent commentators.[25] Through the long retreat from the Vistula, Poland, Berlin, all of Prussia and much of Saxony had been abandoned to the slowly advancing Allies, depriving the French of important resources while granting control to their enemies. In addition to material considerations such as manpower, horses, food and manufactured goods, there were also important psychological and political repercussions. Psychologically, while the seemingly timid and listless French resistance boosted Allied morale, the French and their Rheinbund confederates were disheartened by the endless retreats, confusions in command and poor logistical arrangements. The fact that much of the French retreat had been occasioned by small raiding detachments largely composed of Cossacks only made the situation more humiliating for the French and more encouraging for their foes. Politically, the withdrawal behind the Elbe, as Napoleon had feared, 'brought the war to Germany', exciting France's enemies from the North Sea to the Alps, weakening its alliances and threatening the territory of the Rheinbund with direct invasion. Saxony's wavering allegiance was one sign of the potential threat. Though many in the Allied camp were exhilarated by the concatenation of successes that had carried their arms from the Niemen to the Elbe in three months, Russia and its new partner Prussia could not immediately capitalise on the situation, and it is the actions of the evolving alliance that must be considered next.

Consolidating a Coalition: Factions and Frictions

As Eugène retreated, the political–military situation was changing fundamentally to France's detriment. Through mid-March, the viceroy's only opponents had been Russia's weary forces. Although increasingly recalcitrant if not visibly hostile towards their French 'allies', the Prussians held themselves aloof. Yorck had declared himself neutral as has been seen, and other Prussian commanders were busily recruiting and rearming, allegedly to resume their place as part of the Grande Armée, but actually in preparation for taking the field against Napoleon. Likewise, King Friedrich Wilhelm III had transferred the entire Prussian court – including the French ambassador – from Berlin to Breslau (Wrocław) in late January ostensibly to speed mobilisation on Napoleon's behalf. Thanks to a 24 February 1812 Franco-Prussian agreement, there were no French troops in Breslau or elsewhere in southern Silesia. By removing himself from the area then under French occupation, therefore, the king no longer feared being taken captive and opened the way to closer coordination with Austria and Russia.

Prussia's overtures to Austria yielded little of substance.[26] Metternich in Vienna preferred to maintain the façade of the Franco-Austrian alliance while promoting a policy of armed mediation between the warring parties. Russia, on the other hand, had been pressing Prussia to abandon Napoleon and join 'the common cause'. The tsar's efforts and the urgings of anti-French members of the Prussian court and army finally led to the conclusion of a Russo-Prussian alliance on 27/28 February through the Treaty of Kalisch. The path to this agreement was unconscionably long from the Russian point of view. Friedrich Wilhelm's instinctive caution was one hindrance, but the greatest obstacle was the future of Poland. Prussia argued for the return of Polish lands it had acquired during the partitions of the 1790s but lost when Napoleon created the Duchy of Warsaw in 1807. For Alexander, however, this issue was non-negotiable: Poland must be controlled by Russia. On the other hand, Russia stipulated that 'the immediate goal [of the war] is the reconstruction of Prussia to a proportion that will assure the tranquillity of the two states'. As specified in a secret article of the treaty, this meant 'the complete security and independence of Prussia can only be solidly established by returning it to the true strength it had before the war of 1806'.[27] This pledge included not only the formerly Prussian territories west of the Elbe River (conquered by the French since the Revolution), but 'compensation' for the Polish regions it would have to forfeit to Russia. Such 'compensation', of course, could only come at the expense of the Rheinbund princes, most notably Saxony. Indeed, reporting on his meeting with Tsar Alexander in mid-February, a Prussian envoy recorded that, 'In the course of the conversation, the Emperor Alexander offered me Saxony, saying that Prussia must be aggrandised.' 'Saxony's conduct', observed the tsar, 'made it impossible to treat it otherwise than as a conquered country.'[28] The Saxon king could be compensated in Germany or Italy or elsewhere at some later point. Though this cavalier treatment of Saxony may have made sense in the short term to secure Prussia's signature on the treaty of alliance, it was also, as historian Dominic Lieven notes, 'storing up problems for the future'.[29]

Public announcement of the Treaty of Kalisch was deferred to allow more time for Prussian mobilisation, but with Berlin freed, the French west of the Elbe and ceaseless pressure to act from the Russians as well as from ardent activists within his own court, even the diffident Friedrich Wilhelm could delay no longer.[30] He declared war on France on 17 March. Royal proclamations were released 'To My People' and 'To My Army', Yorck was reinstated, and the pace of mobilisation was increased. Two days later Russian and Prussian representatives signed a convention 'on the subject of the territories of the Confederation of the Rhine' stating that 'the two powers have no other goal than to remove Germany from the influence and domination of France and to invite the princes and the peoples to join in the liberation of their fatherland [*patrie*]'. Following this vague call to action, the very next sentence contained a warning: 'Every German prince who does not respond to this appeal within a fixed time period will be threatened with the loss of his state.'[31]

A public proclamation issued by Kutuzov in the names of the Russian and Prussian rulers on 25 March contained much the same message. It promised 'the return of freedom and independence' from 'the disgraceful yoke' of French power, urging 'every German who wishes to be worthy of the name, be he prince, be he noble or if he stands in the ranks of the people, to join in the liberation plans of Russia and Prussia with heart and mind, with property and blood, with body and life'. It was, however, even more blunt in its threats:

> Their majesties believe they may rightfully expect this attitude, this zeal, from every German after the spirit that Russia's victories over the tottering world dominator have shown so clearly.
>
> And thus they demand faithful cooperation, especially from every German prince, and gladly assume that not one will be found among them who, by being a renegade from the German cause, shall show himself ripe for merited destruction by the power of public opinion or the might of just arms.
>
> The Confederation of the Rhine, that delusive chain that the Prince of Discord recently wrapped around Germany, after first ruining it and even abolishing its name, can no longer be endured as an effect of foreign constraint and an instrument of foreign influence.[32]

The two monarchs thus declared the 'dissolution' of the Rheinbund to be among 'the most specific of their intentions' in the coming war. At the same time, the proclamation took pains to assert that the tsar only aimed to extend 'a protective hand' over Germany and that the shape of the future Germany was to be left 'altogether and alone to the German princes and peoples'. Though aimed at assuaging any concerns on the part of rulers in the 'Third Germany', these words could hardly disguise the menace in the foregoing paragraphs, especially for monarchs who were keen to retain their extant lands and their sovereignty, even if limited, against all outsiders, be they French, Russian, Prussian, Austrian or fiery pan-Germanist in origin. Furthermore, along with its fine sentiments of freedom and independence, the 19 March convention described in some detail how Russia and Prussia intended to divide up 'all the lands that are occupied from Saxony up to the frontier of Holland with the exception of the former Prussian provinces and those of the House of Hanover' [the British royal family's lands] into 'five grand sections'. Each of these 'sections' would be expected to provide supplies to the Russo-Prussian armies as well as military forces consisting of a regular army, a militia (*Landwehr*) and a home guard (*Landsturm*). All was to be managed by a 'Central Administrative Council' of 'unlimited powers' with members appointed by Russia and Prussia; German states that joined the Coalition might be granted representation on this committee on a collective basis at a later stage.

These Russo-Prussian documents stored up several additional, intertwined 'problems for the future'. The first of these was the future political dispensation in Germany. That is, how would the new Germany be organised? To what degree would the major German powers, Austria and Prussia, exercise hegemony over their smaller neighbours? Would the outcome be a new conception of 'Germany', federalised under a constitution as some of the pan-Germanists hoped? Or would the war be another contest of princes, evicting the French but leaving the socio-political order undisturbed? How would Austria and Prussia reconcile their conflicting visions of their future positions in the 'Third Germany'? What role and influence would Russia have west of the Oder? Issues of this nature have less direct bearing on the focus of this study, but these and related concerns certainly informed the thinking of the Rheinbund rulers as they tried to peer beyond the immediate crises of 1813. Second, the schemes sketched in these early agreements incentivised the German princes with promises of 'liberation' from French dominance (and restoration for those who had been deposed by Napoleon), but they also contained powerful disincentives. Most obvious was the absence of any guarantees for the existing lands and ruling houses of the smaller German states. Instead, they were showered with dire threats of dispossession. Even those who joined 'the common cause' could not be certain they would retain what they already had. How were those previously dispossessed by Napoleon to be compensated, for instance, except at the expense of the existing Rheinbund monarchies? There was also the assumption that the German states, under direction of the Central Administrative Council, would support the war effort against France with soldiers and supplies. Departure from the Rheinbund, therefore, would not relieve the smaller German states from the requirement to provide men, munitions and materiel at the behest of 'foreign powers'.

The Coalition's direct appeals to 'the people' of the German states also generated anxiety. The Rheinbund rulers, howsoever enlightened, were all autocrats and all harboured deep fears of uncontrolled and uncontrollable domestic chaos stemming from popular revolutionary movements commonly, if rather imprecisely, termed 'Jacobinism'. Though they might wish to loosen or cut the bonds imposed by Napoleon, the Rheinbund monarchs, their bureaucrats and their officers had no wish to see their countries and societies torn apart by mob violence. Russian and Prussian proclamations that seemed to bypass local rulers and call on populations to rise up in rebellion were thus a cause for instant wariness if not outright alarm. The fact that Heinrich Friedrich Karl vom und zum Stein was appointed to the Central Administrative Council and soon became its de facto head only increased anxieties. Stein had been Tsar Alexander's principal advisor on German matters since June 1812; he had helped create a Committee of German Affairs to promote anti-Napoleon uprisings in Germany and form German military units to fight alongside the Russians (the Russo-German Legion). For many in the German states, indeed for many within the Prussian government, Stein's name was therefore synonymous with radical political and social change; he was a prophet of upheaval and a threat to thrones.[33] The question of popular insurrection as a part of the Coalition war strategy thus became another 'problem stored up for the future'.

The natures of the Allied sovereigns and their governments illustrate the depth of the challenge. The Russian tsar, the Prussian king and, later, the Austrian Kaiser, were all firm monarchical legitimists. These men and their courts had no interest in popular movements that might call their own authority into question; they looked askance at the passionate pan-German patriots promoting uprisings amongst the masses and the possible overthrow of kings, dukes and princes. How then could they threaten fellow monarchs with rebellion without bringing their own legitimacy into question? The planned removal of the King of Westphalia, Napoleon's young brother installed on the invented throne of a composite kingdom, could be explained as restoring the region's previous rulers to replace an alien upstart. But how could such a rationale apply to venerable dynastic houses such as the Wettins in Saxony or the Wittelsbachs in Bavaria? The tension between engaging the common people of Germany (the '*Volk*') against Napoleon without undermining monarchical traditions was never fully reconciled within Coalition councils during the campaigns of 1813, but dynastic legitimacy and popular unrest would influence the decisions made in the courts of the Confederation of the Rhine as they faced the coming storm.

While the Russian and Prussian governments were building foundations for their alliance, military planning and operations continued. Here, too, Russia and Prussia had to resolve differences over strategic approaches to the war. They also had to overcome significant physical limitations. In the first place, the Russians were divided on future operations. Tsar Alexander, full of messianic ardour, envisaged himself leading a grand crusade to defeat

Napoleon and throw the French back across the Rhine. In contrast, Kutuzov, his senior commander, believed that Russia had done enough in destroying the Grande Armée in 1812: further exertions on behalf of romantic notions of European freedom would only weaken Russia and strengthen its rivals, most especially Great Britain. The old marshal's prestige was such that Alexander could not simply push him aside and order a heedless advance.

In any case, the victorious Russian army was exhausted and weakened after the 1812 campaign, it needed time to rest, refit and call up reserves from inside the empire. Thousands of men had to be detached to occupy Poland and besiege or blockade the fortresses on the Oder, on the Vistula and as far south as Zamosc. In addition, some 9,100 men under Russian Lieutenant General Fabian Gottlieb von der Osten-Sacken (hereafter simply Sacken[34]) were assigned to reduce Częstochowa and keep an eye on Poniatowksi. The Russian advance therefore slowed, the main army halting around Kalisch in mid-February to recuperate and prepare for further employment. Prussia also needed time. Its army had been severely limited by Napoleonic restrictions and had to be rebuilt in great haste: regulars reorganised and re-equipped, reserve regiments embodied, a new militia called the *Landwehr* established and a home guard (*Landsturm*) created. All of these factors delayed the Allied advance until late March and thus granted the French some weeks to recover. Eugène was incapable of extending the period of reprieve as his demanding stepfather had desired, but he did preserve the bulk of his tattered forces, while Napoleon, backed by the enormous organisational power of the French state, would bring a large and growing army into central Germany much earlier than his adversaries had believed possible.

Awaiting the Emperor:
Developments in March and April

As described above, in early March Eugène had his army spread in a thin cordon along the Elbe from Dresden to Hamburg. His opponents had previously consisted largely of aggressive raiding detachments backed by several small Russian advance guard corps. Now that a formal Russo-Prussian treaty had been signed, however, the main Allied forces were beginning to cross the Oder and approach the Elbe in accordance with a strategic framework that had been concluded at Kalisch in the first days of March. In broad outlines, this strategy provided for the combined Russian and Prussian forces to advance along two axes. In the north, an army under the command of Russian General of Cavalry Peter Khristianovich Wittgenstein would press from the Oder to the Elbe through Berlin, while Prussian General der Kavallerie

(GdK) Gebhard Leberecht von Blücher would lead a second army from Silesia towards Dresden in the south. Overall command was vested in Kutuzov, whose 'main army' would follow between and several marches behind the other two from its encampments around Kalisch. Although significant forces would have to be detached to observe or blockade the fortresses on the Oder above and beyond the thousands already committed to cover the fortresses along the Vistula, the Allies hoped to compensate for limited numbers by flooding the lands ahead of the regular troops with small, active raiding detachments (*Streifkorps*).[35] These detachments, led by bold and dynamic younger officers, would capitalise on the Allied superiority in mounted troops and the psychological ascendancy they believed they had achieved over the seemingly timorous French.[36]

Initially, there were three principal detachments, all composed of Cossacks supported by some regular Russian cavalry and at most two light guns (*see Chart 3, overleaf*). As the Allies advanced, however, commanders created temporary parties to probe ahead of their main bodies and Prussian mobilisation led to the creation of several additional detachments (known as *Freikorps*), formed from Prussian regulars and volunteers and including infantry as well as cavalry. Swarming through Prussia and Saxony and across the Elbe, these agile, elusive groups spread havoc in the French rear areas, ambushing unwary columns of new recruits, capturing supplies, intercepting couriers, gathering intelligence and exciting local populations.[37] As will be seen, they were a persistent irritant to Napoleon, not only threatening the security of his communications but undermining confidence in his ultimate success, especially among sceptical or hostile portions of German populations.

With Eugène already retreating, the French offered little resistance to either the Allied advance guard corps or the various raiding detachments. Other than some delays in crossing the Oder and occasional scuffles between Russian raiders and French rear guards, therefore, the Allied advance proceeded swiftly and smoothly. The Prussian government accelerated the process by issuing orders for its forces to cross the Oder even before it had renounced its alliance with France. The rehabilitated General Yorck, for example, was placed under Wittgenstein's orders on 8 March and began crossing the Oder on the 12th and 13th, followed by the other available Prussian forces in the north.

By 17 March, the day Prussia declared war on France, the Allied troops were well established between the Oder and the Elbe. In the south, Blücher's Prussian formations were collecting west of Breslau, while his Russian contingent under Lieutenant General Ferdinand Fedorovich Wintzingerode had its main body around Bunzlau (Bolesławice) and its advance guard at

> **Chart 3: Sample Allied Raiding Detachments, March–April 1813**
>
> ### On the lower Elbe, early March 1813
>
> #### Major General Chernishev
>
> | | |
> |---|---|
> | Kazan Dragoons | 2 squadrons |
> | Izum Hussars | 4 squadrons |
> | Don Cossacks | 5 regiments |
> | 1st Horse Artillery | 2 guns |
>
> #### Major General von Benckendorff
>
> | | |
> |---|---|
> | Finland Dragoons | 2 squadrons |
> | Combined Hussars | 4 squadrons |
> | Don Cossacks | 5 regiments |
> | Bashkirs | 1 regiment |
> | 5th Horse Artillery | 2 guns |
>
> #### Colonel von Tettenborn
>
> | | |
> |---|---|
> | Kazan Dragoons | 2 squadrons |
> | Izum Hussars | 4 squadrons |
> | Don Cossacks | 5 regiments |
> | 1st Horse Artillery | 2 guns |
>
> *Total:* approx. 4,000 men
>
> ### West of the Saale River, mid-April 1813*
>
> #### Major von Hobe
>
> | | |
> |---|---|
> | Braunschweig Hussars | I and II Squadrons |
> | Cossack detachment | 61 men |
>
> #### Major von Blücher
>
> | | |
> |---|---|
> | 1st Silesian Hussars | II and IV Squadrons |
> | 2nd Silesian Hussars | III and IV Squadrons, Jäger Detachment |
>
> * These were detached from Blücher's army. Similar detachments of Russian regulars and Cossacks operated west of Wittgenstein.
>   At full strength, the Prussian hussar squadrons should have numbered 150 troopers each plus 200 for the Jäger detachment, so the maximum strength of these detachments was approximately 360 and 800 respectively. Major von Blücher was the general's son.

Bautzen, only some 60–65 kilometres by road from Dresden. A raiding detachment under Major General Alexander Khristofovich Benckendorff observed the French garrison in Wittenberg, while another, under Major General Alexander Ivanovich Chernishev watched the Elbe west of Berlin opposite Tangermünde. In the north, Wittgenstein, whose advance troops had entered Berlin on 4 March and skirmished with the withdrawing French, remained in the Prussian capital and was joined by most of Yorck's corps (some of the

Prussians were watching Stettin or still approaching from the Oder). Of the so-called 'main army', Russian Lieutenant General Mikhail Andreyevich Miloradovich was around Glogau hoping to initiate a formal siege, but the reluctant Kutuzov and the rest of this central force were still at Kalisch, 160 kilometres to the east.

On the very northern edge of the Allied strategic array, Major General Friedrich Carl Freiherr von Tettenborn led yet another Russian raiding detachment. Though his force only consisted of some 1,400 horsemen and two guns, Russian confidence was so high that Tettenborn was given the mission of driving the French out of Hamburg. The situation in this portion of the theatre of war was explosive. French annexation of Hamburg, Lübeck and other Hanseatic territories in 1810 had provoked intense popular dissatisfaction compounded by oppressive actions by local French authorities and the ruination of the region's trade-based economy owing to Napoleon's Continental Blockade. Facing increasing popular unrest and outbursts of violence, the anxious French commandant, GD Carra Saint-Cyr, evacuated Hamburg on 12 March and fled to Bremen with his tiny garrison (at most 2,000–2,500 men). Lübeck, where similar disturbances had erupted, was likewise evacuated.[38] Just east of Hamburg were the Duchies of Mecklenburg-Strelitz and Mecklenburg-Schwerin, deeply discontented members of the Rheinbund that were eager to disavow the alliance and align themselves with Prussia and Russia.[39] Indeed, Mecklenburg-Strelitz had begun making overtures to the Prussian king as early as January 1813.[40] Tettenborn's arrival on 14 March provided an ideal excuse to change sides; by the end of the month, both duchies had joined the Coalition and were busily raising troops to fight against Napoleon 'in the noble struggle'.[41]

Continuing on towards Hamburg, Tettenborn entered annexed French territory and intercepted GD Joseph Morand's small division of Saxon and French troops (2,550) near Bergedorf on the Danish border on 16 March. As noted earlier, Morand's little command had been stationed in Swedish Pomerania and had been belatedly recalled as part of Eugène's general retreat behind the Elbe. Morand and Tettenborn skirmished indecisively on 16 and 17 March, but the French general was able to escape across the Elbe on the 17th before marching for Bremen. On the same day that the Prussian king released his appeals to his subjects and his army, therefore, Morand became the last French commander to cross the Elbe as part of the great retreat from the east. Tettenborn, for his part, rode on for Hamburg, entering the city to a tumultuous welcome on 18 March.[42] Similarly joyous crowds awaited the small detachment of his Cossacks that rode into Lübeck on the 21st.

The same day that Tettenborn entered Hamburg, Eugène was starting to reposition French forces in accordance with repeated orders received from Napoleon. The emperor was thoroughly dissatisfied with the viceroy's cordon deployment behind the Elbe and his attempt to retain Dresden. Napoleon would have preferred to hold Dresden as an anchor for his southern flank while also protecting the Hanseatic cities that had become part of metropolitan France after their annexation in 1810. The available forces were too slender for such an expansive task, however, and Eugène's dispositions left the troops so scattered that both strategic flanks were vulnerable. Napoleon decided to prioritise the northern flank along the lower Elbe, thus shielding the newly annexed regions with their economic and political significance while simultaneously preventing Allied raiders from sparking unrest in fragile Westphalia or pushing on to Holland.[43] He thus commanded a concentration around Magdeburg and a shift in strategic emphasis from Dresden to Hamburg.

Eugène, of course, moved to comply with the detailed written instructions he received, further impressed upon him by the personal visit of one of the emperor's senior staff officers. Davout, whom Eugène had just sent to Dresden, was thus dispatched with reinforcements to restore the situation in the north along the lower Elbe. The marshal set out on 19 March after blowing up part of Dresden's iconic Augustus Bridge, a purely military act, but one that had political repercussions as it infuriated the city's residents and led to a personal protest from König Friedrich August to Napoleon. Davout's departure left only the remains of Reynier's 7th Corps between Dresden and Meissen. This weak force was further reduced when the Saxon division marched off to Torgau on orders of its king. GD Durutte, commanding in place of the ailing Reynier, had no choice but to retreat with his feeble 'division' and Rechberg's Bavarians when Wintzingerode's corps appeared east of Dresden on 26 March. Blücher arrived four days later and the Allies easily advanced west of the Elbe to the Saale River against minimal resistance. Under constant harassment from Allied raiders, the sad remnants of Durutte's two divisions escaped to the west before turning north to join Eugène.

With the withdrawal from Dresden, the southern end of the French line swung back far to the west. Its pivot was the great fortress of Magdeburg, a key bridgehead Napoleon was determined to hold to allow access to both sides of the Elbe and especially to pose a threat to Berlin. In accordance with the emperor's instructions, Eugène moved most of his army to the area west of Magdeburg in the second half of March but crossed back over the Elbe to the east on the 31st in the hopes that the potential of a march on the Prussian capital would draw the Allies north and slow their advance. Eugène did not have his heart in this operation, however, and the straggling series of encounters between 2 and 6 April known as the Battle of Möckern, only resulted in a dreary retreat back across the river.[44] Eugène's opponents, Wittgenstein's Russians and Prussians, had fought with great vivacity and these combats, otherwise marginal, thus became another psychological boost for the Allies who boasted of defeating a French drive on Berlin. The viceroy's men were correspondingly disheartened. Wittgenstein, emboldened by his success at Möckern, pushed south to cross the Elbe at Rosslau and join Blücher on the left bank. Although an attempt to storm Wittenberg on 17 April was thwarted by the alert French garrison, Spandau capitulated on the 24th, releasing the besiegers to join Wittgenstein. By the end of the month, Wittgenstein was thus well across the Elbe, his headquarters in Leipzig and his corps ensconced from that great commercial city to Halle and Dessau. Blücher was just to the south, headquartered at Altenburg. Reconnaissance parties from both armies ranged far to the west, capturing couriers, disrupting Rheinbund mobilisation and repeatedly inflicting small but humiliating defeats on isolated French and German detachments.

The French suffered another embarrassing setback along the lower Elbe in early April. GD Joseph Morand, who had been in Bremen after his escape from Tettenborn on 17 March, had now been ordered to Lüneburg to quell unrest and re-establish French presence in the area. He reached the city on 1 April but was set upon by several of the Allied raiding detachments in a coordinated surprise attack the next day. Despite tenacious resistance by his division, mostly composed of Saxon infantry, he was soundly defeated, and his men were forced to surrender. Badly wounded in the fighting, he died three days later. Davout's advance guard appeared in Lüneburg later that day, but the enemy had wisely retired. Unable to retrieve the situation, the marshal withdrew southwest behind the Aller River on 11 April, while GD Dominique Vandamme, the new commandant in Bremen, covered the line along the Weser to its outlet to the sea.

By late April, therefore, French dispositions in central Germany resembled a vague 'V' with Magdeburg at its apex, most of Eugène's Army of the Elbe gathered west and southwest of the city towards the rugged Harz Mountains with Westphalian outposts stretching southwest beyond that range and a strong garrison in Erfurt on the right. The northwestern arm of this imaginary, canted 'V' was comprised of Davout (including Vandamme) arrayed behind the Aller and Weser Rivers. The army would remain in these general positions until the end of April when the force Napoleon was now assembling south and west of Erfurt arrived on the scene.

As these military moves were taking place and the viceroy awaited the emperor, a political arrangement between Austria and Saxony was threatening to destabilise the Rheinbund. As already mentioned, Friedrich August had fled his capital in February, first to Plauen on the western edge of his realm, then to Regensburg in Bavaria and, finally to Prague inside the Habsburg Empire. Along the way, his advisors had cajoled him into signing a 'convention' with Austria on 20 April that made his kingdom a Habsburg ally and fundamentally contradicted his ties to Napoleon and the Rheinbund. The agreement was secret, but Napoleon was suspicious and recovering Saxony as a confirmed, contributing member of the Confederation would be one of his key political–military goals in the coming campaign.

Saxony was not Napoleon's only worry as far as the Rheinbund was concerned. The Confederation was an important symbol of his empire's prestige, solidity and security as well as a crucial source of men, mounts and material. Moreover, his lines of communication for the coming campaign would cross the lands of the Rheinbund princes, the 'indispensable base for the campaign that was opening' in the words of French historian General René Tournès. The emperor had to be certain of their active cooperation. Minor disturbances in Berg and Frankfurt had been quickly quelled but he was keenly aware of the prevalence of anti-French sentiment.[45] He was thus prepared to be lenient to retain the support of the Rheinbund states, but he could not allow such a major ally as Saxony to slip into putative neutrality or join the Coalition camp lest the entire Confederation edifice begin to crumble. Deft diplomacy was one dimension of his strategy as he moved east that spring but what the strategic situation demanded was a dramatic military victory to reassure his allies, deter Austria, daunt the Russo-Prussian Coalition and bolster the confidence of his own soldiers.

The Russian and Prussian governments were also approaching Saxony as their armies settled into new positions towards the end of April. Having placed their hopes in Austria, however, the Saxons politely turned aside the rather minatory Allied requests just as they had rebuffed Napoleon's demands in flowery but hollow language. This did not stop the Russians and Prussians, of course, from occupying the kingdom. Wittgenstein, as noted earlier, had his command assembled in and west/northwest of Leipzig, Saxony's commercial heart, while Blücher was concentrated more or less between Borna and Altenburg south of the city. Both Prussian and Russian commanders sent numerous raiding detachments to scour the countryside west of the Saale, harassing French and German units, intercepting communications and gathering crucial intelligence as far west as Erfurt and Coburg. One of these, for instance, inflicted an embarrassing surprise on Rechberg's retreating Bavarians at Langensalza on 13 April.

As for the Allied 'main army', Miloradovich's corps was on Blücher's left around Chemnitz and Tormasov's between Meissen and Dresden. The Russian tsar and Prussian king had also arrived in Dresden where they and their generals would have discussions with the Torgau garrison commander, Saxon General Thielmann. The belated arrival of these two corps from the main army (they did not reach Dresden until 22 and 24 April respectively) was the cause of enormous irritation for many Prussians who were urging a relentless pursuit of the injured French forces. The delay was broadly attributed to Kutuzov's distrust of the Prussians and his distaste for engaging in a lengthy war far from Russia's borders. Many subsequent commentators have agreed that a more energetic Allied advance might have crippled Eugène's army and made Napoleon's recovery even more difficult.[46]

However one judges the potential dividends of a more rapid Allied pursuit, Kutuzov, the principal obstacle, was now removed. The old marshal died on 28 April, freeing the tsar and Coalition councils from his cautions, but also presenting the problem of selecting a new overall commander. The choice fell upon Wittgenstein. His aggressive performance in the campaign thus far – including the putative great 'victory' over Eugène at Möckern – and his rather inflated reputation from 1812 made him seem a good candidate.[47] Unfortunately for Allied prospects, he was junior in rank to both Miloradovich and Tormasov, so the two of them would only accept direct orders from the tsar; Wittgenstein could at best invite their cooperation. This hardly boded well for unity of command in the coming campaign.

In addition to the field forces now more or less under Wittgenstein's constrained command, the Allies still had to contend with the many fortresses to the east and other rear area security concerns. Thorn had capitulated on 16 April, but Danzig, Modlin and Zamosc in Poland still held out, as did Stettin, Küstrin and Glogau on the Oder. The Allies could not yet afford to open formal sieges against any of these places, but they all required blockading forces that subtracted men and guns from the field armies west of the Elbe. Likewise, they could not do anything but observe the French garrisons in Wittenberg and Magdeburg, while Thielmann in Torgau, friendly interactions with Allied rulers and officers notwithstanding, continued to deny access to that key fortress. One bit of good news for the Allies was that the Polish garrison in Częstochowa surrendered to Russian General Sacken on 7 April and the bulk of Poniatowski's troops withdrew into Austria. Under a soon to be concluded Austro-Saxon accord, they and the small Saxon detachment that had escaped the Kalisch defeat would be allowed (disarmed) to march through Austria to Saxony. Sacken's division was thus free to join the forces in Germany, but it would not arrive until after the two great battles that were about to erupt between the main armies.

Enter the Emperor: The Battle of Lützen

Napoleon now appears at the head of a large new army and the pace of operations accelerates dramatically. This new army, the 'Army of the Main', had seemingly arisen out of nothing thanks to what Blücher's chief of staff, General Gerhard von Scharnhorst, called Napoleon's 'astonishing activity'.[48] Although it was hastily assembled, just beginning to train, almost devoid of usable cavalry and short on artillery, it was still a formidable force, especially under the emperor's personal leadership. Numbering some 135,000 men and 320 guns, it was divided into 3rd, 4th, 6th and 12th Corps plus the Imperial Guard. Not all of these troops would be available for the opening clash with the Allied army on 2 May, but combined with the 58,000 of 5th Corps, 11th Corps and 1st Cavalry Corps from Eugène's Army of the Elbe, this revived Grande Armée would give Napoleon a substantial numerical advantage over his opponents in the coming battles. As far as German contingents were concerned, Eugène's army only contained two squadrons of fine Würzburg light cavalry with 11th Corps and a small band of dogged Hessian light infantry attached to GD François Roguet's Imperial Guard division. The Army of the Main, on the other hand, included the 39th Division of Baden and Hessian troops in 3rd Corps as well as the Baden light horse, while the 38th (Württemberg) and 29th (Bavarian) Divisions were slated to join the 4th and 12th Corps respectively.[49] A 37th Division composed of Westphalians was also to be created, but it had not yet been assigned to a corps. Some of these Confederation Germans were still en route to their corps when the campaign opened, and, just as in France, many thousands more were being collected, equipped, organised and trained all across the Rheinbund states. They might miss the first battles, but they would not miss the war.

Napoleon's intention was to force a battle west of the Elbe to restore his political fortunes. It was particularly important to retrieve drifting Austria as a true partner (or prevent its desertion to his enemies), pull Saxony back into full cooperation, reassure his other Rheinbund allies and quash the hopes of anti-French German patriots. With luck, he might drive the Allies apart, exacerbating the inherent tensions in Russo-Prussian relations to cause a military–political crisis. He was painfully aware of his inferiority in cavalry and artillery, but his enemies were not fully assembled as far as he could

Spring of Disappointment

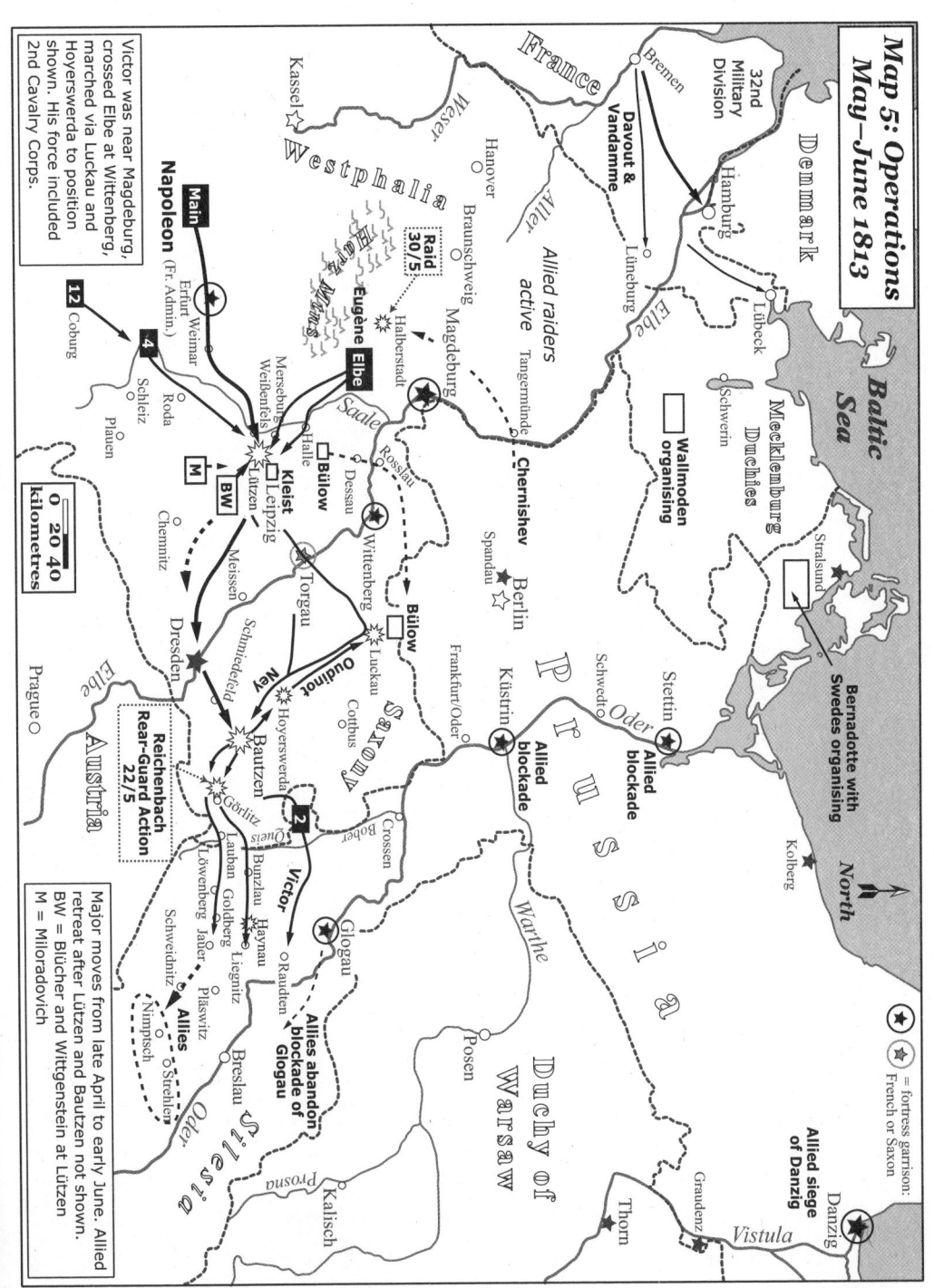

Map 5: Operations May–June 1813

Chart 4: *French Forces at the time of Lützen, 2 May 1813*

Army of the Elbe — *Viceroy Eugène de Beauharnais* — 82,000 men, 146 guns

Imperial Guard Division	GD Roguet	
5th Corps	GD Lauriston	16th, 17th, 18th, and 19th Divisions (17th detached, not at Lützen)
11th Corps	Marshal MacDonald	31st, 35th (French/Italian), and 36th Divisions
1st Cavalry Corps	GD Latour-Maubourg	

Partly formed, not at Lützen

2nd Corps	Marshal Victor	
2nd Cavalry Corps	GD Sébastiani	

Re-forming

Durutte's division		to be new 7th Corps with Saxon contingent

Forming

Polish division	GD Dąbrowski	

Army of the Main — *Emperor Napoleon, commanding in person* — 135,000 men, 320 guns

Imperial Guard	Marshal Mortier	
3rd Corps	Marshal Ney	8th, 9th, 10th, 11th and 39th (Baden/Hesse) Divisions
4th Corps	GD Bertrand	12th, 15th (Italian), and 38th (Württemberg) Divisions
6th Corps	Marshal Marmont	20th, 21st and 22nd Divisions
12th Corps	Marshal Oudinot	13th (French/Neapolitan), 14th, and 29th (Bavarian) Divisions

Other French and Allied Forces

Along the lower Elbe	Marshal Davout & GD Vandamme	26,000 men, 46 guns
In Westphalia	GD von Hammerstein	37th Division forming
In Austria	GD Poniatowski	Polish army with Saxon detachment, to be 8th Corps
Danzig garrison	GD Rapp	later designated 10th Corps
Modlin garrison	GD Daendels	
Zamosc garrison	GB Hauke	
Stettin garrison	GD Grandeau/GB Dufresse	
Küstrin garrison	GB Fornier d'Albe	
Glogau garrison	GB Laplane	
Magdeburg garrison	GD Haxo	
Wittenberg garrison	GD Lapoype	
In Torgau	GL Thielmann	11,000 Saxons, maintaining neutrality

All figures rounded and approximate to indicate 'present under arms'.

Sources: Osten-Sacken, *Geschichte des Befreiungskrieges*, vol. I, pp. 380–94; Caemmerer, *Frühjahrsfeldzuges*, vol. II, Anlage 1.

Chart 5: Allied Forces at the time of Lützen, 2 May 1813

Alexander I, Tsar of All the Russias, Friedrich Wilhelm III, King of Prussia
General of Cavalry Wittgenstein

Unit	Commander	Strength
I Russian Corps	Lieutenant General von Berg	8,000 men, 60 guns
Under Wintzingerode		14,450 men, 90 guns
II Infantry Corps	*Herzog Eugene of Württemberg*	
Cavalry Corps	*Major General Trubetzkoy*	
II Prussian Corps	*General der Kav. von Blücher*	25,480 men, 92 guns
I Prussian Corps	*GL von Yorck*	8,450 men, 40 guns
'Main' Army	*General of Cavalry Tormasov*	16,500 men, 136 guns
III (Grenadier) Corps	*Major General Konovnitsyn*	
V (Guard) Corps	*Lieutenant General Lavrov*	
Cuirassier Corps	*Lieutenant General Golitsyn*	
Under Miloradovich		12,960 men, 94 guns
IV Infantry Corps	*Major General Markov*	
Corps	*Lieutenant General Volkonsky II*	
Jäger Brigade	*Major General Karpenko*	
Cavalry Corps	*Lieutenant General von Korf*	
Prusso-Russian Corps	*GL von Kleist*	6,200 men, 32 guns
Prussian Corps	*GL von Bülow*	6,410 men, 24 guns
Other Allied forces		
En route to Bülow	*Prussian GM von Thümen*	1,900 men, 32 guns
Along the Elster River	*Lieutenant General Gorchakov II*	3,000 men, 12 guns
Along the lower Elbe	*Lieutenant General Wallmoden-Gimborn*	11,630 men, 24 guns; includes raiding detachments of Tettenborn, Chernishev and Dörnberg

En route from Thorn, Russian 3rd Army of the West
    General of Infantry Barclay de Tolly
Russian corps in southern Poland
    Lieutenant General Osten-Sacken
Russian occupation force in Warsaw
    Major General Pahlen
Russo-Prussian blockading forces at Wittenberg, Magdeburg, Stettin, Küstrin, Glogau, Danzig, Modlin and Zamosc

All figures rounded and approximate.

Source: Caemmerer, *Frühjahrsfeldzuges*, vol. II, Anlage 3.

tell, and he was confident that he enjoyed a numerical advantage overall. He hoped to drive the Allied light troops back across the Saale River and use that watercourse to shield his concentration. He could then unite with Eugène and push on for Leipzig where he would be in a position to threaten both Dresden and Berlin. Marching via Erfurt (3rd Corps, Guard, 6th Corps) and through Coburg (4th Corps), the Army of the Main pushed across the Saale at Weißenfels by 1 May. On its left, Eugène shifted to close the gap between the two armies and likewise crossed the Saale with 5th Corps, 11th Corps and 1st Cavalry Corps to assemble west of Leipzig with a garrison at Halle and Durutte's reinforced division west of Merseburg. The Württemberg division destined for 4th Corps and the slowly gathering 12th Corps were further to the rear. Small engagements were necessary to achieve these positions, most notably one fought west of Weißenfels on 1 May that saw the death of Marshal Jean-Baptiste Bessières, commander of the Guard Cavalry. Though his two armies were not as tightly concentrated as he might have wished, Napoleon planned to continue his march on Leipzig during the coming day (2 May) in hopes of precipitating the desired battle.

The Allies too sought a battle. They had already lost several weeks' time and, given French control of the major fortresses on the Elbe and Oder, a retreat would be difficult to halt before the Vistula. Such a retreat would be demoralising for their armies and damaging to their efforts to entice Austria and Saxony away from Napoleon. They knew themselves outnumbered, but believed that the quality of the veteran Russians, the enthusiasm of the Prussians and their great superiority in cavalry would allow them to prevail over the untested army of French conscripts. As it seemed clear the French were making for Torgau via Leipzig, Wittgenstein planned to concentrate the army between Leipzig and Altenburg with the aim of striking the right flank of Napoleon's columns as they marched from Weißenfels towards Leipzig. Believing that a weak flank guard had been identified around a cluster of four villages south of where the Leipzig highway passed through the village of Lützen,[50] Wittgenstein drafted a complex plan to attack on the morning of 2 May. In broad terms this plan envisaged defeating the supposed flank guard around the 'quadrilateral' of villages: Großgörschen (from which the battle takes its name for German authors), Kleingörschen, Rahna and Kaja (or Caja). With this flanking force destroyed, the Allies thought they could exploit their numerous cavalry to outflank Napoleon on his right (west), drive his armies away from their line of communications and force them back into the constricted and marshy terrain formed by the many watercourses around Leipzig.

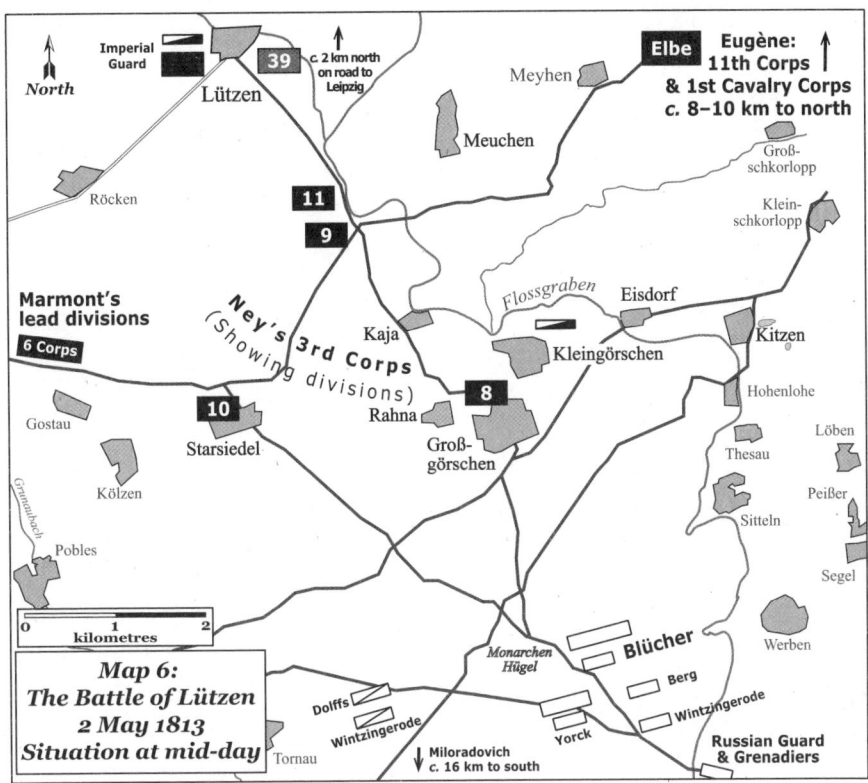

Map 6:
The Battle of Lützen
2 May 1813
Situation at mid-day

With this hopeful concept in mind, the Allies opened their attack on Großgörschen around noon on 2 May. They quickly discovered, however, that their reconnaissance had been faulty: they faced not a small flank guard of 2,000 men as expected, rather the 12,000 infantry of GD Joseph Souham's 8th Division belonging to Marshal Michel Ney's 3rd Corps. Moreover, the rest of Ney's massive corps, totalling some 45,000 men, was bivouacked nearby. On the other hand, Ney and Souham had been shamefully neglectful as far as security was concerned, failing to reconnoitre the local area as Napoleon had directed and, worse, failing to place even minimal outposts around their campsites. The Allies thus achieved complete tactical surprise.[51]

Surprise and the inexperience of the young French troops notwithstanding, the battle that ensued was brutal and bloody. Napoleon, who was near Leipzig with Ney when the sound of cannon fire drew their attention towards Lützen, reacted immediately by ordering the rest of his available forces to assist 3rd Corps: 6th Corps would move up to support Ney's right flank and 4th Corps would advance to threaten the Allied left, while 11th Corps and the 1st Cavalry Corps headed south from Leipzig to overlap the Allied right; Lauriston's 5th Corps was to follow. He took himself to Lützen and ordered the Guard to move forward to support Ney if necessary. The quadrilateral of villages soon became a chaotic charnel house and villages changed hands multiple times as the afternoon wore on. Both sides vied with one another in dogged bravery. Ney took a slight wound while leading the Baden Light Dragoons and Prussian Chief of Staff Scharnhorst was likewise wounded, in his case an injury that would prove fatal. The Prussian king was briefly under fire when he rode forward to check the progress of the fighting and to withdraw his son, the future Friedrich Wilhelm IV, from his post in the ranks of the Royal Guard at Kaja. 'What a sight!' exclaimed the young prince in a letter to his sister three days later, 'The whole village, all the ditches, all the hedges, everything was full of the dead and the dying.'[52] While the appalling carnage amongst the villages raged, both sides tried to gain advantages on the flanks. Allied attempts to press around the quadrilateral towards Starsiedel failed because of poor coordination and the appearance of Marshal Auguste Marmont's 6th Corps on Ney's right. On Ney's left, the Baden and Hessian troops of GD Jean Gabriel Marchand's 39th Division, his last uncommitted formation, advanced up to the Flossgraben opposite Kleingörschen to repulse Russian troops that were trying to press beyond the stream. Similarly, a Russian division sent to outflank the French through Eisdorf halted on encountering Marshal MacDonald's 11th Corps advancing from Leipzig.

Indeed, although the Allies at times thought themselves on the verge of a success, French power was slowly unfolding on both flanks. On the French right, GD Henri Gatien Bertrand's 4th Corps was advancing from the south, while MacDonald's 11th Corps and the 1st Cavalry Corps of GD Marie Victor Nicolas Latour-Maubourg, coming in from the north, began to make their presence felt on the French left. Although these commanders, and Marmont, behaved with excessive caution throughout the day, Wittgenstein could not ignore their menacing approach. From approximately 3 p.m., therefore, the Allied commanders became more concerned with avoiding a catastrophic defeat than achieving a grand victory. Allied prospects dimmed further when Ney retook Kaja and Napoleon, assembling a massive grand battery, launched four brigades of the Young Guard to reclaim the quadrilateral with the dramatic command *'La Garde au feu!'* The Prussians retained a tenacious grip on most of Großgörschen, but the other villages were lost. Likewise, the Russians in Eisdorf, outflanked and under attack, had to abandon that village in the face of MacDonald's overwhelming numbers. They retired to a position just east of Großgörschen as night brought the ferocious fighting to a close.

The day's relentless combat left both armies with horrendous casualty lists: some 22,000 French and more than 11,500 Allied soldiers were assessed as dead, wounded or missing after Lützen.⁵³ Compounding the horror of the high numbers was the fact that most of these men were struck within a confined space of less than five square kilometres from Starsiedel to Eisdorf and Großgörschen to Kaja. Considering these losses, the exhaustion of the army's infantry and the paucity of available reserves as compared to their estimate of the French, the Allied commanders concluded that retreat was their only option. That night, they undertook a long withdrawal that by 8 May would see the Russo-Prussian army across the Elbe and marching for Bautzen.

Napoleon's pursuit, though impeded by the exhaustion of his men, the sluggishness of some of his commanders and, above all, the lack of trained cavalry, kept up the pressure on the retreating Allies. He arrived in Dresden's Altstadt (the 'Old City' on the left bank of the Elbe) on 8 May, received a delegation of municipal officials, established his residence in the Saxon royal palace and immediately initiated preparations to cross the river. French *voltigeurs*, paddling over in boats, seized a bridgehead across the Elbe in the Neustadt (the 'New City' on the right bank) on the 10th and rapid repairs to the stone bridge Davout had destroyed in March allowed the army to begin crossing the very next day. By the evening of 11 May, some 70,000 troops were over the river at Dresden, while Ney had crossed at Torgau with some 45,000. Ney's command was a new sub-army composed of his 3rd Corps plus 2nd, 5th and 7th Corps as well as the barely organised 2nd Cavalry Corps. Reaching a strength of more than 80,000 men over the next two weeks, Ney's army would operate on Napoleon's left flank to threaten Berlin or intervene in Saxony if needed. Eugène, on the other hand, now leaves the scene. Worried about Austria's loyalty, Napoleon had dissolved the Army of the Elbe and sent his stepson to Italy to prepare that kingdom's defences should Austria turn against him.

Militarily, Lützen was a victory for Napoleon, but it was an incomplete one in that the enemy army had performed well and escaped intact. Moreover, his army, despite the undoubted courage and fervour of the soldiers, was showing itself deficient in the agility and speed of movement he expected. Nonetheless, the victory's political consequences were significant. Announced, with no little embellishment, to allies, neutrals and the public at large, Lützen partly rehabilitated Napoleon's reputation. It could not erase the Russian debacle of the previous year, but the battlefield success, conjoined with his ability to create a huge new army seemingly out of thin air sowed doubt among his opponents, encouraged his adherents and shocked the wavering back into obedience. Principal among the latter was König Friedrich August of Saxony. He had been residing in Prague since concluding his 20 April convention with Austria. Now, however, the French victory and a stiff note from Napoleon brought him back to Dresden where he arrived on 12 May. The king's return meant that orders were issued to Thielmann to allow French entry into Torgau and to return the Saxon troops to Reynier's command. Thielmann and his chief of staff, unwilling to join the campaign as French allies, fled Torgau and took service with the tsar, but Saxony's Rheinbund contingent once again entered the ranks of the Grande Armée to serve under French eagles. As Prussian military theoretician Carl von Clausewitz would later lament: 'What one expected from the people and the German princes did not come to pass, and if the edifice of the conqueror in Germany teetered for a moment and threatened to topple, the powerful arm of the emperor knew how to re-establish it quickly.'[54] Or, as partisan leader Major Ludwig Adolph Wilhelm von Lützow would report from his position in the French rear: 'The retreat of the main army thwarted for the moment the real objective assigned to my corps, as I sadly learned that despite all zeal and good will, every attempt to bring a people into revolt must fail without significant blows from the main force.'[55]

What the success at Lützen did not accomplish was the diversion of Austria from its path towards breaking with France and joining the Coalition. Aware of Metternich's increasingly intimate interactions with his enemies (especially after perusing Saxon documents and meeting Friedrich August), Napoleon undertook to at least delay what now seemed an inevitable outcome and gain time for his own rearmament. While prudently dispatching Eugène to Italy as noted above, he met with an Austrian envoy in Dresden to sound out Vienna's intentions. Given the expansive Russo-Prussian demands for peace, Austria's somewhat milder requirements and Napoleon's own excessive expectations, these discussions led nowhere. When the tsar rejected an appeal for direct Franco-Russian discussions, Napoleon concluded that his only hope for acceptable political conditions lay in battlefield victory.

Inadequate Victory: The Battle of Bautzen

The prospects for a decisive battlefield triumph seemed good when Napoleon moved against the Allied main army at Bautzen on 20–21 May.[56] On crossing the Elbe, he had followed the Allies due east with the bulk of the Grande Armée, but he also considered a march on Berlin – a leitmotif that would surface throughout 1813 – and thus sent Ney to Luckau with several corps in case a drive on the Prussian capital seemed feasible and advantageous.[57] When it became clear that the Allies had ensconced themselves in a fortified position along the Spree River at Bautzen, however, he called Ney south. His plan was to hold the Russo-Prussians in place with the 99,000 men of his main

Spring of Disappointment

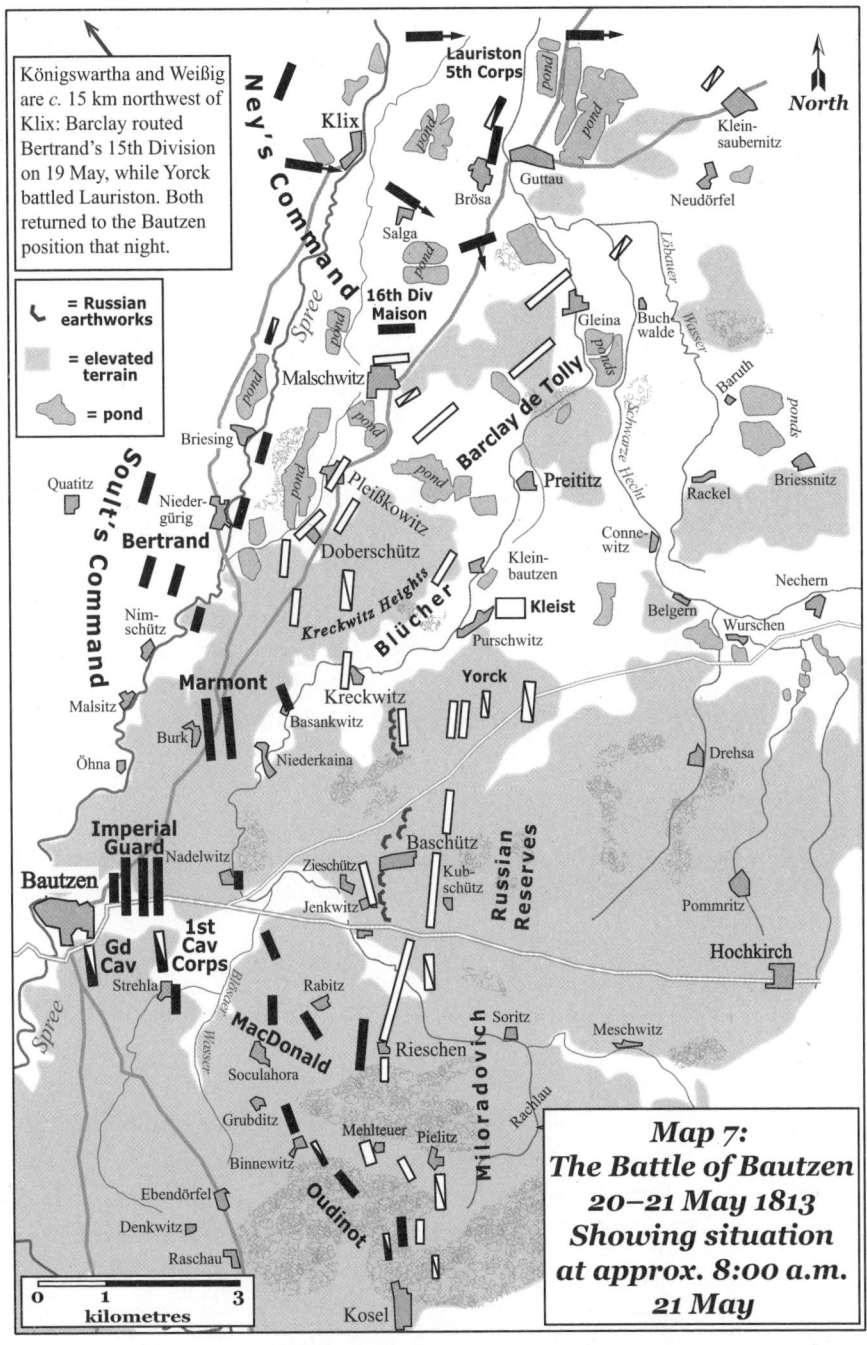

Map 7: The Battle of Bautzen 20–21 May 1813 Showing situation at approx. 8:00 a.m. 21 May

> ### Chart 6A: French Forces at Bautzen, 20–21 May 1813
>
> **Grande Armée** — *Emperor Napoleon, commanding in person*
>
> | | | |
> |---|---|---|
> | Imperial Guard | *Marshal Mortier* | |
> | 4th Corps | *GD Bertrand* | 12th, 15th (Italian) and 38th (Württemberg) Divisions |
> | 6th Corps | *Marshal Marmont* | 20th, 21st and 22nd Divisions |
> | 11th Corps | *Marshal MacDonald* | 31st, 35th (French/Italian) and 36th Divisions |
> | 12th Corps | *Marshal Oudinot* | 13th (French/Neapolitan), 14th and 29th (Bavarian) Divisions |
> | 1st Cavalry Corps | *GD Latour-Maubourg* | 1st (French/Saxon) and 3rd (French/Italian) Light Cavalry Divisions; 1st (French/Saxon) and 3rd (French/Italian) Cuirassier Divisions |
>
> **Under Marshal Ney**
>
> | | | |
> |---|---|---|
> | 3rd Corps | *Marshal Ney* | 8th, 9th, 10th, 11th, and 39th (Baden/Hesse) Divisions |
> | 5th Corps | *GD Lauriston* | 16th, 17th, 18th, and 19th Divisions |
> | 7th Corps | *GD Reynier* | 32nd Division (Durutte) and Saxon Division |
>
> **Approaching (not at Bautzen)**
>
> | | |
> |---|---|
> | 2nd Corps | *Marshal Victor* |
> | 2nd Cavalry Corps | *GD Sébastiani* |
>
> Note: The Saxons had now joined the Grande Armée (1st Cavalry Corps and the revived 7th Corps). Marshal Soult was in effective command of 4th Corps during the battle.

army (the Guard with 1st Cavalry, 4th, 6th, 11th and 12th Corps) and thus set the conditions for Ney to crash into the enemy's open right flank with his huge sub-command of some 65,000 (3rd, 5th and 7th Corps).[58] With both positional advantage and a tremendous numerical superiority, he hoped to cut the Allied line of retreat and crush them against the rugged mountains along the Austrian border. Although weakened by casualties at Lützen and serious attrition from long marches and poor provisioning, the revived Grande Armée had gained by the arrival of numerous replacement columns and reinforcements, among them the Bavarian 29th Division (12th Corps), the Württemberg 38th Division (4th Corps) and the Saxon army from Torgau (7th Corps). Napoleon would thus continue to enjoy a significant numerical edge when the armies next clashed.

The Allied army was in good spirits, but despite the arrival of reinforcements, it was still significantly smaller than the power Napoleon was able to

Chart 6B: Allied Forces at Bautzen, 20–21 May 1813

Allies — Alexander I, Tsar of All the Russias
Friedrich Wilhelm III, King of Prussia
General of Cavalry Wittgenstein

Advance Guard of Left Wing	General of Infantry Miloradovich
II Infantry Corps	Herzog Eugene of Württemberg
Cavalry Corps	Major General Trubetskoy
Lieutenant General Gorchakov II (Miloradovich during the battle)	
I Russian Corps	Lieutenant General von Berg
IV Infantry Corps	Major General Markov
VIII Infantry Corps (part)	
Cavalry Corps	Lieutenant General Uvarov
Russian Reserves	
III (Grenadier) Corps	Major General Konovnitsyn
V (Guard) Corps	Lieutenant General Lavrov
Cuirassier Corps	Lieutenant General Golitsyn
II Prussian Corps	General der Kavallerie von Blücher
I Prussian Corps	GL von Yorck
Prusso-Russian Corps	GL von Kleist
Russian 3rd Army of the West	General of Infantry Barclay de Tolly
Advance Guard	Lieutenant General Chaplits
Main body	General of Infantry Langeron
Reserve	Major General von Sass
Raiding detachments	
Major General Lanskoy	regulars/Cossacks
Colonel Figner	regulars/Cossacks
Major General Platov IV	Cossacks
Major General Karpov	Cossacks
Major Madatov	Cossacks
Major von Hellwig	Prussian regulars
Rittmeister von Colomb	Prussian regulars

All figures rounded and approximate.
Source: Caemmerer, *Frühjahrsfeldzuges*, vol. II, Anlage 9.

wield. Among the reinforcements was General Mikhail Bogdanovich Barclay de Tolly, who outranked Wittgenstein, causing further muddle in the army's leadership and leaving Tsar Alexander as de facto overall commander, a role he thoroughly relished. This was important because the tsar was convinced Napoleon intended to drive the Coalition army away from the Austrian border. He was thus obsessively worried about the Allied left, an anxiety that suited Napoleon's plans perfectly. Indeed, neither the Russian monarch nor any of his senior generals paid any attention to their open right flank. They were aware of French forces to the northwest but dismissed them as too small and too distant to be a serious concern. Barclay and Yorck did conduct a foray to the right on 19 May during which they had a stiff fight with Lauriston's advance guard and inflicted a sharp defeat on GD Luigi Peiri's Italian 15th Division of Bertrand's corps that had neglected its security (engagements at Weißig and Königswartha respectively). The Allies returned to their posts behind the Spree during the night, however, and no further notice was taken of the looming danger from the north.

Instead, Wittgenstein and others relied on earthworks that had been constructed on the hills east of Bautzen and their assessment of their army's qualitative superiority; they even entertained extravagant notions of taking the offensive once the French had committed themselves. The movements during the 19th and the assessment of French intentions left the Allied army arrayed with Russians holding the left and left-centre up to the eastern bank of the Spree, including Bautzen; the Prussians under Blücher's overall command were on the centre-right atop a series of connected hills called the Kreckwitz Heights; the Russian Guards and grenadiers were in reserve and only Barclay's relatively small force of at most 15,000 was left to watch the army's right flank. In all, the Russo-Prussian army numbered approximately 97,000 on 20 May to face the approaching 164,000 of the Grande Armée.[59]

The Battle of Bautzen, fought on 20 and 21 May, was a massive, sprawling affair.[60] Napoleon knew that Ney could not appear in force until 21 May, so the 20th was a preparatory phase. He aimed to lock the enemy in place, get his own troops across the Spree and threaten the Allied left to draw their attention away from Ney's approach. In this he was largely successful. Oudinot's 12th Corps and MacDonald's 11th crossed the river on the French right in the early afternoon, forcing the Russians to evacuate Bautzen and firmly establishing themselves on the eastern bank by evening. Despite tough resistance from the Russians and Prussians, Bertrand on the left and Marmont in the centre likewise secured suitable positions for the next day's battle. A vigorous Russian counterattack at dusk threw back Oudinot's lead division on the far right, but this could only have pleased Napoleon as it demonstrated the enemy's extreme sensitivity about his southern flank. On the other hand, the Allies could also be satisfied with the day's results. They knew they could not hold the line of the Spree against the numerically superior French, but they had fought well, had inflicted no few casualties on their attackers and had restored the situation, as they saw things, on their left. Prussian warnings and worries about Ney's approach and the weakness of the northern flank, however, went unheeded; the tsar and most of the Russian officers remained focused on the south and their fear of being driven away from Austria.

Action erupted early the following morning here on the southern end of the battlefield when Russian troops struck Oudinot's 12th Corps just after dawn. Oudinot's men held their ground and counterattacked, driving their assailants back and penetrating behind the main Allied line. MacDonald, seeing Oudinot in trouble, likewise attacked and made significant progress, pushing back the Russian defenders. These French advances and the dark columns debouching from Bautzen were clearly visible to the tsar and seemed to confirm his fears about the Allied left.[61] Despite Wittgenstein's protestations ('this is a false attack'),[62] Alexander thus ordered twelve battalions of Russian grenadiers from the army's reserve to repel what seemed a dire threat to his left. The two French corps held for a time, but eventually recoiled in the face of this pressure. Oudinot committed part of the Bavarian 29th Division to stem the Russian tide, but he continued to lose ground and appealed to Napoleon for reinforcements. The emperor, who could only have welcomed the Allied reinforcement of their left, sent no help and, by around 2:00 p.m., the situation on the southern flank had stabilised. The 12th and 11th Corps had given ground, but this was of minor consequence for Napoleon as he had invested his hopes in Ney's move from the north.

As Napoleon's intention was simply to pin the Allies in place with demonstrations while awaiting Ney's arrival, action in the centre of the field was limited during the early morning hours. He had instructed Ney to have his 3rd Corps reach Preititz by 11:00 a.m., with Lauriston's 5th Corps advancing on its left (east) to cut the Allied line of retreat. Once the emperor heard the sound of Ney's guns at Preititz, he would order the rest of the army forward in a general attack. For the first hours of the day, therefore, he moved the Guard and Marmont ahead (as the tsar had observed), while Marshal Jean-de-Dieu Soult brought Bertrand's corps across the Spree and Oudinot threatened the Allied left with MacDonald's support. These moves resulted in vigorous artillery exchanges and some tough infantry engagements as Bertrand's French and Württembergers made their way over the river.

Meanwhile, Marshal Ney was indeed advancing on Preititz and, initially, advancing as directed with Lauriston in the crucial position on his left to sever the enemy's route of retreat. The marshal drove off Barclay's outnumbered command and part of his 3rd Corps became involved in a bitter struggle for Preititz, but he first delayed and then allowed himself to become fixated on the Prussian position around the Kreckwitz Heights. Having already detached GD Nicolas Joseph Maison's 16th Division of Lauriston's corps to take Malschwitz on his right, he now called back Lauriston and the bulk of 5th Corps to throw them into the attack on Preititz and the heights.[63] This left a lone division of Lauriston's command to observe Barclay on the left and shoved too many troops into the narrow area between Preititz and Kreckwitz on Ney's right. Any hope of cutting off the entire Allied army thus vanished as Lauriston's battalions dutifully marched off to join the crowd threatening the heights. Nonetheless, these tumbled heights, occupied by Blücher's Prussians, now became the pivot of the Allied line as Napoleon unleashed Marmont and Bertrand. The Prussians stemmed a skilful and courageous attack by the Württemberg 38th Division of 4th Corps, but their situation was quickly deteriorating. With the Young Guard and Marmont advancing on their left, Bertrand in front, Maison charging into Pleißkowitz on their right and Ney advancing from Preititz more or less in their rear, they had no choice but to retreat. This was accomplished speedily and in good order between 3:00 and 4:00 p.m. after a tenacious defence that became the stuff of legend in Prussian histories.

Prussian resistance and Ney's errors notwithstanding, the battle was now clearly lost. The tsar thus turned management of the affair over to the frustrated Wittgenstein and rode from the field while the Allied army initiated a general retreat protected by its numerous horse. The French, lacking effective cavalry and disordered by the jumble of troops involved in the seizure of the Kreckwitz Heights, had only begun to pursue when a terrific thunderstorm brought combat to an end around 6:00 p.m. The Allies, having lost some 10,500 men, retreated into the wet night, while the French, whose casualty count apparently topped 20,000, rested, reorganised and prepared to pick up the pursuit.[64]

The Battle of Bautzen was thus another Napoleonic victory, but not of the scale the emperor both needed and had a right to expect. Oudinot and MacDonald had fought splendidly, and the troops of the Young Guard and Bertrand's corps had conducted themselves with valour and skill, but Ney's limited capacity as an army commander had deprived the Grande Armée of a potentially stunning triumph. Orders to the marshal could have been clearer and could have come earlier, but the basic faults lay in Ney first hesitating and then losing sight of the larger picture and allowing so much of his army to become enmeshed in the fight with the Prussians on the Kreckwitz Heights. Those Prussians, of course, were due the credit they received for their dogged and competent defence of their position, but it is difficult to see how they could have escaped had Ney fulfilled his instructions. Indeed, by maintaining

Lauriston's advance further east as ordered, Ney could have cut off the entire Allied army and driven it into the Bohemian mountains to the south with incalculable consequences for the overall political–military situation. As it was, Napoleon had to be content with another partial success that cost him heavily, left the enemy army intact, and likely would not be sufficient to deter Austria from joining the Coalition.

Pursuit to Armistice

Two weeks of exhausting retreat and pursuit followed the Battle of Bautzen. Without an effective mounted arm and facing an unbroken enemy, however, the best Napoleon could do was attempt to maintain incessant pressure on the Allies. In broad terms, the Prussians and Russians withdrew along two avenues of retreat: a northern through Görlitz, Bunzlau and Haynau (Chojnów) to Liegnitz (Legnica); and a southern through Lauban (Lubań), Löwenberg (Lwówek Śląski) and Goldberg (Złotoryja) to Jauer (Jawor). Napoleon pursued with 5th, 7th and 6th Corps in the north, while MacDonald led 4th and 11th Corps along the southern track; the Guard and Ney's damaged 3rd Corps followed in reserve. The emperor initially left Oudinot's 12th Corps (which had also suffered heavily in the fighting) to clean up the battlefield at Bautzen and chase down Cossacks along the Austrian border. To take Oudinot's place, he called in Marshal Victor with 2nd Corps and 2nd Cavalry Corps. These marched east from near Hoyerswerda north of Bautzen towards Raudten (Rudna) some 20 kilometres south of Glogau but did not participate in any of the combats.

Allied rear guards were both skilful and tenacious, leading to sharp clashes almost every day on both routes. Especially large actions occurred at Reichenbach on 22 May, the day after Bautzen, and on 26 May at Haynau where the pugnacious Prussians punished Maison's division of 5th Corps. Although he was straining the Allies, Napoleon's army was fraying badly, steadily increasing the distance from its support bases and reinforcements. Discipline, already dubious in the hastily built army, deteriorated and the wretched state of logistical arrangements led to a debilitating degree of straggling, sickness and desertion.

The Allied troops were not immune to the wearing erosion of extended daily marches, an alarming lack of provisions and the disheartening atmosphere of retreat, but they were falling back on their lines of communication and gathering in reinforcements as they moved east. The greater problem on the Allied side was the mounting friction between the Prussians and Russians over the quality of the army's leadership and especially over the direction of the retreat. The command issue was eased somewhat when Barclay de Tolly replaced the unsatisfactory Wittgenstein on 26 May, but that did nothing to address the larger political–military concern. Many Russians, including Tsar Alexander, wanted to retreat east of the Oder, perhaps as far as the Vistula, to rest and rebuild before renewing the struggle. For the Prussians, withdrawal beyond the Oder was a death sentence to their country and their cause. This schism caused bitter infighting that almost split the alliance as May turned into June. A compromise of sorts saved the situation for Napoleon's adversaries. After much heated debate and desperate appeals from the Prussian generals to their king, the Allied armies marched south, hugging the Austrian border to assemble in the vicinity of Schweidnitz (Świdnica) before retiring to a position between Strehlen (Strzelin) and Nimptsch (Niemcza).[65] By placing themselves near Austria, they believed they would provide further incentive for Vienna to join the Coalition at an early date, negotiations for which were already under way at Allied headquarters.

Napoleon's weary men continued their pursuit. Victor's advance forced the Allies to abandon the blockade of Glogau and Lauriston entered Breslau as the army occupied the triangle defined by that city, Liegnitz and Jauer by 4 June. That day, however, active operations came to a temporary close. Plenipotentiaries from both sides, in contact since late May, had agreed to a ceasefire on 1 June and signed an armistice agreement at Pläswitz three days later. This was supposed to provide a breathing space for a peace conference. Initially slated to end on 20 July, the armistice period was later extended to 10 August with the provision that either party could terminate it on six days' advance notice. The terms of the agreement fixed a line of demarcation between the two sides, defined a neutral zone to separate the main armies in Silesia, allowed reprovisioning of the fortresses in French hands and required the withdrawal of the Allied raiding detachments across the Elbe.[66] Neither the extant belligerents nor Austria invested any real expectation that the proposed conference would result in a comprehensive peace; instead, all sides bent their energies to bolstering their forces to renew the struggle when the armistice expired in mid-August.

The Armistice at Pläswitz was a blessing for the Allies and Napoleon has been sharply censured for accepting its terms. Although he knew that the Prussians and Russians would recoup much of their strength during the coming reprieve and that Austria would almost certainly turn against him, the erosion of his own army persuaded him that an armistice presented the best means to recover and rebuild before resuming the struggle. He did not perceive the depth of the fissure growing between the Prussians and the

Russians and seems to have calculated that the recuperative powers of the centralised French state, the valour of his soldiers and his own leadership skills would suffice to overcome the numerical superiority his enemies were sure to enjoy when hostilities resumed. Nothing in war can be predicted with certainty, of course, but pushing to the Oder and risking a third major battle in this campaign may have driven a fatal wedge between the Russians and Prussians. In one of his greatest strategic errors, Napoleon chose not to take that risk.

Through Article V of the armistice the Allies agreed to resupply the French-held fortresses.[67] The Allies, hampered by lack of troops and heavy guns, had only been able to undertake two true sieges between March and June, those of Danzig and Thorn on the Vistula. While operations at Danzig proceeded in a rather desultory fashion, the siege of Thorn led that garrison to surrender to forces under Barclay's command on 16 April. All of the other fortresses, however, could only be blockaded or simply 'observed'. As a result, the energetic French commandants were able to launch numerous successful sorties against the weak Allied detachments outside their fortress walls to secure grain, livestock and other victuals.[68] French advances after Bautzen forced the Allied force around Glogau to retreat thus allowing the French to resupply that garrison directly, but the armistice now granted all of the fortresses the ability to restock foodstuffs (as long as the Allies adhered to the terms of the agreement).

While the armistice was taking effect in Silesia and fortresses were being notified, a final combat of the spring campaign was being fought further north. While pushing into Silesia, Napoleon decided to reinforce Oudinot with an ad hoc division under GD Louis Chrétien Carrière de Beaumont: eight squadrons of Rheinbund light horse, two French naval artillery battalions and four guns. Thus strengthened to a total of some 19,000 men, Oudinot was to march north from Bautzen both to protect the increasingly extended French left flank and to test the defences of Berlin. The principal Allied force south of Berlin was a mixed Russo-Prussian corps of approximately 21,000 commanded by GL Friedrich Wilhelm von Bülow, of whom more will be heard in these pages. Where Napoleon wanted Oudinot to contain Bülow and even drive him over the Oder, Allied headquarters hoped Bülow would disrupt the long French line of communications from Silesia back to Dresden. These contending instructions led to a clash at Hoyerswerda on 28 May where the French repulsed a probe by part of Bülow's command. This was followed by a more serious engagement on 4 June at Luckau in which Bülow turned back Oudinot's advance in a small but bloody affray. Bülow pursued the retreating French for several days before the two sides learned of the armistice.[69]

The armistice also halted operations along the lower Elbe. Fortunately for Napoleon, Marshal Davout and GD Vandamme, supported by Danish forces (allied with France from the end of May), had reoccupied Hamburg (1 June) and Lübeck (3 June) just before the armistice came into effect. The Allied forces here had now been placed under Lt. Gen. Ludwig Graf von Wallmoden-Gimborn to provide more coherence to their actions, but these troops were a multinational hodgepodge, a 'military mosaic' in Wallmoden's words, consisting of the old raiding parties combined with new units being raised from the Mecklenburgs and the Hanseatic cities as well as former prisoners of war; incapable of opposing Davout's advance, they retired across the Elbe to complete their organisation and await additional support.[70]

Finally, the terms of the armistice required the Allies to recall the numerous raiding parties they had dispatched across the Elbe. This proved most fortunate for the French as Chernishev and Lt. Gen. Mikhail Semenovich Vorontsov, who commanded the force observing Magdeburg, were planning a major raid on Leipzig. Chernishev had crossed the Elbe north of Magdeburg on 28 May and conducted a successful attack on Halberstadt on the 30th, destroying an artillery park and capturing Westphalian GD Adam Ludwig von Ochs (*see* Chapter 6). He joined forces with Vorontsov near Rosslau, and the two headed for Leipzig with a combined total of more than 6,400 men and 22 guns, arriving on the city's outskirts on 7 June. Leipzig, a massive French supply, replacement and remount depot, had only convalescents and half-trained recruits with no cannon as a garrison. The outnumbered French trainees put up a bold show but were soon overthrown and Chernishev was riding towards the city gates when French Général de Brigade (GB) Auguste Étienne Lamotte appeared with a trumpeter to announce the armistice. The Russians retained Lamotte and several hundred prisoners as hostages until this news was verified, but then dutifully released their captives and returned across the Elbe.[71]

Smaller Allied raiding parties included Prussian Rittmeister Friedrich August Peter von Colomb, who had enjoyed several small successes against French and Rheinbund convoys in Saxony between 8 May and early June but was lucky to escape when he was discovered by a flying column of Westphalian troops near the end of the month (*see* Chapter 6). A party of Prussian volunteers led by Major von Lützow was not so fortunate. His detachment had crossed the Elbe on 29 May and was attempting to make its way back to Allied lines after a brief but not especially successful raid into Thuringia. Having tarried too long, however, his band was attacked and dispersed by Württemberg and French cavalry at Kitzen on the edge of the Lützen battlefield in a controversial action on 17 June. The wounded Lützow and many of his men managed to evade capture, but this minor affair led to formal Allied protests and French responses at the highest levels. Where the French viewed Lützow and his men as criminal freebooters, the Allies painted Lützow as a patriotic hero and chose to see Kitzen as an inexcusable breach of the truce. The Coalition would thus use the incident as a pretext to suspend the resupply of French-held fortresses for several weeks. Kitzen would also have significant repercussions for the Württemberg contingent when the war resumed (see Chapter 4).[72]

While these multifarious actions were flaring along and west of the Elbe, generals were shifting their troops to align with the demarcation lines between the forces stipulated by the armistice terms and diplomats were preparing for the negotiations that were supposed to end the fighting. Rather predictably, these negotiations did not produce peace. With most of the Prussian army intent on waging a sacred war of vengeance, the tsar envisaging himself as Europe's saviour, Metternich seeking simultaneously to restrain Russia and Prussia while confining France, firebrand pan-Germanists urging a 'national' uprising and Napoleon adhering to unrealistic demands, this was hardly surprising.[73] 'The war burning in Europe was a war to the death,' wrote a young Russian officer, 'The armistice of Silesia, far from serving as a road to peace, had therefore been used by both sides only to prepare themselves more ardently for a struggle which was all the more terrible because it was to be decisive.'[74] 'Well, then, we will have war,' Napoleon told Saxon GL Karl Friedrich Wilhelm von Gersdorff, 'the Austrians have declared against me!'[75]

What the armistice period did produce was larger armies and larger coalitions. On Napoleon's side, the emperor employed his phenomenal energy to rest, rebuild, re-equip and reorganise his forces: ad hoc units were incorporated into regular regiments, training was imparted to thousands of recruits, the distant fortresses were revictualled and additional soldiers marched in from France and the Rheinbund states. Furthermore, Denmark abandoned its earlier neutrality to join him as an ally, a small but useful reinforcement that would help protect the vulnerable Hanseatic cities.[76] The extraordinary efforts of the emperor and his agencies succeeded in placing some 442,800 men at his disposal for his field armies with 26,000 more available in fortresses on the Elbe and a further 50,000 locked up in garrisons on the Oder or in Poland.[77] Napoleon also formalised the structure of the Grande Armée, eliminating much of the ad hocery occasioned by its hasty formation in the spring. In addition to fortress garrisons, the army would embark on the autumn campaigns organised into fourteen corps and five cavalry corps with a much-expanded Imperial Guard (*see* Chart 7). Of these, the Danzig garrison constituted the 10th Corps, a new 14th Corps was designated to secure Dresden and the various forces under Marshal Davout were amalgamated as 13th Corps to hold Hamburg and operate on the lower Elbe. Further to the rear, Marshal Augereau was assembling what was to become the 9th Corps in Würzburg and northern Bavaria. Many of these formations contained Rheinbund elements and, despite some shuffling during the armistice, many of the fortress garrisons still included German components as well. Although the French order of battle was now more regularised, it would continue to feature a number of provisional units, especially in rear area locations such as Leipzig. Many of these composite organisations also included Rheinbund troops. Furthermore, Napoleon altered the army's command structure. Viceroy Eugène, as described earlier, had departed for Italy after Lützen in light of Austria's likely change of sides. Now the disastrous defeat of French forces in Spain at Vitoria (21 June 1813) prompted the emperor to send Marshal Soult back to the Pyrenees after his brief participation in the Bautzen campaign. Somewhat surprisingly, however, Marshal Murat, the King of Naples, returned to the army despite Napoleon's anger at his ignominious flight in January.

The increases on the Allied side, of course, were greater. A formal multilateral alliance encompassing all the major Coalition members was not signed until March 1814, but by July 1813, a series of bilateral treaties and agreements bound Austria and Sweden to the existing Russo-Prussian alliance with Britain serving as paymaster and munitions supplier. Sweden pledged 30,000 men for the coming campaign, but the major change was the addition of Austria's 127,000 soldiers, bringing the Allied field armies total to some 512,000 by the end of the armistice with an additional 143,000 in reserve or blockading fortresses.[78] Austria's involvement also meant that Napoleon faced a direct threat on his southern flank along the rugged Bohemian frontier and had to consider the possibility of Austrian forces invading his ally Bavaria or his own Kingdom of Italy. Furthermore, Vienna might renew its covert diplomatic efforts to undermine his alliance with Saxony and could approach Bavaria as well. Beyond the inclusion of the new Austrian and Swedish forces, the existing Prussian and Russian armies expanded dramatically during the summer armistice. The Prussian Landwehr was mobilised, Russian reserves were brought up from the empire's interior, replacements were absorbed, and regiments re-equipped.

Spring of Disappointment

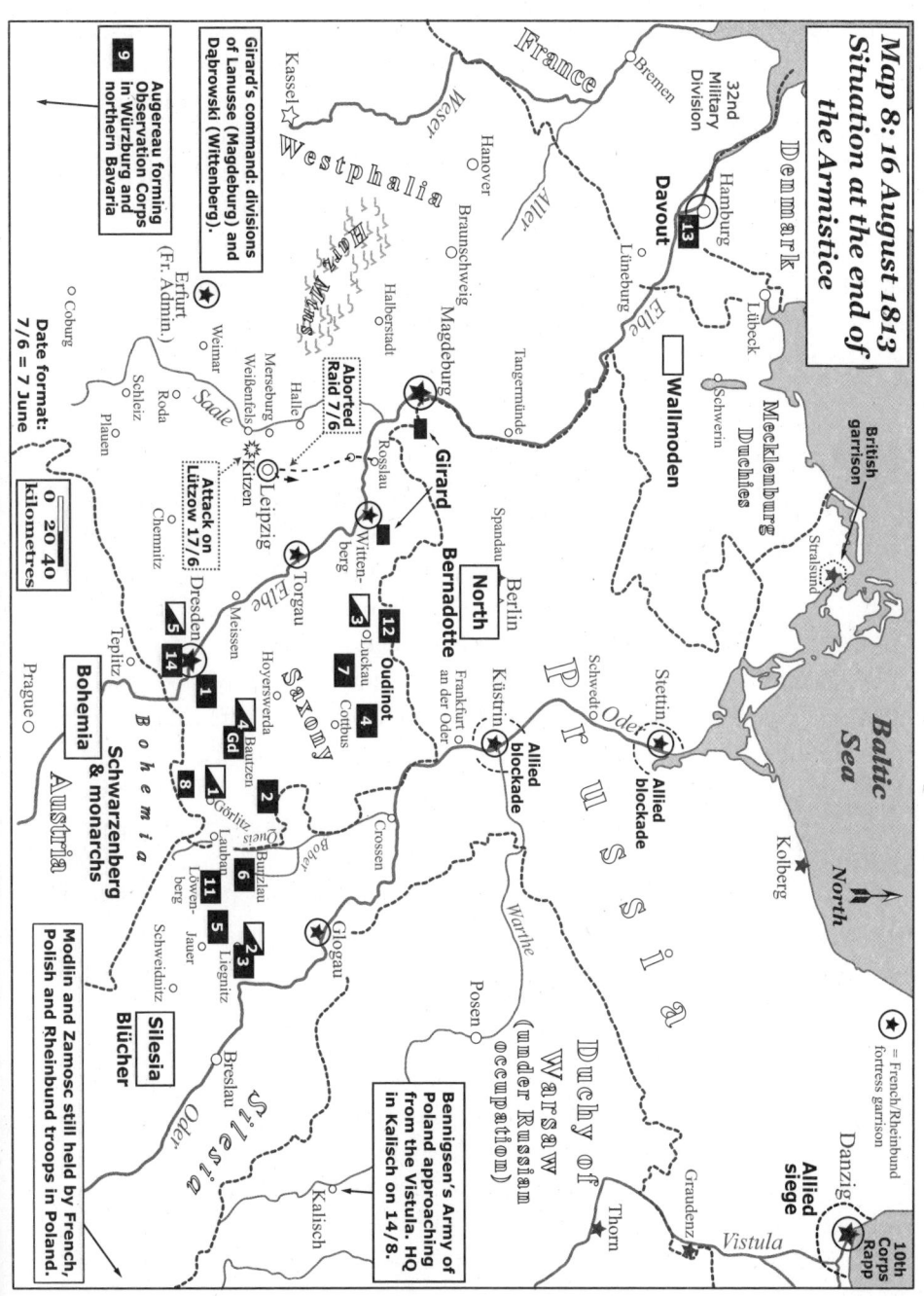

Map 8: 16 August 1813 Situation at the end of the Armistice

The Allied armies also reorganised (Chart 8) and committed themselves to a new strategy. When hostilities resumed in mid-August, most of the vast array of Allied troops would be assembled in three armies. The Army of the North, commanded by Jean-Baptiste Bernadotte, a former French marshal who was now Crown Prince of Sweden, would form the Allied right flank; in the centre was the Army of Silesia, operating out of the eponymous province under the leadership of the fiery Blücher; the left would consist of the Army of Bohemia (also termed the *Hauptarmee* or 'main army') under Schwarzenberg, he who had led the Austrian Auxiliary Corps in 1812. Owing to the size of the Austrian contingent, Schwarzenberg was also to serve as overall commander of Allied forces, an onerous appointment made all the more awkward by the near-constant presence of the Allied monarchs with his army. All of these would be multinational armies, comprised of troops from several nations. Swedes only served in the Army of the North and Austrians in the Army of Bohemia, but Prussians and Russians were present in large numbers in all three. Wallmoden's colourful command on the lower Elbe was also placed under Bernadotte. Far to the rear in south-eastern Poland, General of Cavalry Levin August Theophile Bennigsen was assembling the suitably named Army of Poland (or 'Reserve Army'). Composed exclusively of Russian units at this stage, it would have to detach troops for the blockades of Modlin and Zamosc but would eventually reinforce the Allied armies with a further 59,000 men.[79] In addition to these field forces, second-line troops such as Prussian Landwehr and Russian reserves would blockade the many French-held fortresses along the Oder and in Poland.

The three principal Allied armies were to operate within the guidelines of plans worked out among the military staffs in July. Though commonly known as the 'Trachtenberg Plan', this designation, as historian Michael Leggiere, points out, is something of a misnomer. The actual concept of operations should be more accurately known as the 'Reichenbach Plan' after an outline prepared by the Austrian chief of staff, Feldmarschall-Leutnant (FML) Joseph Wenzel von Radetzy. The basic tenets of this broad plan were that the individual armies, if unsupported, would avoid fighting forces under Napoleon's personal command and would only seek to engage the French emperor if two or more could combine against him. Meanwhile, the other Allied armies would operate against Napoleon's communications, seek to defeat his subsidiary forces, exhaust his armies by forcing them to make repeated long-distance marches, and loose numerous raiding detachments to create havoc in the French rear areas.[80] The expanded Coalition remained susceptible to fracture – some deep differences were barely papered over –

Chart 7: The Reorganised Grande Armée, August 1813

Emperor Napoleon, commanding in person

Unit	Commander	Divisions
Imperial Guard	Marshal Mortier	
1st Corps	GD Vandamme > GD Mouton	1st, 2nd and 23rd Divisions
2nd Corps	Marshal Victor	4th, 5th, and 6th Divisions
3rd Corps	Marshal Ney/GD Souham	8th, 9th, 10th, 11th, and 39th (Baden/Hesse) Divisions
4th Corps	GD Bertrand	12th, 15th (Italian) and 38th (Württemberg) Divisions
5th Corps	GD Lauriston	16th, 17th, and 19th Divisions
6th Corps	Marshal Marmont	20th, 21st and 22nd Divisions
7th Corps	GD Reynier	24th and 25th (Saxon) Divisions, 32nd Division (Durutte)
8th (Polish) Corps	GD Poniatowski	26th and part of 27th (Polish) Divisions
9th Corps	Marshal Augereau	51st and 52nd Divisions (still forming in August)
10th Corps	GD Rapp	7th (Polish/German), 30th and 33rd (Neapolitan) Divisions (besieged in Danzig)
11th Corps	Marshal MacDonald	31st (French/Westphalian/Neapolitan) 35th (French/Italian) and 36th Divisions
12th Corps	Marshal Oudinot	13th, 14th and 29th (Bavarian) Divisions
13th Corps	Marshal Davout	3rd, 40th and Danish Divisions, plus 50th Division (Hamburg garrison)
14th Corps	Marshal Saint-Cyr	42nd, 43rd, 44th and 45th Divisions
Independent	GD Dąbrowski	part of the 27th (Polish) Division
1st Cavalry Corps	GD Latour-Maubourg	1st (French/Italian) and 3rd Light Cavalry Divisions; 1st (French/Saxon) and 3rd (French/Italian) Cuirassier Divisions
2nd Cavalry Corps	GD Sébastiani	2nd and 4th Light Cavalry Divisions, 2nd Cuirassier Division
3rd Cavalry Corps	GD Arrighi	5th and 6th Light Cavalry Divisions, 4th Heavy Cavalry Division
4th (Polish) Cavalry Corps	GD Kellermann/Sokolnicki	7th (part) and 8th Light Cavalry Divisions
5th Cavalry Corps	GD Lhéritier	9th Light Cavalry Division, 5th and 6th Heavy Cavalry Divisions

Notes: GD Gérard commanded 11th Corps while MacDonald led the Army of the Bober. Similarly, Souham assumed Ney's post at the head of 3rd Corps when Ney was assigned broader responsibilities. GD Mouton, Count of Lobau, took command of 1st Corps after Vandamme's capture at Kulm. The 18th Division (5th Corps) was dissolved during the armistice. The 5th Cavalry Corps was split in August (part with Augereau, part with the main army) and not united until later in the campaign.

Source: Amalgamated from Friederich, *Herbstfeldzuges*, vols. I and II; Juhel; and Nafziger.

> **Chart 8:** *The Allied Armies, August 1813*
>
> **The Army of Bohemia**   *FM Schwarzenberg*
>
> **Austrian Troops**
>
> | | | |
> |---|---|---|
> | 1st Austrian Light Division | FML Liechtenstein | |
> | 2nd Austrian Light Division | FML Bubna | |
>
> Right Wing
> *Armee-Abteilung* of — Erbprinz von Hessen-Homburg — 2 infantry divisions, 3 reserve infantry divisions, 2 cavalry divisions
>
> Left Wing
> *Armee-Abteilung* of — FZM Graf Gyulai — 2 infantry divisions, 1 cavalry division
> *Armee-Abteilung* of — GdK Graf Klenau — 3rd Light Division, 2 infantry divisions, 1 cavalry brigade
>
> Note: As shown in the Leipzig outline order of battle, the Austrian army altered its cumbersome organisation after the Battle of Dresden.
>
> **Russian Troops**   *Gen. of Cavalry Wittgenstein*
>
> | | |
> |---|---|
> | I Russian Infantry Corps | Lt. Gen. Gorchakov |
> | II Russian Infantry Corps | Herzog Eugene of Württemberg |
> | Cavalry Corps | Lt. Gen. Pahlen III |
>
> Russo-Prussian Guards and Reserve
>
> | | |
> |---|---|
> | III Russian Infantry (Grenadier) Corps | Lt. Gen. Rayevsky |
> | V Russian Infantry (Guard) Corps | Lt. Gen. Yermolov |
> | *Includes:* | |
> | Prussian Guard Infantry Brigade | Oberstleutnant von Alvensleben |
> | Cavalry Corps | Lt. Gen. Golitsyn V |
> | *Includes:* | |
> | Prussian Guard Cavalry Brigade | GM von Röder |

but when they marched to war again in August, its armies were enlarged, refreshed, re-formed and supplied with a new operational concept that held the promise of success even against 'the very God of War himself'.[81]

Autumn of Blood

When the conflict resumed in mid-August, therefore, the Coalition enjoyed several clear advantages, above all the addition of the large Austrian army to its ranks as well as the modest Swedish contribution. Although the odds were thus increasingly stacked against the French that autumn, the outcome was neither preordained nor ineluctable. At the head of a large army in a central position and enjoying singular unity of command in the face of the fractious enemy alliance, Napoleon could entertain prospects of success. Blunders

Prussian Troops		
II Prussian Corps	GL von Kleist	9th, 10th, 11th and 12th Brigades, Cavalry Brigade
The Army of Silesia	**Gen. der Kavallerie von Blücher**	
I Prussian Corps	GL von Yorck	1st, 2nd, 7th and 8th Brigades, Reserve Cavalry
Russian Corps	Lt. Gen. Osten-Sacken	XI Infantry Corps, Cavalry
Russian Corps	Gen. of Infantry Langeron	VI, IX and X Infantry Corps, I Cavalry Corps
Russian Corps	Lt. Gen. St Priest	2 infantry and 2 dragoon divisions, Cossacks
The Army of the North	**Carl Johann, Crown Prince of Sweden (Bernadotte)**	
III Prussian Corps	GL von Bülow	3rd, 4th, 5th and 6th Brigades, Reserve Cavalry
IV Prussian Corps	GL von Tauentzien	4 infantry divisions, supporting cavalry
Russian Corps	Lt. Gen. von Wintzingerode	3 infantry divisions, 3 cavalry brigades, Cossacks
Swedish Corps	Field Marshal Stedingk	2 infantry divisions, 2 cavalry brigades
On the lower Elbe	Lt. Gen. von Wallmoden-Gimborn	mixed force of Russians, Swedes, Germans and British

Note: The Army of Bohemia was also known as the *Hauptarmee* (or Main Army) and FM Schwarzenberg was accompanied by the three Allied monarchs.

Bülow's subordinate formations are often termed 'divisions' but were equivalent to the 'brigades' in the other three Prussian corps.

Source: Friederich, *Herbstfeldzuges*, vol. I, Anlagen I, II and IV.

by his opponents, his own extraordinary talents and a sizeable portion of good luck might grant him the military triumph that had eluded him in the spring. Indeed, hard marching, tough fighting and his personal tactical touch resulted in a significant victory over the stunned Allies at Dresden on 26–27 August. The benefits of this remarkable achievement, however, were lost almost immediately as his subordinates, left to their own devices on distant battlefields, suffered four demoralising defeats in his absence. These losses, Allied pressure on his flanks and increasing logistical difficulties forced Napoleon to withdraw across the Elbe River in late September, and, as October opened, he was concentrating the bulk of his army east of Leipzig in anticipation of a grand battle that he hoped would restore his fortunes. The resulting Battle of Leipzig (16–19 October), however, was a catastrophe for the French. Forced to retreat after suffering crippling losses, the remains of the Grande Armée made their way towards the Rhine pursued by the Allies and riddled with typhus. His German allies, led by Bavaria, were already beginning to desert his eagles and his only consolation was the repulse he inflicted on a combined Austro-Bavarian force at Hanau on 30 and 31 October. On 2 November he crossed the Rhine heading for Paris. He never returned.

The Iron Dice Are Cast

In addition to reorganising, rearming, training, resting and absorbing thousands of new recruits into their ranks, the corps on the French side of the armistice line had a further task to accomplish before the resumption of hostilities: the commemoration of Napoleon's birthday. German contingents routinely enjoyed special meals and conducted other activities on the birthdays of their sovereigns, but the celebration of the emperor's day involved the entire army. This annual event would normally be held on 15 August, the actual day of Napoleon's birth, but with renewal of the war on the immediate horizon, celebrations were moved up to the 10th to allow adequate time for preparations in advance and rest afterwards. The imminent resumption of hostilities, of course, cast a shadow over the festivities, as Saxon Unterleutnant Friedrich Vollborn noted: 'Everything led to the firm conviction that the campaign would recommence and when Napoleon's Day ... was moved from 15 to 10 August, everyone could see what was coming.' Nonetheless,

> Cannon salutes announced the dawn of 10 August and all were in full dress uniform in the camp, illumination in the evening and grand water- and land-fireworks on the right wing. A colossal **N** set up on a rounded hill was decorated with thousands of colourful glass lamps and illuminated. The towers of Görlitz sparkled like fiery stars through the dark night. In short, there was great jubilation, whose echo sought to push back the approaching storm clouds of war.[82]

Similarly, Martin Carl Ignaz Kösterus, a soldier with the Hessian Leib-Garde Regiment in Ney's 3rd Corps, provided a vivid description of the festivities that day as the army wondered if on the actual birthday 'peace would return to the world or if the torch of war would continue to burn'.

> The festival was therefore moved to 10 August and the grandest arrangements were made many days in advance. The axes of the sappers echoed in the camp again. Trees were cut for this festival, from which an alley was erected through the camp and lined with wreaths of flowers and decorative arrangements of leaves. Seats were placed in the gaps and leafy

Map 9: Major Engagements in the Autumn Phase August–October 1813

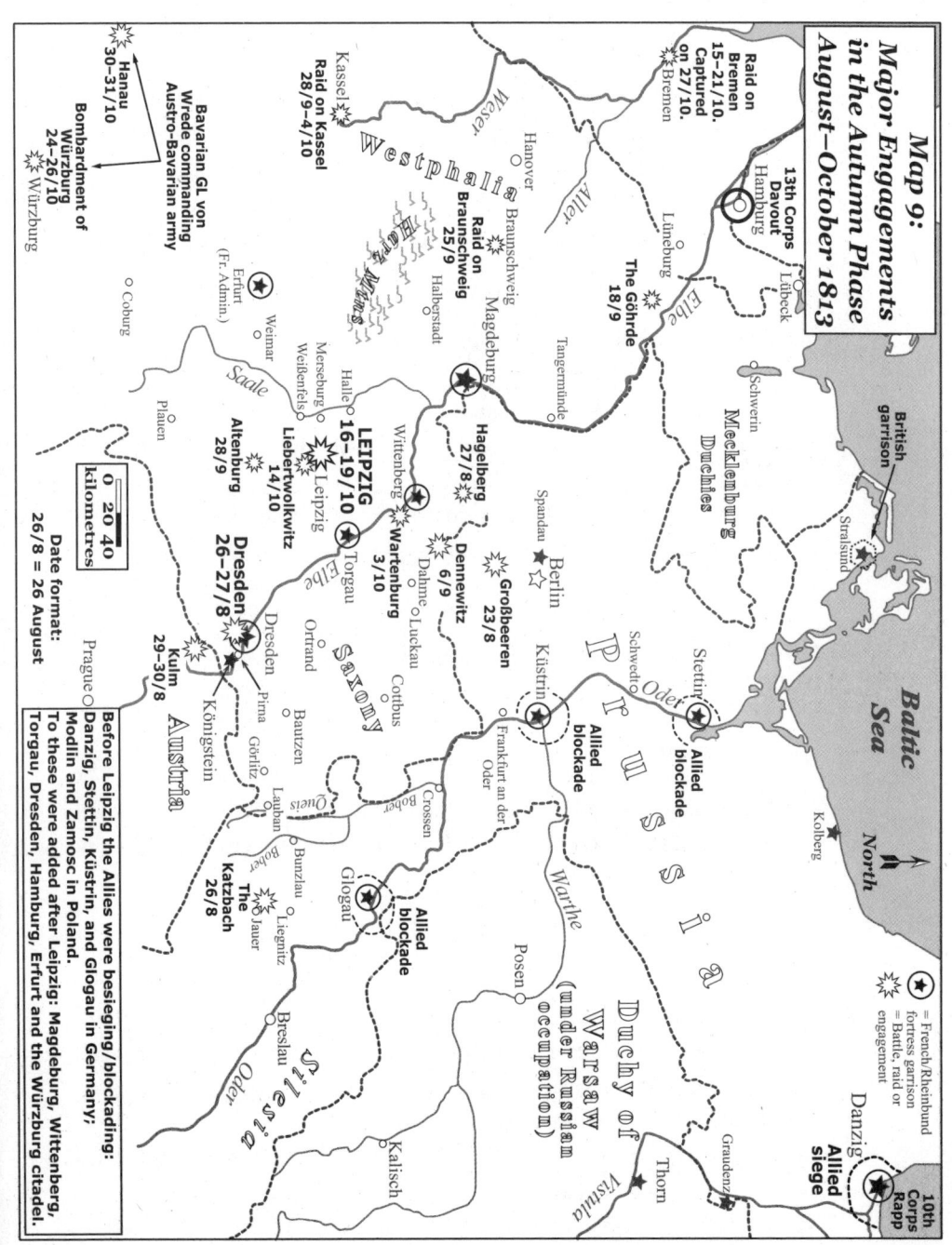

huts and little bosquets were built from the smaller branches; the camp seemed suddenly transformed into a pleasure garden.

One hundred and one cannon shots at set intervals announced the dawn of the festival day. The troops marched out and paraded before Marshal Ney, made a few evolutions and were then placed in a huge square in the middle of which an altar had been constructed from fresh turves, decorated with flowers and surrounded by military emblems.

After the religious service, a triple salvo from the muskets and heavy guns ended the ceremony. Gymnastic games with prizes were set up for the entertainment of the soldiers. Those who did not wish to participate, gathered themselves together: here under the squealing of a lively violin, there, muddling together wildly, singing away the beloved soldier's song from Schiller, or 'Hans Michel' and 'The Dark Brown Girl' with all manner of revisions.

Everyone received two francs and double rations; and fireworks closed the evening along with the loud jumbling of joyous shouts and cheers from the enthused soldiers for the health of the emperor, the grand duke and their beloved commander.

In accordance with an army order, this day of general joy was followed by five days of rest during which neither drill nor any other activity was to be undertaken that might weary the soldiers as, on 15 August, the armistice, after being extended for five days, would come to an end.

'We were near the decision' on peace or war, concluded Kösterus: 'It came, the day of decision, but even before it came, it was a certainty to us that the iron dice would be cast once more.'[83]

One More Victory: The Battle of Dresden

According to the terms of the armistice and subsequent agreements, the temporary peace would come to an end at midnight on 16/17 August. Blücher, however, impatient with what he scornfully termed 'diplomatic buffoonery and letter-writing', decided to move sooner. Seizing on reports of French foraging parties drawing supplies from the neutral zone in Silesia as justification, he ordered his entire army to advance across the line of demarcation on 14 August.[84] The war was on again.

Circumstances, especially Austria's joining the Allies as an active belligerent, forced Napoleon to assume a posture of strategic defence as hostilities opened. During the armistice, he had thus arrayed the bulk of his army in Saxony between Dresden and Silesia with what have been called three 'advance guards' to watch the Allied armies he considered most dangerous: one in Silesia to observe Blücher, one near Zittau to guard the pass out of Bohemia and one south of Dresden along the Elbe. He retained a large reserve between Bautzen and Görlitz, ready to move in any direction, while Dresden remained his centre of operations and logistical hub.[85] Although he would have preferred to take the initiative and open the autumn with an offensive campaign, he was confident that he could use his central position to exploit his enemy's mistakes and defeat the Allied armies *ad seriatim*. At the same time, he did not abandon his interest in an operation against Berlin, hoping thereby to create fissures in Coalition councils, deprive Prussia of significant resources, dampen rebellious sentiment in Germany and set the stage for an advance to the Oder or even to the Vistula. He assigned this task to Marshal Oudinot with an ad hoc army composed of 4th, 7th, 12th and 3rd Cavalry Corps as the 'Army of Berlin'. Davout from Hamburg was to advance in support and another ad hoc command consisting of two divisions under GD Jean-Baptiste Girard would push forward from the Elbe and supposedly connect the two marshals. With Oudinot driving up from the south, Davout from the west and Girard in between, Napoleon hoped to create a concentric threat to Berlin resulting in the defeat of Bernadotte's Army of the North and the seizure of the Prussian capital.

Blücher's advance seemed to offer Napoleon an opportunity to destroy or at least cripple one of the key Allied armies early in the opening campaign. Although he had learned that the main Allied army had crossed to the left (west) bank of the Elbe in Bohemia and would likely advance to threaten Dresden, he trusted that Marshal Gouvion Saint-Cyr with 14th Corps and 5th Cavalry Corps would be able to hold the city while he dealt with Blücher. To Napoleon's frustration, however, the Prussian general, true to the Allied strategic concept, chose to withdraw rapidly to the east rather than accept battle. Moreover, just as he was trying to bring the Army of Silesia to bay, urgent messages from Saint-Cyr complicated Napoleon's situation and drew his attention back to Dresden. Leaving Marshal MacDonald with the newly named 'Army of the Bober' to contain Blücher, Napoleon thus hastened west, leading the Guard and Marmont's 6th Corps on an epic march to Dresden.

Meanwhile, the Allied Army of Bohemia, with two of the monarchs in tow, had indeed crossed out of Bohemia into Saxony well west of the Elbe. Tedious and ill-informed councils of war initially aimed the offensive at Leipzig, but on learning that Saint-Cyr was nearly isolated, the army turned ponderously east towards Dresden, making its weary way along rude mountain trails under constant rain. Saint-Cyr's lone corps could not withstand an army of more than 250,000, but he withdrew as slowly as possible and even launched an aggressive spoiling attack on 25 August when the Allies appeared before Dresden's walls from the southwest.[86] An immediate assault that day would almost certainly have overwhelmed Saint-Cyr's defences to gain at least the Altstadt on the west bank of the Elbe. Dresden's residents were in a state of panic. 'In the city all was consternation and confusion,' wrote one, and people dared not believe the rumours that Napoleon was coming with 100,000 men to rescue their beloved capital.[87] The Allied columns were too slow to arrive, however, and night fell before enough troops were on hand for a concerted attack. Moreover, opinions in the convoluted Allied command structure were divided. Lengthy, testy discussions reached a decision to delay any action until the following day, but the morning of 26 August only brought limited advances followed by vague instructions that ordered the army forward at 4:00 p.m. to test the city's defences. It was all the time Napoleon needed.

Though disappointed at Blücher's uncharacteristically prudent withdrawal, Napoleon saw the coming clash at Dresden as another opportunity for the decisive battle he desired. He thus ordered GD Vandamme to cross the Elbe at Pirna with his 1st Corps and threaten the Allied lines of communication while he took the majority of the available forces directly to the Saxon capital: the Guard, followed by 1st Cavalry Corps, 2nd Corps and 6th Corps. It would take hours for all of these troops to cross to the west bank and for the French commanders to place them advantageously, but Napoleon's rapid decisions and the hard marching[88] of his men completely changed the situation even as the Allies were making their first advances. The emperor entered Dresden at mid-morning to an enthusiastic welcome, not only from his soldiers as usual, but from the city's residents as well.[89] 'The arrival of Napoleon had a magical effect on most of the inhabitants and at once generated for many the hope that the threatening danger would now be averted, even though most of them were his secret foes,' wrote Saxon engineer officer Karl Heinrich Aster,

> Despite this, the personal danger in which they found themselves, not only for life but also for property, meant that even a great number of his enemies did not shy from acknowledging him as their saviour in this moment of crisis, telling one another: 'Napoleon is there! Now things will soon be different!'[90]

Napoleon paid a courtesy call on König Friedrich August and set about making arrangements for a counterstroke. GL von Gersdorff, chief of the Saxon general staff, recorded in his diary that the emperor 'responded with a jovial: "Very well: *à cheval!*"' on learning of the Allied afternoon advance.

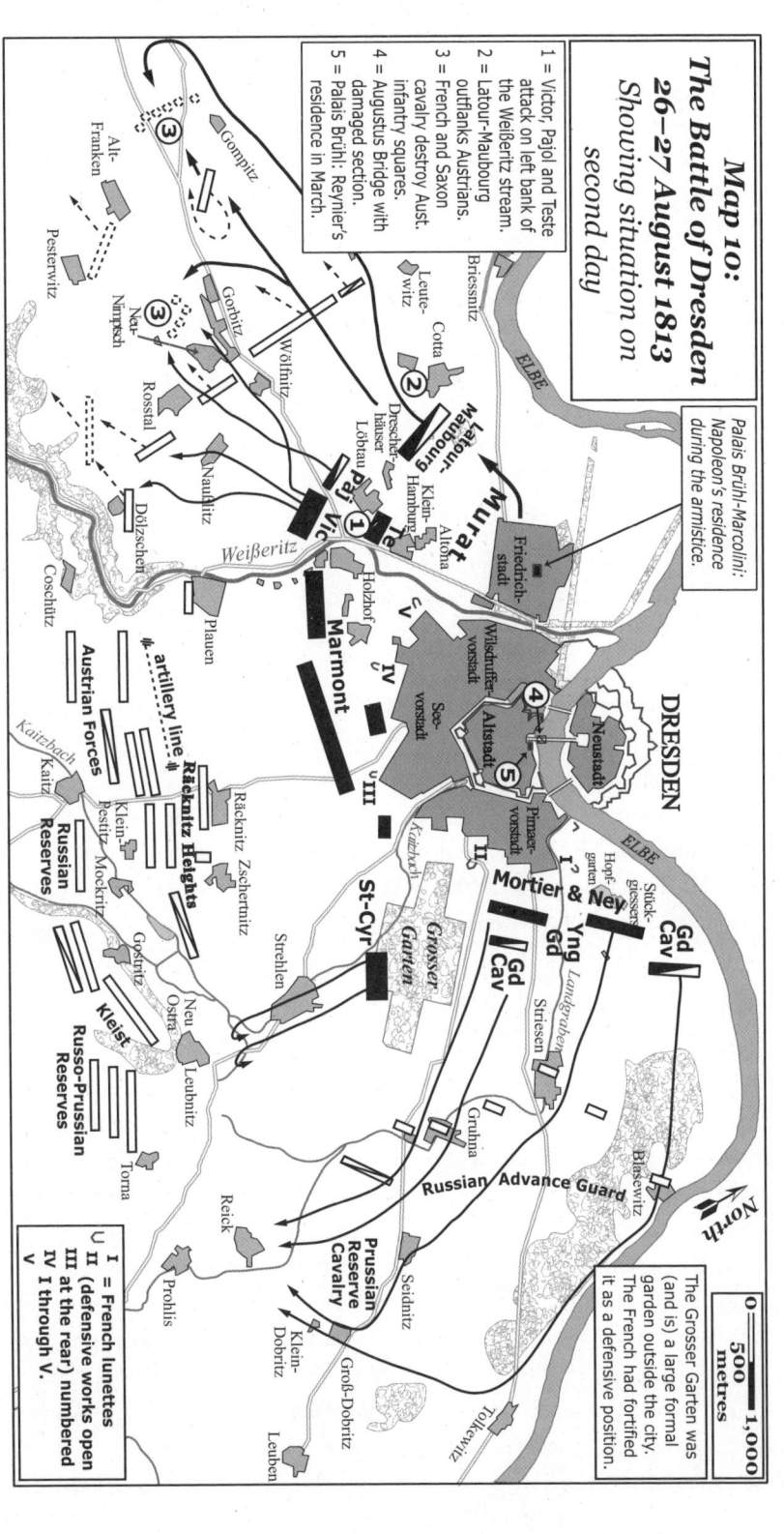

> He mounted his white horse and took himself with his entire suite again to the end of the stone bridge over the Elbe before the royal palace, where gendarmes made a circle around him. He issued his orders with a composure that only the certainty of good results can give. He sent adjutant after adjutant out to the army approaching on the Bautzen highway to urge the troops to hurry. These set themselves at the run and surged in steadily over all three [bridges], but mostly over the stone Elbe bridge. Here he let no regiment pass without saying something to it, to which he usually received a jaunty and jocular reply, and thereby all hunger and weariness were forgotten.[91]

GM Conrad Rudolph von Schäffer, the Baden representative in imperial headquarters, left a similar impression of these moments:

> Around 4:00 p.m., the enemy began to throw bombs and howitzer shells into the city. Fire gripped more or less all the suburbs but did not ignite in the city even though many buildings suffered. The scene became more imposing with every moment; under the thunder of 200 cannon, under the roar of the exploding bombs and shells, the rattle of the collapsing houses, the regiments of the different army corps advanced with Turkish music under flying flags and in exemplary order through the city and onto the fields of honour and death, and the columns greeted the emperor with thousand-fold 'vive l'Empereur!' when they saw him; even the residents of Dresden were encouraged by this grand scene and bore the dangers of the bombardment with stoic composure.[92]

As the French columns hurried across the Elbe into Dresden, the Allies were initiating their preliminary advances: Russians on the right, Prussians against the Großer Garten (Grand Garden) and Austrians on both sides of the Weißeritz Stream. French resistance was spirited and skilled, another sign of Napoleon's presence, but by late morning Saint-Cyr's outposts had been driven in, most of the Großer Garten was in Prussian hands, and the Austrians had cleared the area between the Elbe and the Weißeritz to the edge of the Friedrichstadt suburb. A pause now ensued as the Allied leadership, increasingly persuaded that Napoleon had arrived, once again bickered over their next steps. Disputation notwithstanding, Schwarzenberg gave the signal for the afternoon attack and the Allied battalions, accompanied by thunderous artillery fire, stepped off to assault Saint-Cyr's main defence line. Although the Austrians on the far left beyond the Weißeritz made no progress and the Russians on the right were quickly stymied, by approximately 5:00 p.m., the Prussians from the Großer Garten and the Austrians in the centre had advanced up to the improvised fortifications on the edges of the city's suburbs. The Habsburg troops even succeeded in forcing their way into Lunette III and threatened to break into Lunette IV.

The Allied gains, however, were soon washed away. Sometime between 5:00 and 5:30 p.m., Napoleon unleashed his counterattack. Carefully posted divisions of the Imperial Guard burst suddenly forth from the Altstadt suburbs, surprising and overwhelming the Allied columns. The Russians were thrown back to Striesen, the Prussians lost the Großer Garten, and the Austrians were forced out of the lunette they had captured. Similarly, French troops under Murat's command pushed out of the Friedrichstadt suburb beyond the Weißeritz to reclaim the hamlets and villages the Austrians had occupied in the afternoon advance. Bitter fighting raged deep into the night, but the Allies eventually lost all the ground they had taken during the day. Having acquired room to deploy and bolstered by the arrival of the 2nd and 6th Corps after dusk, Napoleon was well positioned to resume the battle in the morning. The Allies, shaken by the emperor's appearance and the abrupt change of battlefield fortunes, had to absorb even more worrisome news when word came from upstream that Vandamme had crossed the Elbe near Königstein. In a long day's combat, Saxon guns in the fortress had fired in support as he shoved back the Russian corps posted near Pirna, threatening the Allied line of retreat and leading the multinational command to dispatch twelve battalions and ten squadrons from the hard-pressed army opposite Dresden.

After a night of heavy rain, 27 August dawned to fog, more rain and mud. Movement was difficult and the wet weather meant that many muskets would not function, a factor that became significant, especially in the action on the Allied left across the Weißeritz stream. Napoleon opened the second day of battle with attacks on both flanks. While action in the centre was largely confined to mutual cannonade, Saint-Cyr's 14th Corps and the four divisions of the Young Guard drove back the Allied right wing, pushing it away from the line of retreat to Pirna until halted by the threat of Russian–Prussian cavalry and the obstinate Prussian defence of Leubnitz. On the western side of the Weißeritz, Murat led a stunningly successful attack on the isolated Allied left. With 2nd Corps, a brigade from 1st Corps and a large body of horse including the two regiments of Saxon heavy cavalry, he overwhelmed the few Austrian squadrons and broke numerous squares of unfortunate Habsburg infantry whose damp cartridges would not ignite. This success netted the French thousands of Austrian prisoners, including two generals, and drove the Allied left from the field in disarray. In addition

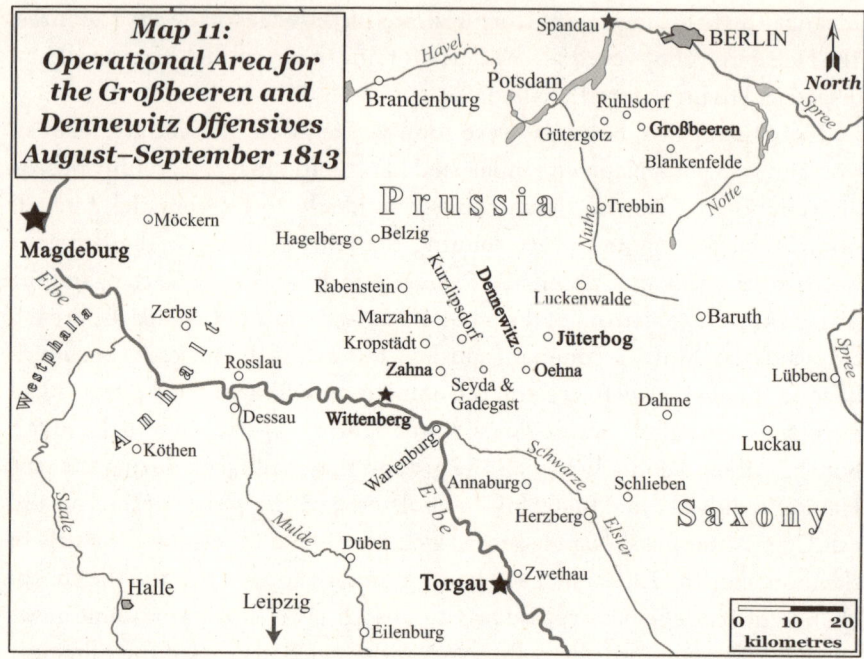

Map 11: Operational Area for the Großbeeren and Dennewitz Offensives August–September 1813

to this calamity on their left, the Allied leaders learned that Vandamme was pressing the Russians at Pirna in their right rear. Considering these tactical concerns along with the army's dismal logistical situation, the dispiriting results of the march on Dresden, and Napoleon's personal appearance on the field, it is hardly surprising that yet another Allied council of war decided on withdrawal to Bohemia.

On the 28th, therefore, the weary Army of Bohemia dragged itself back into the mountains on the same muddy trails it had used to reach the outskirts of Dresden three days earlier. Its losses came to between an estimated 20,000 and 25,000 to which must be added at least 5,000 left behind or captured in the first day or so of the retreat. Given the composition of the army, most of these casualties were Austrians, but the number of prisoners had been substantially increased by 'the tactical destruction'[93] of the left wing across the Weißeritz on 27 August. French losses are not recorded but probably came to 9,000, perhaps as many as 10,000, for the two days.[94] Napoleon regretted that the rainy weather had prevented further action against the Allied centre and right, but he could retire to his quarters in the city with considerable satisfaction for the success achieved.[95] Unfortunately for him, however, hints of decidedly unwelcome developments were already beginning to arrive from other parts of the theatre of war.

A Catalogue of Defeats: Großbeeren and Hagelberg

While Napoleon was achieving his last great victory on Saxon soil, his subordinates elsewhere were faring poorly. Indeed, from late August through early September a tide of defeats washed away the operational and psychological benefits the emperor had gained through the success at Dresden.

The first of these defeats befell Oudinot's Army of Berlin on 23 August. As already explained, Napoleon had tasked Oudinot, much against the marshal's wishes, to lead a force of four corps north from Saxony, overthrow Bernadotte's Army of the North and seize the Prussian capital. Davout from the lower Elbe was to advance in support, while GD Girard was to link Davout and Oudinot by pushing east with GD Pierre Lanusse's French division from Magdeburg and GD Jan Henryk Dąbrowski's Polish division from Wittenberg. The emperor, however, overestimated his marshal and underestimated the magnitude of his mission. Gathering his ad hoc army around Baruth as the armistice ended, the reluctant Oudinot duly marched on 19 August. He first turned west to Luckenwalde, where elements of GD Jean Toussaint Arrighi de Casanova's 3rd Cavalry Corps managed with some effort and confusion to drive off a large detachment of Cossacks. Leaving the Bavarian 29th Division and GD Jean Thomas Guillaume Lorge's 5th Light Cavalry Division behind at Luckenwalde to protect his flank and rear (they would have their own clash with Cossacks on the 20th), the marshal pivoted to his right for the march on Berlin.

The region in which the armies would now operate was generally flat but its soft, loose soil, the numerous criss-crossing watercourses and large tracts of forests and marshes often constricted manoeuvre. Given these features of the landscape and the poor road system, Oudinot decided that his army would advance along three separate axes when it turned north towards Berlin on 21 August: Bertrand's 4th Corps on the right, Reynier with the predominantly Saxon 7th Corps in the centre and Oudinot with his own 12th Corps on the left followed by part of Arrighi's 3rd Cavalry Corps. These three strands would not be able to unite until they emerged from the woods and fens into the open terrain just south of Berlin near the little villages of Großbeeren and Blankenfelde. For the advance on the 23rd, therefore, the various corps under Oudinot's command were more or less isolated as they marched, unable to communicate with each other speedily, let alone support one another should that be necessary. The rainy weather was an additional impediment, rendering passage through the sandy soil a tedious slog.

Oudinot's immediate opponents were Prussians from what was now Bülow's III Corps and one division of GL Bogislav Friedrich Emanuel

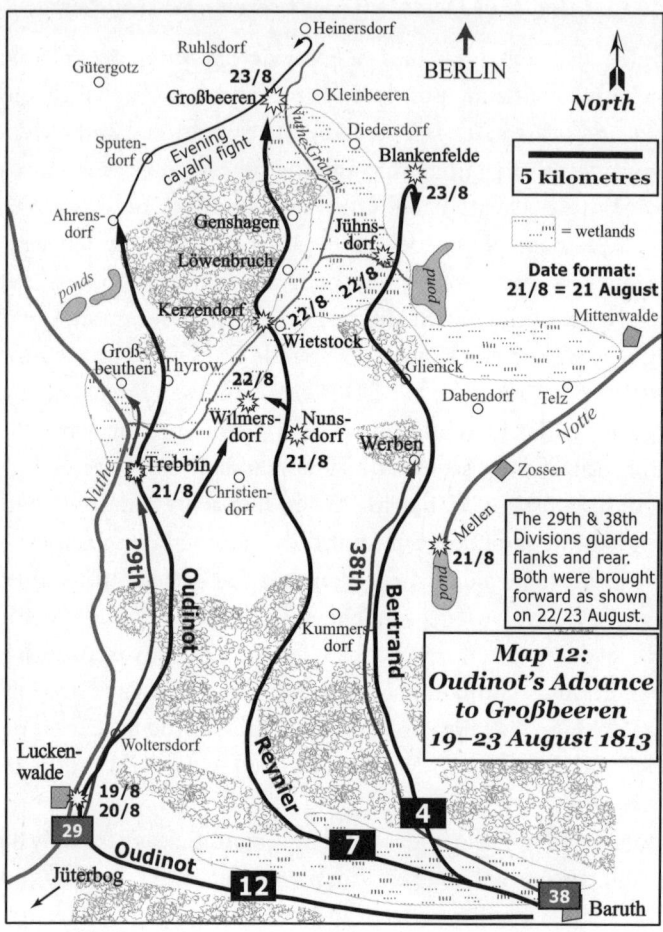

Map 12: Oudinot's Advance to Großbeeren 19–23 August 1813

Graf Tauentzien's IV Corps.[96] Fortunately for Oudinot, the Prussians were scattered and equally hindered by the terrain. Their rear guards, faced with superior numbers of French and Saxon troops, were forced to yield, but the marches of the French corps on 21 and 22 August were repeatedly delayed by sharp skirmishes where their routes crossed watercourses. Resistance at Wietstock on the Nuthe-Graben during the 22nd was especially obstinate, leading to a tough engagement that cost Durutte's division of 7th Corps some 400 casualties and Bülow's Prussians 350 men.[97] As the Prussians withdrew, the Saxons of GL Carl Ludwig Sahrer von Sahr's 25th Division passed over the Nuthe-Graben and through Durutte's ranks to bivouac near Löwenbruch as the lead element of Reynier's corps; Durutte's troops spent the night around Kerzendorf with the Saxon 24th Division of GL Carl Christian Erdmann Edler von LeCoq still east of the stream. To their right, the Italians of the

15th Division in Bertrand's corps camped at Jühnsdorf, having chased some of Tauentzien's Landwehr out of the village in light skirmishing during the afternoon. On the left, parts of Oudinot's 14th Division crossed the Nuthe-Graben at Wilmersdorf against little opposition and stopped at Thyrow, the rest of 12th Corps and 3rd Cavalry Corps halting around Wilmersdorf and Trebbin (*see* Map 12). The Bavarian 29th Division and the Württembergers of the 38th Division were left behind to guard the army's western and eastern flanks respectively. The marshal had little notion of the enemy's dispositions and seems to have expected a more or less unopposed march on the 23rd, telling Napoleon that he hoped to enter Berlin on 24 August.

On the Allied side, Bernadotte expected a battle on the 23rd and deployed his army with Wintzingerode's Russian corps on the right (west) near Gütergotz, his Swedes north of Ruhlsdorf and the Prussians on the left. Although Bernadotte instructed Tauentzien to move to Heinersdorf and Bülow to close in on the Swedes near Ruhlsdorf, the independent-minded Bülow, determined to halt the French before Berlin, modified these orders on his own initiative. He and Tauentzien had already agreed that IV Corps would hold Blankenfelde with its lone available division, that of GM Leopold Wilhelm von Dobschütz. Bertrand would therefore face Dobschütz's men when the French advanced on the 23rd. As for the four brigades of Bülow's III Corps, he left three battalions of GM Karl August Adolf von Krafft's 6th Brigade along with four hussar squadrons and a battery at Großbeeren, collected the 3rd, the 4th and the rest of the 6th around Heinersdorf with his cavalry brigade and called in GM Ludwig von Borstell's 5th Brigade from the east. On the morning of the 23rd, however, Bernadotte ordered Bülow to shift his corps towards Ruhlsdorf so as to close up on the Swedes in anticipation of the battle he was expecting that day. Leaving his small garrison in Großbeeren, Bülow thus marched his men west as directed, but when the sounds of battle began to rumble in from Tauentzien's front later that morning, he urgently appealed for permission to return to the east. Bernadotte made difficulties but eventually agreed and the men of III Corps trudged wearily as far as Licheterade before returning to their former bivouacs around Heinersdorf under a driving rain, arriving around 1:00 p.m.[98] The 5th Brigade appeared shortly thereafter. As the Prussian brigades were the equivalent of divisions in other armies, this meant that Bülow had more than 38,000 men within 5 kilometres of Großbeeren on the afternoon of 23 August. Tauentzien had an additional 13,000 at Blankenfelde. When Reynier's corps of approximately 23,000 emerged from the woods south of Großbeeren later that afternoon, therefore, it would find itself at a significant numerical disadvantage.

The fighting on 23 August, however, began at Blankenfelde, where Bertrand sent the Italian 15th Division forward from Jühnsdorf between 9:00 and 10:00 a.m. The Italians endeavoured to push out of the woods and into the village, but their attack was not pressed with any great vigour and they were repulsed at all points. Although he outnumbered his adversaries, Bertrand was waiting to hear gunfire from his left, hoping that Reynier's advance would outflank the Prussians and force them to retreat. As the wet morning wore away into an equally wet afternoon with no indication that Reynier had arrived, Bertrand thus called off his feeble attack and withdrew to Jühnsdorf around 2:00 p.m. His tentative foray had cost the Prussians some 200 casualties for slightly higher losses in the 15th Division.

Events unfolded very differently in Reynier's sector. Sahr's division, leading the corps' advance, began to emerge from the woods south of Großbeeren between 3:00 and 4:00 p.m., well after Bertrand had concluded his probe.[99] The Saxons quickly evicted the Prussian garrison from the village and drove the Prussian battery from its position on a low knoll called the Windmill Hill just to the west. At this point, Reynier seems to have assumed that his task for the day had been accomplished. Despite misgivings among his Saxon officers, he ordered the corps to encamp for the night with Sahr's 25th Division in Großbeeren and on the windmill hill, LeCoq's men south of the large Neubeeren farmstead and Durutte in between. The corps was thus echeloned slightly from right to left with the Saxon cavalry brigade in the rear. Reynier, however, 'with an unusual insouciance' neglected even the most basic security precautions such as scouting the local area and establishing a proper line of outposts.[100] As a result, he had no idea that Bülow's large corps was concentrated barely 4 kilometres to the north. With the day coming to an end and the rain falling in torrents, his Saxon and French troops went about trying to establish their bivouacs, start fires and prepare their evening meals despite the dreadful weather.

Surprise was thus complete when Bülow's corps loomed out of the rain and gathering darkness as evening came on. Sahr's men scrambled to defend themselves, but their batteries were beaten down by Prussian, Russian and Swedish guns in a ferocious artillery duel and Prussian infantry stormed Großbeeren and the Windmill Hill from the north while Borstell's brigade attacked from the east. What ensued was a tumble of confused combat, much of which was fought with bayonets and musket butts as small arms failed in the downpour. GL von Sahr was among the victims, taking two bayonet wounds as he led the young recruits of the *Low* Regiment in a counterattack. Desperate bravery notwithstanding, Sahr's division soon succumbed to the Prussian pressure,

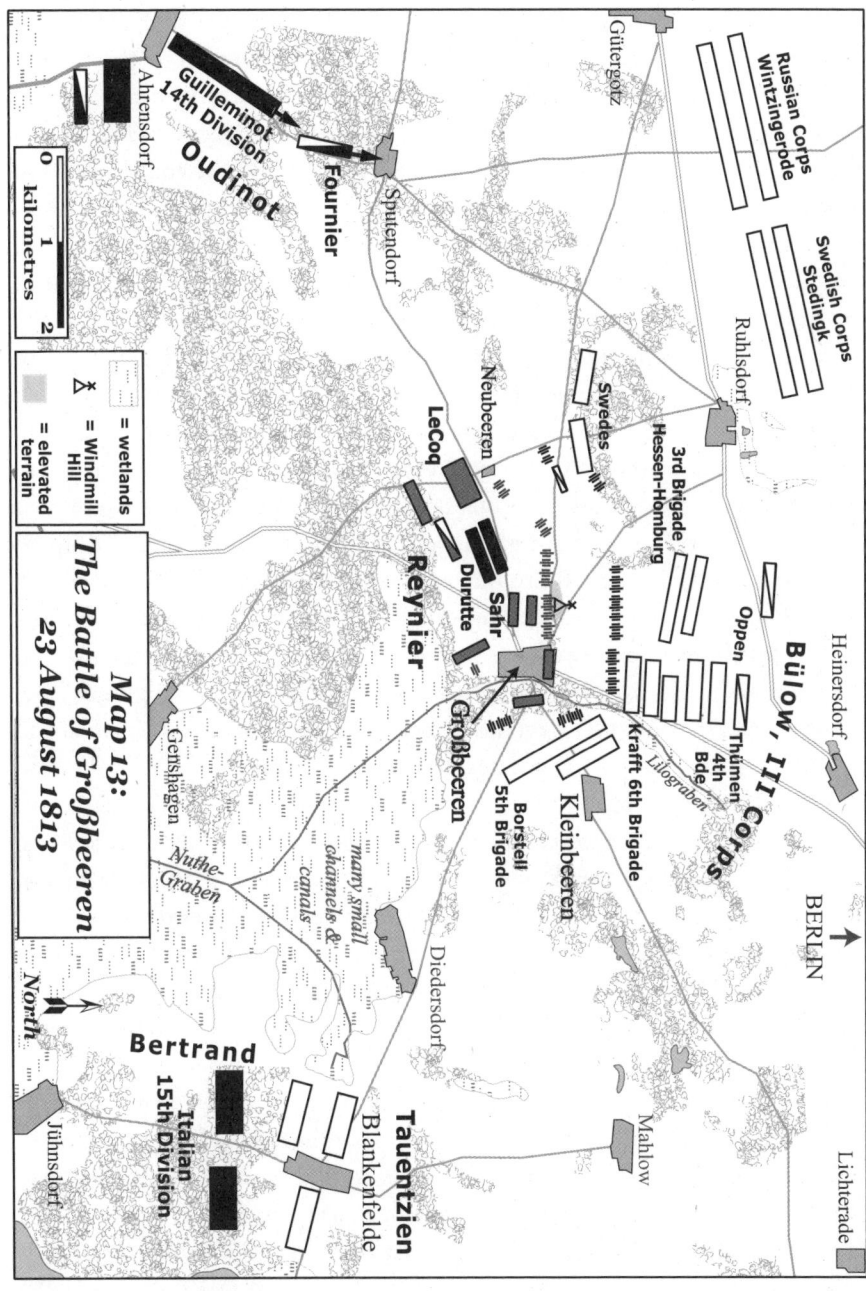

Map 13: The Battle of Großbeeren 23 August 1813

falling back in disarray. This was 'the signal for a general retreat', wrote one of the Saxon brigade commanders, a retreat that 'transformed into a complete rout'.[101] Reynier endeavoured to restore the situation by ordering Durutte against Großbeeren and LeCoq towards the little Windmill Hill, but this attempt collapsed almost immediately. Part of Durutte's division, disordered by fleeing artillery pieces, disintegrated and disappeared into the woods, some of the men throwing away muskets and equipment as they ran.[102] LeCoq engaged in a close fight with the advancing Prussians northeast of Neubeeren but was soon forced back. His division retained enough cohesion to retreat in relative order, but Reynier was fortunate that the fall of night, the drenching rain and Prussian exhaustion prevented any real pursuit. The shaken 7th Corps could thus make its way back to Löwenbruch during the night more or less unmolested.

A final act in this tragedy for Oudinot's Army of Berlin played out on his left flank. GD François Fournier-Sarvlovèse, leading the advance of 12th Corps from Ahrensdorf with his light cavalry division, hastened forward as he heard the cannon fire at Großbeeren and deployed his squadrons in an effort to relieve the pressure on Reynier. It was now after 8:00 p.m. and completely dark, but Prussian cavalry responded, and a wild melee erupted as troopers dashed to and fro in the murk, eventually sweeping past Bülow's astonished infantry in an indistinguishable mass of flailing horsemen. The mounted tumult only began to dissolve when it reached Heinersdorf and the troopers made their ways back to their regiments in small groups. The French 14th Division (GD Armand Charles Guilleminot) had also advanced from Ahrensdorf but with night descending it halted on the edge of the field and did not participate in the action. Likewise, the Bavarians and Lorge, called forward to the area around Trebbin, were not involved in the fighting other than to fend off wandering enemy cavalry detachments. Nonetheless, the sudden appearance of strong French forces near Sputendorf was another reason for Bülow to halt his corps for the night while Oudinot, concerned about his left, called Guilleminot and Fournier back to Ahrensdorf.

Thus ended the Battle of Großbeeren. Losses amounted to approximately 1,000 Prussians as compared to 4,210 men and 13 guns from 7th Corps with another 400 from Fournier's cavalry attack. Reynier had been very severely handled and reported that his command would not be capable of offensive action the next day. The 7th Corps, however, had not been destroyed and Oudinot's other two corps and his cavalry, other than Fournier, had hardly been engaged. The Army of Berlin had certainly suffered a setback, but it was physically intact, and its morale was not broken. What was broken was the marshal's spirit and his willingness to continue with his mission. Believing that 'the losses seem immense', he ordered a retreat on 24 August.[103] Over the following days, the Army of Berlin thus retired towards Wittenberg, fighting rear-guard actions against Prussians and Cossacks on 25, 26, 28 and 29 August in which the Württemberg division figured prominently and favourably (see Chapter 4). Oudinot finally halted the retreat at Wittenberg on 2 September, arraying his army in a semi-circular defensive position just east of the little fortress with 7th Corps and Dąbrowski's division on the left, his own 12th Corps in the centre and Bertrand on the right. Thus ensconced, he awaited further instructions. By now, the army's morale had also declined. 'Such despondency prevailed in the army,' wrote a Westphalian cavalry lieutenant, 'What had happened to the expectations and hopes of conquering Berlin!'[104] Nonetheless, when Bernadotte's subordinates probed the strength of the position on 3 and 4 September, they found it too daunting and desisted from further offensive operations.[105]

The French suffered an additional setback when GL Carl Georg Friedrich von Wobeser's division of Tauntzien's corps joined the somewhat sluggish Allied pursuit. Wobeser had been deployed at Lübben on Bernadotte's far eastern flank but was ordered to Baruth to threaten Oudinot's retreat. Moving south, he attacked and captured Luckau on 28 August along with its small garrison, including an entire Saxon battalion.

It remains to account for the other arms of the abortive French offensive against Berlin. Davout advanced as directed with approximately 27,000 French and Danes to reach Schwerin in Mecklenburg on 23 August. With no information from Oudinot, he dared push no further and retired on Hamburg in early September on learning second-hand of the defeat at Großbeeren.[106] GD Girard was supposed to exercise command of the French division from Magdeburg (GD Lanusse) with a Polish one under GD Dąbrowski from Wittenberg in support of Oudinot. Girard had pushed east with Lanusse's division across the Elbe from Magdeburg on 21 August, but the two divisions were still widely separated when he found himself under attack. While Dąbrowski returned safely to Wittenberg, Girard delayed too long and was caught by Chernishev's Cossacks and a division of Prussian Landwehr under GL Carl Friedrich von Hirschfeld at Hagelberg on 27 August. Girard had some 9,200 men (including three Rheinbund battalions), all new conscripts with little to no training (see Chart 44, Chapter 6). Lax French security measures once again led to complete surprise when Hirschfeld advanced unexpectedly from the north while French attention was focussed on Chernishev's Cossacks to the east. Nonetheless, Girard held his own for several hours against the numerically superior enemy (some 12,000 Prussians plus 2,000–2,500 Cossacks). Hirschfeld's Landwehr were equally inexperienced, but a combination of outflanking moves by the Cossacks and inspired junior leadership among the Prussians eventually broke the French division. As against Prussian losses of 1,750, the French lost more than 6,000, leaving a mere 3,000 demoralised remnants to flee back to Magdeburg. Girard was badly wounded, and his troops arrived in the fortress on 3 September 'in such a state of destitution that one would think they had just conducted a six-month campaign'.[107]

The Hagelberg debacle was the last act of what can be termed the 'Großbeeren operation'. Napoleon had chosen poorly in placing Oudinot in command of the Army of Berlin and directing him to defeat a numerically superior foe en route to Berlin; it was a nearly impossible mission given the resources assigned. The marshal compounded matters by his indifferent leadership and questionable dispositions, especially his decision for an immediate return to Wittenberg after what was a fairly modest affair at Großbeeren. The days of retreat disheartened the troops and frustrated his subordinates[108] while simultaneously encouraging the Allies and supplying them with a propaganda victory that exceeded the material success they had achieved. The Großbeeren operation thus proved to be a damaging exercise in excessive optimism. It would not be the last.

A Catalogue of Defeats: Katzbach and Kulm[109]

On departing Silesia for Dresden Napoleon had left Marshal MacDonald with the 97,000 men of the newly designated 'Army of the Bober' to contain Blücher.[110] The marshal, however, exceeded his instructions, unnecessarily dispersed his forces[111] and was unprepared when he and Blücher collided in an unplanned meeting engagement on 26 August, the same day that major fighting exploded around Dresden. Tactical blunders led to part of MacDonald's army being crushed against a stream swollen by the torrential rains that swept the battlefield, but as at Großbeeren, the greatest losses on the French side, psychological as well as material, occurred during the week of wretched retreat that followed the defeat. By 4 September, the Army of the Bober, weary, dispirited and confused, had dragged itself back 130 kilometres to Bautzen, losing more than 100 guns in the process. Dreadful weather, inadequate logistics and hard marching were the lot of both sides, however, so the casualties suffered by each were not as different as might be supposed: some 22,300 Prussians and Russians as compared to at least 30,000 French.[112] The psychological impact, on the other hand, was enormous. Where the Katzbach victory and subsequent pursuit boosted the Allied Army of Silesia's morale despite its many privations, MacDonald and his army were both demoralised. 'The solders, pale and defeated, most without arms or packs, had the air of walking spectres,' wrote a captain of 3rd Corps, noting that, 'the officers, discouraged by the previous day's unexpected reverse, exhausted by hunger, rain and cold, did not look much better'.[113] The marshal was just as disheartened as his men. In a pathetic letter to Marshal Alexander Berthier, Napoleon's Chief of Staff, he asked to be relieved and declared that 'the indifference of the commanders, the indiscipline, the marauding' and the lack of arms and ammunition made the emperor's presence imperative to restore morale and order. Otherwise, he warned, the army would face 'total dissolution' if it suffered the slightest setback.[114]

While absorbing news of Oudinot's repulse and MacDonald's disaster, Napoleon also learned of another catastrophe, this one suffered by GD Vandamme's 1st Corps at Kulm.[115] This followed from the success at Dresden where the French were now endeavouring to complete the defeat of the Allied Army of Bohemia as it retreated from the Saxon capital. The Allied formations were vulnerable. Struggling over the rugged mountains on poor roads and tracks, the men were tired, hungry, wet, weary, and questioning the indecisive leadership that had thrown them into another repulse. A vigorous, well-coordinated advance likely would have inflicted debilitating losses on the enemy army, but the French bungled the pursuit and Allied good fortune compounded French mistakes. Confusion, lassitude and poor communications on the French side meant that Vandamme, boldly pushing into Bohemia as directed, was left isolated as he clashed with Allied flank guards near the town of Kulm on 29 August. The next day's fighting saw his corps, still unsupported, being driven back when disaster struck in the form of the Prussian II Corps arriving in his rear as it was trying to conclude its own retreat. Outnumbered and surrounded, Vandamme fought on long enough to allow some of his troops to escape, but he and 8,000 to 10,000 of his men were eventually forced to lay down their arms in the presence of the tsar and the Austrian emperor. Total French losses came to as many as 20,000 along with 82 guns, while Allied casualties numbered some 12,000. A pursuit that might have done irreparable harm to the Army of Bohemia thus became another calamity for Napoleon, depriving him of men, guns, an energetic general and considerable prestige, while affording his enemies yet another opportunity to advertise a triumph.[116]

A Catalogue of Defeats: Dennewitz

News of MacDonald's defeat and the allegedly dire state of his army prompted Napoleon to rush from Dresden to Bautzen on 3 September. Leaving parts of the Grande Armée to watch the Allied Army of Bohemia, he put himself at the head of the Army of the Bober and struck east to chasten Blücher. Once the enemy forces in Silesia and Bohemia were defeated or at least contained,

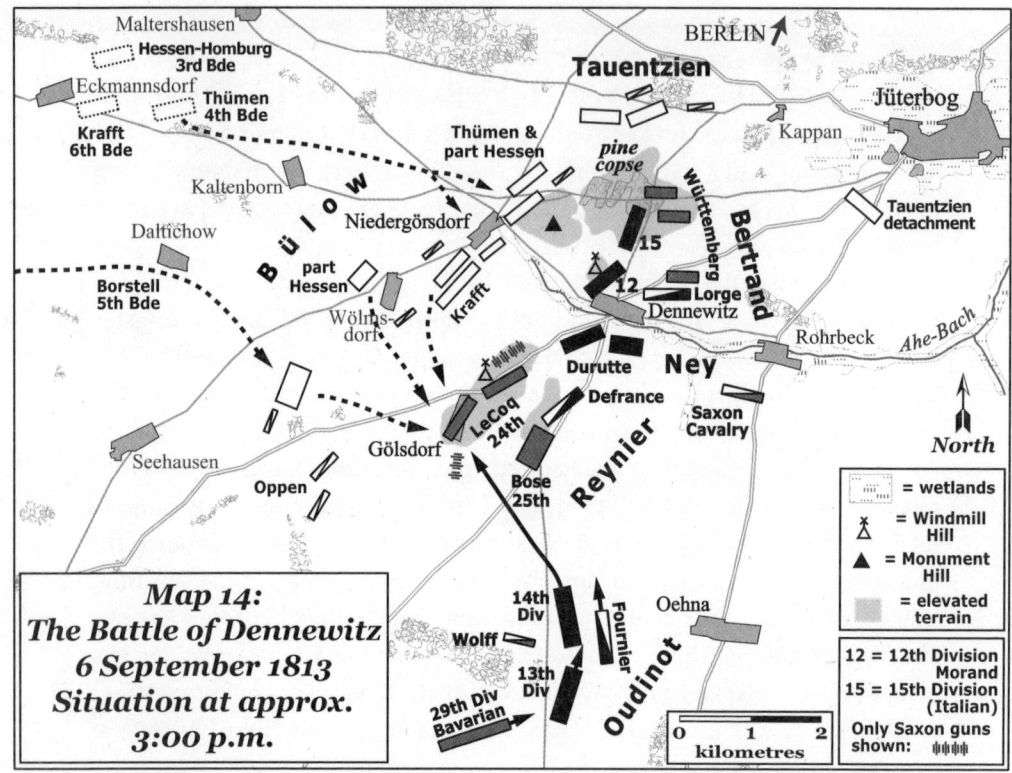

Map 14:
The Battle of Dennewitz
6 September 1813
Situation at approx.
3:00 p.m.

he hoped to turn north and strike at Bernadotte. To this end, he sent Marshal Ney to Wittenberg with orders to take command of the shaken Army of Berlin and march east to reach Baruth on the 6th. Napoleon expected to be in Luckau that day to support a new advance on Berlin. After repulsing Blücher, he wrote, 'I will march on Berlin with all haste.'[117] These decisions led to the next French setback: the Battle of Dennewitz.[118]

Ney arrived in Wittenberg on 3 September and held a review of his new command the following day in the midst of Allied probes against his lines at Thießen and Euper. His Army of Berlin now included a small Polish 'division' under Dąbrowski (only some 2,800 men) but otherwise contained the same formations that Oudinot had led to defeat at Großbeeren. Subtracting losses in this previous operation, the army numbered some 65,000 men with 197 guns. Wasting no time, Ney marched for Baruth as directed on 5 September with 12th Corps in the lead. Oudinot placed his French divisions and one of his Bavarian brigades at the head of his column, kept the other brigade of GL Clemens von Raglovich's Bavarian division in reserve and covered his northern flank with 29th Light Cavalry Brigade, a formation of Rheinbund cavalry jointly commanded by French GD Beaumont and GB Marc

François Jérôme Wolff, a Frenchman in Westphalian service. Oudinot's troops encountered elements of Borstell's and Dobschütz's Prussian formations just west of Zahna and pushed them back in moderately heavy fighting that lasted most of the day. Though the French regarded the Engagement at Zahna as a fairly routine affair, for the loss of perhaps 600 men, they had inflicted 3,000 casualties on the Prussians and severely shaken the Landwehr of Dobschütz's division.[119] The small detachment from Borstell's division retired to the north undisturbed, but Dobschütz conducted an exhausting and discouraging retreat all the way to Jüterbog, 25 kilometres to the northeast. Protected by a Cossack detachment at Rohrbeck ('those loyal guardians of resting armies'[120]), he was joined here by Tauentzien, who had been absent at army headquarters all day. A more vigorous pursuit likely would have crippled Dobschütz, but the French, satisfied with having cleared the road ahead, settled in for the night between Zahna and Seyda on the road to Jüterbog.

The coming battle would be fought on the rolling farmland just west and southwest of Jüterbog. This was a pleasant region of low, gently sloped hills dotted with villages and a few small stands of trees. The soil, however, was loose and powdery, what the chroniclers of the time called 'sandy'. As a result, it quickly created huge clouds of dust when disturbed as it was by a strong wind, not to mention the thousands of horses, guns, wagons and marching feet that crisscrossed the area on 6 September 1813. Blowing dust, combined with the vast billows of smoke attendant upon the firing of nineteenth-century muskets and cannon, would prove a major factor during the battle, obscuring the field and imposing significant limitations on commanders trying to read the enemy's actions and direct their own troops. The weather was dry and hot, making the dust more prevalent and contributing to the enervation of the men and horses on both sides, most of whom would march many kilometres without rest or a chance to drink before being hurled into the most desperate combat. The only watercourse of note was the Ahe-Bach (or Agarbach), a small stream originating near Niedergörsdorf to flow south of Dennewitz and north of Rohrbeck as it made its way east. Though seemingly negligible in size, its marshy banks made it a significant obstacle for troop movement, and it could only be crossed easily at three bridges: one each in Dennewitz and Rohrbeck as well as a third just east of the latter village.

Like Oudinot at Großbeeren, Ney did not expect a battle on 6 September, but the routes he assigned to the three corps and the cavalry essentially had them conducting a flank march across the front of Bernadotte's Army of the North. Although the Russian and Swedish corps were somewhat distant at Rabenstein (31 kilometres from Jüterbog), Bülow had moved to Kurzlipsdorf during the 5th and Tauentzien was around Jüterbog as just described. A clash with the latter was almost inevitable as the French advanced and Bülow, 14 kilometres west of Jüterbog, would be in relatively easy supporting distance. Ney, however, completely neglected to order any reconnaissance and seems to have had little idea of enemy locations. Moreover, a combination of confused orders and errors by several corps commanders meant that the Army of Berlin's constituent elements marched at widely separated distances, such that several hours would elapse before they could hope to act in concert. None of this augured well for Ney's command.

The battle opened shortly before 10:00 a.m. when Bertrand's 4th Corps, leading the Army of Berlin's advance, approached the Ahe-Bach near Dennewitz. Tauentzien, feeling vulnerable at Jüterbog, had decided to shift closer to Bülow that morning. Leaving a detachment in front of Jüterbog, he was marching Dobschütz's division west and had arrived near a pair of small pine copses north of Dennewitz when Bertrand's guns opened up. On Ney's instructions, Bertrand attacked at once, sending the Italian 15th Division across the stream directly against Tauentzien's Landwehr while GD Charles Antoine Morand's French 12th Division peeled off to the west behind Lorge's light cavalry division.[121] Tauentzien attempted to counter by advancing his infantry and guns, but his artillery was overwhelmed, while his inexperienced foot soldiers quickly exhausted their ammunition and fell into confusion under Italian musketry and artillery fire. The Prussian line thus tumbled back as the Italians pushed into the western copse and six Württemberg battalions crossed the Ahe-Bach to deploy north of Dennewitz. Desperate to hold on until Bülow could come to his assistance, Tauentzien launched his cavalry at the advancing enemy. This proved a complete success when the Prussian horsemen, dashing out of the swirling smoke and dust, halted the Italian infantry and overthrew Lorge's cavalry division. The French troopers scattered in discreditable panic, fleeing to the rear to spread fear and confusion as far back as the corps trains northeast of Oehna. Morand's infantry and the formed Württemberg battalions just outside Dennewitz brought the Prussian mounted attack to a halt and the Polish lancers, who had kept their composure, helped drive off the Prussians. The 4th Corps advance then resumed: Morand on the left to what is now the 'Denkmalsberg' ('Monument Hill'),[122] Italians in the centre to the little pine wood, four Württemberg battalions on the right, partly in the woods, partly in the open fields to the east. The other two Württemberg battalions remained near Dennewitz with their horse battery. It was now just after 1:00 p.m., and a brief pause ensued while Bülow's corps began to appear on the French left.

Leading Bülow's advance was GM Heinrich Ludwig August von Thümen's 4th Brigade. Thümen immediately attempted to seize the low Denkmalsberg, but the French had got there first, and his hasty attack was repelled in confusion with no little loss. As the afternoon wore on, however, Morand withdrew from the Denkmalsberg and Thümen's men pushed the Italians out of the pine copse. The four Württemberg battalions in and near the trees were now in a dire situation. Attacked by Thümen's infantry from the woods to the west and by Tauentzien's cavalry and guns from the north, they were trapped and destroyed in bitter hand-to-hand fighting after obstinate resistance. Bertrand's entire corps fell back towards Rohrbeck and retired south of the Ahe-Bach leaving the field north of the stream in Prussian hands.

Ney, however, was not about to give up the fight. Focused on the area immediately to his front and behaving like a corps commander rather than the leader of an army, he looked for fresh troops and found them in Durutte's 32nd Division. Durutte had arrived south of the Ahe-Bach at the head of 7th Corps between 1:00 and 2:00 p.m., anchoring Reynier's right flank while the two Saxon divisions extended his battle line to the southwest towards Gölsdorf. Ney now threw one of Durutte's brigades across the stream but these isolated battalions, cannonaded from two sides, gave way and retired back to the south when Thümen's infantry attacked. A near-simultaneous effort to renew the offensive with Bertrand's shaken command from Rohrbeck likewise faltered and 4th Corps, covered by the remaining Württemberg battalions and a battery, withdrew across the Ahe-Bach in considerable disorder. Eager Prussian infantry occupied both villages.

Reynier's 7th Corps was thus on the field by around 2:00 p.m. while the fight north of the Ahe-Bach was in progress. Struggling through the mass of panicky supply vehicles west of Oehna and annoyed by Cossacks, Durutte deployed just to the southwest of Dennewitz and the stream, while the Saxon 24th Division moved up on his left, opposite the village of Gölsdorf. The 25th Division arrayed itself to the east behind the 24th with GD Jean Marie Antoine Defrance's division of dragoons to its right, partly behind Durutte. Reynier, noticing the presence of enemy cavalry beyond Rohrbeck (part of the detachment Tauentzien had left at Jüterbog), sent the Saxon light horse brigade to hold them in check. Meanwhile, Bülow had brought Krafft's brigade up on Thümen's right south of Neidergörsdorf. What became a vicious and extended contest for Gölsdorf thus developed between Krafft's men and the advancing Saxons of Oberst Alexander Ferdinand von Mellenthin's brigade.[123] As Mellenthin's men mastered the village, Oberst Friedrich Wilhelm August von Brause deployed his brigade on the low 'windmill hill' northeast of the village as support to the Saxon batteries unlimbering there. Faced with the fire of Saxon and French guns from this height, Krafft pulled back to await reinforcements. Reynier, for his part, was also looking for support. He was in a position to threaten and perhaps roll up Bülow's right flank but would need Oudinot's corps to do so.

Unfortunately for the French, the first reinforcements to appear were elements of Bülow's reserve (GM Prinz Ludwig von Hessen-Homburg's 3rd Brigade). These succeeded in wrenching Gölsdorf from the Saxons and soon received welcome support from Borstell's 5th Brigade. The course of the battle seemed about to take a turn, however, when Oudinot's corps arrived on the scene. Reynier convinced the marshal to commit his men to the fight for Gölsdorf and, with support from a French brigade, Mellenthin once again captured the village from the exhausted Prussians. The Saxon and French artillery were dominating the opposing batteries, Borstell's men were showing signs of unsteadiness and the rest of Bernadotte's army was still too distant to assist when two things happened.[124] First, Bülow, alarmed by the turn of events on his right, ordered the entire Prussian line south of the stream to renew the assault on the Saxon position. Second, narrowly focused on what was occurring directly in front of him near Dennewitz, Ney ordered Oudinot to march to the right to support 4th Corps and retrieve the situation along the Ahe-Bach. It was, as a later Prussian historian wrote, 'an almost miraculous shift in the state of affairs'.[125]

It was now approximately 5:00 p.m. and Bertrand's defeated troops were retiring in disorder, when Oudinot, ignoring Reynier's entreaties, decided to obey Ney's instructions even though it was clear that his departure would place 7th Corps in grave danger.[126] The billowing dust clouds stirred up by Oudinot's movement generated opposite reactions on the two sides of the field: the Prussians were encouraged by what seemed to be evidence of the enemy's retreat, while the Saxons concluded that they were being abandoned. Krafft and Borstell thus advanced with revived vigour while the Saxons, despite desperate resistance, lost both Gölsdorf and the windmill hill.[127] Falling back in confusion, the Saxons crashed into Oudinot's march columns and threw them into disarray. Defrance's dragoons imposed some delay on the Prussians, allowing the Saxons to regain a degree of coherence, but Oudinot's 13th and 14th Divisions recoiled to the rear suffering heavily from enemy artillery fire 'that killed many in the ranks'. In the words of the 12th Corps journal: 'Our left was entirely outflanked by the enemy.'[128] Although Oudinot claimed that all three of his divisions retired 'in the best order and in battalion squares', his formations were repeatedly disrupted by Defrance's and Fournier's fleeing troopers, even though the latter had not come into contact with the enemy all afternoon.[129]

For a time, it seemed that some sort of rear-guard defence could be organised on the slightly elevated ground just west of Oehna with the Bavarians and some of the Saxon units, but as the hastily retreating combat troops tumbled back on the parks and trains in that area, all order dissolved. 'Our retreat, or better said, our flight, was so precipitous that there was no way we could deploy into line even once,' remembered GB Louis Bertrand Pierre Brun de Villeret, one of Oudinot's brigade commanders.[130] The Poles and some of the German units retained sufficient composure to provide shelter for Ney and other commanders, but as Russian cavalry arrived to energise the pursuit and enemy shells burst amidst the roiling mass of men, horses and vehicles, the Army of Berlin disintegrated and fled into the forests south of Oehna in a hopeless, helpless jumble enveloped in impenetrable clouds of dust and smoke. The Allied artillery crashing into the disordered moil was such that one Württemberg officer was reminded of the chaos at the Berezina River in 1812. 'Luck had abandoned the French troops, victory their banners!' wrote a lieutenant in the Westphalian Chevaulegers-Garde, 'Ney's mighty army was no more.'[131]

Under such circumstances, it is hardly surprising that the routing elements of Ney's army wandered off in different directions with no overall guidance. Ney had wanted to retreat to Dahme but issuing orders to the army was impossible and both Oudinot and Reynier considered Torgau the only reasonable refuge. With the forces they still controlled and many fugitives, they thus made their separate ways to the Elbe, arriving opposite Torgau during the course of 7 September. Ney, the Bavarians, most of 4th Corps and other elements reached Dahme during the night only to experience another blow the next morning. Bülow's Prussians were too exhausted and battered to pursue as night brought an end to the fighting, but Russian cavalry, Cossacks and one of the ubiquitous Allied raiding detachments scooped up thousands of French, Italian and German prisoners along with guns, caissons, supply wagons and equipment of every description.

If Bülow's men were too weary to take up the chase and most of the Russians and Swedes still too distant, GM von Wobeser once again appeared to compound the French debacle. As described above, Wobeser had been at Luckau since capturing the town on 28 August. Now from Dennewitz, Tauentzien had the good sense to direct him to harass the French rear and intercept their retreat. Marching through the night, Wobeser's division reached Dahme early on 7 September. Ney and the majority of the troops there had already gone, but Wobeser attacked the French rear guard in the town and took some 3,000 prisoners after a desperate defence by the 23ᵉ Ligne.

Fleeing Dahme, Bertrand's corps skirmished with Cossacks while trying to cross the Schwarze Elster at Herzberg only to suffer a final indignity on the morning of 8 September outside Torgau. Covering the Army of Berlin's withdrawal across the Elbe as rear guard that morning, the men, already shaken and drained, fell into an indescribable panic when several thousand Russian cavalry and Cossacks appeared near Zwethau and began lobbing shells into the confused crowd of retreating soldiers, horses and wagons. GL Friedrich von Franquemont, commanding the Württemberg division, managed to extricate most of his remaining men and seek shelter in the bridgehead east of the river, but the bulk of the corps fled to the fortress in disgraceful disorder, a demoralising conclusion to Ney's Berlin foray.[132]

A victory owing almost entirely to Prussian troops,[133] Dennewitz was another calamity for the French, far worse than Großbeeren. The Army of Berlin lost some 22,000 men between 5 and 8 September, or one-third of its total strength at the start of the operation, along with 53 guns and more than 400 vehicles of all sorts. In addition, so many of the French, German and Italian soldiers had thrown away their muskets in their flight that rearming the infantry regiments became a major concern for Ney's subordinates in the days that followed the defeat. The cost was also high on the side of the victors, with Bülow and Tauentzien together losing at least 10,500 men killed, wounded or captured. Once again, however, the psychological impact was as important as the physical: the Allies could celebrate yet another triumph while the French had to endure yet another significant defeat. The Army of Berlin's morale plummeted and, as with Oudinot and MacDonald, so did that of its commander. 'It is my duty to declare that it is impossible to make good use of the 4th, 7th and 12th Corps in their current states of organisation,' Ney reported to Berthier, 'The morale of the generals and of the officers in general is singularly shaken; commanding like this is only to be half in command and I would rather just be a grenadier.' If he could not dispense with the corps commanders and simply have divisional generals under his orders, he asked if Napoleon 'would be willing to withdraw me from this hell'. In another similarity to MacDonald, the sole solution Ney saw was Napoleon's personal intervention: 'In the current situation, only the presence of the emperor can re-establish unity, because all wills cede to his genius and the petty vanities disappear before the majesty of the throne.'[134]

The disaster at Dennewitz also contributed to worsening relations between the French and their German allies. Ney expressed a general distrust of all the non-French troops in his army, telling Berthier that, 'Your Grace should also be informed that the foreign troops of all nations manifest the worst possible spirit, the cavalry that I have with me is likely more harmful than useful.' He reserved specific ire for the Saxons, blaming them for the defeat in his initial report to Napoleon and subsequent communications with Berthier (even though the dusty obscurity meant that he probably could not see that portion of the field).[135] This accusation was repeated in the public account published under his name in the official French *Moniteur Universel* and, worse, in the *Leipziger Zeitung* in late September (*see* Chapter 2).[136] The Army of Berlin's flaws in general and the alleged failings of the Saxons in specific, of course, also supplied convenient excuses for Ney's own errors. Furthermore, as shall be seen, the mistrust went both ways, creating a set of mutually reinforcing recriminations that did not bode well for future operations.

One other consequence of Dennewitz was the reorganisation of the former Army of Berlin. Despite the debacle, the emperor left Ney in command of the forces now recuperating west of the Elbe near Wittenberg. Owing to the losses suffered, however, significant changes were necessary. In the first place, 12th Corps was abolished and Oudinot was recalled to lead a pair of Young Guard divisions. Of its constituent units, the much-reduced Bavarian 29th Division was detached for garrison duty in Dresden, while the 14th Division was disbanded, its regiments being absorbed into the 13th. The re-formed division, placed under GD Guilleminot's command, was then assigned to Reynier's 7th Corps. Similarly, the badly damaged Saxon divisions were amalgamated into one, the 24th, leaving Reynier with two French divisions (13th and 32nd) and only one of Saxons (24th). Bertrand's corps received 29th Light Cavalry Brigade with its Hessian and Westphalian cavalry regiments under the joint command of Beaumont and Wolff (the Bavarian light horse rode off with its division) but was otherwise unchanged. For next several weeks, therefore, Ney's army would consist of 4th and 7th Corps, 3rd Cavalry Corps and Dąbrowski's small Polish division.[137]

A Month of Manoeuvring: September–October 1813

Napoleon received the news of Dennewitz with remarkable calm. Present at dinner with the emperor when a staff general arrived with a detailed account of 'one of the greatest disasters of the campaign', Marshal Gouvion Saint-Cyr recorded that Napoleon 'spoke with a calmness that he could have put into a discussion about news of events in China or in the previous century'.[138] The emperor's overall situation, however, was steadily deteriorating. Although he had quickly revitalised MacDonald's army, Blücher had avoided his stroke in

Silesia and Schwarzenberg's Army of Bohemia was once again stirring. A Saxon general likened Napoleon's predicament to the final act of Shakespeare's *Macbeth*: 'They have me tied to a stake,' says the harried thane, 'I cannot fly, but bear-like I must fight the course.'[139] After several more fruitless forays against these two Allied armies, he abruptly decided to abandon the east bank of the Elbe and transfer his base of operations from Dresden to Leipzig.

While Napoleon was shifting his forces, Blücher saw a chance to energise Allied operations by moving north towards Bernadotte and taking his army across the Elbe. The result of his determination and initiative was a complex series of manoeuvres and clashes in the area between Torgau, Wittenberg, Rosslau and Halle during late September and the first half of October. Bernadotte edged over the Elbe near Rosslau and Yorck's I Corps of Blücher's army gained a crossing at Wartenburg on 3 October after a tough fight with Bertrand's corps that nearly destroyed the thin remnants of the Württemberg division. Napoleon, who had stubbornly kept Dresden as his centre of operations, responded to these developments by leaving the Saxon capital on 7 October to drive north on both sides of the Mulde River. He even pushed some forces across the Elbe for a few days, including 7th Corps. Reynier achieved some handsome successes against Tauentzien and Thümen east of Elbe, and Ney's troops successfully stormed Dessau on 12 October, but Napoleon could not bring Bernadotte or Blücher to bay. The two Allied armies slipped west across the Saale after the French emperor found his attention drawn south by the methodical advances of Schwarzenberg with the Army of Bohemia.

Napoleon had posted Murat with several corps west of Dresden to guard the exits from Bohemia while he tried to trap Blücher or Bernadotte north of Leipzig. Although the Allied Army of Bohemia advanced 'at a turtle's pace',[140] it outnumbered Murat three or four to one and slowly pushed his troops back towards Leipzig. Finally ordered to hold his ground, Murat halted and gave battle at Liebertwolkwitz on 14 October in what was the largest cavalry engagement of the war. Sometimes considered the first day of the Battle of Leipzig, the furious but inconclusive fighting around Liebertwolkwitz was a direct prelude to the coming struggle, halting the ponderous Allied advance and defining what would become the southern end of the French line.

Forces from both sides now streamed towards Leipzig. Napoleon left garrisons in Magdeburg, Wittenberg, Torgau and, controversially, two corps in Dresden (1st and 14th under Gouvion Saint-Cyr) but ordered the rest of the Grande Armée to concentrate around Saxony's ancient commercial centre. Also left behind was the bulk of the Grande Armée's artillery park and baggage train, nearly 7,000 men and more than 600 vehicles escorted by the feeble

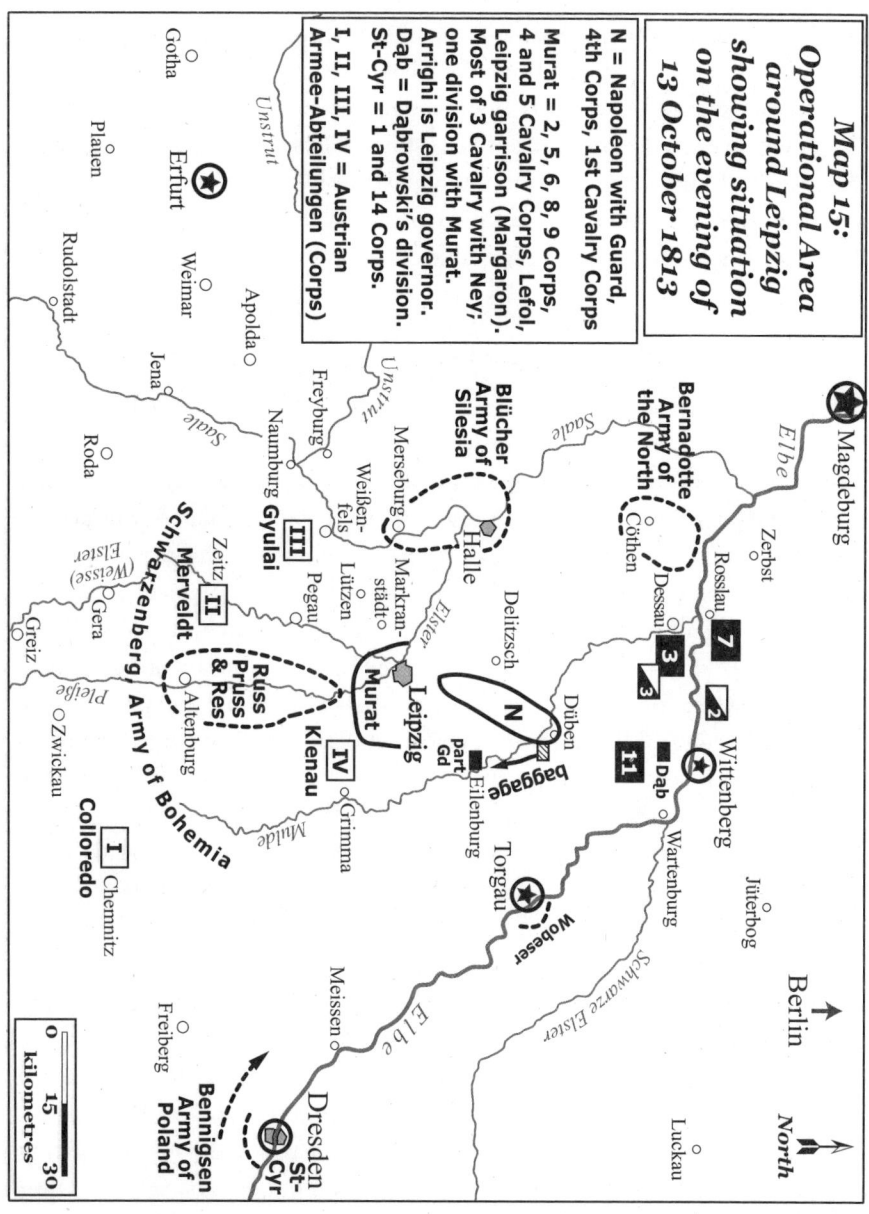

Map 15: Operational Area around Leipzig showing situation on the evening of 13 October 1813

remains of the Bavarian contingent and a Hessian battalion. Napoleon had placed this cumbersome convoy under the command of recently promoted GB Antoine Simon Durrieu and ordered it to halt at Eilenburg to await further instructions.

On the Allied side, the scattered elements of the Army of Bohemia pushed to close up on a long arc stretching from Markranstädt in the west to Grimma in the east. Behind came Bennigsen and the Army of Poland, having left a small corps to observe Dresden. From the north, Blücher drove the Army of Silesia along the right bank of the Elster River with great energy while Bernadotte followed cautiously in his wake. These Allied movements meant that Napoleon would find himself almost entirely surrounded at Leipzig, 'at the bottom of a funnel' in Marmont's memorable words.[141] If he could not win a victory over at least one of the Allied armies in the coming battle he would be faced with a potentially irremediable defeat.

Allied Raiding Detachments: Infesting All the Country, Autumn 1813

Before turning to Leipzig, it is useful to revisit the context in which the battle occurred, specifically the numerous Allied raiding detachments and the havoc they caused in the French rear areas. At the southern end of the theatre of war, the Army of Bohemia, otherwise fairly torpid, launched several such detachments into Saxony at the beginning of September. One under Austrian Oberst Emanuel Graf Mensdorff-Pouilly was to harass French communications between Leipzig and Dresden with a mixed command of some 1,200 Austrian regular cavalry and Cossacks. At the same time, a larger detachment of Austrians, Prussians and Cossacks (2,000 men with two guns) was directed against the principal French line of communications from Leipzig to Erfurt. This group was commanded by Thielmann, the former Saxon officer, now in the service of the tsar as a Russian lieutenant general. Both were troublesome to the French as they intercepted couriers, collected intelligence, overwhelmed small garrisons, captured supply trains and dispersed replacement columns, but Thielmann proved especially effective in this role. By the middle of September, a frustrated Napoleon found it necessary to dedicate more than 8,000 men from the Leipzig garrison and the main army, including a division of Young Guard cavalry under GD Charles Lefebvre-Desnouettes, to suppress the raiders.[142] These countermeasures began to restrict the raiding parties, but Thielmann, reinforced by Mensdorff and additional troops from the Army of Bohemia, managed to inflict a humiliating defeat on Lefebvre-Desnouettes at Altenburg on 28 September. In confused and bitter fighting, the Allied raiders lost 300 men, but the French suffered some 1,400 casualties, including the destruction of four companies of Baden infantry.[143] Despite this success, the additional French troops constrained Thielmann's operations and he was recalled along with the other detachments at the end of September while the Allies prepared to advance on Leipzig.

Even more damaging to Napoleon's cause were forays that struck the principal cities of his youngest brother's Kingdom of Westphalia. Prussian

Oberstleutnant Friedrich August Ludwig von der Marwitz, receiving orders from Bernadotte to launch disruptive raids into Westphalia, crossed the Elbe north of Magdeburg with some 400 Landwehr cavalry and decided to undertake an attack on Braunschweig (Brunswick), the kingdom's largest city. Appearing before the walls on 25 September, he frightened off and dispersed the garrison, captured several hundred Westphalian and Waldeck soldiers and made off with large amounts of money and other loot to the acclamations of the population.

More spectacular still was a raid on Kassel conducted by Chernishev. He crossed the Elbe between Magdeburg and Rosslau on the night of 14/15 September at the head of some 2,500 Russian regulars and Cossacks with four cannon. Learning from captured correspondence that the authorities in Kassel believed the garrison was too weak and that the city was subject to surprise, Chernishev turned towards the Westphalian capital. Making good time despite a convoluted march route, he arrived outside the city on the morning of 28 September. The Westphalian defenders, knowing von der Marwitz had seized Braunschweig two days earlier, panicked and King Jérôme fled the city in haste. Chernishev called off his initial attack owing to reports that significant Westphalian reinforcements were en route but returned two days later to force the capitulation of the city. He made a jubilant entrance into Kassel on 1 October, declared the Kingdom of Westphalia dissolved and remained for two more days before the approach of French reinforcements made withdrawal necessary. For the loss of 70 men, Chernishev's audacity had garnered him 2,000 prisoners (many of whom took service against Napoleon), 30 guns, thousands in currency and all manner of munitions. The psychological impact of his brassy raid, of course, far exceeded these material rewards, providing vivid evidence of the fragility of the Westphalian state and inadequacy of Napoleon's rear-area security measures in 1813.[144]

Dramatic highlights such as Chernishev's Kassel raid or Thielmann's victory at Altenburg are only part of the raiding detachment story in 1813. The proliferation of such detachments, even if small, meant that the entire French rear area, including, as Napoleon had warned Jérôme back in January, much of Rheinbund Germany, was at risk. French reports frequently succumbed to unsubstantiated rumour, exaggerating the numbers of raiders and attributing to them the worst in terms of ferocity, speed and elusiveness.[145] Large columns of replacements and otherwise secure garrisons thus disintegrated or surrendered at the mere appearance of a hundred so of the barbaric and exotic Cossacks or their regular army companions. Exaggerated stories of enemy strengths and movements were granted instant credence, exhausting the defenders with constant alarms and pointless excursions. As Graf Wilhelm von Hochberg, the Baden contingent commander in Leipzig dolefully noted: 'These false rumours reappeared every day which made our duties very strenuous.'[146] In part this was a legacy of the hideous retreat from Russia in 1812, especially as regards the Cossacks, but it also indicated a decline in skill, determination and confidence among many officers and men in the 1813 Grande Armée.

No place seemed safe. French and German reports of the period are replete with references to intercepted communications, captured garrisons and the need to allot thousands of men to escort convoys of flour or columns of recruits. A large ammunition convoy destined for MacDonald's desperate army was attacked and destroyed just west of Bautzen on 3 September, for example, and one reason Oudinot's corps marched to Großbeeren encumbered by their trains was that the commanders feared Cossack raiders would seize their supply wagons if these were left behind. GD Pierre Margaron, the commandant in Leipzig, reported on 16 September that Thielmann's band 'infested all the country' around Naumburg and Weißenfels, 'where he has all the more influence since all the inhabitants are inspired by his presence not to supply the requisitions which are made of them, and that as a result the supplies of this city are made with the greatest difficulty and that the subsistence of the whole army depends on the promptness with which he will be driven out of all that region'.[147] Similarly, Saxon GL von Gersdorff wrote on 6 September that 'the Cossack patrols penetrated through the intervals between the army corps and came as far as the heights above Dresden'.[148] Napoleon even had to warn Baden GM von Schäffer to disguise himself in civilian clothes when travelling back to Karlsruhe 'as I do not want you to be taken'.[149] This pervasive insecurity in the army's strategic rear had important material repercussions – such as the loss of MacDonald's ammunition train – but, once again, the psychological factor was just as important, encouraging Napoleon's enemies across Germany while eroding the morale of his French troops and their German allies.

One final word on these raiding parties, especially their irregular components, is useful before proceeding. The citizens of Germany, Saxony above all, were justifiably wroth at the depredations perpetrated by French soldiery even when operating in the lands of their allies. After recounting how nearby soldiers had 'turned the villages upside down, demanded money from the peasants, taken their horses and looted all the houses', for instance, a French general concluded a report to a fellow commander with a grim warning: 'If such brigandage continues, I have no doubt, my general, that the Saxons will soon become Spaniards.'[150] This is a topic to be revisited at several points in the chapters ahead. At the same time, the marauders from the Allied ranks that haunted the regions behind their advancing armies could be just as pitiless. The Austrian official history repeatedly notes the abuses inflicted on local civilians during the advance on Dresden as poorly supplied soldiers, desperate for food and for shelter from the drenching rain, broke ranks to search for sustenance beyond sodden commissary bread that had turned to mush.[151]

The situation could be just as bad elsewhere. Prussian Landwehr deserters and even some regulars 'plundered and stole on their own hook' in the wake of the Army of Silesia, but the worst and most routine cruelties were blamed on the Russians, particularly the Cossacks.[152] As Radetzky lamented during the period between Kulm and the renewal of the Army of Bohemia's advance:

> The Cossacks pursued their abuses between Prague and the army, plundered the local people and held up the army supply wagons. Everywhere one came upon Russian detachments that had quartered themselves according to their own wishes and which, once they had "eaten out" a district, moved on to begin the game anew.[153]

Local inhabitants, noted Saxon officer Heinrich Aster, regarded the Russians as the worst of their military visitors that fearful year: 'Tales of the crudeness, violence and rapacity of the undisciplined Russian soldiers who were found with the regular troops in Saxony will be repeated from mouth to mouth, to children and children's children for a long time, as one now, after the passage of 30 years, still speaks of them with horror.'[154] As in most wars, therefore, the civilian population suffered dreadfully in 1813, victims of both their supposed allies and their putative liberators.

The Battle of Nations: Leipzig, 16–19 October 1813

The Battle of Leipzig was nineteenth-century Europe's largest military engagement, dwarfing all others in length and in the numbers of forces engaged. For four long days, an immense congregation of troops struggled to determine the fate of Napoleonic Germany. Napoleon commanded more than 190,000 men with units from France, Italy, Poland, Naples, Spain and his Illyrian Provinces as well as elements of seven Rheinbund contingents. Russians predominated on the Allied side (and the tsar was the preponderant voice at headquarters), but the bulk of the Austrian and Prussian armies were present along with Bernadotte's Swedish corps, some small non-Prussian German volunteer units and, curiously, a lone rocket artillery battery representing Great Britain. In all, Napoleon's Coalition opponents brought some 350,000 men to the field. The vast forces assembled by the two sides thus made Leipzig the largest

Chart 9: The Allied Armies at Leipzig, 16–19 October 1813

The Army of Bohemia or Main Army (*Hauptarmee*)
FM Schwarzenberg accompanied by the three Allied monarchs

Austrian Troops

1st Austrian Light Division	FML Liechtenstein
I Austrian Corps	FZM Colloredo
II Austrian Corps	General der Kavallerie Merveldt
III Austrian Corps	FZM Gyulai
IV Austrian Corps	FZM Klenau
Austrian Reserve Corps	General der Kavallerie Hessen-Homburg
Austrian Cuirassier Corps	FML Nostitz

Russian Troops — *General of Cavalry Wittgenstein*

I Russian Infantry Corps	Lieutenant General Gorchakov
II Russian Infantry Corps	Herzog Eugene of Württemberg
Cavalry Corps	Lieutenant General Pahlen III
Cossack Corps	Lieutenant General Count Platov

Russo-Prussian Guards and Reserve

III Russian Infantry (Grenadier) Corps	Lieutenant General Rayevsky
V Russian Infantry (Guard) Corps	Lieutenant General Yermolov
Prussian Guard Infantry Brigade	Oberstleutnant von Alvensleben
Cavalry Corps	Lieutenant General Golitsyn V
Prussian Guard Cavalry Brigade	GM von Röder

Prussian Troops

II Prussian Corps	GL von Kleist	9th, 10th, 11th and 12th Brigades, Cavalry Brigade

Raiding Detachments

Thielmann	8½ Austrian and Prussian cavalry squadrons, 2 Cossack regiments
Mensdorff-Pouilly	3 Austrian cavalry squadrons, 2 Cossack regiments

European battle prior to the First World War while the colourful mix of armies and the issues at stake quickly led observers to refer to Leipzig as the 'Battle of Nations' or *Völkerschlacht*. It is not the purpose here to recount this titanic struggle in detail, but an outline is important to understand the role the various German contingents played in its conduct and outcome.[155]

The battlefield around Leipzig was divided by rivers: the Weiße Elster, Pleiße, Luppe and Parthe. None of these is easily fordable and all present serious obstacles to military operations. The most important of these was

The Army of Silesia
General der Kavallerie von Blücher

I Prussian Corps	GL von Yorck	1st, 2nd, 7th and 8th Brigades, Reserve Cavalry
XI Russian Corps	Lt. Gen. Osten-Sacken	2 infantry divisions, 1 infantry brigade, 3 cavalry brigades
Russian Corps	General of Infantry Langeron	IX and X Infantry Corps, part of I Cavalry Corps
VIII Russian Corps	Lt. Gen. St Priest	2 infantry divisions, 1 dragoon brigade, Cossacks

The Army of the North
Carl Johann, Crown Prince of Sweden (Bernadotte)

III Prussian Corps	GL von Bülow	3rd, 5th and 6th Brigades, Reserve Cavalry
Russian Corps	Lt. Gen. von Wintzingerode	3 infantry divisions, 3 cavalry brigades, Cossacks
Swedish Corps	Field Marshal Stedingk	2 infantry divisions, 2 cavalry brigades, British rocket battery

The Army of Poland
General of Cavalry von Bennigsen

Advance Guard	Lt. Gen. Stroganov	infantry brigade, Cossacks
Main Body	General of Infantry Dokhturov	3 infantry divisions, 1 cavalry division
Attached		
2nd Austrian Light Division	FML Bubna	

Note: The order of battle outlined above reflects the alterations in the Austrian army's organisation since the beginning of the autumn phase of the war. 'Corps' is used here for the official Austrian term of the time '*Armee-Abteilung*'. Bülow's subordinate formations in III Prussian Corps are often termed 'divisions'. Tauentzien and Thümen not present.
Source: Hoen, *Leipzig*, Anhang II; Juhel, Nafziger.

the Weiße Elster (or here simply the Elster, not to be confused with the Schwarze Elster on the right bank of the Elbe), which flows north past the city before turning abruptly west to join the Saale. Paralleled by the Pleiße to the south and the Luppe to the north of the city, the Elster and its sister streams form a nearly impassable tangle of boggy terrain criss-crossed by ditches and rivulets. The Parthe, arching around the battlefield from the east to the northeast before joining the others just north of Leipzig, is smaller but its tortuous track, steep banks and swampy bed made it a significant

Chart 10: The Grande Armée at Leipzig, 16–19 October 1813

Emperor Napoleon, commanding in person

Imperial Guard		
2nd Corps	*Marshal Victor*	4th, 5th, and 6th Divisions
3rd Corps	*GD Souham*	8th, 9th, and 11th Divisions
4th Corps	*GD Bertrand*	12th, 15th (Italian), and 38th (Württemberg) Divisions
5th Corps	*GD Lauriston*	10th, 16th, and 19th Divisions
6th Corps	*Marshal Marmont*	20th, 21st, and 22nd Divisions
7th Corps	*GD Reynier*	13th, 24th (Saxon) and 32nd Divisions
8th (Polish) Corps	*GD > Marshal Poniatowski*	26th (Polish) Division
9th Corps	*Marshal Augereau*	51st and 52nd Divisions (with parts of 53rd and 54th)
11th Corps	*Marshal MacDonald*	31st (French/Westphalian/Neapolitan) 35th (French/Italian), 36th and 39th (Baden/Hesse) Divisions
Independent:		
27th (Polish) Division	*GD Dąbrowski*	
Leipzig Garrison	*GD Margaron > GD Arrighi > GL Graf von Hochberg*	French/Baden/Italian
Provisional Division	*GD Lefol*	(replacement detachments)
1st Cavalry Corps	*GD Latour-Maubourg*	1st (French/Italian) and 3rd Light Cavalry Divisions; 1st (French/Saxon) and 3rd (French/Italian) Cuirassier Divisions
2nd Cavalry Corps	*GD Sébastiani*	2nd and 4th Light Cavalry Divisions, 2nd Cuirassier Division
3rd Cavalry Corps	*GD Arrighi*	5th and 6th Light Cavalry Divisions, 4th Heavy Cavalry Division
4th (Polish) Cavalry Corps	*GD Sokolnicki*	7th (part) and 8th Light Cavalry Divisions
5th Cavalry Corps	*GD Pajol*	9th Light Cavalry Division, 5th and 6th Heavy Cavalry Divisions

Notes: The 12th Corps had been disbanded with the 14th Division being incorporated into the 13th Division and transferred to Reynier; the Bavarian contingent was guarding baggage trains at Eilenburg. 1st and 14th Corps were both immured in Dresden. Other division transfers: 10th from 3rd to 5th Corps, 39th from 3rd to 11th Corps, 13th from 7th to 4th Corps. Poniatowski was elevated to the marshalate on 16 October.

Sources: Amalgamated from Juhel and Nafziger.

barrier along much of its path. These watercourses thus created four sectors that defined the battle: one each west and east of the city, a northern sector between the Parthe and the Elster/Luppe and a difficult wedge of marshy lowlands covered with bushes, undergrowth and the occasional stand of trees that narrowed to a point opposite Connewitz. The challenges involved in traversing this 'labyrinth of ditches and channels' was compounded by the unusually wet summer Saxony had experienced that year.[156] With varying degrees of success, the Allies would attempt advances in all four of these sectors during the coming four days.

Leipzig was a commercial city of approximately 30,000 inhabitants in 1813. Its old defences had long since fallen into disrepair, but its walls were still in place and vehicular access was thus limited to four gates: the Halle to the north, the Grimma in the east, Peter's in the south and the Ranstädt Gate in the northwestern corner of the city's irregular quadrilateral.[157] Several other smaller gates could only be used by riders and pedestrians. As the main entrances into the city from the Allied side of the field, the Halle, Grimma and Peter's Gates would all feature prominently in the fighting on the final day of the battle. Beyond these three gates, Leipzig was encircled by a ring of promenades and parks where the former fortress glacis had been and, beyond this largely open area, a number of suburbs suitable for defence. Many of the suburbs had their own gates (ten in all), so that the Hospital Gate and Outer Grimma Gate, for example, brought a visitor to the boulevard leading inwards through the Grimma suburb and across the green belt of parks and plazas for 600 metres or so towards the (inner) Grimma Gate and the city proper. On the other side of the city, the Ranstädt Gate would be the principal exit for the retreating French. Through this gate ran the road west, carried along an embankment over a series of stone and wooden bridges for more than 2 kilometres before reaching firm ground near Lindenau west of the Elster. The key bridge along this route, 'destined to gain a terrible notoriety' as British military historian Francis Loraine Petre noted, was near the Outer Ranstädt Gate.[158]

Outside the city walls and suburbs, the landscape around Leipzig was largely characterised by low, rolling hills. The tallest of these, such as the Galgenberg and Kolmberg near Liebertwolkwitz were only 150–160 metres high, but in the south these otherwise negligible hills formed a number of ridges advantageous for the French defenders. The villages, stoutly built, would also provide excellent strongpoints for the defence. West of the city, the land was even flatter with no serious hindrance to movement until reaching the Saale River at Weißenfels, 32 kilometres to the southwest. Given the importance of securing the army's rear, the French had constructed several small earthworks south and west of Lindenau and had prepared that town and the nearby villages for defence. These prudent measures proved their worth

Map 16:
The Battle of Leipzig 16–18 October 1813

Showing Allied advances on 18 October with dashed arrows ------------>

Locations as of:

	16 PM	18 AM	18 PM
French:	▭	▨	■
Allies:	▭	▭	▭

Same symbol for Allies on 16PM and 18AM as there was little change in Allied locations from evening 16 October to morning of 18 October. French withdrawals and retreats not shown.

① Combat at Lindenau on 16 October: part of 2nd Baden Bde engaged along with Hessian & Westphalian Chevaulegers.

② Combat at Wachau on 16 October: Saxon heavy cavalry charges.

③ Combat at Möckern on 16 October: Normann's Württemberg brigade engaged.

④ Remains of Württemberg 38th Division posted here at Halle Gates on 16 October.

⑤ General areas of Saxon and Württemberg defections on 18 October.

⑥ Baden/Hessian troops of 39th Div. defend Zuckelhausen & Stötteritz on 18 October.

⑦ Bertrand clears road west on 18 October: including Württemberg 38th Div., Hessian and Westphalian Chevaulegers.

Cr = Crottendorf
Vo = Volkmarsdorf

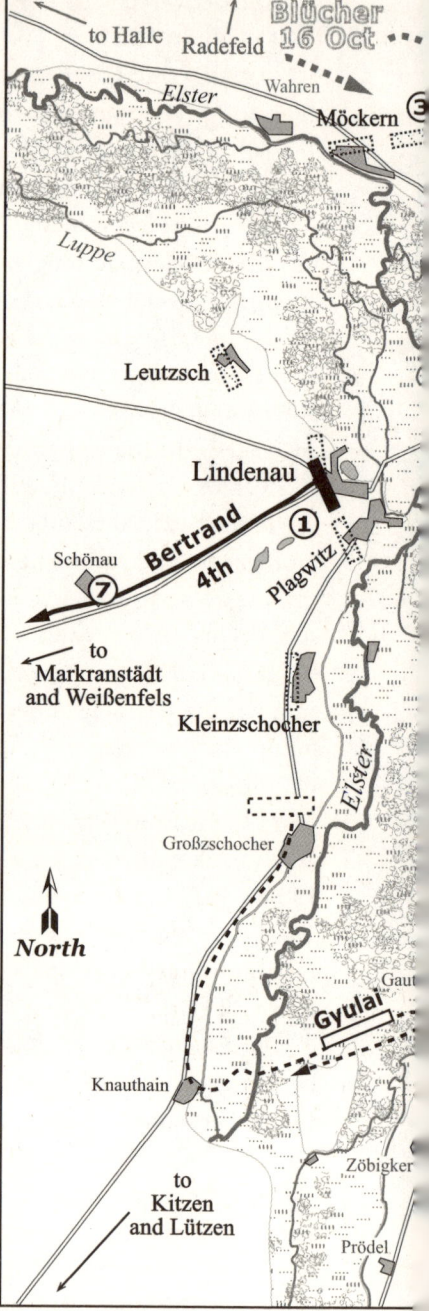

The Battle of Nations: Leipzig, 16–19 October 1813

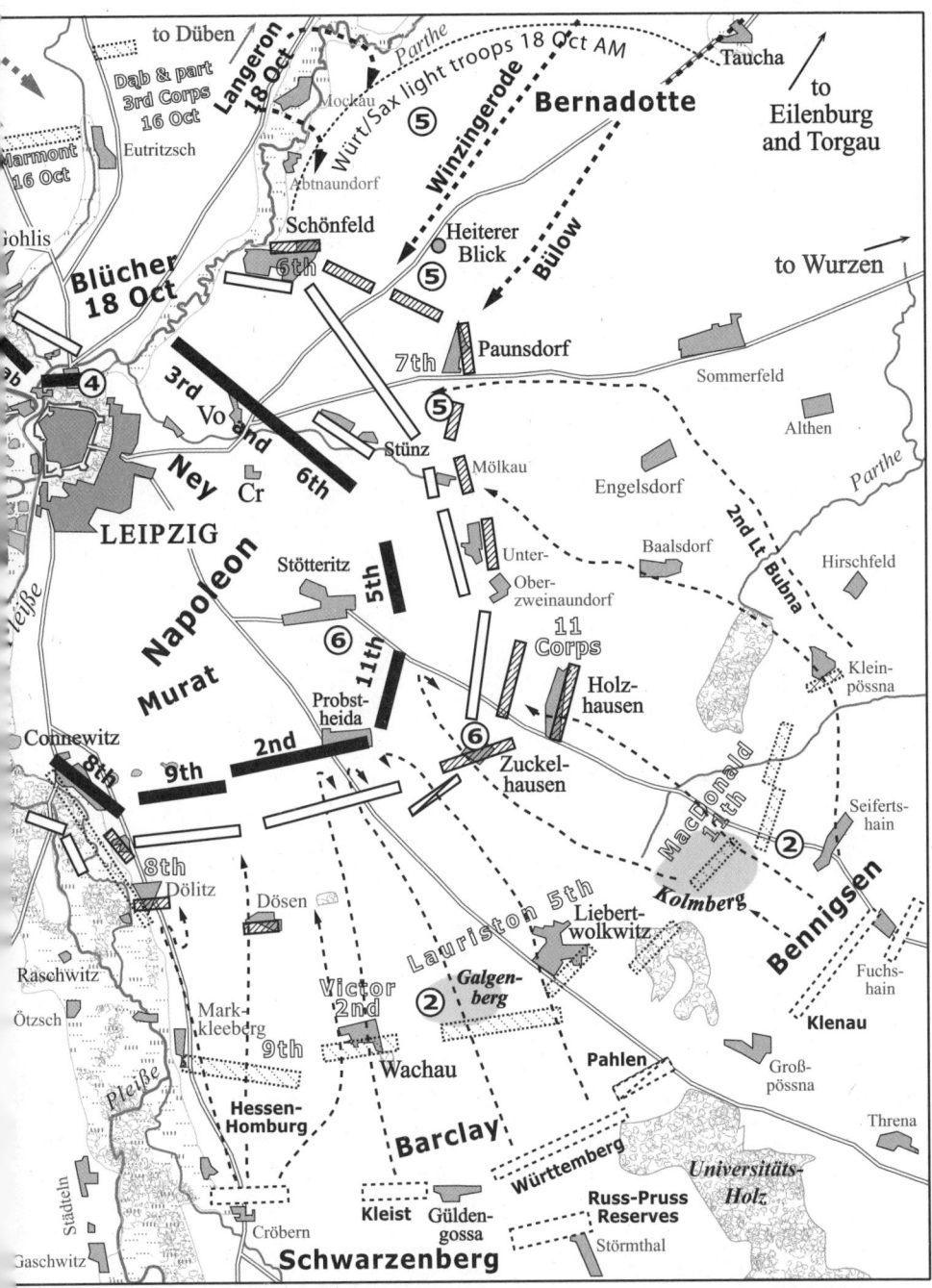

as this would be the route the defeated Grande Armée took when it retreated towards Erfurt on 19 October.

On Friday, 15 October, however, that defeat and retreat still lay in the future. After the initial clash at Liebertwolkwitz on 14 October, the 15th was a day of manoeuvre and preparation with 16 October usually considered the first day of the battle. Napoleon was still awaiting the arrival of 3rd Corps, 7th Corps and Dąbrowski's division from the area around Düben, but his army was otherwise well concentrated around Leipzig that morning.[159] The Allies, however, had now cut his line of communications to the west, leaving only the northeast as an unhindered route of withdrawal. Though he had considered a move back east of the Elbe over the preceding weeks, Napoleon had no intention now of anything but battle. He planned to use a small portion of his army to hold off Blücher in the north while focusing most of his forces on the Army of Bohemia in the south. With luck, he would crush the main Allied army or at least cripple it for an extended period allowing him then to turn on Blücher and Bernadotte.

The fighting on the 16th thus occurred on two 'fronts', so to speak. Napoleon took personal command in the south for what is sometimes called the 'Battle of Wachau' with 2nd, 5th, 8th, 9th and 11th Corps along with the Imperial Guard and four of the five cavalry corps. He prematurely announced a victory, but the result was at best a draw with a slight (and very tactical) advantage to the French. The reinforcements Napoleon had counted on did not arrive in time and a turning movement by MacDonald (whose corps now included the Baden and Hessian troops of the 39th Division) stalled after taking the Kolmberg. Hours of heavy fighting and thousands of casualties thus left the battle lines more or less where they had been when the day began.

The fighting on the northern 'front' was perhaps even more fierce. Here Marmont and the 3rd Cavalry Corps were placed under Ney's overall command and charged with holding off the numerically superior Army of Silesia. In what is sometimes known as the 'Battle of Möckern', Yorck's Prussian I Corps bore the brunt of the combat, pushing back Marmont and inflicting heavy casualties on his opponent, albeit at high cost to his own corps. Dąbrowski and the 9th Division of 3rd Corps, arriving from the northeast, were drawn into the fray as the day progressed, blocking the advance of one of Blücher's Russian corps with especially bitter fighting between the Russians and Poles.

Meanwhile, Austrian Feldzeugmeister (FZM) Ignaz von Gyulai advanced on Lindenau from the west with some 22,000 men in a force consisting of his own III Corps, the 1st Light Division (FML Moritz von Liechtenstein), and the raiding detachments under Thielmann and Mensdorff.[160] The defenders here were the men of Margaron's Leipzig garrison division of 4,300, including a small Baden brigade. Despite the odds, Margaron's troops held on tenaciously until reinforced by Bertrand with 4th Corps. Although Bertrand left the tiny Württemberg 'division' at the Outer Halle Gate (also called the Gerbertor) east of the river, his arrival sufficed to secure Lindenau. A costly counterattack retook Plagwitz and Gyulai withdrew around nightfall.

Napoleon could take only marginal satisfaction in the results of the battle's first day. Margaron and Bertrand had held off Gyulai at Lindenau and, on the southern front, his main force had repelled the opening Allied attacks; but his own offensive in the south had been blunted, while in the north Marmont had suffered a severe defeat at Blücher's hands. His men were exhausted, and food was scarce (the same applied to the Allies), all of his subordinates demanded reinforcements and ammunition was running short. He was not yet completely surrounded since the route east towards Torgau was still open, but he was already outnumbered, and additional enemy forces were on the way. Fortunately for the emperor, the Allies did not attack on 17 October. The characteristic muddles and torpor of Allied general headquarters were compounded by an understandable desire to await the arrival of Bennigsen's Army of Poland, the Austrian 2nd Light Division and the Austrian I Corps. Delays were followed by deferments followed by reconsiderations until it was too late to do anything that day. Sacken's corps of Blücher's army drove the French south of the Parthe, but the old general called off his assault on learning that the Army of Bohemia would not advance until the following morning. Significantly, however, Bernadotte was finally persuaded to move. Though he marched slowly, his Army of the North would cross the Parthe to appear near Taucha on Blücher's left in time for the battle on the afternoon of the 18th.

Other than Blücher's partial success in the north, therefore, Sunday, 17 October passed without major combat. It was a 'lugubrious day', wrote Major Jean Nicole Auguste Noël, 'the sky low and grey, the weather rainy and cold' and 'the battlefield was dreadful to see' after a 'sombre and long October night'.[161] Many remembered a pervasive mood of foreboding. The gaiety of the morning had disappeared, recalled Sous-Lieutenant Frédéric Jacques Louis Rilliet of the 1st Cuirassiers, 'We felt an indefinable malaise similar to that which announces the approach of a thunderstorm.'[162]

For Napoleon, the day brought more grim news. The French had captured GdK Maximilian Graf Merveldt, the commander of Austrian II Corps, during the fighting on the 16th. In an interview with the emperor, Merveldt validated French intelligence that major Allied reinforcements would be in place to attack on the 18th. Worse, he corroborated reports that Bavaria had defected from the Rheinbund and signed a treaty with Austria. Indications from prisoners had already suggested that Bavaria had changed sides, but Merveldt's statements left no doubt. Especially alarming was the likelihood of an Austro-Bavarian army marching to cut the French line of communications in Germany. This dire turn of affairs put the Grande Armée's fate and the future of the entire Rheinbund in jeopardy.[163]

Retreat from Leipzig was more than ever necessary, but Napoleon was reluctant to depart on the 17th lest a withdrawal give the appearance that he had been defeated on the previous day. He sent Merveldt back to the Allied lines with a vague proposal to initiate peace negotiations, but it is doubtful he held out much hope for this mission.[164] More practically, he issued orders that evening sending much of the army's trains and baggage back towards Leipzig and instructed Bertrand to clear a path west towards Weißenfels at daybreak. Guilleminot's 13th Division was attached to Bertrand from 7th Corps for this purpose and two Young Guard divisions were shifted to Lindenau in support.

The rest of the army prepared to defend itself against the Allied assault certain to come with the morning. To account for losses and create a reserve, however, Napoleon contracted his line in the south, pulling back to a position generally running from Connewitz on the right through Probstheida to MacDonald's corps holding the left from Zuckelhausen to Holzhausen. These dispositions placed MacDonald's German units in the first line of defence, while the French, Saxons and Würzburgers of 7th Corps, around Paunsdorf to their left rear, would face Bernadotte's troops in the coming battle.

If Sunday had been largely a day of rest for the armies, the battle resumed with full fury on Monday 18 October. The Allied monarchs, of course, paid no heed to the offer of negotiations delivered by Merveldt. Instead, Schwarzenberg's 'disposition' for the day called for attacks against all facets of the French line. The results, however, were rather less than could have been expected given the tremendous numerical superiority the Allies enjoyed and the fact that the French were now surrounded. The dispersal of the Allied attack columns, poor coordination among them and, above all, the delayed arrival of Bernadotte's army meant that the assault in the south was stymied, the push in the centre stalled in front of Stötteritz and Blücher's Russians could make no impression on the defenders at the Outer Halle Gate north of the city. Only in the left-centre did the French suffer a clear defeat, being pushed back to Volkmarsdorf and Crottendorf in bitter fighting. The French were everywhere skilful and tenacious. At one point, a French counterattack towards Dölitz and Dösen was so successful that Schwarzenberg ordered the

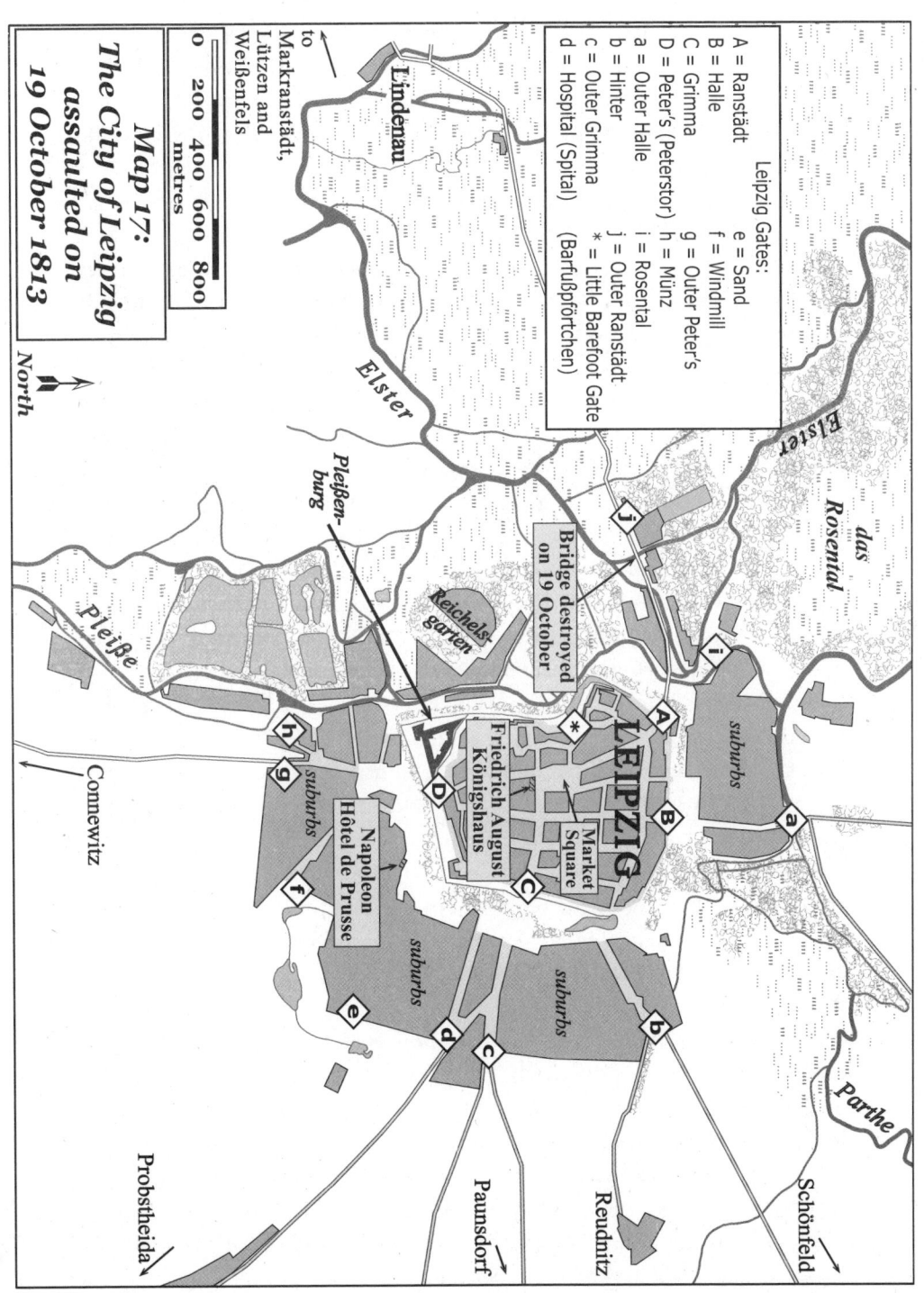

Map 17: The City of Leipzig assaulted on 19 October 1813

panicked recall of Gyulai from across the Pleiße. Gyulai's departure cleared the way for Bertrand to open a line of escape to the west. By evening, he had reached Weißenfels and caused the Austrian detachments along the Saale to withdraw. Liechtenstein, Thielmann and Mensdorf were too weak to do anything but observe his progress from a distance.

In addition to the enervating and costly combat, 18 October also witnessed the defection of two Rheinbund contingents. Late in the morning, GM Karl Friedrich Leberecht Graf von Normann, commander of the Württemberg light cavalry attached to Marmont's 6th Corps, decided to turn his brigade over to Cossacks southwest of Taucha. Though there does not seem to have been any collusion between the two, the Saxon light cavalry brigade deserted around the same time. Late in the afternoon, near Paunsdorf, the rest of the Saxon division likewise changed sides. These controversial betrayals, especially that of the Saxons, were profoundly resented by the French at the time and spuriously used by many then and since as an explanation for the larger defeat. Each of these cases will come under scrutiny in the chapters dedicated to the respective contingents, but for this overview it is enough to note that the defeat of an army of nearly 200,000 in a bitter battle fought over four days can hardly be blamed on the defection of parts of two allied contingents numbering together no more than 5,000 combatants.

The final act of the Leipzig drama played out on Tuesday 19 October with the Allied storming of the city. The French had skilfully withdrawn into the suburbs during the night and Napoleon had designated Marmont (3rd Corps, 6th Corps and Durutte), MacDonald (11th Corps) and Poniatowski (8th Corps and Dąbrowski) as the rear guard to defend the city. Graf Wilhelm von Hochberg of Baden had replaced Margaron and Arrighi as the city's commandant. In addition to French troops, his force included his small Baden brigade and a battalion of Milan Guards as well as the Saxon Guard Grenadiers and the few Saxon regular troops remaining following the previous day's defections. These men with their French and Polish comrades were to protect the withdrawal to Weißenfels and then follow as best they could once the rest of the army was clear of the city.

The Allied assault was late to start and proceeded in a rather blunt and inefficient fashion, leading to vicious fighting in the suburbs against a tenacious defence. Combat around the Outer and Inner Grimma Gates was especially brutal. Napoleon had spent the night just outside the walls (lodged, ironically enough, in the Hôtel de Prusse) and was still in the city when the attacks began. With daybreak, he issued final orders, rode into the city, held a farewell discussion with König Friedrich August and paid a final tribute to the

Saxon Guard Grenadiers standing in formation in the market square before trying to make his way to the Ranstädt Gate. Finding the passage blocked by the confused mass of men, horses and vehicles struggling towards the gate, his Saxon guide led him and his entourage by back alleys to the long series of bridges leading to Lindenau. By the time Napoleon reached the far bank, Leipzig's defences were crumbling. Resistance collapsed when a corporal prematurely detonated the explosives under one of the key bridges, killing hundreds of French and allied soldiers instantly and trapping thousands of others inside the city. Many surrendered and many who sought safety by leaping into the river drowned in the attempt. MacDonald and Marmont managed to escape, but the wounded Prince Poniatowski, who had been made a Marshal of France on 16 October, was among those who succumbed to the Elster's waters. Both Reynier and Lauriston were captured. The Allied sovereigns met in the market square around 1:00 p.m. and stayed long enough to designate the Saxon king a prisoner of war before retiring to celebrate their great success.

It was indeed a decisive victory. Not only did the Grande Armée lose an estimated 72,000 men and 325 guns between 14 and 19 October, but Napoleon now had no recourse but retreat to the Rhine, a retreat that would mean the end of his empire in Germany and the end of the Confederation of the Rhine. It was, however, a success dearly purchased. Total Allied losses came to some 54,000 and the armies were in such a state of confusion and exhaustion that Napoleon's retreating army was able to gain just enough of a lead to evade immediate pursuit.[165] The sufferings of the civilian populace, of course, were also enormous. In addition to the destruction wrought by shot, shell and fire, the region had been devastated by the uninvited presence of more than half a million soldiers and hundreds of thousands of horses for more than a week, plundering, pillaging, ruining roads, tearing up fences and eating everything in sight. These manifold miseries were compounded by the rapid spread of disease in a region encumbered with thousands of sick and wounded soldiers along with further thousands of dead men and horses. It took fourteen days to bury the dead and farmers tilling their fields the following spring frequently unearthed human and animal remains.[166] It is small wonder that the first personal account of the battle by a civilian was entitled *Leipzig during the Terrible Days of Battle in October 1813*.[167]

Sickness, particularly typhus, also ravaged Napoleon's army as it retreated towards the Rhine. Nonetheless, the army held off its pursuers in sharp clashes along the Saale and Unstrut Rivers on 21 October and retained enough cohesion to overcome an Austro-Bavarian army at Hanau on 30–31 October.

This force, quickly assembled after Bavaria had joined the Coalition, was led by Bavarian GdK Karl Philipp Graf von Wrede, a former favourite of Napoleon's. Wrede had marched first to Würzburg, capturing it and forcing the French garrison to lock itself in the Marienberg fortress high above the city, before heading west to intercept the Grande Armée at Hanau. He was defeated and badly wounded during the battle, but Bavaria's shift in allegiance, the debacle at Leipzig and the steady approach of the Allied armies brought about the rapid dissolution of the Rheinbund. Napoleon returned to France for a final, frenetic campaign in 1814, leaving behind tens of thousands of French and German soldiers in garrisons from Hamburg on the North Sea to Danzig and Modlin on the Vistula. Among these were the army's huge baggage train under Durrieu that had taken refuge in Torgau and two entire corps in Dresden. By the end of November, the Confederation's member states had either collapsed (Westphalia, Frankfurt and Berg) or their monarchs had hastened to sign treaties with the victorious Allies, pledging to join the war against Napoleon in exchange for continued political existence. These rulers would now be required to commit their soldiers, in even larger numbers than demanded by Napoleon, to the Allied armies poised to invade France in 1814.

The Confederation of the Rhine thus came to an end only slightly more than seven years after its founding. This had become a possible but by no means inevitable outcome following Napoleon's disaster in Russia. Changes in the pattern of events, such as a truly decisive French victory at Bautzen, could have placed the history of central Europe on a very different trajectory. All was in flux and all of the belligerents had to cope with enormous and enormously frightening uncertainties that endangered the very existence of their states. Leading Prussians, for instance, certainly believed that their national survival was at stake, but perhaps none felt as threatened as the Rheinbund monarchies. Where Prussia had only Napoleon to fear, the emperor's German allies perceived existential dangers not only from the French, but from the Allies (especially Prussia and Austria) and from the spread of radical political ideas ('Jacobinism') among their own subjects as well. The following chapters will examine how the armies of these monarchies, large, mid-sized, small or minute, responded to these changing circumstances while their sovereigns and governments strove to steer safe paths between the contending demands of Napoleon, the Coalition and popular sentiment.

Chapter 2

Saxony: The Price of Loyalty

'I believed I must be an example of the strictest loyalty.'
King Friedrich August to Tsar Alexander,
20 October 1813[1]

THE HOUSE OF WETTIN was one of Europe's oldest, tracing its history back to the second half of the tenth century. The Wettins had been designated as electors of the Holy Roman Empire in the Golden Bull of 1356, but the family split into Ernestine and Albertine branches in 1485 with the electoral title going to the former. The electoral title was transferred to the Albertine branch in 1547, however, because the Ernestines had fought against Holy Roman Emperor Charles V in the Schmalkaldic War. By 1813, therefore, the Albertines had ruled the Electorate of Saxony for more than 260 years, while the various strands of the Ernestine branch were relegated, as they saw things, to small territories in Thuringia that became known as the 'Saxon duchies'. As will be seen below and in Chapter 7, Carl August, Herzog of Sachsen-Weimar and the senior member of the Ernestine branch, would seek to use his alliance with Napoleon to rectify this perceived historic slight. Furthermore, from 1697 to 1763, the Albertine electors had simultaneously reigned as the elected kings of Poland-Lithuania with aspirations to great power status and acquisition of a land bridge through Silesia to connect their German holdings with the vastly larger territory to the east. Frederick the Great's success in his lengthy struggles with Austria for control of Silesia, however, marked the rise of Prussia and ended Saxon hopes for a greater role in continental affairs.[2] Saxony joined the Habsburg opposition to Frederick during most of these conflicts but was occupied by Prussia from 1756 to 1763 during the Seven Years War and found its army unwillingly dragooned into Prussian service. Unsurprisingly, these experiences founded a lasting legacy of Saxon suspicion of its powerful Prussian neighbour. Furthermore, having served as a battleground for many years, the countryside was devastated, and the electorate was on the verge of bankruptcy when peace finally arrived.

For many years thereafter, the state would struggle to restore its finances and political status.

From Kurprinz to König: This Nestor of Monarchs

Saxony's calamitous condition was imprinted on the mind of the boy who would become the new elector and the country's rehabilitation became his first priority when the eighteen-year-old assumed the throne as Kurfürst (Elector) Friedrich August III in 1768. Although the electorate's economy slowly improved, its political situation remained precarious. It was, in the words of historian Dorit Petschel, at best 'half-sovereign'.[3] Not only was Saxony trapped in the Austro-Prussian 'dualism', the rivalry between the two German great powers, but the protections and comfort it had enjoyed within the embrace of the Holy Roman Empire steadily eroded as that institution fell into terminal decline. Friedrich August, imbued with a profound if rather formal conception of duty to his subjects, believed that external stability was essential to assure the welfare of Saxony's people. He thus consistently endeavoured to hew to a path of neutrality in foreign affairs but found that his commitment to the old order compelled him to side with Prussia in the War of Bavarian Succession (1778–9), to contribute a contingent to the imperial armies opposing Revolutionary France in 1793–6, and to align with Prussia in armed neutrality during the War of the Third Coalition in 1805. He joined Prussia again in 1806, this time disastrously. With his Prussian partner crushed and his own army destroyed at Jena, he accepted Napoleon's offer to join the Rheinbund, signing the Treaty of Posen in December 1806 and sending troops to fight alongside his new ally during the 1807 campaign. Admission to the Rheinbund brought territorial expansion and the elevation of Saxony to a kingdom; its monarch thus became König Friedrich August I, the first king of a new and larger realm. Additionally, the 1807 Treaties of Tilsit created a new Polish entity, the Duchy of Warsaw, and unexpectedly placed the sceptre of this revived state in Friedrich August's hands.[4] At a stroke, the subjects under his rule more than doubled from approximately 2 million to more than 4.3 million. These lands and populations, of course, came at the expense of defeated Prussia. The transfer of the Cottbus district, a former Prussian enclave situated inside Saxon territory, was especially painful to the Hohenzollerns and the entire episode left Prussians bitterly resentful of their former junior ally.[5]

By 1813, Friedrich August was 63, regarded by his contemporaries as a '*Greis*' or 'old man', but respected as venerable, 'this Nestor of monarchs' in the words of a French writer at the time.[6] He was a conservative man of the *ancien regime* era, whose sheltered upbringing had left him genuinely religious, with a strong sense of duty to his subjects and office as well as a strong, if rigid, sense of justice and the proper ordering of the world, including the divine rights of monarchs. He harboured none of the grandiose territorial ambitions entertained by his ancestors, leading Charles Maurice de Talleyrand-Périgord to quip that 'he has veritably neutralised his ambition as well as his territory'.[7] Instead, he had been deeply attached to the norms and traditions of the old empire and disliked change, evincing little interest in the new ideas sweeping through Europe since the 1780s. The modernising trends evident in other German states thus found little purchase in his lands such that, 'Friedrich August's principles of governance at his death on 5 May 1827 were the same as at the commencement of his reign on 15 September 1768.'[8] The Saxon court and state reflected the ruler's personality, being characterised by an old-world stiffness and formality. On a personal level, Friedrich August was profoundly cautious, uncomfortable with rapid decisions, rather less than imaginative, and far more content in the company of his family or other small circles than with the demands of public life.[9] He regarded Napoleon with no small degree of wonder and admiration,[10] while the French emperor and most of his compatriots saw the Saxon monarch as a decent and honourable, if not especially inspiring, figure.[11] 'The most honest man who ever wielded a sceptre,' Napoleon would say of him on St Helena.[12] Tied to the Bavarian royal house through his marriage to the king's sister, Marie Amalie Auguste, Friedrich August would face, like his Bavarian counterpart, an existential crisis in 1813, the greatest threat to dynasty and state since the Prussian invasion of 1756.

Although the focus of this chapter is the Saxon army's actions as it coped with the challenges of 1813, this brief overview of the country's history highlights several points relevant to the events under consideration here. First is Saxony's awkward geopolitical situation, caught between the two major German powers, both of which had been both allies and enemies over the preceding five decades. Despite Friedrich August's lack of interest in territorial aggrandisement and his dedication to his realm's internal stability, his efforts to remain strictly neutral were thus undermined by Saxony's circumstances. Second, and linked with the geopolitical situation, was the acquisitive eye Prussia had turned on Saxony in the past, the animosity engendered by the loss to Saxony of what Berlin considered 'its' Polish lands, and especially the transfer of the Cottbus district after 1807. Third was the close historical connection to Poland. Although Friedrich August had not sought the Duchy of Warsaw's crown as his forebears had, he accepted this burden from Napoleon with dignity and took his responsibilities towards Poland seriously. Moreover, even if the new king's commitment to Poland was founded in duty rather than ambition, some members of his court viewed the kingdom's Polish connections as crucial to Saxony's future. Fourth, although the House of Wettin was one of Europe's most venerable dynasties with ancient roots in its particular lands, this antique heritage came under threat when war arrived in the kingdom in 1813. As early as March, the Russians and Prussians were already violating their proclaimed principles of monarchical legitimacy by engaging in cavalier discussions of evicting Friedrich August and his family in exchange for airily imagined and unspecified 'compensations' elsewhere on the continent. All these factors would inform the actions and decisions of the Allies, of Napoleon and of the Saxons themselves as they struggled for survival while their country once again became a battleground for outside powers.

The Saxon Army: From Reform to Russia

Like all the Rheinbund states in this difficult year, and indeed like France itself, Saxony had to determine how to rebuild its army following the Russian disaster: what to retain, what to discard and what to construct anew. Although many regiments had been destroyed in Russia, Saxony had a slight advantage in comparison to its Confederation allies in that the bulk of its troops had been assigned to 7th Corps on the Grande Armée's southern flank. The corps suffered horrendous losses but was not as devastated as the formations that had marched to Moscow and back. It was weak but still intact when it retreated through Poland towards Saxony as 1812 ended and 1813 began. Nonetheless, the once fine army was in ruins and had to be reconstituted from the ground up. As outlined below, all of the infantry regiments and a substantial artillery component would eventually take the field as the campaigns progressed, but the desperate straits of 1813 meant that only half of Saxony's cavalry regiments from 1812 could be reformed for this new war.

The Saxon army had undergone a major transformation in its first years as a French ally.[13] When Saxony joined the Rheinbund in December 1806, its army was a relic of the previous century, appearing to contemporaries like an antique, outdated in everything from its stiff uniforms and tactics to its pedantic administration and command style.[14] As demonstrated at Jena, its soldiers showed no lack of fortitude, but the ponderous formality of its actions was unsuited to the swift, seemingly breathless operational tempo of the new age. Individual units, especially the cavalry, did well enough in 1807 but its first performance as a united corps two years later in the 1809 war with Austria was generally poor. The cavalry was often commended for its skills and the corps tried to innovate in the midst of the war, but it faltered badly at Wagram, leaving a negative impression in the minds of many French officers, including Napoleon. Again, there was no dearth of courage, but weaknesses in tactics, leadership and unit cohesion led to collapse and flight at the centre of the French line on 6 July 1809, albeit under extraordinarily demanding circumstances.[15]

The army's experiences in the 1809 war led Saxony to undertake a series of thoroughgoing reforms the following year.[16] This programme touched almost every aspect of Saxony's military establishment including the creation of a general staff for the first time, the publication of new drill manuals for all branches, the introduction of conscription, the retirement of overaged officers,[17] and the altering of officer promotions to emphasise merit rather than seniority, as well as a variety of other major administrative changes. To enhance the durability of the individual units, four of the old line regiments were disbanded and their personnel used to increase the strength of the remaining eight as well as the king's Leib-Grenadier Regiment. The number of cavalry regiments was likewise reduced from nine to eight. At the same time, two light infantry regiments and a small Jägerkorps were formed to address the lack of light troops that had been painfully evident during the 1809 war.[18] On the material side, the clumsy and diverse artillery equipment of the past was replaced with a more modern set of guns and vehicles, while the artillery train and supporting functions were militarised.[19] The entire army also received new, more practical uniforms. Remarkably, most of these changes were accomplished in little more than a year, so that the army that marched into Russia in the summer of 1812 was substantially more flexible, capable and durable as compared to its pre-1810 antecedents.

Something that did not change was basic uniform colours. The new uniforms issued to the remaining eight line infantry regiments thus retained the traditional Saxon white with the regiments differentiated by their facings and button colours. The new light infantry and Jägers also adhered to tradition, being given the dark green jackets, black leather gear and hunting horn emblems associated with many German light troops. Unlike the dark blue common in most other armies, however, the Saxon artillerymen continued to wear dark green with red facings and buff leather gear, another tradition from the old electorate; their comrades in the new train battalion had light blue jackets with black facings trimmed in red. In stark contrast to these subdued hues, the Leib-Grenadiers retained their bright red coats with yellow facings, a striking combination that led them to be nicknamed 'the King's Buttered Lobsters' ('*des Königs Butterkrebse*'). Unlike the bicorne hats worn prior to

1810, shakos were now standard issue throughout the army, including the Leib-Grenadiers, but for parades and other special occasions, these elite soldiers were also distinguished by large bearskin bonnets similar to those of the French Imperial Guard.

The three Saxon chevaulegers regiments that rode off to Russia also wore red, as did the *Prinz Clemens* Uhlans, the kingdom's lone lancer regiment, converted from chevaulegers in 1811.[20] The other component of the light cavalry was Saxony's Hussar Regiment, decked out in traditional hussar garb of dolman, pelisse and breeches in light blue with extensive trim in white (troopers) or silver (officers). All of these light cavalry units wore shakos with tall plumes for parades and oiled leather covers for field duty. The heavy cavalry on the other hand, Leib-Cuirassiers and *Zastrow* Cuirassiers, had plumed brass helmets and blackened cuirasses over white jackets trimmed in red and yellow respectively. A third heavy cavalry regiment, the Garde du Corps with its helmets and handsome straw-coloured jackets, was destroyed in Russia and never rebuilt. Organisationally, the Hussar Regiment was divided into eight squadrons (1,067 men) but all of the other regiments, light and heavy, were structured into four squadrons for a total of 768 men each plus a staff of 18. As will be seen, however, the losses in Russia meant these numbers were never attained during 1813.

Infantry organisation was similar to many European armies. Each line infantry regiment consisted of two battalions, each of four companies plus two grenadier companies for an authorised total of 2,073 officers and men. As in Austria and Prussia, however, the grenadiers were habitually detached to form separate combined grenadier battalions known by the names of their commanders. Each of these consisted of four companies from two sister regiments who shared facing colours. The *Anger* Grenadier Battalion, under the command of Major Carl Friedrich Anger, was thus composed of the grenadier companies from the blue-faced *Prinz Anton* and *Low* Regiments. Apparently influenced by the French model, the Saxons also returned to the idea of adding two 4-pounder cannon to each line regiment destined for the 7th Corps in 1812 such that the contingent marched into Russia with 20 of these small pieces.[21] The regimental guns would thus be present at the Battle of Kalisch in February as the contingent marched back from Russia, but scarcities of manpower and equipment meant that they would not be revived when the army reorganised in March and April.

The light infantry regiments had neither grenadiers nor cannon, but the two regiments were likewise each composed of two battalions of four companies for a total of 1,652 men each. In the Leib-Grenadiers, on the other hand, all

Chart 11: Saxon Units, 1812–13

Unit	Coat colour	Facing (buttons)	Bde/Div./Corps in 1812	Div./Corps, autumn 1813
Prinz Friedrich August Infantry	white	green (yellow)	1/21/7	24/7 two battalions
Prinz Clemens Infantry (*Steindel* Infantry in 1813)	white	green (white)	1/21/7	25/7 two battalions
Liebenau Grenadiers	white	green	1/21/7	24/7
Prinz Anton Infantry	white	blue (white)	2/21/7	25/7 two battalions
1st Light Infantry *LeCoq*	dark green	black, red trim	2/21/7	24/7 two battalions
König Infantry	white	scarlet (yellow)	1/22/7	25/7 one battalion
Niesemeuschel Infantry	white	scarlet (white)	1/22/7	25/7 one battalion
Brause Grenadiers	white	scarlet	1/22/7	25/7
2nd Light Infantry *Sahr*	dark green	black, red trim	2/22/7	25/7 two battalions
Anger Grenadiers	white	blue	2/22/7	25/7
Spiegel Grenadiers	white	yellow	2/22/7	24/7
Prinz Clemens Uhlans	red	light green	21/7	7th Corps Cavalry Brigade
Polenz Chevaulegers	red	light blue	21/7	(not re-formed)
Hussar Regiment	light blue	light blue	21/7	7th Corps Cavalry Brigade
Garde du Corps	straw	blue	22/7 to 4th Cavalry Corps	(not re-formed)
Zastrow Cuirassiers	white	yellow	22/7 to 4th Cavalry Corps	1st Cavalry Corps
Prinz Albrecht Chevaulegers	red	dark green	22/7 to 3rd Cavalry Corps	(not re-formed)
Prinz Johann Chevaulegers	red	black	9th Corps	(not re-formed)
Low Infantry	white	blue (yellow)	28/9	25/7 two battalions
Rechten Infantry	white	yellow (white)	28/9	24/7 one battalion
Prinz Maximillian Infantry	white	yellow (yellow)	Morand in Pomerania	24/7 one battalion
Leibgarde Cuirassiers	white	red	Saxony	1st Cavalry Corps
Leibgrenadiers	red	yellow	Saxony	24/7 one battalion
Jägerkorps	dark green	green, red trim	Saxony	24/7

the soldiers were grenadiers, so there were no separate grenadier companies; each battalion consisted of four companies amounting to 1,666 officers and men for the regiment. The common soldiers in the light infantry were called 'Schützen' (loosely 'sharpshooters'), and the same designation was applied to the 45 men each line battalion was to train for skirmishing and other light infantry tasks. The unique Jägerkorps was a company-size unit recruited from trained hunters and woodsmen with an authorised strength of 126.[22]

As shown in Chart 11, almost all of the units described above participated in the war against the tsar.[23] Left behind in Saxony were the Leib-Grenadiers, the Leib-Cuirassiers and the Jägerkorps along with a garrison company in the Königstein fortress (205), three 'half-invalid' or sedentary companies and small depots for each of the regiments in the field.[24] The *Prinz Maximillian* Infantry Regiment and an artillery battery, stationed in Pomerania under GD Joseph Morand, also escaped the miseries of the Russian war. As for the regiments that went to Russia, the bulk campaigned with 7th Corps under Reynier, but substantial elements fought under other headquarters in other parts of the theatre of war. The 7th Corps sent home several thousand men who were sick, wounded or otherwise unfit for duty during the course of the campaign and it returned to Saxony with most of its regiments decimated but still intact. Almost all of the other Saxon units, however, were destroyed in Russia. Of the 628 men in the *Prinz Albrecht* Chevaulegers, for example, only 14 officers and 12 troopers initially returned home; 12 men and 4 horses of the Garde du Corps came back and 16 men with 3 horses from the *Zastrow* Cuirassiers. Losses among the detached infantry regiments were equally gruesome. As a result, Saxony in 1813 was never able to return its army to the strength and organisation it had possessed before the Russian campaign. Although some provisional chevaulegers squadrons were hastily thrown together for a short time in the spring, none of these regiments would be reformed in full. Instead, their depots would be drained to fill out the Uhlans and hussars. Similarly, the Garde du Corps was never rebuilt. These gaps in the order of battle notwithstanding, this 1810–12 background is important as it provides the template that informed the decisions the kingdom made while it attempted to reconstruct its forces in the aftermath of the Russian disaster.

Retreat from Russia: The Battle of Kalisch

The Battle of Kalisch, fought on 13 February 1813, is widely considered 'the last battle of the 1812 campaign'.[25] This is an entirely apt designation but, as French historian Camille Rousset noted, Kalisch was also 'the veritable junction point of the campaign of 1812 and that of 1813'.[26] Moreover, beyond this linkage and the year in which it occurred, the battle has a place in this study owing to its significance for the Saxon contingent's future evolution.[27]

The withdrawal from Russia had left 7th Corps reduced but still intact and the first days of February 1813 found it in and around Warsaw, sheltered behind a screen provided by Schwarzenberg's Austrian Auxiliary Corps. To the rear were Prince Poniatowski and the remnants of the Polish 5th Corps as well as a host of new levies produced by the Duchy of Warsaw's scrambles to raise a new army. At this point in the campaign, the Saxon infantry element of 7th Corps was still divided into two divisions (21st and 22nd of the Grande Armée or 1st and 2nd Saxon), but the 22nd Division had effectively only one brigade as its 1st Brigade had been surrounded and captured after an obstinate fight at Kobrin (Kobryn) in July 1812. Also absent were two battalions that had been detailed to the garrison in the fortress of Modlin north of Warsaw: II/*Prinz Friedrich* and the *Niesemeuschel* Battalion, the latter a combined unit made up of the survivors of the Kobrin disaster. The remaining men of *Prinz Friedrich* and other cadres were then sent back to Saxony along with a convoy of some 3,500 sick and injured to help rebuild the army.[28] The corps was also sadly deficient in cavalry as four of its seven original regiments had been detached early in the Russian campaign.

In addition to the Saxon troops, GD Pierre François Joseph Durutte's 32nd Division had been assigned to the corps in late October. This curious formation consisted of five French regiments assembled from draft-dodgers and other dubious elements, 'one of the worst in the French army' in the words of one caustically sharp Saxon general.[29] It also included three battalions of the Würzburg Infantry Regiment. As with the Saxons, Durutte's command had been diminished by two battalions detached to the Modlin garrison (I/133^e Ligne and IV/Würzburg) before departing Warsaw. Although the Würzburg troops generally enjoyed a good reputation, standards and discipline among the French regiments were often poor, setting a negative example for their German allies. The 32nd Division would remain a major component of 7th Corps throughout the battles of 1813 and would often display surprising tenacity in battle despite its unpromising composition.

Except for a brief interval in the spring, GD Reynier would also remain associated with the Saxon contingent during the 1813 campaigns. Swiss by birth, Jean Louis Ebénezer Reynier had entered the armies of Revolutionary France in 1792 as a volunteer gunner and soon rose through the ranks, being promoted to *général de brigade* in 1795 and *général de division* in 1798. During two decades of extensive service in Holland, Germany, Egypt, Naples, Portugal and Spain, he had shown himself intelligent, honest, capable and

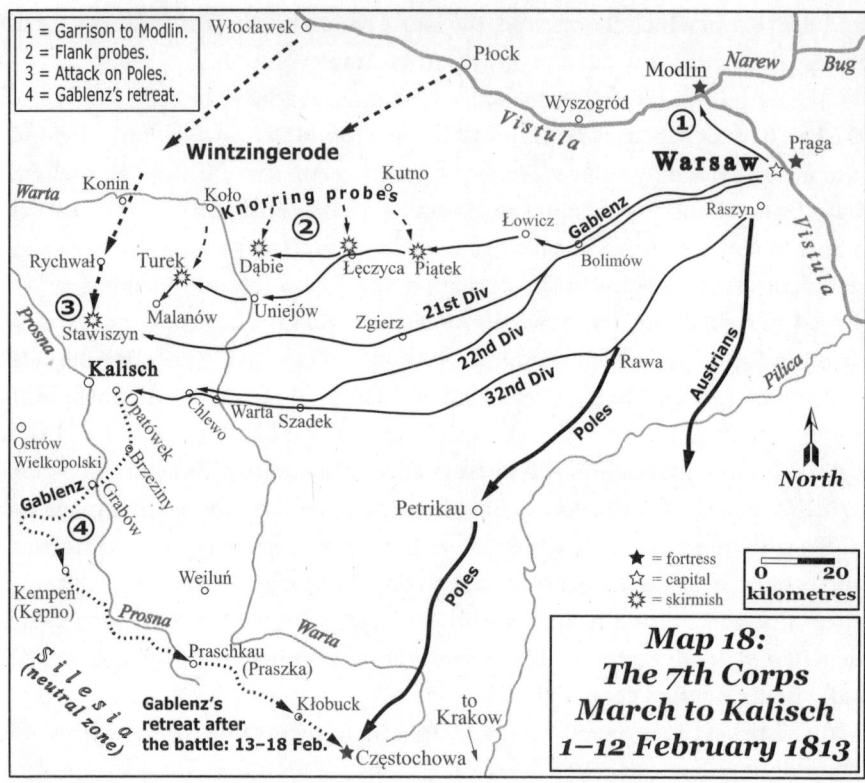

Map 18: The 7th Corps March to Kalisch 1–12 February 1813

courageous on the battlefield, but 'he lacked the faculty to elevate his men and communicate to them his ardour'.[30] The Saxons first came under his command in July 1809 just after their harrowing trial by fire at Wagram. Opinions in such cases are almost always mixed, but his new charges appreciated his unruffled demeanour, his broad grasp of military affairs, his intellectual acuity and the attention he devoted to the care and wellbeing of the Saxon troops. At the same time, he was consistently characterised as taciturn, cool and distant. As one officer observed after describing his skills during 1812: 'Nature had denied him the great art of inspiring soldiers, so that while he could – rarely enough – reassure the great mass through his calm silence, he was too cold, too inwardly focused, too uncommunicative, in a word, too restrained for the common soldier.'[31] Nonetheless, Reynier gradually earned the enduring respect and admiration of his Saxon subordinates. 'The venerable General Count Reynier, whose memory will always be dear to every Saxon soldier', as one officer described him.[32] His experience and manifold talents notwithstanding, he would exhibit a surprising degree of tactical laxity at several points during 1813. One of these points was the Battle of Kalisch.

As part of the general withdrawal of the Grande Armée's southern wing, 7th Corps retreated from Warsaw over several days in early February.[33] Reynier aimed for Kalisch as directed while Schwarzenberg's Austrians retired to the southwest towards Krakow and Poniatowki's Poles shifted to Petrikau (Piotrków Trybunalksi). Delayed by bad weather, dreadful roads, the exhaustion of the troops and the belief that his mission required him to wait for Poniatowksi, Reynier did not move as rapidly as he might have done.[34] As a result, the lead elements of the corps did not reach Kalisch until 12 February and most of the corps was not assembled in and around the town until the following morning 'after a very difficult night march as a thaw had set in that rendered the roads bottomless'.[35] His flank guard, under Saxon GM Heinrich Adolf von Gablenz, had sparred repeatedly with Maj. Gen. Karl Bogdanovich Knorring's Russian cavalry brigade from 7 February and experienced an especially sharp fight at Turek on the 11th. The vigour of these repeated clashes combined with other intelligence that a Russian corps under Wintzingerode had already crossed the Vistula between Płock and Włocławek in some strength indicated that an enemy attack was likely in the offing. Reynier reported the Russian cavalry activity to Eugène and issued a special order of the day praising the troops of Gablenz's command for their steadfastness at Turek, but he seems to have entertained an unwarranted degree of confidence that his corps would not be disturbed on 13 February.[36]

Kalisch in 1813 was a town of approximately 8,300 souls and the seat of the eponymous department of the Duchy of Warsaw. Still walled, it was situated on an island formed by the arms of the Prosna River as it flowed north through a fairly broad valley towards the Warthe. The Swędrnia stream joined the Prosna just south of the town after snaking its way through a shallow but noticeable valley. These two watercourses formed the boundaries of the coming battle on the west and southeast respectively, while its northern edge was defined by an extensive forest that hid the approaching Russians but also channelled their advance. In between, the low rolling hills were dotted with windmills and a few small villages that afforded some degree of shelter and sustenance for the soldiers of both sides. In general, however, the terrain was open, gently sloping and devoid of serious obstacles: perfect for the mounted arm in which the Russians were decidedly superior. Even though it was mid-February, 'the weather was very mild, the sun rose very brightly, and it was a lovely spring day' remembered Feldwebel Friedrich Vollborn.[37]

The Saxons were dispersed among these villages on the morning of the 13th, seeking such rest and refreshment as they could after their trek from Warsaw. To the northeast was GM von Gablenz with his flank guard

Chart 12: 7th Corps at Kalisch, 13 February 1813

GD Reynier

		bns/sqdns	present under arms
Flank/Rear Guard	GM von Gablenz		
Polenz Chevaulegers		4	208
Hussar Regiment		7	134
1st Light Infantry *LeCoq*	(detached from 21st Division)	2	625
French voltigeur companies	Major Cailhassou (132ᵉ Ligne)	5 companies	627
Polish Krakus and Uhlans		–	?
2nd Horse Artillery Battery	Hauptmann Hiller	–	128
21st Division (1st Saxon)	GL LeCoq		
1st Brigade	GM von Steindel		
Prinz Clemens Infantry (future *Steindel*)		2	651
Prinz Clemens regimental guns		–	41
Liebenau Grenadier Battalion		1	346
2nd Brigade	GM von Nostitz		
Prinz Anton Infantry		2	428
Prinz Anton regimental guns		–	43
1st Foot Artillery Battery	Hauptmann Brause	–	96
22nd Division (2nd Saxon)	GM von Sahr		
2nd Brigade	GM von Sahr		
2nd Light Infantry *Sahr*		2	665
Eychelberg Grenadier Battalion		1	282
Anger Grenadier Battalion		1	314
Spiegel Grenadier Battalion		1	218
3rd Foot Artillery Battery	Hauptmann Bonniot	–	87
Prinz Clemens Uhlans		4	130
32nd Division	GD Durutte		
1st Brigade	GB Devaux		
35ᵉ Léger (former 1ᵉʳ Mediterranean)		2	815
36ᵉ Léger (former Belle-Île)		2	763
2nd Brigade	GB Maury		
131ᵉ Ligne (former Walcheren)		2	1,106
Würzburg Infantry Regiment (II, III)		2	605

around Zelazków and Zborów. He had found the surrounding hamlets full of Cossacks on his arrival that morning; these had mostly withdrawn, but the presence of Russian cavalry at Tykadłów prevented him from occupying that village as he had planned. GL von LeCoq had posted GM Carl Friedrich Ernst von Nostitz at Borków with six companies of *Prince Anton* Infantry and two regimental pieces to provide a link with Gablenz. He established his own headquarters in Kokanin with the other two *Prince Anton* companies,

Graf Wilhelm von Hochberg and the Baden Brigade covering the crossing of the Berezina in November 1812. The brigade's self-sacrificing stand, including the 'death ride' of the Baden Hussars and Hessian Chevaulegers, helped save much of the fugitive Grande Armée. The youthful Wilhelm would return to the field in the autumn of 1813 (after Feodor Dietz).

Württemberg Leutnant Christian von Martens's impression of the Cossacks that terrorized the Grande Armée during its wretched retreat in 1812 and would often continue to inspire panic in 1813.

Saxon line infantry: Saxon line infantry grenadier in the simple white uniform introduced in 1810. Regiments were distinguished by colours of lapels, collars and cuffs, here the blue of the *Low Infantry* that suffered severely at Großbeeren.

Saxon light infantry: Wearing the dark green typically associated with light troops in the nineteenth century, the Saxon light infantry battalions were considered an elite, frequently employed as advance and rear guards or given other special tasks.

Saxon Garde-Grenadier: known to Dresden's citizens as 'the king's buttered lobsters' for their showy uniforms, the grenadiers were also combat troops, fighting in all the major battles of 1813. They usually wore shakos in the field not the costly bearskin cap shown here.

Saxon hussar: this large regiment of eight squadrons performed well as part of the Saxon contingent's light cavalry. The officer shown here is turned out for parade and would look less brilliant on campaign.

Saxon Uhlan: the *Prinz Clemens* Uhlan Regiment had been converted from chevaulegers in 1811 and wore the traditional red of Saxony's chevaulegers; all the latter had been destroyed in Russia and were not re-formed until after Napoleon's defeat at Leipzig.

Saxon *Zastrow* Cuirassier: though re-formed with raw recruits after destruction in Russia, this regiment with its black cuirasses earned great renown alongside the Leib-Cuirassiers for their actions at Dresden in August.

Saxon horse artillery at Bautzen, 21 May: Hauptmann Probsthayn's battery rushes into action at Napoleon's orders, temporarily losing one piece that tumbles over as the drivers hurry their teams across a ditch. Probsthayn's skill and energy under Napoleon's eye would earn him the Legion of Honour.

Bavarian line infantry: Bavaria uniformed its infantry in a unique cornflower blue jacket with regimental distinctions on the lapels, collars and cuffs, here the 11th Infantry. Bavaria retained the tall *Raupenhelm* even after other armies had converted to shakos.

Bavarian artillery: dressed in the dark blue with black and red trim typical of this arm in much of Europe, Bavaria's artillery performed well. Poor security, however, cost them five of the six guns they had laboriously dragged back from Russia.

Bavarian chevauleger: clad in the green of light troops with the ubiquitous *Raupenhelm*, each of the country's six regiments contributed one newly raised squadron to the combined regiment that campaigned with the Grande Armée in 1813.

GL Carl Christian Erdmann Edler von LeCoq (1767–1830): the veteran LeCoq led the 21st Saxon division in Russia and brought the remnants home from Kalisch to take over the 24th Division in the reorganised army.

GL Heinrich Wilhelm von Zeschau (1760–1832): a competent general, Zeschau was deeply loyal to his king and painfully embarrassed when the Saxon division defected at Leipzig despite his efforts to hold it to its duty.

Dresden bridge, mid-March: Saxon troops escort Lieutenant Colonel Stepan Khrapovitsky, the blindfolded Russian parliamentaire, past the damaged span for his meeting to discuss a temporary ceasefire.

Plundering Cossacks, 20 October 1813: Allied soldiers often engaged in looting and other abuses such as these Cossacks ransacking the dead near Leipzig's Grimma Gate the day after the battle in this print by contemporary Leipzig artist Christian Gottfried Heinrich Geißler.

Dresden bridge, mid-May: with the main bridge repaired and two new wooden spans constructed, French and Rheinbund troops surge across the Elbe.

Above: Battle of Großbeeren, 23 August: Saxon gunners struggle to repair their piece in the rain and under fire as they attempt to cover the retreat from Großbeeren while cavalry suffers on the right in this painting by Albrecht Schuster.

Left: Napoleon and Friedrich August outside Dresden: the emperor's visits to the Saxon capital afforded opportunities for talks with his loyal Saxon ally, such as the ride in the Großer Garten depicted in this painting by Christian Friedrich Sigmund Trochold.

A Saxon heavy cavalry trooper's helmet of the type worn by both the Leib-Cuirassiers and *Zastrow* Cuirassiers in 1813.

Leipzig, 19 October: Napoleon bids farewell to the Saxon Guard Grenadiers in the market square, urging them to 'Guard your king well!' Murat is visible behind the emperor, looking 'the same as always' in his 'fantastic outfit', as Württemberg legate Kölle recalled. König Friedrich August, whom Napoleon has just left, observes from a balcony while citizens peer from other windows.

Top: Christian Geißler's rendering of Leipzig's Roßplatz showing the broad open space between the suburbs and the city proper (this area had been the glacis when Leipzig was a fortress). Much of the fighting on 19 October took place in this relatively open area of markets, trees, gardens and promenades.

Above: The Battle of Hanau, 30–31 October 1813. Bavarian General von Wrede led a combined Austro-Bavarian army to intercept the battered Grande Armée's retreat from Saxony. The attempt failed, however, as the Imperial Guard smashed through to permit the retreat to continue and Wrede himself was badly wounded. Note Bavarian infantry with French prisoners on the right, Austrian grenadiers advancing from the left.

3rd Brigade	GB Jarry		
132ᵉ Ligne (former Île-de-Ré)		2	713
133ᵉ Ligne (former 2ᵉ Mediterranean)		2	797
Artillery (two batteries)		–	233
West of the Prosna (not engaged)			
6th Squadron, Hussar Regiment (HQ escort)		1	66
2nd and 4th Saxon Foot Artillery Batteries			
	Hauptmann. Sonntag, Hauptmann Weisser	–	138
Prinz Friedrich regimental guns		–	46
Saxon Sapper Company		–	62
König Infantry		2 companies	76
French Artillery Park		–	343
Polish troops	GB Żółtowski		
2nd Infantry Regiment		2	920
7th Uhlans		4	306
Krakus		–	c. 300

7th Corps Strength

Infantry:	9,031 (3,605 Saxon, 4,821 French, 605 Würzburg)
Cavalry:	538 (Saxons not including Poles)
Artillery, Sappers and Train:	1,217 (641 Saxon, 576 French)
Total:	10,786 with 66 guns (including regimental pieces)
Poles	c. 1,500
Grand total (Saxon, French, Würzburg and Polish)	c. 12,300

Saxons: The official 'Situations' for 10 and 15 February list this small remnant of the *König* Infantry as present with the corps. Assuming the Situations are not in error, it is possible that these men were assigned as guards for the baggage and artillery park.

Poles: The 5th Polish Chasseurs-à-Cheval were allotted to Gablenz through 11 February. Ponatiowski recalled them on 11 February, but left the Krakus and 'several hundred' men of the 7th Uhlans with the Corps (*Sachsen und seine Krieger*, p. 77 and Baranowski, *Bitwa pod Kaliszem*, p. 116).

Source: Pierre Juhel, 'Kalisch', *Tradition*, no. 201, June 2004. For 1 February figures, see Reboul, *Campagne de 1813*, vol. II, Annex 8.

the regiment's other two guns and the *Liebenau* Grenadier battalion. Of these, the two *Prince Anton* companies were stationed on the northern side of the village, one grenadier company (2nd) was held in the village churchyard and the other three companies of grenadiers were posted just on the southern side of Kokanin as a ready reserve. To assure his connection with Kalisch, LeCoq placed GM Friedrich Gottlob von Steindel in Pruszków and Pawłówek with *Prinz Clemens* Infantry (soon to be *Steindel*), its four regimental guns and the divisional 6-pounder battery under Hauptmann Johann von Brause. GM von Sahr's division (five battalions and an artillery battery), had left Chlewo at daybreak and marched through Opatówek to arrive in the vicinity of Winiary in the early afternoon just before the combat opened. Between Sahr and LeCoq, GB Henry Maury's brigade of Durutte's division, including the two Würzburg battalions, held Skarszew as support for Gablenz. The rest of Durutte's division was behind Kalisch along with the artillery park, the Saxon bridging equipment and most of the trains (some elements had already headed west towards Glogau). A substantial number of Polish troops were also present. GB Edward Żółtowski commanded a mixed brigade of approximately 1,500 infantry and cavalry that participated in the fighting: 2nd Infantry, 7th Uhlans and the newly-created 'Krakus' or 'Polish Cossacks'.[38] A Saxon corporal described the Krakus as 'a sort of Landwehr composed of young persons, who, armed with lance, sabre and two pistols, were to join with us in defending their fatherland'.[39] Additionally, Kalisch was the base for a number of Polish regimental depots and as many as 5,000–6,000 men were being organised in the area. Consisting of depot troops and brand-new recruits who were untrained and unequipped, however, they were totally unsuited for combat. Żółtowski wisely sent many of them west on the 12th.[40]

The morning of the 13th passed quietly, a welcome respite for the men who had been marching, often at night, in weather that alternated between cruelly freezing temperatures and sudden thaws that turned the roads into muddy sloughs.[41] The Saxon Hussars, however, did engage in minor skirmishing with Russian dragoons, a development that led Gablenz to conclude that new Russian forces had arrived on his front. He immediately dispatched an officer to report this worrisome news to headquarters. Sometime between 9:00 and 10:00 a.m., as this young officer was trotting off to find Reynier and most of the men were moving into position and seeking something to eat, Reynier rode to meet LeCoq in Kokanin. According to the principal Saxon account, LeCoq warned Reynier that an attack was to be expected and urged him to draw the corps into a tighter defensive stance on the heights just east of Kalisch. Reynier, convinced that the only enemy nearby were Cossacks and small cavalry reconnaissance detachments, dismissed these concerns. His casual reaction is difficult to understand. Perhaps he had grown accustomed to constant harassment by roving bands of Cossacks and thus saw little danger. Perhaps he wanted to ensure all his troops had billets in villages and would not have to bivouac yet again in the raw weather.[42] Whatever his reason, he compounded his errors from the Saxon perspective by directing LeCoq to have Steindel's men take up their quarters for the day, an order that LeCoq

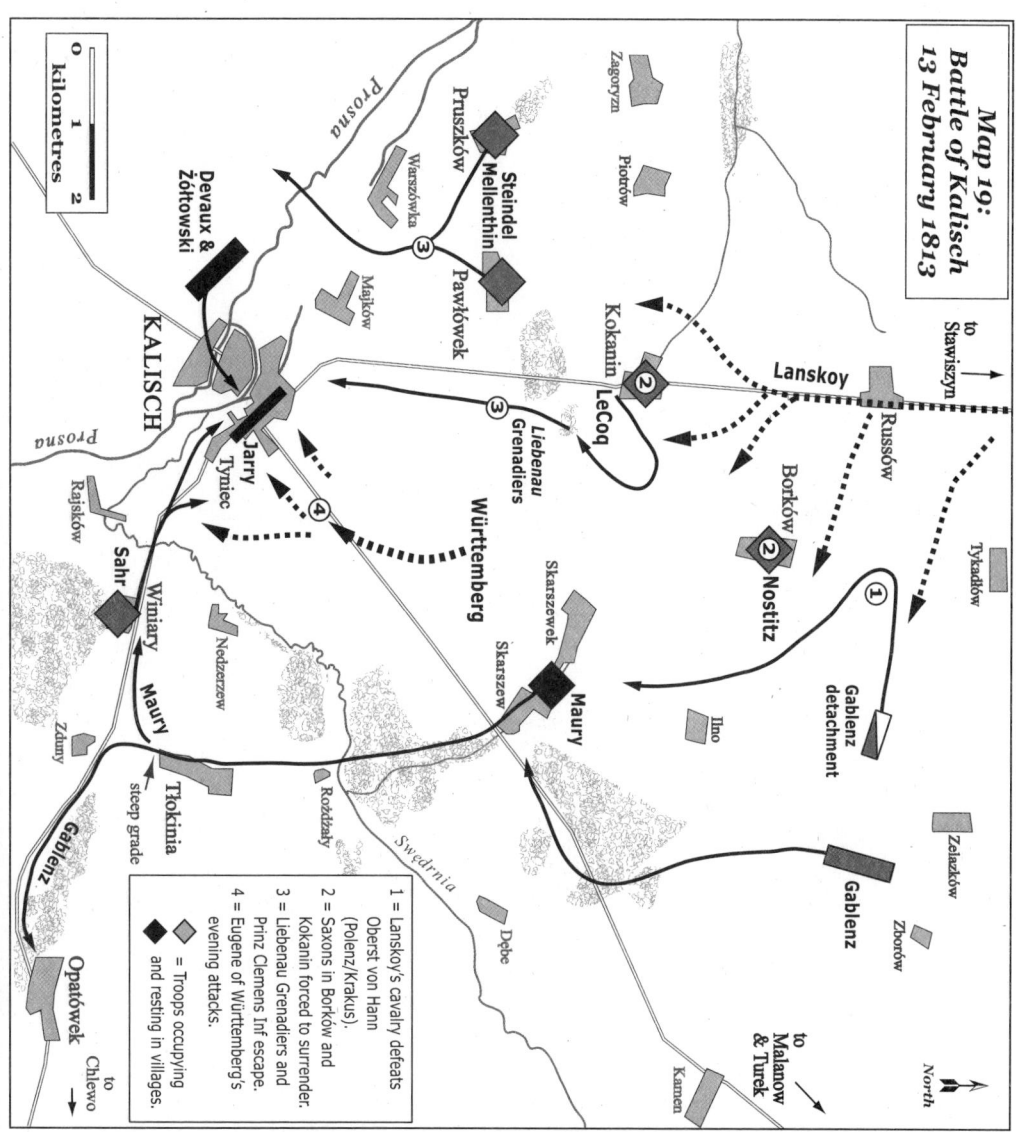

Map 19: Battle of Kalisch 13 February 1813

relayed with the quiet caveat that Steindel should remain as concentrated as possible and alert for enemy action. Reynier concluded the exchange by ordering LeCoq to borrow some cavalry from Gablenz and push the enemy out of Russów before nightfall.[43] Just as Gablenz received this order his officer returned from headquarters to report that the troops should draw ammunition as usual but that a Russian attack was hardly to be expected that day.[44]

Preparations and coordination for this minor attack on Russów apparently took some time and the day was creeping towards mid-afternoon before Gablenz's cavalry arrived. These men, the *Polenz* Chevaulegers and two

Chart 13: Russian Forces at Kalisch, 13 February 1813

Lt. Gen. Wintzingerode

		bns/sqdns
Advance Guard	*Maj. Gen. Lanskoy*	
20th Jäger Regiment (detached from 3rd Infantry Division)		2
Alexandriskii Hussars		8
Byelorusskii Hussars		8
Liflanskii Jägers		4
Don Cossacks		5 regiments
(Grekov III, Grekov IX, Grekov XXI, Kuteinikov IV, Sutsherinov)		
3rd Ural Cossack Regiment		1 regiment
7th Horse Artillery Battery		–
Col. Davydov Raiding Detachment		
Detachment of Akhtyrsky Hussars		–
Cossack detachment		–
Don Cossack Regiment Popov XIII		1 regiment
1st Bug Cossack Regiment		1 regiment
II Infantry Corps	*Lt. Gen. Eugene of Württemberg*	
3rd Infantry Division	*Maj. Gen. Shakhovsky*	
Muromskii Infantry Regiment		2
Revelskii Infantry Regiment		2
Chernigovskii Infantry Regiment		2
Reserve battalions		3
1st Heavy Artillery Battery		–
4th Infantry Division	*Maj. Gen. Pyshnitsky*	
Tobolskii Infantry Regiment		2
Volynskii Infantry Regiment		2
Kremenchugskii Infantry Regiment		2
4th Jäger Regiment		2
Reserve battalions		3
6th Light Artillery Battery		–

companies of the new Polish Krakus, perhaps something more than 500 or so in all, had just passed GM von Nostitz's position at Borków when they were suddenly set upon by Russian hussars and Cossacks. A brief but desperate melee left Oberst Johann Joseph von Hann of the *Polenz* Chevaulegers a prisoner as well as 65 of his fellow Saxons and an unknown number of Poles dead, wounded or captured (Hann himself had taken three minor lance wounds). The rest fled back towards Skarszew in confusion.

These Russians were part of Wintzingerode's Advance Guard commanded by Maj. Gen. Sergey Nikolaevich Lanskoy. Having crossed the Vistula early in the month, Wintzingerode was supposed to intercept the retreating 7th

II Reserve Infantry Corps	Maj. Gen. Bakhmetyev	
34th Reserve Infantry Division	Maj. Gen. Talyzin 1	
Reserve battalions		7
33rd Heavy Artillery Battery		–
35th Reserve Infantry Division	Maj. Gen. Zapolsky	
Reserve battalions		6
75th Ship's Company		–
7th Light Artillery Battery		–
Cavalry Corps	Maj. Gen. Trubetskoy	
Brigade	Maj. Gen. Witte	
1st Ukraine Cossack Regiment		1 regiment
3rd Ukraine Cossack Regiment		1 regiment
Brigade	Maj. Gen. Olenin	
Reserve squadrons		8
		(1 Jäger, 4 dragoon, 3 hussar,)
Brigade	Maj. Gen. Knorring	
Tatarskii Uhlans		8
Litovskii Uhlans		2
Sumskii Hussars		2
8th Horse Artillery Battery		–
Total strength	c. 15,000 infantry, 72 guns	

Not included: Detached Don Cossack Regiment *Sementchikov* and 9 guns.

Source: Osten-Sacken, *Geschichte des Befreiungskrieges*, vol. I, Beilage XXIV.

For organisation and additional details as of 5 January 1813, see Baranowski, *Bitwa pod Kaliszem*, pp. 103–6.

Corps but he had moved rather methodically at first, more or less paralleling Reynier's march.[45] Learning that he had an opportunity to catch Reynier at Kalisch, however, he reached Rychwał on 12 February with his main body and pushed Lanskoy's Advance Guard south to Stawiszyn from which place his men evicted the ill-prepared Polish 7th Uhlans, taking between 250 and 350 prisoners. Wintzingerode had approximately 13,500 to 15,000 men under his command along with 72 guns, so his overall numerical edge over Reynier's 10,000 or so men and 66 guns was of little significance, especially as Reynier could draw on some of the Polish recruits in the town.[46] However, 6,500 to 7,000 of the Russian troops were mounted men, regular cavalry and Cossacks, vastly superior to the 980 Saxon troopers available to the 7th Corps along with some number of raw Polish recruits. Moreover, cavalry would have a considerable advantage over infantry in the open terrain east of Kalisch making withdrawal from the villages where Reynier's soldiers were posted a risky proposition, a point that Wintzingerode specifically recognised in his battle report.[47]

The Russian superiority in mounted strength immediately made itself felt. When LeCoq saw Lanskoy's horsemen descend on the Saxon chevaulegers and Polish Krakus, he ordered the three *Liebenau* Grenadier companies in reserve behind Kokanin to assist Oberst Hann's outnumbered little band. The lead grenadier company advanced in open order, but as the Saxon and Polish horsemen tumbled back in disarray, they and the following two companies found themselves isolated in the open terrain in the face of the victorious enemy cavalry. Fortunately for the grenadiers, a nearby stand of birch offered some protection. The 1st and 4th Companies hastened to the temporary safety of this coppice while holding off the Russian horse with skirmish fire. Forming a combined square, these two companies marched for the main road to Kalisch. The 3rd Company, only some 40 or so men strong, was somewhat delayed but also managed to form its own tiny square and withdrew along with but slightly separated from its fellows. Halting periodically to repel repeated cavalry attacks, the grenadiers even maintained their formation when the Russians unlimbered two guns to shower them with canister shot. Fortunately for Premierleutnant Friedrich Maximilian von Mandelsloh and his company, 'Owing to the close proximity in which the guns had unlimbered, they mostly overshot us so that the balls rattled among the bayonets, but few reached their targets.' The Russians, however, then repositioned their pieces and fired more effectively. The battalion commander, Oberstleutnant Friedrich Christian von Liebenau, was badly wounded in this artillery fire and wanted to be left behind, but the grenadiers refused to leave him. 'The appearance of this little square was strange indeed', wrote Mandelsloh, 'as its little space was more than full with the horses of the major and his adjutant, the officers' servants and their packhorses and the wounded, who were all taken along, and even offered protection to a pair of *cantinières*.' The men thus brought their commander and all but their most seriously wounded comrades to safety, joining the corps' battle line on the heights east of Kalisch after an hour-long retreat.[48] At the conclusion of what had been a superb display of fortitude and tactical ability despite seemingly overwhelming odds, the three much-reduced companies remained in the firing line to contribute to the defence of the town for the remainder of the afternoon. They left behind 57 of their comrades, dead, captured or too seriously wounded to move.

Other elements of LeCoq's division were not as fortunate as Liebenau's grenadiers. Russian cavalry had quickly flooded the field and surrounded Kokanin and Borków. LeCoq had escaped with the grenadiers, but the three companies in Kokanin were overwhelmed. Corporal Carl Buhle, on outpost duty some distance towards Stawiszyn, dashed back to the village when 'an immense body of cavalry sprang upon us'. Although the little regimental guns kept the horsemen at bay for a time, a Russian battery appeared 'and bombarded Kokanin village so heavily with every kind of ammunition that in about a quarter of an hour neither man nor horse was left to draw breath by our two cannons, all lay about killed or mangled by the enemy guns'. Buhle and other infantrymen tried manning their regimental pieces, but with the arrival of Lanskoy's Jäger Regiment, the defenders were driven back into the village churchyard and forced to surrender when their ammunition was consumed.[49] A similar fate befell Nostitz in Borków. Hoping that Gablenz would arrive to support him, the general decided to stand fast in the village and thus missed his only chance to make a safe retreat as the grenadiers had done. 'The guns were pulled back into the village and the infantry defended itself behind hedges and walls,' recalled one of the regiment's gunners, 'We already heard the hurrahs behind and around us and the enemy masses came ever closer.'[50] Encircled and beyond assistance, Nostitz and his 319 men held out for several hours, rejecting four calls to surrender before capitulating late in the afternoon when ammunition ran low and the enemy threatened to bombard the village.

The flood of Russian cavalry also threatened to engulf the *Prinz Clemens* Infantry and the division's artillery battery. The suddenness of the onslaught caught the regiment unprepared. Unterleutnant Eduard Franz von Wolffersdorff had just sat down to enjoy some dumplings with his commander, when they heard shots and hurried outside to organise a defence.[51] As with the *Liebenau* Grenadiers, however, the Saxons on this part of the field responded to their desperate situation with cool professional competence. Although GM von Steindel was present, real leadership here seems to have emanated from Oberst von Mellenthin, the commander of the *Prinz Clemens* Infantry, with the general merely approving what the *Oberst* recommended.[52] Under heavy pressure, Mellenthin managed to unite his two battalions near Pawłówek and form them into two squares with Hauptmann von Brause's battery and the four regimental guns in between. Once assembled, the Saxons began a slow and orderly withdrawal west of the main road towards Kalisch, repelling the constant attacks by the Russian cavalry with well-directed musketry and cannon fire. Feldwebel Vollborn remembered the impact of several shots from the 6-pounder battery on a mass of enemy on a hillside nearby: 'the effects were so visible that it looked as if a gateway had been opened' in the Russian ranks. The Russians brought up several howitzers to shell the Saxons, but Mellenthin astutely shifted his squares 50 paces forward to place them largely inside the arc of the Russian fire.[53] Nonetheless, casualties were mounting. Two of the regimental pieces were disabled and an exploding ammunition caisson, hit by a shell, caused hideous burns among the gun crews: 'a gruesome sight only made somewhat bearable by the familiarity with similar scenes of horror'.[54] Twice the infantry had to detail men to take the place of dead or wounded gunners. One Russian shell created a moment of vulnerability when it badly wounded a battalion commander's horse. The major disentangled himself from the stirrups safely but the frenzied beast, trailing a stream of blood, crashed through one side of the square, injuring several soldiers in its agonised passage. Vollborn believed the battalion fortunate that the enemy cavalry did not take advantage of the havoc the wounded horse wrought in the square.[55]

The regiment had now been conducting its fighting withdrawal for some three hours and night was coming on; an officer sent for orders was captured and Kalisch seemed beyond reach. Mellenthin and Steindel thus decided to wait for night and then seek safety by crossing the Prosna north of town under the cover of darkness. Christian Friedrich Frenzel, a private soldier, described one of the charges the regiment had to endure during its ordeal that long afternoon:

> But now the mass of cavalry attacked us. With fury from three sides [they came] but paying no attention (to either their hurrahs or their madly brave onslaught) we let them get very close to us until we had them totally in our sights. Then we fired and they collapsed together in heaps. Man and horse, they were in the greatest disorder. They had to retreat. And the canister and shells gave them an escort. Our colonel stood in the middle of the square and said to us: 'Men, we are indeed cut off from the corps, but will not want to give up, because where my soldiers stand, there stand I and where I stand, my soldiers stand too.' With one voice we answered: 'No, colonel, no giving up, we would rather go through the Prosna.' [The colonel]: 'Bravo, comrades, that is my desire too. But as long as it is daylight, we must defend ourselves against the enemy with brave hearts.' We knew our colonel, and what he said, he stood by.[56]

The Russian cavalry seems to have charged at least four times raising 'a battle cry that would have made our hair stand on end'.[57] At one point, a knot of Uhlans broke into the Saxon defences and began dragging away one of Brause's howitzers. Feldwebel Vollborn and seven other volunteers, however, dashed from their square, killed or wounded several of the Uhlans, drove off the rest and rescued the piece (Vollborn was promoted to Unterleutnant for this act and several of his comrades received awards for valour). With enormous effort, the soldiers then manhandled the howitzer to the Prosna where the battery was in the process of crossing. Shielded by the darkness and a chain of skirmishers, the infantry broke the thin and rotten river ice to wade through chest-high frigid water past floating chunks of ice before clambering up the steep and slippery bank on the far shore. 'Icy in our soaked clothes, the cold shook through us,' recalled Wolffersdorff, 'as tired as we were, however, we could not rest, but had to run around to warm ourselves up.'[58] Wolffersdorff regretted the loss of all his possessions, left behind with the dumplings in his haste to join the regiment, but Steindel, Mellenthin, Brause and their men could take great pride in the execution of an exemplary withdrawal under heavy pressure.

While the *Prinz Clemens* Infantry was conducting its epic withdrawal, the Russian advance continued elsewhere on the field. Delayed by the need to traverse the large forest between Rychwał and Stawiszyn on a single road, Wintzingerode's infantry were now appearing and pushing against the outskirts of Kalisch. GB Antoine Anatole Gédéon Jarry's small brigade was responsible for the defences here and Durutte reinforced him with two guns and II/35e Léger as the Russian pressure increased. The Polish 2nd Infantry became involved in this fighting as well.[59] Nonetheless, the Russians were able to gain a foothold in the eastern suburb of Tyniec and their artillery belaboured Jarry's men and the Poles. Fortunately for Reynier, Sahr's brigade had arrived in Winiary from Opatówek in the early afternoon. Thinking themselves secure behind friendly lines, the brigade was surprised to be fired upon by rows of troops on the high ground to the north.[60] In the fading light, Sahr at first thought these to be Poles and ordered his men not to return fire. When it became clear they were facing the enemy, he sent the *Anger* Grenadier Battalion to clear a path to Kalisch while the rest of the brigade occupied the Russians with feints, skirmishers and cannon fire. Although they were only seeking to slip past into Kalisch, the presence of the Saxons forced the Russians to evacuate Tyniec, easing the strain on Jarry's hard-pressed troops. This timely intervention proved crucial as Russian attacks soon intensified. Although the evening was rapidly progressing towards full night, Wintzingerode was determined to master the town. His infantry were now all up and, against the advice of his key subordinate, Eugene of Württemberg (nephew of König

Friedrich of Württemberg), he ordered an assault. The French, Saxons and Poles stood firm, however, and, as Eugene later wrote 'despite all the effort, it was impossible to dislodge them'.[61] Though more fortuitous than planned, therefore, Sahr's arrival had been key to halting the Russian advance and retaining control of the town. As the Saxons withdrew through the outskirts of the town across the river, the two trailing companies of the *Anger* Battalion exploited a final opportunity to inflict an unpleasant repulse on a Russian column they caught by surprise in the stygian streets. Cautioning his men to silence, Hauptmann Gideon Carl Caspar von Geibler led them close to but unnoticed by the enemy column, loosed a sudden volley and then charged with the bayonet, scattering the Russians and opening the path for the two companies to gain safety in the town.[62]

It remains to account for Gablenz, Maury and the Saxon Uhlans. On hearing the gunfire occasioned by the Russian attack, Gablenz had assembled his remaining men and headed towards Kalisch, encountering 'the first unfortunate harbingers of this day' in the form of 'the ruins of the *Polenz* Dragoon [sic] Regiment that had been detached from us and overthrown by the enemy's superior numbers as well as the newly formed Polish Cossacks that had been provided as support'.[63] Fortunately for the Saxons, the Russians, focused on Kalisch, had not pursued Hann's retreating chevaulegers. Gablenz thus had time to rally his small command around Maury's brigade in Skarszew but, finding the way to Kalisch blocked by the flood of Russian troops, he was forced to turn south towards Tłokinia in the hopes of rejoining the corps via Winiary. Maury and the Polish troopers followed in his wake. Before reaching Winiary, however, Gablenz spotted Cossacks and guns on the high ground to his right front. The evening's gathering gloom did not permit a clear view of the enemy and his men held off their probes, but he became convinced that he could not reach Kalisch without suffering heavy casualties. He attempted to locate a crossing over the Prosna south of the town but found the way blocked by flooded streams, so he turned back to Opatówek and ended up reaching Brzeziny at 2:00 a.m. on 14 February after an exhausting 30-kilometre march. Maury, on the other hand, had been delayed by the struggles Gablenz's artillery experienced in climbing a steep hill just outside Tłokinia. By the time his brigade made the turn towards Winiary, Sahr's advance had cleared off the Russians and Maury reached Kalisch that evening 'without the loss of a single man'.[64] The Poles and some elements of the *Polenz* Chevaulegers reached safety by attaching themselves to Maury's column.

The *Prinz Clemens* Uhlans, on the other hand, missed the fight entirely. Having been misdirected that morning, the regiment waited all day in the wrong location before its commander, Oberstleutnant Wilhelm August von Thümmel, decided to make for Kalisch. An adjutant somehow found them while en route and guided the Uhlans past nearby Russian positions in total darkness. Thümmel and his men thus returned safely, their only loss being members of an outpost who could not locate the regiment and ended up joining Gablenz.[65]

Combat continued in the darkness until around 9:00 p.m. while Reynier slowly pulled the remaining elements of his corps across the Prosna and destroyed the bridges in Kalisch.[66] The cessation of firing in the direction of Borków led the Saxons to conclude that Nostitz and their comrades there had succumbed but there was no word from Gablenz. Taking stock of the situation that night therefore, the Saxons could be well satisfied with the courage and tactical skill they had demonstrated during the battle. Indeed, the next day, Russian General Lanskoy sent a *parlementaire* to compliment the Saxons on their bravery.[67] The cost, however, had been heavy: at least 1,000 Saxons were dead, wounded or captured and six of their regimental guns had been lost along with two flags. While the men of *Prinz Clemens* proudly saved their standards and all but two of their guns (the two that had been lost were both disabled), the *Prinz Anton* Infantry had been wiped out. Losses in Jarry's brigade and II/35ᵉ Léger, the only French formations to be seriously engaged, came to 212.[68] The absence of Gablenz meant that the corps was deprived of an additional 1,000 men, meaning that the overall strength of the remaining Saxon contingent with 7th Corps was reduced by about half.

It had been a battle of isolated engagements with no evidence of overarching direction from Reynier except for the direct defence of the town itself. Once the Russian cavalry was unleashed, higher management of the fighting would have been nearly impossible in any case given the separation and surrounding of the corps' various components. This placed a premium on lower level leadership, especially among the brigade, regimental and battalion officers. As the Saxon contingent's campaign diary noted: 'These were anxious hours, during which each had to operate according to his own perception and at his own risk.'[69] With the possible exception of Nostitz missing his brief chance to escape Borków, in most cases the Saxons and their French comrades performed very well once past their initial shock.

Why had the corps allowed itself to be shocked in the first place? The depiction above is the sequence of events as recorded by Clemens Franz Xaver von Cerrini, a generally reliable observer who was at that time a major on LeCoq's staff and thus possibly present for the Saxon general's morning exchange with Reynier. Frédéric Reboul, a careful historian, casts doubt on this outline of events, citing 'the insufficiency of the intelligence gathered by the Saxon cavalry' and 'the poor tactical dispositions of General LeCoq'. It is possible that both are correct in their own ways. Reynier, as will be seen at Großbeeren, sometimes displayed an overly casual attitude towards tactical security as he seems to have done here. For his part, LeCoq was likely responsible for what Reboul castigates as the tactical placement of his division in three groups with 'at least 1,800 to 2,200 metres distance between them ... individually very weak and too separated from one another to offer assistance'. As corps commander, of course, Reynier could have chosen to alter LeCoq's arrangements, but elected not to do so, probably owing to his conviction that the corps faced little serious danger that day. As for the 'insufficiency of intelligence', Reboul acknowledges that the impenetrable screen of active Cossacks 'deprived the cavalry of the 7th Corps of all means to reconnoitre' the heavily forested area north of Stawiszyn. It seems reasonable to assume that driving off the enemy and learning more about his movements to the north motivated Reynier to order the abortive advance on Russów before the close of day.[70] The Russians also deserve credit for masking their movements. 'It was evident that the enemy did not believe a considerable corps was on his flank', reported Wintzingerode after the battle, 'Orders were therefore given to show only the Cossacks, so as to hide our true forces from him and not alarm him too soon for fear that he might escape us.'[71] This clever ruse no doubt contributed to Reynier's complacency.

Wherever the fault lay, two additional points are worth noting before closing this review of the Battle of Kalisch. First, the Saxons neither surrendered nor deserted despite ample opportunity to do so. Instead, they fought with great determination and, when they could escape entrapment, persevered in the face of daunting odds until they reached the safety of their own lines. Second is the significance of the interaction of arms and how the Allied superiority in mounted troops not only offered advantages in gathering intelligence but could also be the deciding factor on the battlefield. Here Reboul's analysis deserves citation:

> During the day, the inferiority of the French forces owing to their weakness in cavalry was affirmed for the first time: the leadership, lacking intelligence and seemingly stunned by the attack, by the swirl of horsemen, was constantly inclined to judge the enemy more dangerous and more numerous than they really were and to take, as a result, hasty decisions; the detachments of infantry, enveloped, isolated from one another, acted on their own account or lost their sangfroid; these were natural phenomena,

consequent to the lack of cavalry, that could be observed during the days before the combat at Kalisch and during the course of the combat itself.

Although Reynier's 7th Corps was one of the last intact components of the 'old' Grande Armée of 1812, the experience at Kalisch was thus a foretaste of the cavalry problems the 'new' Grande Armée of 1813 would face. Already mentioned in the overview chapter above, the debilities of the French mounted arm and the manifold effects these frailties had on the Rheinbund armies will continue to be a theme of this narrative.

Back to Saxony

Heading back to Saxony, the 7th Corps, accompanied by large numbers of Polish depot troops and convoys of material from the regional magazines, left the heights east of Kalisch on the morning of 14 February.[72] The losses in the battle had effectively reduced the Saxon contingent to Steindel's and Sahr's brigades, so these were combined into one division under LeCoq with a total of only some 2,400 men.[73] The weather had turned bitterly cold again and the men of *Prinz Clemens* moved 'as if armoured in ice' as they began what proved to be five days of wretched marching over bottomless roads.[74] The column reached Glogau on 18 February untroubled by the enemy, however, and went into quarters east of the fortress for several days of much-needed rest. 'No words can describe the blissful feeling that came over us as we were so suddenly transferred from the greatest suffering and deprivation of war to the greatest peace and security and found the long-missed bed, a well-set table and educated company,' recalled Mandelsloh.[75] Marching again on 22 February, the corps reached Bautzen on 1 March but retired to Dresden when Reynier learned that Eugène had abandoned Berlin. What was left of the Saxon contingent thus arrived in their capital on 7 March 1813, but the trial at Kalisch and the separation of Gablenz's detachment meant that it counted only some 1,436 infantry and 92 Uhlans present under arms on its return.[76] Losses notwithstanding, a Saxon officer-historian noted that,

> The Saxons who returned out of Poland at this time still displayed an attachment to the French; they had also retained their military bearing as a result of their strictly exercised discipline. They arrived in Dresden on 7 March fully armed and in good order as proven, capable warriors, albeit much diminished in numbers, but they at once perceived there an entirely different attitude towards the French among their countrymen.[77]

As he withdrew towards Saxony, Reynier requested support from the troops that had been left behind in the kingdom during the invasion of Russia (*see* Chart 14). He hoped these would at least guard the main roads out of Silesia while the remnants of his corps tried to recover from their extraordinary exertions. Saxony, however, had little beyond recruits to offer and claimed it could not send those owing to their unready state and the needs of home defence.[78] Moreover, the kingdom was at this point unwilling to commit more troops without evidence of direct French support as was bluntly stated in a personal letter Reynier received accompanying a message from the king:

> The viceroy's [Eugène's] position and yours prove that you neither wish to nor can you defend the line of the Oder ... The Saxon Army is ruined ... and I can assure you that it is useless to hope to be able to reorganise the Saxon Army before an army arrives that can reassure us regarding the defence of our country.[79]

Such undisguised frustration notwithstanding, the authorities in Dresden could not entirely ignore Reynier's request, so this task was assigned to GL von Thielmann. Formerly one of the most dedicated adherents to the French alliance, Thielmann was viewed as an experienced field commander who was close to Napoleon. He was thus charged with reorganising the army after his return from Russia and now assembled several hastily constructed new units between Hoyerswerda and Cottbus on 21 February in response to Reynier's pleas: a brigade of heavy cavalry (Leib-Cuirassiers and the reformed *Zastrow Cuirassiers*) with a horse artillery battery, three raw provisional squadrons of light cavalry and a provisional battalion of infantry recruits, perhaps 2,500 men in all.[80] This proved a very short-lived move. The infantry and light horse duly marched for Halbau (Iłowa) on 25 February, but the heavy brigade, under GM Eugen Dietrich Moritz von Liebenau, returned to Dresden, detaching two squadrons of the Leib-Cuirassiers west to Plauen to escort the king (*see below*).[81] At the same time, Thielmann was reassigned to take command in Torgau. The infantry were recalled shortly thereafter. Most of these men, along with the remains of the Saxons from 7th Corps, would soon end up in Torgau, where the Saxon army was to be reconstructed under Thielmann's guidance.

While the remains of 7th Corps were making their way west to Saxony and Thielmann was trying to cobble together new formations, Gablenz was heading south. Contact with Reynier was re-established on 15 February, but the French general forbade Gablenz to march through Prussian Silesia to rejoin the corps. As noted earlier, a Franco-Prussian convention of 24 February 1812 prohibited French entry into the southern portions of Silesia and Reynier feared that the Russians would use Gablenz's passage as an excuse to violate

> **Chart 14: Saxon Reserve Forces, as of late February 1813**
>
> The following Saxon formations were available in addition to the remnants of 7th Corps retreating from Poland, and Gablenz near Krakow.
>
> **Infantry**
>
> | | |
> |---|---|
> | Leib-Grenadier Regiment | 1st Battalion in Torgau, 2nd Battalion in Dresden and Königstein |
> | Jägerkorps | Torgau |
> | 1st Provisional Battalion | Torgau, formed in mid-1812 |
> | 2nd Provisional Battalion | Dresden, formed in 1812, shifted to Torgau in early 1813 |
> | 3rd Provisional Battalion | Torgau, formed in 1812 |
> | 4th Provisional Battalion | Torgau, formed in January 1813 |
> | 5th Provisional Battalion | Torgau, formed in February 1813 |
> | Provisional Light Battalion | Torgau, formed in February 1813 |
>
> **Cavalry,**
>
> Heavy Cavalry Brigade   *GM von Liebenau*
>   Leib-Cuirassiers
>   *Zastrow* Cuirassiers   re-formed after Russia
>   Horse Artillery Battery   *Hauptmann Probsthayn*
> Light cavalry   February
>   *Polenz* Chevaulegers Squadron
>   *Prinz Clemens* Uhlan Squadron
>   Hussar Squadron

the zone as well.[82] Instead, he directed Gablenz to seek safety with the Poles and Austrians. The Saxon general thus turned south, reached Poniatowksi's headquarters in Częstochowa on 18 February and marched on the following day to join the Austrian corps, now commanded by FML Johann Freiherr von Frimont (Schwarzenberg had been recalled to Vienna for employment on a diplomatic mission to Napoleon).[83] Warmly received by Frimont, by the end of the February, Gablenz was able to place his little detachment of slightly more than 1,000 men into winter quarters around Krakow. Here they would remain in a sort of politely interned status until mid-April.

Flight to Neutrality

By the time the Saxon soldiers returned to Dresden, their king was no longer present in his capital. Apprehension about the safety of the royal family had been accumulating since late January when the first Cossacks had been sighted on the kingdom's northeastern borders. The wretched state of the French army, the loss of Warsaw, the clash at Kalisch, the breaching of the

Oder River line and the Russian raid on Berlin accelerated Saxon anxieties. As early as 22 January the Austrian ambassador reported to Vienna that the alarmed court was packing for an imminent departure.[84] Events did not move with quite such haste, but Friedrich August sent most of his family members west on 22 February, following with Queen Amalie and their daughter, Maria Augusta, three days later. They were accompanied by his closest advisors, a large train of royal baggage, two squadrons of Leib-Cuirassiers and part of the 2nd Battalion of Leib-Grenadiers. The destination assigned to this cavalcade was Plauen, a small city in the far western corner of Friedrich August's realm. Here the family and court would remain for the coming month, despite an invitation of residence in Mainz or Strasbourg from Napoleon and an offer of refuge in Prague from Austrian Kaiser Franz. The king released a decree asserting his faith in 'the strong support of our great ally' and empowered an 'Immediat-Commission' of four senior civilian officials to manage day-to-day affairs in his absence. 'It is the king's intention', the commissioners were told, 'to remain true to the French cause; therefore, nothing should be granted [to the Allies] that would displease the Emperor Napoleon.'[85] As his carriage trundled west, his recovering army was divided between Dresden (Reynier with the remains of 7th Corps and Liebenau's cavalry brigade) and Torgau (garrison and trainees under Thielmann). With the Saxon king separated from his capital and his army, the narrative must now switch back and forth between the court's several locations and the banks of the Elbe to outline the events of the next several months.

Once ensconced in Plauen, the Saxon government was temporarily safe in a physical sense but found itself entirely insecure as far as its foreign policy was concerned.[86] The stakes were high, indeed existential, as a misstep could lead to Friedrich August's dethronement and the dissolution of his monarchy. In addition to the preservation of the throne and Saxony's territorial integrity, the king sought to minimise the burdens of war on his subjects while averting any threat to the kingdom's paternalistic social order. Moreover, Friedrich August and his advisors – particularly his foreign minister, Friedrich Christian Ludwig Graf Senfft von Pilsach – maintained a persistent interest in the Duchy of Warsaw. This interest stemmed not only from the king's rather formal sense of duty to his Polish subjects, but also from a desire to be sufficiently strong to balance Prussia. If Poland could not be retained under the Saxon sceptre, the court hoped to gain compensation elsewhere, specifically casting its eye on Erfurt (administered directly from France) and the various Thuringian micro-states: the so-called Saxon Duchies ruled by the Ernestine branch of the Wettin clan as well as the Reuß, Schwarzburg and Anhalt principalities.[87]

Saxony, however, was too weak to sail alone on its sea of troubles. As in the past, it needed the support of a major state to secure its interests.[88] Between March and May, therefore, the peripatetic king and his court would tack back and forth within a triangle of great powers as they travelled from Saxony to Bavaria and then to Bohemia. On one side of this triangle was France. Not only was Saxony formally allied with France, but Napoleon had been the only leader willing to guarantee Saxony's territorial integrity. Moreover, on a human level, Friedrich August continued to admire the French emperor, even after the Russian disaster, and he valued the genuine courtesy, respect and friendship Napoleon consistently displayed in their correspondence and interactions. Adherence to the French alliance also reflected Friedrich August's conception of loyalty and the sanctity he assigned to his personal pledges. At the same time, anti-French sentiment was widespread in Saxony and was evident even in the correspondence among senior government officials. In a letter to Senfft, for instance, Joseph Woldemar von Zezschwitz, one of the members of the king's Immediat-Commission, described the relationship with France as 'an imprisonment, not an alliance, and we must free ourselves from it'.[89] In addition to feeling confined and burdened by the alliance, Napoleon's defeat in Russia had convinced many that French power would not be able to protect the kingdom from the advancing Russians and Prussians.

The Russo-Prussian bloc, the second side of the triangle, generated dread rather than hope from the court's perspective. The popular attitude towards the Allies was largely favourable as many Saxons seem to have hoped that the disappearance of the French meant their land would be spared the ravages of war. Russian troops were generally greeted with a mixture of relief and curiosity when they first arrived in Saxon villages and the Allied monarchs, especially the engaging tsar, received a genuinely warm welcome when they reached Dresden on 24 April.[90] As their armies advanced, however, Allied generals issued proclamations calling on the Saxon people to rise up and join in a pan-German revolt against Napoleon. Some Saxon officials, enthused by this anti-French vision, eagerly embraced the Allies and urged their compatriots to do likewise, but most did not and the popular mood could certainly fluctuate, as evident in a report submitted to Stuttgart by a businessman who served as a Württemberg government informer: 'How the inhabitants of Dresden are disposed, I cannot truly tell, I do not think they even know themselves; one day they cheer Tsar Alexander and praise the Russians to the skies, the next they shout "*Vive l'Empereur!*".' Allied officials such as Stein were thus soon complaining about the lack of selfless support for 'the good cause' among the

Saxons: 'The great mass of people is devoted to their king and demand his return, but it is not to be expected that these weak worriers, so attached to their property, will be capable of an uprising or resistance.'[91]

In the meantime, Allied actions were exciting anger and outrage at court while generating resentments among the populace at large. The threatening Kalisch declarations had already caused particular alarm, leading the Saxon court to perceive the numerous subsequent proclamations issued by various Allied generals as sinister attempts to foment rebellion and divide Friedrich August from his subjects. Denunciation of the French and warm words of brotherhood did nothing to mitigate the negative impact of such statements.[92] One distributed by Wittgenstein on 23 March, for example, prompted the distressed Zezschwitz to protest to General Wintzingerode (who was seen as more sympathetic) about the wisdom of such statements: 'The true German will do his uttermost before he deviates from his prince's view or is disloyal to him.' Senfft also responded angrily. 'This proclamation comes from the pen of a general who serves an emperor not a *comité du salut public* [Committee of Public Safety: a reference to the reviled French Revolutionary government]', he wrote, it was 'an attack on the founding pillar of the throne upon which his own sovereign sits and if he himself [the tsar] approved such speech, it is a neglect of his own worth that does not bode well for the cause itself.' Throwing themselves into the arms of new foreigners like 'giddy insurrectionists', he continued, 'would be a new slavery, the most wretched ... That would be literally to lay aside the crown or at least the sceptre.'[93] Pamphlets published by known Allied propagandists heightened Saxon indignation by insulting Friedrich August personally and hinting at his replacement by Carl August, Herzog von Sachsen-Weimar-Eisenach from the Ernestine branch of the Wettin family.[94] Furthermore, for many Saxon leaders, pressure from an unruly populace had forced King Friedrich Wilhelm III of Prussia to act against his will in deserting Napoleon. They feared this Prussian 'Jacobinism' would spill over into Saxony. The Saxon public, prompted by Allied proclamations and the obloquy directed at their king, might then become radicalised and escape the control of the government with unnerving consequences for the socio-political order. For the deeply conservative Saxon monarchy, such as outcome would be, of course, an abomination.[95]

Fears of material and territorial loss also haunted the Saxon ruler and his advisors. The Allied armies, though generally well-disciplined at first, nonetheless made what seemed to the Saxon regime extravagant demands for food, clothing, horses, fodder and services. Most threatening, however, was the prospect of future domination by a restored, vengeful and avaricious Prussia that would surround Saxony geographically.[96] The Cottbus district, ceded to Saxony by Prussia in the treaties of 1807, was the most sensitive issue. As soon as Blücher's troops entered the area on 23 March, Prussia declared it once more under Prussian sovereignty, a unilateral move that Friedrich August saw as an abrupt and unseemly violation of a formal treaty.[97] Combined with the almost certain loss of the Duchy of Warsaw to Russia and the declared Allied aim of returning Prussia to its former position and influence, the Saxons feared their own future status would be diminished by a Russo-Prussian victory while the country's lands were desolated by Allied armies in the interim. As the king's adjutant, GM Friedrich Carl Gustav von Langenau, pointedly remarked on 8 April: 'Breaking the chains that oppress us is my innermost wish and the duty of every German; to exchange them would be foolishness.' Or, as he later told Thielmann: 'I do not want to be a French slave, but neither a German one.'[98]

In these difficult circumstances, Friedrich August and his advisors sought a third way, an alternative policy that would relieve them of the onerous burdens of the French alliance without committing them to a war whose goal was the revival of Prussian power and a radicalised populace. They believed they had found this alternative in Austria. Metternich, endeavouring both to make Austria more independent and to break Napoleon's hold on Germany, was quietly extending offers to the key Rheinbund states on Austria's borders: Bavaria, Württemberg and Saxony. This Austrian policy was the origin of the invitation for the king to take refuge in Prague. Beyond a safe place for the court, however, Vienna proposed a pact under which Saxony would join Austria in armed mediation between the two warring parties in an effort to achieve a rapid and lasting peace. Austria thus represented the third side of the triangle, but the sceptical Saxons were still debating a response to this Habsburg proposition when military developments along the Elbe prompted significant changes in the policy calculus at court.

The Capital's Renowned Ornament

Reynier and the remnants of 7th Corps, as described, had returned to Dresden by 7–8 March as part of the general French withdrawal west of the Elbe. He took lodgings in the Brühl Palace in the Altstadt on the left bank and initiated what measures he could to defend the city with the limited forces he had in LeCoq's and Durutte's feeble divisions while Rechberg's Bavarians (also under his orders) covered the crossing at Meissen. He knew he would not be able to hold the eastern shore, however, and thus issued instructions to begin preparing Dresden's famous stone bridge for destruction. Saxon army sappers and civilian miners under the direction of Chef de Bataillon Paul Clément François Gatte, Durutte's chief engineer, started digging on the night of 9/10 March, but work was interrupted on the 10th when a crowd of outraged citizens gathered to protect what was considered a Saxon national treasure. Throwing the workmen's tools into the river, they abused a Saxon lieutenant until his nationality was revealed and then turned on Gatte, assaulting him and trying to push him into the Elbe. His hat went over the balustrade, but a Saxon officer who chanced by rescued him and escorted him to the nearest guard post. The angry mob then rushed the Brühl Palace shouting anti-French slogans and hurling rocks through the windows. Durutte, furious at what he called 'the weakness of the Saxon generals', wanted to use his French troops to restore order, but Reynier, fearing violent consequences, 'obstinately' refused. Indeed, all Saxon accounts record that Reynier retained his characteristic calm during these outbursts and a combination of Saxon soldiers and city watchmen eventually dispersed the crowd 'without a sabre being drawn or a shot fired'.[99] The city fathers apologised to Reynier the following day, several ringleaders were carted off to imprisonment in the Königstein fortress and work on the bridge resumed on the night of 11/12 March without further disturbance.

This bridge incident highlighted the conflicting sentiments among Saxony's soldiers. Combined with anger at the prospect of the span's destruction was embarrassment and shame at the assault on Reynier's residence and the insults hurled at a commander they had come to trust and respect. Similarly, a desire to break with the French was mingled with loyalty to the king and worries about popular revolution. As one lieutenant noted in his journal:

> Let people think what they will: it requires only love for order and enmity to all disorder to find such behaviour completely criminal. As long as the King of Saxony stays true to his alliance, as he has publicly proclaimed, only one mode of conduct is legitimate; if he takes up an opposite policy, then in that instant the opposite becomes legitimate. Until then the act of wanting to throw an officer of an allied army into the river because he is doing his duty for a strictly military measure as commanded remains unheard of and almost without precedent.[100]

Marshal Davout now entered the drama. As noted in the introductory chapter, Viceroy Eugène had sent Davout to Dresden to hold the line of the Elbe between Torgau and Dresden with parts of two French divisions (some 9,700 men) and the 6,500 or so Saxons, Bavarians and French under Reynier's command. The marshal, preceded by his reputation for adamantine sternness, arrived on 13 March and Reynier left the next day for Paris via Plauen, ostensibly to recover the exertions of the Russian campaign, but perhaps because of prickly relations with Davout.[101] Uncharacteristically for such an undemonstrative personality, Reynier's attachment to his corps seems to have been on visible display at his departure: 'The Saxons had won not only Reynier's respect but also the love of this seemingly heartless man and he laid aside his command overcome by a degree of emotion that he, despite all his self-control, could not completely master.'[102]

Durutte thus assumed command of 7th Corps. Much of the Saxon cavalry, however, departed. The Saxons did not consider Liebenau's cuirassier brigade to be part of 7th Corps, so the cuirassiers rode off to join the king in Plauen, followed by the depots of the light cavalry regiments.[103] The remaining Saxon troops stayed in Dresden under Durutte, participating in a reconnaissance to the east on 14 March that involved some skirmishing with Russian cavalry. Davout praised the Saxon troops for their performance in this small action but rebuffed an appeal from city officials to spare the bridge. Leaving only 100 Saxon *Schützen* on the eastern bank, the French and their allies evacuated the Neustadt in the early hours of 19 March and ignited the charges under 'the capital's renowned ornament'.[104] Watching with fearful curiosity, one of Dresden's citizens described 'the frightfully majestic eruption of a volcano' as 'a dense pillar of earth and fire climbed to the heavens with a roar of thunder, throwing a rain of stones up and down into the Elbe . . . and the noble one [the bridge], that had braved so many enemies, bent its grey neck under the yoke of these iron times'.[105] Despite great anxiety on the part of Dresden's residents, the explosives had been prepared so expertly that only the two designated arches of the bridge were destroyed and no damage was inflicted on the rest of the structure or on the nearby buildings.[106] Davout, called north to take command along the lower Elbe, departed that night with his two French divisions, leaving Durutte behind with the meagre 7th Corps (his own 32nd Division, LeCoq's Saxons and Rechberg's Bavarians) to guard more than 100 kilometres of river line against the approaching Allies.

The destruction of the Dresden bridge evoked fury across Saxony and was a major factor in the court's next policy decisions. What Davout, Eugène and Napoleon regarded as an ordinary military necessity, the Saxons took as a pointless and spiteful offence that ignored the bridge's antiquity and symbolic significance. Davout had already upset the Saxons, including Friedrich August, by burning (rather than dismantling) the renowned wooden bridge at Meissen on the night of 11/12 March, and the king had sent personal letters to Davout, Eugène and Napoleon asking that the span in Dresden be preserved. Although the missive to Napoleon was only sent on 15 March, too late to save the structure, the fact that the king himself signed these messages is an indication of the importance attached to the bridge. Condemning what he termed Davout's 'barbaric caprice', Senfft wrote to the Saxon ambassador in Paris that, 'The king is rightly indignant at the unforgiveable act that has been permitted with respect to him, and we all mourn this beautiful bridge that brings glory and delights to the capital.'[107]

Indeed, the bridge's destruction prompted Friedrich August to send his first letter of complaint to Napoleon. 'My ambassador in Paris will inform Your Imperial and Royal Majesty's minister of everything that I did to oppose this act of violence against my kingdom & which was as senseless as it was harmful to my capital,' he wrote, adding that 'Your Imperial and Royal Majesty's sense of justice & the friendship that you have always shown me allow me to hope confidently that you will not refuse me in disapproving of the behaviour of the Marshal Prince of Eggmühl [Davout] & in withdrawing him from any command that would bring him contact with my state or my troops.' Such frank language, almost routine from the pugnaciously blunt Friedrich of Württemberg, was completely outside the normal correspondence of Saxony's monarch. The sharp change in tone, albeit restricted to this lone communication, not only reflected the deep sense of injury he and other Saxons felt over the destruction of the bridge, but it would also have consequences for Saxon policy. Christoph Friedrich Karl Kölle, the Württemberg legate with the Saxon court, recalled that when the king and his entourage arrived in Bavaria, 'Prussia's treaty with Russia and the related declaration of Kalisch became known here, and here the royal family's bitterness over the destruction of the Dresden bridge was used to prepare for a closer association with Austria.'[108]

Napoleon was also displeased by Davout's destruction of the Dresden bridge. He initially seems to have perceived some advantage in taking down the structure under certain circumstances, but he soon changed his mind. 'I still hope that the Prince of Eggmühl [Davout] will not have blown up the bridge,' he told Eugène on 24 March, unaware that the span had already been destroyed. Two days later, with news of the explosion in hand, he expressed his annoyance in another letter to his stepson: 'I saw with the greatest sorrow that the Prince of Eggmühl blew up the Dresden bridge. This cannot fail to attract the enemy there. Especially if he blew up a pillar, that will exasperate the inhabitants and, consequently, the Saxon army. This conduct therefore shows a great deal of inconsideration on the part of the Prince of Eggmühl.' Unsurprisingly, Napoleon attempted to minimise the bridge's significance in his correspondence with Friedrich August and hoped that Reynier's return to the Saxons 'would repair, as quickly as possible, the blunders of the Prince of Eggmühl'. He told the king that he was 'angry at the untimely destruction of the Dresden bridge', but his final comment that 'after all, it is just a matter of a few hundred thousand francs' could only have excited further Saxon fury.[109]

Other bilateral frictions were arising as well. First, GL LeCoq at Dresden was proving obstinate about obeying Durutte's orders, causing the French general to write directly to Friedrich August for help in clarifying the command relationship. Instead, the king instructed LeCoq to remove his small remaining contingent from Durutte's command and march to Torgau to join the rest of the reassembling Saxon army.[110] Only 100 Saxon cavalrymen were left behind to supplement the tiny group of Bavarian chevaulegers in 7th Corps. LeCoq's announcement of his departure left Durutte outraged at 'this sudden defection', undermining his hopes of defending the river and deepening his suspicions that LeCoq had orders' to observe the strictest neutrality'.[111] Second, Thielmann in Torgau was displaying a disturbing truculence in his dealings with the French. Though maintaining a degree of haughty civility, he refused a request to send guns to Wittenberg, allowed a captured Russian major to wander about the fortress, denied all entry to French forces, exaggerated enemy strength in his reports and was generally almost aggressively uncooperative. 'I was displeased with the attitude of this general,' wrote Davout after meeting Thielmann in the city on 21–22 March, 'he likes to accept and spread all the nonsense that malevolent people spout'. The marshal suspected that Thielmann could only behave in this contrary manner if he had instructions to do so and noted that the Saxons in Torgau were evincing 'a very marked distrust' towards their French allies.[112] Davout would have been even more suspicious had he known that Thielmann had sent an officer to Mainz in disguise to assess the strength of the rebuilding French army and was in frequent contact with Allied officers.[113]

The Saxons had complaints of their own. French indiscipline was a particular aggravation. As one of many examples, a mid-March letter from GM von Langenau described the population's 'righteous indignation at the poor behaviour of the French troops and the demanding presumptions of their generals' as contrasted with what he termed 'the moderation and prudence' of the enemy forces.[114] Complaints of this nature increased as the war progressed.

As for Durutte, the absence of both Davout and LeCoq meant that 7th Corps contained at best some 2,844 officers and men with 18 guns.[115] He could not stay in Dresden with such numbers. Bold Cossacks under Colonel Denis Vasilievich Davydov appeared outside the Neustadt on 20 March, and a Russian officer with a white flag rode up to one of the gates the following day brashly demanding the city's immediate surrender. Exaggerating their numbers by clever ruses and verbal bluffs, the Russians seem to have intimidated the city authorities with dark threats and lofty promises reinforced by the fearsome reputation that rode with the Cossacks that spring. Durutte did not detect the weakness of Davydov's force (perhaps 500 Cossacks with no infantry or guns), but the arrival of these Russians provided him an opening to withdraw safely and with honour. An initial exchange with Saxon officers resulted in Davydov sending Lieutenant Colonel Stepan Khrapovitsky to be rowed across the river blindfolded, for a meeting with Durutte, LeCoq and the Immediat-Commission (*see image*). Long negotiations brought a local ceasefire agreement under the terms of which Durutte withdrew the Saxon *Schützen* from the eastern shore on the 22nd to allow Davydov's men uncontested access to the Neustadt.[116] Four days later, on learning that the Russians had crossed the Elbe north and south of the city, Durutte decided to retreat to the west and by 1:00 a.m. on 27 March the French and their Würzburg, Saxon and Bavarian allies had left the city.[117] While LeCoq's Saxons had retired towards Torgau on the night of 21/22 March, Durutte went west to Rochlitz with the 32nd Division, Rechberg's Bavarians and the 100 Saxon light cavalrymen LeCoq had agreed to leave behind. Marching via Altenburg, they reached Gera on 31 March where the Saxon troopers were released to join their depot at Plauen; the tiny 'corps' then continued to Jena, where it turned north to link up with Eugène between the Harz Mountains and Magdeburg on 6 April (*see* the description of Rechberg's division in Chapter 3).[118]

Hopes for Habsburg Help

Friedrich August and his court were also about to move. With the Russians across the Elbe, the king transferred his temporary residence to Regensburg in neighbouring Bavaria. Coinciding with the general lull in fighting on the main battlefront, the Saxon court's sojourn in Regensburg saw a shift in policy as the king's advisors gradually persuaded the reluctant monarch to enter into an agreement with Austria.[119] Foreign Minister Senfft and royal adjutant Langenau were particularly persistent in nudging their master towards this change. They enjoyed enthusiastic support in their endeavours from members of the Immediat-Commission such as Zezschwitz, and from the Saxon ambassador in Vienna, GM Karl Friedrich Ludwig von Watzdorf. Thielmann in Torgau, on the other hand, urged a union with the Russo-Prussian alliance and favoured Allied requests as far as he dared, pressing at the boundaries of his nominally 'neutral' status. The king and his close councillors, however, regarded Prussia as anathema and brushed off a haughty 9 April letter from Friedrich Wilhelm III with flowery platitudes.[120]

Doubts and suspicions about France and the Russo-Prussian bloc thus led Saxony to the third side of its policy triangle: Austria. For the key decision-makers around the king, the Habsburg Empire seemed to offer numerous advantages in this political crisis, a viable 'third way' between the two contending sides. Although efforts to craft a pact that included Bavaria and Württemberg as well as Saxony and Austria failed, the idea of a bilateral Austro-Saxon arrangement took root and flourished.[121] The Habsburg court, in the person of Metternich during long discussions with Watzdorf, appeared receptive to Saxon concerns and, unlike Prussia, had no avaricious designs on Saxon territory. Indeed, the Saxons hoped that Austria would use its influence with the Allied powers to moderate their military exactions, prevent the loss of hereditary Saxon lands and provide territorial compensation should the Duchy of Warsaw be forfeited in an Allied victory. Also comforting was Austria's clear opposition to the sort of 'revolutionary' ferment that threatened to bubble out of Prussia to the horror of the Saxon regime. Moreover, no other Rheinbund states had as yet deserted the alliance[122] (the Mecklenburgs, when they went, were regarded as irrelevant) and the proclaimed Austrian stance of 'armed mediation' comported well with Friedrich August's longstanding personal predilection for neutrality, peace and conservative status quo stability.

While negotiating with Austria, however, the Saxons sought to avoid an open break with Napoleon. With Austria still – technically at least – an ally of France, they convinced themselves that they could conclude a satisfactory agreement with Vienna without violating their treaty obligations to the French emperor and the Rheinbund. Only a few voices argued that such a move would simply poison relations with both belligerents.[123] In short, the Saxons sought to have it both ways. This proved an illusory hope. Nonetheless, stung by the French destruction of the Dresden bridge and Prussia's seizure of Cottbus, the court and king eventually acceded to Austria's seemingly appealing approach and Watzdorf signed a 'convention' with Metternich in Vienna on 20 April. The king left Regensburg for Prague the following day and ratified the convention on reaching Linz inside Habsburg territory. Their policy course set, Friedrich August and his entourage travelled on to enter Prague on 27 April, while his cavalry brigade, marching by a different route, arrived somewhat later to be quartered in the surrounding area.

For a little more than two weeks, this 20 April agreement was the centrepiece of Saxon policy.[124] In the eyes of Friedrich August and his advisors, it fulfilled their key concern by gaining Austria's pledge to guarantee Saxony's territorial integrity. With a cloud of doubt surrounding the outcome of the imminent combat and the attendant uncertainty concerning Napoleon's future in Germany, this was a vital Saxon objective. Less satisfactory was the reference to compensation for the likely loss of the Duchy of Warsaw. The best the Saxon negotiators could achieve was an ambiguous Austrian promise to help Saxony obtain 'an adequate indemnity in territory as circumstances permit' (which the Saxons hoped would come through absorption of some or all of the small Thuringian states). The document also mentioned that the Austrian Kaiser would use his 'good offices' to urge the return of Cottbus to Saxony, but this was a feature Metternich had no intention of pursuing with Prussia.

At the same time, the convention contained some startling provisions. In the first place, at its core was Saxony's adherence to Austria's efforts at armed mediation. Should that mediation fail, however, Saxony was obligated to supply 30,000 men who would join the Austrian army under overall Austrian command (that is, 10,000 more than required under the Rheinbund). Second, Article VI specifically stated that the two contracting parties would regard the convention 'as equivalent to a treaty of alliance'. Third, a secret article stipulated that Saxony would 'renounce all participation, both direct and indirect, in the next campaign' and that the two sides would conclude a separate military convention to cover operational contingencies. How any of this could be consistent with the kingdom's membership in the Rheinbund is difficult to comprehend. Although Senfft hoped that Napoleon would not misunderstand the convention, no amount of Saxon sophistry could disguise the separation from France.[125] Moreover, in private there was no ambiguity. 'We have irrevocably broken with France,' wrote the exultant Senfft to Zezschwitz on 30 April.[126]

Unfortunately for the proponents of the alignment with Austria, tying Saxony to Austria's putative peace efforts also meant committing the kingdom to the prospect of war against Napoleon. As Senfft learned to his dismay when he travelled incognito to Vienna after the agreement had been signed, Metternich was principally interested in gaining time for the Austrian army to mobilise.[127] As there was little expectation that any of the belligerents would accept Austria's armed mediation initiative, Saxony faced the appalling likelihood of being drawn into a war a central purpose of which was the aggrandisement of Prussia – exactly the opposite of the court's desires in entering into the convention in the first place.

Are You Friends or Enemies?

While the Habsburg and Saxon courts were engaged in these feverish exchanges, Napoleon was gathering his new army and moving east. He was also losing patience with Saxon intransigence. The emperor had both tactical and strategic concerns vis-à-vis Saxony. On the tactical side, he made two specific demands of his ally. First, given his dire shortage of mounted troops, he wanted the Saxon cavalry accompanying the king to be dispatched at once to join the new Grande Armée. Second, he wanted the fortress of Torgau to be opened to French forces with the troops there coming under Reynier's command in a revived 7th Corps. These specific requirements, of course, were nested in the larger context of Saxony's status: was the kingdom an ally or not? Saxon defection from the Rheinbund would not only complicate his military operations and deprive him of resources, it would also be a severe blow to the alliance as a whole.

From early March through the end of April, therefore, Napoleon sent seven personal letters to Friedrich August, supplementing these with messages from Berthier, from Ney and from his ambassador, Baron Charles François Serra, as well as through the Saxon ambassador in Paris. Reacting to Durutte's complaints about LeCoq, for instance, he pressed his foreign minister, Hughes Bernard Maret, for explanations and lambasted Serra for not keeping him informed. Maret was to tell the Saxons 'how much all these difficulties upset and annoy me'. Baffled and irritated, he asked rhetorically, 'What can the Saxons gain by having the rest of their country ravaged by the Cossacks?' In addition to apprising Friedrich August of his progress in assembling the Grande Armée, four of the personal letters as well as the missives from Berthier and Ney addressed the urgent desire for the Saxon cavalry. Berthier was instructed to write 'that I desire that the king give positive orders so that all the uncertainties that have arisen no longer occur, and that the fortress [Torgau] and the troops come under my orders without the least reluctance'. Similarly, Serra was to tell the king that Napoleon considered a refusal to send the cavalry as the beginning of a change in Saxony's alliance policy. Ironically, three of Napoleon's letters (dictated at different times during the day) were composed on 20 April, the same day the Austro-Saxon convention was signed in Vienna. He had just listened to a report from one of the officers charged to deliver letters to the Saxon government and had received a Saxon officer with an empty reply from Friedrich August. As a result, the emperor took an increasingly sharp tone. 'Your Majesty's letter hurt me', he wrote, asking if Friedrich August's former amity had vanished, blaming 'the enemies of our cause that may be in your cabinet' and reiterating his 'need for all your cavalry and all your officers'. He concluded this brief note, however, with the words 'whatever eventuates, Your Majesty may count on the esteem you inspire in me and which is invulnerable to harm'.[128] This short letter neatly encapsulates Napoleon's view of the situation: Saxony was behaving badly, disregarding orders, creating obstacles at Torgau and denying him vital cavalry, but he maintained his personal affection for Friedrich August, attributing these irritating problems to the 'many intrigues around that respectable sovereign'.[129]

A further irritation arose when the Saxons arranged with Austria for the return of Gablenz's detachment and Poniatowski's Polish troops (still being described as '5th Corps') from their cantonments near Krakow. Metternich and Watzdorf had signed an agreement on 8 April to allow transit of Habsburg territory.[130] This convention regulated details of food, fodder and billeting, but required the soldiers to deposit their weapons in wagons that would follow the march columns. Napoleon was furious. In his view, this stipulation was not only a dishonour to the Poles but entirely inconsistent with Austria's status as an ally. How could Friedrich August's escorting cavalry retain its arms when the Poles, French and Saxons returning from Galicia were forced to march without theirs? The fact that a small number of French troops were involved only intensified his ire: 'The emperor would prefer that the French battalion attached to the 5th Corps fight and be sent to Siberia rather than that it be disarmed to traverse Austrian lands.'[131] Larger matters soon absorbed his attention, but this transit agreement thus became another source of imperial suspicion vis-à-vis his Saxon allies.

Through this entire period, the Saxons fended off Napoleon's requests, irritating the emperor with florid but hollow expressions of fealty and transparent excuses about the requested cavalry. 'Those are fine phrases', the emperor told the Immediat-Commission when he reached Dresden, 'that do not touch on the substance of the issue.'[132] The obvious evasions concerning the cavalry's state of readiness were not without some foundation as the untrained depot troops often lacked the most basic equipment and the ranks of the newly re-formed *Zastrow* Cuirassiers were entirely filled with raw recruits. Nonetheless, the anxious effort to avoid sending off the mounted regiments was unmistakable. Furthermore, the king's several replies to Napoleon and Berthier made no mention of Torgau and, of course, did not address the covert negotiations under way with Austria – a matter that Napoleon had already begun to suspect.[133] Napoleon continued to hold Friedrich August in high regard personally, but by the time he reached Weimar on 28 April, his tolerance for this sort of equivocation had been exhausted. He thus directed Weimar's duke, Carl August, to send a letter to his cousin Friedrich August highlighting the danger of continued evasion:

> The emperor appeared to have doubts about the sentiments of Your Majesty and expressed the desire that you explain yourself frankly – HM ordered me, sire, to transmit to you his own words: 'That the King

of Saxony tell me frankly if he is for me or against me. He has nothing to complain about as far as I am concerned because I have done so much for him. Write that I did not believe anything, but that the conduct in Torgau was suspicious. Let him declare himself, then I will know what I have to do. If he is against me, then he will lose all he has; I am hurrying to come and save Saxony.'[134]

Carl August's letter arrived in Prague on 3 May but evoked only more ornate assertions of gratitude and a reference to Friedrich August's previous letters. Generally content with the Austrian agreement and safely ensconced in Prague, the Saxon court worried about the wellbeing of the monarchy's populace, but seems to have believed all was going to plan even though pressure was also mounting from the Russians, from the Prussians and from the Allies' administrative factotum Stein. Thielmann had visited the Allied monarchs in Dresden on 25 April (*see below*) in the course of which the tsar had told him personally that neutrality was impossible even if Saxony tied itself to Austria. Furthermore, following a conference with Stein and others, a message was sent to the Saxon court on behalf of the Russo-Prussian rulers proposing Saxony's adherence to the Allied cause. In this, the Allies pledged to guarantee Saxony's dynasty and territory, while Saxony would promise a large monthly financial payment, provide logistical support for the Allied armies and supply a troop contingent of 12,000 regulars plus 20,000 Landwehr. Torgau was to be immediately 'utilised for the common cause ... not against the Coalition powers, rather in a hostile manner against France'. Should Saxony fail to agree to these terms it would 'immediately come under martial law' and the Allies would accomplish their goals 'through the people' even though they would prefer to work through the government.[135] For the Saxons, this was further proof of the dangerously 'revolutionary' intentions of the Allied powers and their disregard for their revered king.

The Saxon leadership, however, was so confident in its new Habsburg ally that Friedrich August replied to these promises and threats with letters both to the tsar and, more pointedly, to Friedrich Wilhelm III announcing his convention with Austria and his neutral stance. The king also used this opportunity to note that Saxony's neutrality did not permit 'hostile treatment of my lands and subjects', and he again boldly stressed the return of the Cottbus district to his control.[136] The Allied monarchs had left Dresden before these notes arrived, but the Saxon messenger was coldly received by the respective foreign ministers and left in no doubt that the Russian and Prussian governments would not acknowledge Saxon neutrality.[137] Nonetheless, the Saxon court's attitude remained firm, as was evident in orders sent to

Thielmann on 5 May: he was to maintain strict neutrality and was specifically enjoined to deny entry to the French even 'if the fortunes of war should lead the French army back to the Elbe' unless ordered by the king in consultation with the Austrian Kaiser.[138] Events on the battlefield, however, soon brought a reversal of these instructions.

Although the Saxon army was not involved in the Battle of Lützen, the outcome of the war's first major clash had a decisive impact on the monarchy's policy. Reports of the battle were at first ambiguous, especially because the Allies initially announced a victory. Rumours of a possible French success seem to have reached Prague late on 5 May or early on the 6th, but definitive news of Napoleon's victory only arrived on the 7th. Indeed, Senfft had to pen a postscript to a letter he was composing to Watzdorf: 'I have just received a message from Dresden that rectifies the notions we had formed about the latest military events in Saxony. Instead of obtaining advantages over the French army, that of the Allies is taking a retrograde direction.' In quick succession, Ambassador Serra, a municipal official from Leipzig who had met Napoleon when the emperor passed through the city after Lützen, a report from the Saxon liaison officer with French headquarters and, finally, an urgent message from the Immediat-Commission all arrived in Prague.[139] All these communications contained the sharpest possible warnings that Saxony would be treated as enemy territory and Friedrich August would cease to reign if he did not comply at once with the demands Napoleon had been making since the beginning of April regarding the Saxon cavalry, the troops at Torgau and the king's personal adherence to the stipulations of the Rheinbund alliance. Imperial displeasure burned through these communications, fuelled by Napoleon's knowledge that Thielmann had rejected Ney's request to enter Torgau 'as a consequence of an intimate treaty of alliance with HM the Emperor of Austria'.[140] 'Gentlemen, are you friends or enemies?' Napoleon demanded when he met the Immediat-Commission, 'It is time to speak clearly!'[141]

Friedrich August, the recipient of these stern warnings, was now in a dreadful dilemma. The court initially temporised, hoping that a Habsburg *deus ex machina* would arrive rapidly to deliver salvation in the form of public and unequivocal support for Saxon neutrality and territorial integrity. Unfortunately for the anxious Saxons, Metternich's envoy, Johann Phillip Graf von Stadion, was delayed en route. He did not appear in Prague until 9 May and departed after a brief and inconsequential audience with the king. Even had Stadion arrived on 7 or 8 May, it is unlikely he could have rescued the Saxons from their desperate situation. His lengthy instructions from Metternich were focused on his upcoming meetings with the Russians and Prussians; the Saxon mission was secondary, and Stadion's brief said nothing on the issues the king and his court considered vital.[142] At best, he could have conveyed Saxon concerns to the Allied monarchs – now retreating east from Dresden – and returned some days later with a likely negative reply.

In Stadion's absence, Friedrich August, feeling abandoned by Austria and threatened by both France and the Russo-Prussian alliance, concluded that his only option in these 'completely unexpected circumstances' was a rapid return to the Napoleonic fold.[143] On 8 May (the same day that Napoleon entered Dresden and the Allied monarchs departed), he composed an appropriately submissive letter acceding to all of Napoleon's demands and stating his intention to travel to Dresden as soon as the roads were clear. GL von Gersdorff carried this letter to Dresden along with orders for Liebenau's cavalry to return and for Thielmann to place Torgau and his troops under Reynier's command.[144] Along the way he encountered an imperial aide-de-camp as well as a Saxon civilian official, both of whom were bearing additional severe injunctions from the emperor. The king had already reversed course, however, and these latest messages only served to reemphasise in Saxon perceptions the elevated temperature of Napoleon's ire.[145] Friedrich August penned an explanatory note to Kaiser Franz and set out from Prague on 10 May, returning to his capital on the 12th to be greeted with cannon salutes, church bells, crowds of well-wishers and all the military pomp Napoleon could muster. Exuding charm and warmth, the emperor embraced his aged ally in the Großer Garten outside the city. 'Magistrates! Love your king: see in him the saviour of Saxony,' he told the group of royal officials gathered to receive their king before the two monarchs retired for the first of many face-to-face exchanges they would have over the coming weeks. Watzdorf felt 'ineffable bitterness' at the king's return but remained at his post in Vienna, while Senfft and Langenau resigned from their positions and took service with the Habsburgs.[146] As far as is known, Napoleon never again mentioned the abortive Austro-Saxon convention the trio had worked so hard to achieve.

If Friedrich August was relieved to end months of tense indecision and return to what he regarded as proper adherence to his solemn commitment to the Rheinbund, much of Saxony's population was dismayed. Most Saxons had hoped the trip to Prague presaged an end to the French alliance, an end to the exactions and uncertainties of war and the removal of all armies from their lands. Furthermore, many feared the French would wreak a terrible vengeance on their country for the sympathy they had shown towards the Coalition in March and April. The reaffirmation of the union with France thus created the first crisis of confidence between the monarch and the people in Friedrich August's 45-year reign.[147] This by no means meant that most Saxons were prepared to abandon their king and leap into the arms of the Allies. It did mean that nascent hopes were dashed, and that disappointment and anxiety were widespread. These sentiments were broadly shared within the army. For the purposes of this study the significance is that many officers came to believe that their king was not at liberty to make independent decisions and that his move to Prague and the abortive pact with Austria indicated their monarch's true desires regardless of his numerous subsequent pronouncements reasserting his loyalty to Napoleon. This perception of the king's circumstances and the lingering hope in the Habsburgs would become factors for many officers when they decided to desert the Grande Armée five months later at Leipzig.

Thielmann and Torgau

A major factor in both sides' demands of Saxony was the fortress city of Torgau. In addition to providing the occupying army with a protected permanent bridge over the Elbe, Torgau was the assembly point for the bulk of the Saxon army, a body of men that numbered roughly 11,000 by late April. Even though most of these were new recruits and many others were in hospital, this was a force that the Allies could not leave unchecked in their rear as they advanced west of the Elbe and one that Napoleon rightly regarded as his to command under the terms of Saxony's Rheinbund obligations. Beyond these practical military considerations, Torgau also acquired symbolic value as an indicator of Saxony's commitment to one side or the other in the war. Indeed, owing to the personality of its commander, GL von Thielmann, Torgau became a test case for Saxon loyalty, emblematic of the pressures faced by officers and men across the Rheinbund in 1813.[148]

Thielmann was an intelligent, energetic and competent officer, who had displayed considerable skill in small-scale warfare during 1809 and led the Saxon heavy cavalry brigade at Borodino with great distinction. He was also proud, ambitious, vain and prickly, convinced of his own self-importance and given to bombastic statements and histrionic gestures. Previously among Napoleon's admirers, he had turned against the emperor and France after 1812, bitter that, 'They have not only ruined us, but also deprived us of the means to rebuild ourselves.'[149] Now, as governor of Torgau, Thielmann found himself at the centre of the contest for Saxony's allegiance in the spring months of 1813.

When he was appointed to command in Torgau on 24 February, Thielmann's orders specified that he was to turn his troops over to Reynier should

> **Chart 15: Saxon Troops at Torgau, 29 March 1813**
>
> *GL von Thielmann*
>
> 1st Brigade   GM von Steindel
>   I/Leib-Grenadier Regiment
>   2nd Regiment   Formed from 3rd and 4th Provisional Battalions
>   *Prinz Anton* Battalion
>   *Low* Battalion
>   3rd Regiment   Formed from 2nd Provisional Battalion
>   *Prinz Friedrich August* Battalion
>   *Steindel* Battalion
> 2nd Brigade   GM von Sahr
>   Combined Grenadier Battalion
>   1st Regiment   Formed from 1st and 5th Provisional Battalions
>   *König/Niesemeuschel* Battalion
>   *Max/Rechten* Battalion
>   Light Battalion *Le Coq*   ⎰ Both *Le Coq* and *Sahr* formed from
>   Light Battalion *Sahr*   ⎱ the Provisional Light Battalion
> Cavalry
>   1st Squadron   Hussars and Uhlans
>   2nd Squadron   Combined Chevaulegers
> Jägerkorps

the French general arrive in the fortress. A 14 March letter from the king contained similar instructions. It was not until 18 March that Langenau sent him a letter specifying he should accept orders from no one but the king.[150] In the interim, Thielmann had already begun to demonstrate unmistakable obduracy in response to French requests. He hosted a meal for Gérard and his officers when the French division crossed the Elbe on 10 March, for instance, but had a temporary bridge thrown across the river so the French would have no reason to enter his fortress. Other French requests included: supplying some Torgau guns to arm Wittenberg, providing Reynier with reinforcements, accepting a French garrison, permitting establishment of a French magazine and allowing Polish troops into the fortress. Thielmann refused them all. His behaviour was motivated by his own increasingly anti-French outlook, his belief that 'France's humiliation' would soon force Saxony to adopt a different policy and his fear that anti-French sentiment in the population at large would result in an explosion of rebellion. 'The outraged feelings of the people against the unparalleled repression and insults to national honour are appearing in our ranks,' he told Langenau on 19 March, adding that he had 'no doubt at all about great military success against the French'.[151] He received support from the court's view that Saxony's fortresses and their garrisons were separate from the kingdom's Rheinbund contingent, but he took most of these actions on his own initiative.[152] Thielmann thus largely made his own policies and decided for himself that he was free to accept or reject French demands according to his interpretation of Saxon interests.

After the Russians and Prussians arrived on the Elbe, Thielmann's pro-Allied inclinations became more pronounced. Although he declined to turn over the fortress to the Allies as proposed by several fellow generals in early April, he was already making barely disguised anti-French statements to his officers in late March and his actions vis-à-vis the Allies made his attitude clear to the entire garrison as was, indeed, his intention.[153] In the first place, he was in constant and cordial written communications with Allied commanders, sent officers to report to them and frequently met senior enemy generals personally (such as on 18, 21 and 22 April). His outposts concluded a local ceasefire with the Allies after which they were 'the best of friends', as one officer recalled, 'we spent many enjoyable hours together'.[154] Furthermore, he contrived to arrange for Cossacks to capture a number of boats to support Allied river-crossing efforts, showed Allied officers his correspondence with the French and personally guided several of them on tours around the city's defences. Though inclined to comply, he turned down a request to send cannon to assist the Allied siege of the French garrison in Wittenberg but he did dispatch a map of the little fortress along with one of his officers who had helped construct its fortifications. In contrast, he proudly reported his rejection of French requests and described how he had 'coldly' assured Davout that he was impervious to intimidation.[155]

Another action seen as a sign of his personal desires and the kingdom's future was a visit he paid to Dresden on 25 April at the invitation of the Allied monarchs. During long, friendly audiences with both Alexander and Friedrich Wilhelm III as well as a testy meeting with Stein and other key leaders, Thielmann declined to commit his troops or open the fortress but urged the dispatch of a messenger to his king in Prague as discussed above. Unlike the monarchs who treated him with great courtesy, Stein displayed disgust when Thielmann refused to defect with his troops. For his part, Thielmann allegedly replied 'I am no General Yorck' as Stein and others pressed him to act.[156] He also continued to spurn the impassioned importunities of the pro-Allied Saxon enthusiasts around Stein who plied him with a fervid correspondence. His private rejection of desperate entreaties from what he called 'revolutionaries', however, did nothing to diminish the impression that he favoured Saxon commitment to the Allies. His simple arrival in the city as Alexander's guest and especially his public appearance at a parade of the Russian Imperial Guard alongside the tsar were hardly the actions of a general whose kingdom was allied with France and could only be taken as significant indicators of an impending shift. Although he repeatedly stressed his loyalty to Friedrich August, he also made extravagant claims for his monarch and led the Allies to believe that Saxony would inevitably change sides. His personal desire that this switch occur soon was entirely obvious. Indeed, considering his words and actions, the Allies had every reason to think that Thielmann and his troops would join them in short order even if the king dithered or remained with Napoleon.[157] In a 16 April letter to Prussian GL von Kleist, for instance, Thielmann referred to the Russians and Prussians as his 'so-called enemies' and transmitted a lengthy and rather pompous memorandum outlining his personal perspective, including the notion that loyalty to his sovereign had its limits. Referring to himself in the third person, he declared: 'If his king, which is impossible in the current state of things, wants to declare himself definitively for France, he would then regard the bond between prince and subject as dissolved.' In a letter to Prussian GL von Bülow on 1 May, he wrote of 'our common cause' and expressed his regret that he could not comply with the request to send troops and guns to assist in the siege of Wittenberg. 'Count on me!' he exclaimed in a 10 May note to Stein.[158] None of this, of course, was consistent with any definition of 'neutrality'.

Thielmann did report his many interactions with the Allies to Friedrich August and the court, including his visit to Dresden, but it seems clear he concealed the degree of intimacy these exchanges had attained and the extent to which he made his own preferences apparent to his Allied interlocutors. He was certainly trying to nudge the 'weak, vacillating' court towards a change in policy, however, and some of his letters aroused suspicions among the king's councillors. Generals Sahr and Steindel, his two brigade commanders in Torgau, also became concerned about his behaviour and the fissures he was generating within the officer corps.[159] The king's direct replies repeatedly extolled Thielmann for his steadfast assertions of neutrality and, once the convention with Austria was concluded, instructed him to maintain 'the independence of the fortress of Torgau' and not to permit access to any of the belligerents without the express orders of the king in consultation with the Austrian Kaiser (19 April). As mentioned, Friedrich August later (5 May) emphasised that Thielmann was to refuse the French even if 'the fortunes of war' brought them to his gates. At the same time, other communications from the court contained warnings. The king, for instance, praised him for not sending guns to support the Allied siege of Wittenberg as Bülow had requested, an indirect hint that Thielmann should not exceed his instructions. Senfft was more blunt in cautioning that 'any unauthorised uprising in mass or individually for any military purpose' would incur the king's 'greatest displeasure', while Langenau warned that 'whoever takes a step forward without the king's permission must, in my view, be stricken from the rolls of the nation forever'.[160] Having invested their hopes in Austria and deeply apprehensive of Prussian intentions, the court did not want Thielmann to initiate any action that might upend their plans for neutrality.

Meanwhile, the barracks, coffee houses and inns of Torgau bubbled with rumours. 'We are all extremely keen to see which side our king will take,' wrote Major Heinrich Carl Ferdinand Friedrich von Hausen to his brother on 14 April. He lamented the 'thoughtless' destruction of the Dresden bridge and related the stories he had heard about the king possibly going to Prague to arrange an alliance with the Austrian Kaiser. 'The attitude among our officers and our men is becoming ever more anti-French,' he continued, prompted by 'the indiscipline of the French army that we had enough opportunities to observe in the previous campaign and which now shows itself again among the troops in Saxony, as they treat our population not as allies but as enemies; furthermore, the unnecessary destruction of the Elbe bridge at Dresden has fed the bitterness even more'.[161]

Matters came to a head in Torgau on 27 April at a most curious venue: a luncheon hosted by the garrison's senior officers to celebrate Thielmann's 48th birthday. Rumours had circulated that Thielmann would make some dramatic announcement at this event and the general, arriving at the crowded dining site, signalled his intentions to the gathering by having ostentatiously omitted his French Legion of Honour and his Order of the Westphalian Crown from his array of decorations. Towards the end of the meal, with the group rather loud and raucous, Thielmann arose to offer several toasts. The first was a simple 'To the king!' but the second was preceded by a magniloquent oration in which he lauded the Allies' 'high, sacred cause' and pledged never again to draw his sword on behalf of France. It is unclear how many of the chattering, boisterous gathering heard Thielmann, but GM von Sahr certainly did. When Thielmann called for glasses to be emptied in hopes the Saxons would soon 'join the ranks of the high Allies' to fight 'the common foe', Sahr stood up. He had cautioned Thielmann privately earlier in the day and now spoke up to counter Thielmann's speech: 'Yes, general, we will fight, and with the greatest possible courage, with the French against the Russians and Prussians, with the Russians and Prussians against the French – as our king desires! No politics!

Nothing but long live our king!' Sahr's impassioned declaration ignited a general tumult. Thielmann tried to undermine his subordinate's words, while Sahr, supported by Steindel, cut through the din of voices to assert their strict interpretation of loyalty to their monarch. The group dispersed in a chaos of contending opinions and clusters of officers continued debating events and options throughout the afternoon. The day concluded with a ball in Thielmann's honour organised by the town's citizens. In another indication of the general's inclinations, one of the guests was a Prussian officer with whom Thielmann had a long and lively interaction. There were no French present.

Sahr's intervention at the birthday luncheon broke Thielmann's pro-Allied momentum. The following day, Sahr drafted a written version of his luncheon interruption to put his stance on record. In a clear rebuke to Thielmann and incorporating the royal guidance concerning the concord with Austria, he wrote that obedience to duty consisted solely in four points:

1. Taking no offensive step against *anyone* pending further royal orders.
2. Defending the fortress to the uttermost against *everyone*.
3. Calmly waiting to see which side our venerable King will take according to his wisdom, and
4. Entering into no premature negotiations with foreign generals that might anticipate His Majesty the King...

Sahr delivered this statement to Thielmann on 28 April, adding in a cover note:

> I have never fought for the French happily and of my own free will; and I wish, as every German, that it will never again occur, and that I would instead, *at my king's orders*, take up arms against them. Should our king order differently, however, I will, true to the duty I owe my sovereign, fight on behalf of France as in the cause of my king.

To forestall any unauthorised action by Thielmann, Sahr and Steindel issued orders of the day to their brigades specifying that the king had prohibited opening the fortress to anyone without explicit orders 'in conjunction with His Majesty the Kaiser of Austria' (Thielmann had thus far chosen not to announce the Austrian arrangement to the garrison).[162] Sahr's firm and lucid declaration summarised his own view and, as far as can be discerned at this remove, the attitude of the majority of the Saxon officers. Though many had hoped their king would chose the Coalition, 'most concurred with the generals' opinion that the king's orders should be awaited before speaking out'.[163] At the same time, it also represents a tidy encapsulation of the conundrum faced by many Rheinbund officers in 1813, illuminating the importance of local, particularist loyalties in determining how those officers would respond to the choices they faced in this crucial year.

Driven by external developments, events in Torgau now moved rapidly towards a conclusion. When a Saxon courier bearing news of Napoleon's victory at Lützen arrived in Torgau, he was sent back with a brief reply from Oberstleutnant Ernst Ludwig von Aster, Thielmann's chief of staff, melodramatically proclaiming that the general 'would rather see himself buried under the ruins of his fortress' than open its gates without specific royal instructions. The king's 5 May order to deny entry to the French reinforced Thielmann's determination. Arriving on 8 May, this order fully justified him in rejecting requests from Ney and Reynier as they advanced towards the Elbe after Lützen. He likewise rebuffed a member of the Immediat-Commission Napoleon had sent after his arrival in Dresden. On 10 May, however, Friedrich August's letter announcing his return to the Rheinbund reached Thielmann. He reacted with uncharacteristic calm, turning command over to Steindel and sending the king a two-sentence notification that he was concluding his thirty-two years of Saxon service before departing that evening with Aster to request commissions from the tsar.[164] Thielmann would reappear in the autumn as a Russian general leading a raiding detachment in the French rear while Aster earned numerous awards serving with Russian cavalry units.[165] The twelve-week drama in Torgau thus came to an end with the fortress and the entire Saxon army at the French emperor's disposal. Major von Hausen expressed disappointment with his king's decision and claimed 'the majority' of his fellow officers felt likewise. He depicted his comrades as being 'very distressed and disheartened by this outcome' as they bid Thielmann farewell 'with deep emotion', but they remained faithful to their oaths and embarked on the new campaign once again as allies of the French under Reynier's command.[166] For some, however, the experiences in Torgau reinforced their conviction that their king secretly desired a break with France, a conviction that would provide a convenient rationale for changing sides in their moment of desperation at Leipzig.

Once More with Eagles

Having recounted the events surrounding Thielmann, Torgau and the abortive attempt at neutrality, the narrative must now briefly step back in time to return to the rebuilding of the Saxon army, before addressing its actions in the remainder of the spring campaign. When Thielmann relinquished command to Steindel on 10 May elements of the kingdom's army could be found at Prague and Krakow as well as Torgau. There were veterans of 1812 among these groups, but most were new troops raised since the opening of the Russian campaign. One component of the pre-1812 army, however, was missing while Saxony's generals attempted to re-establish their army: the original *Prinz Max* Infantry Regiment under Oberst Friedrich Franz von Ehrenstein and the foot artillery battery of Hauptmann Johann Christian August Essenius.[167]

Calamity at Lüneburg[168]

It will be recalled that the *Prinz Max* Infantry and Essenius's battery had been assigned to GD Joseph Morand's small division in Swedish Pomerania to guard the coastline after the invasion of Russia opened. Ordered west as the French forces withdrew towards the Elbe in early 1813, Morand left Stralsund on 9 March. His mixed command included some French soldiers, sailors and customs officers, but the heart of his little 'division' was the Saxon regiment and its accompanying artillery, more than 1,600 of his 2,550 soldiers and six of his twelve guns. As the column approached the great river, the French and Saxons first came into contact with Cossacks and Russian regular cavalry on 15 March. They fought a minor skirmish with the Russians the following day but were able to cross the Elbe successfully on 17 March despite heavy pressure from their pursuers. Morand was so pleased with the performance of what he called 'the Pomeranian Column' that he issued a congratulatory order of the day and authorised an extra ration of food and brandy for the men.[169] He did not linger on the opposite shore, however, but linked up with Carra Saint-Cyr's garrison from Hamburg and marched west to reach Bremen on 22 March.

The little command did not remain long in Bremen either.[170] Annoyed that Morand had 'made the mistake of quitting the left bank of the Elbe', the viceroy ordered him to move to Lüneburg to observe the lower reaches of the river where some 300–400 Cossacks had reportedly crossed.[171] Morand thus departed Bremen on 25 March and pushed slowly east, scattering small bands of Cossacks and armed civilians as he cautiously advanced. His division had shed its sailors and some of its French guns but had acquired two battalions of the 152^e Ligne, two 4-pounders and a handful of horsemen to supplement his Saxons and customs officers. These additions gave him a total of approximately 3,000 men but left him severely deficient in mounted troops as he faced a lively enemy well supplied with Cossacks and regular cavalry. Furthermore, though the region had nominally become part of France after its annexation in 1810, the population was hostile and actively supported the enemy raiders.

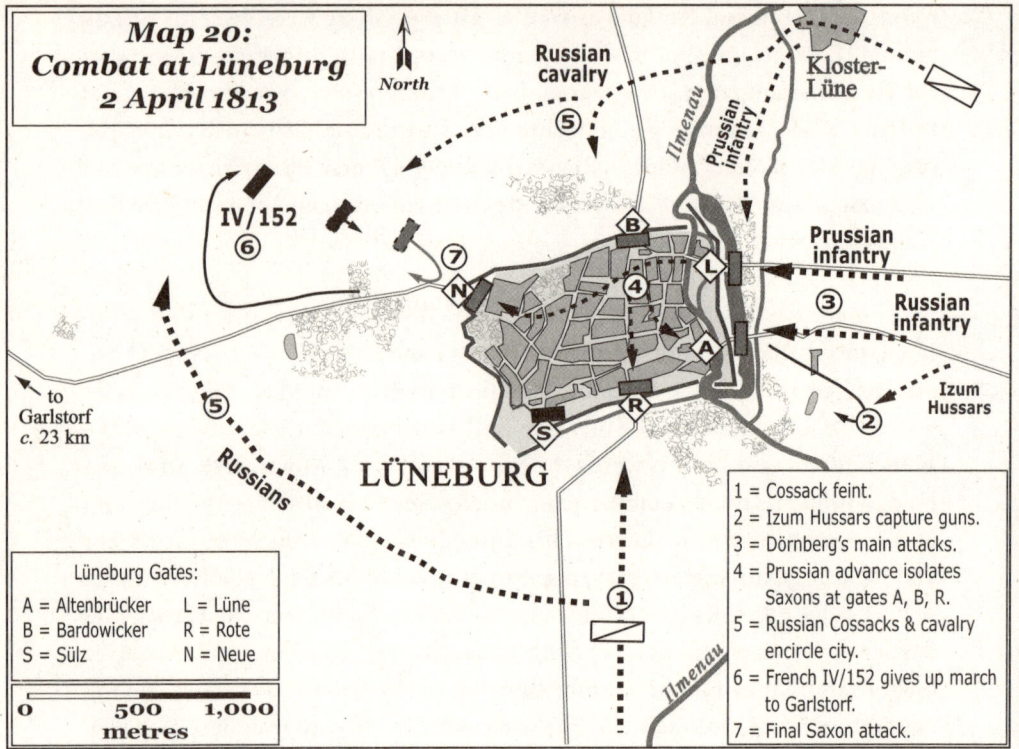

Nonetheless, leaving I/152ᵉ Ligne behind to protect his communications with Bremen, he advanced to Lüneburg on 1 April and captured the town after brief resistance by armed citizens. The ease with which his small force had chased off the local militia volunteers and Cossacks seems to have made Morand complacent. After subduing civilians who had continued to fire on his men from windows and rooftops, he ordered his troops to be dispersed to routine billets and only posted small guards of fifty men each at the town's six gates. He established no outposts, sent out no patrols and seems to have done little to inform himself about the local situation. He thus had no inkling that several Allied raiding detachments totalling more than 4,000 men were gathering just several kilometres to the east. His opponents, on the other hand, allowed their own preconceptions to distort their judgements in mistakenly assuming that the 'the morale of Morand's troops is quite poor'.[172]

Lüneburg in 1813 was a town of 10,000 encircled by a medieval wall that retained its defensive value despite its antiquity. The Allied attackers would therefore focus their initial attention on the six gates. These attackers were composed of Russian and Prussian regulars, Cossacks and several hundred locals (mostly unarmed) under the command of Major General Wilhelm

Freiherr von Dörnberg, a former Westphalian officer who had rebelled against King Jérôme in 1809 before taking service with Great Britain. He had 820 infantry, 3,000 cavalry and 10 guns at his disposal. Morand, having deposited one of his French battalions in the rear, had 2,150 infantry supported by seven cannon and two howitzers, but his 'cavalry' consisted of a mismatched assortment of regulars, gendarmes and mounted customs officers totalling only 70 men. The Allies thus enjoyed an overall edge in numbers and, as usual, a dramatic superiority in mounted troops, though Morand's advantage in infantry should have proven decisive in defending the walled town. Sadly, for the French general, this would not be the case.

Dörnberg planned a direct attack on the two gates along the city's eastern face, but he detached two Cossack regiments and several guns to his left to approach Lüneburg from the south as a diversion. This feint proved successful. As Cossacks showed themselves and opened a distracting fire some time between 9:00 and 10:00 a.m. on 2 April, the defenders assumed it was just another quotidian annoyance from the Russian irregulars. Covered by Morand's miniscule 'cavalry', two guns were thus ordered to a small knoll southeast of the city to drive off the Cossacks. Unbeknownst to the French and Saxons, however, Dörnberg's main body had arrived east of the city, its march screened by low hills and trees. As Prussian artillery opened up on Morand's pair of guns, a sudden charge by the Izum Hussars quickly scattered the French horsemen and captured the two pieces. This was just the beginning of Morand's troubles. Apparently apprehensive about his line of communications, he had sent his French battalion back to the village of Garlstorf, 23 kilometres to the west, shortly after 9:00 that morning. This left the defence of Lüneburg in the hands of the Saxon troops with II/*Max* in reserve and I /*Max* distributed among the gates, supplemented by the customs officers and some French gunners. They were soon under heavy pressure after Dörnberg launched his infantry against the two eastern gates, while more Cossacks and cavalry swung around to the north. The Saxons defended themselves stoutly, but requested reinforcements only arrived after Dörnberg's Prussian battalion had already broken into the city through the Lüne Gate (Lüne-Tor). Disordered by the troops retreating from the gate, the reinforcements tumbled back through the streets and alleys, constantly outflanked by the exuberant Prussians and suffering significant losses. Several brief stands delayed the attackers, but the Saxons and their French allies were soon retreating through the city's western gate (Neue-Tor or New Gate). Morand and Ehrenstein both received minor wounds in the process. The rapid Prussian advance left the Saxons at the other three gates cut off and

Chart 16: Forces at Lüneburg, 2 April 1813

		bns/sqdns	present under arms
French/Saxon	*GD Morand*		
Prinz Maximilian Infantry	*Oberst von Ehrenstein*	2	1,492
Saxon Artillery Battery	*Hauptmann Essenius*	–	170
IV/152ᵉ Ligne	*Major Palis*	1	468 + 1 × 4-pdr
French Customs Officers (foot)		–	247
French Customs Officers (mounted)		–	25
French artillery (8th Foot Regiment)		–	193
Cavalry and gendarmes		–	45
Staff		–	7
	Total		2,647

Note: I/152ᵉ Ligne was also part of Morand's command but was detached in the rear (50 kilometres to the west) to secure his line of communications back to Bremen.

		bns/sqdns	present under arms
Russian/Prussian	*Maj.-Gen. von Dörnberg*		
Prussian			
Fusilier Battalion/1st Pomeranian Infantry			
	Major von Borcke	1	520
Artillery half-battery		4 guns	74
Russian	*Maj. Gen. Benckendorff*		
2nd Jäger Regiment	*Major Essen*	1	300
Finland Dragoons		2	
Grodno Hussars		2	
Don Cossacks (Melnikov IV, Andriev II)		2 regts	1,400
Bashkirs		1 regt	
Cavalry and artillery		2 guns	
Maj. Gen. Chernishev			
Riga Dragoons		2	
Finland Dragoons		2	
Izum Hussars		4	see below
Don Cossacks		4 regts	
(Ilovaysky XI, Zhirov, Vlasov III, Grekov XVIII)			
Artillery half-battery		4 guns	
Combined cavalry and artillery		–	1,800
	Total		4,094

Plus approx. 350 local volunteers, mostly unarmed. One Prussian company and some Cossacks were detached to guard flanks and rear.

Source: Cazalas, pp. 30, 37.

under attack from both inside and outside the city. 'Every group fought for its existence' wrote Ehrenstein, but their prospects of rescue were dim.[173]

It was now approximately 1:00 p.m. and the fighting moved outside Lüneburg's walls. The French battalion, finding its road to Garlstorf blocked by Cossacks and several Russian guns, had returned towards the city around the time that the Saxons were retreating through the Neue-Tor. Morand was thus able to unite his force on the low hills west of Lüneburg but vacillated for several hours trying to decide what to do while his men fended off a charge by the Izum Hussars and kept the multitudinous Cossacks at bay with lively skirmish fire. His situation was dire. He was completely surrounded in open country by an enemy with a decisive advantage in cavalry. The presence of the few Russian guns covering the road towards Garlstorf and the numerous enemy cavalry seem to have daunted him from trying to escape west and he probably did not want to abandon those of his men who were still resisting inside the walls. He finally decided that his only option was an attack to regain the city. Around 3:00 p.m., therefore, he rode to the front of the remaining Saxon troops, waved his hat, called out '*Vive l'Empereur*!' and led the regiment forward with support from the two Saxon guns that were still operational. The attack was surprisingly successful at first, but lost momentum as it neared the Neue-Tor. Unfortunately for Morand, the French battalion failed to support the advance and the Saxon attackers, reduced to only some 480 men and their two guns, were insufficient to overcome the defenders.[174] Worse, the French side lost all of its key leaders at this crucial point. In a matter of minutes, Morand, Ehrenstein and the French regimental commander, Major Joseph Palis, were all wounded, in Morand's case a wound that would prove mortal. Assuming command of the entire force in this crisis, Ehrenstein attempted to save what could be saved by negotiating a ceasefire with Dörnberg that would have allowed the remaining troops to retire with weapons and baggage. By the time this agreement had been reached, however, the encircled division's fate had been sealed. Cossacks and Russian cavalry had closed in on the troops, inserting themselves between the French ranks and leaving no option but surrender. Although battle losses were similar on both sides at around 350 each, the remainder of Morand's force, some 2,300 men with nine guns and all of their baggage, fell into Allied hands. It was a small but crushing defeat that provided another psychological boost for the Allies.

Lüneburg was a remarkable engagement in several ways. The Allies benefited from energy, good leadership and no small amount of good luck, as well as a numerous cavalry that provided a crucial advantage once the combat shifted to the open terrain outside the city. Morand, on the other hand, was lax about security and lapsed into indecision when a determination either to defend the city or strike out for Garlstorf might have saved his command. He and his men also suffered from several doses of misfortune such as the near-simultaneous loss of so many key leaders. At the same time, this little battle illustrates an interesting and perhaps surprising aspect of the Rheinbund armies in 1813: a dedication to their conception of military honour, professionalism and adherence to their monarch's commitments that did not permit consideration of capitulation except as a last resort. Oberst von Ehrenstein provides one example in his effort, albeit abortive, to save the command by concluding an arrangement for safe passage with arms and equipment. Likewise, the junior Saxon officers charged with defending the gates only surrendered when trapped and out of ammunition. Leutnant David August von Döring, commanding the small force at the Rothe-Tor on the southern wall, went even further. Though cut off when the Prussians burst into the city at the Lüne Gate, he and his men continued to resist until a French officer brought word of the division's capitulation. Even then, he would not give in until he was permitted to visit the badly wounded Ehrenstein to confirm that the force had surrendered.

Displays of this sort of defiant determination would not always be the case among Rheinbund troops in 1813 and they declined in frequency as Napoleon's star dimmed, but they occurred more commonly than is often assumed. Furthermore, the Saxons remained doggedly defiant as prisoners. Shuffled about in Prussia, they were subjected to months of cajoling, intimidation, and threats of imprisonment in Siberia. Many escaped on their own, but the others, guided by their officers, repeatedly rejected appeals and threats to side with the Allies. They specifically rebuffed the detested Prussians. The situation only changed at the end of June when an energetic recruiting officer for the Russo-German Legion managed to separate the men from their officers through a ruse and thereby persuaded approximately 500 of the remaining 880 Saxons to enrol in the Legion's 6th Battalion. Even then, one-third of the men refused the offer and only two officers elected to change sides.[175] Lüneburg and the fate of the *Prinz Maximilian* Regiment were thus but one example of a phenomenon that will be encountered repeatedly as this narrative progresses.

Rebuilding the Army

The loss at Lüneburg deprived Saxony of one of its last remaining bodies of trained soldiers. The captured officers and NCOs would be especially difficult to replace while the kingdom was endeavouring to rebuild an army decimated by the Russian campaign, short of equipment and riven with divided loyalties.

The king's move to Prague had sparked hopes that Friedrich August would abandon the French alliance and an equal degree of disappointment arose within the army and the general population when he decided to return to the Napoleonic fold. Nonetheless, the press of the campaign meant that available soldiery would be hastened into combat at once whatever their mood or state of readiness. As Gablenz's small detachment in Poland would not return until the armistice, the Saxon troops involved in the remaining weeks of the spring campaign consisted of two groups of existing units: those that Thielmann had been charged with organising in Torgau and the cavalry that had accompanied Friedrich August on his trek to Plauen, Regensburg and Prague.[176]

The troops in Torgau would form the core of the reconstituted army. Napoleon ordered them to be incorporated immediately into a new 7th Corps under Reynier, along with Durutte's 32nd Division, as part of Ney's larger command. Reynier, however, called the corps 'not at all organised' when he arrived in Torgau on the morning of 11 May. Although he found approximately 11,500 men on the rolls in and around the fortress, some 3,200 of these were on the sick lists and, after deducting 1,850 who would have to remain behind as a garrison, he was left with only 5,441 Saxons available to take the field (see Chart 17). These 'lack many items', he told Berthier, particularly basics needed for field operations such as bivouac gear, artillery spares, medical personnel and equipment, victuals wagons and more. On top of these deficiencies, 'the armaments are in poor condition'. Leadership at all levels – officers and NCOs – was another serious problem. In the senior ranks Reynier replaced Steindel (aged and ill, he was soon retired) with Sahr ('who performed very well during the campaign') as commander of this ad hoc Saxon division and assigned two colonels 'who also performed well' to lead the brigades. Sahr and these two men, Mellenthin and Carl August von Bose, were all soon promoted at Reynier's request. Mid- and junior-grade officer and NCO requirements could be met partly by shifting men among units and promoting promising young subordinates, but these steps could not make up all the deficits and commanders would complain about the paucity of qualified leaders for the remainder of the war. Durutte's division laboured under similar shortages and the entire corps needed administrative staff, sappers and a full complement of artillery.[177] Nonetheless, Sahr's and Durutte's men found themselves marching west on 15 May to join the offensive against the Allied position at Bautzen. Reynier, hoping that he and his command would receive due imperial recognition, wrote directly to Napoleon on 19 May asking that he be allowed 'to distinguish himself in your eyes' and prove his 'zeal and devotion' (unlike 1812 when he was far from Napoleon).[178] His request would soon be granted.

Chart 17: Saxon Field Forces, mid-May 1813

Re-formed 7th Corps, GD Reynier (15 May 1813)

		bns/sqdns	present under arms
Saxon Division	*GL von Sahr*		
1st Brigade	*GM von Mellenthin*		
Jäger Company	*Premier-Leutnant von Petrikowsky*	–	144
I/Leib-Grenadier Battalion	*Major von Jeschki I*	1	381
Prinz Friedrich August Battalion	*Major von Brand*	1	603
Steindel Battalion (former *Prinz Clemens*)	*Oberstleutnant von Seydewitz*	1	627
1st Light Battalion *LeCoq*	*Major von Rade*	1	454
1st Foot Artillery Battery	*Hauptmann. Kühnel*	4 × 6-pdr, 2 × howitzer	138
2nd Brigade	*Oberst von Bose*		
Combined Grenadier Battalion	*Major Anger*	1	784
Prinz Anton Battalion	*Oberst von Ryssel*	1	368
Low Battalion	*Major von Schmieden*	1	631
2nd Light Battalion *Sahr*	*Major von Jeschki II*	1	665
2nd Foot Artillery Battery	*Hauptmann Rouvroy II*	4 × 6-pdr, 2 × howitzer	138
Cavalry	*Oberstleutnant von Lehmann*		
1st Squadron: Hussars and Uhlans	*Major von Feilitzsch*	1	160
2nd Squadron: combined Chevaulegers	*Rittmeister von der Planitz*	1	137
Sappers		–	65
Pontooneers		–	11
Artillery park	*Oberstleutnant von Raabe*	–	135
32nd Division	**GD Durutte**		
1st Brigade	*GB Devaux*		
35ᵉ Léger	*Capitaine Devilleu*	(one company)	95
IV/36ᵉ Léger	*Colonel Baume*	1	663
IV/131ᵉ Ligne	*Colonel Maury*	1	750
IV/132ᵉ Ligne	*Colonel Triboulat*	1	673
2nd Brigade	*GB Jarry*		
IV/133ᵉ Ligne	*Colonel Menu*	1	824
Würzburg Infantry Regiment (II, III)	*Oberst Moser von Filseck*	2	1,179
Artillery		3 × 6-pdr, 1 × howitzer	59
Grand total	3,064 French, 1,179 Würzburg and 5,441 Saxon = 9,684		

Also en route to Bautzen were the cavalry units that had followed the king to Bohemia. The Leib-Cuirassiers were a fine regiment of long-service troopers, but the others were struggling to form. The *Zastrow* Cuirassier Regiment 'cannot ride and are frightful' wrote an observer after watching them at a review in early March and many of the light cavalry recruits were still in their civilian clothes when they rode for Plauen, many lacking even saddles,

Serving in 1st Cavalry Corps, GD Latour-Maubourg

		bns/sqdns	present under arms
In 1st Cuirassier Cavalry Division	*GD Bordessoulle*		
3rd (Saxon) Brigade	*GM von Lessing*		
Leib-Cuirassiers Regiment	*Oberst von Berge*	4	626
Zastrow Cuirassiers	*Oberst von Ziegler*	4	408
2nd Horse Artillery Battery	*Hauptmann Probsthayn*	4 × 6-pdr, 2 × howitzer	95
In 1st Light Cavalry Division	*GD Bruyère*		
3rd Brigade	*GB Jacquet*		
1st Italian Chasseurs	*Major Sardieux*	4	704
Saxons	*Oberst von Thümmel*		
Hussar Regiment	*Major von Fabrice*	4	404
Prinz Clemens Uhlan Regiment	*Major von Berge*	4	364
Total Saxons			1,865

Notes:

(1) These firgures are from the 15 May French report submitted by 7th Corps on 28 May. Titze gives a substantially higher total of 6,296 for the Saxons (only) on 11 May before the division left Torgau.

Left behind to garrison Torgau were *c*. 1,300 men of the *König/Niesemeuschel* and *Max/Rechten* Battalions (these would expand to four full battalions over the coming weeks) along with 550 artillery personnel and sappers, pontooneers, etc. for a total of *c*. 1,850 fit for duty. Additionally, there were some 3,200 men in hospital in the fortress.

(2) Five more French battalions (3,843) were marching with 6th Corps as a temporary brigade en route to Durutte.

Sources: 7th Corps, 'Situation' and 'Situation Sommaire', 15 May 1813,
'État de la Composition de la Division Saxonne formée à Torgau le 12 Mai',
all SHD, 2C541;
Titze, *Sachsen im eigenen Land*, pp. 13–14, 174; Titze, *Chevaulegers*, pp. 24–5; Titze, *Husaren-Regiment*, pp. 26–8.

stirrups and other basic horse furniture. Like the French cavalry, *Zastrow* and the light cavalry also suffered from a paucity of experienced officers and NCOs. Whatever their state of readiness, however, the Saxon cavalry units left Bohemia on 11 May to reach assembly areas inside Saxony four days later: the cuirassiers and artillery near Dresden, the light troopers south of Königstein. The two heavy regiments and Hauptmann Friedrich Gottlieb Probsthayn's

2nd Horse Artillery Battery, totalling around 1,034 horsemen and 95 gunners, now came under the command of GM Heinrich August von Lessing and were assigned to GD Étienne Tardif de Bordesoulle's 1st Cuirassier Division of the 1st Cavalry Corps led by GD Latour-Maubourg. Separated from their compatriots under Reynier, they would remain with Latour-Maubourg for the remainder of the war, the only Rheinbund troops incorporated into one of the five French cavalry corps. The light cavalry were also attached to 1st Cavalry Corps for the spring campaign. Hastily uniformed and equipped, with no time even to complete proper regimental rolls, they were organised into two regiments, one of hussars and one of Uhlans, each of four squadrons. Numbering 768 officers and men, they were brigaded together under Oberst von Thümmel and detailed to GD Pierre Joseph Bruyère's 1st Light Cavalry Division.[179]

The Saxon cavalry provides another example of the army's ambivalence at this stage of the war. On the one hand, some of the men reportedly declined to hail Napoleon with the customary *'Vive l'Empereur!'* when he and Friedrich August reviewed them in Dresden on their way to Bautzen. On the other, an ardently pro-Allied Saxon official dispatched by the tsar was firmly rebuffed when he attempted to suborn the cavalry commanders while they marched from Bohemia back to Saxony.[180]

Bautzen and Beyond[181]

Both Saxon elements now moved towards Bautzen within the embrace of Napoleon's larger plan: the cavalry brigades with the emperor and the main army, the 7th Corps with Ney's outflanking force. Marching via Luckau and Hoyerswerda, Reynier's regiments arrived on the battlefield at Klix around 3:00 p.m. on 21 May and marched past Preititz towards Belgern in support of Lauriston's advance. The Saxon batteries earned Ney's praise while participating in bombardments of the Allied positions near Belgern and Wurschen in the late afternoon and the small cavalry component seems to have conducted some charges, but the infantry were not engaged, and the corps took few casualties.[182] The men bivouacked around Nechern that night, having moved from the trailing position to the lead of Ney's command. The cavalry regiments manoeuvred with the rest of Latour-Maubourg's troopers but were not committed to combat. Hauptmann Probsthayn's horse battery, on the other hand, was ordered to join a French gun line on the heights west of Basankwitz not far from where Napoleon was observing the battle. Their target was the Russian fieldworks southeast of Kreckwitz. Two guns were damaged as the battery galloped into position, but they were quickly repaired and went into action with the other four pieces. 'We moved with the greatest precision and order,' Probsthayn proudly recorded in his diary and Napoleon was impressed enough to award the captain the Legion of Honour for his performance.[183]

The Allies greeted the dawn of 22 May with a cannonade directed at the Saxon bivouac around Nechern, and, as the closest to the enemy, the 7th Corps would serve as the army's advance guard for the next two days along the northern pursuit route. This task involved repeated manoeuvres and attacks to lever the skilful foe out of well-chosen rear-guard positions. With Lauriston's 5th Corps on their left and Latour-Maubourg's cavalry corps on the right, the Saxons led the 7th Corps advance along the highway towards Görlitz. In constant fighting, they first forded the Löbauer-Wasser to force the enemy back from Weißenberg and then turned southeast, crossing the Schwarzer Schöps between Meuselwitz and Schöps to drive on Reichenbach. The Russians under Eugene of Württemberg had established a strong defence along the hills north and east of the town, but Mellenthin's brigade, Leib-Grenadiers and Jägers in the lead, managed to seize the town with support from Lauriston's men on their left. Meanwhile, cavalry from Latour-Maubourg's corps and the Imperial Guard were approaching through Sohland am Rotstein, the troopers offering the numerous Russian artillery on the hills a dense target as they squeezed between fences to reach the stream. A vicious mounted engagement ensued in which the recruits of Thümmel's light cavalry brigade, 'masters of neither their horses nor their weapons', suffered heavily and GD Bruyère, their division commander, was mortally wounded. Despite their losses, French GD Édouard Colbert, was relieved to see the Saxons arrive. His outnumbered brigade of Guard Lancers (including the squadron of Berg Lancers) was unsupported and in trouble 'because the enemy's artillery was doing it tremendous harm'. 'Finally', wrote Colbert, 'it was freed from its difficult situation by a brigade of Saxon cavalry ... General Bruyère, who commanded the Saxon cavalry disengaged the lancers through many well conducted charges and was killed by a cannon ball.'[184] The Saxon light cavalry eventually retreated with loss just as Bordessoulle's division advanced on its right. The heavy cavalry did not become entangled in the melee, but its arrival caused the Russians to pull back and gave the light division time to recover.[185] Reynier's infantry, on the other hand, were in the low ground between Reichenbach and the stream and had to form squares to protect themselves from the victorious Allied horsemen.

The loss of the town and Lauriston's outflanking move, however, had the desired effect and the Allies, having delayed their pursuers for several hours and having severely handled the French cavalry, retreated to a new position between Reichenbach and Markersdorf. It was now 4:00 p.m. and Napoleon rode up to the 7th Corps position on the hill above Reichenbach. He offered GL von Sahr effusive praise for the performance of the Saxon troops and ordered them to continue their advance despite Reynier's protest that his men had been in constant action for almost twelve hours. With powerful support from French batteries, therefore, the two Saxon brigades formed into columns and advanced again, but the Russians only held their position for a short time before retiring behind the Weißer Schöps. 'Napoleon directed the movements himself', wrote Major Cerrini, the Saxon chief of staff, 'and drove the advance with his usual intensity.' Under the emperor's eye, the Saxons occupied the village of Markersdorf and the adjoining houses of Holtendorf but were unable to capture the bridge over the Weißer Schöps before night brought an end to the combat.[186] The light infantry battalions and the tiny Jäger Company had especially distinguished themselves throughout the day.

The Saxons were again in the lead on 23 May. The *LeCoq* Light Battalion crossed the Neisse near Görlitz by wading and using small boats to claim a bridgehead on the eastern bank but repairs to the bridge at Holtendorf delayed the bulk of the corps until noon and it only advanced some 10 kilometres beyond Görlitz before halting for the night. Combat, however, was again heavy and the Saxon light infantry were once more at the forefront of the action. The two light battalions and the Jägers captured Leopoldshain, set ablaze by the retreating Russians, but were thrown back when they allowed their enthusiasm to overcome good sense and stormed towards a large wood to the east. Reynier reinforced them with the *Friedrich August* and *Steindel* Battalions as well as Mellenthin's battery, however, and they returned to the attack to clear the enemy from the woods. Sahr was close to the action, even riding up to the skirmish line to scold the *Schützen* of his regiment for not taking enough advantage of cover as they fought. With balls flying all about, a corporal chided back: 'But general, if we are supposed to take cover, you should not be here on horseback!' The popular Sahr dismissed this concern with a phrase that became part of the light infantry's legend: 'O! the king can find a general like me every day but not such *Schützen* as you are!' Beyond such jocular battlefield exchanges, Sahr did not neglect to praise his men in his official reports, writing on 25 May to the king that, 'Despite the shortage of provisions, these troops, almost all newly organised, led to the battlefield so hastily and unprepared, have fought like the best, most experienced, hardened warriors, always holding the same courage, composure and order in the toughest, most exhausting engagements.'[187]

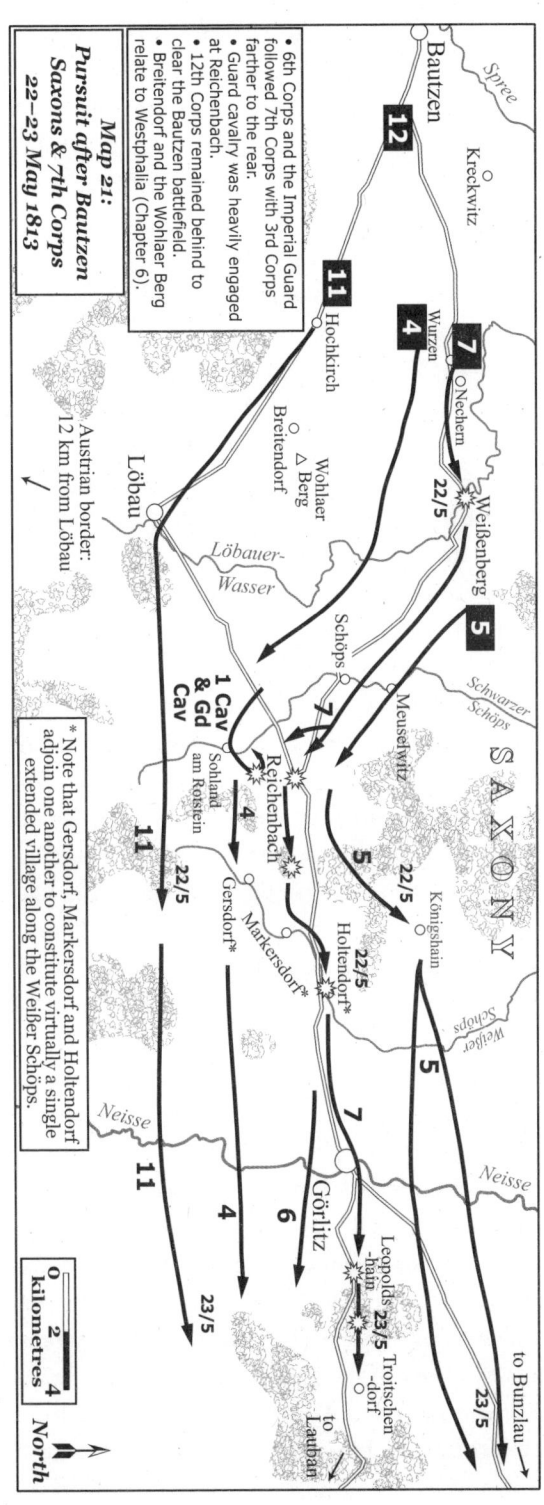

Map 21: *Pursuit after Bautzen Saxons & 7th Corps 22–23 May 1813*

Reynier's wish to have his corps in action under Napoleon's personal supervision was thus fulfilled, but the cost for the three days of combat from Bautzen to Görlitz had been high: 38 dead, 248 wounded and, at 453, a high number of missing. In contrast, Durutte's division suffered about half as many casualties. As for the Saxon cavalry with Latour-Maubourg, the two light regiments, heavily engaged at Reichenbach on the 22nd, lost 114 men killed or wounded and another 48 missing, while their cuirassier compatriots and the artillery battery had none killed and only 17 wounded.[188]

Active operations continued for another two weeks, but 7th Corps was no longer part of the army's advance guard and the Saxon regiments with 1st Cavalry Corps saw no major combat. Other than periodic skirmishing and small actions, therefore, the remainder of the spring campaign was a time of marching, manoeuvres and privations for the Saxon troops. Reynier's men moved from Görlitz through Liegnitz to conclude the campaign encamped west of Breslau, while the cavalry found itself just north of Pläswitz between Jauer and Breslau. Here they remained until shortly after the declaration of the armistice when both groups withdrew to their respective assembly areas: the 7th Corps to Görlitz, the two cavalry brigades to Sagan.

Space does not permit a detailed account of each minor action or incident in which the Saxons were involved during the spring campaign, but several general points are worth noting. First, as with many armies, the light infantry played a crucial role in pursuits, skirmishing, seizing advanced positions or undertaking any mission that required swift movement, initiative and independent operations. Second, the light cavalry with Latour-Maubourg suffered from the rawness of its troops and lack of officers, but Thümmel submitted a favourable report after their initial action. 'I have every reason to be satisfied with the behaviour of the brigade under my command,' he wrote, mentioning that both Latour-Maubourg and Bruyère had been pleased with the Saxon cavalry and that the troopers had retained their composure under the heaviest artillery fire he had ever experienced. He credited 'the good spirit of the troops' to 'the superb example of the officers' who had distinguished themselves in spite of 'unbearable exertions and the poor provisions while constantly in danger of death'.[189] The two squadrons with Reynier also performed well despite being small in size and recently thrown together. Third, poor provisions meant that the Saxons were not above stripping their own country of food and fodder. Quite understandably, officers and men would revile the French for ravaging the countryside, but as Leutnant Ferdinand Heinrich August von Larisch of the *Friedrich August* Infantry ruefully recorded in his diary for 28 May, the Saxons could inflict similar depredations: 'I was the officer of the day and as a result had to lead a requisitions detachment, or better said a plundering detachment; bacon, flour, peas, barley, chickens, fruit and lard were our booty.' Fourth, the Saxon sappers and pontooneers also contributed to the pursuit after Bautzen. Between 22 May and 1 June, the sappers built or repaired at least five bridges along the corps' route of advance. The bridge at Görlitz was constructed under fire and when Napoleon demanded two more crossings there, the pontoon company used their clumsy equipment to erect a floating bridge as well (French engineers built the third).[190]

Finally, despite the widespread anti-French sentiment in the kingdom and despite many material handicaps, the Saxons acquitted themselves well after their sudden and, for some, unexpected and unwelcome, return to the French alliance. Additionally, there seem to have been few desertions.[191] Napoleon and his generals had no cause for complaint and Sahr could justly report to his king on 2 June that the health and physical condition of the troops had declined, but that 'great daily exertions and lack of provisions have not yet had any negative influence on the courageous endurance of the old or young soldiers'.[192]

While the army generally performed in a competent and professional fashion, the anti-French mood prevalent among much of Saxony's civilian population occasionally burst into the open. When Prussian Major von Lützow was attempting to lead his partisan band past Leipzig to the Elbe after learning of the armistice, for instance, he sent a lieutenant into the city to negotiate with GD Arrighi, the French commander responsible for the area. A crowd of burghers swiftly gathered as news of his arrival spread. They greeted the lieutenant with loud hurrahs, then manhandled and insulted the French soldiers who tried to disperse them. After the defeat of Lützow's force on 17 June at Kitzen, local citizens open-handedly supplied food and clothing to the captives and actively assisted partisan fugitives to escape (possibly with the passive assistance of Württemberg guards who looked the other way).[193] The barely disguised efforts to abet the enemy, combined with a press item praising Colomb's Prussian raiders and numerous other subversive activities, led the French authorities to impose a harsh 'state of siege' (*Belagerungszustand*) from 20 June along with a hefty financial penalty. 'His Majesty the Emperor Napoleon is very displeased with the conduct displayed by many individuals of this city during the recent political events,' read a proclamation.[194] The restrictive measures were not lifted until 16 July after Napoleon had personally visited the city and persuaded himself that the residents had learned the appropriate lesson.

Chart 18: Reorganised 7th Corps, 17 August 1813
GD Reynier

		bns/sqdns	present under arms
24th Division (1st Saxon)	**GL von LeCoq**		
1st Brigade	Oberst von Brause		
I/Leib-Grenadier Battalion	Hauptmann von Dreßler	1	723
1st Light Infantry Regt. *LeCoq*	Major von Rade	2	1,247
Combined Regiment	Major von Wittern		
1st Battalion (*Prinz Maximilian*, assigned to garrison Luckau)		1	579
2nd Battalion (*Rechten*)		1	609
Jäger Company	Premierleutnant von Zychlinski	–	136
2nd Brigade	GM von Mellenthin		
1st Grenadier Battalion	Major von Spiegel	1	668
(Grenadiers of *Max*, *Rechten*, *Friedrich* and *Steindel*)			
Prinz Friedrich August Inf. Regt.	Major von Brand	2	951
Steindel Infantry Regiment	Oberst von Seydewitz	2	1,152
1st Foot Artillery Battery	Hauptmann. Kühnel	6 × 6-pdr, 2 × howitzer	172
2nd Foot Artillery Battery	Hauptmann Rouvroy II	6 × 6-pdr, 2 × howitzer	183
12-pounder Artillery Battery	Hauptmann Rouvroy I	6 × 12-pdr, 2 × howitzer	211
Train		–	97
Sapper Company		–	78
25th Division (2nd Saxon)	**GL von Sahr > Oberst von Bose** (*after Großbeeren*)		
1st Brigade	Oberst von Bose		
2nd Grenadier Battalion	Major von Sperl	1	680
(Grenadiers of *König*, *Niesemeuschel*, *Anton* and *Low*)			
2nd Light Infantry Regt. *Sahr*	Major von Selmnitz	2	1,167
Combined Regiment	Major von Bose		
1st Battalion (*König*)		1	501
2nd Battalion (*Niesemeuschel*, guarding corps trains)		1	554
2nd Brigade	Oberst von Ryssel		
Prinz Anton Infantry Regiment	Major von Holleufer	2	1,086
Low Infantry Regiment	Major Anger	2	1,089
3rd Foot Artillery Battery	Hauptmann Dietrich	6 × 6-pdr, 2 × howitzer	108
4th Foot Artillery Battery	Hauptmann Zandt	6 × 6-pdr, 2 × howitzer	177
Train		–	75

The Autumn Campaign: From Defeat to Defection

The armistice brought yet another reorganisation for Saxony's army. The two cuirassier regiments remained with Bordessoulle in the 1st Cavalry Corps, but Thümmel's brigade and Probsthayn's battery rode off to join 7th Corps around Görlitz. The hussars and Uhlans were filled out by emptying the depots of

		bns/sqdns	present under arms
Light Cavalry Brigade	*GM von Gablenz*		
Hussar Regiment	*Oberst von Lindenau*	8	730
Prinz Clemens Uhlan Regiment	*Oberst von Thümmel*	5	796
1st Horse Artillery Battery	*Hauptmann Birnbaum*	4 × 6-pdr, 2 × howitzer	176
2nd Horse Artillery Battery	*Hauptmann Probsthayn*	4 × 6-pdr, 2 × howitzer	151
Main Artillery Park	*Major von Großmann*	–	271
32nd Division	*GD Durutte*		
1st Brigade	*GB Devaux*		
35ᵉ Léger (I and detachment/II)		1+	1,003
131ᵉ Ligne (III, IV)	*Colonel Maury*	2	1,558
132ᵉ Ligne (III, IV and detachment/II)	*Colonel Triboulat*	2+	1,521
2nd Brigade	*GB Jarry*		
36ᵉ Léger (IV and detachment/III)	*Colonel Baume*	1+	820
133ᵉ Ligne (III, IV and detachment/II)	*Colonel Menu*	2+	1,404
Würzburg Infantry Regiment (II, III)	*Oberst Moser von Filseck*	2	961
Artillery		–	439
Grand total	14,367 Saxon, 6,745 French and 961 Würzburg = 22,073		

Notes:

(1) The Saxon pontooneers were attached to a French engineering train during the armistice and did not rejoin the corps.

(2) En route to Durutte were: IV/35ᵉ Léger (698), I/132ᵉ Ligne (887) and I/131ᵉ Ligne (1,004), but these were diverted elsewhere: I/131ᵉ to escort prisoners via Dresden, the other two to the Leipzig garrison (SHD, XP3).

(3) The brigades of Durutte's division seem to have changed by the time of Dennewitz as Würzburg histories uniformly assign their regiment to Jarry.

(4) The Würzburg Regiment may have received a replacement detachment before embarking on the campaign as it is listed with 1,145 in 15 August returns (SHD, XP3)

Sources: 7th Corps 'Situation', 1 August 1813, SHD, 2C541; 7th Corps 'État des Pertes', 23 August 1813, SHD, 2C154; Titze, *Sachsen im eigenen Land*, pp. 24–6; Juhel, *Aout 1813*, pp. 21–2.

the old chevaulegers regiments and Gablenz's detachment also returned from Poland to add much-needed veteran officers and NCOs.[195] These additions and thousands of recruits allowed the expansion of the Saxon contingent into two divisions (24th and 25th of the Grande Armée) with a fine light cavalry brigade and a strong complement of artillery. Combined again with Durutte's 32nd Division, they would constitute the 7th Corps for the autumn campaign.

One of those marching back to Saxony through Austria was Corporal Carl Buhle of the *Prinz Anton* Regiment. Captured at Kalisch, Buhle had escaped and survived many travails to reach Austrian Galicia where a Habsburg colonel had tried to recruit him. Buhle, however, replied that, 'If I had wanted to take service in a foreign country, this could have been done in Russia where we prisoners were invited to do so; instead, I have risked my life in order to serve my fatherland again.' The generous colonel, impressed by this reply, obliged him with a pass permitting travel through the empire. He came upon Poniatowski's column in Moravia and journeyed part of the way with the Poles to reach Saxony 'with tears of joy and nostalgia' but also to find the country in ruins after the passage of the armies. Re-joining his regiment, he was soon drilling new recruits in preparation for the renewal of hostilities.[196] Recounting his experiences *after* Napoleon's defeat, on the other hand, Hauptmann Friedrich von Dreßler und Scharffenstein of I/Leib-Grenadiers described the column as marching 'silently and discontented towards its fate'. In his post-Leipzig view, there was none of 'the eagerness for battle or the best of spirits with which the French bulletins so liberally sought to encourage the troops'.[197]

Beyond 7th Corps and the cuirassier brigade, Saxons played important roles in a number of support functions. The pontoon detachment was attached to a French pontoon train near Glogau during the armistice and returned to Dresden in September where it joined pontoon troops from the depot in Torgau to build, maintain and dismantle bridges along the Elbe. Small numbers of engineer officers and sappers also made crucial contributions to the defence of Dresden in supervising fortification work and manning the lunettes before, during and after the battles in August.

Dresden: Rivals in Bravery[198]

In the absence of 7th Corps, there were very few Saxon troops in Dresden when the Allied Main Army lumbered out of Bohemia to threaten Friedrich August's capital after the armistice. Other than II/Leib-Grenadiers serving as the king's personal guard and some 250 artillery and train personnel, there were only a few engineer officers, sappers and pontooneers in and around the city.[199] The huge force Napoleon brought to contest the Allied advance, however, included Lessing's brigade of Saxon cuirassiers. These arrived in the mid-afternoon of 26 August and deployed near the Friedrichstadt suburb along with the rest of 1st Cavalry Corps. Here they came under Marshal Murat, who Napoleon had entrusted with command of the troops on the western side of the Weißeritz Stream. Although the men had to mount up late in the day when it seemed the Austrian left wing might advance, the heavy

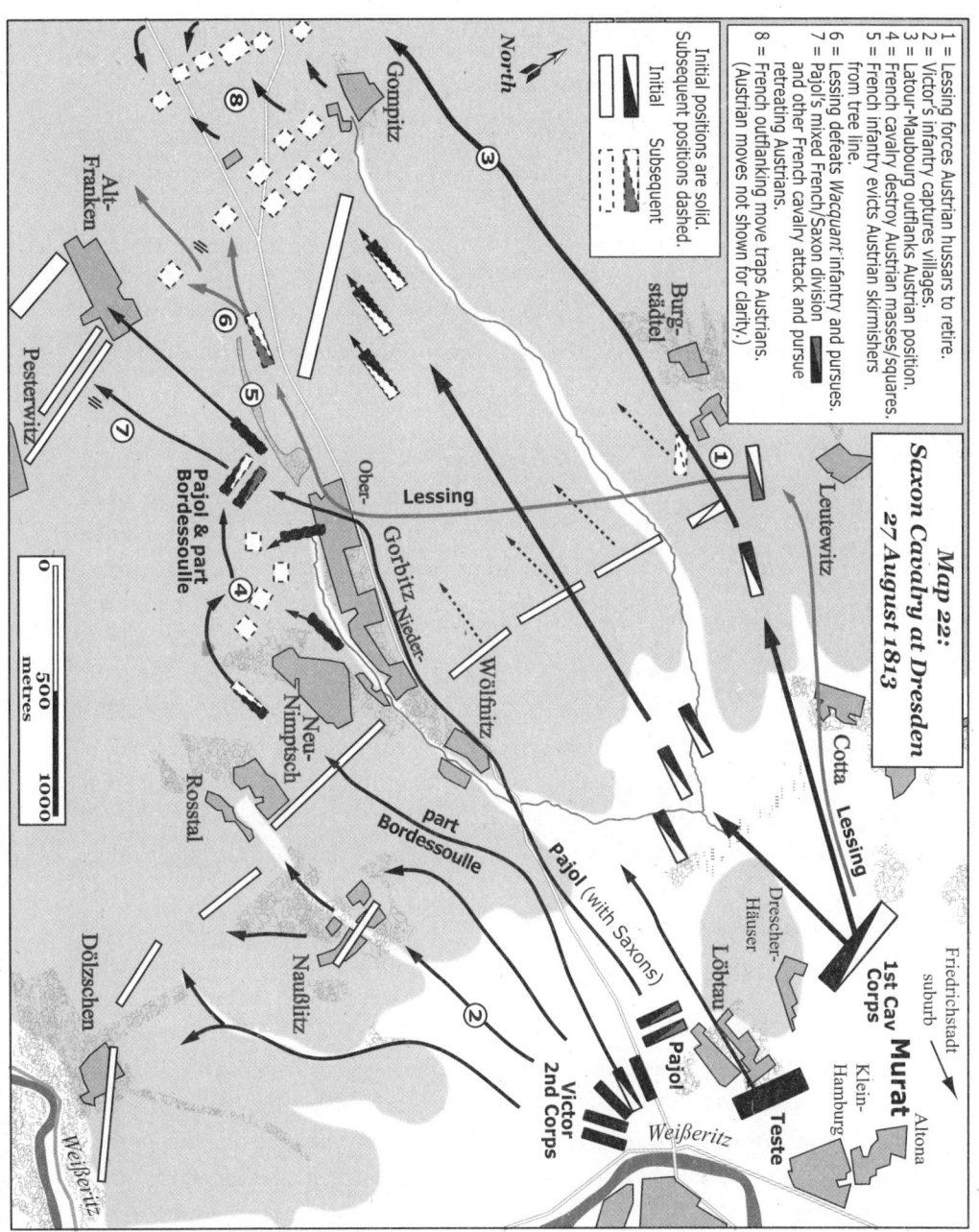

Map 22: Saxon Cavalry at Dresden 27 August 1813

regiments were not engaged, and the night passed quietly if miserably under the rainy weather.

Riding out early on the morning of 27 August to conduct a pre-battle reconnaissance, Murat took a squadron of the Saxon Leib-Cuirassiers as his personal escort. The regiment's remaining three squadrons were assigned to GD Claude Pierre Pajol's 10th Light Cavalry Division assembling near Löbtau. Pajol was in the left centre of the French line with Marshal Victor's 2nd Corps on his left bordering the Weißeritz and a brigade of GD François Antoine Teste's 23rd Division to his right behind Löbtau; Latour-Maubourg's cavalry corps with the other Saxon cuirassiers constituted the right of the line. In all, this large mass probably numbered more than 40,000 men, some 10,000 or 11,000 of those being cavalry. The Austrians opposite counted perhaps 20,000 in their ranks, but only some 560 of these were cavalry, hussars of the *Erzherzog Ferdinand* and *Palatinal* Regiments. Murat, obvious in his gaudy costume and plumed cap, now trotted back from his reconnaissance, returned the Saxon escort squadron to Lessing and set the entire force in motion. It was about 10:00 a.m.

Opposite the French, the Austrians had withdrawn from their previously advanced positions to a line on the high ground roughly from Dölzschen through Naußlitz and Gorbitz towards Leutewitz. By the time the French advance began, almost all of the Habsburg squadrons had been pulled across the Weißeritz to join the centre of the Allied army. This left the defence of the sector to a few artillery batteries and white-coated infantry battalions whose muskets had been rendered nearly useless by the heavy rain.

As Victor's and Teste's infantry attacked towards Dölzschen, Naußlitz and Wölfnitz, Murat sent the 1st Cavalry Corps to outflank the Austrian line. Lessing's five squadrons (*Zastrow* and the squadron of Leib-Cuirassiers that had escorted Murat) initially deployed to a position on the far right between Leutewitz and Burgstädtel that placed them behind the Austrian left. The five squadrons of hussars that held this end of the Austrian line, quickly pivoted back and sent skirmishers forward to harass the Saxons. Lessing also detached troopers to skirmish but as the Saxon squadrons made preparations to launch a charge, the Austrians turned about and dropped to the rear, taking themselves out of the action for the remainder of the day. The French outflanking move was thus able to proceed unopposed and unobserved to swing around past Gompitz (Compitz) and attack the Austrian line from behind.

The Saxons were not involved in this manoeuvre or in the direct approach adopted by some of the French units. Instead, Lessing led his men diagonally across the field behind the advancing French to Ober-Gorbitz before turning right and using a shallow ravine to appear on the left of the French cavalry line. Straight ahead of him was an Austrian battery flanked by two battalion masses of the *Wacquant* Infantry No. 62 (analogous to a square in other armies, the 'mass' or '*Bataillonsmasse*' was a uniquely Austrian infantry formation used to defend against cavalry). Fortunately for the Saxons, the Austrian gunners were aiming high and most of their shot and shell passed over the heads of Lessing's troopers. Austrian skirmishers tucked among trees and shrubs on his left, however, were knocking men out of their saddles. In another stroke of good fortune, a French infantry column appeared from Gorbitz at this point and its commander happily acceded to Lessing's request to clear the troublesome Austrians from their covered positions.[200] This nettle removed from his flank, Lessing proceeded to charge. The Austrian battery quickly limbered up and departed, losing only one gun to pursuing Saxon troopers. The *Wacquant* Infantry masses, however, lost cohesion and surrendered after bravely withstanding two attacks. An Austrian battalion adjutant, Leutnant Theodor Binder von Bindersfeld, described the scene as resistance collapsed:

> The masses had dissolved into little knots and alternately attacked the so-called iron men, whose courage was all the more enlivened by the conviction that no musket could fire. A general slaughter ensued. The cuirassiers fired their pistols into our clumps, our men chased them back a few paces again with the bayonet while another cavalry section attacked our men from the rear, scattered them and cut them down.

Two thousand men and two standards thus fell into Saxon hands in addition to the cannon, a fine prize for their determination and tactical skill. According to the Austrian regimental history, Oberst Adolf Gottlob von Ziegler, commanding the *Zastrow* Cuirassiers, took time to honour his opponents after their capture: 'Comrades! You fought like lions; I regret your fate!'[201]

Meanwhile, the three Leib-Cuirassier squadrons with Pajol were also acquiring battle trophies. French infantry and cavalry had already forced the capitulation of four Austrian masses between Neu-Nimptsch and Ober-Gorbitz when Pajol's column rode through Wölfnitz and Gorbitz to deploy south of the latter village. The Austrians had then fallen back to the area between Alt-Franken and Pesterwitz, but French artillery bombarded Alt-Franken and French infantry stormed the village, chasing out the defenders. Pajol's troopers, combined with one of Bordessoulle's brigades, took up the pursuit of the retreating Austrians with the three Saxon squadrons capturing two Austrian guns in the process before dispersing to hunt down more fugitive Habsburg infantrymen. For a combined loss of 9 dead, 38 wounded and 25 missing, the two Saxon heavy regiments thus made an appreciable contribution to the defeat of the Austrian left wing on 27 August and fully justified the praise they received in Murat's report: 'The Saxon cuirassiers rivalled the French cuirassiers in bravery in all the charges they undertook; they took two of the standards among the twelve that we have in our hands.'[202] The two regiments received fifteen crosses of the Legion of Honour for their actions and Napoleon would remember them when he encountered them personally at Leipzig two months later.

Großbeeren: Defeat in a Downpour[203]

While the Saxon cuirassiers were 'covering themselves in glory' as Napoleon told Friedrich August, their compatriots in 7th Corps were retreating from the defeat at Großbeeren.[204] As noted in the introductory chapter, Napoleon had placed Reynier's command under Marshal Oudinot as part of the Army of Berlin for a drive on the Prussian capital when the armistice concluded. Setting out from its encampments around Görlitz, the corps reached Luckau on 17 August. Here the 12-pounder battery was attached to the 24th Division, the *Niesemeuschel* Battalion was assigned to escort the corps' baggage train and the *Prinz Maximilian* Battalion was detached to bolster the small French garrison in Luckau. Reynier and his men then headed north on 18 August as the central column of Oudinot's three-pronged advance. The next day, 'we entered a sandy, monotonous and exhausting terrain which promised little for the sustenance of the troops,' wrote Hauptmann Friedrich von Dreßler of the Leib-Grenadiers.[205] Occasional skirmishes with Cossacks dogged the corps' progress, but the Saxon light infantry and artillery drove the Prussians out of Nunsdorf on 21 August and the gunners successfully supported Durutte's capture of Wietstock on the 22nd while Oberst von Brause's brigade assisted the French 14th Division in its attack on Wilmersdorf (*see* Map 12). Reynier was displeased with Oudinot's arrangements, believing the marshal should have placed himself and the 12th Corps in the centre of the army's advance, but it was too late to make any adjustments even if such were suggested. Reynier thus made his own plans for the next day's march, holding Durutte in Kerzendorf with LeCoq behind on the eastern side of the Nuthe-Graben and Sahr's division pushed ahead towards Löwenbruch. Sahr would therefore lead the corps' march to Großbeeren on 23 August.

That night the 1st Saxon Division 'bivouacked in concentrated columns behind burning Wittstock [*sic*]', as Mandelsloh recalled. 'Everything indicated that we would have a hard clash with the enemy on the next day and no one doubted that the next evening would find us in Berlin. We officers amused ourselves around our fire with the marvels of Berlin and made plans of how we would take advantage of the pleasures of the capital.' A defiant rejoinder from a captive Prussian Uhlan, however, caused Mandelsloh to ponder the different sort of spirit motivating the enemy army, while on the French and Rheinbund

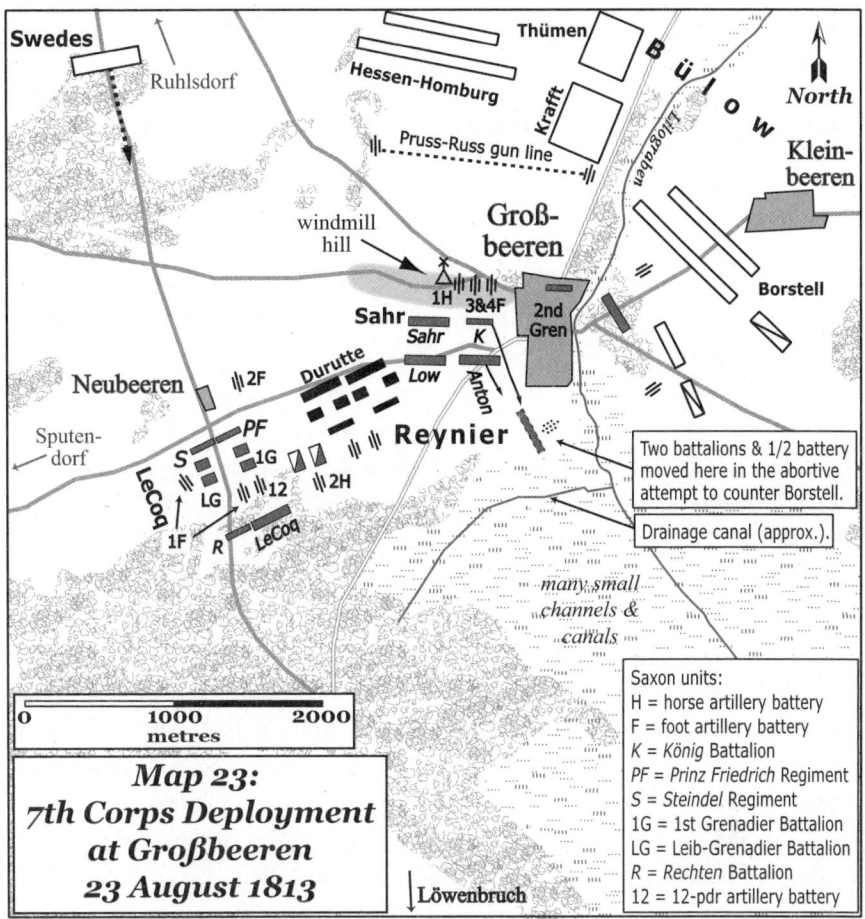

**Map 23:
7th Corps Deployment
at Großbeeren
23 August 1813**

side 'hopes of victory were rooted solely in the genius of our commander-in-chief'.[206] In other words, as many French and Rheinbund officers would observe, all depended on Napoleon. Nonetheless, the Saxons had 'hopes of victory' that night, hopes that would be dashed when they indeed experienced a 'a hard clash' with their Prussian foes.

Großbeeren was a Saxon battle. Oudinot's dispositions left his three corps advancing on separate axes, so Reynier's men were isolated when they emerged on the northern side of the forest just west of the village after a tedious march in driving rain. Sahr's division took the lead as the corps slogged north through the mud on this grey and wet 23 August, followed by Durutte and the light cavalry. Next came the corps baggage train, inserted into the march column because the swarms of roaming Cossacks made the rear area insecure. LeCoq brought up the rear. Clearing the woods and peering through the sheets of rain, Reynier and his officers could discern the little town and a low hill distinguished by a prominent windmill only about 1½ kilometres to their right front. The town was held by three battalions of Prussian infantry while four guns on the windmill hill, protected by Cossacks and Prussian cavalry, opened fire as soon as the Saxons appeared in the open. The hour was now approaching 4:00 p.m. and Reynier ordered Sahr to take the village and hill before the corps settled in for the night.

As the rain prevented musket fire, Major Christian Gottlob Wilhelm von Sperl's 2nd Grenadier Battalion stormed Großbeeren with the bayonet, driving out its defenders, while two Saxon batteries forced the Prussian guns to limber up and leave the hill. Three of Reynier's batteries (1st Horse, 3rd and 4th Foot) soon took their place on this little prominence where the miller later claimed that six Saxon officers had clambered atop his shed to wave handkerchiefs from their swords while calling out ribald greetings to the ladies of Berlin in anticipation of the coming night's lodgings.[207] To the right of these brash and hopeful men, Sperl's grenadiers occupied the town and the small wood on its eastern side towards Kleinbeeren. The rest of Sahr's infantry deployed in two lines in the low ground west of Großbeeren with the cavalry brigade and Durutte to their left rear in two brigade squares. LeCoq held the corps left flank. He had shoved past the baggage wagons during the march when the cannon fire became audible and veered off to the west on a smaller track towards a large farmstead called Neubeeren. Arriving on Durutte's left as the afternoon waned, he arrayed his men in a large square, open at the back with skirmishers forward and along the woodline to his rear.

Despite warnings from Saxon officers that large enemy forces were gathering to the north and especially to the east beyond Großbeeren, Reynier was content with his position. He seems to have thought that he was only facing an enemy advance guard and told his apprehensive staff, 'Ah, it is nothing, they will not come.'[208] It was already late on a gloomy, dark day, so perhaps he believed there were not enough hours of daylight left for a serious action. He also expected Oudinot's corps to appear on his left at any moment as the marshal had planned. Whatever his decision process, he ordered no reconnaissance and allowed his men to begin preparing their camps for the night. His negligence thus compounded the dangers his outnumbered corps would face over the next several hours.

Reynier's opponent, Prussian GL von Bülow, displayed no such complacency. Aggressively energetic, he launched his III Corps into an attack as soon as it was assembled, leading with a powerful line of artillery. The brigades of Krafft and Hessen-Homburg followed close behind with Thümen and the cavalry in reserve. Sometime after 5:00 p.m., therefore, a violent artillery duel erupted between Bülow's guns and the three Saxon batteries on the windmill hill. The Saxon gunners scored considerable success, dismounting at least five of the enemy pieces, but a Swedish battery unlimbered on their left and GM von Borstell added 12 guns on the Saxon right from beyond the little stream, increasing the weight of iron the Allies could bring to bear. The Saxon batteries were crammed tightly on the narrow hilltop, making an inviting target. Outclassed in numbers and calibre, they soon began to suffer heavily from this harrowing crossfire. Sahr's infantry, reduced to five battalions owing to the detachments in and south of Großbeeren, also took casualties as Allied rounds flew over the low ridge to fall among their ranks.

While this artillery exchange raged, Borstell deployed his brigade east of Großbeeren and advanced on the little wood held by the Saxon grenadiers. Reynier, whose attention had been focused on his centre and the artillery battle, belatedly recognised the threat to his right. He quickly dispatched two battalions (*König* and II/*Prinz Anton*) and half a battery from the windmill hill to cover the space south of the village, but it was too late. The half-battery, spattered with canister fire as it tried to unlimber, was put out of action immediately and the infantrymen took casualties without being able to reply. The situation rapidly deteriorated. Borstell's artillery set Großbeeren afire, and his infantry stormed the little wood and the village, while Krafft's brigade attacked from the north on the western side of the Lilograben stream. The lone Saxon grenadier battalion offered brave but brief resistance before being forced out of the burning village and back towards the two battalions on the south side of the town. Breaking out from among the buildings, the Prussians charged the three Saxon battalions initiating what became an especially bitter struggle. The *König* Battalion escaped, and the Saxon gunners saved their four pieces, but the 2nd Grenadiers and II/*Prinz Anton* were broken. Only five or six of their muskets had discharged when they tried to greet the Prussians with a volley, and they were thrown back across a large drainage canal in disorder after a brief but vicious hand-to-hand melee. Most were able to flee to the safety of the woods, but some men drowned in the canal and many others, trapped in the mud, were helplessly bayoneted where they stood or, if lucky, simply taken prisoner.[209]

With Großbeeren lost, Reynier ordered Durutte to block the Prussians advancing out of the village and told Sahr to evacuate the windmill hill and withdraw into the woods. Again, it was too late. Four of the Saxon guns had been dismounted and losses of men and horses meant they could not be saved. Meanwhile, GB Devaux of Durutte's division seems to have misunderstood Reynier's instructions. Instead of advancing on Großbeeren, he pulled his brigade back towards the forest. Chaos ensued. Their ranks disordered by Saxon batteries hurrying to the rear, Devaux's confused men were then charged by Prussian cavalry against which they could not defend themselves. As noted earlier, several Saxon accounts describe many of the French soldiers 'dispersing by the hundreds and throwing away their equipment and arms' and Devaux apparently appealed to Oberst Thümmel for Uhlans to help herd the scattered French back into their ranks. Jarry's brigade, on the other hand, received praise from Reynier for 'marching in very fine order among the battalions and squadrons of the enemy'.[210] Whatever the behaviour of Durutte's men, though barely engaged, they fell back into the forest with heavy losses and did little to hold off the Prussians.

Sahr's infantry also dropped back in haste when they saw numerous Prussian battalions looming out of Großbeeren and cresting over the little hill. With confusion behind and the enemy encroaching on his centre and right, Reynier attempted to gain time for an orderly withdrawal by directing Oberst Xaver Gustav Reinhold von Ryssel to launch a counterattack with the *Low* Regiment. The regiment was retreating, but Ryssel and Sahr placed themselves at the front of its two battalions, turned them about and led them against the four Prussian battalions streaming down at the run from atop and around the windmill hill. Surprised, the onrushing Prussians halted, and, for a few brief moments, the two sides stood facing each other with levelled bayonets in the pouring rain while their officers encouraged their men to stand firm. Suddenly, Major Carl Adam von Gagern, commanding the 5th Prussian Reserve Infantry, spurred forward and slashed his opposite number, Major Carl Gottlob von Schmieden of I/*Low*, in the face with his sabre. As Schmieden fell from his mount badly wounded, the temporary tension broke. 'Forward', shouted Gagern and the Prussians attacked yelling 'At them! At them! No quarter for the Wittstockers!' I/*Low* broke for the rear and, in Gagern's words, 'the enemy column dispersed, the individual fugitives were bayoneted or taken prisoner'.[211] Sahr was also grievously injured, taking two bayonet wounds as he tried to rally his men. The general was carried to safety, but most of I/*Low*, including Schmieden, thus went into captivity. The Saxons, however, had also chased off one of the other attacking Prussian battalions and II/*Low* was able to retire to the woods in good order, covered by Sahr's steady light infantrymen who had been wisely posted along the woodline. The Prussians, themselves now disordered, broke off the pursuit at the appearance of the Saxon Uhlans on their right flank.

The arrival of the Saxon Uhlans was timely. Shifted to the east with Probsthayn's battery from their position next to LeCoq to help cover the retreat from the windmill hill, they repelled an effort by Borstell's cavalry to intercept the fleeing French and Saxon infantry. Chasing their quarry too far, however, the Saxon troopers were in turn sent flying by a Prussian countercharge that overran Probsthayn's guns. It was now dark and distinguishing friend from foe in the stygian confusion was nearly impossible. Probsthayn's gunners were thus only able to get off one shot before the enemy troopers were upon them. 'We retired towards the forest without having time to limber up and found the woodline already occupied by Pomeranian Uhlans who encircled us and took many of us prisoner,' lamented Probsthayn.[212] The Prussians made off with three of the pieces as well as Oberst von Thümmel of the Uhlans, but in confused fighting between isolated groups of Prussian and Saxon horsemen, a band of rallied Saxon troopers was able to recover the other three guns, more by luck and grit than considered intention.[213] The fall of night brought an end to the Prussian pursuit and the disordered bits and pieces of Sahr's and Durutte's divisions slowly stumbled back through the sodden forest to their previous bivouacs near Löwenbruch and Kerzendorf.

GM von Gablenz and the Hussar Regiment were already in the rear. As it became apparent that the corps would have to retreat, Reynier had sent Gablenz back to Wietstock to ensure the safety of the bridge. Plagued by encounters with Cossacks that cost the hussars several dozen men, the regiment reached its objective and secured the bridge. The withdrawal of the corps' baggage wagons, on the other hand, created a massive tangle in the dark, dank wood. Reynier's personal intervention helped to sort out the mess and the retreat continued across the Nuthe Graben after a few hours' rest.

Also retreating, of course, was LeCoq's division. At the same time that he ordered Durutte's men towards Großbeeren, Reynier had called LeCoq to the right. The situation on that side of the field, however, was totally masked: 'The continuing misty rain and the low-lying powder smoke from the cannonade blocked all observation,' noted the Leib-Grenadiers' journal.[214] Moreover, by the time this order reached the Saxon general, the windmill hill was already lost, and the corps was in full retreat back to the woods. Reynier therefore rescinded his initial instructions and directed LeCoq instead to withdraw along the path from Neubeeren to Wietstock thereby protecting the corps' left flank. LeCoq thus turned his division around and assigned Oberst von Brause the task of covering the withdrawal with the 12-pounder battery, the *Rechten* Battalion, I/*Friedrich* and the light infantry. Hessen-Homburg's brigade was advancing towards Neubeeren and elements of LeCoq's division had brushes with the Prussians on both sides of the farmstead in the gathering darkness. These brief encounters did not delay the Saxons and the withdrawal was carried out in perfect order with little disturbance from the enemy. The only glitch for LeCoq was that the *Rechten* Battalion, thrown into disorder by fleeing Frenchmen, lost its way in the forest gloom and ended up at Ahrensdorf rather than Wietstock.[215] With LeCoq's arrival at Löwenbruch, the corps withdrew across the Nuthe-Graben, burned the bridge and established itself on the far bank to reorganise with the coming day.

Großbeeren was a serious setback for 7th Corps and the Saxon contingent. Casualties came to 2,110 for the Saxons and 2,010 for Durutte's French and Würzburg battalions. As would be expected, almost all the Saxon losses were from Sahr's division, especially the 2nd Grenadier Battalion (216), *Prinz Anton* (301) and *Low* (831); this last regiment was therefore reduced to a single battalion for the remainder of the war. Beyond personnel casualties, the Saxons left behind 7 guns (4 from the 3rd Foot Battery and 3 of the 2nd Horse) as well as 57 caissons and supply wagons, most stuck in the mud along the forest road back towards Wietstock.[216] An additional 7 pieces were taken from Durutte's division for a total of 14 guns captured by the Prussians. More than 80 per cent of the Saxon losses were in missing or captured, but this troubling figure appears to have resulted from the peculiarities of the battlefield circumstances – the surprise, rain, confusion and closing darkness – not from large numbers of soldiers deserting to the Prussians or giving up at the first opportunity. Moreover, as Reynier noted when filing his casualty list, 'The number missing or taken prisoner is less considerable than in the present chart, and many have returned during the preparation of the table.'[217] Indeed, the outnumbered troops had generally performed well despite the dreadful situation imposed on them by Reynier's surprising negligence and what the Saxons (and Reynier) regarded as lack of support from Bertrand and especially from Oudinot. 'The 7th Army Corps', wrote Leutnant Vollborn, 'was, in the truest sense of the word, left in the lurch by Marshal Oudinot, & was as exhausted as it was discontented.'[218] Despite the defeat, most Saxons were angered at the lack of support from Oudinot and surprised at the marshal's decision to call off the offensive: 'We could not explain to ourselves this over-hasty retreat as neither the 12th nor the 4th Corps had suffered serious losses,' Major Hausen told his brother. Furthermore, even Hausen, who had regretted his king's decision to stand by the alliance with Napoleon, displayed frustration at the defeat when 'a unified advance towards Berlin probably would have led to victory'.[219]

The entire Army of Berlin now turned back towards Wittenberg on the Elbe. Under constant observation and in frequent skirmishes with Cossacks and Allied cavalry, the 7th Corps 'therefore had to march cross-country in columns alongside the roads to always be ready for deployment with the artillery and trains in between'. An officer of the Leib-Grenadiers compared the tactics to those used to fight against the Turks and recorded that 'our constant companions the Cossacks' not only 'passed their time with us in actions but even with words, as they would boldly approach our scouts and ask in broken German: "Say, lads, don't you want to go to Berlin?"'[220] Retiring through Jüterbog and Dennewitz – a region the Saxons would soon revisit – Reynier's men repelled a more significant Allied thrust in an extended engagement near Kropstädt on 29 August. Oudinot, however, had abandoned any thought of further offensive operations. The retreat thus continued to Wittenberg where the marshal had decided to establish a defensive arc northeast of the fortress on the right bank of the Elbe. The Saxons were assigned a position on the left-centre of this line and gradually withdrew to this position early on 3 September. On their left, Dąbrowski's Poles from the Wittenberg garrison guarded the gap between 7th Corps and the river, while 12th Corps extended the line on their right to the 4th Corps positions towards Thießen and Euper. Russians under Vorontsov harassed the Saxon rear guard and probed the new position that very morning before launching a more serious attack from Schmilkendorf against Ryssel's brigade shortly after noon. With support from two of LeCoq's battalions, one of Durutte's Würzburg battalions and a horse battery, Ryssel was able to fend off his tormentors after two hours of combat while the Italians and Württembergers clashed with their Prussian pursuers at Thießen. Although the Württemberg 38th Division fought a tough and costly action against Dobschütz's Prussians at Euper the following day, the Saxons were able to use 4 September to rest and recover somewhat.[221] There was even sufficient time and calm for Marshal Ney to review the corps. All these Allied attempts were repulsed, but the Army of Berlin would enjoy only a brief respite before being hurled into action again.

A curious incident occurred on 29 August near Kropstädt during the minor engagements that flared while the corps was retreating to Wittenberg. Oberst von Bose had directed three companies of the *Sahr* Light Infantry to hold a small village about a kilometre ahead of his division's main battle line. The nearby Saxon cavalry were repulsed and the light infantry companies in the village found themselves surrounded by enemy Cossacks, line cavalry and artillery when Major Heinrich von Bünau arrived and assumed command based on his seniority over the company commanders. Assembling these three officers, Bünau remarked that, 'As we cannot retreat and cannot count on support, the fate of the troops will be captivity. Would it not be advisable', he then asked, 'to attempt to gain a favourable capitulation from the enemy?'

The three company commanders were astounded to hear such a proposal from an otherwise brave and respected officer. They unanimously rejected his suggestion and declared that, barring other orders, they would fight on as long as they had ammunition to shoot. Shortly thereafter, the companies were recalled and retreated safely to their division despite enemy artillery fire and the numerous Russian cavalry looming close at hand.[222] Though rebuffed in this instance, Bünau's intention to find a pretext for defection was evident. He would soon try again with greater success.

The defeat at Großbeeren was not the only calamity the Saxon army suffered in August. As noted, the *Prinz Max* battalion had been left in Luckau when 7th Corps marched towards Berlin. Combined with a number of French and Italian sappers and gunners as well as 30 Saxon Uhlans, they constituted a garrison of slightly more than 1,000 officers and men under French Major Delavigne. Unfortunately for the garrison and Delavigne, they became a target for GL von Tauentzien in the wake of Großbeeren. Tauentzien, operating semi-independently on the Army of the North's eastern flank, assigned the task of taking the town to GL von Wobeser whose 7,000 Prussians arrived at Luckau around 11:00 a.m. on 28 August. Wobeser quickly surrounded the town but his attempt to rush the defenders failed and Delavigne refused several demands to surrender. Wobeser thus opened fire with his artillery while his *Schützen* sniped at anyone they could see. The *Prinz Max* Battalion commander, Major Ferdinand Anton Ludwig Erasmus von Könneritz, was badly wounded in this fire and his men began to waver. After Wobeser's howitzers set many buildings ablaze, the city's citizens began loudly abusing Delavigne and demanding that he surrender to stop the shelling. With heavy casualties, his troops uncertain, no hope of rescue, and the citizens threatening insurrection, the major agreed to an honourable capitulation. After resisting all afternoon, therefore, the battalion and the rest of the garrison went into captivity, some 600 Saxons in all, making the *Prinz Maximilian* Regiment perhaps the most luckless unit of the Saxon army in 1813. The only redeeming aspect of this miniature disaster was that the local population helped many of the Saxon soldiers to escape their captors during the night to make their way back to Torgau.[223]

In addition to losing the battalion at Luckau in August, the Saxons lost a significant amount of funds on the 18th when a roving band of Cossacks intercepted a treasury convoy that had been destined for the contingent. Some 142,000 thalers and the escort of 50 or 60 Leib-Grenadiers all fell into enemy hands. Cossacks also captured a large wagon train transporting bread for the Saxon troops, leading LeCoq to report that he was 'in the unfortunate anxiety of not being able to satisfy even the current distribution'. This incident also highlighted the generally poor state of logistics even at this early stage of the autumn campaign. Comparing the situation with his experiences in 1812, LeCoq wrote that the circumstances thus far 'could only offer us the gloomiest views of the future'.[224]

Dennewitz: Disaster in the Dust[225]

There was neither time nor need for the Saxons to make major organisational changes during the brief halt outside Wittenberg. Battle casualties and illness, however, made some alterations imperative. Oberst von Bose was thus designated to replace the badly wounded GL von Sahr as division commander and the light cavalry came under Oberst Adam Friedrich August von Lindenau from the Hussar Regiment when sickness forced Gablenz to retire to Dresden. The only order of battle adjustments were the consolidation of the *Low* Regiment into a single battalion and the reduction in the corps' artillery component owing to the losses at Großbeeren. The major change for the entire Army of Berlin, of course, was Ney's appointment to overall command and Oudinot's relegation back to 12th Corps.

Ney reached Wittenberg on the afternoon of 3 September and wasted no time complying with Napoleon's intentions. The Saxons were involved in minor actions against probing Allied patrols in which the *Prinz Anton* Infantry, I/*Low* and a Würzburg battalion gamely repulsed the enemy thrusts with the support of a horse battery. Some skirmishing took place on the 4th as well, but that did not deter the marshal from reviewing the troops as described above. He also altered the Army of Berlin's organisation, attaching the 2nd Polish Infantry of Dąbrowski's division to Durutte, and adding several Polish cavalry squadrons to his order of battle before leaving the Wittenberg area for Baruth on 5 September with his entire force. The 7th Corps with some 18,000 men under arms, including approximately 11,600 Saxons, was not engaged in the fighting around Zahna that day but marched with great caution owing to the persistent danger posed by the swarming Allied cavalry.

That same caution was applied the following day as the corps headed towards Dennewitz. In stark contrast to Großbeeren, 6 September was hot and dry. The men thus marched along sandy tracks raising billowing clouds of dust that parched their throats and made it almost impossible to distinguish friend from foe at any reasonable distance. Bertrand's corps led the army's advance and had already been engaged north of the Ahe-Bach for about three hours when Reynier's troops began arriving on the field between 1:00 and 2:00 that afternoon. Bertrand's situation was precarious. Grappling with Tauentzien to his front, he now discerned Bülow's troops

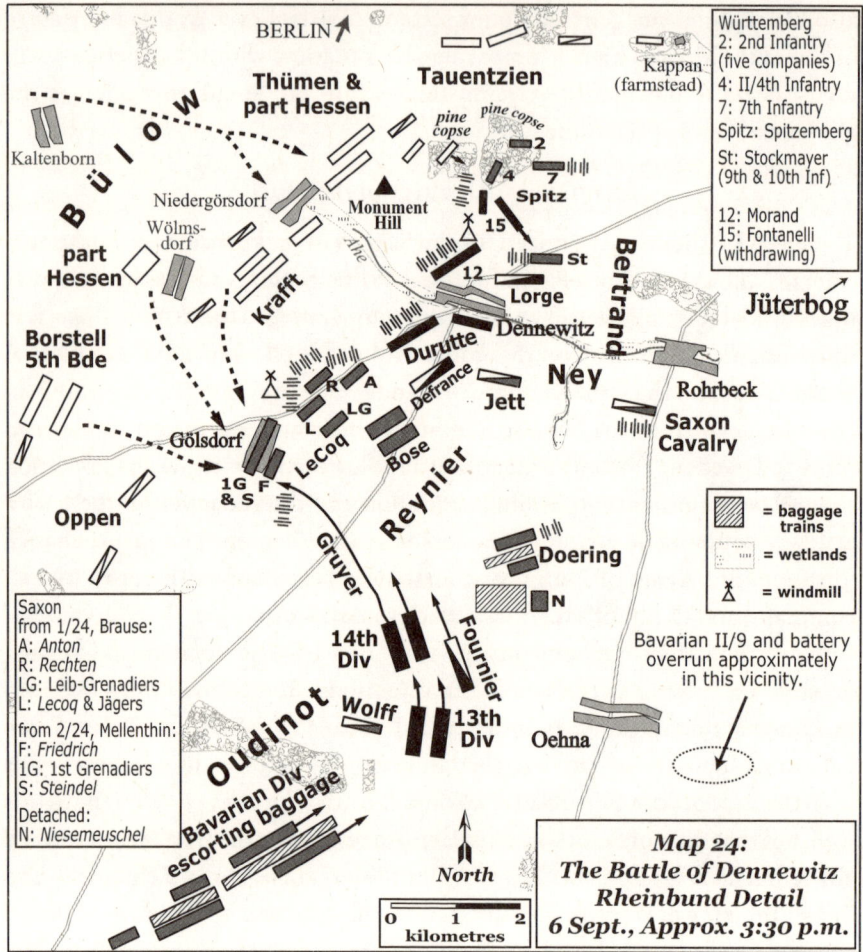

Map 24:
The Battle of Dennewitz
Rheinbund Detail
6 Sept., Approx. 3:30 p.m.

advancing to threaten his left towards what would become the 'monument hill'. Chaos reigned in his rear as Lorge's fleeing cavalry division and other fugitives spread panic among the corps trains. Reynier's arrival, though delayed by Ney's march dispositions and individual decisions by Reynier and Oudinot, was thus timely. His battalions steadily forged their way through what Cerrini called 'this stream of confusion',[226] Durutte with an attached squadron of hussars marching to Dennewitz to shore up Bertrand's left while the two Saxon divisions peeled off to the left towards Gölsdorf. The Saxon cavalry, on the other hand, trotted to the right towards Rohrbeck to block the menace of Allied cavalry north of the Ahe-Bach around Jüterbog. The dust was so thick that a Prussian battery and accompanying cavalry only knew they were near the enemy when a Saxon battery showered them with canister. The Saxons were equally surprised when Prussian guns took them under fire in the 'impenetrable dust' as they waited on the road before turning left to Gölsdorf.[227] 'Only the cool composure of the Saxon commander [Reynier], supported by the excellent discipline in the corps, allowed the battalions to be led (amidst a rain of balls from the enemy guns) through that indescribable tangle of baggage and retreating cavalry against the enemy in good order,' recalled a soldier in the *Prinz Friedrich* Regiment.[228]

The 25th Division had led the march to Großbeeren, but this time Durutte's 32nd Division was in the van. It was thus Jarry's brigade of French and Würzburg troops that Ney called forward to shore up the 4th Corps' left flank. LeCoq's 24th Division was next in the line of march and, as Durutte moved towards the monument hill, Mellenthin's brigade swung left towards Gölsdorf. This village, at the far right of Bülow's line, was held by the Fusilier Battalion of the 3rd East Prussian Infantry from Krafft's brigade. Mellenthin cleared the Prussian battalion out of Gölsdorf with the 1st Grenadiers and *Steindel*, while Brause's infantry unfolded along the low ridge to the right (north) of the village in support of a line of guns. Like many other bits of relatively high ground in this region, the 'ridge' was topped by a distinctive windmill which soon became a prominent battlefield landmark for the Saxons (a replica stands there today). An impressive and deadly array of artillery soon appeared around this windmill. The gun line initially included both of LeCoq's 6-pounder batteries and the 12-pounder battery, but a battery from Bose's 25th Division soon joined while Bose's other guns unlimbered on the southern side of Gölsdorf. The *Prinz Friedrich* Regiment was held in support just outside the village and Bose's infantry were posted slightly further to the east to LeCoq's right rear. To the right of the Saxons, Jarry's men conducted a 'well-executed' advance but were forced to withdraw south of the stream owing to the retreat of 4th Corps.[229] This retrograde shift left Durutte behind Dennewitz with Defrance's dragoon division covering the space between his ranks and the Saxons while his battery added to the weight of iron opposing the Prussians in this sector. Fournier's squadrons deployed to the southeast to protect 7th Corps' left flank.

The time was now approaching 3:00 p.m. and the Prussians, worried by the Saxon move against their weak right and spying the clouds of dust in the distance that presaged the arrival of new enemy forces, launched an attempt to retake Gölsdorf. Borstell's brigade was approaching from the west, but the attack did not await his arrival. Seven Prussian battalions from Krafft and Hessen-Homburg thus stormed up the gentle slope and pushed the defenders back into the middle of the tiny village. Mellenthin threw *Prinz Friedrich* into the fray and a lengthy, costly close-quarters struggle ensued, with the

Prussians more or less west of the village's central street and the Saxons to the east. Curiously, a tacit zone of peace seems to have been recognised around the village fountain. Wounded men of both sides sought refuge there and soldiers would dash over to slake their thirst or fill a water bottle unharmed before returning to the vicious fight.[230] The Prussians eventually prevailed and Mellenthin withdrew into the open ground east of Gölsdorf. The Saxon 6-pounder batteries also pulled back slightly but remained in action repelling half-formed Prussian efforts to push beyond the village. Borstell's brigade, no longer needed to attack Gölsdorf, deployed west and southwest, but the Saxon artillery, reinforced by a French battery, curtailed his attempts to advance.

The dust the Prussians had observed was generated by Oudinot's men. In response to Reynier's urgent requests, the marshal sent his lead brigade towards the southern end of Gölsdorf while the rest of his parched men trudged up behind. Commanding this lead brigade was GB Antoine Gruyer of Guilleminot's division and, as Gruyer's infantry and battery deployed, Mellenthin exploited the arrival of this welcome support to return to the attack. The Prussians, surprised and disorganised after the confused struggle to take the village, were once again ejected. The loss of Gölsdorf forced Borstell to retire slightly and provided a solid pivot for a broader French advance.

The crisis of the battle had arrived. Oudinot's corps was ready to enter the action and the entire Prussian right seemed in danger. Indeed, a frustrated Saxon officer later wrote: 'At a time when the 12th Corps could have made the greatest contribution to the outcome of the affair, it marched by its right to the army's right wing on Marshal Ney's orders.' Bülow responded by ordering a renewed advance, but the possibility existed that his right would be defeated before the distant Russians and Swedes could arrive to shift the numerical balance in the Allies' favour. Instead, as Major Maximilian von Schreibershofen, chief of staff of Bose's 25th Division, wrote in his report: 'In this moment, when the 12th Corps could have given the most splendid decision by a rapid advance, it marched off to the right by platoons to the right flank where it had been directed by Marshal Ney's orders.'[231] A 'most splendid decision' was hardly a foregone conclusion, but Ney's orders and Oudinot's obdurate obedience forfeited whatever chance the Army of Berlin had for a victory that day.

Rather than marching to victory, Ney's army collapsed. Oudinot disengaged Guilleminot's division with difficulty and marched off towards Rohrbeck as ordered. All he would leave behind in response to Reynier's pleas was a battalion (II/9) and a battery from the Bavarian division. Given the battlefield conditions, of course, Oudinot's battalions raised enormous clouds of dust as they turned about and tramped away behind Reynier's men. The Prussians took the dust as a sign of a French retreat and launched themselves at Gölsdorf and the adjoining windmill height with renewed vigour. The Saxons and Gruyer offered tenacious resistance. 'The bayonet and the musket butt were the quietest, deadliest weapons', according to Vollborn, and as ammunition ran low 'each side took from the cartridge pouches inside the houses & fought like madmen'. His experience also illustrates the deadly nature of the fighting. On pulling back from Gölsdorf, he found that the basket of his sword hilt had been smashed, a musket ball had driven into his officer's gorget, two had passed through his shako and five through the hem of his overcoat.[232] The Saxons outside Gölsdorf were also under heavy fire. Standing in a battalion square adjacent to the village, Leutnant von Larisch saw several of his fellow officers wounded and took two holes in his shako that he attributed to Prussians firing from the church tower. As Vollborn indicated, however, LeCoq's two brigades and the Saxon artillery were nearly out of ammunition and the Prussians were able to seize the area around the windmill.

The Saxon position quickly became untenable. Pressed in the front by Prussians trying to advance out of Gölsdorf and with their left flank denuded owing to Gruyer's withdrawal with the rest of 12th Corps, they now saw that Durutte too had been forced back, jeopardising their right flank as well. Moreover, the dust stirred up by Oudinot's move aroused confusion and apprehension.[233] Some Saxons thought this meant the French were abandoning them on the field of battle; others feared that enemy cavalry were rushing to attack them from the rear. Afraid that they would be cut off and cut up, they began to withdraw. Some retired in good order. Reynier reported to Napoleon that Oudinot had formed his 12th Corps into squares and that the Saxons passed through the gaps between these to re-form on the far side. The 1st Light Infantry and the Jägers, for example, conducted a counterattack to blunt the Prussian push on the windmill height and fell back in fine style. Other elements, including most of the artillery pieces with their now-empty caissons, hastened to the rear in a degree of disarray. Defrance's cavalry made some effort to stem the enemy advance with what Reynier described as 'a fine charge' by his brigade of dragoons.[234] In contrast, the Saxons complained that the charges were half-hearted and left them vulnerable to the Allied horse.

In any case, Defrance could do nothing to restore the overall situation. Indeed, the French squadrons were soon tumbling back, and the retiring Saxon infantry found itself disordered as these horsemen and their own batteries crashed through their ranks in their hurry to escape (the fleeing troopers apparently included a squadron of the Westphalian Chevaulegers-Garde who had also been sent to assist). Oudinot's men were also thrown into confusion, a matter he blamed on the Saxons who 'broke and fell upon four of my battalions which caused a moment of disorder'.[235] Fournier's division, which had not been engaged at all, was 'more concerned with saving itself than in maintaining order', in the words of a bitter French brigade commander, and contributed to the growing chaos when it fled after receiving a few Prussian shells.[236] 'Few of the charges of our cavalry had any success,' reported one Saxon officer, 'These troops did not endure the artillery fire and were the first to abandon the field of battle where they had done almost nothing but occupy the intervals' (that is, between the infantry units and artillery batteries).[237] With Prussian cavalry appearing suddenly out of the dust, the Saxons formed small squares as they retreated towards Oehna and the hoped-for safety of the forests behind. Even units that managed to form square found themselves in danger owing to the murk and confusion as Reynier related: 'A body of enemy cavalry entered the square of the Saxon 1st Light Infantry in the darkness and sabred some of them before they could tell if they were friends or enemies.'[238]

Other retreating units also had difficulties. As the battle diary of Mellenthin's brigade recorded, the men of the *Steindel* Infantry found a welcome caisson of infantry ammunition as they withdrew from Gölsdorf and,

> The eagerness with which the men and NCOs tried to refill their cartridge pouches in order to face the enemy once again was laudable ... but all the efforts of the officers to conduct this business in an orderly fashion were in vain ... despite the enemy canister fire, the regiment was indeed partly re-formed, but before a square could be created, it was broken up by enemy cavalry.

Nonetheless, 'Given the many recruits who had only been trained in the camp around Görlitz, what had been achieved up to that point was admirable.' Now, however, many were 'carried helplessly away as if by a flood'.[239]

The circumstances of the ensuing retreat are as shrouded in contradiction as the battlefield was in dust. Both at the time and later, Rheinbund Germans and French accused each other of retreating in disarray as contrasted with the disciplined order of their own troops. What is clear is that the scene between the Ahe-Bach and Oehna as evening approached was one of panicked flight in which only a few units of any nationality managed to maintain their cohesion.[240] Leutnant Albrecht von Holtzendorff, LeCoq's adjutant, attempted to describe what he witnessed:

> When one looked over the battlefield, one saw a vast sea of ruins; cannon, often only pulled by two horses, ammunition-, equipment-, administrative- and forage-wagons tangled together or crossing the columns of marching troops; riderless horses, isolated groups of fugitives, generals without troops, all covered the broad plain and one had to be very pleased in this great confusion – Reynier called it an avalanche – that our troops still marched in relative order and always obeyed orders. During the later pursuit, this order was threatened and often disrupted by shellfire, terrain difficulties, ignorance of the roads and the arrival of darkness; but with all this the battalions always remained prepared for action.[241]

Holtzendorff may have been overly generous in his praise of his countrymen, but the Saxons, Poles ('following with outstanding composure and steadiness') and at least some of the Bavarians seem to have retained their discipline as well as if not better than many of the French regiments. Parts of the Saxon contingent and the Bavarian II/9 Infantry, for example, briefly delayed the Allied pursuit on a slight elevation near Oehna before being overwhelmed, while Reynier employed the Saxon Hussars, the 2nd Grenadier Battalion and Hauptmann Carl Moritz Birnbaum's horse battery to cover the retreating army's left. Similarly, though his 25th Division had been dragged away in the confusion of the general retreat, Oberst von Bose was able to impose a modicum of order, helped by Defrance's dragoons in a renewed charge. Nonetheless, the *König* Battalion lost its flag before it could gain the safety of Bose's formation.[242]

Leutnant von Larisch left a vivid description of the infantry's travails:

> We reached a little rise; here square was formed again, then it was over into closed company columns. The various bodies of troops crowded together ever more, so that the march continued with multiple columns next to each other. Pursued by enemy guns, all accelerated to a speed and length of stride that almost exceeded human strength.

Larisch and other officers in the rear of the columns called out to slow the pace but were merely told to keep up. An enemy battery pelted them from one side, and they noticed behind them a fairly large body of cavalry that they took to be Württembergers. They were soon disabused of this happy notion.

> Suddenly there arose a loud clash of arms; the column received a blow that shoved it some 20 paces sideways to the right. In the first moment, it was thought that the cause was our battery slamming into us with its horses;

but in the steadily rapid march one soon learned that it was occasioned by the attack of the enemy cavalry that had been following us for so long and that we had misidentified... the rearmost of us thereby jammed into those ahead; stepped on their gaiters and shoes; many fell, were cut to bits, stabbed and trod upon by the horses and, before one was even aware of what was happening, separated from the mass by the excessive pace of the unrelenting march. The disorder was even greater when the columns, pursued by the enemy artillery, came upon the park- and wagon-columns all jammed together near the woods. Separations occurred and the march proceeded in large and small sections according to whim and individual best judgement; in the main, however, all hurried through Herzberg and Annaburg towards Torgau.[243]

Night and Prussian exhaustion brought welcome relief. Unlike Larisch's column, some 'left the battlefield without seeing another enemy' to arrive in Torgau on 7 September as an anonymous Saxon recalled 'with his little band completely untroubled'.[244] Though the pursuit was not pressed with the vigour some expected, all four French corps lost heavily in the disordered retreat through the darkness. Efforts by Reynier and other officers to slow the flight and cobble together a coherent rear guard were swamped by the fleeing, leaderless masses. Men, guns and vehicles of all descriptions fell into Allied hands during the night. Coats and faces covered with dust, the soldiers gave up inquiring about one another's regiments and simply asked in exhaustion: 'Are you Saxon?' In a case that illustrates the rampant confusion that encumbered all sides, a Prussian raiding party surprised Hauptmann Carl Anton Ludwig Dietrich's battery in the darkness and seized his eight guns but had to abandon them when it discovered itself surrounded by large numbers of retreating enemy units. Likewise, Saxon hussars escorting Reynier's personal baggage rode unnoticed through a Prussian-occupied village to make a quiet escape.

When the mobs of men and horses reached Torgau on 7 September, 'the great haste and disorder of this retreat' was unmistakable to Saxon Oberst Johann Anton Friedrich von Birnbaum who was posted in the fortress. The shattered army gradually began to make its way to the western side of the Elbe on 8 September but came under enemy fire as it did so, igniting utter panic among the fearful fugitives. 'The tumult in the city during that day', reported Birnbaum, 'was beyond any description as the wounded were lying about on the streets without any food or help, the streets themselves were jammed with innumerable vehicles and everyone wanted to crowd into the fortress.' French GB Brun agreed. 'Our men were so demoralised that they did not even fight back,' he would later recall, 'Five columns pressed together wanting to enter the citadel at the same time. The disorder was unbelievable.'[245]

As 7th Corps passed through this chaos on 8 September to assemble on the western bank of the Elbe, Reynier considered his losses in the latest failed attempt to prepare an advance on Berlin. Having marched to Dennewitz with approximately 11,600 men under arms, the Saxons had lost 3,290 between 5 and 7 September, leaving only 8,373 fit for duty in the contingent's 10 September report. Losses were almost evenly split between the two divisions, suggesting that the 25th Division contributed to the rear-guard fighting while the corps attempted to withdraw at the end of the battle. Two-thirds of the men on the casualty rosters, however, were listed as missing. Most of these were almost certainly captured during the chaotic retreat, but it is impossible to know how many in this number deserted, how many were genuinely captured and how many had been left behind dead but unrecorded. Some percentage would also return to the ranks in the coming days and there were some, such as lightly wounded soldier Frenzel, who struggled to keep up with the retreating battalions to avoid capture: 'I thought it better to escape with the big group than to drag along behind alone and give myself up as a prisoner.' Durutte's division was in even worse condition. He probably had some 4,600 men when the corps departed Wittenberg, but Dennewitz left his command with only 2,593 present under arms a week later. The battle also cost the Saxons twelve guns, all from the foot batteries that had been engaged on the windmill height near Gölsdorf. Muskets were another problem as many men had thrown theirs away on the retreat. LeCoq thus issued a stern order of the day on 8 September stipulating that 'every soldier who returns without his weapon shall be punished with 40 blows on the rear if he cannot display a significant wound. No excuses will be accepted'.[246]

Dennewitz also added to Franco-Saxon tensions. In their reports to Napoleon and Berthier, both Ney and Oudinot specifically blamed the Saxons for the defeat. Their tendentious portrayals of events also influenced GD Anne Charles Lebrun, Napoleon's personal representative, in his post-battle reports. Ney was especially keen to designate the Saxons as scapegoats for a loss that mostly resulted from his own failings. His knowledge of Durutte's complaints about Saxon recalcitrance back in March/April and his personal experience with Thielmann's truculence may have left him predisposed to mistrust the Saxons, but his comments after Dennewitz were particularly pointed. While denigrating his senior officers and all allied troops in general, he reserved special accusations for the Saxon contingent which 'appeared weak'. 'The battle was won', he wrote, 'but the 7th Corps beat a retreat carrying with it part of the 12th Corps' so as to leave a gap in the line. In addition to his official reports, Ney shared his demeaning view of the Saxons with fellow officers while in Torgau after the battle. 'He had remarked during the course of the campaign that we could not place much confidence in the Saxons,' wrote GB Brun. 'On departing [Torgau], he ordered me to have all the Saxons leave and to send them to General Reynier.'[247] This, of course, did not happen (not that Brun did not try), but it indicates Ney's state of mind vis-à-vis the Saxon contingent.

French mistrust was obvious to the Saxons in Torgau at the time as Birnbaum related to Gersdorff on 10 September, but friction increased when Ney's ire was made public. An edited version of his account of Dennewitz was published in *Le Moniteur Universel*, the official French paper, on 20 September and later carried by the principal Saxon paper, the *Leipziger Zeitung*. Although this published report only mentioned that 'two divisions of 7th Corps failed' rather than citing the Saxons by name, Ney's assertion that Durutte's division had 'performed well' left no doubt that his obloquy was directed at the Saxons.[248] Ney's report did not appear in the Leipzig paper until 29 September, but it seems likely the Saxon officers knew of his disapprobation much earlier.

Whatever the timing, Ney's denunciations prompted LeCoq to protest to Reynier and Reynier to Napoleon. Directly addressing the thinly veiled condemnation of the Saxons in Ney's published report, Reynier disputed 'these false assertions' and assured Napoleon that he would 'prove to Your Majesty that the 7th Corps and its commander did everything they were supposed to do in this instance'. He then outlined his version of events: the 7th Corps retired in good order between the squares of the 12th, re-formed and established itself between the other two corps until the French cavalry on the left (Fournier) and the directionless baggage train sowed disorder in the ranks. He maintained that his corps had suffered fewer losses than the other two 'even though it was the most engaged'. While asking the emperor to have confidence in his own devotion as well as that of his troops, he also made his distaste for Ney unmistakable: 'I will execute well any operation you charge me with directly or that may be ordered by other commanders.' Reynier shared his letter with LeCoq, telling the Saxon general that, 'Your troops retired in good order and showed fine form after having conducted yourselves very well in the attacks on Gölsdorf.'[249]

For the Saxons, Dennewitz was another example of the 'disunity, insubordination and incapacity' among the French corps commanders that denied them an otherwise certain success, as Major von Hausen wrote to his brother on 13 September. If the 12th Corps had arrived as intended, he

Chart 19: Saxon Troops in 7th Corps, 10 September 1813

		bns/sqdns	present under arms
24th Division (1st Saxon)	*GL von LeCoq*		
1st Brigade	*Oberst von Brause*		
I/Leib-Grenadier Battalion	Hauptmann von Dreßler	1	–
1st Light Infantry Regiment *LeCoq*	Major von Rade	2	–
Rechten Infantry Battalion	Major von Hausen	1	–
Jäger Company	Premierleutnant von Zychlinski	–	–
2nd Brigade	*GM von Mellenthin*		
1st Grenadier Battalion	Major von Spiegel	1	–
(Grenadiers of *Max*, *Rechten*, *Friedrich* and *Steindel*)			
Prinz Friedrich August Infantry Battalion	Major von Brand	1	–
Steindel Infantry Battalion	Major von Larisch	1	–
3rd Foot Artillery Battery	Hauptmann Dietrich	6 × 6-pdr, 2 × howitzer	–
Train		–	–
Sapper Company		–	–
25th Division (2nd Saxon)	*GL von Zeschau*		
1st Brigade	*Oberst von Ryssel*		
2nd Grenadier Battalion	Major Anger	1	–
(Grenadiers of *König*, *Niesemeuschel*, *Anton* and *Low*)			
Prinz Anton Infantry Battalion	Major von Holleufer	1	–
Low Infantry Battalion	Hauptmann Roos	1	–
2nd Brigade	*Oberst von Bose*		
2nd Light Infantry Regiment *Sahr*	Major von Selmnitz	2	–
König Infantry Battalion	Major von Bünau	1	–
Niesemeuschel Infantry Battalion	Major von Bose	1	–
4th Foot Artillery Battery	Hauptmann Zandt	6 × 6-pdr, 2 × howitzer	–
Train		–	–
Light Cavalry Brigade	*Oberst von Lindenau*		
Hussar Regiment	Major von Feilitzsch	8	–
Prinz Clemens Uhlan Regiment	Major von Trotha	5	–
2nd Horse Artillery Battery	Hauptmann Probsthayn	4 × 6-pdr, 2 × howitzer	–
Reserve Artillery			
1st Horse Artillery Battery	Hauptmann Birnbaum	4 × 6-pdr, 2 × howitzer	–
12-pdr Artillery Battery	Hauptmann Rouvroy I	6 × 12-pdr, 2 × howitzer	–
Main Artillery Park	Major von Großmann	–	–
Total		–	**8,373**
Saxons remaining in Torgau		40 sappers, 380 artillerymen, 451 in depots	

Note: Artillery distribution is as shown in the 7th Corps 'Situations' but it is possible that all four foot batteries remained, only with three guns and one howitzer each (Titze, *Artillerie-Korps*, pp. 24–6).

Source: Cerrini, *Feldzüge der Sachsen*, pp. 273–5. Saxons in Torgau: 10 September 1813 report to Gersdorf, Sächsisches Hauptstaatsarchiv SHSA, Generalstab, 11339, Nr. 285.

asserted, 'the victory would have been ours'. Instead: 'We are, it is said, betrayed and sold out, and our bitterness against the French has reached the boiling point.'[250] The discouragement that followed the loss of two battles in quick succession and the sense that they had been abandoned and accused after doing their best, of course, was layered atop a foundation of pre-existing anti-French sentiment. Leutnant von Larisch, for example, wrote that 'It was distressing to hear an otherwise brave senior officer, Maj. von T. [Major Ernst von Tiling], in exaggerated enthusiasm for the German cause, express his joy at the enemy's victory [at Dennewitz].'[251]

Ney's belatedly published report on Dennewitz, though damaging, was not the sword that 'cut the last band through which the Saxons believed themselves tied to Napoleon's fate', as General Funck assumed.[252] It was indicative, however, of the mounting problems in the relationship – problems that would only grow more evident during the coming weeks with sullen murmurs, outbreaks of disaffection and even defection becoming more common as the army headed for Leipzig and the end of the alliance with France.

The March to Defection:
Approaching Ruin with Giant Steps

The losses incurred at Dennewitz forced yet another reorganisation of the Saxon contingent. This came as part of the larger reorganisation in which Oudinot was reassigned to the Imperial Guard, his 12th Corps was dissolved, and his two French divisions were merged as the 13th under Guilleminot.[253] The two Saxon divisions were likewise combined into one as the 24th Division of the Grande Armée with GL Heinrich Wilhelm von Zeschau in command. Although the consolidation of the two divisions into one was viewed as logical if regrettable, LeCoq's recall surprised and dismayed many in the contingent. Mellenthin was reassigned at the same time. 'This was a great loss', noted an officer, 'as both generals were held in high regard by the soldiers.' Reynier was also unhappy. He tried without success to have the decision reversed and LeCoq departed with a personal note of gratitude from the king. For officers and soldiers who had been through the Russian campaign, LeCoq was a father figure who had sustained the Saxon corps through the worst trials. Zeschau, on the other hand, was an unknown quantity. Though competent, experienced and loyal, he was characterised like Reynier as cold and distant, not one to earn the soldiers' trust and affection quickly.[254] Coming in the wake of two stinging defeats, poor logistical arrangements and numerous frictions with the French, LeCoq's unexpected departure seemed another reason for Saxony's soldiers to be discouraged about the present and worried about the future.

With this new configuration and new commander, the Saxons participated in the series of fruitless manoeuvres along the Elbe from mid-September through mid-October, including a brief foray across the river to the eastern shore. Frequent patrols and reconnaissance missions sparked occasional skirmishes, but the Saxons were not involved in any major engagements during this period. Anger towards the French, however, continued to mount. As noted earlier, Ney, fearing allied treachery ('the Saxons manifest the worst possible attitude'), attempted to remove all the Saxons from Torgau. This measure irritated the Saxons and prompted another rebuttal from Reynier: 'This news has the worst possible effect on the minds of the Saxons, who are already very affected by the latest events and the conduct of the troops in their country.' It also earned the marshal an imperial rebuke: 'The Emperor charges me to inform you that he is dissatisfied with the measures which have been taken in relation to the Saxons and which can only upset them,' wrote Berthier on 11 September, 'His Majesty's intention is that all the depots of the Saxon corps remain in Torgau and that we have respect for the Saxons. Give the necessary orders for this.' There were disputes over foraging with the French complaining that Saxon troops returned requisitioned livestock to local people while the Saxons were furious at the devastation their putative allies wreaked upon their homeland. The cattle incident provoked one of Ney's most quoted remarks. He saw the act of removing livestock the French had requisitioned and distributing it among the nearby Saxon villages as 'a sort of insurrection'. 'Such is the spirit of the Saxon army', he told Berthier, 'and it is not to be doubted that these troops, particularly the cavalry, will turn their arms against us at the first opportunity.' Ney also complained that the Saxons exaggerated enemy strength in their reporting and all the French allies panicked when faced with a few Cossacks.[255]

As these examples illustrate, the key challenge for Zeschau and his officers in these weeks was coping with threats to morale and discipline rather than combat. The most serious of these challenges arose only one day after Zeschau's assumption of command. During the night of 22/23 September, Major von Bünau, commander of the *König* Battalion, defected to the Allies, taking his 360 men with him. The battalion, temporarily attached to the light cavalry brigade, had been on outpost duty and Bünau, whose behaviour right after Großbeeren had hinted at such inclinations, took the opportunity to switch sides. He seems to have been inspired and abetted by one of the company commanders, but it seems unlikely that the other officers or his men knew of the plan as the conspirators told the cavalry outposts that they had been instructed to make a reconnaissance towards the enemy's positions around

Dessau. Compounding the embarrassment for the Saxons, a combined patrol of 50 Uhlans and hussars was surprised, surrounded and largely captured by Cossacks and Swedish dragoons later that same day.

Zeschau was appalled at Bünau's defection. He had served with Bünau in the same regiment for many years and had 'always known him as a man of honour'. 'Nonetheless,' he wrote to Friedrich August, 'I find myself forced to report that he has been unfaithful in his duty to Your Majesty, his country and the principles of honour.' He took immediate corrective action. Visiting each brigade, he recounted 'the infamy of this action', had the officers renew their oaths of loyalty to the king, and instructed them 'to employ every means so that this miserable example will have no influence on the troops'. Each of the brigade commanders later sent a personal letter to the king reasserting 'their loyal attachment to Your Majesty and their disgust at this dishonourable step'. Reynier was equally shocked at the desertion of 'a highly esteemed officer who seemed devoted to us', but informed Berthier that, 'The Saxon generals and officers are deeply chagrined by this event and indignant at the conduct of these two officers [that is, Bünau and the company commander].' Major Cerrini later wrote that the 'general disapproval' the battalion had earned was heightened because its commander had acted 'without considering the attitude and fate of those remaining behind'. The battalion had thus 'secretly left its comrades in arms in the lurch and thereby committed a crime against the spirit of comradeship which had allowed the Saxon army to uphold its discipline even in the most unfortunate circumstances'. Leutnant von Wolffersdorff lamented that, 'This incident increased French mistrust of us and was disapproved of by all Saxons under these circumstances; as an individual officer may never make his own politics and leave his comrades vulnerable to all the evil consequences thereof.'[256]

For his part, Friedrich August issued a proclamation to the army on 26 September reminding the officers and men of his paternal care for 45 years of rule and assuring them of his faith that they would hold fast to their king and their flag: 'A strict sense of duty will lift you over everything that could make you falter in the fulfilment of your obligations.' A royal decree released the following day adjured all his subjects to remain true to their king in accordance with 'the most sacred laws' and warning those who allowed themselves to be misled by Allied propaganda that they would be regarded as criminals and 'punished with unrelenting severity' as 'rebels and traitors'. Bünau, tried and convicted *in absentia* by court martial on 5 October, was declared an outlaw. Even though it was the regiment that carried his royal title, Friedrich August never wore its uniform again.[257]

Chart 20: Saxon Troops in 7th Corps, 21 September 1813

		bns/sqdns	present under arms
24th Division	*GL von Zeschau*		
1st Brigade	*Oberst von Brause*		
1st Light Infantry Regiment *LeCoq*	Major von Rade	1	767
Rechten Infantry Battalion	Major von Hausen	1	312
Prinz Friedrich August Infantry Battalion	Major von Brand	1	595
Steindel Infantry Battalion	Major von Larisch	1	637
1st Grenadier Battalion	Major von Spiegel	1	339
(Grenadiers of *Max, Rechten, Friedrich* and *Steindel*)			
Jäger Company	Premierleutnant von Zychlinski	–	77
2nd Brigade	*GM von Ryssel*		
2nd Grenadier Battalion	Major Anger	1	329
(Grenadiers of *König, Niesemeuschel, Anton* and *Low*)			
König Infantry Battalion	Major von Bünau	1	309
Niesemeuschel Infantry Battalion	Major von Bose	1	546
Prinz Anton Infantry Battalion	Major von Holleufer	1	609
Low Infantry Battalion	Hauptmann Roos	1	257
2nd Light Infantry Regiment *Sahr*	Major von Selmnitz	1	716
Artillery			
3rd Foot Artillery Battery	Hauptmann Dietrich	6 guns	137
4th Foot Artillery Battery	Hauptmann Zandt	6 guns	137
1st Horse Artillery Battery	Hauptmann Birnbaum	4 guns	(incl. with 2nd)
2nd Horse Artillery Battery	Hauptmann Probsthayn	4 guns	215
12-pounder Artillery Battery	Hauptmann Rouvroy I	6 guns	180
Artillery Park and train	Major von Großmann	–	552
Sappers and Pontooneers		–	68
Light Cavalry Brigade	*Oberst von Lindenau*		
Hussar Regiment	Major von Fabrice	8	623
Prinz Clemens Uhlan Regiment	Major von Trotha	5	638
Total		–	8,043

Note: I/Leib-Grenadier Battalion en route to Dresden to join Imperial Guard.

Source: Cerrini, *Feldzüge der Sachsen*, pp. 284–6. A 14 September report from Berthier to Napoleon gives the Saxons approximately the same number of cavalry but only 4,842 infantry.

Ney, of course, saw his mistrust vindicated. 'The worst possible spirit reigns among the Saxon generals and officers and even among the soldiers', he wrote, 'and it is much to be feared that all this will entail and cause the defection of the other allied troops.'[258] In fact, however, Bünau's example inspired indignation rather than emulation. An appeal Bünau issued several days later calling on Saxon soldiers to join a Swedish–Saxon legion garnered almost no response.[259] Bertrand noted that some Saxons who had deserted in the wake of Dennewitz had taken service with the enemy after being 'menaced with Siberia' but had 'thrown aside their arms on seeing our troops' and escaped. Even regimental histories written in the late nineteenth century during the peak of anti-French, Prusso-German nationalism regarded his defection as a deed that 'from the standpoint of the soldier must be most harshly condemned'.[260]

It is hardly surprising that Bünau's act sparked intense discussion in the Saxon ranks. Anger at the French was intermingled with adherence to military honour and loyalty to the king.[261] Newly promoted Leutnant August Kummer of the *Prinz Anton* Infantry thus recalled that, 'The greater part of the corps regarded this act as an infamous betrayal, the lesser part would have happily followed his example as we had every reason to be dissatisfied with the French business because the French behaved in Saxony as if they were in enemy territory.' Similarly, Leutnant Vollborn poignantly described the contending emotions he and his compatriots experienced as they faced their uncertain future in the light of this latest development:

> The observer could not miss the indignation at such an undertaking, but from the depressing circumstances of our troops as well as the sad conditions of the other Rheinbund and French who were operating together with us to oppose an enemy crossing the Elbe, he would also persuade himself that everything was approaching ruin with giant steps. Weather, continual marching back and forth from Torgau to Dessau to defend the left bank of the Elbe; lack of bread, other victuals & shoes; steady reduction of strength on this side, continual rush to arms on the other side; on this side, provinces sucked dry and ruined villages, the potato fields uprooted & spoiled; on that side, relatively regulated supplies & protected provinces in the rear; defeat & dissatisfaction; in short, everything united to our misfortune and signalled an early dissolution of all. And if the gloomy question was raised among us around the meagre watchfire of how this all might end? Then the individual must not act egoistically & rather go down together than save oneself from the chaos through such an honourless act as that of Major v. Bünau, through which this wretch exposed those left behind to mistrust, mockery & shame.[262]

Bünau's defection also had an effect on operations in that Reynier immediately withdrew the Saxons from outpost duty, a move Ney claimed he had been urging for some time. The contingent as a whole thus now remained

The Autumn Campaign: From Defeat to Defection 219

in the second line behind the two French divisions of 7th Corps. Nonetheless, Saxon units continued to conduct reconnaissance and screening missions. Saxon light cavalry patrols captured more than 40 Prussians and a number of vehicles on 13 October, for example, and Kummer's men not only seized two Prussian soldiers during a patrol, but, doubtless more important as far as the men were concerned, a considerable haul of beef cattle and sheep.[263] There are no reports of serious desertion problems, let alone defection to the enemy, on these or any similar expeditions. Other than such occasional patrols and foraging duties, this period was one of fatiguing marching between Torgau and Dessau as Vollborn mentioned. The Saxons participated in the corps' brief excursion across the Elbe during 11–14 October but did not engage in any major combat until they reached the field of Leipzig on the 17th.[264]

Before marching to Leipzig, however, the 7th Corps underwent an imperial review. The corps was near Eilenburg on 9 October when it was instructed to assemble for the emperor's inspection. Napoleon, well aware of the discontent in the Saxon contingent, hoped to use the opportunity to raise morale and encourage fidelity. Gathering all the officers and NCOs, he addressed them in French translated by GD Armand Caulaincourt, Grand Master of the Palace and one of his most trusted senior officers. He highlighted the apposite themes – the threat from Prussia, his desire to expand Saxony, loyalty to their king, fighting for Saxony – and stated that anyone who wanted to join the Allies was free to leave the ranks at once. Unfortunately for the emperor, Caulaincourt's German was poor and the translation awkward. The Saxons, for instance, had to stifle laughs when Napoleon's intended phrase that he was there 'to place himself at their head and lead them to victory' was rendered as asserting he planned 'to sit on their heads'.

Whether or not the Saxons offered the customary *Vive l'Empereur* as their French comrades did at the end of his exhortation is unclear. As historian Roman Töppel observes, it is difficult to penetrate the clouds of post-Napoleonic Prusso-German nationalism that informed subsequent accounts. Some memoirists stress that the Saxons were sullenly silent when called upon to cheer, leaving Napoleon to ride off sour and suspicious, but others, such as Oberstleutnant Ernst Otto Innozenz von Odeleben, Napoleon's Saxon escort officer, simply noted that Napoleon's effort to inspire the Saxon troops was unsuccessful. Major von Hausen, for example, in a 12 October letter to his brother, merely mentions that the review occurred and that five crosses of the Legion of Honour were awarded to each battalion, including to him and to four others of the *Rechten* Infantry. He says nothing of a failure to cheer. Vollborn even claimed that 'At the end of this address there came an echoing cry of *"Vive l'Empereur"* at which our drawn sabres – for so we stood before the emperor – were swung about.' It is also possible that the cheer was offered but only in a perfunctory fashion at the anxious urgings of the officers in response to a plea from the respected Reynier.[265] Whatever the case at the particular moment, the review and Napoleon's address did not ameliorate the widespread resentment and restiveness within the contingent, sentiments that would manifest themselves in action only nine days later.

Leipzig, 16–17 October: Cuirassiers and Guardsmen

Other than depots, garrisons, the sick and a few artillery and engineer troops, the entire Saxon army was now headed for Leipzig.[266] The battalion of the Leib-Grenadiers that had been campaigning with 7th Corps had been called to Dresden as part of the reorganisation after Dennewitz. It departed on 19 September to arrive in the capital on the 21st where it paraded before Friedrich August. The king, apparently motivated by Bünau's defection, convened a private audience for the officers several days later during which he 'asserted his complete satisfaction with how they had thus far fulfilled their duties'. Combined with drafts from II/Leib-Grenadiers to bring it up to strength, the 1st Battalion was incorporated into the French Imperial Guard as a special honour on 4 October.[267] The Saxons thus became part of the 2nd Old Guard Division under GD Philibert Jean-Baptiste François Curial in a brigade commanded by GB Henri Rottembourg that included a Polish Guard Battalion and the lone remaining battalion of the Westphalian Füsilier-Garde. The 1st Battalion and the remaining two companies of the 2nd left Dresden with the king on 7 October and marched via Eilenburg to arrive outside Leipzig on the evening of the 14th. Rottembourg's brigade, allotted a spot near Holzhausen, bivouacked under miserable conditions:

> The night was cold and uncommonly stormy, an uninterrupted rain streamed down, there was no material to build huts at all, no watchfire would burn, so that the men ran back and forth just to keep their bodies warm. There was a complete lack of provisions, and the troops were limited to sparse foraging.

The guardsmen of the 1st Battalion were doubtless envious of their comrades in the two companies of II/Leib-Grenadiers who had accompanied the king into Leipzig and thus spent the night in relative comfort.[268]

Friedrich August, whom the grenadiers had been escorting, arrived in Leipzig on the afternoon of 14 October, the anniversary of the Battle of Jena seven years earlier that had led to his alliance with Napoleon. The journey had been slow and arduous for the old king. Napoleon had offered him the choice of staying in Dresden and some of his advisors had recommended the safety of the near-impregnable Königstein fortress, but Friedrich August elected to maintain his proximity to his ally. In part he was motivated by his personal loyalty to Napoleon, in part by a desire to avoid being trapped in Königstein or in Dresden with a French marshal in command of the city and in part because he thought he would have more freedom if he was physically closer to Napoleon (and in the place where the Allied monarchs would soon be gathering). 'Königstein would certainly protect me personally', he told Gersdorff, 'but Saxony would be even more exposed.'[269] He also declined to ensconce himself in Torgau owing to the prevalence of disease in that stronghold. He thus set out on the 7th with his wife and daughter; his brothers Anton and Maximilian remained in Dresden with their households and a royal commission to manage affairs in the king's absence. To protect Friedrich August and his family during their travel to Leipzig, Napoleon had assigned a large detachment from the French Imperial Guard as a supplement to the Saxon Leib-Grenadiers. Many Saxons (at least in their subsequent recollections) took the presence of this substantial French escort as evidence of their sovereign being a captive of the French, an ironic conclusion in that Napoleon doubtless meant it as both a ceremonial honour and as a practical security measure to ensure the king's safety given the Cossack bands and other Allied raiding parties that infested the region the royal cavalcade had to traverse.

Napoleon was near the highway when the king's entourage approached on the 14th. Capitaine Charles Parquin, commanding Napoleon's personal escort that day, recalled that the emperor:

> ...walked some fifty paces down the road and would have walked right up to the king. But the King of Saxony had already alighted and with his hat in his hand he came straight to greet the emperor. I can still picture the king: a tall, handsome old man with powdered wig and long queue. He was wearing a white uniform and the chains of two watches hung at his sides. He hastened to take off his gloves and offer his hand to the emperor, but the latter embraced him, calling him his brother.

The two then proceeded to the royal coach, where Napoleon exchanged a few pleasantries with Queen Amalie and Princess Augusta before taking his leave to return to operational affairs.[270] Friedrich August and his family continued on into Leipzig to take up residence in the 'Königshaus' (or 'Thomashaus') on the city's market square.

The heavy cavalry brigade was also en route to Leipzig. Like the rest of Latour-Maubourg's corps, the two Saxon regiments had endured exhausting forced marches, back and forth from the Silesian border to the Dresden area in September and during the fruitless attempt to intercept Blücher west of the Elbe in early October. Other than an unfortunate small encounter with Cossacks on 19 September near Ortrand (between Cottbus and Dresden, see Map 9) that led to the capture of Oberst von Ziegler, commander of the *Zastrow* Cuirassiers, however, they had seen little combat since the Battle of Dresden in late August. Like the grenadiers, the heavy regiments arrived in the Leipzig area on the night of 14/15 October.[271]

The 15th passed quietly, but the regiments of the 1st Cavalry Corps were on the move early on 16 October after a cheerless night around Schönfeld. Leading the column, the two Saxon regiments unexpectedly came upon Napoleon who smilingly greeted the troopers. With his customary personal touch, he reminded them of their courage at Friedland in 1807 and urged them to show such bravery once again. Proceeding on, the corps trotted into its assigned position just behind Wachau, the Saxons on the right of the line. Here they remained until mid-afternoon, suffering badly from Allied shot and shell as the battle raged to their front. The Saxons took especially heavy losses when a caisson exploded near their ranks. 'This artillery fire was so constant that one could detect no pause and individual shots could not be distinguished,' recalled Rittmeister Christian Gottlob Friedrich Eckhardt of the Leib-Cuirassiers, 'rather the fire of entire batteries crashed together like a battalion volley.' Despite the enemy artillery, much of the men's attention was devoted to the cavalry battle to their right front where Polish regiments, the French Imperial Guard Dragoons and GD Sigismond Frédéric Berckheim's 1st Light Cavalry Division were engaged in a violent clash with Allied regiments between Wachau and Markkleeberg. The Saxons may have indulged in some *Schadenfreude* to see the French Guard Dragoons discomfited as a certain animosity had developed between the two regiments over frictions in bivouacs during the campaign and because many Saxon troopers, like their fellows in 7th Corps, had long been dissatisfied with the French alliance.

While observing the spectacle and waiting under this punishing fire, the *Zastrow* Cuirassiers suddenly received an order to assist Berckheim's men who were tiring after their lengthy struggle with the Allied horse. The regiment immediately swung to the right and headed off but as it trotted past Dösen it came under musket fire from Austrian infantry. 'This caused the regiment some casualties', reported Rittmeister Franz Ludwig August Meerheim, 'but as conditions on the battlefield we were to reach demanded haste, no one concerned himself further with the garrison in the village.' The regiment arrived just as the French were being hurled back after yet another charge 'so that they crashed partly through, partly around the approaching Saxon regiment in wild flight'. The Saxons retained their cohesion, rejected a call by the opposing Austrians of the *Somariva* Cuirassiers to defect and launched a charge of their own only to be overwhelmed and overthrown. 'Friend and foe intermingled, the chase now ran over field and stone at the gallop' until the wild roil of horsemen came upon a French square that opened fire on the Austrians. In an instant, the French and Saxon horsemen halted as if by magic, turned about, captured 80 Austrians and pursued the rest back the way they had come.[272]

Around 3:00 p.m., as this engagement was coming to an end, Murat personally led Bordessoulle's division with the Leib-Cuirassiers in an attack on the Allied centre. The division's specific targets were several large Russian batteries in front of Guldengossa. With the Saxons on the right, the French 2nd, 3rd and 6th Cuirassiers on the left in the first line and the 9th, 11th and 12th Cuirassiers following in reserve, this imposing mass of heavy regiments surged forward. Terrain hindrances forced the regiments to halt and realign several times, but they ignored the increasingly heavy enemy artillery fire and rode past nearby infantry columns to charge the guns as ordered. The Russians managed to drag off some of the pieces, but most fell into the cavalry's hands after a brief and hectic melee. The gunners had taken most of their horses when they fled, however, so the Saxons, in an exposed position and unsupported, could not bring back any of their prizes. They thus rode back to the French lines with only one caisson and a long casualty list as evidence of their success. Rittmeister Eckhardt regretted the absence of 'the cold-blooded courage and judgement' of Latour-Maubourg, who had been badly wounded before the charge. 'Given the bravery with which our side advanced, things must have gone differently had we been able to attack again with the entire line supported by reserves.' The opportunity passed, however, and the Leib-Cuirassiers took no part in the day's remaining actions. Reunited with their sister regiment towards evening, they retired to Stötteritz with the rest of 1st Cavalry Corps, where they stayed through 17 October.[273]

Although the Saxon heavy cavalry regiments thus saw considerable combat on 16 October, the Leib-Grenadiers were not committed to action. They remained in reserve throughout the day, first behind Liebertwolkwitz, then being shifted towards Connewitz in the afternoon to support Poniatowski's tenacious defence of the French right. Here they remained through a night that was 'again very rainy and cold, the slippery earth practically dissolved, a complete lack of straw as well as provisions, but the battalion received some bread, rice and brandy from the supplies of the French Guard the next day'.[274]

Leipzig, 17–18 October: The Division Defects

While some of their compatriots were present around Leipzig for the combat on 16 October, the bulk of the Saxon contingent was still en route to the battlefield where they would both fight and defect two days later. This defection did not transpire all at once. Rather, as outlined below, some elements switched sides deliberately, some surrendered with conditions when surrounded, some were simply captured in combat and others remained with the French. Although several key aspects are lost in the fog of history, the general progress of events is fairly clear.

The Saxons of 7th Corps had marched to Eilenburg on 16 October along with the rest of Reynier's command. Arriving around the town in the evening, the men hoped for a rest and, in the absence of straw, scraped holes for themselves in the earth to construct field shelters.[275] As far as the corps artillery park and baggage train were concerned, Eilenburg would be their home for the next several days. Here they would encamp with the Grande Armée's huge baggage column and come under the authority of GB Durrieu, the French general in charge of the army's park. Left behind by the rapid movements of the armies, the parks and trains would never get to Leipzig. Instead, the long convoy of wagons would trundle off to the relative security of Torgau on the 18th and 19th escorted by the *Low* Battalion (450), a detachment from *Friedrich August* (51), and two 6-pounders loaned by the Bavarian brigade at Durrieu's request.[276] Their fate is described in Chapter 8. In contrast, the respite for the Saxon combat elements (approximately 5,000 men and 22 guns) on the evening of the 16th was painfully brief. A few hours after dispersing to their bivouacs, they were called back into formation and marched through the night on a road 'teeming with soldiers and guns' to reach Taucha at 4:00 a.m. on 17 October. Halting amidst potato fields, the men quickly availed themselves of the opportunity to make a meagre breakfast of potatoes roasted in hot coals in the dawn chill before continuing on towards Leipzig.[277]

All seemed calm, but as they neared a farmstead called 'Heiterer Blick', they were surprised by an explosion of artillery fire towards Schönfeld and the Parthe River. Reynier, expecting battle, swung the corps to the west to face the stream, Saxons in the middle with Durutte on the left and Guilleminot on the right. Deploying as ordered, the men found themselves surrounded by a disordered mass of French cavalry from Arrighi's 3rd Cavalry Corps fleeing an engagement with Blücher's horse on the far side of the Parthe.

The 7th Corps remained steady despite this temporary tumult, the Saxons regarding the routing squadrons with disdain as they watched them flee past 'just as cowardly and in confusion as at Dennewitz and Gölsdorf'. Some of the Saxons at first thought they were being abandoned by the French and a few men whose families lived in the vicinity used the opportunity to sneak off.[278] Zeschau, concerned at the impression created by the disorder among the French, took a moment to address the troops, assuring them of his confidence in their steadfastness and reminding them of their duty. 'In these days we will fight for our king in the truest sense,' he told them, 'his fate, our fate hangs on the outcome of the battle; every true Saxon thus has reason to exert all his strength to fulfil his duty. Are you determined to do so?' Answered with a loud '*Ja!*', he offered a cheer for the king and set about ordering the division for the expected attack convinced that 'a good spirit animated the lads'.[279]

The anticipated attack, however, did not occur, the French cavalry regained its composure and Reynier resumed his march towards Leipzig. His assigned position was in and around Paunsdorf. Here he placed the Saxon infantry with Durutte's battalions, each division receiving an attached squadron of Saxon hussars. Most of the Saxon light cavalry brigade, however, was posted to the north towards Plösen and the Parthe supported by Birnbaum's battery and the *Sahr* Light Battalion. To Reynier's intense frustration, orders arrived during the night detaching Guilleminot's 13th Division to join Bertrand's 4th Corps at Lindenau for the push west towards Weißenfels in the morning. He objected and sent a letter to Ney just after midnight recommending that it would be better to send the entire 7th Corps to support Bertrand rather than 'to slice it up and leave less reliable troops almost alone in this position'.[280] His protest was to no avail, and he was once again left with only the Saxons and Durutte under his command to face the coming day.

On the morning of the 18th, however, Reynier brought surprising orders to his Saxon subordinates: the corps was to turn about and march east to Torgau. On 16 October, before marching to Leipzig, Reynier had sent Saxon Major von Schreibershofen to update Napoleon on the corps' situation and request instructions. However, he had also charged Schreibershofen to report to Friedrich August in Leipzig. In his memoirs, Schreibershofen called this latter mission a 'confidential' one that demonstrated Reynier's 'benevolent attitude' towards the Saxon contingent. According to his account, Reynier 'instructed me that if I saw that the Allies were victorious, I was to tell the king that he (Reynier) was prepared to place the Saxon troops at his [the king's] disposal'. Now, between 7:00 and 8:00 a.m. on 18 October, that is, two days later, Reynier told Zeschau that the Saxons were to march back to Torgau.

Chart 21: The Saxon Division at Leipzig, 17–18 October 1813

		bns/sqdns	present under arms
24th Division	GL von Zeschau		
III/Hussar Regiment		1	c. 62
1st Brigade	Oberst von Brause		
1st Light Infantry Regiment *LeCoq*		1	477
Rechten Infantry Battalion		1	159
Prinz Friedrich August Infantry Battalion		1	574
Steindel Infantry Battalion		1	346
1st Grenadier Battalion	Major von Spiegel	1	221
Jäger Company		–	44
2nd Brigade	GM von Ryssel		
2nd Grenadier Battalion	Major Anger	2 companies	181
Niesemeuschel Infantry Battalion		1	300
Prinz Anton Infantry Battalion		1	280
2nd Light Infantry Regiment *Sahr*		1	718
Artillery	Oberstleutnant Raabe		
6-pounder Artillery Battery	Hauptmann Dietrich	8 guns	193
1st Horse Artillery Battery	Hauptmann Birnbaum	4 guns	(incl. with 2nd)
2nd Horse Artillery Battery	Hauptmann Probsthayn	4 guns	184
12-pounder Artillery Battery	Hauptmann Rouvroy I	6 guns	144
Sappers		–	45
26th Light Cavalry Brigade	Oberst von Lindenau		684
Hussar Regiment (IV, V, VII, VIII)		4	
Prinz Clemens Uhlan Regiment		3?	
Detached			
I/Hussar Regiment to corps staff duties		1	c. 62
II/Hussar Regiment to Durutte		1	c. 62
VI/Hussar Regiment to Guillleminot		1	c. 62
2nd Grenadier Battalion guarding baggage	Major Anger	2 companies	187
Total		4,985 men	22 guns

The origin of these instructions is wrapped in mystery. It is nearly impossible to imagine Reynier issuing such orders without Napoleon's approval, but no such order is found in the French archives and Schreibershofen makes no specific mention of Torgau in his memoirs. In fact, he recounts that Berthier's orders recalling 7th Corps to Leipzig had already been dispatched when he reported to imperial headquarters on the 16th. He even sent his orderly back to Reynier to relay this order before proceeding to the king's residence in the city.[281] As he rode to report to his royal master that evening

Distribution by evening, 18 October

Remained with Zeschau

	men	guns
Prinz Friedrich August Infantry Battalion	104	
Anger Grenadier Battalion	181	
Niesemeuschel Infantry Battalion	281	
Prinz Anton Infantry Battalion	92	
Sappers	35	
I & II/Hussars	c. 124	
Total remaining in Leipzig	c. 817	0

Defections and Combat Losses

	men	guns
Losses	375 (est.)	3 (damaged: 1 × 12-pdr, 2 × 6-pdr)
Total defected	c. 3,791	19

Notes:

1. Number of Uhlan squadrons may have been reduced to three by this time. The four detached hussar squadrons numbered 248 officers and men in total, but it is not clear how many were in each squadron. The 6th Squadron attached to Guilleminot re-joined the light cavalry brigade on the evening of 17 October when Guilleminot departed.

2. The *Low* Battalion and a detachment from *Friedrich August* were escorting the artillery park and baggage to Torgau (approximately 300 infantry and 500 men for the park/baggage for 800–1,000 total).

(16 October), however, he concluded that the prospects for release from the French alliance were not good. 'Everything that I saw and everything I heard from the king's entourage showed that a separation from the French was not to be thought of,' he noted, 'nonetheless in the report I made to the king I mentioned that Reynier's attitude was favourable to the king's interests.' He also stated that Reynier himself had an audience with Friedrich August on 17 October. Unfortunately, Reynier's meeting with the king is another lacuna in the historical record.

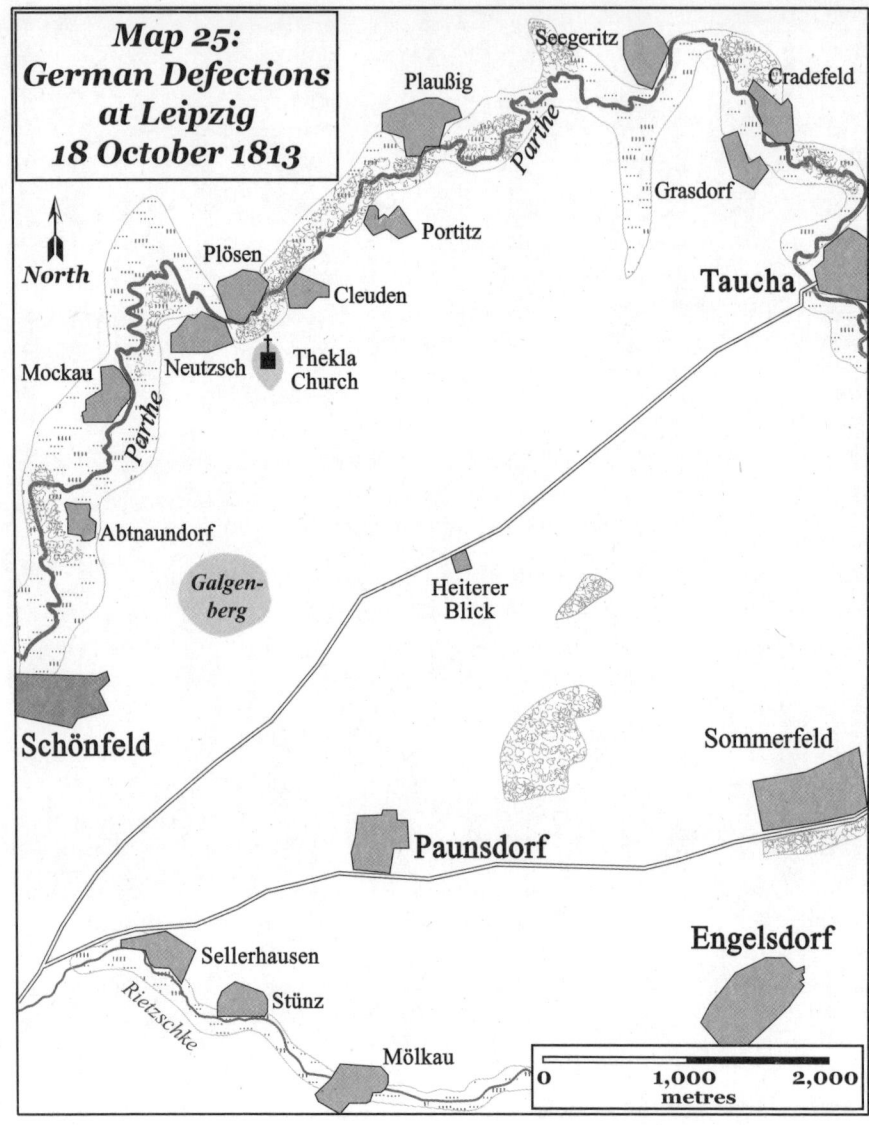

Map 25: German Defections at Leipzig 18 October 1813

Just as the origin of these new orders is enigmatic, the intention behind the purported shift to Torgau is also unclear. Schreibershofen and other Saxons assumed it was because Napoleon knew from his own experience and from Reynier's most recent report that the sullen Saxons had grown increasingly unreliable, but a French order along these lines seems unlikely given the unyielding responses to other Rheinbund requests for release. Other sources suggest the division was to provide a more robust escort for the enormous baggage train that GB Durrieu had assembled some 16 kilometres away around Eilenburg. With only the remains of the Bavarian 'division' and a lone Hessian battalion (II/Garde-Fusiliers) – barely 2,500 infantry – to guard it, Durrieu's column was in grave danger in the open terrain dominated by the numerous Coalition cavalry. In his midnight missive to Ney, Reynier had warned that the 7th and 6th Corps were too weak to sustain themselves against the Allied hosts and suggested sending their baggage to Torgau rather than risking a major portion of the army in what was likely to be a futile attempt to rescue the lumbering wagon train. Marching to assist Durrieu was thus a logical assumption on the part of Saxon participants and historians, but again there is no confirmation in the French (or any other) records. Berthier's orders to Reynier (16 October) only instructed him 'wherever this present order finds you' to march the 7th Corps to Leipzig at once. Ney sent two letters to Reynier before the crisis (one at 5:30 p.m. on the 17th one at 5:00 a.m. on the 18th) but neither of these ordered 7th Corps to Torgau. Reynier was only directed to put himself in communication with Durrieu and then informed that Durrieu should displace to Torgau if the cumbersome convoy could not reach Leipzig.

Whatever the origin and rationale of Reynier's orders to Zeschau that morning, the Saxon division thus moved to the Heiterer Blick farmstead in preparation for departure for Torgau. 'This news spread rapidly through our ranks and created general joy at the prospect of separation from the French and occupation of our own national fortress,' wrote Mandelsloh.[282] Saxon hopes for this outcome, however, were soon dashed. Riding to the low knoll surmounted by the Thekla-Kirche to reconnoitre, Reynier could see that it was already too late to escape: parts of Blücher's army were approaching the Parthe from the west and advance troops from Bernadotte's army had already occupied Taucha. The road to Torgau was closed. The Saxon infantry and artillery thus returned to a position between Paunsdorf and Stünz around 9:00 a.m. They were oriented generally southeast with Durutte on their left and one of Durutte's battalions along with two companies of *LeCoq* Light Infantry detailed to hold Paunsdorf. Marmont's 6th Corps, stretched from Schönfeld along the Parthe to the northeast, initially covered Reynier's left. By mid-morning, however, General of Infantry Louis Alexander Andrault Langeron's large Russian corps from Blücher's army had deployed on the northern side of the Parthe and was clearly preparing to cross. At the same time, Cossacks from Bennigsen's army were approaching from the southeast and Bernadotte's advance guard was massing around Taucha. Marmont thus swung his divisions back, pivoting on Schönfeld, so that his line now extended from that village to Durutte's division on the 7th Corps left flank. In front of both corps were their light cavalry brigades: GM von Normann's Württemberg horsemen for Marmont and Oberst von Lindenau's Saxons for Reynier. Normann had his attached horse battery while the *Sahr* Light Infantry Battalion and Birnbaum's guns supported Lindenau.

It was soon apparent that these Rheinbund light horse between the Heiterer Blick farm and the Parthe were in trouble. On one side, large numbers of Langeron's Russian cavalry were crossing the Parthe between Mockau and Plösen; on the other, Bennigsen's Cossacks were trotting up from the southeast. The Saxons charged the Russians advancing from the Parthe but were overwhelmed and thrown back towards the Galgenberg. Although they were able to rally behind the *Sahr* Light Infantry, they were now badly outnumbered and nearly surrounded. Some of the officers thus perceived this moment as a good opportunity to change sides. For them it seemed a case of defection or destruction under the sabres and lances of the Russian horse. Oberst von Lindenau's role in what transpired is unclear, but some group of his subordinates apparently decided to act with or without his approval. They first sent officers to Zeschau to request permission to defect, but only received decidedly negative replies. They then took matters into their own hands.[283] For some reason, they concluded that Birnbaum's battery should not defect and deployed their squadrons to cover his retreat back to the division south of Paunsdorf, escorted by a squadron of Uhlans. The rest then rode towards the looming Russians masses with sheathed sabres. After halting and shouting a Russian style 'Hurrah', they were warmly welcomed into the Allied ranks.

Nearby French cavalry, astonished that the Saxons were advancing to what seemed a suicidal attack, watched in dismay as their allies were enveloped by the enemy with a great deal of shouting. They turned about to support the Saxons only to retreat in haste when they were peppered with canister fire.[284] Langeron, on the other hand, at first feared an enemy ruse but was reassured when he rode up and heard the Saxon officers express their enthusiasm for joining the fight against the French immediately. Langeron refused this offer, however, and sent the two regiments to report to Yorck's Prussian corps in the rear. As Bruno Colson notes in his history of Leipzig, Saxon ardour for instant employment cooled decidedly when they were assigned to the detested Prussians.[285] Lindenau, the brigade commander, was either unable or unwilling to halt the defection but he and several others refused to participate and rode back to report to Zeschau.

The *Sahr* Light Infantry, trapped by Russian squadrons near the Parthe, somehow managed to arrange a friendly capitulation. The officers may have pledged to join the Coalition, but whatever the details, the men were allowed to retain their arms and were not treated as prisoners of war.[286] They were marched off behind Bernadotte's ranks. Between approximately 10:00 and

11:00 a.m., therefore, the entire Saxon detachment, with the exception of the artillery battery and one Uhlan squadron, had defected to the Allies. The Uhlan squadron, leaving Birnbaum's guns with the division, likewise soon found a way to turn itself over, in their case to the Swedes. Although there is no indication that the two brigades colluded in their actions, the Württemberg brigade also went over to the Allies around the same time.

As the Rheinbund horsemen were changing sides, Austrian FML Ferdinand Graf Bubna von Littitz's 2nd Light Division, approaching from the south, attacked the French and Saxons in Paunsdorf and took the village only to lose it to a counterattack. A renewed Austrian advance once again secured it at 1:00 p.m., but this time Reynier concluded that the village was too exposed to hold. He withdrew his men to their main position from the Taucha road to Stünz where the Saxon artillery was heavily and successfully engaged with Russian and Austrian batteries. Zeschau now received 'the entirely unexpected news' that the light cavalry had gone over to the enemy. 'From this moment on,' he wrote in his journal, 'I noticed an unusual tension among many of the senior officers.' Indeed, his two infantry brigade commanders, GM von Ryssel and Oberst von Brause, were agitating to change sides at once. They not only pressed Zeschau and Oberstleutnant Gustav Ludwig Ferdinand Raabe, the artillery commander, but Ryssel sent an officer to the Allied lines to alert the opposing officers to the intended action even as he was importuning his division commander. Zeschau, however, would not act without the king's approval. Raabe gave a similar answer to these urgings. Zeschau thus sent Hauptmann Gustav von Nostitz, one of his staff officers, into Leipzig to request instructions from Friedrich August. The exact nature of Zeschau's communication to the king is unknown, but Nostitz apparently spoke excitedly about the desertion of the cavalry in the morning and asserted 'how the infantry, under General Ryssel, was determined to do the same in case the king did not immediately renounce the French alliance and how, therefore, His Majesty's final decision was awaited'.[287] Around 2:00 p.m. Nostitz returned with a cryptically ambiguous royal reply:

> Dear General-Leutnant von Zeschau! I have always placed my trust in my troops and do so in the present moment more than ever. They can only prove their attachment to me by fulfilling their duties, and I am sure that you will do your utmost to encourage them to do so. I herewith ask God to take you into his holy protection.[288]

The opacity of this note notwithstanding, for Zeschau, the king's intentions were clear: the division should remain aligned with the French.

Indeed, there is little doubt as to the king's wishes. 'Could and should the king sanction in this moment a step that went against the general principles of honour and all international law?' wrote a court official, noting that no other course was possible given 'the king's strict sense of what was right'. Ryssel, on the other hand, vehemently protested, alluding to what he pronounced as a boundary between duties to the sovereign and to the vision of a pan-German fatherland.[289] In any case, he and Brause saw the king as a hostage to Napoleon and decided that this vague message was sufficiently open-ended to serve as pretext for what they planned to do anyway. They would defect at the first opportunity.

By now it was afternoon, and the Saxons were engaged in a fierce artillery duel. 'It rained shot and shell all around us', recalled Oberkanonier (senior gunner) Friedrich August Wilhelm Böhme of Dietrich's battery, 'A cannon ball tore away the head of a gunner who was standing near me in such a way that the head remained in his shako.' 'Only those who have been in similar situations can truly imagine how I felt', he continued, especially as he and his comrades were unable to remove the corpse from the battery 'even though it lay in our way'. The Saxon artillery stood under heavy fire until approximately 2:00 when this diminished somewhat, but this 'hail of shot swept many of us away, some overwhelmed in their struggle with death, some still fighting against it'.[290]

Someone suggested marching the entire division into Leipzig to protect the king. Parts of the division actually made some moves in this direction, but the jammed roads, the blocked gates and the presence of thousands of French troops nearby soon led the Saxons to return to their previous position. The fact that such an unrealistic – one is tempted to say absurd – notion could have been taken seriously is an indication of the level of desperation within the officer corps: both on the part of the two brigade commanders who saw defection as their only salvation and on Zeschau's side for apparently seeking an alternative to what he considered gross disloyalty.

In the meantime, Ney had appeared on the scene and ordered the recapture of Paunsdorf. Reynier objected and a heated exchange ensued which ended with Ney giving the order to Durutte directly. Durutte's men successfully accomplished this task, but soon lost the village for a final time to the Prussians of Bülow's corps which had now reached the battlefield via Taucha. With the French fully occupied holding off Bülow and with no desire to defect to the Prussians, the Saxons who wished to march to the Russians or Austrians had a clear but brief moment to do so. The artillery moved first even though the unfortunate Raabe was emotionally torn between his sense of loyalty to his king and his fear that he and his guns would be subjected to 'the rage and revenge' of the French and would be 'unquestionably lost to the fatherland' should the battle end in defeat as seemed likely.[291] These worries and unrelenting pressure from Ryssel – who seems to have deceived Raabe concerning the nature of the king's message – finally persuaded Raabe to act. Shortly after 3:00 p.m., his gunners limbered up and moved off, first at the walk but soon at the trot, men and horses breathless at the pace. Zeschau, who had just conveyed an order from Reynier to withdraw the 12-pounder battery, at first thought his instructions had been misunderstood and sent an adjutant to correct the presumed error. He was soon disabused of this impression when he saw Brause's and Ryssel's brigades beginning to advance. Suspecting what was going on, Zeschau dashed up to order them to halt and return to their positions. The columns dutifully halted, but as Zeschau rode away both brigades resumed their movement towards the Allied lines, now at double time. Zeschau galloped back in a fury. Catching up with Ryssel's men and the *Friedrich August* Battalion of Brause's brigade, he relieved Ryssel of command and ordered him to report to Reynier. After a few angry words, however, Ryssel spurred away, waving his handkerchief to urge his men to follow his example.[292]

In the midst of this confusion, the enemy intervened. Durutte's division had been holding the line to the left of the Saxons, but Prussians and Austrians, pushing out of Paunsdorf, drove the French back in disorder, their flight hastened by hissing Congreve rockets launched by a British rocket battery nearby (the lone British unit at the battle). Parts of the *Prinz Anton* and *Prinz Friedrich* Battalions became entangled in the confused French rout. Many men from *Prinz Friedrich* surrendered to pursuing Russian cavalry but they did not wish to be considered defectors or deserters and thus gave up their weapons and packs to be led away as prisoners of war.[293] Zeschau himself was caught up in the moil of fleeing men, horses and vehicles for a few precious moments. Reynier, like Zeschau, at first thought the movement towards the Allied lines was the result of misunderstood orders. As he later told a Saxon friend, he was well aware of the sullen mood in the contingent but never thought that the men would desert on the field of battle. Now, aghast at the turn of events, he tried to reach the hurrying Saxon artillery only to be turned back by heavy enemy fire. According to the annotations in the French edition of Odeleben's memoirs, when Reynier rode up, the Saxons, fearing for his safety, urged him to retire at once. His chief of staff rode to the corps' left and had Durutte's guns open fire on the Saxons, but it was too late. In contrast, French cavalry on the corps' right flank, thinking the Saxons were attacking, offered up hearty cheers of *'Vive l'Empereur!'* It was, as a modern Saxon historian writes, a scene of 'confusion without end'.[294]

Most of the NCOs and common soldiers seem to have been unaware of the plan to defect that Ryssel and Brause had concocted.[295] Schreibershofen explicitly stated that the men could be counted on but they had not been informed in advance. Some of the junior officers seem to have been equally ignorant when it became evident that what they thought to be a march to attack was in actuality a march to defection. They knew nothing of Nostitz's mission nor of the message from their king in reply, and they had no time for pondering their action when they were ordered forward. Indeed, it seems likely that Ryssel and Brause, rightly assuming that they had a receptive audience, implied that their action had the king's blessing. Though it is necessary to keep in mind that he wrote well after the fact, Frenzel of the *Steindel* Infantry offers a view of these events from the rank and file:

> That our Saxon generals from the artillery, infantry and cavalry were in agreement and all officers concurred was only too certain. But we common soldiers knew nothing other than what we could notice in the behaviour of our superiors who always viewed the French very resentfully. And they knew the attitude of the soldiers as the men had often expressed themselves out loud. If only there was an opportunity, we would all go over. So it was with the soldiers. When an officer heard such talk, he turned aside and said nothing. No one was called to account. When we began to change sides, as generals and adjutants dashed ahead and waved white handkerchiefs, our officer said to us: 'Now keep together tightly, we are going over.' The closed column kept itself as tight as a wall ... We soldiers would have gone against the French at once. But General Riessel [*sic*] gave no orders for this.[296]

If the common soldiers did not know in advance what their commanders had in mind, they no doubt noticed the intense discussions among the officers. Mandelsloh and his fellow subalterns, for example, were aware that some of their seniors were agitating to defect. They were engaged in a lively debate over this dramatic option: 'Some saw the salvation of the fatherland in joining the Allied host,' others did not deny this interpretation, but claimed that 'at least now, during the battle, would not be the time to leave the ranks of the French army'. Though still undecided, in the emotional chaos of the hour, he and his comrades found themselves caught up in the momentum generated by Ryssel and Brause. They thus ignored Zeschau and rode or marched with their men in the wake of their excited brigade commanders. It was only after they had been led to safety behind Allied lines 'where we were suddenly transferred from the battle to peace that we had time to consider the step we had taken'.[297]

Led by Ryssel and Brause, the bulk of the Saxon division thus marched through fire from both sides to Bennigsen's lines south of Paunsdorf where they were greeted with cheers and salutes. 'A cloud of Cossacks, who seemed prepared for our arrival, enclosed us and brought us in triumph into the ranks of the Allies,' wrote artillery Hauptmann Probsthayn. Indeed, on seeing the Saxons making friendly gestures, Major Karl von Wedel, one of Bennigsen's staff officers, had carried orders for the Cossacks to welcome and protect the approaching Saxons. Ryssel soon galloped up in advance of the column. Bennigsen, however, regarded the defection with some suspicion and received the excited Ryssel 'with an icy cold demeanour'. Ryssel apparently asked to be employed at once, but Bennigsen demurred, suggesting to the somewhat deflated Ryssel that the Saxon infantry go into reserve. Bennigsen only wanted some of the Saxon guns to support his depleted batteries. Most of the Saxons were thus escorted to a bivouac site near Engelsdorf, where they were issued a ration of brandy and treated as friends and comrades.[298] Sous-Lieutenant Rilliet, a young French cuirassier officer who watched the Saxon defections from his position with the 1st Cavalry Corps, summed up the attitude towards the Saxons displayed by both Langeron and Bennigsen in his rather mordant fashion. The Allies may have welcomed the Saxons with loud hurrahs because 'one takes advantage of a perfidy at all times and especially in the middle of a battle', he wrote years later, but one does so 'without relying too much on traitors; they were sent a league to the rear of the army'.[299]

Though often inflated in later French accounts, the number of Saxons who deserted on 18 October was relatively small, especially given the titanic scale of the battle. Deducting estimated casualties and the men who remained behind with Zeschau, the total amounts to approximately 3,790 officers and men (Chart 21). This was not an entirely trivial number, and their departure did open a momentary hole in an important part of the French line. Napoleon thus rode over personally to survey the situation and employed part of his Guard to cover the unexpected gap in the line while Ney brought up one of his reserve divisions to fill the void. Nonetheless, the Saxon defection was not sufficiently significant to alter the overall course of the struggle.

The defecting troops took with them 19 artillery pieces (three had been disabled or lacked horses). Some of these, as Bennigsen requested, were soon turned against the French. As his compatriots headed off to rest, therefore, Hauptmann Birnbaum assembled three 6-pounders and a howitzer and joined the Allied artillery line, a decision that later earned him a sharp rebuke from Raabe. Wedel, however, was pleased to report that, 'This artillery was... immediately used against the enemy with good effect.'[300] Before being withdrawn and before being wounded, Birnbaum's guns engaged in the mutual cannonade and helped repel a French counterattack; the lone howitzer was also used to bombard Stünz when the Allies stormed it as evening descended. Additionally, the Saxons supplied their new Austrian and Russian colleagues with some artillery ammunition as the Army of Poland's reserve artillery park had not yet arrived.[301]

Ryssel and Brause, meanwhile, were called to meet the Allied monarchs. They received the appreciation of the three rulers as well as assurances that their action had preserved the integrity of the Saxon kingdom (although Friedrich Wilhelm III of Prussia apparently grumbled aloud that the Saxons had taken too long to make this move).[302] The Saxons asked that their troops not be employed until Friedrich August's desires were known, a request the Allied monarchs also granted. Birnbaum's battery was therefore withdrawn when Ryssel and Brause returned, and the Saxon division was not involved in the fighting on 19 October.

On the other side of the field, the distressed Zeschau, having failed to hold his division to its duty, requested Reynier's permission to withdraw. As evening came on, he assembled the small remnant of his command near Sellerhausen and retired to the area around the Grimma Gate. He then reported to Friedrich August. 'With a greatly pained feeling', he recorded, 'I entered his room, and I was so shaken that I could barely speak the words: "I come to Your Majesty in this moment with the conviction that I have fulfilled my duty, but from the corps entrusted to me I bring back only a few faithful".' Zeschau was deeply touched when the king took his hand and replied, 'So much greater then is the worth of those who remained true.' 'I found him much moved by the events of this day, but totally composed,' wrote Zeschau, noting that the king's 'greatness of soul' reinforced his attachment to his monarch. With only 800 or so men remaining from the division, Zeschau relinquished command and stayed with the king, sending a message to notify Reynier and to take his leave, trusting that Reynier would testify that he had always acted as 'a man of honour and probity in these disastrous days'.[303] In his reply, Reynier wrote: 'It is unfortunate for the honour of the Saxon troops, that I have commanded with pleasure as they have conducted themselves perfectly during the recent campaign, that a part of these troops can be stained by the unworthy action of passing over to the enemy during a battle.' He praised Zeschau for his performance and recommended that the remaining Saxon infantry who had 'shown themselves loyal servants of their sovereign' be taken into the royal guard.[304] Thus ended Reynier's long association with the Saxon army. Remaining in Leipzig with Durutte's division and parts of 3rd Corps, he would be captured by the Allies near the Halle Gate on 19 October and would die in Paris in February 1814 shortly after being exchanged.

Zeschau may have taken some small comfort from the actions of Leutnant Friedrich August von Lindenau who had been assigned to support two French guns on the flank with a half-company of the *Friedrich August* Infantry. On seeing the Saxon division defect, a French colonel told Lindenau that he and his men were free to go. Lindenau, however, declined the offer and earned the respect of the French colonel by marching his tiny command back to Leipzig.

The Narrow Path of Duty

Reviewing the defection on 18 October in later days and decades, Saxon participants cited a number of motivating factors. In the first place, the decision to change sides was informed by years of dissatisfaction with the French alliance. The miseries and anxieties of 1813 accentuated these feelings, as a Württemberg general noted while traversing western Saxony in late September: 'The mood in all Saxony is highly tense, one cannot wait for the complete downfall of the French army,' wrote Württemberg GM Joseph Ignaz von Beroldingen, 'It is impossible to describe the troubled spirit that prevails in all Saxony.'[305]

References to 'throwing off the French yoke' or 'hatred of the French' (*Franzosenhaß*) are thus common in the memoir literature and there is no doubt that widespread hostility towards France in general and Napoleon in particular was a central element of the backdrop against which the Saxon officers at Leipzig decided to desert the alliance. Interpretations must be tempered, however, by considering that many of these memoirs were written and published during an era dominated by the Prussian narrative of 1813 and the concomitant Prusso-German hyper-nationalism founded on animosity towards France as the 'hereditary enemy'. Moreover, as the acerbic but trenchant GL von Funck observed in 1815, beyond a general war-weariness, 'few knew what they wanted'. Indeed, what most Saxons found objectionable, even if they did not recognise it as such, was what seemed to be the Saxon court's reflexive submission to every French request, whether it came formally from Napoleon and his government or spontaneously from a general on campaign. Rather than try to ameliorate or even decline French demands, Saxon officials would acquiesce and then cite Napoleon and his regime for the imposition of unpopular measures. Funck was keenly aware of the strength and scope of anti-French sentiment in Saxony, but in his view much of the friction stemmed from the Saxon court's responses to French requests rather than from the requests themselves.[306]

The catastrophe in Russia compounded extant anti-French attitudes. In addition to the shock at the horrendous casualties and the epic scope of the defeat, Saxon officers repeatedly complained that their efforts had not been acknowledged. Reynier, for instance, was disappointed that the Saxons had not received any crosses of the Legion of Honour despite demonstrating 'great bravery, steadfastness and enthusiasm in the service of His Majesty the Emperor' during the Russian campaign. 'This withholding of honours on account of His Majesty's satisfaction with the troops, who have behaved in the most excellent manner, has the most adverse effect, especially at the present moment, when German minds are strongly preoccupied with the events and by the intrigues of the Prussians,' he told Eugène in a 9 March letter from Dresden.[307] Leutnant von Holtzendorff neatly summarised the resentment this alleged lack of recognition engendered: 'The so completely failed Russian campaign, which did not provide a rewarding end to the great efforts and achievements, not even due recognition, laid the foundation on which Thielmann built so industriously and not without success.'[308] Such carping and desire for reward, of course, sit in rather uneasy contradiction to assertions of all-consuming enmity towards Napoleon and his army, but the frustrations of 1812 provided fertile ground for subsequent outrage when French commanders blamed the Saxons for the defeats at Großbeeren and Dennewitz.

The frictions that emerged during 1813 must be viewed against this general backdrop. The overbearing behaviour and perceived presumptions of the French were constant sources of irritation and occasional intra-allied fisticuffs. Formerly admired for their military skills and record of victory, the French after Russia were increasingly seen as unworthy of emulation. To the Saxons, the Grande Armée of 1813 was characterised by appallingly bad discipline, a logistical system that had ceased to function and generals who seemed operationally inept. There were two broad consequences to these frictions. First, Saxon troops saw themselves being led to repeated defeats by squabbling French marshals and then suffering ignominious and unfair blame for the losses. Second, the Saxon soldiers, poorly fed and supported even in their own country, had to watch as their putative allies ravaged the land. Whether wilful or ordered or simply the result of slothful neglect on the part of the French administration, the devastation visited upon Saxony caused more outrage in the ranks than any other French offence. As most of the men came from peasant backgrounds, they immediately sympathised with villagers who lost livestock, crops and homes in the course of the conflict. Furthermore, as Saxons, they were the first to hear the doleful lamentations and angry protestations of the local people. As Vollborn noted, the depredations of the French contrasted poorly with what the Saxons imagined to be more orderly and clement requisitions by the Allies.[309] Odeleben, on the other hand, offered a rather more realistic appraisal when he later commented that, 'The evils with which Saxony was burdened came to it from all the armies of Europe; they were inevitable in a territory so constricted; but the unfortunates who suffered accused Napoleon.'[310] French generals and the emperor himself were clearly aware of the problem, but the many attempts to curb the excesses were inadequate given the young army's indiscipline and the abysmal logistical situation.

Marching arm in arm with anger towards the French was an alleged desire to save Saxony – not only from the French, but from the Allies (especially the mistrusted Prussians) and from the general miseries of war. On the one hand, Napoleon no longer seemed capable of protecting their country, indeed, his army was contributing to its destruction. On the other hand, officers and men alike feared that the victorious Allies would treat the kingdom as a conquered land, not only imposing all manner of painful exactions but possibly breaking it apart and deposing their venerated king. As Major von Hausen wrote to his brother on 24 October in reference to the defection: 'Oberst von Brause and many other officers now asked General von Zeschau to leave the French army with the division, in the hope that the Allies would then treat the king and fatherland more leniently.'[311] Some officers were at least partly motivated by pan-German visions: Bünau, Ryssel and Brause, all of whom later entered Prussian service, were in this category. As shall be seen, Ryssel's younger brother was of a similarly impassioned disposition. He too would later join the Prussian army. Some, or perhaps all, of these officers may also have been motivated by expectations of greater career opportunities with the larger and seemingly victorious Prussian army. Most of the officers on the field at Leipzig, however, were primarily concerned with the fate of Saxony: their country, their king and their countrymen.

Saving the army was an essential element in saving Saxony. For reasons of professional and personal pride, of course, no one wanted to be on the losing side, but this concern for the kingdom's future drove a strong impulse to preserve the army. The string of recent French defeats, the insulting bravado of the ubiquitous Cossacks, and the enemy's evident numerical superiority made the coming battle look hopeless.[312] Furthermore, the departure of Guilleminot's division the night before and the obvious preparations for withdrawal led many Saxons to suspect that they would be abandoned or that adherence to the French alliance could result in a long retreat westward even beyond the borders of their country.[313] The spectre of Napoleon sending Rheinbund troops to Spain loomed large for some, prompting fears that they too would be dragged across the Rhine in French service. Others worried about direct repercussions. Raabe, as noted above, feared that his artillery 'would be subject to the rage and revenge of the French and would be entirely lost to the fatherland if the battle had an unfortunate outcome,' especially if he and his men were left behind after the infantry deserted. Schreibershofen was more explicit in his post-war analysis, noting that on 17 October,

> The Saxon troops had the opportunity and the time to review and consider their situation. After all the armies of the Allies had arrived near Leipzig and encircled the French position, their disproportionate superiority made it impossible to imagine a victory for Napoleon, and what use would it have been?! What consequences would a French defeat have for Saxony?![314]

Exhaustion doubtless contributed to the discouragement amongst all ranks. The 7th Corps had marched some 280 kilometres during 5–18 October and, despite the day of relative rest on the 17th, the men were weary, wet and ill-fed. Moreover, they had slogged through scenes of chaos on their way to Leipzig that only served to confirm their fears for the future.[315] As Frenzel observed in his naïve fashion:

> Quite a number of ammunition and other wagons that belonged to the trains were left behind by the corps marching to Leipzig and destroyed by the Cossacks, as well as dead horses and broken-down men ... It seemed more like a flight, rather than an ordered march. All this awoke grim forebodings.[316]

Buhle, in the *Prinz Anton* Battalion, left a similar impression:

> For 14 days before the battle we had had little or no bread; raw vegetables from the fields were our only nourishment as the enemy who harassed us day and night left us no time for cooking or preparation of what we had. And in the villages through which we marched there was hardly a living creature, let alone an inhabitant, to see. Thus, we children of a fatherland that was being ruined by foreigners had to suffer from hunger before we were led to the great battle as if to the slaughterhouse.[317]

On the eve of Leipzig, therefore, the prevailing mood in the Saxon contingent was desperation, an urgent desire to find some escape from what they perceived to be an impending catastrophe.[318] For the anxious officers, 18 October seemed the last chance for their intact division, 'armed and combat capable', to change sides 'and that this must occur to save the honour of the Saxon name and the independence of Saxony'.[319]

Desperation led to rationalisation. The officer corps knew that Zeschau was also frustrated, and those like Ryssel who were keen to defect at once assumed their commander would concur and collude with them. Beyond assumptions about Zeschau, there was a widespread belief among all ranks that their king was a captive of the French, unable to make independent decisions. The experiences of the spring were fresh in the minds of most senior officers as they had participated in the lively debates about Saxony's stance between the belligerents and their monarch's wishes while ensconced in Torgau. Given their sovereign's flight to Bohemia, the orders to Thielmann about 'neutrality', and the April pact with Austria, many told themselves that Friedrich August would *tacitly* approve of their plans to cut the odious bonds to France even if he could not issue a direct order to do so. They also persuaded themselves that they could desert the French alliance without breaking their oaths to the king. Given the sanctity of these solemn oaths in contemporary military culture, the Saxons, officers and men alike, were acutely aware that they were risking disgrace by defecting without formal approval from their sovereign.

Furthermore, desertion in the face of the enemy was a capital crime in the Saxon army as in all armies of the age. Funck, who had two sons serving as junior officers in the contingent, thus warned them not to dishonour themselves if it came to defection; he summed up this attitude by observing that, 'The Saxons left Napoleon's banners without ill will towards Reynier and not to separate themselves from their beloved ruler, rather in the firm belief that by changing sides they would purchase freedom for him and for the fatherland as well as the friendship of the Allies.' This line of reasoning was not entirely illogical, but it was infused with a large dose of wishful thinking as anxious officers under the pressure of events sought a rationale for an action they were convinced was both urgent and unavoidable. This reasoning also illuminates the continued Saxon hope that Austria would provide the 'third path' for their country to escape its ties to France without throwing itself under Prussian dominance. Indeed, Ryssel and Brause made special, though ultimately ineffectual, appeals for support to Kaiser Franz and Schwarzenberg during their visit to Allied headquarters on 18 October and in later audiences.[320] Unfortunately for Saxony, the results did not match these exaggerated hopes.

Whatever the Saxons were thinking, the French reacted to the defection with outrage and exaggeration. The outrage is entirely understandable, especially as the defection occurred in the middle of a hard-fought battle. The tale grew in the telling, however, and this exaggeration only served to make the action appear more momentous than it was. Although imperial headquarters at first tried to suppress knowledge of the defection, news quickly spread in the ranks, but 'instead of inspiring the least disquiet, it only excited the rage of the soldiers'; indeed, as a Guard artillery officer recalled, 'Indignation, exalting the courage of the troops who had witnessed this cowardly betrayal and those who were sent to fill the gap in the line, only augmented the ferocity of the defence.'[321] On the other hand, French veterans at the time and subsequent historians almost unanimously lauded Friedrich August. 'The Saxons abandoned us,' wrote Capitaine Jean François de Gouttes of the 11th Cuirassiers, 'their loyal but unfortunate king undoubtedly hoped for a better treatment of our enemies' but he 'was disgracefully taken to Berlin as a prisoner and his states treated as conquered lands'.[322]

This sense of perfidy was perpetuated and inflated in the later memoir literature, the Saxons firing on their former comrades being the subject of particular fury and disgust. GD Jacques Alexandre François Allix de Vaux, for instance, a hardened French artillery officer in Westphalian service during 1813, regarded it as 'one of the most odious monuments that history can present for our consideration'.[323] Before riding over to assess the situation, Napoleon had received the unwelcome news with his customary equanimity even in the eyes of his Saxon escort officer Odeleben. Speaking to Odeleben two days later at Weißenfels, he calmly referred to the 'treason' on the 18th but listened attentively to Odeleben's attempt to explain – though not excuse – his countrymen's actions.[324]

The report published in official French papers just after the battle, however, attributed considerable significance to the event:

> At 3:00 in the afternoon, the victory was ours on the front against the Army of Silesia as on the front where the emperor was facing the main army. But at that moment the Saxon army, infantry, cavalry and artillery along with the Württemberg cavalry all passed over to the enemy. This treason not only made a hole in our lines but delivered to the enemy the important position that had been entrusted to the Saxon army which pushed its infantry to the point of immediately turning cannon against Durutte's division.[325]

Similarly, Napoleon, in exile on St Helena, described the defection 'as the infamous and disgraceful treachery of the Saxons, who, though they were serving in our ranks and were our companions in danger and glory, suddenly turned to fight against us'. In his retelling, this 'unlooked-for treachery' meant that 'the whole Saxon army, with a battery of sixty guns, occupying one of the most important positions of the line, passed over to the enemy and turned its artillery on the French ranks'.[326] For many French, the fact that the Saxon action occurred near Bernadotte's army only made the defection more infamous as Bernadotte was widely considered a traitor 'who did not remember that he had been born French'.[327]

The exaggerations incorporated into such narratives – most commonly inflating the number of men and guns involved – were largely exercises in excuse-making. Nonetheless, these erroneous portrayals have been accepted uncritically by some subsequent historians, thus perpetuating a distorted account.[328] This is not to say that the sudden creation of a gap in the line was irrelevant. Napoleonic veteran and military historian Guillaume de Vaudoncourt overstated the case in writing that, 'It was not possible to repair completely the harm caused by the desertion of the Saxons,' but the unexpected gap did jeopardise Durutte's division and endanger Marmont's flank.[329] Napoleon was forced to commit part of the Guard and some of Ney's reserve to fill the void. These diversions were not decisive to the overall outcome, but neither were they minor matters. In other words, although the loss of the battle cannot be laid at the doorstep of the Saxon contingent, the defection did have local tactical impact. In a larger sense, one of Napoleon's concluding observations on St Helena was representative of the way many French and not a few Saxons viewed the defection: 'Whatever might be the fatal effects of their desertion, the disgrace attached to themselves is greater than all the mischief they caused us.'[330]

Leipzig, 19 October:
From Accolades to Fusillades

The final day of battle began with an effort at diplomacy rather than combat. Napoleon, in collaboration with Gersdorff, authorised the dispatch of Saxon emissaries to the Allies in what was likely a combination of altruism and cynical practicality: to spare Leipzig the horrors of an assault and to gain time for as much of the Grande Armée as possible to escape. Two delegations of respected senior civilians thus attempted to leave the city early on the morning of the 19th: one to Schwarzenberg and one to Bernadotte. Both groups immediately ran into trouble as all the access roads were jammed with traffic and, worse, the battle was already beginning. 'The actual street was completely blocked with incoming wagons,' wrote Johann Carl Gross, one of the delegates, as 'cannon balls and shells flew over our carriage'. Finding progress impossible, both groups turned back. 'Our carriage turned around and drove back to the Grimma Gate,' continued Gross, 'As this was closed to all vehicles, however, we had to get out and, to get into the city, Dufour and I had to creep under the lowered barrier behind which stood Baden soldiers with cocked muskets.' A junior member of each delegation managed to reach the tsar and Blücher (not Bernadotte) on horseback, but the Coalition leaders snubbed both. Blücher merely told his emissary that Leipzig had nothing to fear from his troops; while the tsar dictated stern conditions but only granted half an hour for the rider to reach the Saxon king and return with an answer – nowhere near enough time to reach the city's centre, leave alone return with a considered reply. Both missions thus failed as did a subsequent initiative by Oberst Anton Friedrich Carl von Ryssel, GM von Ryssel's younger brother.[331]

On the military front, the defections and combat of the previous day left the elements of the Saxon contingent scattered about the region around Leipzig on the morning of 19 October: most of the light cavalry attached to Yorck's Prussian corps, the *Sahr* Light Infantry and an Uhlan squadron with Bernadotte's Army of the North along with much of *Friedrich August* (the last temporarily as captives), the bulk of the division east of Engelsdorf. In addition to these 3,790, slightly fewer than 2,000 others remained under the king's orders in Leipzig: those Zeschau had brought back from 7th Corps and the Leib-Grenadiers. The remaining troopers of the two heavy cavalry regiments (*c.* 200) found themselves west of the Elster at Schönau.

Ryssel and the bulk of the units that had defected held themselves aloof from the fighting on the 19th. He refused a request for artillery support from Bennigsen and likewise declined Bernadotte's invitation to be incorporated into the Army of the North, citing his intention to await orders from Schwarzenberg. These did not arrive until the afternoon, after the city had fallen. Ryssel was thereby directed to march his men to Pegau but it was too late in the day to reach that destination and the remaining Saxons bivouacked around Connewitz for the night.[332]

The heavy cavalry experienced their own miniature odyssey on 18–19 October. GM von Lessing, the brigade commander, had learned of the division's defection shortly after Ryssel and Brause led their men to the Allied lines on 18 October. Like Zeschau, Lessing immediately sent to the king for instructions and, also like Zeschau, he received in answer a note stating that 'the cuirassiers have always known how to do their duty', which he correctly interpreted as meaning that he and his men should hold true to the French alliance. His brigade thus remained with 1st Cavalry Corps throughout the 18th, 'Even though,' as one officer noted, 'we too, recognising the circumstances, did not find in our hearts the devotion to the French to be as strong as before.'[333] The two cuirassier regiments were not involved in any combat that day but did undertake an exhausting march from Stötteritz through Leipzig to Schönau with the rest of the corps, a journey of perhaps 11 kilometres that took them seven hours owing to the confusion and congestion in the city. In what strikes the modern observer as a remarkable dereliction of duty, Lessing chose to remain in Leipzig and allowed other officers to do likewise. Five officers elected to stay at their posts and rode with the brigade to Schönau where they bivouacked for the night.

Lieutenant Auguste Thirion of the 9th Cuirassiers had served with the Saxons throughout the spring and autumn campaigns. He summed up the French attitude towards these regiments in his memoirs, describing them as 'a *corps d'élite* who had always conducted themselves admirably during the course of the campaign and whose men, at the moment of their army's defection, gave proof of their loyalty and of the sentiments of honour that animated them'. When the Saxons learned that they were being recalled to their king:

> The officers, led by their colonel, came to the officers of each French regiment in the bivouac at night to say their farewells ... They wanted to win our esteem as they assured us of theirs. This noble language, this handsome conduct, was keenly felt; embracing, we said our farewell and the next day these friends of yesterday were forced by orders to become our enemies. This is an episode of military life which proves that this rage of destruction which animates the sovereigns passes to the soldier, that from one moment to the next these men who were friends became enemies by order of their sovereign and passed from accolades to fusillades.[334]

The two regiments were now reduced to a combined strength of only 200 or so, and the following morning their French commanders initially told them their king had agreed that they would have to give up their horses to the artillery and continue their service on foot. These instructions instantly aroused understandable anger and indignation among the troopers which was only contained by the exertions of the remaining Saxon officers. Fortunately, Oberst von Lindenau, the former commander of the light cavalry brigade, arrived and appealed to GD Bordessoulle. Bordessoulle, who had gained the respect and affection of the Saxons during the campaign, sent Lindenau to find a higher authority who could change his orders. Further, he and other French officers personally informed the regiments of this request and assured them of the esteem in which they were held by their French comrades in arms. Lindenau's mission seems to have succeeded, as some hours later, Rittmeister Adolf von Gutschmid, the senior remaining officer, was called to imperial headquarters. Napoleon praised the regiments, inquired after the wellbeing of specific officers and declared that troops who had consistently performed with such distinction should not be subjected to the indignity of losing their mounts. On Gutschmid's return, Bordessoulle formed the regiments, announced Napoleon's decision and lauded the men for their conduct and comradeship. The officers, however, were required to report to Caulaincourt, who rather brusquely informed them that they had to sign a pledge not take up arms against the French for a year.[335] This was a common enough measure at the time, but the officers were annoyed as it meant an extended separation from their units. Despite their irritation, all five signed, and the two regiments were released from French service. Directed to Merseburg, the Saxons encountered Russian outposts from Blücher's army en route, received a warm welcome and bivouacked with their hosts for the night. The two regiments continued on to Merseburg on 20 October and, minus the five officers who had reluctantly signed the pledges, joined the re-formed Saxon army towards the end of the month.

While the heavy cavalry's future was decided outside Leipzig, the Guard Grenadiers were witnesses to the drama taking place in the city's market square. The 1st Battalion had remained on the field with the Imperial Guard throughout 18 October where Major Charles Pierre Lubin Griois, passing by with a battery, described it as 'composed of very fine men dressed in white [sic] and well turned out'.[336] Released from service with the Guard on the 19th to 'form the guard of HM the King of Saxony', the soldiers of I/Leib-Grenadiers left the battlefield and struggled through the jam of men, women, horses and vehicles to reach their sovereign's residence in the Königshaus on the southern side of the square around 9:00 a.m. Here the battalion joined the two companies that had remained with the king since Dresden.

The grenadiers had just reassembled themselves in an orderly fashion before the entrance to the Königshaus when Napoleon arrived to see the king. During their half-hour meeting, Napoleon offered Friedrich August the option of accompanying the Grande Armée to Erfurt, an offer the Saxon king politely declined in order to stay with his subjects and share their fate. The French emperor spoke harshly of Queen Amalie's brother, Max Joseph of Bavaria, warning that he would regret his decision to break with the Rheinbund and align himself with the Allies. 'It is that scoundrel your brother who has caused all my problems,' he told the queen.

Although they could not hear the words exchanged, curious observers outside in the square watched as this remarkable discussion unfolded. 'I saw him [Napoleon] standing there in the bay window between the king and the queen and speaking in a lively fashion,' recalled the merchant J. G. Trefftz, 'The queen seemed very upset and dried her tears with a white cloth.'[337] In general, however, this brief interaction seems to have been characterised by courtesy and respect between two monarchs who genuinely liked one another. Their final farewell was thus quite poignant as Napoleon then took his leave.

Returning to the market square, Napoleon 'mounted and rode over to the Saxon Guard Grenadiers' formed in ranks on the cobblestones. The battalion commander, Major Friedrich von Dreßler und Scharffenstein, described the ensuing scene:

> He directed numerous questions to me, that were for him in this moment completely irrelevant, but which demonstrated that this great man, even in this permanent twist of fate, did not lose his equanimity and strength of mind. These questions were the following: If this was the battalion that had stood with his guard? If it had lost many men? Whether those were from cannon or musket fire? If it had been present at the fusillade around Stötteritz?
>
> The emperor took another look at the men, raised his right hand and closed with the words '*Gardez bien votre roi!*', at which he and his entourage rode towards the Ranstädt Gate followed by the assembled [French] Guard. My soldiers farewelled him with a lusty '*Vive l'Empereur!*' Other than my dialogue with the emperor four days earlier at Holzhausen, I experienced here the most sublime moment of my career and was certain that this meeting would be remembered even two hundred years on.[338]

Württemberg legate Kölle was watching as the emperor and his entourage rode off through the crowds and confusion. 'He wore the renowned little hat, the plain grey overcoat, and looked calm but very aggrieved,' he recalled, 'Fatigue lay especially heavily on Berthier. All, man and horse, looked very worn out. Only Murat, in his fantastic outfit with carefully curled locks, was the same as always.' As the imperial entourage rode off and ever more French soldiers pressed into the square trying to escape, it seemed to Kölle 'as if I heard the rustling of a page of the vast book of fate above my head as it was being turned over'.[339]

Sometime after Napoleon departed to make his agonisingly slow passage to Lindenau, the remaining Saxon troops from Zeschau's division arrived in the marketplace and formed up in columns near the grenadiers. Zeschau himself appeared and instructed the officers that they should greet any approaching Allied troops in a friendly fashion with white flags and await further developments. When Prussian light infantry charged into the square in the early afternoon, therefore, they were welcomed with waving bits of white cloth and a cheer from the assembled Saxon battalions who stood with their muskets inverted, muzzles towards the pavement and stocks in the air.[340] As the Prussians dashed off in pursuit of the retreating French, however, Oberst Anton von Ryssel, younger brother to the brigade commander who had led the defection the previous day, appeared on horseback in front of the ranks with his sword drawn. The junior Ryssel, no less fervent and excited than his brother, had just returned from his abortive mission to beg clemency from the Allied monarchs. Having delivered his report to the Königshaus, he now decided for himself that there was nothing to do but lead the available Saxons against the French as quickly as possible. Without awaiting definitive orders, he rushed back into the square and 'seemed to take over command of the Saxon troops there, said something about Germany's liberation and set off with them towards the Ranstädt Gate'. They had not got far when a Prussian officer intervened, telling the Saxons that they would receive orders when it was time to march. Exactly what happened next is unclear. Perhaps the lead Saxon unit, the *Anger* Grenadier Battalion, either did not receive or chose to ignore these sardonic instructions. Or a Prussian officer may have led a number to the gate. Alternatively, the leader was a former Saxon officer, now in Austrian service. Some Leib-Grenadiers may have been involved as well. Whatever the precise details, a small group of Saxons, probably no more than a company in strength, opened fire on some French troops beyond the gate shortly before the bridge over the Elster was destroyed. Other than Birnbaum's four guns on 18 October, this is the only clear instance of Saxon troops firing on the French at Leipzig.[341]

The scene in the city was one of shifting chaos. A mob of French soldiers and vehicles was trying to jam through the lone open gate while incoming howitzer shells crashed all about and a press of Allied soldiers rushed through the streets to the exuberant cheers of citizens hanging from their windows and balconies. The cheers redoubled on the appearance of the Allied monarchs with their large suites of followers. The victors, however, evinced no interest in speaking with Friedrich August. Several Allied officers apparently paid brief calls at the Königshaus and Bernadotte stopped to exchange friendly words with the king, but the Allies had spurned several attempts to discuss sparing the city that morning (such as Oberst von Ryssel's mission) and the

Russian and Prussian monarchs pointedly ignored their fellow ruler when they rode into the market square.[342] Colonel Louis Victor Léon, comte de Rochechouart, a French émigré on Alexander's staff, was 'stunned by the treatment, if not cruel, at least ungenerous, of the Russian emperor towards the old man with the crown, who seemed to me rather saddened than humiliated by this reception'.[343] Likewise, Kaiser Franz, in whom the Saxons invested so much hope, spent a few hours in Leipzig, but made no effort to see the king. When a Saxon emissary requested meetings with Alexander and Friedrich Wilhelm III, he was bluntly informed that the tsar believed such a meeting would be 'disagreeable';[344] Prussia's king did not deign to reply at all. Similarly, personal letters dispatched to the Kaiser and the tsar brought no relief. Franz sent a courteous but empty response; Alexander was decidedly cold and chose not to see the king even though he called on Queen Amalie on 21 October. Discussions with Stein and Allied foreign ministers were equally discouraging and a session with Metternich only produced more hollow sympathy mixed with condescending admonitions regarding Saxony's earlier policies. At the insistence of the Russian and Prussian sovereigns Friedrich August was thus declared a prisoner of war and Russian guards replaced the Saxon grenadiers outside the royal residence. Although the Austrians would have preferred to see the defeated king exiled to Prague, there is no evidence to indicate Kaiser Franz attempted to alter the stern position adopted by his allies.

On 23 October, therefore, Friedrich August, his queen and their daughter along with a small entourage were sent to Berlin escorted by Cossacks and under close surveillance.[345] They would remain Prussia's prisoners until 1815, their expenses paid from Saxony's treasury and the kingdom under first Russian, later Prussian, administration. Given his status as a prisoner, the king was not permitted to attend the Congress of Vienna, but his kingdom, along with his former Duchy of Warsaw, were objects of bitter contention during that gathering: Prussia sought to annex Saxony in its entirety and Russia was determined to rule all Polish lands. Opposition from Austria, Britain and Bourbon France preserved Saxony and Friedrich August's position as its royal ruler. Kaiser Franz duly invited the king to a castle outside Vienna in February 1815 where he was given the option of either agreeing to his kingdom's partition or seeing Saxony vanish into Prussia. Determined to preserve what he could, Friedrich August accordingly ratified a treaty in May by the terms of which the kingdom lost half of its territory and approximately half of its population to Prussia. He also abandoned any claim to Polish lands. There would be, of course, no 'compensation' for the loss of the Duchy of Warsaw.[346]

The army, meanwhile, stood in a sort of stateless limbo. The French governor released the Saxon troops in Torgau on 24 October and the remains of the division – temporarily under Ryssel's command – awaited instructions in Zeitz south of Leipzig. All was clouded in doubt, misgivings and mistrust. The king to whom the officers and men had sworn their oaths had been escorted off as a Prussian prisoner, their immediate past was disconcerting, and the continued survival of their country uncertain. The depth of their disorientation is portrayed in Cerrini's prolix but pointed depiction:

> The situation of the Saxon corps in the course of time just mentioned is undoubtedly one of the rarest, as well as one of the most perplexing and therefore most unfortunate, in which the concurrence of imperative, irreconcilable circumstances can bring such an association of brave warriors, tried and tested in adversity and death, and it would, indeed, have required a higher spirit, descending from the source of light, in order to guide us, without evil consequences, through this highly emotive sea of opinion.[347]

The Allies contributed to apprehension in the Saxon ranks by placing Thielmann (as a Russian general) in command. As some anonymous grenadiers recorded in 1815, many officers and men regarded him as a traitor 'who had broken his oath and loyalty to king and fatherland' and 'injured the duty of the honest soldier and grateful subject'.[348] Similarly, Kummer wrote that 'he had shown himself an open enemy of the king and of his Saxon fatherland' from the time he left Torgau.[349] Although most were glad to be free of Napoleon and had no qualms about taking up arms against the French, this satisfaction was mixed with doubts about the future, deep scepticism about Thielmann and bitterness that their perilous action on 18 October had not earned them the expected reward of security. 'We are all very depressed,' wrote Major von Hausen on 24 October, 'as our very existence seems under extreme threat.' Hauptmann Probsthayn expressed similar anxieties in his journal, while Leutnant von Wolffersdorff observed that his soldiers, 'faithful adherents of the royal house' and usually 'lively and in good spirits', now revealed their apprehensions through 'their dull silence, their gloomy mood'. 'The situation of the troops at that time', he recalled, 'was among the most hopeless and therefore unfortunate that can befall a band of warriors who have proven themselves through thick and thin.' Raabe, whose batteries had led the way across the field from the French side to the Allies at Leipzig, never seems to have reconciled himself entirely to an action taken under pressure from Ryssel. He found himself 'misled' to 'grasp every means for its preservation and to choose the lesser of two evils, even though my inner voice disputed the legitimacy of this undertaking'. 'The interests of the king and the fatherland', he wrote years later, 'may have misled me into taking improper steps.' Leutnant Vollborn, assigned to the detachment guarding the trains headed for Torgau, was not present at Leipzig and accounted himself 'pleasantly reassured that I had not gone over to the enemy', but asked 'How did this help us? The king remained in Leipzig & was declared a prisoner by the Allies.' Leutnant von Holtzendorff, who had participated in the defection, ruefully commented that the Saxons had paid a high price for their desperate act, 'which threw such an unfavourable light on them from a military point of view,' and concluded that it had been 'completely in vain' and had come 'rather at their own painful loss'.[350]

With this mood in the background, the reassembled Saxon contingent participated in the siege of Torgau with Thielmann in command. The *König* battalion that had defected with Major Bünau joined the rest of the contingent outside the fortress but 'their reception from our side was a rather cold one', noted Mandelsloh, 'just as their attitude displayed a certain reticence, a relationship that did not recover in later times'.[351] These internal tensions notwithstanding, the Saxons now found themselves engaging the French and Rheinbund troops in the fortress. The *Anger* Grenadier Battalion, for instance, fought with its former friends south of Torgau during a sortie by the garrison on 5 November. Likewise, the light cavalry that had defected skirmished with the retreating French on 21 October near Freyburg as part of Blücher's advance guard before being released to join their compatriots at Torgau.[352] The entire army was soon called away, however, and departed on 14 November to play a minor role on the margins of the 1814 campaigns in Belgium as part of III German Corps under Herzog Carl August of Sachsen-Weimar.[353] Disaffection grew steadily, however, while their king remained under arrest in Prussia and Thielmann's actions clearly demonstrated that he hoped Saxony would soon be absorbed into the Prussian kingdom. The pro-Prussian sympathies of Ryssel, Brause and a few others were also obvious and Thielmann's arbitrary, authoritarian command style ('a tyrannical person' noted one officer) further inflamed the smouldering anger prevalent among his subordinates. Back in Saxony, officers like Scheibershofen could barely contain their fury when confronted with 'the brutal, arrogant behaviour that many Prussians permitted themselves vis-à-vis the Saxons'.[354]

Months of discontent culminated in a riot in May 1815 when the men were told that Prussia's forthcoming annexation of half the country meant the Saxon army would be divided, with half to remain Saxon, the other half to be merged with the Prussian army. This was just prior to the Waterloo campaign, and the Saxons were under Blücher's overall command. On hearing what to them was intolerable news, a mob of Saxon grenadiers stormed Blücher's headquarters in Liege, hurling stones, breaking windows and shouting abuse. A tense calm was eventually restored, but Blücher, with no desire to have the Saxons in his army on the eve of facing Napoleon again, ordered exemplary punishment. The offending battalions were disarmed, seven ringleaders were executed (after the battalions had been threatened with decimation) and the flag of the Guard Grenadiers was publicly burned. The Saxons were then marched deeper into Germany where they were divided into Prussian and Saxon contingents in June. The remaining Saxon elements, reinforced to a strength of 16,000, were finally assigned to Schwarzenberg's command to support the blockades of Schlettstadt and Neuf-Brisach in Alsace as the 1815 campaign wound down. A small detachment remained in France until 1818 as part of the Allied occupation force following Napoleon's second abdication.[355]

The grenadiers in Belgium were not the only angry Saxons. Back in Saxony, some Leipzig citizens erected an 18-metre-high wooden cross near Probstheida on 19 October 1814 in the presence of the Russian military governor to commemorate the Allied victory. It was decorated with a poem celebrating the city's 'rescue' by the Allies and a collection box was attached to raise money for the reconstruction of the village church (which had been destroyed by Allied artillery fire). The monument, however, did not enjoy a lengthy existence. When news spread that half of Saxony was to be detached to Prussia, unknown persons sawed the cross down during the night, and it disappeared without a trace. Left behind was a bitterly satirical poem: 'If the Prussian can steal our land from us/The devil's hand can take this cross.'[356]

*

The Saxon defection at Leipzig was one of the most dramatic events involving the Confederation of the Rhine during 1813. It was, however, only one point on the spectrum of Rheinbund reactions to Napoleon's impending defeat and the end of the alliance. The heavy cavalry's actions during the same battle sit on another point of the spectrum: regiments that performed loyally, competently and courageously despite being imbued with the same sort of anti-French resentments evident among their compatriots. Indeed, the entire contingent fought well until the very end, enduring relentlessly grinding marches and demonstrating disciplined, steadfast behaviour on the battlefield even in very trying circumstances such as the withdrawal from Gölsdorf at Dennewitz. Moreover, in addition to and despite anger towards the French, there was a clear underlying desire for victory as evident in the disappointment over the perceived lack of support at Großbeeren and Dennewitz or the heavy cavalry's regrets that Latour-Maubourg was not present to coordinate a more successful series of charges at Wachau on 16 October. Major von Tiling may have momentarily moaned for an Allied victory at Dennewitz, but Schreibershofen's frustration at the loss of an opportunity for 'a most splendid decision' was more representative of the contingent's attitude.[357] The Saxons naturally rejected the accusations that they had caused the defeats at Großbeeren and Dennewitz as unfounded insults to their personal and professional pride, libel against their courage and competence as soldiers. It is not idle to wonder how a successful drive on Berlin under Oudinot or Ney might have influenced Saxon attitudes. Or what might have eventuated if Napoleon had committed sufficient resources and his own person to gain an unquestionable victory over Bernadotte's army?

Whatever the Saxon views of the French by 1813, the Saxon soldiers placed a high value on maintaining a reputation for skill and valour at the individual, unit and national levels, qualities that received validation in the award of honours from their king and especially from the French emperor – as was evident in Saxon complaints about not receiving due recognition in 1812. Thielmann may have discarded his Legion of Honour as emblematic of a desire to change sides, but he was unusual in this regard. The attachment to these symbolic acknowledgements of bravery was strong. A captive French officer in Leipzig thus had a surprising encounter in the complete chaos in the market square on 20 October 'amidst uniforms of every nation'. Left to wander by his Russian escort, he encountered a Saxon officer with whom he was acquainted. The Saxon immediately opened his coat to show his concealed cross of the Legion of Honour and said, 'our generals have dishonoured us, but this sign will remain by my heart till death'.[358]

Two other points are worth mentioning before shifting attention from Saxony to Bavaria. First is that some Saxons, like Oberstleutnant von Raabe, seem to have carried a burden of unease if not guilt about the defection for the rest of their careers. For many, the fact that the division's defection meant betrayal of their respected corps commander added to their discomfort. Leutnant Larisch, for one, reflected this regret in his account of his experiences: 'How I wish I could have seen Reynier, who had led the Saxons for so long and in such a caring manner, spared this insult.' Likewise, Schreibershofen, who was on the scene, could not bring himself to join the initial defection despite his desire to break with the French. 'Personally, it was very difficult for me, morally and practically, to join my comrades and follow them to the Allies', he would write, 'It was impossible for me to leave right in front of General

Reynier, whom I held in high esteem, who had shown me every confidence up to that moment and at whose side I was during the advance of our troops.' 'All of us believed we had acted for king and fatherland,' Mandelsoh would write, 'and none of us imagined that we would one day regret this step that did little for the fatherland, but left us subject to many reproaches.'[359] It is unlikely that those who took Prussian service experienced such lingering reservations, but Wolffersdorff doubtless captured the emotional anguish of many when he later wrote 'Shall I say what was happening in my heart at the time? ... It was the thought of going against the will of our king, of having made our own politics!' He upheld 'the incorruptible sense of what is right and the loyal fulfilment of duty' on the part of the Saxon army and rued that this was taken by Saxony's German 'opponents' as 'parochialism and incorrect calculation of the great needs of the time'. Thus, he claimed, he first came truly to understand the lines from Friedrich von Schiller's drama *Wallenstein's Death* that conclude with: 'Safe is the narrow path that duty treads.'[360] As shall be seen, most Rheinbund officers would face similar ethical challenges during the course of these campaigns.

The second concluding point is the centrality of leadership. As in almost any military endeavour, the quality of leadership was crucial to attitudes and outcomes. From the evidence cited here, the rank and file in Bünau's battalion and the men of Brause's and Ryssel's brigades do not seem to have been aware of the intended defections and, if some of the French accounts are accurate, junior officers displayed chagrin when Reynier arrived, begging him to distance himself from the columns so as not to be captured. Bünau, Brause and the Ryssel brothers, on the other hand, were ardently convinced of the necessity of their actions. Although they 'represented a small minority in the Saxon corps, where the majority orientation was Saxon-national rather than German-national', they were ultimately persuasive enough by position and personality to implement their plans.[361] Zeschau was a loyal and capable officer, but with only one month in command, he was unable to divert the momentum towards defection before it began and too late to alter events once the columns started to march. It is not idle to wonder what might have transpired if the better known and highly respected LeCoq had been left in command.[362]

Chapter 3

Bavaria: The First to Fall

'It is that scoundrel your brother who has caused all my problems.'

Napoleon to Queen Amalie of Saxony, Leipzig, 19 October 1813[1]

BAVARIA WAS THE LARGEST and most important Rheinbund state.[2] It had allied itself with France through a bilateral treaty in the autumn of 1805 almost a year before the establishment of the Confederation of the Rhine and its soldiers had served under Napoleon's eagles in all the major wars across central Europe from Vienna to Moscow (with Spain being a notable exception). The close Franco-Bavarian association during those years had served the interests of both states. For Napoleon, Bavaria was the cornerstone of the trans-Rhine buffer zone on France's western borders and bolstering Bavaria was a key component of his effort to supplant Austria in Germany while containing Prussia. A stronger, more coherent Bavarian state, of course, would also be better able to supply the troops and resources he sought from all his Rheinbund allies. Moreover, Bavaria was under the sceptre of the Wittelsbach dynasty. With a history as Bavaria's dukes and prince-electors dating back to the eleventh century, the Wittelsbach family was one of Europe's oldest ruling houses and presented attractive marriage prospects for Napoleon as he endeavoured to strengthen his own family's legitimacy. His stepson Eugène was thus duly wedded to Princess Auguste Amalie of Bavaria in January 1806, a political union that produced a deeply happy marriage. An additional family connection to Napoleon's hierarchy, though less loving, was created in 1808 when the emperor's chief of staff, Alexander Berthier, was pushed into a marriage with Max Joseph's niece, Maria Elisabeth, Herzogin in Bayern. The marriage lacked the warm intimacy of that between Eugène and Auguste, but the personal link to Max Joseph meant that Berthier corresponded regularly with Bavaria's ruler, his letters often taking the place of direct communications from Napoleon.

From Bavaria's perspective, alliance with France likewise offered manifold benefits, both to the state and the dynasty. Foremost among these was protection against the avaricious intentions of Habsburg Austria. Austria had presented the principal threat to Bavaria for more than a century, especially during the reign of Kaiser Joseph II (r. 1780–90) who had manoeuvred assiduously but unsuccessfully to annex all or most of the Wittelsbachs' south German territories.[3] Highlighting the underlying enmity, the War of Austrian Succession (1740–48) and the War of Bavarian Succession (1778–79) saw the two states on opposite sides, including – much to the horror of the Habsburgs – the brief stint of a Wittelsbach, Charles VII, as Holy Roman Emperor in 1742–45, the first time in three centuries that a non-Habsburg had occupied that sacred seat. Austria remained a danger as the eighteenth century turned into the nineteenth and its invasion of Bavaria in September 1805 as part of the War of the Third Coalition prompted the hesitating Kurfürst Max IV Joseph to sign an alliance with Napoleon in late September of that year. By joining Napoleon Bavaria secured enormous rewards in territory and population in the wake of the French victory at Austerlitz. Gains included the Tyrol and Vorarlberg (from Austria) as well as most of Franconia (from Prussia) for a total increase of nearly 20,000 km^2 and 608,000 new subjects to underwrite Bavaria's long-desired elevation from an electorate to a kingdom on 1 January 1806. As the first to ascend to this royal dignity, the former *Kurfürst* thus became Max I Joseph, König von Bayern. All this history was very recent and relevant in Bavarian minds as the kingdom faced the challenges of 1813.

The Monarch in Munich: I Am a Bavarian

Bavaria's accession to the Rheinbund as a founding member in July 1806 certainly constrained its sovereignty in external affairs and tied it to Napoleon's military enterprises, but it had enjoyed only restricted foreign policy independence under the Holy Roman Empire, so the arrangement with France did not seem a drastic sacrifice in exchange for security against the Habsburgs, a dramatic expansion in size and the acquisition of a royal crown. Joining the Rheinbund was also a protective measure as it meant Napoleon was unlikely to chop up Bavaria to satisfy the desires of its German neighbours, especially the acquisitive Friedrich of Württemberg.

Just as important from Munich's perspective were the advantages to be gained on the domestic front. The Bavarian leadership, eager to pursue a dramatic reform agenda, had been hindered by the strictures of the old *Reich* that buttressed internal opposition. Alliance with Napoleon granted the king greater internal authority and thus cleared the way for a sweeping state modernisation programme. The leading figure in this Enlightenment enterprise was Maximilian Graf von Montgelas, the king's most trusted advisor and, after Max Joseph, the single most powerful figure in the monarchy. Montgelas introduced comprehensive changes across almost all aspects of national life under an increasingly centralised state bureaucracy, including the promulgation of Bavaria's first constitution in 1808 (modelled after that of Westphalia).

Napoleon seldom meddled in these domestic matters. Chiefly concerned with the external aspects of the alliance, he saw no need to interfere in the internal workings of a state like Bavaria that seemed well managed and dutifully fulfilled his requirements for troops, resources and political support. Napoleon's economic policies, on the other hand, were a significant burden. Both the Continental Blockade aimed at Great Britain and tariff schemes that advantaged French products harmed the Bavarian economy and generated increasing popular displeasure towards the French alliance. Many people, rightly or wrongly, also blamed increased tax burdens on the French alliance as being caused by the need to maintain the army and participate in Napoleon's wars.[4] Conscription, too, was often imputed to the French even though Bavaria had instituted its conscription law on its own initiative in 1804 before it was under any alliance obligation to France. Montgelas and other key Bavarian reformers, however, were convinced that Napoleon's hegemony would be a transitory phenomenon, unlikely to endure beyond his lifetime.[5] Restrictions in foreign policy and frictions over commerce or other issues could therefore be tolerated in the short term to exploit Napoleon's protection against the traditional Habsburg enemy. Behind the French shield, Munich's leaders could pursue longer-term interests by creating an expanded Bavarian state that was modernised, centralised, geographically unified and elevated to a higher plane in European affairs. Montgelas would later characterise the relationship as always maintained 'in a respectable and dignified manner, according to existing practice and on the footing of complete equality'.[6]

Franco-Bavarian political frictions, however, accumulated over time. Even though Bavaria accrued net gains in territory and population as reward for its participation in the 1809 war against Austria, for instance, some in Munich were dissatisfied when Napoleon removed the southern districts of the Tyrol from Bavarian control because he had concluded, quite correctly, that over-zealous imposition of Bavarian reforms had been a major factor behind the region's rebellion during the war. Napoleon's marriage to the Habsburg Archduchess Marie Louise in 1810 was especially disappointing as it tied the emperor personally to the traditional Austrian adversary and foreclosed any prospect of further Bavarian expansion at Austria's expense. The emperor's wedding and birth of his son in 1811 also curtailed Wittelsbach dynastic ambitions because it made it unlikely that Eugène, and with him Auguste, would ascend to the imperial throne as Napoleon's heir. With Napoleon at least temporarily reconciled with the Habsburgs, Bavaria lost much of its former significance as a French ally against Austria and, for many in Munich, the burdens of the alliance began to weigh more heavily than the benefits.[7]

With little prospect of further territorial growth, the king and Montgelas were deeply sceptical of the looming war with Russia. Regardless of the outcome, they and others in Munich feared that the consequences would be detrimental to their hopes for Bavaria: a Russian success might bring the tsar's troops to Bavarian soil, while a Napoleonic triumph could remove all constraints from the French emperor's behaviour and leave Bavaria subjugated, diminished or even broken apart.[8] There was also a royal family link to the Russian imperial house as Tsarina Elizabeth Alexeievna was one of Bavarian Queen Caroline's younger sisters. Nonetheless, Max Joseph could not evade Napoleon's summons. The Bavarian army duly marched for the Niemen and performed well during the campaign only to be shattered in the process as recounted in the Prologue. The horrifying results of the Russian disaster shocked the court, the army and the population at large, erasing 'the remaining sympathies in Bavarian public opinion'.[9] As Queen Caroline told the Prussian ambassador in Munich in January 1813: 'One could only shudder at the thought of the thousands of dead, who were sacrificed, not in the interests of the state, but rather solely to the ambition and the "*bon plaisir*" of a single individual.'[10] With the entire European political situation in flux, the early months of 1813 thus saw Bavaria in crisis: its army destroyed, its French benefactor gravely weakened, the Coalition powers advancing from the east and a tide of anti-French anger growing among its own people.

Like their counterparts in Saxony, Bavaria's leaders therefore found themselves struggling to navigate a sea of uncertainty and reconsidering their alliance with France even as they endeavoured to conjure up a new army to replace the one lost in the maelstrom of war beyond the Niemen. Three men would determine how Bavaria would cope with this crisis: Max Joseph, Montgelas and General Wrede. The burden of decision, of course, rested on the king's shoulders. Max Joseph was 57 in 1813, imbued with the ideas of the Enlightenment and cherishing a strong attachment to France. As was the case with many others, he also stood in awe of Napoleon, remarking that 'he has accustomed us to wonders' even as he expressed his reservations about the invasion of Russia.[11] For his part, Napoleon held Max in high regard, viewing him as a friend and model monarch.[12] Indeed, the two remained on genuinely cordial terms until the very end.

Portrayals of Max Joseph often describe him as 'anxious' and sometimes exhibiting physical symptoms of stress; he could be hesitant, impatient with details and uncomfortable with difficult decisions. At the same time, he was possessed of a 'sure political instinct' and an extraordinary personal charm such that he was equally at ease with peasants, tradesmen, courtiers and kings. He also held to a strong belief in personal honour, including loyalty to one's oaths. Like his brother-in-law on the Saxon throne, therefore, he would view the prospect of breaking with France as 'a betrayal of which I am incapable'.[13] Part of his affinity for France derived from his early years with his French tutor, from the appeal of Enlightenment ideals and from spending twelve years as a French officer before the Revolution. Close familiarity with military affairs led him to accord a high priority to modernisation of the Bavarian army when he became prince-elector in 1799 (the same year that Napoleon became First Consul by coup).[14] Army modernisation, however, was only one facet of the sweeping reforms Max Joseph and Montgelas introduced to increase the authority of the centralised, secular state, strengthening Bavaria domestically to underwrite a greater role in the international arena. Deeply committed to his state and dynasty, Max Joseph sought to preserve all that he and his minister had accomplished over the years since his ascent to the throne and feared Bavaria would be 'revolutionised' by pan-German extremists or whittled into insignificance, even expunged, by the whims of the great powers.

Montgelas, the second crucial figure, was a brilliant stateman and skilled bureaucrat. He had been closely associated with Max Joseph since 1795 and, as one Bavarian historian points out, it is often difficult to discern which of the reform ideas originated with the monarch and which with the minister. Indeed, the king hardly ever changed the draft texts he received from his advisor. Subsequent nationalist writers would condemn Montgelas for not being an ardent Prusso-German 'patriot', but he, like his king, saw himself as solely dedicated to Bavaria's welfare. He had little patience for what he perceived as vague and dangerously 'revolutionary' pan-German notions that would limit Bavaria's expansion, annul its achievements and diminish its independence.[15] In 1813, he was both Foreign and Interior Minister as well as nominal head of the Finance ministry. These offices and his influence with the king would make him one of the central players in the forthcoming drama.

The third critical person was GdK Carl Philip Freiherr von Wrede. Wrede was in many respects similar to Saxony's GL von Thielmann. Ambitious, proud, sensitive to perceived slights and brimming with self-assurance, he was also an energetic and competent general long favoured by Napoleon. By the time of the invasion of Russia in 1812, however, Wrede believed he had fallen into disgrace with the French emperor. He thought Napoleon should have intervened on his behalf in land disputes involving his estates in former Austrian territory and he resented not being awarded the Grand Cross of the Legion of Honour, the order's highest degree. He also saw himself as the victim of multiple personal indignities inflicted by French officers who he considered his peers rather than his superiors. As the campaign in Russia progressed, his irritations with his French counterparts multiplied and he twice requested to be relieved of command. Napoleon, on the other hand, continued to hold him in high regard. Towards the end of the campaign, for instance, a combination of circumstances left Wrede in charge of a composite corps that included French, Westphalian and Hessian regiments as well as his few remaining Bavarians. This force eventually came to number some 10,000 men and represented the only time in the entire Napoleonic epoch when a non-French general commanded a corps-level formation. Though his unique position was in part a result of the army's dire situation in October and November 1812, it was also indicative of the emperor's faith in Wrede as a field commander.[16]

Wrede does not seem to have drawn this conclusion. When he returned home in early 1813, he was weary, frustrated and incensed at what he perceived as the persistent mistreatment he and his men had received from senior French officers. In this mood, he 'suddenly discovered his Germanness' and became a determined proponent for ending the alliance with Napoleon.[17] Stopping in Württemberg territory on 17 March on the road back to Munich, for instance, he read the Prussian king's proclamation to his people and remarked: 'Well written and very true and not at all a rant!'[18] Carl Eduard von Löwenberg-Hruby und Geleny, the Austrian representative in Munich, summarised his impressions of Wrede several days later in a 23 March report to Vienna: 'General Graf Wrede, full of the bitterest gall from aggrieved ambition, eagerly desires an opportunity to make France feel his worth, of which he is most convinced, and therefore advises negotiations with Saxony and even with Württemberg in order to act independently at once in case of an even greater failure of French arms.'[19] Although he submitted a memorandum arguing for neutrality in the spring, Wrede only came to the forefront in the autumn when he would work relentlessly to push Max Joseph towards the Allies and thereby become the most important factor in the speed with which the Bavarian shift occurred. Like his king, however, Wrede was first and foremost concerned with Bavaria's status, not some dubious form of pan-German unity under Prussian or Austrian aegis.[20]

Importuning from the outside during Bavarian policy debates in 1813 was Crown Prince Ludwig, a vehement opponent of Napoleon. Where Max Joseph, Montgelas and Wrede were contemplating a break with France for practical reasons of state, Ludwig was motivated by an emotional attachment to romantic images of a Germany that had been sullied and oppressed by France. Ludwig, Max Joseph's son by his first wife, had been born in Strasbourg where Max Joseph's French regiment was garrisoned. Twenty-seven in 1813, he was full of passionate intensity, hating Napoleon as the despotic inheritor of the French Revolution and dreaming of a 'Teutschland' (as he and other pan-German patriots spelt the name) free of all French influence. Opposed to policies his father and Montgelas pursued towards France, he made no secret of the lively detestation with which he regarded the French and their emperor. He lamented French victories in 1805 (wishing Strasbourg to be 'a German city again'), toasted Napoleon's death with the Austrian ambassador in Munich during the winter of 1808/9 and penned perfervid poetry to express his angers and his hopes.[21] An 1807 poem, for example, entitled 'An die Teutschen' ('To the Germans') began with: 'Up you Germans! Up and break the chains/A Corsican has laid upon you!'

Ludwig and his small coterie of followers were on the extreme fringes of the spectrum of opinion in Bavaria until 1813, but he pressed his views so fervently, so loudly and so frequently that spring that he became tiresome. 'Your hatred of the emperor is your *idée fixe* and all of your thoughts are subordinate to it,' Max Joseph wrote to his strident son on 25 May, 'I beg you never to talk about politics with me again.' The king did try to placate Ludwig in their extensive correspondence, but he had no interest in his eldest son's pan-German visions and repeatedly asserted his local loyalties in his letters. 'Believe me, I will not neglect the interests of Bavaria or my house for a single minute ... I am neither French, nor Russian nor Prussian nor Austrian – I am Bavarian,' he wrote in mid-September.[22]

Queen Caroline, Max Joseph's second wife, was another figure at court who opposed Napoleon. She would urge her royal husband that autumn 'to march against France', but her degree of influence on policy was likewise limited.[23] Although she and Ludwig represented a certain element of elite opinion, therefore, Montgelas and Wrede were the real influences and, in the end, Max Joseph would decide on his own.

The Army in Russia No Longer Exists

With the exception of depot units, fortress garrisons and part-time National Guard battalions, the entire Bavarian army marched to Russia in the spring of 1812. Incorporated into the Grande Armée as the 6th Corps (19th and 20th Divisions) under then General Gouvion Saint-Cyr, this fine force totalled some 25,000 men divided into 12 infantry regiments, 6 light infantry battalions, 6 light cavalry regiments and 10 batteries of artillery. Replacement columns dispatched during the course of the war would bring the Bavarian commitment to more than 30,000 by the end of the year. Very few of them would ever see their homes again. As Hauptmann Johann Michael Antelsperger recorded when he arrived with a replacement column in mid-January: 'the army in Russia no longer exists'.[24] Although most of its soldiers vanished in Russia, this 1812 establishment would form the template for the new army the kingdom would raise to meet the crisis of 1813.[25]

Several points are worth noting before describing the constituent elements of the Bavarian army in 1813 as they illustrate the intersection of military and political considerations while the kingdom charted its course in this period of frightening uncertainty. First, there was never any question of re-forming the army after the Russian catastrophe. Whether it remained true to its alliance with Napoleon, crafted a neutral position or joined his enemies, Bavaria would need an army of sufficient size to give military weight to its political decisions.[26] Debate in Munich thus focused on how quickly and efficiently the army could not only be rebuilt but reinforced. Second, the rebuilding and reinforcing process was inhibited by severe deficiencies in finances, trained soldiers, trained horses, and above all, by the dearth of suitable officers and NCOs. Problems in these areas would have a deleterious impact on all the formations outlined below. Third, doubts about the French alliance were already evident in the first three months of 1813, manifesting themselves in a firm determination to commit only the absolute minimum number of troops to Napoleon until the strategic situation clarified. While the ragged remnants of its regular army reassembled in Poland, therefore, Bavaria would exert itself to re-create a respectable military force to be held within its borders but would exaggerate its difficulties, erect administrative obstacles and create excuses to avoid sending additional troops to the Grande Armée.

The 12 line infantry regiments were the core of Bavaria's active army. Each of these was supposed to consist of 2 battalions for an authorised field strength of 1,835 officers and men, but the manpower shortages in 1813 made this figure unattainable. Nonetheless, each battalion was still to retain its old organisation: a grenadier company, a *Schützen* company and four fusilier companies.[27] In addition, each regiment had left behind a reserve battalion (*c.* 600) of four companies in its home garrison when it marched to the Niemen the previous year; classified as 'National Guard First Class' (*National-Garde I. Klasse*) until 1810, these battalions would be crucial to the army's reconstruction after Russia. Whether in the regular or reserve battalions, all of these infantrymen were uniformed in distinctive Bavarian style with unique cornflower blue coats and wearing the tall, crested Bavarian *Raupenhelm* for headgear. As the 12th Infantry had disgraced itself in 1806, that number had been stricken from the army's rolls, so the twelve regiments in 1813 were numbered 1st through 11th, each of which also bore the title of an *Inhaber* or proprietor, plus the 13th which carried no special title. They were differentiated from one another by the colours of the lapels, collars and buttons on their uniform coats as shown in Chart 22. The two 'royal' regiments (*König* and *Kronprinz*) were further distinguished by special decorative braid across their lapels, in white and yellow respectively.

The six light infantry battalions had a similar organisation to their line counterparts, each consisting of six companies for a full-strength total of 924 officers and men, not including two reserve companies (*c.* 300) that were intended to remain in Bavaria. As with the line regiments, this 1812 figure was beyond Bavaria's capacity in early 1813 and company strength was correspondingly reduced to 121 rather than 150. Battalion organisation was also similar to the line units with one company of *Schützen* and four of fusiliers, but instead of grenadiers each light battalion had carabiniers for its second elite company. As was common in the era, the light infantry soldiers all wore dark green jackets with black lapels and red trim and were only differentiated from one another by the colours of their collars and buttons.

The losses incurred in Russia combined with the confusion and haste surrounding the army's re-establishment meant that these authorised models of infantry organisation could not be maintained in 1813. The result was an unusual order of battle for the infantry during the coming campaigns. To establish some sort of regularity, in early March the army decided that the infantry elements still in the field (that is, in Poland at the time) would be designated as the '1st Battalion' of each line regiment, regardless of its original 1812 organisation; fresh recruits and men culled from the regiment's reserve battalion would then form the regiment's new '2nd Battalion' in Bavaria. As a special honour, these new '2nd Battalions' were issued new regimental standards 'decorated with the colours of their Fatherland' to replace those lost in Russia.[28] Even if severely weakened by drafts to the new 2nd Battalions, the Reserve Battalions remained in place (four companies each) to serve as organisations for new recruits and those unfit for field duty.[29] The 13th Infantry, immured in Danzig, was an exception as both of its original battalions were still intact (*see below*) and it had retained its standards during its retreat. The four companies of its Reserve Battalion, as shall be seen, would therefore take the field with the Grande Armée.[30]

The same organisational concept was applied to the light battalions. Those still in the field organised their remnants into three companies, one of carabiniers and *Schützen* combined and two of fusiliers; these were designated the battalion's '1st Division'. At the same time, a '2nd Division' was created for each battalion in Bavaria, similarly organised with one combined carabiniers/*Schützen* company and two companies of fusiliers.[31]

The Bavarian cavalry's challenges were just as daunting, compounded by the difficulties and expenses involved in procuring and training appropriate mounts. Each of the kingdom's six chevaulegers regiments was supposed to be composed of six squadrons, four for field service and two as reserve plus a depot. Unlike Saxony, Bavaria decided to re-form all six regiments, but owing to the dearth of men and horses after Russia this could only be accomplished in slow, sequential fashion: one squadron per regiment at a time. As a result, the troopers who joined the Grande Armée that spring would be organised into an ad hoc composite unit mixing squadrons from each of the kingdom's regiments. These men wore traditional light cavalry uniforms consisting of dark green jackets with distinctive colours shown on their lapels and collars along with the ubiquitous – at least for Bavaria – *Raupenhelm*.

Paucity of horses and men also hampered the re-creation of the Bavarian artillery. This arm, always one of the army's strong points, was organised into 20 numbered companies: 12 foot (1 through 12), 4 reserve (13 through 16) and 4 light (1 through 4). Each company supplied one battery of six pieces, normally four guns and two howitzers, 6-pounders for the foot batteries, 12-pounders in the reserve batteries and 6-pounders for the light batteries in which all of the men were either mounted or rode on the battery's vehicles. Two foot batteries would accompany the division that took the field with the Grande Armée in 1813, but the French apparently requested an organisation along French lines, so for the first time each of these two Bavarian batteries would be equipped with eight pieces: six 6-pounders and two howitzers.[32] Similar to many other armies, Bavaria's artillerymen wore dark blue coats with black lapels and red distinctions while their comrades of the train were dressed in grey with light blue trim; both also wore the *Raupenhelm*.

Although not involved in combat as part of the Grande Armée in 1813, Bavaria's militia was also a crucial component of the kingdom's rearmament

Chart 22: Bavarian Units in 1813

Unit	lapels (trim)	collars (buttons)
1st Infantry *König*	red	red (white)
2nd Infantry *Kronprinz*	red	red (yellow)
3rd Infantry *Prinz Karl*	red (white)	red (yellow)
4th Infantry *Sachsen-Hildburghausen*	yellow (red)	yellow (white)
5th Infantry *Preysing*	rose	rose (white)
6th Infantry *Herzog Wilhelm*	red (white)	red (white)
7th Infantry *Löwenstern-Wertheim*	rose	rose (yellow)
8th Infantry *Herzog Pius*	yellow (red)	yellow (yellow)
9th Infantry *Ysenburg*	yellow (red)	red (yellow)
10th Infantry *Junker*	yellow (red)	red (white)
11th Infantry *Kinkel*	black (red)	red (white)
13th Infantry	black (red)	red (white)
1st Light Battalion	black	red (yellow)
2nd Light Battalion	black	red (white)
3rd Light Battalion	black	black (white)
4th Light Battalion	black	black (yellow)
5th Light Battalion	black	yellow (white)
6th Light Battalion	black	yellow (yellow)
1st Chevaulegers	red (red)	green (white)
2nd Chevaulegers *Taxis*	red (red)	green (yellow)
3rd Chevaulegers *Kronprinz*	black (red)	black (yellow)
4th Chevaulegers *König*	red	red (white)
5th Chevaulegers *Prinz Leiningen*	light red	red (yellow)
6th Chevaulegers *Bubenhofen*	black (red)	black (white)

after Russia. Established by the 1808 constitution as the 'National Guard Second Class' (*Nationalgarde II. Klasse*), the militia was formed into nine 'Mobile Legions', one for each of Bavaria's nine districts (*Kreise*). Each legion was to carry the name of its district and consist of four battalions (e.g., I/Isarkreis was the 1st Battalion of the Isarkreis Legion) some or all of which could be mobilised in case of national emergency.[33] Most important for the circumstances of 1813 was that the constitution specifically stated that the mobile legions would not serve outside Bavaria, a stricture that was reinforced by the 28 February decree that called them into existence; this included the royal assurance that 'the National Guard would never and under no circumstances be employed beyond the borders of the kingdom'. Max Joseph also made certain that Napoleon knew of this constraint, highlighting it in a 3 March letter to the emperor. Eighteen of these mobile legion battalions were formed as the result of a royal decree, soon followed by orders directing the creation of a volunteer National Guard cavalry regiment, the 'National-Chevaulegersregiment', with the same restrictions on employment outside the kingdom.[34] The authorities in Munich, particularly driven by Montgelas, deliberately designed these National Guard units to address two requirements. First, despite gross deficiencies in officers and NCOs as well as training and equipment, they were a means to increase the size of the available military force at relatively low cost as compared to the expenses involved with resurrecting and expanding the active army. Second, the constitutional prohibition against employment outside the kingdom appealed to new recruits and provided a convenient excuse to fend off French requests for more troops in the main theatre of war. Munich could therefore claim with some truthfulness that it was doing its utmost to repair the damage of 1812 while strictly limiting the troops dispatched to join the new Grande Armée. The mobile legions, whatever their defects, thus served Bavarian purposes very well.

January–April: The Long Road from Russia

While the authorities in Munich were contending with the kingdom's military and political challenges, most of Bavaria's active regulars were still in the field far from home. With the exception of the 13th Infantry in Danzig, the Bavarians, as explained previously, had constituted the 6th Corps under Gouvion Saint-Cyr in 1812. The corps was assigned to protect the main army's left flank in concert with Oudinot's 2nd Corps. To the great annoyance of the Bavarians, however, the six cavalry regiments were detached to the main army; they fought well at Borodino and marched to Moscow but were utterly destroyed during the ensuing retreat. Meanwhile, the bulk of the contingent distinguished itself in two battles at Polotsk (August and October) that year but suffered heavily from disease as well as combat casualties. Among those casualties were Saint-Cyr (wounded) and the senior Bavarian general, Bernhard Erasmus von Deroy (killed), losses that led to Wrede assuming command of the few remaining Bavarians and, eventually, a substantial multinational corps as noted above. The strength of Wrede's brave band steadily ebbed away, however, and when he made contact with 'the whirling human river' that had been the Grande Armée on 6 December, more than half of his remaining men vanished into 'the defenceless mass of half-frozen, half-starved creatures staggering by in a wild jumble'.[35] Two days later, with only some 1,000 men under his command, Wrede became the army's rear guard, holding off Cossacks and refusing demands to surrender when surrounded, only to see his remaining troops dissolve on reaching Vilna. All Wrede could do was direct the survivors to the 6th Corps' designated rally point, Płock on the Vistula in Poland, and make his own way there as best he could.

Fortunately for Wrede, on the way to Płock he was joined by the 6th Corps rear depot. The depot had not only maintained a substantial amount of equipment but had collected some 1,200 men (albeit mostly without weapons) during the course of the previous weeks. Individuals and small groups of stragglers also found their way to Płock, but most important were five replacement columns that had been dispatched from Bavaria during the autumn and were only now arriving in the theatre of operations. These replacements were shocked by what they encountered on meeting their countrymen in frozen Poland. Hauptmann Antelsperger, one of the fresh officers, noted in his diary that the condition of the survivors from Russia was 'indescribable': 'some had frozen hands or feet, some were sick or wounded, pale countenances, ragged bits of clothing'.[36] The newcomers may have been stunned by horror and pity, but Wrede made good use of these men and the supplies they brought with them. In addition to some 5,000 replacement troops, the five columns delivered such large quantities of food, medicaments, clothing and shoes that the entire contingent could exchange its tattered rags for new uniforms. By mid-January 1813, therefore, the tireless Wrede was able to assemble a revived '6th Corps' with himself as its commander. Although the 'corps' was, in reality, a combined arms division, this was no small achievement and Major Ludwig von Seiboltsdorf wrote with justifiable satisfaction that the division 'after 14 days on the banks of the Vistula was again equipped, clothed and constituted the only solid mass of the army'.[37]

Wrede's reconstructed command had a 'present under arms' strength of approximately 6,000 infantrymen in two small brigades formed by merging the survivors from Russia with the newly arrived recruits, each soldier allotted to his original unit of assignment (i.e., light battalion or regiment).[38] The light battalions were arranged into three companies (rather than six) and the men of each line regiment were amalgamated into a single battalion (as noted above, the army administration in Munich would later designate these the 1st Battalion of its regiment) with two of these composite battalions making a combined regiment. Each of the brigades thus included three reduced light battalions and three of the combined line regiments; to promote cohesion, units of the former 19th Division went to 1st Brigade, those of the former 20th

Division to the 2nd. As for the other arms, Wrede had enough horses to mount an ad hoc cavalry regiment of around 300 men and to create four artillery batteries with a total of 20 guns. Though most of these men were brand new recruits from Bavarian depots and more than 800 were without arms, this was a respectable force, especially in the desperate conditions prevailing at the time. A contemporary French officer-historian referred to the Bavarian division as 'the truly effective part of the army' ('*la partie réellement effective de l'armée*').[39]

On the negative side of the ledger, there was a severe shortage of NCOs, there were not enough muskets for the available soldiers, and sickness was rife, leaving 500 men in the Płock hospitals, many of whom would die of their ailments. Also worrying for the Bavarian commanders was the morale and inner resilience of the men. Although harsh measures had restored discipline, the cheery and confident attitude that had buoyed the troops in the past was absent. Even the replacement columns had spent two months on the march from Bavaria, the first three columns suffering considerable loss to sickness and exhaustion as their untried recruits had trudged over bad roads through snow squalls and bitter cold 200 kilometres beyond the Vistula in search of 6th Corps before learning of the disaster and turning towards Płock. It is thus unsurprising that a later Bavarian historian observed: 'One could hardly speak of confidence and martial enthusiasm among men who had experienced such frightful misery or who were witness to its consequences and whose situation was even now highly uncertain and by no means hopeful.'[40] This apprehensive attitude, of course, did not augur well for the division's future performance.

Wrede and his men stayed in Płock for two weeks, incorporating the replacement detachments, organising, outfitting and sending back to Bavaria over 1,000 excess officers and NCOs along with those too ill to continue service.[41] One of these was Hauptmann Joseph Maillinger of the 1st Infantry Regiment who departed on 18 January with his brother Fridolin, an *Unterleutnant* from the 8th Infantry. Both were afflicted with typhus but 'we preferred to die along the way rather than fall into captivity and suffer the mistreatment that so many of our comrades in arms had to endure'. The Maillinger brothers were representative of many sick, wounded and exhausted Rheinbund officers struggling to make their ways home in those early months of 1813: contending with difficulties, sometimes nearly overwhelming, in securing transport, clothing, lodgings and food in Poland, but finding better, almost comfortable, conditions once they reached German-speaking regions, despite the obvious ferment, animus and abuse often encountered in Prussia. For these men, it was a welcome relief finally to cross into another Rheinbund state where more regular arrangements for the quartering of passing troops could be expected. Both Maillingers survived the journey to tread once more 'the soil of the beloved fatherland with tears of gratitude' on 17 March.[42] Many of their comrades were not so fortunate, surviving the ordeal of the Russian campaign only to succumb to illness, injury or enervation on the long road home.

Back in Płock, Wrede received unwelcome, and to him outrageous, orders on 15 January: he was to detach 3,000 men to serve as garrison in the fortress of Thorn. The 4th Light Battalion (281 men) had already been sent to Thorn on the 11th despite his protest, now he was to dispatch half of the division he had taken great pains to form into a respectable force. He was furious. He complied by assigning the mission to GM Friedrich von Zoller and the 2nd Brigade, but to him this was 'unpleasant and harmful for the service as well as for the administration of my corps'.[43] Moreover, he saw it as further evidence of French disregard for their Bavarian allies in general and for his own person in particular. Wrede and his adjutant, Hauptmann Eduard von Völderndorff und Waradein, blamed Davout, who was collecting the sad ruins of the 1st and 8th Corps in Thorn. They averred that he promoted the employment of the Bavarians in the garrison so that he could withdraw his French troops from the barely defensible fortress and sacrifice the Bavarians who could then be made scapegoats should it be lost. Wrede and Davout had clashed prior to the invasion of Russia and the marshal was not reluctant when it came to harbouring dark suspicions about France's allies, including the Bavarians.[44] In this case, however, there is nothing to suggest that he either advocated defending Thorn or recommended the Bavarians as its garrison. Indeed, the evidence of his correspondence points in the opposite direction. In the first place, although he viewed it as a useful bridgehead 'for the next campaign', he advised against defending Thorn unless the line of the Vistula was to be held and a mobile force was provided on the west bank to support the garrison at need. Otherwise, any troops committed to its defence would simply be lost for little gain. Second, he did not have the authority to order the Bavarians to Thorn and indeed specifically argued against assigning this task to them:

> If one does not have the certainty of going to the aid of Thorn if it is seriously attacked, in the current state of affairs one should not think of its defence: this would be to compromise the troops, since there is no protection, and I dare to say that at the first simulacrum of an attack, the Bavarians, worked upon by the inhabitants who do not care to see their city burned, will force the hand of the general in command, whatever his strength. And what effect will not the news of the capture of these 3,000 Bavarians have in Bavaria, men who perhaps will be in the enemy

ranks within a few months? [Note that Davout was not singling out the Bavarians; he was suspicious of the loyalty of all foreign contingents and offered similar warning about the Poles in the same letter.]

Once Zoller and his brigade arrived, however, Davout was reassured. 'I shall leave in Thorn General von Zoller, of whom I have heard the highest praise' he told Eugène on 20 January. He seemed quite confident the following day, writing to his friend Poniatowski that, 'The garrison that I have left in Thorn is very strong. It is animated by the best of spirits. The Bavarian general who commands these troops is a man of honour and very reliable.'[45] Leaving behind some 500 French infantry and artillery as part of the garrison, the marshal then departed for Posen to meet Eugène and receive new instructions.

Wrede's aggravation at seeing his just-organised Bavarian division broken apart is understandable (from his perspective it was a sequel to the cavalry regiments being sent away during the Russian campaign), but his flaring indignation seems misplaced in this instance. Having dispatched Zoller's brigade to Thorn on the 16th, he set the rest of the division on the road towards Gnesen (Gniezno) two days later but rode off to Posen ahead of the men in a state of high dudgeon to ask Viceroy Eugène to countermand the offending orders. In this he failed. Eugène apparently agreed to reduce the number of Bavarians to 1,000 (rather than the entire brigade), but it was already too late to implement even this relatively minor concession: Zoller had already arrived and Davout had departed by the time this decision was made. Wrede, however, believing Eugène had issued the necessary orders to Davout, reported that the French marshal had deliberately disobeyed these instructions and had a stiff confrontation with Davout when they met in Gnesen on 24 January.[46] Wrede 'explained himself with that frankness and emphatic vigour that the French marshals had had occasion to experience', wrote Seiboltsdorff, 'Nonetheless, the brigade – at least for this campaign – was to be considered as lost.'[47]

This entire affair was probably just another case of misunderstanding, poor communications and headquarters confusion on the French side at this early, chaotic stage when Chief of Staff Berthier was gravely ill and Eugène had just assumed command from the hastily departing Murat. For Wrede, however, it was another example of the French dismissing their ally's concerns, this time a dishonourable scheme concocted by the devious Davout. Deeply bitter, he turned his attention to his remaining men who were now beginning to arrive around Gnesen where they were to form the link between Thorn and the small observation corps Eugène was assembling east of Posen.[48]

Wrede did not remain long at Gnesen. He already had Max Joseph's permission to return to Bavaria and now, with no chance to reunite his two brigades, he turned over command of the Bavarian 'division' to GM Joseph von Rechberg on 7 February and set off for the kingdom. It was his last day as a French ally. Feeling angry, resentful and personally offended, he would soon be charged with creating a new Bavarian army to fight against Napoleon. In the meantime, the events of January 1813 had left the Bavarian troops in the field dispersed in three distinct locations. The mobile division, now under Rechberg, was around Gnesen, approximately 50 kilometres east of Posen as part of Eugène's small *corps d'obsérvation*, Zoller's brigade, soon to be isolated, held Thorn and the 13th Infantry was part of the Danzig garrison. As each of these elements would operate on its own for the remainder of the spring campaign, the following pages shall examine their activities separately while keeping in mind that the authorities in Munich consistently sought to bring all of them back to Bavaria. As for the men who had already left Płock to become cadres for the re-forming army, they found only icy hostility in the Prussian lands through which they passed and, on returning home, were adjured to restrain their accounts of the Russian campaign's horrors so as not to arouse anxiety or incite anti-French attitudes among the Bavarian populace.[49]

The 13th Infantry: From the Daugava to Danzig[50]

Unlike the rest of the Bavarian contingent, the 13th Infantry was weakened but intact when 1813 began. The regiment, along with two guns from the 2nd Foot Battery, had been one of several Rheinbund units sent to join the garrison of Danzig in March 1811 at Napoleon's request. When the Russian campaign opened, therefore, the 13th and what was effectively its regimental artillery had already been in the great fortress for more than a year. As a result, although it was considered part of 6th Corps on paper, it never served with the rest of the Bavarian contingent. It did, however, participate in the invasion of Russia. Assigned to GD Grandjean's 7th Division, it was part of Marshal MacDonald's 10th Corps, advancing from East Prussia into Latvia to operate on the far left flank of the great French offensive. It saw little combat in this role and was thus spared the destructive battles and appalling privations that decimated the other elements of the kingdom's army. Indeed, Oberst Kajetan von Butler was pleasantly surprised when he was transferred from Polotsk to take command of the 13th in the autumn of 1812: 'I found the regiment in the best condition. The men are healthy and fairly well supplied with equipment. What a contrast with the regiments I have just left.' The regiment also earned a favourable reputation with its French allies. MacDonald wrote that he was 'very pleased with its order and discipline',

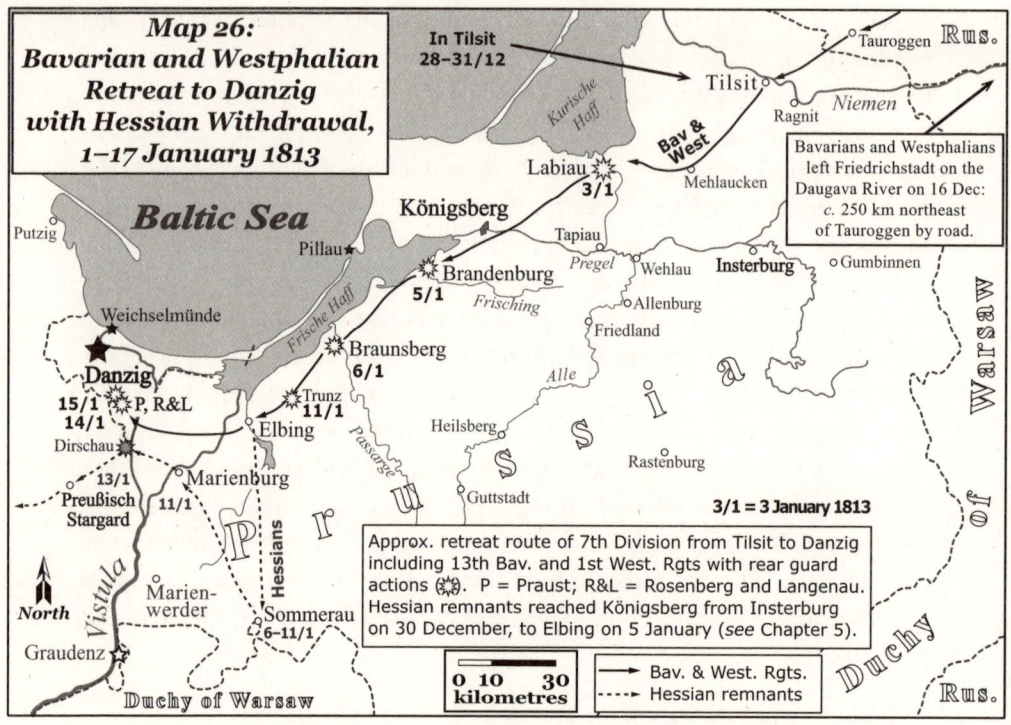

while its brigade commander, GB Étienne Pierre Sylvestre Ricard, described 'its fine appearance and its discipline, the excellent spirit that animates it' in a letter to Max Joseph.[51]

The 13th Infantry had been posted at Friedrichstadt (Jaunjelgava) on the Daugava (or Düna) River for several relatively uneventful weeks when the shocking news of the main army's disastrous retreat from Moscow caused MacDonald to begin falling back towards the Prussian border on 16 December 1812. Withdrawing in fine order, the 7th Division reached Tilsit (Sovetsk) on 28 December, but MacDonald ordered a hasty departure on the last day of the month when he learned of the Prussian defection at Tauroggen. Moving by forced marches with little rest under execrable weather, the 13th arrived in Labiau in the early morning hours of 3 January having left 165 men in Tilsit with cold weather injuries and losing almost half its remaining strength to march attrition during the gruelling retreat. The corps moved on again later that same day after only a few hours' rest with the Bavarians joining the 10th and 11th Polish Infantry Regiments to constitute the rear guard under GB Gilbert Désiré Joseph Bachelu. The regiment was soon in action. Initially placed west of Labiau in support of the Poles, the Bavarians lost 59 men as they repeatedly switched places with their Polish allies as Bachelu's command slowly withdrew '*en echelon*' from position to position in an extended engagement. The 7th Division's journal credited the Bavarian *voltigeurs* (*Schützen*) with performing 'prodigies of valour', but the fighting on 3 January was only the beginning.[52] The regiment would remain in this rear-guard role almost every day for the coming two weeks, burnishing its reputation and earning MacDonald's 'particular respect and confidence' during these enervating combats but suffering a steady drain of casualties.

Helping to cover the retreat to Danzig, Butler's regiment and its tiny artillery detachment were thus involved in further rear-guard actions on 5, 6, 11, 14 and 15 January at Brandenburg (Ushakovo), Braunsberg (Braniewo), Trunz (Milejewo), Langenau (Łęgowo), and Praust (Pruszcz Gdański) respectively (*see* Map 26). Most of these engagements involved the Poles and Westphalians as well as the Bavarians and all of them imposed a cost in blood. As shown by an incident at Brandenburg on the 5th, the Bavarians and their partner units had to contend with the hostile East Prussian population as well as the pursuing Russians. A detail from the 13th was attempting to burn a bridge over the Frisching River that day when a lieutenant was slightly wounded by a civilian shooting from a nearby house. The Bavarian soldiers, enraged to see their officer hit by what was considered a cowardly and unlawful act, stormed across the burning bridge and would have set the local buildings afire had Oberst von Butler not intervened to restrain them.

The regiment's rear-guard trials ended when it marched into Danzig on 17 January in parade style with flags flying. In the one month from the beginning of its retreat on the banks of the Daugava to its entry into Danzig, the 13th Infantry had covered more than 600 kilometres and solidified its reputation for reliability and courage. It had lost 12 dead, 82 wounded and 114 missing or captured in the process; an additional 162 were entered on its rolls as stragglers (*traineurs*) and 371 were listed as sick. These losses notwithstanding, the 13th was intact, well-led, adequately supplied and undefeated. Moreover, the men had not personally experienced the shock of witnessing the wreckage of the Grande Armée and had not become engulfed in its miseries. When Oberst von Butler led his command through Danzig's gates, therefore the 13th Infantry and its artillery attachment still had 1,135 officers and men fit for duty (140 of whom were detached). The men were all veterans with campaign experience and their colonel was a paragon of military correctness as well as a skilled and courageous combat leader. He and his men did not know it yet, but this would be the start of a new trial, one that would put the regiment to the test for the next eleven months as part of Danzig's polyglot garrison before they again marched out through those gates (*see* Chapter 8).

Within the Walls of Thorn[53]

Approximately 150 kilometres south of Danzig, a second group of Bavarians was also engaged in defending a fortress on the Vistula. This was Zoller's 2nd Brigade, detached from the reorganising Bavarian division in Płock to Wrede's great fury. Departing Płock on 17 January, Zoller and his eight battalions arrived in Thorn on 20 January to join the 4th Light Battalion which, as described, had been sent to the city on the 11th.

Thorn, home to some 7,000 people in 1813, was an old city, founded by the Teutonic Knights in the 13th century. It was situated on the right or northern bank of the Vistula at a point where the river ran almost east to west and was connected to the southern shore by two long wooden bridges which met on a small island in the middle of the river. In addition to the walls and bastions that encircled the city proper, a permanent defensive work had been constructed on the island, but the southern end of the bridges was only protected by an abatis around the few houses clustered there. Also on the southern bank and considered a part of the city's defences was an old and partly ruined castle called Schloß Dybow (Zamek Dybów) about a kilometre downstream from the bridge. The Vistula was 800 metres wide at this point in its course and a formidable obstacle in most seasons, but it was completely frozen over that winter with ice thick enough to permit an infantry assault against the decrepit walls along the city's riverfront. This vulnerability would remain until the ice began to break up on 22 February.

As a fortress, however, Thorn was ill-prepared when war came to its walls in the late winter of 1813. Long neglected, it was in poor physical condition despite a refurbishment programme that Napoleon had initiated after his conquest of Poland in 1806–7. Compounding the deficiencies of the works, the city was surrounded by a ring of hills on both sides of the river. Though low, these sandy hills were higher than the fortress walls and edged close to the outer works, thus offering considerable advantages to an attacker. As the French artillery commander during the siege reported, not only were the defences 'in a bad state of maintenance' but 'the hillocks, sometimes as close as 200 metres to these first works, dominated them on all sides'.[54] Furthermore, the available artillery was inadequate for a fortress of Thorn's size. The garrison had 50 artillery pieces, but many of these were outdated antiques, and there were only two dubious mortars to disturb prospective siege trenches. The lack of artillery pieces was compounded by the fortress' limited stock of artillery ammunition, sufficient for only a relatively brief defence. On the other hand, there was an adequate supply of infantry ammunition and the city was well provided with food, albeit mostly old stocks of legumes and salted meat.

The garrison numbered some 4,660 men when Davout left on 21 January. The principal component was Zoller's brigade of 4,044 Bavarian infantrymen, but there were also 300 French infantry from the 85^e and 108^e Ligne along with 188 French and 76 Polish gunners to serve the fortress guns plus perhaps 50 additional French staff officers, sappers and others.[55] Unfortunately, there was no cavalry detachment to conduct reconnaissance or contend with the numerous Allied horse who would soon appear. Lack of cavalry was not the only problem in the garrison's composition. The overall strength was barely adequate for the size of the fortress and numbers would soon drop dramatically as sickness rampaged through the ranks. Furthermore, the sturdiness of the Bavarian brigade was questionable. Unlike Butler's men in Danzig, Zoller's command consisted of an unpromising mix of shattered survivors of the Russian catastrophe and inexperienced recruits hastily sent from Bavaria as replacements. Wrede and others had accomplished a great deal in welding these disparate elements together during the few weeks in Płock and the troops made a favourable impression on Thorn's inhabitants when they entered the city, but the new brigade was as yet untested. Given these circumstances, the quality of the leadership provided by the garrison's officers would be of paramount importance in shaping the brigade's performance during the trials in the weeks to come.

As the garrison was to be almost entirely Bavarian, Davout had offered command to Zoller, but the general demurred, citing his ignorance of the

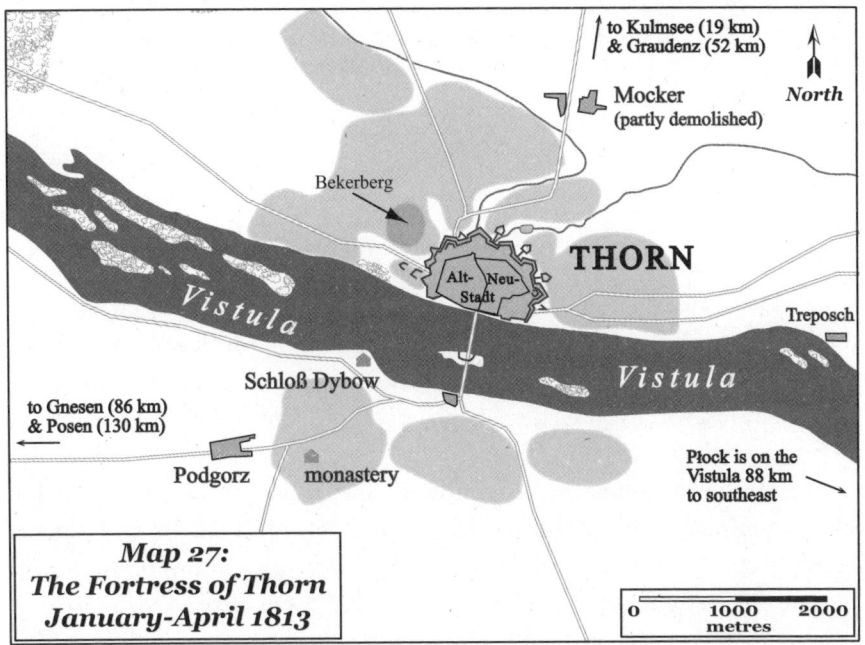

Map 27:
The Fortress of Thorn
January–April 1813

Chart 23: The Thorn Garrison, 20 January–18 April 1813

Governor: *GB Poitevin de Maureillan* Commandant: *Oberst von Hoffnaaß*

Strength figures as of 25 March 1813

		bns/sqdns	present under arms	in hospital
Staff and administration		–	30	–
French infantry	Col. Piat			
85ᵉ Ligne		–	123	15
108ᵉ Ligne		–	133	12
2nd Bavarian Brigade	GM von Zoller			
2nd Light Battalion		1	79	73
4th Light Battalion		1	85	133
5th Light Battalion		1	91	166
1st Combined Infantry Regiment				
2nd and 6th Infantry Regiments		2	444	380
2nd Combined Infantry Regiment				
3rd and 7th Infantry Regiments		2	481	530
3rd Combined Infantry Regiment				
5th and 11th Infantry Regiments		2	486	505
French sappers		–	19	0
French artillery and artillery artisans		–	169	32
Polish artillery		–	73	3
French cavalry (1st Chasseurs)		–	7	2
Total Bavarian, French, Polish			2,220	1,851
Total Bavarian only			1,676	1,787

Note: The figure for staff/administration includes 10 Bavarians. The Bavarian Ministry of War considered the line infantry battalions listed above to be the 1st Battalions of their regiments.

Source: Hößlin/Hagen, 'Verteidigung von Thorn', pp. 58–9.

---

fortress and its surroundings as well as the lack of specialist artillery and engineer officers on his small brigade staff. Though Zoller had solid military reasons for declining command, Wrede, suspicious of the French, was relieved because he feared the Bavarians would be blamed if the city fell. He thus applauded Zoller's action: 'I give my complete approval, my dear general, to your decision not to accept the government of Thorn, so that in the future you will have a witness [i.e., the French governor] who will be in a position to do justice to the behaviour of your troops.'

In addition to expressing his doubts about the French, however, Wrede's letter illuminates themes that were core values for most Rheinbund officers during 1813: national honour, loyalty to the sovereign and military renown. Despite his extreme aggravation at seeing his corps dispersed, therefore,

Wrede warned Zoller to maintain the army's good reputation 'and show that Bavarian troops, wherever they are, know how to earn the emperor's esteem'. His letter thus continued:

> I therefore request, my dear general, that you say to your troops that the eyes of the king, of the fatherland and of their comrades are upon them.
>
> The troops that you now command, my dear general, are the cadres of the regiments that comprised my old division over a long string of years. Never did I have reason to be dissatisfied with them.
>
> I am certain that you will lead them to new fame and that, under your orders, they will only continue to bring honour to their king and to the nation to which they belong.[56]

As Zoller had declined the post, Davout appointed a French engineer, GB Jean Poitevin, Baron de Maureillan, as Thorn's governor. This proved a felicitous choice. Maureillan was not only a skilled and experienced professional who had most recently served as chief engineer in Marshal Ney's 3rd Corps during the Russian war, he was also exceptionally able, energetic and resourceful. Furthermore, he knew how to inspire similar activity and enthusiasm in the troops. Under his direction, the garrison immediately set about preparing for the siege that was sure to come: strengthening the works, conducting reconnaissance patrols, evacuating to Posen as many of the sick as possible and painting logs to mount on the walls as dummy guns to conceal his weakness in artillery.[57] The respected Oberst Ferdinand von Hoffnaaß of the Bavarian 2nd Infantry was appointed as the fortress commandant to support Maureillan.

Maureillan's preparations also included sending out detachments to collect intelligence and as much fresh food as possible before the city was surrounded. Livestock was a special target of these expeditions. Numerous Bavarian reconnaissance and foraging parties thus ventured far out into the countryside north and south of the Vistula during late January and early February. These detachments varied in size from a few dozen to a few hundred men depending on their missions and the anticipated threat. On 22 January, for example, fairly large detachments were sent downstream on both sides of the river, each consisting of a light battalion accompanied by a grenadier company for a total of perhaps 200 to 300 men per column. The few Cossacks they saw tried to keep out of range: 'No sooner had we spotted them, but they sprang away' wrote Hauptmann Antelsperger of the 2nd Infantry. These two groups were also typical in that their tasks were accomplished in a single day, the men marching out 10–12 kilometres to gather cattle and information before returning to the fortress. In a few other instances, however, the detachments remained away for several days, such as Hauptmann Carl Baron Lilgenau's company of the 11th Infantry that was sent 20 kilometres to the southwest on 25 January and did not return until 2 February.[58]

These early forays encountered nothing beyond scattered Cossack bands who showed no interest in engaging the garrison's infantry. In the first days of February, however, the Cossacks became bolder and regular cavalry began to appear, sparking minor skirmishes with the Bavarian reconnaissance detachments. Hauptmann Antelsperger's diary entry for 4 February gives us a picture of these missions outside the fortress walls:

> On the 4th, I participated in the 2nd sortie, which Oberst von Rott [Wilhelm Rodt, 11th Infantry] led in the strength of 800 men towards Kulmsee [Chełmża, 20 kilometres north of Thorn] to bring cattle into the fortress. The Cossack outposts which had blockaded the fortress since our arrival pulled back. But they were noticeably reinforced so that after a time they had grown to several hundred, among which were some sections of dragoons. We marched in three groups: advance guard, main body & rear guard. Every group was formed into a square. As the Russians were without infantry, we proceeded on our march untroubled, [and] reached some villages from which we took away numerous cattle & sheep. On our return we were totally surrounded by enemy cavalry and the skirmishing was rather lively. The Cossacks followed us up to the range of the fortress guns. We had only a few wounded from the 5th Rgt., while the Russians lost many men and horses.[59]

Skirmishes also occurred south of the river on the 4th and 5th, these actions gaining Oberst Rodt warm praise from Chef de Bataillon de la Roche, the overall infantry commander in the garrison.[60]

The first indication of a serious threat to Thorn came with the arrival of enemy infantry on the southern bank on 7 February. These were men of the Russian Third Western Army's Advance Guard under Lieutenant General Yefim Ignatievich Chaplits who had crossed the Vistula below Thorn earlier in the day. The Bavarians surprised the blockading force when they sallied out against the Russian position on the heights that night to gauge the enemy's strength and intentions. The Russians soon returned and resumed work on their positions, so Oberstleutnant Carl von Theobald of the 4th Light Battalion recommended another foray. Some 500 Bavarians thus attacked in the predawn hours of 9 February, but this time the enemy was not caught unawares, and the Bavarians took 43 casualties before withdrawing to the protection of the fortress again (Russian losses are unknown).[61] Though not as effective as the first, this second sortie again demonstrated the garrison's aggressive determination while gathering intelligence and disturbing the enemy's preparations. The defenders' resolve was also evident in Maureillan's instant rejection of another surrender demand, a refusal which led Chaplits to bombard the city ineffectually on 10 February. To the surprise of the garrison, however, Chaplits departed that very night. His sudden move was the result of a change in the strategic situation. Russian headquarters, learning that Eugène was withdrawing from Posen, had ordered Chaplits west in pursuit and Bavarian patrols thus found the enemy gone when they probed towards the hills from the bridgehead the next day.

Four days passed before new Russian troops appeared, this time on both banks of the Vistula. These were other elements of Barclay de Tolly's Third Western Army: Lt. Gen. Alexander Lvovich Voinov's command on the left bank and Langeron's division on the right, each group approximately 4,000 men strong. As with Chaplits's departure, this move was prompted by Eugène's retreat from Posen. With a mobile French force west of the Vistula, a siege of Thorn had not seemed viable (as Davout had concluded), but with Eugène pulling out, capture of the city became useful, practicable and politically desirable given the tsar's interest in dominating Poland. By 16 February, therefore, Thorn was encircled, but the Russian commanders, having failed to attack while the city was still vulnerable to an assault across the frozen Vistula, would now need to reduce the fortress through a formal siege. For this they required proper siege guns and those could only come from Prussian arsenals once the kingdom became an open ally.[62] Several weeks of waiting thus ensued during which action was limited. Skirmishing flared as the garrison continued its practice of conducting forays to gather intelligence and livestock, outposts occasionally nattered to one another, the garrison endeavoured to hinder the besiegers' activities with artillery fire and the Russians frequently bombarded the city at night, provoking replies from the fortress guns. The Russians also sought to secure the garrison's surrender through intimidation and propaganda. For example, the fortress journal recorded the following for 15 February: '... a Russian *parlementaire* appeared at the outpost line with a letter for the governor, he was sent away without a reply. He returned an instant later with a new summons to which the fortress replied with a few cannon shots.'[63] Otherwise, the two sides spent the time from mid-February to late March in preparing for a formal siege: the prospective attackers accumulating materials and selecting positions while the defenders industriously applied themselves to strengthening the works.

The tiny band of French and Bavarian soldiers in Schloß Dybow demonstrated especial verve. Cut off from the city when ice broke the bridge from the island to the south bank in late February, the castle's garrison only numbered some 40 men with a single howitzer and a pair of ancient wall guns. Led by a dynamic French captain named Savary, however, the defenders rejected all Russian appeals, used signal flags to maintain communications with the main fortress and deterred assault with a lively and imaginative use of clever ruses.[64]

While the garrison awaited the opening of the formal siege operations, however, the situation inside the fortress deteriorated. All Maureillan's energy could not counter the scourge of sickness, particularly typhus, that ravaged the ranks of the defenders. Although some men recovered and returned to duty, the numbers in hospital and those who succumbed to disease were enormous. Maurellian believed that Bavarian habits helped propagate sickness because 'the garrison was mostly composed of new Bavarian soldiers accustomed to overheating their houses at home and not allowing the necessary air into their rooms'.[65] By 15 March, the count of fatalities had climbed to more than 600 of the original 4,000 in the Bavarian brigade. The tally for 25 March was typical of the status from late February to the end of the siege: against 1,666 Bavarian officers and men fit for duty (not including staff), there were 1,787 in hospital, almost all victims of disease rather than wounds. On what seems to have been the worst day for the Bavarians, 22 March, 123 men died of illness and the average over the entire period of their stay in Thorn was 21 deaths per day from sickness alone. The grim situation meant that a burial detail had to be included in the roster of daily duties to be performed inside the fortress.

Despite its steadily ebbing strength, the garrison remained active and defiant. The reduced number of troops fit for duty meant larger forays could no longer be considered, but the defenders launched small sorties, maintained forward positions outside the fortress walls, repaired damage, and responded to Russian bombardments with active fire from the fortress guns. They even constructed two small gunboats and contemplated using boats to evacuate the garrison down river by night. Moreover, morale remained surprisingly good. Maureillan continued to reject demands for surrender and his men stayed true to their colours in the face of continual Russian efforts to undermine their determination. Russian *parlementaires*, for example, assiduously plied the garrison with leaflets urging surrender as well as recent newspapers featuring embellished accounts of French setbacks and Coalition advances. These notices failed in their effect. 'Vain effort!' wrote one Bavarian officer and another later recounted, 'Even in the context of the highly unfavourable circumstances and prospects,' these pamphlets and gazettes 'had no influence on the spirit' of the garrison. 'Although the German soldier had become alienated from the French cause since the catastrophe in Russia, in these moments of danger, he regarded the fulfilment of his duties as more important than the prevailing opinion.'[66] Likewise, the attitude of the population, clearly negative towards the French and fearful for their city, does not seem to have engendered discouragement among the soldiers. There were almost no desertions and the troops continued to conduct spirited counterattacks until the very end of the siege.

As March turned into April, however, the garrison's days were numbered. Prussia had now joined Russia in the war and 60 siege guns and mortars were soon on their way to Thorn from the Prussian fortress of Graudenz (Grudziądz), adding to the 13,200 men and 96 guns of Barclay's army.[67] Barclay only committed a portion of this force to the siege, but his Russians and their new Prussian allies dramatically outnumbered the much-weakened defenders. Although he maintained close personal oversight of the coming operations, Barclay assigned Langeron the day-to-day tasks associated with reducing the fortress. Under his supervision, the siege, skilfully prosecuted by the Russian engineers, proceeded rapidly despite the garrison's vigorous defence. Bombardments increased in frequency, the first parallel was opened on 8/9 April and Russian infantry secured the heights north of the city on the night of 14/15 April. Maureillan and his men remained defiant. On the night of 11/12 April, for example, Hauptmann Johann von Fleischmann of the 3rd Infantry earned the Bavarian Max Joseph Order and the Legion of Honour by leading 50 men in a brilliant counterattack to regain a lost outpost on the crucial Bekerberg just outside the city's walls.[68] Smaller local ripostes were conducted along other parts of the outpost line as well.

Viewing the swift progress of the Russian siegeworks and pressured by the city's inhabitants (as Davout had predicted), however, Maureillan could see that the end of resistance was near.[69] He therefore agreed to send emissaries to discuss terms of surrender with Lt. Gen. Ivan Vasilievich Sabaneyev, Barclay's chief of staff. Three meetings, including one in which Zoller participated personally, were held on 15 April without result. The French and Bavarian representatives argued for the right to retain their arms and were especially keen to avoid the term 'prisoners of war' in the wording of the capitulation document. Nonetheless, although they threatened to defend their post until the city was left nothing but a 'heap of stones', the French and Bavarians had run out of options. Artillery ammunition, already dangerously low, had been further diminished when a lucky Russian shot caused a powder magazine in a tower to explode and innovative efforts to convert infantry ammunition for use by the guns proved too slow and inefficient.

A white flag thus appeared on the fortress walls again and a fourth meeting led to a capitulation on 16 April, the terms of which required the men of the garrison to surrender their arms but allowed them to retain their baggage and to return to their respective countries under a pledge not to fight against the Allies for a year. Leaving 1,027 sick behind in Thorn's hospitals, on 18 April Zoller and the remaining 2,020 Bavarians fit to march thus departed the fortress they had so stoutly defended along with their French and Polish comrades in arms.[70] The brigade's total losses during its three-month stint in Thorn amounted to 7 killed in combat, 40 captured, deserted or otherwise missing and 922 dead from disease.

Several aspects of the siege are worth highlighting before leaving Thorn. First, the garrison remained resilient despite the isolation of the fortress, the sullen citizenry, the appalling sick lists and the ghastly backdrop of the Russian disaster. This sturdy resilience manifested itself in the determined defence throughout the blockade and siege, in the repeated forays beyond the city's walls and in the ability to launch resolute counterattacks such as Fleischmann's right up to the end. Perhaps most significant was the absence of desertion. Despite numerous opportunities and repeated Russian inducements, only 16 soldiers were listed as deserting during the entire three-month period; even if the 12 missing are added, the total only comes to 38 men out of an initial 4,000, or less than 1 per cent of the brigade. No officers changed sides. Even the cynical private Josef Deifl, publishing his memoirs of Thorn in the midst of the nationalism-drenched nineteenth century, repeatedly condemned the idea of desertion: 'Better to die a Bavarian!' he wrote.[71] There is no indication of recalcitrance on the part of Zoller's men and no suggestion that Maureillan worried about the reliability of his Bavarian troops. Indeed, the French commander showed no hesitancy in routinely sending Bavarian detachments 12–20 kilometres away from Thorn to forage, gather intelligence and probe the enemy's positions. Langeron claimed in his memoirs that Zoller quietly disparaged the French and expressed his hope that Bavaria would soon change sides when the two met during the surrender proceedings, quoting him as saying 'Farewell, general, in three months we will meet together against these rascals.' That may have been Zoller's secret hope, but if so, it was not reflected in his leadership during the siege or in the behaviour of his men.[72]

Second, as in most military operations, the quality of the garrison's leadership was crucial. Maureillan performed superbly in his role as governor.

His drive, ingenuity and intelligence as well as the respect with which he evidently treated his Bavarian subordinates were thoroughly repaid by the men of the garrison. His success as a leader, of course, would not have been possible without the unstinting cooperation of Zoller, Hoffnaaß and the rest of the Bavarian officer corps as well as the obedient loyalty of the NCOs and soldiers.[73] Maurellian paid full tribute to his Bavarian subordinates in his summary report. 'General von Zoller was always perfect in the required movements: during the night of 11/12 [April] he himself directed the attack against the enemy's reconnaissance,' he wrote, adding that 'One must give Oberst Hoffnaas, fortress commandant, the highest praise for the manner in which he conducted the affairs of the fortress from the start and for the activity he deployed in all the aspects of his service.'[74] He also named the commanders of the 2nd and 4th Light Battalions for their contributions to the defence. Together these officers and their French comrades in arms presented the Russian high command with a formidable obstacle, as Maurellian's chief of staff recorded in his journal of the siege:

> Despite the conviction one had of the weakness of the fortress and the materials available for defence, and despite the composition of the garrison, seven-eighths of whom had little direct interest in the preservation of the fortress, a rare spirit of unity prevailed among its diverse components during the entire time of the blockade and siege under the most trying circumstances. The entire garrison rightly attributed the preservation of the same [i.e., holding the fortress] to the confidence which the governor had known how to earn for himself.

'Only this unity of outlook and effort', he concluded, could explain how a relatively minor fortress with so many disadvantages could 'occupy the enemy for three months' and force them to undertake the sort of extensive preparations and exertions that would have been required to capture a first-rate fortress.[75]

Finally, the experience at Thorn is another example of the importance the Bavarian and other Rheinbund contingents attached to their conceptions of national and personal honour. From Wrede's first objections, to Zoller's insistence that his men retain their weapons and not be considered prisoners of war, the preservation of Bavaria's military honour was a central theme for the contingent's commanders. The individual soldiers also engaged in a symbolic act of defiance and personal dignity by holding on to their bayonets even as they stacked their muskets prior to leaving the fortress. They thereby contravened the strict terms of the capitulation, but the Russians, apparently content with their victory, did not bother to correct the infraction. The Bavarians also took pride in comments from Sabaneyev during the lengthy negotiations leading to the surrender. Responding to the French and Bavarian demand that the garrison be permitted to retain its arms, Sabaneyev reportedly asserted that he had specific instructions from Tsar Alexander to deny such requests because the dogged tenacity of the defenders had tied down an entire Russian corps and required the conduct of a formal siege.[76] Despite the shifting political circumstances and the numerous miseries endured by the garrison, therefore, the stalwart defence of Thorn acquired a special place of honour in Bavarian military history.

It remains to account for the two-month journey from Poland back to Bavaria, the final leg on an odyssey that for Zoller and some of his brigade had begun in March 1812, when they had left their homeland to join the great Napoleonic array on the Russian border. The men were relieved that the ordeal of the siege was over, but many harboured 'a certain unease at the thought that perhaps we would be led off into the depths of the Russian empire as prisoners of war after the capitulation'.[77] Nonetheless, unarmed but unbowed, they departed Thorn in fine military form, deposited their arms at the arsenal and marched through Poland into hostile Silesia to reach Bunzlau on 12 May escorted by a Russian staff officer and a detachment of Cossacks. Here they halted for ten anxious days, growing increasingly suspicious of their escort's intentions all the while. These apprehensions were confirmed when the column finally moved again: their assigned route of march crossed the path of the confused mass of the Allied army retreating from the Battle of Bautzen and their Russian escorts ordered them eastwards deeper into Silesia instead of south towards Austria as promised. Maureillan and Zoller, learning that the Allied authorities planned to intern them in a Prussian fortress contrary to the terms of their capitulation, defied their instructions and led the column on a forced march to safety in still neutral Austria so that only a few isolated men were captured and held by Prussian Landwehr. There followed a long march through Bohemia to enter Saxony on 4 June, the same day that the armistice went into effect. Here the 1,747 Bavarians in the column parted from Maureillan and the 712 remaining French with whom they had shared the trials of the blockade and siege.[78] Heading for home, Zoller and his men crossed the Elbe south of Dresden on the 6th and finally returned to Bavaria on 16 June.[79] 'It was for us an indescribably joyous moment when we saw the barrier with the white and blue of our national colours,' wrote Antelsperger.[80]

Rechberg's Retreat[81]

The third Bavarian element in the field that January was the so-called 'division' at Gnesen east of Posen. After detaching Zoller's brigade to Thorn, Wrede had moved the rest of the kingdom's contingent from Płock in administrative marches to arrive around Gnesen in batches between 24 and 27 January. Now part of the small mobile force Eugène was collecting east of the Oder River, the Bavarians were able to rest and reorganise while enjoying several days of decent quarters and food undisturbed by the enemy. Part of the reorganisation was a reduction in the division's artillery component. The viceroy deemed 20 guns to be too many for the small force at Wrede's disposal while the paucity of personnel, horses and ammunition made the extra pieces more a burden than a benefit. He thus directed the return of 14 guns to the contingent's depot in Görlitz to reconstitute the Bavarian artillery, an order that Wrede later amended to send them back to Bavaria where they arrived safely on 23 February.[82] This change left the division composed of the 1st Brigade's infantry along with the ad hoc cavalry regiment and a lone artillery battery for a total of approximately 3,000 men present under arms along with six guns (see Chart 24).

Wrede himself was in a sense excess to requirements. Not only was he genuinely too senior to command what was essentially a reinforced brigade, but with his proud and ambitious nature he likely regarded this subordinate post under Eugène as an affront to his dignity. As had been apparent in the later months in Russia, he believed he merited an independent command under Napoleon's personal direction. Having already received the king's permission to return to Bavaria, he thus turned over command to the senior remaining general, GM von Rechberg, on 7 February and set out for Munich.

Rechberg was a veteran officer, well-known at court, but the composition of force he inherited was problematic. As with Zoller's detached brigade, the division comprised a few discouraged veterans and a large number of recruits who had been in uniform for less than a year. Moreover, they had just watched 4,000 of their compatriots march off to a seemingly hopeless assignment in Thorn. The artillery battery generally maintained that arm's strong tradition of competence and the infantry demonstrated courage and resilience in several small encounters when well led, but vigilance was generally lax and morale poor. The consolidated cavalry regiment was especially weak, so dangerously inept and so likely to be surprised by the enemy that it could not perform traditional outpost and scouting duties. Infantrymen had to undertake these tasks in the place of their mounted brethren with significant degradation in field security and tactical intelligence. To make matters worse, Rechberg's command, unlike the Thorn garrison, seems to have lacked strong and active leadership. Without in any way minimising the challenges of his assignment, Rechberg, despite his experience, does not seem to have had the capacity to instill in his troops the vigour and determination supplied by Butler in Danzig and by Maureillan, Zoller and Hoffnaaß in Thorn.

The division's deficiencies were evident as soon as Russian cavalry began probing its positions around Gnesen. Bavarian cavalry outposts and patrols were repeatedly surprised and scattered in a number of small encounters during 5–10 February and the troops were subjected to constant harassment from the mobile and elusive Russian horse. As at Thorn, Rechberg's men were also recipients of numerous leaflets distributed by their foes. Like their comrades elsewhere, however, these proclamations 'did not make the least impression – and not a single man went over to the Russians'.[83] In this respect, leadership seems to have been firm, likely reinforced by the widespread fear of suffering abuse or transportation to the imagined distant and frigid reaches of the tsar's domains should they fall into Russian hands. Moreover, despite its many frailties, the division was an important element of Eugène's command in the context of early 1813 as Hauptmann Friedrich Winther of the 1st Infantry proudly recorded in his journal: 'Although this army corps had suffered extraordinary losses from the northern climate, the unusual severity of the cold and the dearth of provisions, it was nonetheless one of those in unbroken, serviceable condition, able to face the enemy as is proven by the honourable tasks it was assigned.'[84]

After two weeks at Gnesen, the Bavarians were ordered west. As part of his withdrawal to a cordon defence behind the Oder, Eugène directed Rechberg to Crossen while the rest of the French mobile troops shifted back to Frankfurt an der Oder. Badgered by Cossacks, the Bavarians left Gnesen on 11 February, reached Posen the following day and marched on at midnight of 12/13 February after fending off another Cossack attack. Finally free of their mounted tormentors, they arrived undisturbed at Crossen on the 16th, but bad weather and the strains of the marches, many made at night, took a toll on the division's manpower. Sickness and exhaustion meant that Rechberg could only count on 2,366 officers and men fit for duty while the number of sick and injured rose to 1,298. Curiously, in some cases, the number of available men increased. The roster of artillerymen, for instance, was augmented slightly despite the prevailing illnesses as stragglers and convalescents were welcomed back to the battery. 'This retreat from Gnesen to Crossen, conducted mostly at night and in forced marches, could be nothing other than very arduous for men who were already totally exhausted,' recorded Seiboltsdorff, 'Nonetheless, only 81

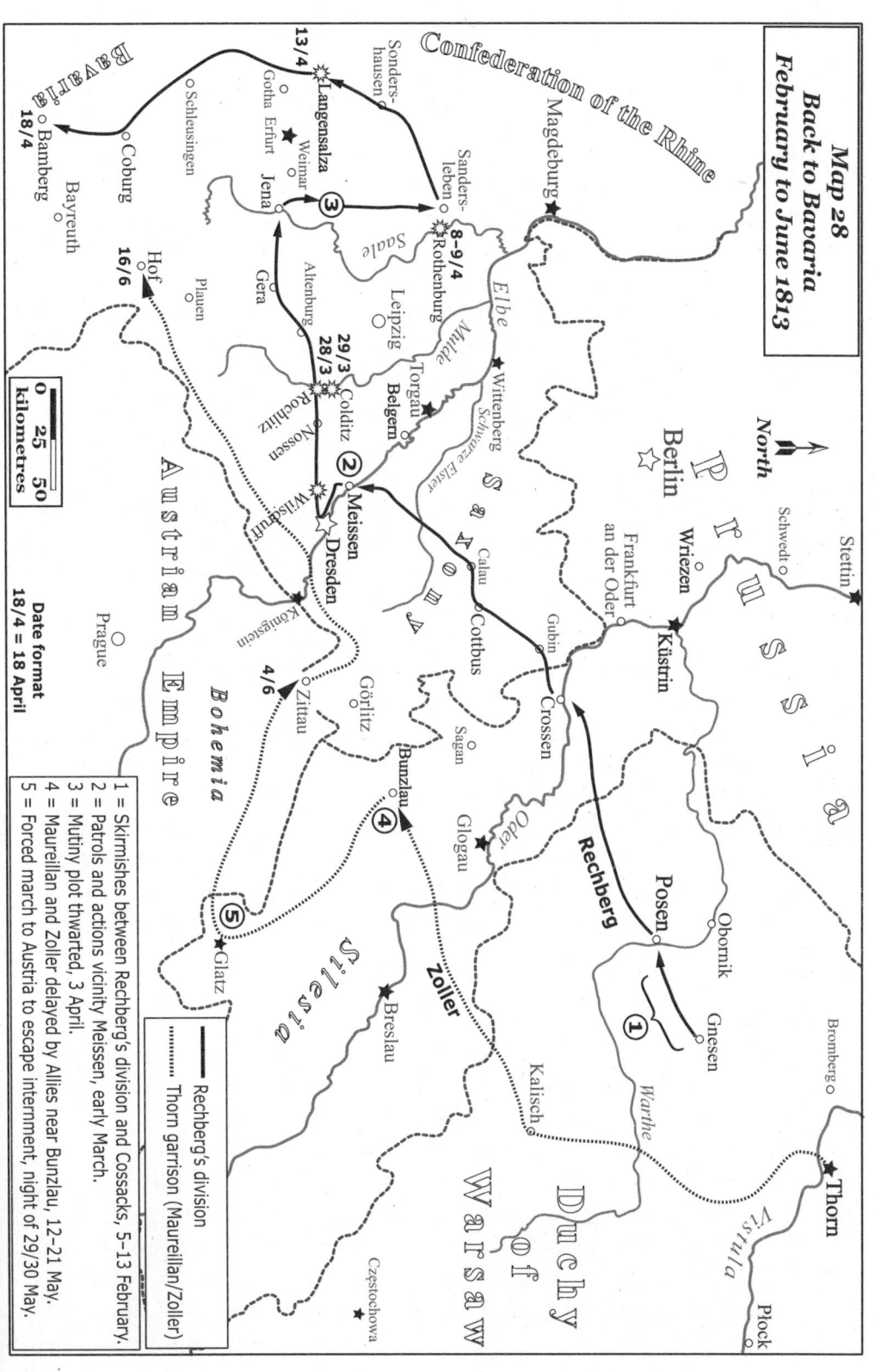

sick men were left behind owing to lack of wagons – and many of these dragged themselves along to rejoin at Crossen in the following days as the Cossacks did not follow on the last two marches.'[85] Overall, however, the picture was grim. Unable to sustain his outposts east of the river, for example, Rechberg was granted authorisation to withdraw to the western bank on 21 February. Even here he remained anxious about maintaining 'the good reputation of the division and the fulfilment of our duty before the enemy'. He requested immediate recall to Bavaria, reporting that he feared his division would face 'general dissolution' should it encounter the enemy in its current condition.[86] Such permission was not forthcoming. Instead, the division was assigned to Reynier's 7th Corps and ordered to Meissen on the Elbe. Rechberg and his men thus left Crossen on 27 February to arrive at Meissen on 9 March.

The Bavarians remained in and around Meissen for the next two weeks, covering some 50–70 kilometres along the Elbe as far north as Belgern. To Rechberg's dismay, his division now fell under Davout's orders. He praised Reynier, reporting that his men had been well cared for, intelligently posted and adequately supplied during 'the rather difficult retreat from Crossen to the Elbe'. His view of Davout was entirely different: 'Davout, whose attitude towards the Bavarian troops has long been negative, now began by separating the cavalry from the division and commanding my weak force to an extended cordon along the riverbank.'[87] Davout had the then-famous wooden bridge at Meissen burned on the night of 12/13 March causing 'a great sensation' among the angry and disconsolate local population whose livelihood was tied to the span.[88] Furthermore, in an anxiety-inducing reminder of the Bavarian mounted regiments being detached in 1812, the marshal ordered the chevau-legers regiment to Dresden on 14 March, leaving Rechberg for the moment with only 25–30 cavalrymen for courier and escort duties. Durutte, assuming command of what remained of 7th Corps after Davout's departure, then called the entire Bavarian division to Dresden on 23 March to replace LeCoq's Saxons who had marched north on the way to Torgau.

In the meantime, the Bavarians had reorganised Rechberg's little command. According to two royal decrees issued in early March, the three light battalions were reduced to one company each and combined into a single unit (termed a 'division'), while each line battalion was consolidated into two companies. Despite these drastic reductions, the affected units retained their titles in order to seem larger than they were: a single company would thus still be listed as a 'battalion' even though it might number no more than 100 officers and men. The purpose in this shell game was not to fool the enemy, but the French. The Bavarians wanted to recall as many officers and NCOs as possible

Chart 24: Rechberg's Division

Strength figures as of 1 April 1813

		bns/sqdns	present under arms	detached
1st Infantry Brigade	**GM de la Motte**			
1st Light Battalion	Oberstleutnant von Hertling	1	69	5
3rd Light Battalion	Major Waible	1	109	8
6th Light Battalion	Oberstleutnant Palm	1	88	6
1st Combined Infantry Regiment	Oberst von Treuberg	2	408	44
1st and 9th Infantry Regiments				
2nd Combined Infantry Regiment	Oberst von Rummel	2	401	20
4th and 10th Infantry Regiments				
3rd Combined Infantry Regiment	Oberst von Hausmann	2	178	69
8th Inf. Regt and 13th Inf. Regt. replacements				
Combined Chevaulegers Regiment	Major von Hertling	3	136	98
9th Foot Battery and train	Hauptmann Wagner	4 × 6-pdr, 2 × howitzer	62	28
Total			1,451	278

Source: 7th Corps 'Situation' for 1 April 1813, SHD, 2C541. Demmler gives a total of 1,551 as of 17 March ('Neubildung', pp. 99–102), not including the cavalry which were detached to Dresden at that time.

to help rebuild the forces inside the kingdom but worried that giving their field contingent a more accurate designation, such as 'regiment', would prompt the French to treat it as such and perhaps consign the remaining troops to some forlorn fortress garrison or other detached duty out of Bavarian control. Of course, the designation as a 'division' meant that the Bavarians were assigned duties they could not fulfil, leading the officers to fear for 'the reputation and honour of Bavarian arms'.[89] A number of men were sent home as cadres on 17 March, but, to further this deceit, Rechberg also kept fairly senior officers in place as unit commanders even though Napoleon had agreed to the king's request that excess officers return to Bavaria. All these changes, implemented on 15 March, left Rechberg with three light and ten line companies along with his lone battery for a total of between 1,450 and 1,550 men fit for duty when he headed for Dresden on 23 March to join his detached cavalry regiment.[90]

The assignment to Dresden was welcome as it allowed Rechberg to unify his little command, but it did not last long.[91] Concerned that the Meissen area was not covered by the Saxons, Durutte ordered Rechberg to send a detachment back north. This mission was undertaken by the 'battalion' of the 8th Infantry with two guns early on 26 March. The outnumbered battalion confirmed that

Russians had crossed the river and retired to the southwest before rejoining the division the following day. Leaving the light infantry and the 1st Infantry in Dresden, Rechberg was ordered to Meissen as well later that same day, but his men had hardly reached the town when he was redirected to Wilsdruff where they were joined by what was left of Durutte's 32nd Division along with the light troops and 1st Infantry (the Bavarian light infantry may have been the last troops to evacuate Dresden). Marching off that very night the Bavarians formed square to deter attacks by Russian cavalry but lost a dozen or so men captured when isolated outposts were overwhelmed.[92] Followed by the now wary Russian horse, the division made its way through Wilsdruff to Nossen (27th), then to Rochlitz on the 28th where further skirmishes with Cossacks occurred. A detachment of light infantry (322), two guns and 25 chevaulegers sent to Colditz was the object of a more serious attack. Despite warnings from its outposts, the detachment allowed itself to be surprised by 250–280 Russian cavalry on the afternoon of 29 March. The Russians burst into the centre of the town, but the Bavarians regained their composure, nearly trapped the intruders in the narrow streets and chased them off with loss. At a cost of 1 killed and 16 wounded, the detachment inflicted an estimated 50 casualties and thus managed to eke out a small success in spite of the initial setback. Durutte, who seems to have trusted the Bavarians, was very pleased, writing later that the detachment 'gained great honour' in this minor affair.

Durutte and Rechberg continued west for the next several days without enemy contact.[93] On reaching Jena on 2 April, the happy rumour arose that the division would continue on to return to Bavaria. The men were now closer to home than they had been for many months or, in some cases, for over a year, and hopes sparkled brightly in the ranks. The next day, however, the column turned north in order to join the right wing of Eugène's army near Magdeburg. Struck as they were with dark disappointment, new rumours immediately spread among the soldiers that the division, after all its losses and tribulations, was to be assigned to isolation and misery in the Magdeburg fortress garrison just like Zoller's brigade had been consigned to oblivion at Thorn. In desperation, some of the men planned a mutiny for the night of 3/4 April. Urgent intervention by the Bavarian officers forestalled what could have been an ugly episode and calm was restored, but the possibility of such an outburst highlighted the fragility of the contingent's morale at this stage of the war. After months of sickness, endless marching, harassment by the ubiquitous Cossacks and seeming neglect from their home government as well as their French allies, fears for the future were close to the surface and the soldiers quickly hearkened to rumours both hopeful and horrible.[94]

The crisis of a potential mutiny averted, Rechberg's men continued north with Durutte's tiny French 'division' (which at this point could 'only be considered cadres').[95] The Bavarians fought their last engagement with the Russians on 8 and 9 April when they destroyed the bridge over the Saale at Rothenburg. Though the fire was often lively, this minor affray only occasioned a few contusions among the Bavarian troops from spent balls and perhaps one man wounded on the enemy side. That night the long-awaited permission to return arrived and a relieved Rechberg turned his column south on 10 April to arrive in Langensalza (now Bad Langensalza) on the 12th. 'The division lost a number of men left dead on the road during these two days as everyone put forth the greatest possible effort not to remain behind when practically on the borders of the fatherland and at least not to fall alive into disgraceful captivity,' wrote Seiboltsdorff of these marches.[96] The men were only three days' march from home.

Unfortunately for the Bavarians, they would suffer a final humiliation before their travails came to a conclusion. The officers were acutely aware that Prussian raiding detachments were active in the region through which they were marching and Rechberg had hurried his pace and altered his route to minimise the danger and avoid some of the most likely trouble spots. His initial plan was to make a wide swing through Westphalia's capital, Kassel, but he heard that King Jérôme was retaining any troops that appeared in the city, so he opted for the more direct, but more parlous route through Langensalza.

Halting for the night, however, the Bavarians again neglected their security procedures. In particular, to satisfy the town's citizens who claimed to fear an explosion if the ammunition caissons were parked in the town, they moved their six guns and their ammunition caissons just outside Langensalza's walls under inadequate and apparently inattentive guard. Thanks to information from local inhabitants, this opportunity came to the attention of Major Friedrich von Hellwig, one of the boldest Prussian partisan leaders. His band only consisted of some 90–100 men from the 2nd Silesian Hussar Regiment so he could not take on the entire Bavarian column of perhaps 1,700, but he was determined to capture their guns. With stealth, skill and great audacity, his raiders attacked in the early morning hours of 13 April, overwhelmed the surprised pickets and made off with all six pieces before the Bavarians could react. One of the 6-pounders was lost in a ditch during the escape, but the remaining five pieces became Hellwig's trophies for his well-planned and daringly executed strike. In addition to the artillery pieces, the Bavarians lost several caissons, some 30 horses and a dozen men; Hellwig's casualties also came to a dozen or so troopers killed, wounded or captured.

For the Bavarians, of course, the loss of the guns was deeply embarrassing, especially so close to home and to such a small enemy detachment. The incident cast a gloomy pall over the remaining men of the division, sentiments that were heightened by the months of huge effort the gunners had devoted to hauling these pieces back safely from the banks of the Daugava River, through the terrors of the retreat in Russia and then the exhausting withdrawal from Poland.[97] The Bavarians recovered the gun that Hellwig's men had left in the ditch, but this was small consolation for the loss of the other five.[98] 'The painful impression is hardly to be described,' wrote the disheartened Seiboltsdorff.[99]

Rechberg compounded the division's disgrace by failing to launch his cavalry in an immediate pursuit. The chevaulegers regiment still counted some 200 men in its ranks at this point and thus (although the Bavarians could not know it) outnumbered Hellwig two to one. Though man and beast were certainly weary from the long retreat, they offered the best chance to recapture the lost guns, caissons and horses. Like many other officers and officials at this time, both French and Rheinbund, however, Rechberg grossly overestimated the strength of the raiding party and hesitated to commit his fatigued troopers on their tired mounts to pursue an enemy force of unknown size into the darkness. His overriding concern remained simply returning what was left of his command to Bavarian soil. Skirting Gotha (which had also been hit by a Prussian raid) the crestfallen men resumed their anxious marches later on the 13th. They encountered French and Baden outposts as they neared Bavaria and 'crossed the border of the fatherland which excited widespread joy' near Coburg on 17 April.[100] They reached Bamberg on the 18th (the same day that Zoller's men left Thorn) where the division was disbanded the next day. Rechberg, promoted to *General-Leutnant* by an order of 24 March, rode off to join the army Wrede was creating in southern Bavaria; he would lead a division in the campaigns against his former allies come the autumn. As for his officers and men, about two-thirds were sent to their regimental depots, while 458 were reassigned to an 'observation corps' being formed under GL von Raglovich. This new 'corps', soon to be the 29th Division of the Grande Armée, was assembling in Bamberg and Bayreuth to fulfill Bavaria's Rheinbund commitment and its story will be told later in the chapter.

Between Hammer and Anvil:
Bavarian Politics, March–May[101]

While Bavaria's soldiers endured sieges, sicknesses, combats and seemingly endless marches, their king and his advisors were struggling to craft a policy suitable to the kingdom's situation. This would be a hedging policy, similar to Saxony's, an effort to avoid committing fully to France, to Austria or to the Russo-Prussian alliance until the likely victor in the coming struggle was clearer. As such, it did not totally satisfy any of these external powers, but it sufficed to limit Bavaria's contribution to the Grande Armée and allowed it to rebuild its army at home while awaiting further developments. It was a period of great tension and constant pressure on the king and his advisors. 'One sensed the approach of great events,' wrote Montgelas in his memoirs, 'old passions awoke, and previously repressed attitudes threatened to become dangerous. This arrangement of men and things could have a significant impact on the country and in a single day, rob it of all that had been achieved with so much effort over many years.'[102] It is not surprising, then, that Bavaria's policy did not emerge all at once in some full-fledged and consistent form. Rather it evolved between March and May in a slow, hesitant process full of starts, stops and reversals.[103]

Compressing this evolution through the spring months, Munich's policy can be described as arising from a set of overlapping perspectives largely shared by Max Joseph and Montgelas and informed by the anxieties of a middle power caught between great powers at war. In the first place, the leadership recognised that a middle power such as Bavaria – like Saxony – required a great power patron to maintain, never mind enhance, its position in the European system. The king and his minister, however, had little faith in any of their prospective protectors. They feared isolation and imagined all manner of ways in which the monarchy might be vulnerable to the actions of the continent's major actors. Max Joseph, for instance, worried that Napoleon might sacrifice Bavaria in order to re-establish his alliance with Austria or that the French emperor might turn on Austria and Bavaria after reaching some accommodation with Russia and Prussia (there is no indication Napoleon ever entertained any such notions). Reports reaching Munich in March indicated that the tsar was already attempting to lure Vienna with offers of Bavarian territory including the possible dismemberment of the kingdom and displacement of its monarch, while some in Prussia seemed intent on reclaiming Franconia (Franken) which the kingdom had lost to Bavaria between 1802 and 1810. There were also worries that Saxony and Württemberg, known to be in contact with Austria if not the Russo-Prussian Coalition, might make deals with Vienna at Bavaria's expense. From Munich's perspective, therefore, the foreign policy landscape that spring was bleak, with dreads looming in every direction and little opportunity for reliable support in the monarchy's critical circumstances. Any hope for succour from Russia evaporated given the reporting that Tsar Alexander seemed unconcerned with the dynasty or the kingdom and was prepared to discard Bavaria in what Munich perceived as a most cavalier fashion. An approach to Prussia, which initially seemed promising, was abandoned when its ambassador delivered a brusque ultimatum demanding Bavaria join the Coalition at once or face insurgency in Franconia. This crude diplomacy led Bavarians to link Prussia with Stein and revolutionary upheaval, prompting Max Joseph to comment to Ludwig that he would rather see 200,000 Russians in his realm than any Prussians.[104]

Fears concerning Russia and Prussia left France and Austria as prospective pillars of support for the Bavarian state and dynasty. Bavaria had gained a great deal from France, both directly in territory and subjects as well as indirectly in that French protection had allowed Max Joseph and Montgelas to pursue their internal reform objectives. Both men were keenly aware of these benefits. 'King Maximilian Joseph did not step back lightly from an alliance that he had concluded with deliberation and from which he had drawn many advantages for a long time,' wrote Montgelas later.[105] Moreover, the king remained in awe of Napoleon's genius despite the Russian catastrophe. The emperor had the advantage of unique unity of command as compared with the disputatious Coalition and he was once again demonstrating his and France's colossal capacity for generating military strength as he raised an enormous new army seemingly out of nothing. As Montgelas commented in a wide-ranging 25 April memorandum, 'It will always be difficult to predict what the sword wielded by a skilled hand can produce.' At the same time, the quality of the new French army was in doubt while all Europe now seemed to be rising up against Napoleon, including, most worryingly, a dramatic majority of Bavarians across all districts of the realm and among all social strata.[106] Although most Bavarians no more wanted war *against* France than they wanted war *on France's behalf*, this heated anti-French sentiment constituted a threat to the throne that the king and his advisors could not ignore. The leadership in Munich also had to weigh Napoleon's political aims against his military capacity, its perception pithily summarised by historian Michael Doeberl on observing that Napoleon was unlikely to accept any peace that the rest of Europe would consider reasonable, but lacked the military strength to enforce a peace on his own terms.[107] If these considerations argued for breaking with France at the earliest possible moment, the presence of thousands of French troops within the kingdom's borders (it was the transit route for many marching north from Italy and west from the Rhine), the memory of past benefits, doubts about the Coalition's intentions and Max Joseph's sense of loyalty were all potent counter-arguments. Thus, neither outright opposition

Saxony's König Friedrich August (1750–1827): at 63, Friedrich August was considered an 'old man' (*Greiß*), 'the Nestor of monarchs' in 1813. After vacillating in the spring, he stolidly adhered to his alliance with Napoleon. The Allies would deprive him of half his kingdom for this display of loyalty.

Bavaria's König Max I. Joseph (1756–1825): a French ally in 1805 and a founding member of the Rheinbund in 1806, Max Joseph was popular with his people and favoured by Napoleon, but Austria pressured him to defect in 1813, seconded by persistent voices within his own family and army, most notably Wrede's.

'French Troops plundering and firing a village': although this is a British propaganda piece published in 1817, it reflected the reality often experienced by local populations, especially in Saxony (even if most fires were accidental rather than intentional). Such common French indiscipline alienated civilians in the war zone and had a negative impact on the morale and motivation of Rheinbund troops.

GL Johann Adolf Freiherr von Thielmann (1765–1824): a former protégé of Napoleon's, the vain and ambitious Thielmann turned against the emperor in 1813, holding Torgau against the French until after Lützen. Defecting to the Russians, he led a raiding detachment during the autumn and commanded the Prussian III Corps in the Waterloo campaign.

Maximilian von Montgelas (1759–1838): this skilled statesman of the Enlightenment was Max Joseph's closest advisor and thus a central figure in Bavaria's domestic and foreign policy decisions. He helped push the king towards the break with France in 1813 and remained a powerful voice in Munich until his opponents persuaded the king to dismiss him in 1817.

Kronprinz Ludwig (1786–1868): Bavaria's crown prince detested Napoleon and pestered his father with proposals to sever the Rheinbund alliance. Among many grand projects during his controversial reign as king (1825–68), he commissioned the 'Liberation Hall' to celebrate France's defeat in 1813 and the 'Walhalla' to honour notable German personalities.

Bavarian GM Joseph von Rechberg (1769–1833): Rechberg led the Bavarian remnants during the withdrawal from Poland in early 1813 only to lose most of his guns just before returning home. Promoted to GL, he would lead a division against the French in 1814.

Bavarian GL Clemens von Raglovich (1766–1836): Napoleon had asked for Wrede to lead the Bavarian division in 1813. Instead, Raglovich did well at Dennewitz but seems to have been overwhelmed by the lack of support from home.

Bavarian GdK Karl Philipp Graf von Wrede (1767–1838): Napoleon had valued Wrede for his military talents, but the ambitious and self-important Bavarian general turned against the emperor after Russia and actively pushed his king to dissolve the French alliance in 1813.

The Meissen bridge aflame on the night of 12/13 March: in addition to the furore over the damage to the stone bridge at Dresden, Saxons were also angered by Davout's decision to burn what was considered the beautiful wooden bridge at Meissen.

13 April: Prussian Major von Hellwig's raiding detachment surprises Rechberg's Bavarians at Langensalza, capturing five of the remaining six Bavarian guns. Having dragged these pieces all the way back from the Russian frontier, their loss was especially humiliating for the Bavarian troops.

The Battle of Bautzen, first day: Bavarian infantry in their distinctive Raupenhelms cross the Spree River on the army's right flank on the afternoon of 20 May. The enormous battle at Bautzen would be the first time under fire for most of the Bavarian division's men.

Allied raiders plagued Napoleon's rear areas. Here Prussian Rittmeister von Colomb's men destroy guns and vehicles of an ambushed French artillery convoy.

Saxon heavy cavalry at Dresden make their successful charge against the helpless Habsburg infantry (in this case a Hungarian regiment) under the clouds and rain on 27 August.

The front half of a blackened metal cuirass of the design worn by both the Saxon Leib-Cuirassiers and *Zastrow* Cuirassiers in 1813.

The Battle of Großbeeren, 23 August: Saxon infantry (in white uniforms on left) in hand-to-hand combat with Prussian Landwehr in the heavy rain that rendered most muskets useless during the afternoon's fighting.

GD Jean Louis Ebénézer Reynier (1771–1814): Reynier first commanded the Saxon contingent in 1809 and then led the 7th Corps into Russia in 1812. He retained this command through 1813 and, despite his cold and distant manner, earned the loyalty of his Saxon soldiers. Captured at Leipzig, he died in Paris in February 1814 only weeks after being exchanged.

Marshal Nicolas Charles Oudinot (1767–1847): the Bavarians were pleased to serve under the experienced and considerate Oudinot. The marshal was generally satisfied with the Bavarians, and was gratified by the awards he and some of his staff received. As shown in the Großbeeren operation, however, army command was beyond his grasp.

Bavarian infantry on the march in 1813. In addition to the Raupenhelms with their huge crests, note the soldier in the right centre carrying his squad's cooking pan, an essential piece of field gear for armies of the era.

Having finally decided to abandon Dresden, the emperor crossed the Elbe for the last time on 7 October using a bridge of boats near Meissen. The Saxon king left his capital the same day.

Leipzig: Christian Geißler's drawing shows the 'Heiterer Blick' farmstead with the village of Taucha in the background beneath the clouds on the left. The Saxon and Württemberg light cavalry were deployed near this compound when they defected to the Russians on 18 October.

Saxon troops serving in Belgium under Blücher in May 1815 were uneasy about the fate of their kingdom and army. On learning that their regiments were to be divided between Prussia and Saxony, they rioted and attacked Blücher's headquarters in Liege as shown here. The unrest was quelled, and summary punishments were applied: seven ringleaders were executed. Half of the Saxon troops were duly absorbed into the Prussian army in June despite the violent protest.

to Napoleon nor unquestioning acceptance of the terms of the Rheinbund alliance seemed a prudent policy and Bavaria, like Saxony, continued to seek a third path in these tense and desperate months.

Austria, of course, was another major factor in Bavarian calculations. Itself in the process of transitioning from an ally of France to a new stance as an armed mediator between the belligerents, Austria provided both an opportunity and a threat for Bavaria. On the favourable side, Metternich carefully nurtured the contacts that had begun in March. He was clear that the Tyrol, the Vorarlberg and other Austrian borderlands must return to the Habsburg crown, but he promised adequate compensation (including but not limited to Würzburg) and expressed Austria's commitment to Bavaria's territorial integrity and its status as a kingdom. Equally important was his opposition to the sort of insurrectionary movements that the Bavarians associated with Prussia and Stein. Schwarzenberg conveyed these intentions in person during cordial discussions when he passed through Munich in late March on his way to resume his ambassadorial post in Paris. Subtle Habsburg diplomacy notwithstanding, decades of suspicion and antipathy were not easily cast aside. Indeed, coming from the ambassador in Vienna, the Russian offer to Austria vis-à-vis Bavaria's future kept the traditional mistrust very much alive, reinforced by Austrian plots concerning the Tyrol. Though Munich shared a certain 'commonality of interest'[108] with Vienna, therefore, deep-seated Bavarian misgivings, rooted in the past and revived in the present, would impede collaboration during the spring phase of the war.

Compounding these external concerns was a deep dread at the possibility of internal unrest and 'revolution'. The prominence of Stein and 'the sect of Stein adherents' in the Coalition camp was particularly alarming. 'These people are ready to set all Germany afire', wrote Bavaria's ambassador in Vienna, Aloys Franz Xaver von Rechberg und Rothenlöwen (elder brother of General von Rechberg). Montgelas agreed. He and others, including Max Joseph, saw Saxony's case as a warning. In his reply to Rechberg Montgelas thus wrote 'To avoid such a great evil as a popular uprising, it is above all necessary for central and southern Germany to spare itself and its subjects such inflammatory proclamations as have been directed at the King of Saxony.'[109]

As historian Daniel Klang has observed, however, there is an important nuance in Montgelas's perception of the 'revolutionary' threat. In addition to the violence and chaos Europeans of the day associated with 'Jacobinism', Monetgelas feared that Stein and his ilk would overthrow all that Bavaria – and others – had accomplished over two decades to impose some re-crafted version of the old order of things from the days of the dissolved *Reich*, what Montgelas called 'an aristocracy disguised with popular forms'.[110] Seeing the kingdom as 'a citadel of modernity and universal values', Montgelas prized 'the absolute sovereignty he had won for Bavaria' and rejected both 'the assertion of all-German loyalty as appealing to a dead past' as well as Stein's 'impassioned leadership'.[111] By inciting people against their legitimate monarchs, Stein and his backers in the Coalition threatened to ignite unpredictable and likely uncontrollable popular passions, with the aim of weakening the power of the existing German princes and reforging the chains that had trammelled rulers in ages past. 'While an enemy power that was already considerably weakened [France] could have been combatted with normal means,' Montgelas would later write, Stein preferred to employ 'an unusual tool' [insurrection] to 'transform a diplomatic war into a crusade'.[112] Montgelas and many others in Rheinbund capitals thus feared not only a diminution of the territory and status they had gained under Napoleon but a deliberate programme designed to undermine Bavaria's independence and the Enlightened socio-political order they had worked so hard to build.

The immediate danger for Bavaria and others, however, was the outbreak of rebellion inspired by the Coalition advances and their incendiary propaganda. Some of the Bavarian depictions of internal dissent were exaggerated to excuse the kingdom from dispatching its full contingent to the Grande Armée, but Munich's anxiety was genuine and there were legitimate reasons to be concerned.[113] Having gained much of its territory and population through Napoleon's largesse between 1805 and 1809, Bavaria felt especially vulnerable to insurrectionary threats in these newly acquired regions. As Max Joseph told Berthier on 23 April: 'The public mood is very bad in Franconia and in the Tyrol.'[114] Passive and sometimes vocal resistance to Munich's authority were regarded as part of the price for incorporating the Tyrol and the Vorarlberg into the kingdom, but incidents grew in frequency and intensity in 1813, especially during efforts to enforce conscription. Credible reports that Austrian Archduke Johann was attempting to foment unrest in these restive regions only amplified Munich's anxieties.[115]

Where king and court seem to have reconciled themselves to the eventual loss of these quondam Habsburg lands – in return for fulsome compensation, of course – their attitude towards the former Prussian districts in Franconia was different. These they were determined to hold despite widespread popular discontent. This discontent was becoming increasingly open and disquieting. As early as 2 March, for example, a senior official from Nuremberg reported that if Russian troops entered Franconia 'they would tread upon volcanic soil and, perhaps against their intentions and their orders, give the signal for popular uprisings and other disorders'.[116] Enthusiastic reports of uprisings in East Prussia resonated widely in these former Hohenzollern domains while a wave of fiery Coalition proclamations, poems and broadsheets aimed at arousing opposition to Munich's rule exacerbated the volatile situation. It is important to note that being anti-French in these areas did not necessarily mean being pro-Prussian. Although many former Prussian bureaucrats now serving as royal Bavarian officials may have yearned for a return to Hohenzollern suzerainty, most people and most soldiers simply wanted a release from the French alliance, an onerous union that they associated with commercial stagnation, taxation, conscription and war. Nonetheless, Munich had no doubt as to the origin of these propaganda pieces and their malevolent prevalence served to drive a deep wedge between the Bavarian and Prussian governments. Montgelas, for example, reading some of these materials, expressed his disgust and alarm at 'all the indecency and danger of this insurrectionary doctrine' in a letter to Ambassador Rechberg: 'Rivers of blood have been spilled to destroy Jacobinism only to come back to the same formula after 20 years.'[117] The fact that Berlin papers published a call to 'shake off the yoke of French slavery' that was signed by sixteen former Rheinbund officers, including several Bavarians, excited further outrage against Prussia in Munich.[118]

It was not only the new acquisitions that ignited anxieties, however. Rumblings of dissatisfaction with the monarchy's policies, above all its alignment with France, percolated even into the traditional regions of Altbayern (Old Bavaria), deeply loyal to the House of Wittelsbach and previously favourably inclined towards the alliance with Napoleon. Max Joseph cited domestic unrest as a rationale for keeping Bavaria's troops in the kingdom in a 3 March letter to Napoleon while the emperor complained that Bavarian journals were gleefully publishing negative stories about French setbacks and Coalition successes.[119] Munich's apprehensions about internal security became so acute that Bavaria approached Saxony regarding a pact whereby each would assist the other if confronted with internal insurrection. The proposal to Dresden quickly proved abortive and the appeal to Napoleon backfired when the emperor offered a brigade of French troops to ensure internal tranquillity. More French troops being the last outcome Bavaria wanted, Montgelas had to decline the offer hastily but politely by claiming that the threat was not so grave as to necessitate French intervention.[120] Nonetheless, fears of a domestic explosion remained a crucial factor in policy decisions until the kingdom formally joined the Allies in October. This worry was especially important in Munich's perception of Vienna as Austrian interlocutors had repeatedly stressed adamant opposition to popular upheaval. Concerns about Austrian territorial aspirations remained prominent, but Bavarians welcomed Habsburg abhorrence of 'revolution' or 'Jacobinism'. This mutual interest in opposing radical movements would be a central feature of the future Austro-Bavarian alignment.

These critical but conflicting considerations led Bavaria to weigh a variety of policy options as external and internal demands for a definitive decision mounted from March through May. In addition to pressure from Austria, Prussia, Russia and France, the king had to contend with impassioned missives from the crown prince and the queen's desire to see Bavaria turn against France. 'I do not hide from you', he wrote to Berthier on 23 April, 'that this moment of crisis is terrible.'[121] With the fate of the kingdom at stake, however, none of the available courses of action seemed sufficiently secure to embrace. Max Joseph and Montgelas thus strove to avoid committing the kingdom too early; in Montegelas's words: 'We are encircled on all sides – we are not ready, we must wait to play for time.'[122] Although initial discussions with Prussia seemed promising, for instance, Munich, as noted above, rejected the heavy-handed Prussian ultimatum despite the arrival of Russian and Prussian raiding detachments in Hof by early April. Neutrality seemed another option and some in Munich, avidly supported by Crown Prince Ludwig, urgently advocated such a course. 'We are atop a volcano', wrote Ludwig from Innsbruck on 7 April, 'where from one moment to the next we are in danger of being engulfed if we do not soon remedy the situation, and the only way is to remain neutral for the rest of this war.'[123] Somewhat surprisingly given his preference for hedging, Max Joseph actually approved neutrality as the kingdom's policy in response to Montegelas's 25 April memorandum. This happy illusion, however, collapsed almost immediately. The Russians and Prussians would not have recognised Bavarian neutrality and Napoleon would have regarded such as declaration as a flagrant breach of the Rheinbund alliance.[124] Vague notions of a neutrality pact among southwest German states proved equally illusory and, as we have seen, discussion of some bilateral arrangement with Saxony quickly foundered.[125]

Nor would Munich align itself unequivocally and publicly with Vienna. At several points, Bavaria seemed on the verge of finalising an agreement with Austria, but Max Joseph would not commit. Metternich eventually lost patience with the king's equivocations, but neither his threats nor his attempts at persuasion could produce a definitive decision from Munich. As April melted into May, Austria's evident intention to join the Coalition as a belligerent bolstered Bavaria's reluctance.[126] As Max Joseph explained to his son, 'It is no longer a question of neutrality but of marching against France ... You see, my dear Ludwig, that if I delay in deciding it is so that I will not find myself between the hammer and the anvil. Up to now I have had a fairly secure and successful tactic and the older I get, the calmer I become.'[127]

As for Bavaria's formal ally, the uncertainties of the coming campaign and Max Joseph's sense of loyalty militated against an immediate desertion of France. Even years later, Montgelas would comment that France at this stage remained 'the most natural pillar of support' for Bavaria against Prussian and Austrian territorial ambitions.[128] At the same time, the king and his advisors were determined to recall all their units in the field and to avoid any future French requests for troops to join the Grande Armée. Napoleon accepted that Bavaria would not be able to meet its full treaty obligations at once, but he left no doubt that he expected the kingdom to complete its contingent as soon as possible. Indeed, the correspondence between the two allies through March and May dealt almost solely with the return of GL von Rechberg's small command and the formation of a new Bavarian field contingent.[129] Munich was successful in finally gaining the release of Rechberg's sad remnant, but it could not evade Napoleon's demands for troops entirely and, as outlined in the next section, a new Bavarian contingent was in the process of assembling even as policy debates dragged on. Neither Lützen (which the new Bavarian division missed) nor Bautzen (where it fought) altered Bavaria's decision to limit its contribution to Napoleon's field army. Nor did these Napoleonic victories convince the king to tie his kingdom more closely to France in general. On the contrary, Bavaria effectively employed the threat of Austria to excuse itself from deploying any additional forces beyond its borders.

The relatively new French ambassador, François Joseph Charles Marie Mercy d'Argenteau, reported from Munich on 3 May that, 'The Bavarian minister for some time seems to have been struck by the idea that Austria will not be long in changing her system,' adding that, 'The king, who speaks to me at every opportunity, does not seem to doubt that this power will eventually declare against us.' Bavaria, he concluded, would be reluctant to send more troops until it was 'perfectly tranquil regarding Austrian intentions'.[130] Metternich, eager to deprive the French of Rheinbund troops, cleverly contributed to Bavaria's excuse, telling Ambassador Rechberg in Vienna: 'Keep your troops in your own hands, do not let them be abducted; through our mobilisation we will provide you with the most effective rationale'.[131]

Napoleon may have suspected this was more a ruse than a rationale, but the claim was not entirely hollow, and he did not elect to press the issue.

Instead, he exploited Berthier's family connections to the Bavarian court to ply Max Joseph with embellished accounts of the Grande Armée's strength and the scope of its victories; Viceroy Eugène reinforced these favourable impressions in person on 15 May as he passed through Munich en route to take up command in Italy. The Bavarian court doubtless discounted much of this as exaggeration – it was clear, for example, that Napoleon's cavalry was 'incontestably inferior to that of its enemies' – but there was no denying the numbers Napoleon had assembled with astonishing speed.[132] With many of these troops in Bavaria or on its borders, caution was the order of the day vis-à-vis France: maintaining the façade of a steadfast ally while trying to create space for greater flexibility in protecting Bavaria's interests in the future.

The meandering course of Bavaria's policy deliberations during the tense spring months meant that the kingdom's stance was still ambiguous when the armistice was announced in early June. Where Napoleon seems to have accepted the need to guard the kingdom's borders with Austria and the resultant limits on Bavarian troop contributions to the Grande Armée, the Coalition partners perceived insufficient zeal for the 'good cause' in Munich's behaviour. Nonetheless, unlike their avaricious attitude towards Saxony, the Russians and Prussians were more interested in enlisting Bavaria than conquering it and they remained open to a change of policy even as they grew impatient with Munich's seeming indecision.[133] Austria, too, hoped to detach Bavaria from Napoleon and with it the rest of the states of southwestern Germany. Given its pronounced aversion to the sort of radical pan-German visions represented by Stein and its determination to forestall Prussian expansion into southern Germany, Vienna had a strong interest in sustaining Bavaria as a stable, monarchical bulwark on its western frontier. Metternich might have been frustrated with Munich's failure to enter into a formal agreement during the spring months, but he could wait, especially since Napoleon's May victories threatened to unravel the entire Allied enterprise.

On the Bavarian side, Max Joseph continued to harbour deep suspicions about Austria, what Montgelas termed 'a certain mistrust towards the court in Vienna that cannot be remedied',[134] but the relative moderation of Austrian demands, its reasonable diplomacy during their negotiations and the strong mutual interest in opposing 'revolutionary' movements created a foundation for the collaboration that would be realised in the autumn. In the meantime, Max Joseph's policy of temporising had largely paid off, at least for the short term. He experienced a growing sense of vindication when Napoleon strode from success at Lützen, to the occupation of Dresden and the victory at Bautzen, while French troops under Davout re-entered

Hamburg.¹³⁵ He viewed the proposal for a peace conference to be convened in Prague as especially encouraging. None of these events, of course, shifted his determination to keep his commitments to France to a minimum. Though frequently condemned for hesitancy and indecision, by refusing to commit fully to any side he had managed to walk a thin line between the contending parties, minimising the direct support provided to Napoleon and thus allowing the army to rebuild at home without utterly alienating the Russians, the Prussians or, most importantly, the Austrians. He had wavered at times during these several months and the situation was hardly ideal when the armistice was declared, but by remaining focused on Bavarian interests he had averted existential threats to his monarchy and dynasty from both sides and had retained enough flexibility to align the kingdom according to circumstances as the war marched on into the summer and autumn.

A Thrown-Together Division: Bavaria's Army in March and April

The above discussion has jumped ahead chronologically somewhat to outline Bavarian political developments during the spring. Napoleon's counter-offensive, however, was unrolling at the same time and Max Joseph, as he stuck to his hedging strategy, could not avoid dispatching a minimal contingent to join the emperor in Saxony. Hastily constructed from dubious materials, this force would become the Grande Armée's 29th Division under GL Clemens von Raglovich zum Rosenhof. Other than the 13th Infantry in distant Danzig, it would constitute Bavaria's principal contribution to the Rheinbund alliance for the remainder of the war.

As almost all of Bavaria's active soldiers had been committed to the Russian war, there were only some 17,000 uniformed and organised men within the kingdom on 1 March to serve as a basis for its army in the aftermath of the disaster across the Niemen. These troops consisted of the reserve battalions of the line infantry regiments, a 'division' or half-battalion for each light battalion, three reserve squadrons for each of the chevaulegers regiments as well as the artillery and train personnel left behind when the contingent marched for Russia. Only 14,400 were considered truly available for the coming campaign, however, as one third were either unfit for field duty or were at the end of their terms of service.¹³⁶ Horses were another issue as 1,200 of the 1,706 animals on hand were totally untrained remounts. The government attempted to remedy these problems by issuing an edict on 18 March for the conscription of 14,845 men (in effect doubling the number of available soldiers) and embarking on a purchasing programme to bring 3,000 cavalry and draft horses into service by the end of April. These measures were largely successful as far as horses were concerned, but draft evasion and desertion in Franconia and the Tyrol reduced the number of men entering the ranks. As these raw recruits arrived at their unit depots they had to be clothed, equipped, trained and, above all, led. Grave shortages of qualified, experienced officers and NCOs, however, hampered the army's ability to impart proper training, discipline and unit cohesion to the thousands of new inductees. Nor were there enough veterans on hand to provide a sturdy framework within which the conscripts could learn the basics of soldiering. Most of the men already in the reserve battalions, half-battalions and squadrons had less than six months of service, some 9,000 having only been brought in during November and December 1812. Serving officers were reassigned, junior men promoted – even from the ranks – and old, sometimes infirm, men were appointed, but these expedient solutions could not repair the deficiencies in terms of either numbers or quality. As one case, the battalion of the 10th Infantry 'has only four officers for company commanders', reported Raglovich, 'two of whom are very young men completely inexperienced in service'. 'The great lack of NCOs is especially noticeable', he lamented, 'as seldom does a company count more than one experienced NCO, those appointed in the present emergency have hardly served more than half a year.'[137] As Bavarian historian Heinrich Demmler concluded, greater exertion by the kingdom probably could have produced more recruits but the leadership deficit would have remained.[138] Bavarian commanders would thus have to contend with severe challenges in leadership, training, morale, staff work and even such military fundamentals as accountability and adherence to uniform regulations as they rushed to prepare their contingent to take the field with the Grande Armée.

Napoleon expected Bavaria to fulfil its complete treaty obligation of 30,000 men eventually. As in 1812, these would be formed into two divisions (28th and 29th) and incorporated into the Grande Armée as a separate corps, in this case, the 9th. For the beginning of the spring campaign, however, he reduced his immediate demand by one-half in recognition of Bavaria's difficulties in raising a new army at once. A 2 March letter thus requested thirteen battalions to be united in the kingdom's north-eastern corner 'with as much cavalry and artillery as possible'. The emperor also expressed his desire to see Wrede command this force and asked for details on the strength, commanders' names and march dates of the division as well as updates on the status of Bavaria's fortresses. He concluded with yet another mention of his need for mounted troops: 'I can only recommend that Your Majesty make every effort to complete your contingent and above all your cavalry and your artillery.'[139]

Napoleon's request and details provided by the French ambassador would have resulted in a division of some 15,000 men in three brigades with several artillery batteries and a substantial cavalry component of 1,000–1,200 that the emperor hoped would soon rise to 2,000 or even more. These numbers were never attained, and Napoleon had to abandon his plan to have a corps of two full Bavarian divisions take the field in 1813.[140] The number '28' was therefore dropped and Bavaria's troop contribution would enter the Grande Armée's order of battle as its 29th Division with an authorised strength of just 9,712 officers and men organised in two infantry brigades with two artillery batteries and a lone cavalry regiment.[141] Given Munich's determination to minimise the troops it provided to the Grande Armée, no replacements were ever dispatched, and the units allotted to the requested third brigade were diverted to the restive Tyrol. Furthermore, one of the original battalions (II/4th Infantry) and a company of II/10 were left behind for fortress garrison and internal security duties in Franconia when the division departed home soil in late April, thereby reducing the authorised strength to 8,809. This was approximately half of Napoleon's request and less than one-third of Bavaria's treaty obligation. Most of the units, however, never reached authorised strength and the division would leave the kingdom with 7,850 'effectives', which included the sick, the injured and those on detachment. Once these categories were deducted, the present under arms strength would be only 7,143 even before any combat or serious marching.[142] In addition to the small size of the division, the French were disappointed in Bavaria's choice for its commander. Claiming that Wrede's health did not permit him to assume a field command, Max Joseph assigned the division to Raglovich.

Raglovich managed to collect most of his new command around Bamberg and Bayreuth by the beginning of April, but a number of serious weaknesses were immediately apparent. In the first place, in addition to being under-strength, the quality of the troops left much to be desired. As with Rechberg's command and similar to the French units Napoleon was stamping out of the earth, most of Raglovich's men were young, completely untrained inductees. In a typical example, 255 of 540 men in the Reserve Battalion of the 13th Infantry were brand new recruits. Soldiers who had been in uniform for nearly a year were the 'old timers' of their units. Raglovich conveyed his concerns to Wrede in a letter on 31 March, opening with a sardonic line:

> The state of the troops is not the most splendid. There are battalions without staff officers, companies with no officers, sergeants who have only served for ten months. Very few are complete. The skirmishers cannot

Chart 25: Raglovich's Division

Showing present under arms strengths at the beginnings of the campaigns

		bns/sqdns	3 May	31 July
1st Brigade	GM von Beckers > GM von Maillot de la Treille in August			
Combined 3rd/4th Light Btn	Maj. von Fortis	1	669	463
1st Combined Regiment	(Vacant)			
II/3rd Infantry	Oberstleutnant von Sarny	1	571	357
Reserve/13th Infantry	Hauptmann Laib	1	527	371
2nd Combined Regiment	Oberst von Hausmann			
II/8th Infantry	Major von Hannet	1	627	448
II/4th Infantry	Major von Vincenti	1	—	—
2nd Brigade	Oberst von Maillot de la Treille > GM von Habermann in August			
Combined 5th/6th Light Btn	Oberstleutnant Palm > Major Abele	1	645	423
1st Combined Regiment	Oberst von Habermann			
II/5th Infantry	Major von Flad	1	591	447
II/7th Infantry	Major Golfen	1	835	605
2nd Combined Regiment	Oberst von Rummel			
II/9th Infantry	Major von Treuberg	1	798	508
II/10th Infantry	Major von Ribaupierre	1	688	561
Combined Chevaulegers Regt	Oberst Seyssel d'Aix			
1st Division	Oberstleutnant Niedermeyer	2	255	137
1st Sqdns of 1st and 2nd Chevaulegers				
2nd Division	Oberstleutnant von Weise	2	252	130
1st Sqdns of 4th and 5th Chevaulegers				
3rd Division	Rittmeister von Hetzendorf	2	258	125
1st Sqdns of 3rd and 6th Chevaulegers				
Artillery and Train	Major von Marabini			321
10th Battery	Hauptmann E. Weißhaupt	6 × 6-pdr, 2 × howitzer	94	
12th Battery	Hauptmann Pamler	6 × 6-pdr, 2 × howitzer	93	
Reserve and Train			240	
Total present under arms			7,143	4,896
Detached			328	580
Hospital			377	1,178
Prisoners of war/missing/deserters			2	524
Grand total of 'effectives' (which included all of the above)			7,850	7,178

Notes: (1) Although technically assigned to combined regiments under the senior battalion commander, the infantry functioned as individual battalions with little regard for this adminstrative arrangement. (2) Initially part of 1st Brigade, II/4th Infantry remained on fortress duty in Bavaria. (3) The 8th Fusilier Company of II/10, also left behind on fortress duty at first, joined its regiment in July from Bavaria.

Sources: Divisional strength reports for 3 May and 31 July 1813, BayHStA, 495a.

skirmish, the cavalry cannot ride; how difficult it is to have such troops under one's command will not escape Your Excellency's insight.[143]

Although he praised the artillery and found the morale of the infantry and cavalry good, Raglovich despaired of instilling 'the spirit of earlier days' in his men.[144]

Compounding this lack of training and experience was a second problem: men from formerly Prussian and Austrian districts of Bavaria, inspired by the French disaster in Russia and other faults appearing in the Napoleonic edifice, were actively resisting Bavarian authority. Recruiting in these areas could only be carried out by force and the refractory men were prone to desert. The king was partly exaggerating for effect when he told Berthier that, 'All my soldiers from the Bayreuth area and even the Upper Palatinate are deserting,' but collecting conscripts in these regions and keeping them in the ranks was clearly a major concern.[145] Furthermore, many military men from across Bavaria displayed a decidedly negative attitude towards their French allies as the Nuremberg official cited earlier wrote in his 2 March report:

> I now come to the attitude towards our allies, the French: this is atrocious indeed!!! ... The worst aspect is that the royal military – officers as well as soldiers – is of the same mind as the people, perhaps even more embittered towards the French nation than are the people – I may even say enraged.

The government in Munich disseminated several protocols to curb open expressions of discontent such as one dated 13 March with the bureaucratic title 'Prohibition on military individuals to refrain from all narratives and utterances about the state of public affairs through which ill-will, anxieties and unrest are spread'.[146] Such proscriptions were evidently only partially effective as Raglovich would have to issue similar orders later in the campaign.

A third major deficiency was leadership. At all levels of command there were simply not enough officers and NCOs to fill authorised positions, and those who were on hand were often incompetent, ignorant, or infirm. The NCOs of his 'thrown-together division' Raglovich wrote, were 'for the most part completely useless'. 'As raw and unpractised as the common soldiers', they could neither impart practical knowledge nor serve as role models. The junior officers, mostly 'as young in experience as they are in years', were equally incapable of instructing and managing the men. Even the more experienced officers, through 'exhaustion or sullenness', were lackadaisical.[147] Indeed, many who had survived the Russian campaign seemed numb and indifferent, hardly bestirring themselves when reprimanded. Officers in the artillery regiment had to be admonished to wear their uniforms and turn up

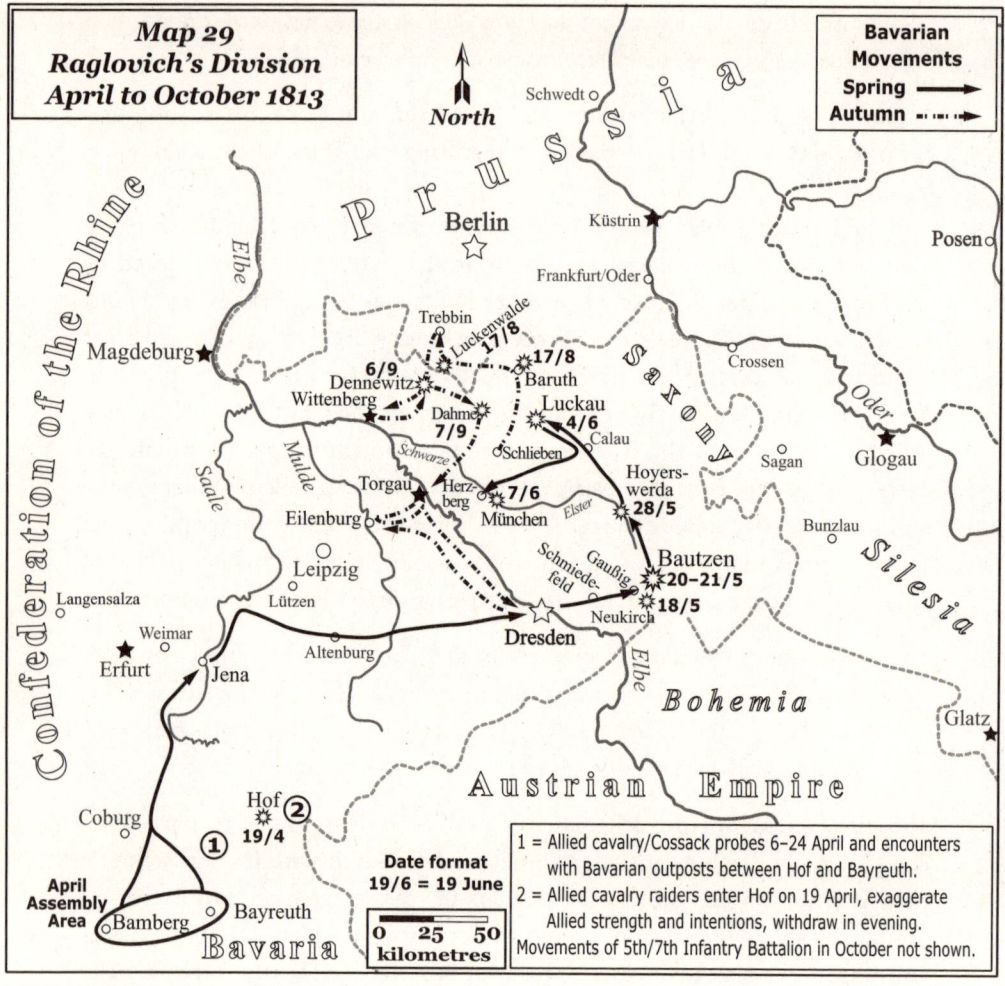

for training while the men indulged in all manner of indiscipline.[148] The senior officers were little better, and many soon discovered that they were physically unfit for active campaigning. Raglovich's gloomy outlook deepened when he considered that his weak chief of staff and the near total lack of experienced division staff officers hampered command and administration.[149] Finally, he was entangled in a bitter personality clash with one of his brigade commanders, GM Karl August Graf von Beckers zu Westerstetten. Raglovich had been barely two weeks senior to Beckers before his promotion to *General-Leutnant* on 24 March 1813 and Beckers evidently resented both the promotion and serving under someone he considered a peer.[150] As a further awkward complication, Beckers, owing to his seniority, would assume command of the division for a time when Raglovich fell ill in mid-April.

Furthermore, Raglovich himself seems to have been unsuited to his post. Tall and slender, he had already seen more than a quarter century of military service, had often demonstrated his talents as a chief of staff and had earned a reputation for probity, modesty, obedience and strict discipline towards himself and the men under his command. Despite these fine qualities, he seems to have been very uncomfortable in his role as an independent field commander. Apprehensive before the division even left Bavaria, the 'strains and cares' of the campaign soon began to tell on the 47-year-old general, manifesting themselves in frequent illness, repeated requests for relief and a growing despondency in his correspondence with his king.[151] It is not clear whether Raglovich was specifically informed of his government's decision to minimise its commitment to Napoleon, but as an experienced officer he must have suspected. The shortage of cavalry and artillery, the diversion of the division's third brigade to the Tyrol and his appointment to command in place of Napoleon's stated desire for his protégé Wrede, were all clear indications that the government was reluctant to invest its resources in the enterprise Raglovich was to lead. 'I am alone', he wrote to his sovereign on 12 May, having evidently concluded that his command did not have the kingdom's full support.[152]

April Aggravations

April brought exchanges of fire with the enemy as Russo-Prussian cavalry patrols probed towards the Bavarian border and a band of raiders even briefly attacked Hof in June as described later in this chapter. None of these encounters amounted to anything serious but the Bavarian troops repeatedly had to make minor shifts in position to counter these dangers and Raglovich, overestimating the enemy like everyone else on the French side that season, contemplated possible withdrawal should the pressure increase.

His next challenge, however, came in the form of another Franco-Bavarian contretemps rather than enemy action.[153] Consistent with the effort to keep all Bavarian troops inside the kingdom. Munich had designated Raglovich's command an 'observation corps' with the implication of a solely defensive mission and a degree of independence. Raglovich was forbidden to cross the border without explicit instructions from the Bavarian authorities and specifically instructed not to allow his cavalry to be separated from the division.[154] The French, on the other hand, quite reasonably regarded his command as part of Bavaria's Rheinbund contingent and expected to incorporate it into the Grande Armée, as had been the practice in every previous campaign over the past eight years. The command hierarchy, however, was murky, at least as far as the Bavarian officers and officials were concerned. Napoleon initially attached the Bavarian division to Ney's corps, authorising him to communicate directly with the Bavarian monarch and urging him to press the Bavarians 'to assemble as much cavalry as possible'. Raglovich therefore duly communicated with the marshal, but he avoided acknowledging that he was under Ney's orders and even refused to provide routine strength reports until he had approval from Munich.[155] This behaviour was annoying for the French, but matters escalated when GD Bertrand attempted to coordinate his operations with Raglovich on 8 April. Bertrand was marching his 4th Corps from Italy through Bavaria to Saxony and wanted the Bavarians to shift their positions so as to cover his right flank. This request conflicted with Raglovich's instructions from Munich, leaving the general in a quandary. Bertrand, on the other hand, uncertain and fretful in his new position as a corps commander, quite understandably expected Bavarian support and wrote to Munich to complain. This confusion led to an awkward and unpleasant meeting between the two generals when Bertrand arrived in Bamberg on 16 April. To Bertrand's evident consternation, Raglovich declined either to be included in 4th Corps or to advance beyond Bavaria's frontiers without further orders from his king; he would only agree to some small adjustments in the Bavarian unit locations. Max Joseph dismissed Bertrand's demands ('he has nothing to say to us') and subsequent Bavarian historians deride Bertrand's behaviour, claiming he used 'a brusque and presumptuous tone' in making his demands.[156] Whether such descriptions are accurate or not, the meeting between the two generals was clearly confrontational and Bertrand departed in frustration to communicate his surprise and displeasure in a report to Berthier.

The result of these disagreeable misunderstandings was immediate intervention from army headquarters and the emperor himself. Even before Bertrand had met Raglovich, his complaints about the Bavarians and the insecure tone of his correspondence prompted a reproving reply from Napoleon: 'It would have been much better to address yourself to the Prince of the Moskva [Ney] rather than to upset the Bavarians who are already anxious enough,' he wrote on 14 April.

> You must have known that the Bavarian general was under the orders of the Prince of the Moskva; it was therefore quite useless to write to Munich. You would have had plenty of time to instruct the Bavarians to make a retrograde movement when you knew that the enemy cavalry had arrived in Bamberg; and, certainly, the Bavarians would have known to do so without you telling them: all this smacks of weakness. The allies

have so little firmness, that one should try to give them some, instead of undermining it even more by vain precautions.[157]

As for the Bavarians, the emperor was 'greatly surprised at the conduct of the Bavarian general' when he received Bertrand's account of the 16 April meeting. He instructed Bertrand to 'give orders in my name' for Raglovich to assemble his division and advance at once to 'take up a militarily sound position to dominate the Saale'. He also had Berthier address both the general and the king. In a stiff note to Raglovich, Berthier specified that as part of Napoleon's larger plan the Bavarians were to come under Bertrand's orders and participate in the advance into Saxony. He concluded with a definitive rebuke: 'The emperor, general, commands his army in person and His Majesty hopes that all the hesitations shown by the allies in recent times concerning the unity of command will no longer occur.'

Berthier also wrote to Max Joseph to stress that Napoleon was commanding in person, to provide a general operational overview and to convey the same message he had given Raglovich, albeit in more circumspect and solicitous terms:

> Your Majesty knows how important it is in the present circumstances that there be no hesitation in the minds of the generals on the subject of unity of command. I can only urge Your Majesty to give precise orders to the general commanding the Bavarian troops in this respect, as it seems that there was some uncertainty at the beginning.

A personal letter from Napoleon, borne by one of his general officer ADC's, similarly asked the king 'to give his generals such orders that there is no reluctance on their part and that they obey my orders without any reservation'. Both the emperor and his chief of staff expressed the desire that Max Joseph 'send General Wrede to command his troops if there is no reason to the contrary' and Napoleon concluded (again) with a plea for mounted units: 'I cannot recommend too highly that Your Majesty push forward all the cavalry that you can.'[158] A report from Hauptmann von Völderndorff of Raglovich's staff created additional pressure on the Bavarians. Sent to brief Napoleon on the Bavarian division and receive orders, Völderndorff had an hour-long audience with the emperor during which Napoleon stated that 'he would never forget' the King of Saxony's refusal to send the requested cuirassier regiments (an aggravation that was prominent in his mind at that point in late April).[159]

In reply to these requests, Max Joseph assured Berthier that he had given orders for Raglovich to obey Bertrand but tried to excuse the hesitation by averring that it had been occasioned by uncertainty as to who would command his troops. He also took the opportunity to highlight (again) the external and internal threats to Bavaria: 'It cannot therefore be considered wrong that I have forbidden my generals to leave my lands.' He regretted that Wrede's health still did not permit him to take up a field command and mentioned the purchase of horses. Despite the threat the Bavarians perceived in Napoleon's comments to Völderndorff, however, Max Joseph made no promises about sending cavalry. Throughout this note, as in all his correspondence with Napoleon and Berthier that year, the king stressed two themes: the need for immediate peace and Bavaria's incapacity to contribute more than it was already providing as far as military power was concerned.[160]

With Max Joseph's instructions to Raglovich, this momentary misunderstanding passed. Raglovich acknowledged his attachment to Bertrand's corps (with the punctilious reminder that his king wanted the cavalry regiment to remain under the division) and Napoleon was able to write to Ney on 26 April that, 'The King of Bavaria has removed all the difficulties the Bavarians were causing.'[161] Bertrand, however, was no longer in the picture as his corps was divided up with two of its French divisions and the Bavarian contingent being detached to form the 12th Corps under Marshal Oudinot. The manner in which this brief dispute was resolved, however, meant that Bavaria was left with no option but to send part of its army into the consuming maelstrom of war beyond its borders; the option of remaining on the defensive or pursuing some sort of disguised neutrality had vanished for the moment. Moreover, rightly or wrongly, the incident reinforced for many Bavarians the image of French arrogance and imperious treatment of their ally. Raglovich felt compelled, for example, to issue a stern order of the day on 2 May after meeting with Oudinot:

> The marshal has observed to me, that many officers have allowed themselves expression regarding the unpleasantness of this war, which has caused much agitation. I warn everyone who is sensible and devoted to the will of our king to refrain from such expressions... In general, I cannot ask the commanders enough to order their subordinates to show the utmost tolerance towards the imperial French troops, the necessity of which cannot escape anyone's insight.

For many French, of course, the opposite was true since Raglovich's initial reaction and cases of casual insolence (such as an artillery officer who rebuffed Oudinot's chief of staff when he was delivering instructions to Raglovich) only confirmed a perception of Bavarian recalcitrance.[162] The seemingly minor incident with Bertrand thus illuminates some of the fissures in the alliance, cracks that could be repaired or at least covered over in previous years, but which were now more likely to widen than lessen.

To Bautzen and Beyond: Military Operations in May and June

Now incorporated into the 12th Corps as the *'corps bavarois'* or, officially, the 29th Division of the Grande Armée, the Bavarians marched into ducal Saxon territory on 28 April. Having left II/4th Infantry and the 8th Fusilier Company of II/10th behind as fortress garrisons, it listed 7,143 officers and men on its rolls as 'present under arms'. They were organised into nine infantry battalions, six cavalry squadrons and two eight-gun artillery batteries. Despite the division's manifold deficiencies, its month-long posting along the border had provided an opportunity for some training and organisation. Raglovich was therefore pleased with the 'good will' the men displayed in their first encounter, albeit very minor, with enemy scouting parties on 2 May south of Jena. He was also relieved to be placed under Oudinot. The two men knew each other from Russia, where Oudinot's 2nd Corps and the Bavarian 6th Corps had campaigned together in and around Polotsk. In addition to mutual respect at the personal level, the marshal had developed a favourable opinion of the Bavarian troops during the trying days of 1812 and detailed some of the Bavarian chevaulegers to serve as his staff escort. He thus welcomed the contingent into his command and proved solicitous to Raglovich's concerns.[163] When he visited the Bavarians on 7 May, however, Oudinot was troubled to find the camp disorderly with the outposts neglectful of due vigilance and a general absence of proper military appearance. The marshal's complaints and Raglovich's own observations led to a series of strict instructions on every topic from the proper wearing of uniforms to camp security and the casual firing of muskets.[164]

In addition to lax discipline and ignorance of military standards, logistical problems manifested themselves as soon as the division left Bavaria. Raglovich urgently requested medicines, shoes and, above all, bread wagons from Munich as early as 2 May, but these were long in arriving largely because of lassitude and excessive frugality on the part of the kingdom's War Ministry. These Bavarian national failings compounded the Grande Armée's widespread shortfalls in logistical support during 1813. Inadequacy of transport and supply would therefore dog the division for the remainder of the war, eroding strength and sapping morale with all the attendant deleterious effects on discipline.

The Bavarians and 12th Corps reached Jena on 2 May where they could hear the rumble of the guns from Lützen but were too distant to participate. Instead, Oudinot's command became involved in Napoleon's drive to the Elbe following the battle, turning east to head for Dresden via Naumburg ('all the houses and all streets full of wounded soldiers' from Lützen) and Freiberg. Administrative annoyances accumulated along the way, adding to the burdens borne by the soldiers and contributing to Franco-Bavarian frictions. Young artillery Unterleutnant Ferdinand Sigmund von Praun, for instance, recorded that he rode into Freiberg through steady rain to seek quarters for himself and his men. He reported to division headquarters soaked to the skin only to be told that he would have to bivouac in the open because 'French cavalry had already taken over all the quarters in the town'. 'Full of resentment towards the French who always enjoy the advantage and pick out the best quarters for themselves, I threw myself on my tired and almost exhausted horse and rode back to my men full of anger.' This was a typical case, the sort of quotidian frustration experienced by many Rheinbund soldiers, but hardly unusual in any military operation involving any nation in any era.[165] Other Bavarians, after all, seem to have been quartered in the town. Whether or not situations of this sort represented intentional disregard of their Bavarian allies, Praun and many other Germans certainly perceived such incidents as evidence of French arrogance and presumption, especially when the recipients of the seeming neglect were tired, wet and hungry.

Such annoyances notwithstanding, the Bavarian division reached the outskirts of Dresden on 12 May, practicing square formations along the way owing to the superiority of Coalition cavalry as experienced at Lützen.[166] Napoleon reviewed the division the following day and, apparently at Oudinot's suggestion, presented Oberst Max Graf Seyssel d'Aix, commander of the composite cavalry regiment, with a belated award of the Legion of Honour for his performance at Borodino the previous year. The Bavarians greeted the emperor with the obligatory cheers and Raglovich reported that 'he seemed very satisfied' and 'spoke very kindly with me'. Napoleon would later pronounce himself '*très content*' with the appearance of the division.[167] No one knew it yet, of course, but this would be the last time Napoleon would review a Bavarian formation.

The Bavarians spent the next week following the main army on the road east from Dresden towards the Russo-Prussian position at Bautzen to bivouac near Gaußig on 18/19 May. Other than brushes with Cossacks and patrolling detachments, there was limited contact with the enemy. Seyssel's attention to his chevaulegers regiment, however, paid off in several small encounters. One squadron was attached to each of the two French divisions of 12th Corps during the advance and one of these had the better of scouting Cossacks on 16 May while a squadron detailed to GB Gruyer's brigade of the 14th Division earned the marshal's praise two days later by helping to clear enemy cavalry from the French flank near Neukirch along the border with Bohemia. The Bavarian composite cavalry regiment thus demonstrated what good leadership could accomplish even with new recruits and Oudinot expressed his satisfaction in an order of the day on the 19th: 'The Bavarian chevaulegers justified the confidence placed in them by conducting several fine charges as well as veteran soldiers would have done.'[168] The 1st Brigade conducted a reconnaissance to Gnaschwitz on the morning of 19 May, pushing a company and some chevaulegers east to chase off Cossacks near Schlungwitz hard by the Spree before returning to Gaußig. Oberstleutnant Peter Palm's light infantry battalion of the 2nd Brigade also had an encounter with the omnipresent Coalition raiding parties. The men were settling into their bivouac near Gaußig and preparing their evening meals as the sun set on the 19th. Many had already undressed to clean their uniforms when Cossacks suddenly appeared in their rear. Hastily grabbing their muskets and cartridge boxes, the light infantrymen, many still in their underclothes, dashed towards the enemy and opened fire. The Cossacks took flight, especially after a nearby French battery, the gunners likewise at best half-dressed, greeted them with canister rounds.[169]

Courage and Perseverance at Bautzen

The minor affairs of the 16th and 19th were followed by the gigantic Battle of Bautzen on 20 and 21 May. This was an entirely different experience for the majority of the men in Raglovich's division. Although the Bavarians played only a small supporting role, this huge affray provided the young soldiers with a sudden and rude introduction to the scale, scope and violence of a major Napoleonic battle.[170]

Oudinot's task in Napoleon's plan for Bautzen was to draw Allied attention to their left while Ney swept in from the north to outflank them on their right. Ney, however, would need time to arrive, so 20 May was to be a day of preparation to set the stage for the decisive action on the 21st. The 12th Corps therefore crossed the Spree south of Bautzen around midday on the 20th with the two French divisions in the lead, GD Michel Marie Pacthod's 13th Division on the left and GD Guillaume de Latrille Lorencez's 14th on the right. The Bavarian division, having left II/10th Infantry at Schmiedefeld to secure the main road to Dresden, followed in reserve with an estimated

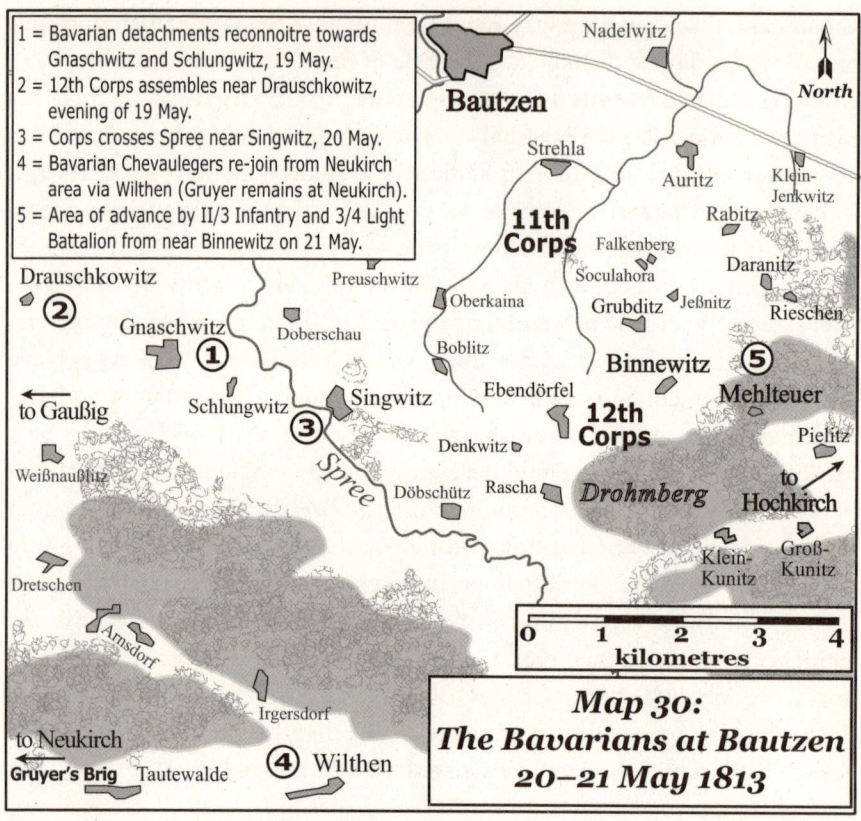

Map 30: The Bavarians at Bautzen 20–21 May 1813

5,350 infantrymen and its two artillery batteries. Owing to the threat of Coalition cavalry the French and Bavarian infantry made most of their moves in square formation. The young French soldiers made good progress, reaching Jeßnitz, Mehlteuer and Pielitz before the evening counterattack by grenadiers from the Russian reserves pushed them back to a line running roughly from Grubditz to Binnewitz and the Drohmberg. Oudinot, however, was unsure of how the Bavarian division's partly trained recruits would perform in their first combat.[171] He thus elected to hold Raglovich's men in a supporting position around Ebendörfel. Momentarily separated from the division, the combined Chevaulegers Regiment, 630 strong, had been sent south to help clear the way for Gruyer to join the corps from Neukirch. They clashed with Cossacks east of Wilthen during the day but rode up to join the 12th Corps right flank near Denkwitz that evening.[172]

As Napoleon was intent on keeping enemy eyes focused to the south, Oudinot renewed his attack early on the morning of the 21st. The French infantry pressed as far as Rieschen on the left and once again seized Pielitz on the right while the Bavarians, formed in squares, remained in their reserve position near Ebendörfel with Major Wilhelm von Fortis's combined 3rd/4th Light Battalion slightly forward towards Binnewitz. Here they suffered their first casualties of the battle when Russian artillery fire fell among their ranks. Friendly artillery eventually silenced the enemy guns, but the Bavarians soon found themselves under fire again as the French attacks faltered. Although Russian counterattacks threw the advancing French infantry back in confusion, the marshal still chose to keep most of the Bavarian division in reserve, sending only two of the 1st Brigade's battalions to assist Pacthod on the left.[173] It was near midday as these two, II/3rd Infantry and Major von Fortis's 3rd/4th Light Battalion, arrived to assist Pacthod, the general reportedly shouting 'Bavarians, save the position that has been lost!' as he urged the men forward. The Bavarians advanced into the wooded high ground north of Mehlteuer and, despite being disordered by the difficult terrain, pushed as far as Rieschen before being forced to withdraw. Fortis, wounded in the neck by a spent ball, lost his voice and had to be led or carried by his men, but they held on stoutly before slowly falling back to Grubditz.[174] The rest of the division remained around Ebendörfel to cover the retreat of the disarrayed French infantry, but the Schützen Company of II/8 and the half-company of Schützen from the 13th Infantry's Reserve Battalion took considerable losses protecting a French battery from Russian infantry attack.

Enemy pressure eased as Oudinot swung his corps back to the line from Grubditz to Ebendörfel. Facing towards the southeast with a strong artillery line of French and Bavarian guns, the Bavarians presented a formidable front that the Russians declined to attack. Russian shot and shell continued to fall among the ranks, but the tsar's gunners were disadvantaged by the terrain and Bavarian casualties were relatively minor. 'It was lucky for us', wrote Leutnant Friedrich Mändler of the 6th Light Battalion, 'that the cannon balls did not ricochet or bounce but rather came down from the hill [the Drohmberg], bored into the earth and stuck fast where they landed, and that the numerous shells which the enemy threw at us, especially towards the end of the battle, mostly flew over our heads.'[175] Russian cavalry also threatened the corps' right flank from south of the Drohmberg, but the French and Bavarian guns and their Bavarian infantry supports evidently looked steady enough to forestall any serious attack. 'The well-directed fire of the artillery under my command was able to confine the advance of the enemy masses, composed of Russian Guard according to precise information, to the heights they had taken,' reported Raglovich.[176] Shielded by the Bavarians and the guns, the disordered French infantry were thus able to re-form and resume their place in the line. The Bavarian after-action account exaggerated in claiming that the division's stand saved the army's right wing and perhaps allowed Napoleon's overall plan to succeed, but its role, while hardly decisive given the 'inactivity of the victorious, very superior enemy', was not an insignificant contribution to the eventual victory.[177]

From the 12th Corps perspective that afternoon, however, victory seemed a remote prospect. Outnumbered and hard-pressed by elite Russian formations, the men felt they were barely hanging on. There was no question of further advance, and all were quite taken aback when an officer from imperial headquarters arrived between 2:00 and 3:00 p.m. to announce that the battle was won, as Mändler recalled:

> We looked at one another in doubt, and did not know if we should trust this news more than our own eyes. Because we noticed neither a movement to the rear nor any other change in deployment along the entire enemy battle line. Before long, however, we saw how the Allies, under heavy French artillery fire, formed many columns and, behind the protection of their artillery, pulled back in the greatest order as if on the exercise field.[178]

From his more elevated perspective, Raglovich waxed almost lyrical in his official report as he described 'the imposing view' afforded by the closing moments of the battle:

> The immensely long line of battle on both sides was covered with artillery pieces that fired ceaselessly. The burning villages along the length of the front, as the Russians fired every village that they had to leave, the town of Bautzen, spared from the general misfortune, uniquely illuminated by the sun breaking mightily through the clouds and powder smoke, all these features presented a dreadful/beautiful whole.[179]

As this spectacle faded with the setting sun and the approaching rain, the Bavarians and the rest of 12th Corps followed the retreating enemy to bivouac for the night around Hochkirch.

The Bavarian Chevaulegers Regiment came into action in the area south of Ebendörfel around noon when it was assigned to GB Marc-Antoine de Reiset's French dragoon brigade. Ordered to scout the road towards Hochkirch and maintain liaison with Gruyer's brigade, the brigade advanced with the Bavarians in the lead. An attack on a superior body of Russian horse over unsuitable terrain, however, was repulsed. The Bavarians were thrown back and the Russians fell upon the French brigade. The melee with the dragoons allowed the Bavarians time to recover and Seyssel led his squadrons back to the attack to relieve his French comrades-in-arms.[180] This minor clash had no impact on the outcome of the larger battle but did serve to demonstrate that the Bavarian troopers were learning their trade in the harsh school of combat.

Indeed, despite inexperienced troops, lack of officers and NCOs, desertion, and numerous other problems, the division had done well in its first major engagement. Raglovich, who had certainly not stinted in expressing frank complaints to his king, concluded his report with warm regard for his men:

> Furthermore, Your Majesty, I cannot praise enough the courage and perseverance of the troops under my command, especially manifested in the coolness and calm of the young soldiers, which is usually only seen in older troops, particularly during the marshal's fine retrograde movement after the loss of the heights on the right flank [Drohmberg], as well as the activity and effectiveness of the artillery.

Based on his account, the War Ministry commended the division for displaying 'glorious bravery' despite being mostly composed of 'newly raised conscripts'. Raglovich was not alone in lauding his men. Oudinot, expressed his satisfaction to the general after the battle and included due acknowledgement in his after-action report: 'The Bavarians supported these movements [the French advances] with the courage that has always distinguished these brave allies; their artillery also rendered good service.' Similarly, the description published in the official French journals could not praise enough 'the bravery, constancy and coolness of the Bavarian troops, amidst such heavy fire even though the greater part of the force was composed of young soldiers'. 'The artillery responded perfectly to what was expected of it', ran the French account, and 'The 1st Regiment of Chevaulegers withstood with great courage several very sharp attacks by the enemy cavalry.'[181]

Given their fairly limited participation in the fighting, the cost to the Bavarian division was modest, especially compared to the severe casualties suffered by their French allies. According to the report submitted by 12th Corps on 25 May, the Bavarians lost 58 killed, 248 wounded and 195 missing for a total of 501. These losses were concentrated in a few units. Having been thrown forward to support Pacthod, for instance, the II/3 Infantry suffered 116 casualties and dissolved its 6th and 8th Companies so the men could be distributed to the other four to keep them up to strength and compensate for the lack of officers. In contrast, the lone brigade from Lorencez's 14th Division lost 1,776 men and overall French casualties came to 5,547 for the corps (thus 6,048 with the Bavarians added).[182] Where the French could expect replacements for some of their losses, however, Raglovich would receive none. His only hope to rebuild his division's strength would be stragglers returning to the ranks or convalescents sufficiently recovered to re-join their units.

Hoyerswerda, Desertion and Luckau

The losses suffered by the 12th Corps and the pernicious plague of enemy raiding parties led Napoleon to leave Oudinot in the area around Bautzen while the rest of the army pursued the retreating Allies. An ad hoc mixed 'division' of Rheinbund cavalry and French infantry under GD Beaumont was placed under his orders; but Beaumont, who had been covering the French flank northeast of Dresden during the push towards Bautzen, would not join Oudinot until 27 May. The Bavarians thus stayed in the vicinity of Bautzen from 24 to 26 May, clearing the gruesome battlefield, escorting convoys and performing other rear area tasks. Raglovich had hoped to use this break to train and restore his division's lax discipline. The men thus drilled every day from 7:00 to 9:00 a.m., but this welcome respite from combats and marches came to an end when the corps headed north on 26 May. Napoleon, underestimating the forces under Prussian GL von Bülow, had ordered Oudinot towards Berlin 'to contain Bülow and to throw him beyond the Oder'.[183] The marshal, on the other hand, overestimated Bülow's strength and would exercise great caution during his hesitant and abortive march towards the Prussian capital.

Unfortunately for Oudinot, he found himself deprived of several units when he set out on his independent mission towards Berlin. Among these were two Bavarian battalions left behind to garrison Bautzen until they could be relieved by the Westphalian 8th Infantry Regiment from Dresden. Beaumont's ad hoc division was also delayed as it took a day to assemble its scattered components and several French battalions that were supposed to join 12th Corps from Magdeburg were likewise not ready (they would not arrive at all).

The absence of these units reinforced Oudinot's innate hesitancy, but Napoleon's orders were clear, and he duly marched on the 26th. The Bavarian light horse, his only cavalry until Beaumont caught up, led the way and surprised a detachment of Cossacks at Hoyerswerda on the first day of the march, capturing 47 of the enemy in a tidy action that earned Oudinot's praise.[184] The marshal, however, mindful of his missing battalions, was convinced that he was grossly outnumbered. Even after Beaumont arrived on the 27th, Oudinot believed his 14,000 men faced 36,000–40,000 Prussians/Russians.[185] He thus wanted to assemble all his available troops before proceeding and kept most of his corps south of Hoyerswerda on the 27th, sending only the 13th Division with a squadron of Bavarian chevaulegers somewhat to the north.

Oudinot's opponent, GL von Bülow, was operating under the opposite assumption: he believed Oudinot was advancing with only 7,000 men and thus sent just two of his brigades under Borstell to surprise the French at Hoyerswerda. Franco-Bavarian security and reconnaissance were poor. Scouts had returned that morning to report no enemy anywhere nearby, so the corps relaxed. Indeed, the Bavarians, posted to the rear, were in the process of preparing meals and distributing soldiers' pay. Borstell was therefore able to gain an initial advantage when he attacked on the morning of 28 May. He soon discovered his error, however, and withdrew after some brisk combat. The Bavarian 2nd Brigade, four guns and a cavalry squadron were involved in this engagement, entering the battle line in support of the 14th Division on the French left while the 1st Brigade remained in reserve guarding the corps' baggage. Bavarian casualties were minimal, 18 wounded or missing out of the 400–500 lost by the corps in repulsing Borstell's ambitious advance. Oudinot once again praised the Bavarian troops and Raglovich wrote to the king that he could not do justice to the 'courage and endurance' of his men.[186]

As the gunfire faded away on 28 May, Raglovich found time to compose a comprehensive report on the division for his king. According to this report, the Bavarian division now numbered 5,817 officers and men present under arms including the two battalions from Bautzen (which re-joined their comrades at Hoyerswerda on 29 May).[187] Another 503 were on detached duty in various locations, 961 were in hospital and 284 were listed as prisoners of war. The accompanying letter to Max Joseph again illustrated Raglovich's pessimistic outlook as he pleaded for replacements, especially officers and NCOs to provide the necessary supervision of the men and correct some of the division's discipline problems. He also informed the king of his rather surprising decision to send two cannons and two howitzers back to Dresden owing to what he claimed was an insufficiency of artillery personnel; from this point on, therefore, each of the batteries would consist of five guns and one howitzer.[188]

These late May strength figures also offer some clues regarding the extent of desertion in the Bavarian contingent. Adding all together and including generals and staff officers, the division's total strength on 28 May came to 7,580 officers and men, that is 270 fewer 'effectives' (not 'present under arms') than had been carried on the rolls in late April on leaving Bavaria (7,850). To arrive at a gross figure of possible desertions, we can add the 284 listed above as 'prisoners of war' to this 270-man deficit for a rough total of 574 men who were no longer in the ranks but who were not part of the known tally of wounded, sick or detached. Deducting the recorded 58 combat deaths results in a figure of 516 soldiers as the pool of men who *might* have deserted. In actuality, of course, some, perhaps many, of these were probably men who had not deserted, that is, those whose battle deaths had not been recorded or who had expired in hospital or who were genuine prisoners of war; but even assuming that all 516 were deserters only yields an approximate desertion rate of 5–7 per cent.[189] While hardly admirable figures, such percentages do not seem to justify terms such as 'massive' used by subsequent Bavarian historians, nor are they very different from what seem to have been the levels of desertion among French units in 1813; indeed, they were likely lower. Though only one data point among many, this helps provide some context for the loyalty, discipline and reliability of the Rheinbund troops in this stressful, challenging year. As noted above, however, the problem of steadily diminishing strength was essentially irremediable for the Bavarians because Munich had decided not to send replacements to Raglovich's division.

The Bavarians were not alone in suffering from desertion and discipline problems. Oudinot attempted to curb these ills among his French regiments with severe orders and punishments, including executions, as he gathered his corps around Hoyerswerda after the engagement on the 28th. Enmeshed in apprehensions and uncertainties, the marshal loitered here for several more days, only heading northwest towards Berlin on 31 May after being prodded again by Napoleon. Oudinot's renewed advance brought on a second engagement with Bülow's corps at Luckau on 4 June. The 13th Division bore the brunt of this bitter combat since the marshal held most of the 14th Division and the Bavarians in reserve. The Bavarians, at least according to Unterleutnant von Praun's testimony, were tired of sitting out the combat: 'with vehemence and impetuosity we Bavarians demanded at last to be led into the fight'.[190] Oudinot, however, was not interested in expanding the engagement and the only Rheinbund involvement came in the early evening when four of Oberst von Seyssel's chevaulegers squadrons and the Hessian Garde-Chevaulegers were entangled in a Prussian cavalry attack on the French right flank. Caught by surprise, two of the Bavarian chevaulegers squadrons were overthrown and apparently fled through a nearby French battery, preventing the guns from firing and scattering the gunners. The French infantry hastily formed squares and opened fire, causing casualties among the retreating Bavarian and Hessian horsemen but the battery lost three cannons to the charging Prussians in the confusion. Fortunately, Seyssel led his other two squadrons in a countercharge to repel the enemy and recover two of the three lost guns.[191] Despite this small success, the fight at Luckau was a setback that put an end to the 12th Corps' advance on Berlin and seemed to confirm Oudinot in his cautious appraisal of his circumstances. He withdrew that night in the general direction of Torgau, falling back to the southwest behind the Schwarze Elster near Herzberg in a miserable march under drenching rain. Recounting the corps' discouragement, Praun recalled that, 'Bad roads and worse weather exhausted our horses, which we did not have time to feed properly, yes, numerous misfortunes combined to make our bad situation worse.' Some '60 to 80 men are left behind on every march', lamented Raglovich, distressed that these stragglers 'then make no effort to catch up'.[192]

Minor outpost clashes continued after the corps' arrival on the Schwarze Elster. The 1st Division of the Chevaulegers Regiment, for example, had two men wounded in a skirmish with Prussian cavalry near München on 7 June in what would be the final Bavarian action of the spring campaign.[193] Both sides learned of the armistice the following day and moved to new positions over the coming week to comply with its provisions. For the Bavarians this meant a shift to bivouacs and billets in the vicinity of Herzberg and Schlieben where they would remain until the resumption of hostilities in August.

Armistice Anxieties[194]

The Bavarians, like the rest of the army, welcomed the armistice. The men not only enjoyed a break from exhausting marches and the dangers of combat, but, initially at least, also benefited from better provisions in a region that had not suffered the depredations inherent in the passage of multiple armies. Lack of fodder for the horses caused Raglovich great concern, but the men could rest in regular billets and encampments instead of shifting from one hasty bivouac to another every day on the road. An energetic quartermaster with the appropriate name of Mathias Schnell managed to put together a transport of shoes and clothing in Dresden which reached the division on 18 June. Tardiness on the part of the Bavarian bureaucracy and fears of Allied raiding parties delayed supplies from home, but a convoy of biscuit and shoes arrived on 10 July under escort of the 10th Infantry's 8th Fusilier Company (previously withheld for fortress duty in Bavaria). This transport also included sufficient medicines and medical personnel to allow the division to establish its own field hospital as Raglovich had been requesting for weeks.[195]

Raglovich was especially grateful for the ceasefire, gloomily reporting to Max Joseph that the division might have soon dissolved had it not been given this unexpected respite.[196] Despite the genuine satisfaction he displayed in his accounts of the division's battlefield performance, his letters during the armistice period are crowded with doleful worries, grim predictions and repeated pleas for support. He intended to use the armistice period to drill the division and instill 'the spirit of veteran troops' in his young conscripts, but he was deeply troubled about the quality of leadership in his command and associated problems of discipline as well as his inability to provide adequate victuals for man and beast. As far as animals were concerned, losses among the division's horses and the paucity of fodder were such that Raglovich had to resort to employing local animals, including oxen, for his transport wagons. In contrast, the food supply for the men was initially good, indeed, better than that provided to the neighbouring French formations. The situation soon deteriorated, however, and Raglovich feared that the harsh means required to collect food on a daily basis 'are harmful to the morality of the soldiers in the most detrimental fashion'. 'This predatory routine, which has been elevated to a system in the army, tempts many a man to unauthorised actions,' he wrote on 18 June, citing the poor example set by the French and 'Italian' regiments.[197] Given the circumstances, he also sympathised with the local population in 'this most pitiable land'.

> The country must be in despair. Country people as well as townsmen see their livelihoods taken by force, their cattle and horses are no longer their own possessions, the green fodder no longer shared out. From these causes the deep popular hatred for the French and their allied armies is easily explained.[198]

In Raglovich's view, his officers and NCOs were often incapable or unwilling to address these deficiencies in discipline. In the first place, there were not enough of these key leaders (as seen with II/3) so that 'many companies are commanded by lieutenants who are themselves embarrassed by their positions'. Furthermore, their attention to basic responsibilities such as supervision and accountability was 'almost totally absent or only partial', he complained.

> The NCOs, as raw and inexperienced as the common soldiers, have neither the knowledge nor the standing to be effective. Most of the officers, as young in experience as they are in years, are unable to give the men the proper attention as a large part of those who have served longer, either ignorant themselves or, as is beginning to become so general, rendered idle by exhaustion and disaffection, neither support them nor properly hold them to their duty.[199]

He even took the fairly drastic step of criticising some of the battalion commanders and other more senior officers by name and regretted that he could not dismiss them for lack of replacements.

These discipline worries were not without their humourous aspects. Oberst Nikolaus Hubert von Maillot de la Treille, commander of the 2nd Brigade, for example, found it necessary to issue a lengthy order chastising his men for the quality of their Raupenhelms. Some of these were ridiculous, he complained, so large that the wearer had trouble keeping the swaying helmet on his head, some bore incorrect chin scales with unauthorised piscine images of every description or were equipped with all manner of crests when wool was prescribed, and some were simply dirty and unpolished. Some officers appeared on parade without the proper uniforms or neglected to wear their rank insignia at all times, while some men were too casual in dress or failed to attend to basic requirements of personal cleanliness and hygiene. How successful Maillot and the other commanders were in their effort to address these issues is unclear, but the armistice certainly afforded an opportunity to tighten military discipline and appearance while recuperating from the opening campaign and training diligently for the next.[200]

These weeks also brought a few improvements in the leadership situation as some regiments did receive a reinforcement of officers, if not of men, during the armistice. The II/5 Infantry provides an example. Each of its six companies should have been commanded by a *Hauptmann*, assisted by an *Oberleutnant* and an *Unterleutnant*, but when the armistice was announced, the battalion had only one *Hauptmann* fit for duty and not a single *Oberleutnant*; their slots were filled by *Unterleutnants*, the army's most junior officer rank. Nine officers, including three of *Hauptmann* rank, arrived to take posts with the battalion in early August, but this addition still left it short of appropriate commanders for two of its companies and only gave it one *Oberleutnant* rather than six.[201] Another improvement, at least from Raglovich's perspective, came with the departure of Beckers. Promoted to *General-Leutnant*, he was recalled to command a division in the kingdom. Oberst Maillot de la Treille, promoted to *General-Major*, took Beckers's place at the head of the 1st Brigade while Georg Josef Baron Habermann of the 5th Infantry, also newly promoted, assumed command of the 2nd as a *General-Major*. Raglovich certainly regretted the general shortage of officers and wished some replaced, but he could at least take comfort in the departure of this disagreeable subordinate.

As for himself, Raglovich clearly felt isolated if not abandoned. Having received no reply to any of the four reports he had submitted during May, he feared that they had been intercepted by the Cossacks and raiders that infested the army's rear areas. He even considered routing his messages through neutral Prague rather than allied Saxony.[202] As far as is known, this was not the case. All or most of his letters seem to have reached their destination and received brief annotations from the Minister of War or other officials. The roads back to Bavaria were certainly insecure, but rather than insecurity of the roads, the lack of response was an indication of his government's priorities: Munich was focused on the forces being reconstituted under Wrede at home; Raglovich's division was a regrettable sacrifice to the exigencies of the Rheinbund alliance.

Off in Saxony, of course, Raglovich also had to contend with the challenges of the French alliance. On the one hand, he wrote that he 'could not praise enough the most friendly distinction' afforded to the division by Oudinot and his entourage. He suspected that a desire to be awarded the Max Joseph Order accounted for much of the courtesy shown by the marshal and his leading staff officers, but references to Oudinot's 'paternal care' appear repeatedly in his correspondence. On the other hand, he felt compelled to report his perception of the frictions with the French as well as the larger debilities afflicting the Grande Armée: 'There seems to have been an increase in insolence and rudeness, in disrespect and contempt for foreigners, as well as in disorder and licentiousness, together with a complete lack of discipline, more than has ever been observed at other times.'[203]

In addition to these larger alliance issues, Raglovich had to contend with more immediate challenges. Oudinot, for instance, impressed upon him the need to replace the division's losses and bring it to full strength. Although he dutifully relayed this entirely reasonable request to Munich and pledged 'to do everything possible' to comply, it placed Raglovich in an embarrassing position as he likely knew that no replacements, let alone reinforcements, would be forthcoming.[204] The Bavarian general was especially apprehensive when Oudinot informed him in early August that the Chevaulegers Regiment was to be detached from the division and assigned to GB Wolff's cavalry brigade. This was a sensitive matter for the Bavarians as they, in common with all Rheinbund members, were determined to keep their contingents united under national command, especially after the bitter experience of having the six fine mounted regiments separated from the rest of 6th Corps in 1812. Raglovich immediately protested to Oudinot and received the marshal's promise that the regiment would be carried as part of Wolff's brigade for reporting purposes but that it would remain *de facto* under Raglovich's orders.[205] This may have been Oudinot's intention, but his pledge would prove misleading. At the time, however, it was the best Raglovich could hope to achieve.

Oudinot's attention to and praise for the Bavarians, especially for Raglovich as their commander, was genuine, but he also had concerns. In addition to his general doubts about the division owing to its inexperience and lack of training, he commented that the Bavarians were slow on the march and displayed little skill in patrolling or outpost duties.[206] The last was an old criticism, dating to at least 1809 when Marshal François Lefebvre, commanding the Bavarian contingent as 7th Corps of the Army of Germany, had voiced similar complaints. By 1813, however, it was also an ironic objection given that Napoleon's other allies and most notably the French themselves were repeatedly victims of surprise owing to poor security practices and inadequate reconnaissance.

Raglovich's worries and the division's deficiencies notwithstanding, the Bavarians put in a good performance when Oudinot reviewed them in detail on 30 June. The marshal declared himself extremely pleased after inspecting the men closely and his chief of staff, GB Louis-François Lejeune, recalled that, 'General Raglovich's Bavarian division came on to the ground in the very finest condition, evidently well-prepared to take the field again.'[207] There were also crosses of the Legion of Honour to distribute, but Leutnant Mändler was surprised and disappointed when his commander, Oberstleutnant Palm, turned back the four offered to the 5th/6th Light Battalion because 'everyone had simply done his duty'. 'Another commander would certainly have regarded it as an honour to count four more members of the order in his battalion!' exclaimed Mändler. Several weeks later, the Bavarians, like the rest of the army, celebrated Napoleon's birthday with a parade and religious service, cannon salvoes, banquets, toasts, a ball for the officers and sporting competitions with prizes for the men. 'All was given over to joy that day,' reported Raglovich.[208] One week later, the 5,700 officers and men of the Bavarian division were once again on the march.[209]

The halt in military operations during the armistice was matched in Bavaria's case by stagnation on the diplomatic–political front. Entertaining vain hopes for peace from the congress that was supposed to convene in Prague and other diplomatic activity, the king even proceeded on his annual holiday to take the waters at a spa in Baden-Baden. Although he would have preferred a genuine form of neutrality, this was clearly impossible as Montgelas explained to the crown prince in a 24 July epistle. For the moment, Max Joseph remained suspicious of Austria as a potential threat and continued to view France as the buttress that supported Bavaria's territorial expanse and its extant dynastic order. He was satisfied that his hedging strategy had preserved the kingdom's existence during the spring crisis, avoiding a rush to an unsustainable declaration of neutrality or to the Coalition's dubious embrace and allowing him to assuage his sense of honour by remaining – at least formally – a French ally. Even Ludwig became quiescent.[210] Thus convinced, Max Joseph saw no reason to change course even as the ramshackle peace efforts collapsed, and war resumed in the middle of August.

For the Bavarian army, Munich's policy meant that the urgent rebuilding at home would continue to keep troops out of Napoleon's immediate reach, while deterring Austrian adventurism and establishing a viable armed force that would give weight to Bavarian interests as the country charted its difficult course into the future. As mentioned above, this rebuilding included the creation of new 'national guard' or militia units as well as the reconstitution of the regular regiments. Placed under Wrede's command, these troops were assembled in a large training camp outside Munich starting in June and slowly accrued strength and competence during the summer. As this corps had the ostensible purpose of fending off an Austrian advance, the Bavarians portrayed it as part of the kingdom's Rheinbund contingent, a characterisation that the French seem to have more or less accepted. Wrede had some 17,000 on hand in early June, a figure that would rise to roughly 25,000 by mid-September, allowing Max Joseph to assert that he had not only met, but exceeded his treaty obligation.[211] Raglovich, meanwhile, was left bereft of reinforcements.

Napoleon welcomed the formation of this corps near Munich. He certainly wanted to see Raglovich's division brought up to strength, but he was also concerned about the growing likelihood that Austria would join his enemies at the end of the armistice. As the summer progressed, therefore, he took steps to secure his strategic right flank along the Austro-Bavarian border. He viewed this area as divided into two zones separated by the Danube.

For the northern bank of the great river, he placed Marshal Augereau in charge of the troops along his line of communications from Mainz to Bamberg and Bayreuth as 'The Observation Corps of Bavaria'. Augereau's principal tasks were rear area security and preparing new units to join the main army, but his presence would also serve to dissuade Austria and reassure Bavaria. As his area of responsibility included the northern districts of Bavaria, Berthier informed Max Joseph that the emperor classed the Bavarian troops as part of Augereau's observation corps and asked him to have Wrede correspond with the marshal.[212] At the same time, Napoleon was annoyed at 'the poor situation of the Bavarian army' that could not put 4,000 cavalry in the field despite its large population. He compared what he viewed as Bavaria's meagre efforts unfavourably with those of its smaller neighbour Württemberg that managed to muster 2,000 horse and concluded that Bavaria thus left itself exposed to 'becoming the prey of the enemy's light troops or the least body of partisans'.[213]

These apprehensions notwithstanding, he had no choice but to entrust the defence of the second zone, south of the Danube, to Bavarian forces. 'The emperor has charged me to inform Your Majesty that he sees with pleasure that you have formed a camp at Munich and that General Wrede will command it,' wrote Berthier to Max Joseph on 17 June, 'The emperor desires to be informed of the strength of this camp, infantry, cavalry and artillery.'[214] Napoleon even considered the possibility of Wrede's corps invading Bohemia in conjunction with an advance by Viceroy Eugène from Italy into southern Austria.[215] This imperial interest corresponded neatly with the Bavarian desire to keep as many of its men as possible on home soil. The kingdom thus exerted itself to establish Wrede's corps (rather confusingly, this was also titled an 'observation corps') and happily dispatched staff officers to provide the requested data – along with exaggerated estimates of Austrian forces across the border.

Always thinking of the offensive, Napoleon's strategic considerations had several implications for Bavarian policy. First, the requirement to establish a force in the Danube valley provided Munich with a strong rationale to demand the immediate return of Raglovich's division. 'If hostilities recommence,' wrote Max Joseph to Berthier on 15 June, 'it would be very useful to me to return General Raglovich's division. Believe me that I would not make this request if I were not completely convinced that I have the greatest need: 7,000 men less will mean nothing to the emperor; in any case, they will serve the same cause.'[216] Though unsuccessful in gaining the release of the division, the danger from Austria at least allowed Bavaria to deny replacements to Raglovich and to recall officers and NCOs as his division diminished during the course of the autumn campaigns.

Second, the threat posed by a belligerent Austria placed Bavaria's strategic predicament in sharp relief. With at most 20,000–25,000 men fit for duty, Bavaria's forces by themselves were utterly inadequate to cover a frontier stretching from Hof near the Saxon border to Bozen (Bolzano) on the southern side of the Brenner Pass. From Napoleon's perspective this was not a major concern. He was prepared to give up terrain in southwestern Germany on a temporary basis as he knew that the war would be decided by his contest with the principal Allied armies along the Elbe. He hoped the presence of Augereau and Wrede would suffice to deter any adventurous Austrian notions in the first place, but if the enemy did attack, it would only be with secondary forces. In such a case, the French and Bavarian 'observation corps' only had to contain the enemy thrusts, falling back as necessary to the north and west even as far as Württemberg or Mainz until events in the main theatre of war forced the Allied intruders to withdraw. As Berthier told Augereau,

'You will understand, marshal, that if the enemy thus weakens himself by a corps of 30,000 men against the Bavarians and a corps of 25,000 against Würzburg, these would be promptly recalled by the operations of the Grande Armée.'[217] In an abstract sense, this strategy was entirely reasonable, but it did not account for the precarious state of the Franco-Bavarian alliance or the prevailing mood in the Bavarian court.

Napoleon, of course, did not communicate this broad concept to Munich, but the situation was obvious and only served to excite Bavarian fears. From the Bavarian perspective, their country was vulnerable to Austrian invasion, occupation and, even worse, annexation, especially in areas such as the Tyrol where ferment was already widespread. As Mercy d'Argenteau reported on 16 August, the distance between Augereau's corps and the Bavarian forces 'leaves a considerable gap that causes the greatest disquiet here regarding the possibility of an imminent invasion against which one sees little means of resistance'.[218] From this viewpoint, France was on the verge on reneging on its pledge to protect the kingdom from Habsburg avarice and the situation only grew more alarming when military developments along the Elbe during the autumn caused Napoleon first to weaken Augereau's corps and then transfer it entirely away from Bavaria and into central Saxony. In addition to understandable anxiety about invasion and genuine fear of being abandoned by France, however, there was also what might be termed an 'instrumental' aspect to Bavarian interpretations of the strategic situation. That is, those in Munich who were trying to nudge the king towards deserting the Rheinbund could cite the absence of French troops as putative evidence that Napoleon was not abiding by his commitment to protect his ally. Combined with a genuine fear of Austrian attack, therefore, Napoleon's seeming neglect of Bavaria's security also served as a convenient excuse for those who saw a break with France as the only pragmatic solution to the kingdom's existential crisis.[219]

There is one more skirmish to address before leaving the period of the armistice. This was the lone combat action of II/4 Infantry, that had been left behind when Raglovich marched off to Saxony. It occurred during a raid conducted by Lützow's *Freikorps* against Hof on 8–9 June. As his band roamed through western Saxony and the Saxon Duchies, Lützow detached a squadron of 100 Uhlans, 50 Cossacks and some 300 'infantry' (recently captured local militia from Sachsen-Gotha-Altenburg) to attack Hof. The Bavarians in the town consisted of the grenadiers and three fusilier companies of II/4 Infantry. Their commander, Major Theodor von Vincenti, had learned of Lützow's proximity and wisely gathered the companies together, but the garrison was surprised when the raiders dashed into outlying areas late on the afternoon of

8 June. Seven Bavarians were taken prisoner and one killed, but the attackers were unable to capture Hof despite an engagement that lasted for three hours.

Bavarian reinforcements arrived the next day (the Schützen Company of II/4 and I/2nd Chevaulegers), but after a tense standoff, Vincenti was able to convince the raiders that the armistice had been signed. No further fighting occurred and Lützow's men withdrew with an unknown number of casualties.

This minor affair is of interest for several reasons. First, it is yet another example of the insecurity that plagued the Grande Armée's rear areas during the war, the sort of activity that made Raglovich wonder if his correspondence was being intercepted. Second, along with a few Rheinbund deserters, Lüzow's 'infantry' was composed of new enlistees from the Thuringian states whom he had captured and persuaded to enroll in his band over the preceding week.[220] Finally, though surprised, the Bavarians quickly overcame their initial panic and neither surrendered nor joined Lützow's troop. Nor did Lützow's men find much sympathy among the local population. Indeed, local citizens took considerable risks to help Bavarian officers escape capture during the initial moments of shock at the raiders' sudden appearance.[221] Despite the romance associated with these *Freikorps* and their undoubted boldness, therefore, this particular escapade must be counted a disappointment and one that could have gone badly for the raiders given the additional Bavarian troops that appeared on the second day.

Last Actions as an Ally

The Bavarians, like the rest of 12th Corps, had drilled constantly during the armistice, including target practice with shooting competitions featuring cash prizes for the best marksmen. The days after the commemoration of Napoleon's birthday, however, saw Oudinot beginning to assemble the army he had been assigned for his thrust towards Berlin. By 16 August, on the eve of the resumption of hostilities, he had gathered 12th Corps and two of the divisions from Arrighi's 3rd Cavalry Corps in the vicinity of Baruth. The 14th Division, now under Guilleminot in place of the badly wounded Lorencez, was just to the north while Pacthod's 13th and Raglovich's 29th Division camped on the southern side of the town. The Bavarian division totalled some 5,300 officers and men present under arms in its infantry and artillery components with an additional 400 in the Chevaulegers Regiment with Beaumont's and Wolff's 29th Light Cavalry Brigade.[222] As would be the case through most of this brief campaign, the division was designated to guard the corps' artillery park and baggage train. Owing to the shaky state of the French cavalry,

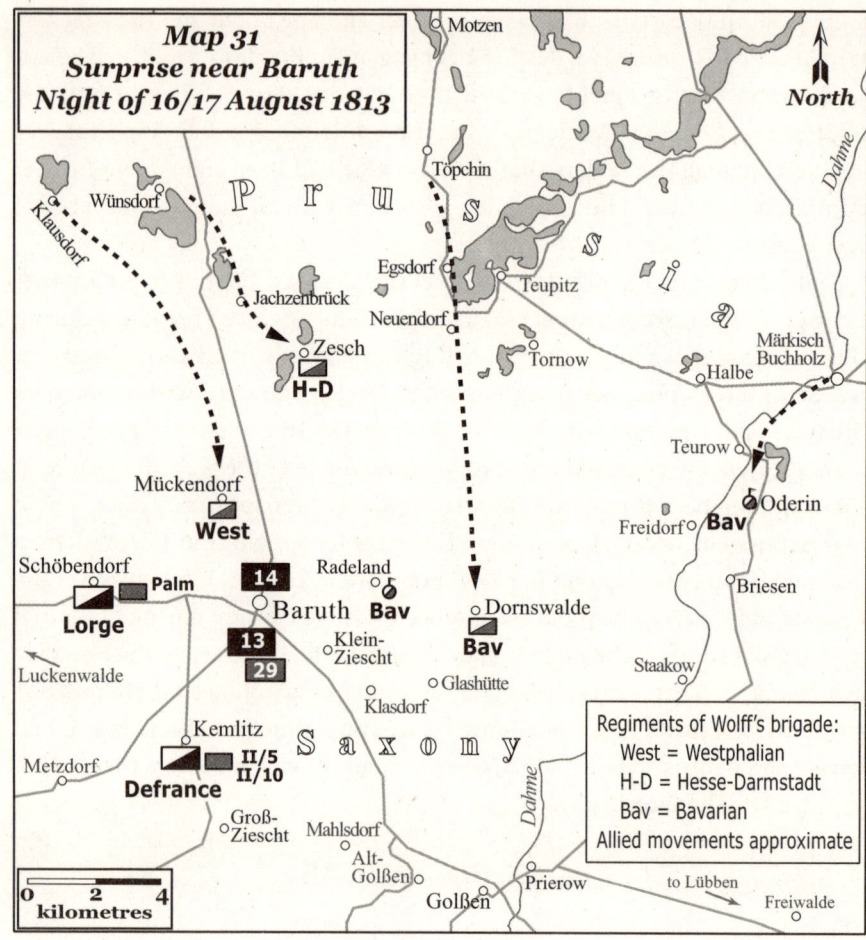

however, Oudinot detached three Bavarian battalions to support the divisions near Baruth: II/5 and II/10 to GD Defrance's division at Kemlitz to the south and Palm's 5th/6th Light Battalion to the west at Schöbendorf with GD Lorge. Rather than the more numerous but unreliable French horse, Oudinot chose the Rheinbund cavalry of Wolff's brigade to cover his deployment, posting the three regiments in an arc from Mückendorf on the left (Westphalians) to Dornswalde and Oderin on the right (Bavarians) with the Hesse-Darmstadt Light Dragoons in the centre at Zesch (now Zesch am See), 10 kilometres north of Baruth.

On the Sidelines at Großbeeren

Unfortunately for the marshal's new command, this notionally prudent disposition left the Rheinbund horse dispersed in an unknown, heavily wooded landscape with no infantry support and too far away to be quickly reinforced. General von Raglovich and Oberst von Seyssel, worried that local citizens would guide enemy attackers, both urged a reconsideration of this extended and unsupported outpost line but to no avail. As a consequence, Oudinot's independent operation against Berlin would begin with a rude setback when Prussians from Borstell's brigade attacked around 1:00 a.m. on the night of 16/17 August. The advance by the Pomeranian Hussars, 1st Pomeranian Infantry and some Cossacks was part of a general reconnaissance conducted by Bernadotte's Army of the North that night to gauge French reactions and capture prisoners. In Wolff's sector it met every Allied expectation. Owing to the disadvantageous position, the lack of support and the lax security measures characteristic of the Grande Armée that year, all three of the Rheinbund regiments were surprised and suffered heavily (*see also* Chapters 5 and 6). The Bavarian loss was especially grievous as Oberst von Seyssel fell into Prussian hands. Hearing the alarm caused by the sudden attack on Dornswalde, Seyssel had ridden out alone to investigate when he was surrounded and captured by Prussian hussars after taking two serious wounds to the head. A lieutenant and 40 other Bavarian troopers along with 86 horses were also captured and Borstell subsequently enjoyed riding Seyssel's former mount whenever he reviewed the Pomeranian Hussars. Prussian losses were minimal.[223] Oberstleutnant Joseph Niedermeyer took over the reins of the Chevaulegers Regiment.

Raglovich, writing to Oudinot that day, regretted a 'most unfortunate accident that deprived me of an excellent cavalry officer' and expressed his concern that the incident 'made a very negative impression' on the cavalry regiment and 'on the rest of my division'. He also took the opportunity to remind Oudinot of the pledge 'that my cavalry will never be separated from my infantry and would always be under my orders'. He requested therefore that the Chevaulegers Regiment be returned to his division. Doubtless to the general's frustration, however, Oudinot replied that it was not in his power to make alterations in the emperor's decisions. Although he promised to ask for a change in organisation 'by the first courier' it is not evident that he ever did so and the likelihood of success would have been small in any case.[224] The Bavarian worry that the cavalry would be detached thus came partly true and the Chevaulegers Regiment would remain with Wolff's brigade until 12th Corps was broken up in September.

Small encounters continued while Oudinot slowly made his way towards Berlin. Raglovich and Lorge were the trail formations in the 12th Corps' column, tasked with guarding the trains and protecting the flanks of the march. Reaching Luckenwalde on 19 August, for instance, Raglovich and Lorge were instructed to 'occupy and defend' the town while the rest of the corps turned north towards Trebbin (*see* Map 12). As part of this mission, II/8 accompanied the French 15th Light Cavalry Brigade on a 2:00 a.m. reconnaissance south towards Jüterbog on the 20th.[225] They found no enemies there, but Cossacks harassed the outposts around Luckenwalde later that morning. The evening brought a more serious clash when an estimated 2,000 Cossacks attacked around 6:00 p.m. Maillot's 1st Bavarian Brigade and Hauptmann Franz Pamler's battery were sharing outpost duty with one of Lorge's brigades and several French guns, while the remainder of Maillot's infantry were stationed at each of the town's gates; the other Bavarian brigade and the rest of Lorge's division bivouacked behind the town. When the Cossacks charged, however, the French brigade was thrown into panicked flight and stampeded through Luckenwalde to Lorge's great embarrassment. Raglovich reported 'without exaggeration' that the French horse were only saved from 'complete dispersal and destruction' by the steadiness of Maillot's infantry and the effect of the Bavarian and French artillery pieces. The French troopers were able to rally and Lorge expressed 'his liveliest thanks' for the protection afforded by Maillot's men. The incident having demonstrated that the outposts were too extended, Raglovich and Lorge tightened their position on the 21st, but the day passed without further enemy attacks.[226]

The Bavarians moved north to Trebbin on 22 August and Raglovich pushed Habermann's 2nd Brigade forward to Großbeuthen the following day. There were minor brushes with enemy cavalry on both days and on the 23rd the men could hear the heavy cannon fire from Großbeeren that rolled on for several hours after sunset. They were surprised, however, to receive orders to retreat and escort the corps' park and train on the withdrawal towards Wittenberg. The next several days were spent making the slow shift through Luckenwalde and Jüterbog to the Elbe. The constant presence of Allied cavalry resulted in several skirmishes and the infantry frequently conducted their movements and their bivouacs in squares as the inept French cavalry were unable to disperse the Allied squadrons and Oudinot was unwilling to risk any further offensive operations. In at least one instance, Hauptmann Eduard von Weißhaupt of the Bavarian 10th Battery joined mounted French horse artillerymen in an impromptu charge to chase off Cossacks who were trying to drag away wagons from the baggage train. A serious engagement seemed in the offing at Jüterbog on the 27th and 28th (*see* Chapter 4) and there were exchanges of fire on the 30th and 31st near Marzahna, but these resulted only in momentary delays in Oudinot's retreat. There was even time to announce to the troops that Napoleon had won a great victory at Dresden and to lift three rounds of *'Vive l'Empereur!'* in celebration. The Bavarians exchanged infantry fire with the enemy on several occasions and their artillery batteries helped chase off probing Allied detachments. Major Fortis's 3rd/4th Light Battalion, for instance, drove enemy troops out of Malterhausen west of Jüterbog on 29 August and Bavarian howitzer shells chivvied them into the nearby woods. In general, however, the Bavarians were held in reserve or detached to cover the baggage train and were therefore only peripherally involved in these minor clashes. One regimental history characterised the actions as 'falling in the category of a military pastime during the pause in a campaign'.[227] Likewise, when they halted east of Wittenberg on 3 September, Raglovich and his men were placed in reserve and not engaged in the fighting that day or the next when Bernadotte's subordinates tested Oudinot's defensive position.

Despite the lack of large-scale combat, this was a period of considerable stress as the troops endured unremitting harassment by Allied cavalry and the frequent threat of attack by major formations of all arms. Raglovich described 31 August, for example, as a day of 'unceasing tension' and he was almost captured by Cossacks while he rode to review the positions of the other corps on 2 September. He was pleased, however, with the manner in which his men responded to the pressure. 'I occupied a wood in front of us with the battalion of the 10th Regiment and immediately thereafter the enemy cavalry made numerous attempts to push back my posts,' he reported. 'The latter, however, well aware of the advantages that calm, steady infantry has over cavalry, especially in constricted terrain, coolly received the enemy and quickly drove him off.' He was also happy with the supply situation when the division reached the banks of the Elbe near Wittenberg, claiming that his units were well victualled while the two French divisions of the corps had to endure 'shortages of the most important necessities'. On the other hand, Raglovich regretted to inform Max Joseph that the Chevaulegers Regiment was not only still separated from his division but had been assigned to 4th Corps. Even though Bertrand expressed a very favourable opinion of the Bavarian cavalrymen, the regiment's transfer to an entirely different corps was galling as far the Bavarian commander was concerned. Overall, however, Raglovich was satisfied with his men. Although they had not yet experienced a serious encounter with the enemy, they had endured a great deal on their marches and in constantly being under arms. 'I am very fortunate to be able to tell Your Royal Majesty that all of this has so far had no noticeable influence on the number of sick in the division nor on its spirit,' he proudly wrote, concluding with his observation that 'the name *Bavaria* is spoken with the greatest respect by every French soldier'.[228]

The Chevaulegers Regiment also performed well during this period. Under yet another new commander, Oberstleutnant Caspar Joseph von Weisse of the 1st Chevaulegers (Niedermeyer, promoted to *Oberst*, had been recalled to Bavaria to take over a different regiment), it was now attached to Bertrand's 4th Corps with the rest of the 29th Light Cavalry Brigade. Bertrand offered the three Rheinbund regiments particular praise for their actions in repelling the Prussian attacks on the defensive position around Wittenberg on 3 and 4 September. In the action around Thießen on 3 September, for instance, the Bavarian riders charged into the open ground between the village and the woods and helped drive back a battalion of the Prussian 1st Pomeranian Infantry that had ventured too far forward (*see* Map 37 in Chapter 4).[229]

Determination and Disintegration at Dennewitz[230]

The Bavarians learned of Oudinot's replacement by Ney on 4 September and underwent a brief inspection by the marshal that same day. The review seems to have been rather perfunctory and Ney appeared grim, but his arrival inspired an improvement in morale. 'Everyone stood in hope that this courageous warrior, still in the best years of his life, would shortly enter the enemy capital at the head of his troops', recalled Unterleutnant Praun.[231] Indeed, the division immediately noticed a new level of urgency and Raglovich hastened to issue ammunition and four days' rations in preparation for a renewal of the offensive.

Ney set his new command in motion early on 5 September and 12th Corps, leading the advance, soon encountered Prussians just west of Zahna. These were Dobschütz's men from Tauentzien's command north of Bülzig and a detachment of Borstell's brigade straddling the road to Woltersdorf. Oudinot deployed his corps with Guilleminot's 14th Division on the left, Pacthod's 13th on the right and the 1st Bavarian Brigade in the centre. The other half of Raglovich's division, Habermann's 2nd Brigade, was held in reserve to protect the trains. By mid-afternoon, the outnumbered Prussians had been pushed back seven kilometres to Zallmsdorf and the day would end with a small but clear French victory. The Bavarian artillery and skirmishers contributed to the success, but the French infantry and especially the artillery bore the brunt of the fighting and neither of the two Bavarian brigades was heavily engaged. As the Prussians escaped towards Jüterbog during the night, the Bavarian division settled into bivouacs around Gadegast four kilometres beyond Zallmsdorf and just northwest of Seyda.

The Rheinbund cavalry brigade under Beaumont and Wolff was also involved in Oudinot's advance, trotting along in support with the

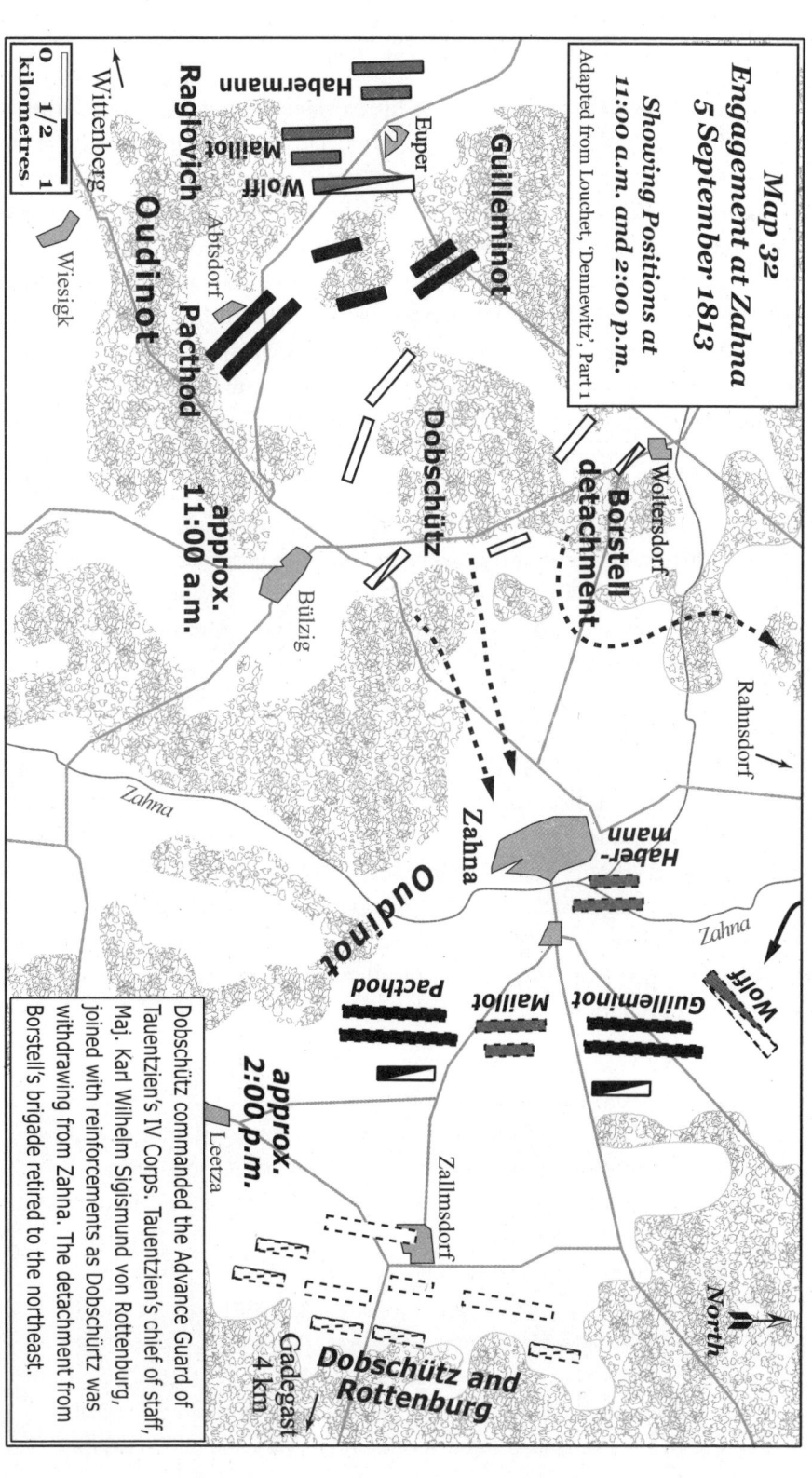

Westphalians initially in the lead. As his battle line passed Zahna, Oudinot detailed the brigade to cover his left flank. Here the German cavalrymen managed to hustle a Prussian detachment out of Rahnsdorf before returning to participate in the concluding actions near Zallmsdorf. The Bavarians contributed by charging the withdrawing Prussians, seizing more than 40 prisoners and then enduring a rain of artillery and musketry as they held a hill until the arrival of infantry support. Pleased with the performance of his men, GD Beaumont concluded his report of the affair with a warm accolade: 'I cannot praise enough the troops that I command who in this situation as in all the preceding ones have never ceased to distinguish themselves.' They also received plaudits from Raglovich. He commended Wolff's three regiments as the only active cavalry on the field, a stark contrast in his view with the shameful passivity of Arrighi's French regiments.[232]

Again assigned to guard the 550 vehicles of the 12th Corps baggage train and artillery park, the Bavarians formed the tail of Ney's Army of Berlin when it resumed its march on 6 September. Raglovich's division was thus the last formation to arrive on the field of Dennewitz where the 4th and 7th Corps had already been heavily engaged for several hours. Deployed in squares to the front, sides and rear of the great mass of the corps' trains, the division emerged from the woods south of Oehna sometime after 4:00 p.m. just as the French situation was beginning to deteriorate. The Bavarians had begun their march full of confidence after the success on the 5th, 'but we had only been on the road for a few hours when the rapid succession of cannon shots announced to us the beginning of the unhoped-for calamity that I would prefer to pass over in silence,' wrote Praun.[233] 'We were entangled in the combat as soon as we debouched from the woods', recalled Leutnant Mändler with Palm's 5th/6th Light Battalion:

> We had barely deployed our columns when a numerous enemy cavalry swarmed around and attacked us from all sides. Raglovich had squares formed by battalion and advanced in this formation. I can relate little of the course of the fighting; we could see nothing of the movements and attacks that happened as the dust and smoke were so thick and dense that one could not see or discern anything beyond a distance of 20 paces...this dreadful dust, that made breathing difficult, shrouded everything before our eyes like a curtain. For this reason, no coherent and coordinated action was possible along the entire battle line. This dust arose largely from the powerful masses of enemy cavalry that now here, now there stormed at our separate squares across the dry, dusty fields seeking to break through. But our squares stood in echelon, and we could thus fire at the

enemy cavalry from all four sides without hitting or hurting our nearby squares.[234]

As he was trying to take in this discouraging situation, Raglovich received repeated orders to close up on the battle line with his division and the trains he was escorting. The general, seeing the growing disorder on the left wing, objected and apparently had not yet responded to these instructions when one of Oudinot's artillery officers dashed up and directed him to send forward a battery of French 12-pounders and a Bavarian battery with appropriate supporting infantry. The French battery and Weißhaupt's 10th Bavarian Battery hurried to the front accompanied by Major Eginard von Treuberg's II/9th Infantry. They trundled into a storm of dust, fire and confusion. 'Soon we arrived at the scene of a bloody battle', wrote Praun, one of Weißhaupt's officers, 'the balls caused a lot of destruction and in a short time a large number of our cannoneers were killed or wounded; within a quarter of an hour, two of our cannons were disabled ... Death conducted his tragic business everywhere!' Ney and his staff were nearby, rallying and encouraging the shaken army, but 'all for nothing'. In the chaos and obscurity, the French guns opened 'a dreadful fire' on their own men, taking them for Prussians, a hideous error that killed or wounded more than the enemy's guns and compounded the growing disorder. Fortunately for Praun, Weißhaupt directed him to take the two disabled cannons to the rear. He was thus spared when the French guns and the remaining four Bavarian pieces were overwhelmed by a whirlwind of canister and cavalry somewhere southeast of Oehna.[235] Exact circumstances and location are unclear (the fate of the French battery is unknown), but the Bavarian gunners managed to find shelter in the square Major von Treuberg hurriedly formed with his battalion. Showered with canister from the front and charged from the rear by the Pomeranian Hussars, the battalion withstood two attacks and inflicted considerable loss on the Prussians before succumbing to a third charge. With Treuberg and all his officers wounded and ammunition running out, the square collapsed. The remnants of II/9 surrendered, the four guns were lost and only 30 men escaped to relate their defeat to Raglovich. *Schützen* of the Pomeranian Grenadier battalion were also involved in the battalion's demise with this Prussian infantry unit claiming one of the Bavarian guns, their standard and two dozen of the prisoners. The Pomeranian Hussars 'cut up a Bavarian battalion and three cannon, made a complete massacre and captured them all', boasted Borstell.[236]

'This final movement occurred at the moment that the confusion on the left wing spread to the right and later to the entire line,' reported Raglovich. He

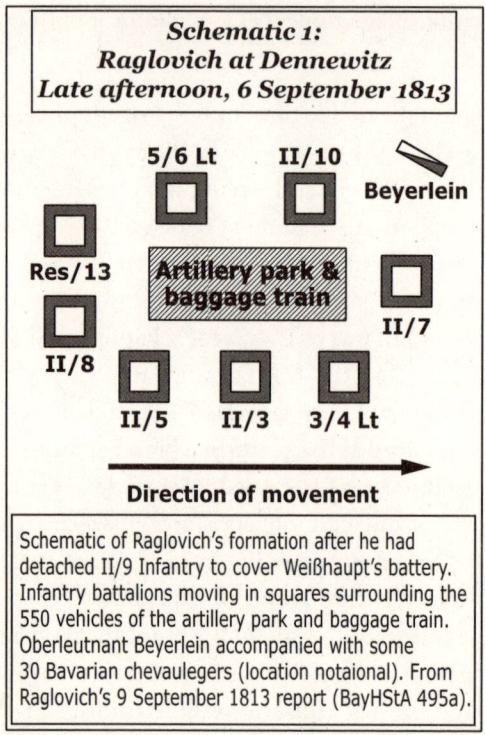

was convinced that his entire division would have suffered the same fate as the unfortunate Treuberg had he obeyed the order to advance that was 'completely contrary to the situation'. When one of Ney's couriers somehow found him in the murk and chaos with orders to fall back on Dahme, however, the need for an immediate retreat was painfully obvious. It was now some time after 5:00 p.m. and the Bavarian division was the only intact major formation on the field when Raglovich turned his command away from Oehna and towards the promising safety of the woods to the rear. 'Despite the ever-increasing mass of fugitives, especially the heavy cavalry that rode over everything ... despite the monstrous confusion,' the division and the cumbersome jumble of vehicles that constituted the train made its ponderous way southeast through the disorder, dust and growing darkness towards Dahme. With infantry battalions arrayed around the baggage wagons and partly screened by an Oberleutnant named Wilhelm Beyerlein with a small detachment of some 30 men from the Chevaulegers Regiment that had somehow re-joined the division, Raglovich and his men held off repeated enemy attacks and reached the woods south of Oehna as night was falling.

Leutnant Mändler left a vivid impression of this phase of the combat:

> In the last moments of the battle the confusion was so great that in the end we did not know which way to turn without falling into the enemy's hands, as the thunder of the guns roared at us from almost every direction. It was an incomparable chaos. In their hopeless cowardice, the French train soldiers, who had cut the traces and left their cannons and caissons standing, wanted to push into our squares and we had to shove them away with our bayonets. French infantrymen, too, without their muskets, crept into the square between our feet to seek shelter. It was late evening; dusk had already fallen as we left the battlefield and the mutual cannonade gradually ebbed away.[237]

Up to this point, the Bavarians had performed admirably, maintaining their cohesion, holding off the enemy and protecting the bulk of the baggage train despite enemy artillery fire and cavalry charges, a welter of panicked fugitives, an exploding ammunition wagon and disarray in the Army of Berlin's leadership. As their commander, Raglovich had demonstrated good tactical sense and superb control over his division of young conscripts. On arriving under the trees south of Oehna, however, the bonds of discipline began to dissolve. 'A panic of terror came over every soldier,' recalled Praun, 'everyone thought only of his own safety.'[238] Seeking water to quench their desperate thirst, caught up in the prevailing confusion, falling behind from exhaustion, disheartened by the obvious disaster, or simply lost in the dark wood, soldiers dropped out of the ranks in large numbers. From just the two companies of the 5th Light Battalion, for instance, 99 men and six horses were left behind owing to exhaustion (the companies also lost all their records). A few took off for other reasons. One such was an NCO from the 5th/6th Light Battalion who was insubordinate towards Major Carl Abele, who had taken Fortis's place as battalion commander. When threatened with punishment, he fled into the gloom to join the Prussians pursued by shots from his former comrades; they could not tell if any of their rounds stuck home but they heard no more of the sergeant 'who had forgotten his duty'.[239]

The rain that rolled in late that night only deepened the men's miseries, quelling the dreadful dust but turning the roads and forest tracks into muddy sloughs. Raglovich subsequently counted himself 'more than lucky to reach Dahme with my entire division' at 1:30 a.m. on 7 September, but by the time his command had covered the 30 kilometres to Dahme it was a 'division' in name only. When he turned to Habermann to charge the town and evict the tiny Prussian garrison, for example, the 2nd Brigade commander could only call on some 350 men with a lone drummer from the 5th Infantry.[240] Nevertheless, helped by some Württemberg cavalrymen Oberleutnant Beyerlein's few chevaulegers surprised and overwhelmed a Prussian picket outside Dahme, captured 20 and learned that some 200 to 300 Prussians were in the town. The garrison, now alerted, barricaded the gates, but fled when Habermann's infantrymen stormed the walls and forced their way in. The Bavarians thus secured Dahme in short order and gained a brief but welcome rest.[241]

The division did not remain long in Dahme, but some of the officers of the 5th/6th Light found time to enter the first decent home, enjoy a coffee and cleanse themselves of at least some of 'the horrible dust'.[242] There was also time for a few stragglers to make their way back to their units in the early hours of the day. As one example, the 3rd/4th Light Battalion counted only 37 men on arrival but was able to depart that morning with 150.[243] Raglovich was thus able to collect at least some of 'the exhausted men who had been left behind owing to unprecedented fatigue'.[244] Nonetheless, it was a drastically reduced division that he led on the retreat to Torgau on 7 September: four guns and 47 wagons had been lost, II/9 was destroyed and large numbers of men from the other battalions were dead, wounded or (mostly) missing when the weary Bavarian column arrived outside the fortress at 9:00 that night. The men, hungry, thirsty and utterly enervated after three days of dust, rain, marching and battle with little rest, were infuriated when the fortress commandant denied them access to stockpiled supplies of firewood.[245] Deciding to help themselves, they began tearing down the wooden palisades around the Torgau bridgehead until the commandant relented and delivered the desired fuel.

The Chevaulegers Regiment had also made its way to Torgau. Leaving its bivouac at Seyda around noon on the 6th, the regiment had formed the corps' rear-guard, charged with sweeping up stragglers and preventing surprise. As it approached the battlefield, however, it was threatened by swarms of enemy cavalry and only managed to re-join Wolff with great difficulty. Engulfed in the confused combat and apparently left without orders when Beaumont and Wolff withdrew with the rest of the brigade, the Bavarians held their ground but were struck by Allied horse as they were wheeling about to retreat. Overwhelmed and scattered, the regiment tumbled to the rear. Oberstleutnant von Weisse and at least 59 other officers and men were taken prisoner in the process. The next senior officer, Major Franz von Hetzendorf of the 6th Chevaulegers, took charge and led the survivors back to Torgau during the night while Oberleutnant Beyerlein with some 30 men managed to make his way to Raglovich as just described.[246]

The division crossed over to the west bank of the Elbe on 8 September, shouldering its way through the disorderly crowd of French soldiers who had been panicked by the appearance of a thousand Cossacks and a few cannon at Zwethau. 'There was much confusion,' remembered Praun, 'all rushed towards the bridge for fear of being caught by the Cossacks or of being killed, the French cavalry especially, seized by a panic, forced their way through with their sabres in their fists.'[247] The Bavarian Chevaulegers were initially deployed to counter the Allied cavalry threat but crossed over separately after losing a few men and horses to artillery fire. They joined Raglovich the next day (9 September).

Once on the far bank, Raglovich learned that firewood was not the only administrative and logistical problem. The Bavarian supplies, commissaries and paymasters had been left behind in Wittenberg when the corps embarked on the offensive towards Berlin. The insecurity in the rear areas meant that these officials and their wagons could not be sent to Torgau at once and were shunted off to Leipzig instead. The general, collecting his command around Eilenburg on 9 September, thus found himself 'in the greatest embarrassment' in providing his tired troops with shoes, clothing, food and pay.

In addition to supply deficiencies, of course, Raglovich had to contend with the intertwined issues of troop strength, morale and relations with the French. In terms of strength, the division was in a deplorably diminished condition. The Chevaulegers Regiment, for example, now under Major von Hetzendorf as its fourth commander in a few weeks, had been reduced to a single squadron with around 100 men in the saddle. Similarly, the division's infantry and artillery mustered a mere 2,210 officers and men at Eilenburg.[248] Combined, these made a sad total of 2,304 or roughly half of the 5,700 Bavarians who had been available under arms when the autumn campaign had opened less than a month earlier. This number hardly qualified for designation as a 'division' and Raglovich knew that no replacements would be forthcoming. In consultation with his two brigade commanders and pending his king's approval, he thus provisionally reorganised the division into four combined battalions, each of only four companies (rather than the regulation six) and made plans to send the surplus officers and men back to Bavaria to assist in reconstituting their units. He intended, however, to retain the designation 'division' for as long as possible. Although he did not specifically state his reasons, this was doubtless for fear that any lesser formation title would diminish Bavaria in the eyes of its French ally and, more pragmatically, might lead Napoleon to assign the Bavarian contingent to some hopeless fortress garrison or other onerous duty.

Raglovich was also unsure of the contingent's morale. On the one hand, he told Max Joseph that he was proud to stand at the head of the division 'in these times of danger, of renunciation, and of such unhappy results after such extensive exertions'. The preservation of so much of the corps' train, he reported, was ascribed to 'the order and composure of my division'. On the other hand, he was apprehensive about the impact of the Dennewitz defeat on his men and expressed his worry that 'one more small shock' would cause his weak command to 'dissolve entirely'.[249]

His assessment of the French army contributed to his concerns about the future of the campaign. In the first place, the senior leaders seemed maladroit and uncommitted to the war. Raglovich viewed Ney's entire operation as an 'extraordinarily dangerous' flank march across the front of a numerically superior enemy about whose positions and movements the French were in 'complete ignorance'. The debacle at Dennewitz was a result of this poor planning, he wrote, and it now seemed to him that, 'We will not be able to undertake anything major easily and will be incapable of any kind of offensive operation.' 'Fortunately, the enemy did not exploit the total dissolution of these four corps' to inflict even greater damage, but 'the losses must be extraordinary'. In addition to evident operational ineptitude, Raglovich was repelled by what he saw as corrosive indiscipline that undermined any realistic hope for success in the war.

> The morale [*Stimmung*] of the French army grows steadily worse; the common soldier compares the carelessness with which the healthy and the sick alike are treated with the indulgent pomp, affluence and greediness of his superiors and feels himself miserable and discontented to the highest degree.
>
> The peasant, from whom everything is robbed and whose home is often devastated and given over to the flames, supports out of desperation the activities of the more humane enemy...
>
> This is the situation in which this army, through its own behaviour, digs itself ever deeper.[250]

For Raglovich, the operational bungling and pervasive indiscipline were a departure from the past that not only set a repugnant example to his own men (who were not above taking what they needed or wanted from the local population) but vitiated confidence in the French as allies.[251] French treatment of their German confederates reinforced these negative images. He could not praise Oudinot enough, but 'There are also so many frictions, so many unpleasant incidents – and all one's efforts cannot prevent that the unity of both allied powers is not only very often disturbed but turns into decisive hatred.' Contributing to the increasingly difficult relationship was the Bavarian soldiers' sense of self-worth. Regarding themselves as no less brave than the French, they 'could not endure the arrogance' of what he termed these 'degenerate warriors'.

Frictions with the French, concerns about morale and heavy losses notwithstanding, Raglovich repeatedly stressed two themes that were common to most of the Rheinbund contingents: loyalty to the king and preservation of the army's and the monarchy's honour. In his private letter to Max Joseph on 9 September, he thus wrote that everyone in his command would do everything possible, bear any burden, to fulfil the king's intentions and expectations. Similarly, in both the private letter and the formal report that day, he assured Max Joseph that Bavaria's reputation for courage, steadiness and reliability was intact:

> Staff and senior officers as well as the common soldiers have supported me gloriously in my efforts, through endurance in battles and exemplarily strict discipline and care of entrusted equipment, to maintain the respect for the Bavarian name that has not only been a pillar of support for those under the pressure of war but has also always impressed French generals and soldiers up to now.[252]

Reorganised, Reassigned and Released

The division set out from Eilenburg (which the men would soon see again) on 11 September and arrived outside Torgau the following day. Here they remained until the 19th when they learned that 12th Corps was being disbanded, and its constituent elements redistributed. While Oudinot's French infantry went to 4th Corps along with the Hessian and Westphalian cavalry of Wolff's brigade, the Bavarians, including the remnants of the Chevaulegers Regiment, were assigned to the Dresden garrison.[253] They set out for the Saxon capital on 20 September, but before leaving the area around Torgau, Raglovich wrote Oudinot a heartfelt letter expressing 'our regrets and the general sadness' felt by the division's officers and men on hearing of their separation from the marshal's command.[254] Hetzendorff penned a similar farewell message to GB Wolff and received a flattering reply lauding 'the bravery of the Bavarian nation' and commending the regiment for its service under his command. As Oudinot rode off to assume a position with the Imperial Guard (taking with him his Bavarian Chevaulegers escorts) and Wolff joined Bertrand's corps, the Bavarians turned towards Dresden 'like a wandering nomadic people'.[255] The much-reduced division arrived in the Saxon capital on 24 September where they were reviewed by the garrison commander, GD Antoine Jean Auguste Henri Durosnel, and found a welcome improvement in billets and provisions. They also found an unsettling contrast between the condition of those fit to

Chart 26: Bavarian Reorganisations, September–October 1813

As a 'Division' under GL von Raglovich (from 9 September)

	bns/sqdns	present under arms as of 14 September
1st Brigade GM von Maillot de la Treille		
1st Combined Regiment	1	460
II/3rd Infantry and 3rd/4th Light Battalion		
2nd Combined Regiment	1	415
II/8th Infantry and Reserve/13th Infantry		
Half-Battery	3 × 6-pdr, 1 × howitzer	
2nd Brigade GM von Habermann		
1st Combined Regiment	1	587
II/5th Infantry and II/7th Infantry		
2nd Combined Regiment	1	419
5th/6th Light Battalion and II/10th Infantry		
Half-Battery	3 × 6-pdr, 1 × howitzer	
Combined Chevaulegers Squadron	1	92 (plus 430 detached)
Artillery and Train personnel	–	269
Total		2,242
Detached (including the 430 chevaulegers)		691
In hospital		578
Prisoners of war/missing/deserters		142
Grand total of 'effectives' (which included all of the above)		3,653

Notes: (1) The number of prisoners/missing/deserters is clearly incorrect. (2) The discrepancy in the cavalry figures is a result of losses to the regiment's horses; only some 200 were still fit at this stage: approximately 100 each with the division and detached. Most of the detached men were likely sent to remount depots to await new horses. (3) As of 19 September the half-batteries each consisted of two 6-pdr and one howitzer.

fight and those consigned to the city's many hospitals: 'At this time, Dresden presented a picture of the greatest luxury and simultaneously the greatest misery. Coming out of a coffeehouse in which a surfeit of luxury prevailed, in which French and other officers lost huge sums in gambling, one saw only unfortunate miserable men, who were near death and who counted themselves lucky when they received a loaf of black bread to still their hunger.'[256]

Several changes in the contingent's organisation were instituted during this relatively stable period from early September into early October, one of which had political implications that highlighted Franco-Bavarian differences. First, during the halt at Eilenburg, Raglovich decided to release the officers and men he considered excess to the reduced size of the division. He thus

As a 'Brigade' under GM Maillot (from 4 October)

		bns/sqdns	present under arms as of 5 October
1st Combined Regiment	Oberstleutnant von Bach		
1st Combined Battalion		1	443
3rd/4th Light Battalion and II/3rd Infantry			
2nd Combined Battalion		1	416
II/8th Infantry and Reserve/13th Infantry			
Half-Battery		2 × 6-pdr, 1 × howitzer	
2nd Combined Regiment	Oberst von Rummel		
1st Combined Battalion		1	516
II/5th Infantry and II/7th Infantry			
2nd Combined Battalion		1	360
5th/6th Light Battalion and II/10th Infantry			
Half-Battery		2 × 6-pdr, 1 × howitzer	
Combined Chevaulegers Squadron		1	115 (plus 276 detached)
Artillery and Train personnel	–		252
Total			2,102
Detached (including the 276 chevaulegers)			516
In hospital			679
Prisoners of war/missing/deserters			(not listed)
Grand total of 'effectives' (which included all of the above)			3,297

    Note: See opposite for explanation of the cavalry numbers.

    Sources: Divisional strength reports for 14 September and 5 October 1813, BayHStA, 495b.

sent 67 officers, 103 NCOs and 110 soldiers back to Bavaria. He had told the 12th Corps chief of staff of his decision, but he had not received approval from general headquarters and thus earned Oudinot's annoyance for this unilateral action.[257] Indeed, after personally selecting the officers, he directed them to leave in small groups and at night so as not to come to the attention of either the French or the various Allied raiding parties in the army's rear.[258] Owing to a lack of horses and artillerymen, he also deposited two of the division's 6-pounders at Torgau against a receipt issued by the fortress commandant. This left the Bavarians with a total of four 6-pounders and two howitzers divided into two half-batteries with one assigned to each of the miniature brigades.

Second, while in Dresden, Raglovich received permission to return home himself. He had requested reassignment in his 9 September letter to Max Joseph, claiming that continuing with this campaign was an 'impossibility'. Citing his many campaigns and his five wounds, he thus asked to be allowed to return to Bavaria where he could assume duties consistent with his state of health. This now granted, he redesignated the contingent as a 'brigade' (each of the former 'brigades' became a 'regiment'), issued a farewell order of the day to the men, turned over command to GM von Maillot on 4 October and departed for Bavaria via Leipzig two days later.[259]

Third, before relinquishing command, Raglovich attempted to march the entire division back to Bavaria. He had recommended withdrawal in a letter to the king on 16 September and asked Max Joseph to write to Berthier explaining the urgency of this measure 'to at least save something' when the 'possibility of complete destruction or dissolution' seemed 'so certainly imminent'. In response, the king sent orders for Raglovich to march his men home, but these were accompanied by rather unhelpful instructions to obtain the division's release 'through clever negotiations'.[260] For his part, Raglovich wrote to his immediate superior, Durosnel, to explain that the king wanted the remains of the division returned so it could 'cover a part of its own country menaced by the armies of the enemy' while being brought up to strength, re-armed and re-equipped. He therefore requested marching orders, but he was keenly aware of the political sensitivities involved and understood that Saxony's wavering in the spring and recent Westphalian defections cast a shadow over any suggestion that a Rheinbund army would remove itself from the theatre of war. A Bavarian withdrawal, even for purely military reasons, he noted, could be considered a political act. As he told Max Joseph on 3 October: 'It could be concluded that the policy had changed according to the circumstances of the time, which would give a different interpretation even to military intentions.' In an attempt to smooth the path to acceptance of his proposal, he and the Bavarian ambassador in Dresden collaborated in approaching French Foreign Minister Maret as well as Durosnel. Raglovich, for example, wrote to persuade Durosnel that the division's completion would benefit the larger war effort:

> His Majesty, my sovereign, having only the good of the service and the interest of the armies and of the Confederation of the Rhine in mind with this request, I dare to ask Your Excellency to kindly place before his [Napoleon's] eyes the king my master's request in terms suitable for assuring His Imperial Majesty of all the devotion of the King of Bavaria and of the loyalty of his troops to the common cause.

Predictably, the appeal was denied. Durosnel seemed inclined to accept but Maret wrote that Napoleon was 'very surprised' by the request. In the current circumstances, he told the two Bavarians, 'this could only give substance to a rumour about a change' in Bavaria's policy and Napoleon 'had expressed a desire that the request in question should not be acted upon'. As Raglovich had feared, therefore, what he wanted to portray as a simple military act generated immediate political implications. It was also problematic from a military standpoint as evident when Berthier, replying on behalf of the emperor, sternly informed Raglovich that the letter was 'contrary to military subordination'.

> As part of the army commanded by the emperor, it is not for you to make this request. If the king, your master, wished to make some changes in the destination of his troops, he would address the emperor or he would inform His Majesty's minister [the French ambassador] of his dispositions. The Bavarian contingent is part of the army because of foreign relations and treaties, and it is by the same channel that it could cease to be a part. You would then have received the necessary orders not from Munich but from general headquarters. You have already sent back cadres and, although that was well done, you should only have done so by my order.

Although Berthier concluded this stiff note by approving the new command arrangement and Raglovich's personal return to Bavaria, Maillot and the brigade would remain in Dresden under undisputed French command.[261]

This brings the narrative to early October when Napoleon left the Saxon capital for what proved to be a futile attempt to trap and defeat Blücher and Bernadotte north of Leipzig. As part of this shift north, Maillot and the Bavarian brigade left Dresden on the night of 6/7 October with 2,102 officers and men present under arms. Although the brigade was assigned to guard Napoleon's baggage train, the battalion composed of the 5th/7th Infantry (516 strong) was almost immediately detached to the specific task of escorting the Imperial Guard's supply wagons. Both groups of Bavarians reached Eilenburg on the 10th and spent the next several days moving between Eilenburg and Düben with the lumbering vehicles. The 5th/7th Infantry battalion followed the Guard to Leipzig on 14 October and would remain separated from its compatriots until they all returned home following Napoleon's defeat. The bulk of the brigade, on the other hand, returned to Eilenburg on the 15th. Maillot, named the commandant of a position to which 'the emperor attaches great importance', seems to have been impressed by 'this mark of confidence' and promised 'to do whatever honour and rectitude dictate' to hold the town and protect the large baggage park.[262]

The next several days were filled with anxious uncertainty for Maillot. The thunder of the guns at Leipzig was clearly audible in Eilenburg, but he had no instructions from Munich, direct communications with imperial headquarters had become impossible, and the surrounding countryside swarmed with Cossacks. Two officers sent to gain information were captured, for example, and GB Durrieu commanding the French trains asked Maillot to loan two guns to the Saxons who were escorting the 7th Corps baggage and other wagons to Torgau (as related in Chapter 2). Unterleutnant von Praun received this mission, departing on 18 October to join 'the endless convoy' of vehicles as Durrieu shifted the cumbersome baggage train safely to Torgau during the night of 18/19 October.[263] The Bavarian brigade remained at Eilenburg, more mobile in the absence of the clumsy wagons, but more or less on its own as the Russians continued to press. A few shells from Hauptmann Pamler's howitzers sufficed to chase off swaggering Cossacks on the 18th and musketry discouraged scouting parties that probed Maillot's position on the 19th, but a reconnaissance patrol brought back news that Napoleon had lost the great battle and a Russian officer sent by Bernadotte arrived to demand that Maillot cease resistance because Bavaria had joined the Allies. A second officer, a Russian major, rode up to the Bavarian outpost line on the 19th bearing threats: Maillot should send an officer to Bernadotte, but 'measures would be taken' if Eilenburg's defenders did not submit.[264]

Under pressure, Maillot retained his composure and sought to gain time. In his words: 'I could not be convinced of the changed state of affairs other than through official channels as military history provides so many examples where excessive credulity in such a delicate situation ends in dishonour.'[265] Or, as his chief of staff, Hauptmann von Völderndorff recounted, 'General Maillot, as a man of honour and duty, had to have definitive orders from the king his master in hand or receive other sufficient proofs in order to attach himself to the Allies as was demanded.' Maillot thus refused to meet the Russian major but did promise to send an officer to Bernadotte. His concerns mounted, however, as was evident in a letter to Durrieu, his immediate superior. Reminding Durrieu that he only had 'three feeble battalions', he stated that he would be unable to protect the road to Leipzig and would have to restrict himself to holding the village.

> Will you be able to rescue me? My men are exhausted from fatigue. Would it not be prudent to retire to Torgau? I would be able to contribute to the defence of the fortress and not risk compromising myself.[266]

Durrieu was indeed trying to decide on the safest course of action for the enormous train of 540 vehicles and Torgau was foremost in his mind. With no word from the Grande Armée and Russian officers demanding surrender, he contacted GD Louis Marie Jacques Amalric de Narbonne-Lara, the governor of Torgau, to solicit advice. In a brief exchange of correspondence, the two French generals agreed that Durrieu should move the cumbersome wagon train to the open ground west of Torgau while they awaited word from imperial headquarters. Durrieu thus moved out on the night of 18/19 October to reach the outskirts of Torgau on the 19th. From here he wrote to inform Berthier that he had 'at least avoided increasing the enemy's trophies' and expressing his hope 'that the emperor will deign to approve' his actions.

Maillot, designated as the rear guard, had remained behind temporarily. He had also contacted Narbonne, a highly respected officer-diplomat who had been ambassador in Munich, and 'was known to the Bavarians as an honourable man imbued with the most refined sense of duty'. Sending Völderndorff to Narbonne in advance to explain his predicament, Maillot, his brigade, and the remaining wagons thus slipped away during the night of 19/20 October and met Narbonne outside the fortress walls the next morning. To Maillot's relief, the French general advised him to send an officer to Bernadotte: if the officer returned with sufficient proof that Bavaria had changed sides, Maillot was free to leave; if not, the Bavarians would join the French in the defence of Torgau. The Bavarians could occupy a requisitioning area nearby while they waited for an answer. Völderndorff, entrusted with this mission, returned with convincing evidence of Bavaria's new alignment, including a personal letter signed by Tsar Alexander. Maillot's clear task was now the swift return of his command to Bavaria, and, in a courteous meeting, Narbonne released the brigade 'with gracious acknowledgment of the Bavarians' loyal service and bravery'. Durrieu likewise praised his Bavarian allies, writing in his report to Berthier that 'General Maillot has shown great loyalty' during those tense and confusing days.[267] Numbering 1,226 officers and men, the brigade with its guns (including the two loaned to the Saxons under Praun) and baggage duly departed Torgau for home on the night of 22/23 October.

'Thus, the Bavarians separated themselves, and separated themselves with joy, from those in whose ranks they had unhappily fought against their German brothers,' wrote Völderndorff when composing his history of the war some years later. The joy Völderndorff described was doubtless true at the time, but the reference to fighting against 'German brothers' was likely an ex post facto embellishment to suit subsequent sentiments. His next few sentences, however, are worth quoting at length as they illuminate a key feature of the Bavarian memory of their service under Napoleon. 'Loyalty took precedence over their own inclination; faith in their king's wisdom over their own cleverness', he wrote, 'No passion, no example, could lure them from their duty.' The soldier who thinks otherwise is mutinous, he asserted, 'and turns the bayonet against the order he is called upon to execute'. On one hand, these brief sentences show how the Bavarians contrasted themselves with other former members of the Rheinbund in later years: 'that not a single Bavarian at that time left the French army until he had received a definitive order from his king'.[268] The reference to the Saxons and others is obvious. At the same time, Völderndorff provides a sense of the deep obligation many Rheinbund soldiers felt to steadfast obedience to their monarchs' wishes and thus helps illuminate their attitudes and actions in the trying campaigns of 1813.

Two days after most of Maillot's men marched off from Torgau, the brigade's lone remaining battalion also broke away from its former allies. As noted above, the 5th/7th Infantry Battalion had turned for Leipzig with the Imperial Guard when the other elements of the brigade went back to Eilenburg. Arriving on 15 October, the battalion was not involved in the fighting, but protected the Guard's baggage wagons and, on the 18th, was assigned the curious task of sending unwounded malingerers back to the battle line. It is not clear how successful they were at this unusual duty, but the men headed for Erfurt at 5:00 that evening with the trains. As they were passing through Lindenau, a captured Austrian officer handed the officers a printed flyer announcing the Treaty of Ried by which Bavaria had joined the Allies. This could hardly be considered an official document and the battalion's officers, consulting together, decided to stay with the French until they received formal notice from Munich. They thus marched west with the retreating Grande Armée. One company, however, was held back to help defend the crossing of the Unstrut River at Freyburg on the 21st. This tiny band of perhaps 80 men seems to have been trapped by Allied cavalry and forced to surrender when their rain-soaked powder would not ignite; only a few fugitives escaped to meet up with Maillot on his way back to Bavaria.[269] The other three companies reached Erfurt on 23 October, learned of Bavaria's new status and left for home at 2:00 a.m. on the 24th. There seems to have been no notification or farewell, the men simply marched off under the cover of darkness. Berthier did issue an order formally releasing the battalion from service later that day, but this was evidently intercepted by Cossacks and never reached the battalion commander:

> The king your master, sir, disregarding that which the emperor has done for him, has declared war on France; in similar circumstances, the Bavarian troops who find themselves with the army should be disarmed and declared prisoners of war; but this is contrary to the confidence which the emperor wants the troops under his orders to have in him. As a consequence, sir, the intention of the emperor is that you assemble your battalion. You will be given four days of rations and you will depart from here to go to Bamberg via Coburg where you will come under the orders of the minister of His Majesty the King of Bavaria.
>
> It would be equally contrary to all sentiments of honour and loyalty for you to take up arms against France. As a consequence, the intention of the emperor is that you and your officers give your word of honour that neither you nor your soldiers will serve against France for one year.[270]

Noteworthy in both this case and in regard to Maillot's men is that the French did not treat the Bavarians as prisoners of war or even disarm them. Instead, they were permitted to march off with arms, baggage, banners and honour.

This last battalion reached Nuremberg safely on 30 October with 229 men fit for duty, but contrary to custom and French expectations, these men and Maillot's would soon find themselves in action against their former allies. After a welcome week to begin recovering from the campaign, the battalion received urgent orders to march to Bamberg. These instructions came from Maillot, who had arrived in Bamberg on 8 November.[271] The general and his men, however, were only granted the briefest of respites: on 11 November they moved out to join the Bavarian troops under Wrede who were approaching the borders of France.

The Wine Is Poured, It Must Be Drunk[272]

It is now necessary to step back in time once again to outline how Bavaria came to break with France. While Raglovich and his men marched and fought in Saxony, deliberations on Bavaria's future continued in Munich where the façade of alliance remained in place during the summer and the first weeks of the autumn campaign. In a late July letter to Berthier, for instance, Max Joseph touched on his usual themes: the recall of Raglovich because 'I have a very great need for my troops to guard my frontiers' and the importance of immediate, comprehensive peace. At the same time, he reiterated his commitment to Napoleon and his worries about his kingdom's security:

> My attachment to the emperor and the cause of France will never vary for an instant. You may thus be sure that I will do the impossible to satisfy

the desires of His Imperial Majesty. I only ask that you not lose sight of the interests of my kingdom and come to my rescue in the case of war with Austria.[273]

An internal memorandum expressed similar sentiments. 'War seems to be near,' wrote the king to the State Secretary for War. 'As it is my firm intention to remain in the French system, I therefore order you herewith, in coordination with Minister Graf Montgelas and General Graf Wrede, to take all measures to conduct this war with honour and to the satisfaction of Emperor Napoleon.'[274]

Despite the king's attitude, Bavarian policy was in turmoil when hostilities recommenced. The intensity of the debate, however, was unknown outside a small circle of royal advisors, Montgelas and Wrede being the two most important. Though mostly disgruntled at having been dragged out of their civilian lives, the soldiers gathered in the training camp that Wrede had established outside Munich thought, for example, that they had been conscripted to fight on France's behalf after the catastrophe of 1812, a common belief that contributed not a little to the surly recalcitrance in the ranks.[275] Shifted from Munich to the Inn River in mid-August, the men would even fire celebratory cannon shots to announce Napoleon's victory at Dresden that month (after courteously warning the Austrians, of course). Unbeknownst to all but a few of them, however, their country was by then on the verge of a complete shift in alignment.

The reversal in Bavaria's stance was a process that extended over nearly two months, in part because of the inherent torpor of horse-bound communications, but mostly because of the difficulties Montgelas and Wrede experienced in overcoming their king's hesitations. Early indications that Munich was at least leaving the door ajar came on 18 August with the departure of Habsburg envoy Hruby. Although Austria's declaration of war against Napoleon had transformed it into an enemy of the Rheinbund, Rechberg, the Bavarian ambassador to Austria, remained in Vienna under the pretense of illness along with his entire staff, while Hruby was treated to a cordial farewell audience with Max Joseph and a courteous letter from Montgelas expressing friendship for the Austrian ruling house and regret at the coming hostilities. A meeting with Wrede on the way to the border only reinforced Hruby's sense that Bavaria would be receptive to the right offer. This was not long in coming. Forwarded by FZM Heinrich XV Fürst zu Reuß-Plauen, the Austrian commander opposite Wrede, a 31 August letter from Tsar Alexander arrived in Munich on 5 September conveying flowery greetings and seemingly solemn, if rather imprecise, promises to the king.[276]

News of Napoleon's victory at Dresden temporarily bolstered Max Joseph in his adherence to the French alliance, but Dresden's glory was soon tarnished by the string of defeats which the tsar had not neglected to highlight in his letter. Max Joseph remained reluctant, wanting a formal treaty with definitive pledges of compensation for the lands he knew he would forfeit to Austria. Privately, he entertained illusory hopes for some form of neutrality that would mollify the Allies but avoid an irreparable break with Napoleon. Such a solution was no more possible in September than it had been in May, but he clung to it for a surprisingly long time despite opposition from his advisors.[277] Nonetheless, Alexander's missive was enough for him to authorise direct communications between Wrede and Hruby. In a clandestine discussion with Wrede (Hruby arrived in an Austrian uniform as 'Major Renner'), Hruby heaped flattery on Bavaria but also hinted at the dire consequences of delay.

Ten days passed, however, before Max Joseph answered Alexander and the reply, from the Allied point of view, was unsatisfactory. Montgelas prepared two drafts for his monarch, one proclaiming continued allegiance to Napoleon, the other indicating a shift towards the Coalition. The king, at this point in September, was congratulating himself on his choice of a hedging policy thus far. Marching at once against France as his queen urged would have been an act of treason in his mind and he did not trust the Allies. As he told Ludwig on 12 September:

> The two emperors have agreed to tell me that they need sacrifices on my part against compensations, but without saying anything as to what the one and the other must consist of. I require that they tell me in advance; I want to be sure of my actions. It is permissible to be distrustful in the century in which we live and in which the word *loyalty* is crossed out in all languages.[278]

The disaster at Dennewitz, news of which reached Munich on 14 September, seems to have driven him to a decision. 'I have lost two-thirds of my corps, and it seems to have been the only one to conduct its retreat in good order,' he lamented to Mercy d'Argenteau, 'My corps is reduced to 1,150 bayonets; equipage and cannons are lost. God knows what will become of this! Farewell, my good count, *have pity for me!*'[279] In this mood, he signed the draft favouring the Coalition on 15 September. Hesitancy, however, continued to reign. Although the letter to the tsar for the first time openly expressed Bavaria's *intention* to break with Napoleon, promised to recall Raglovich, and reiterated that Wrede had 'long had the precise order to abstain from all offensive movements', it did *not* constitute a disavowal of the Rheinbund or definitive adherence to the Coalition.[280] Harried and anxious, the king endeavoured to hold to his own course. 'I will do all I can to save as much as I can from the shipwreck,' he wrote to Ludwig after signing the reply to the tsar, 'I am overwhelmed with work and worry.'[281]

In the meantime, Wrede and Reuß had concluded a formal ceasefire between their respective commands on 17 September. The two sides had not been engaged in active hostilities and had essentially concurred on a tacit ceasefire as early as 22 August.[282] To the annoyance of the French, they were also courteously exchanging deserters, line-crossers and patrols that inadvertently wandered into one another's territories.[283] At the same time, the Austrians categorically threatened Bavaria with invasion and insurgency. Writing to Wrede on 16 September, Reuß noted darkly that 'the entire Prussian nation' was aroused with revolutionary fervour with the implication that such disturbance could spread to Bavaria. The king, he added, had to act immediately while Austria could still influence events 'before the Prussian and Russian armies break into Franconia and Vandamme's defeat becomes known in the Tyrol'.[284]

The formal ceasefire agreement provided further evidence of Munich's friendly intentions but also served to ease Bavarian security concerns by forestalling Russo-Prussian invasion and by curbing Austrian intrusions into the Bavarian portions of the Tyrol. Combat had already begun between Habsburg troops and Franco-Italian forces along the borders of Napoleon's Kingdom of Italy, including the Tyrolean districts under that kingdom's rule, but the Austrians were also sending patrols into the Bavarian Tyrol and unabashedly providing support and sanctuary to prominent leaders of the region's 1809 revolt in anticipation of a renewed insurrection. To the Bavarians, these men were the worst sort of villains, brigands and disloyal subjects of the king. Despite his urgent desire to split with France and the bonhomie he enjoyed with Hruby and Reuß, Wrede thus penned angry notes to other Austrian generals reproving them for harbouring these Tyrolean 'bandit chieftains'.[285]

Tensions in the Tyrol lingered, but Austrian activity had abated by the time answers to Max Joseph's 15 September letter arrived on the 27th. This time there were three missives: not only from Tsar Alexander, but from Kaiser Franz and, one day later, from King Friedrich Wilhelm III as well. The florid prose of these letters intensified the flattery lavished on Bavaria, to include the promise to place Reuß's Austrian corps under Wrede's command for combined operations against Napoleon's line of communications. At the same time, the Allied monarchs also made unmistakably clear that time was rapidly running out for Bavaria. Max Joseph, cleaving to his conception of loyalty, remained painfully reluctant to change course. He outlined his thinking in a 1 October letter to Ludwig:

> Three days ago, I received letters from the Emperors Alexander and Franz and one from the King of Prussia. The first tells me clearly that I must make sacrifices and makes me understand that I must give up immediately what is asked of me and wait until the peace for compensation. This is contrary to my dignity and would be a great loss for my finances. That of the Emperor of Austria is honeyed and the letter of the Prussian polite and even friendly. But all three demand that I march at once against the Emp. Nap. [Emperor Napoleon]. I will send Wrede precise instructions tomorrow and will enjoin him in a personal letter to do everything on earth to obtain neutrality, if that is not possible, he should declare that I will not take a step before I apprise the emperor of my change in policy. To go behind his back like a traitor would be a cowardice which does not suit the loyalty of my character.[286]

Nonetheless, the letters from the three sovereigns, buttressed by stern words and threats of invasion from Hruby (this time menacing Bavaria with Bennigsen's Army of Poland that was just arriving in Bohemia),[287] gave Montgelas the support he needed to gain the king's approval for new instructions to Wrede. Max Joseph had not entirely jettisoned his hopes for neutrality, but the general, now equipped with plenipotentiary powers, was to negotiate a treaty that would bring Bavaria into the Coalition. Wrede was to insist that the accord be a formal document and that it specify in detail the compensation Bavaria would receive for any territory lost in the post-war settlements. In contrast, the working draft presented by the Austrians was merely a *preliminary* treaty with vague assurances of Bavarian sovereignty and fair compensation; all specifics were to be determined in a final treaty after the war. This Austrian text, almost unchanged despite days of discussion, would become the basis for the agreement signed on 8 October.

What followed was a week of hectic activity as couriers dashed back and forth between the royal residence outside Munich, Montgelas's home just northeast of the city, and the small town of Ried where Wrede was conducting the negotiations with the Austrians. Most Bavarian historians depict these exchanges as a conflict between personal sentiment and reasons of state (*Staatsräson*).[288] On one side was Max Joseph, uncomfortable with finally severing his ties to Napoleon, fundamentally opposed to an alliance with untrusted Austria, and enmeshed in uncertainty concerning the future of his kingdom owing to the airy Allied promises and the preliminary nature of the Austrian proposal. Indicative of the king's attitude was his extreme reluctance to accept one of Metternich's central stipulations: a specific Bavarian statement disavowing the Rheinbund. Although separation from the Rheinbund would be an obvious consequence of siding with the Allies, Max Joseph resisted making such an unequivocal commitment. He also worried about the fate of his daughter Auguste and his son-in-law Eugène should Napoleon fall.[289] On the other side were Montgelas and Wrede. The general, who Max Joseph thought 'pressed too much', was 'the true motor' behind the swift policy shift.[290] He portrayed Bavaria's critical situation as entirely the result of the French alliance and urged an immediate change. Montgelas, equally determined but in his much subtler manner, likewise worked to alter the kingdom's course. Crown Prince Ludwig also yearned for change, but his role seems to have been peripheral. Max Joseph was well acquainted with Ludwig's passions and positions; he would make his own decision based on counsel from Wrede and Montgelas.

The denouement came at a meeting of the three principals at the minister's villa on 7 October. The Austrians, increasingly impatient, had threatened to break off the talks and advance into Bavaria if an appropriate answer was not received within 36 to 40 hours. This ultimatum prompted the alarmed Wrede to hasten back in a final effort to move the king. In this, he and Montgelas succeeded. What finally convinced Max Joseph to concede is not entirely clear. The threat of Austria discontinuing the negotiations was probably most important, but he was under pressure from his two key advisors and, justly or not, felt abandoned by Napoleon.[291] He thus relented, relinquished his hollow hopes for neutrality and agreed to join the Coalition. Though he had little real choice at this stage of the war, he was distraught in the wake of his decision, feeling cast loose from all support as neither France nor Austria nor his brother-in-law the tsar was likely to stand reliably by Bavaria. Expressing his pessimism in a letter to his son, he wrote:

> I met this morning with Wrede at Montegelas's home. I signed the convention that he has made with Prince Reuß. He will set himself in march towards the Main tomorrow or the day after with 30,000 Bavarians and 35,000 Austrians under his orders. The convention stipulates neither indemnity nor cession. But judging from appearances it leaves [us] neither the Hausruck and Innviertel, nor Salzburg nor the Tyrol nor the Vorarlberg, that is to say, they want to have everything that was taken from them. You see that they are always the same. It remains to be seen what we can perhaps wrest from them through the treaty that is being prepared in

Prague and what the Emperor of Russia can obtain in our favour, but I confess that I do not count much on that. We will gain independence from France out of all this but only by returning to the Austrian yoke, because with the military line that she wants to have, provided at best that this remains the situation, we will not be able to fart without her permission, because the Russians, once back home, are unlikely to leave it any time soon. With our relations with France in disarray, our neighbours will make cabbages and turnips of us. Here is a profession of faith, my dear Louis, carefully keep this letter as sooner or later you will be obliged to say my old father was right. Do not speak about it anymore. The wine is poured, it must be drunk.[292]

His king's intimate discouragement notwithstanding, Wrede hurried back to Ried that night. Arriving at 3:00 a.m. on 8 October, he signed the preliminary alliance agreement with Austria later that day. Bavaria, an ally of France since 1805 and a founding member of the Rheinbund, was now an enemy of its former benefactor and a friend of its former foe.

This Inconceivable Defection[293]

Bavaria's defection came as an unpleasant surprise to Napoleon. Although he was aware of rumours to this effect, he had refused to give them credit. In a lengthy 5 October audience with GM von Beroldingen, the Württemberg liaison officer at imperial headquarters, for instance, the emperor asked if Beroldingen had heard stories of Bavaria declaring itself neutral. When Beroldingen replied in the affirmative, Napoleon answered 'I assure you, there is no truth in them.' As late as 9 October, he told Murat 'Do not believe the news of the defection of Bavaria nor anything else claimed by the enemy.' Although doubts had arisen in the communications surrounding Raglovich's request for release, it was only on 13 October that the veracity of 'this inconceivable defection' was confirmed. Napoleon's subsequent interview with the captured Austrian GdK Merveldt provided verification and led him to excoriate Max Joseph in his farewell conversation with the king and queen of Saxony. Napoleon's choler towards his former ally was held in abeyance but did not abate as the remnants of the Grande Armée struggled back to France. The Bavarian action 'presaged the defection of the other princes and made the emperor decide to return to the Rhine', recounted one of the army's bulletins, '[an] unfortunate change as everything had been prepared to operate based on Magdeburg'.[294] Unsurprisingly, he had bitter words for his ambassador and Bavaria when he met Mercy d'Argenteau in Mainz after his victory at Hanau:

> They fooled you in Munich; it is disgraceful. The king is guilty of a cowardly treason. I have just killed their Wrede and passed through the entire body of the Bavarian army. The king will see me again next year, and he will remember it! As to the rest, it is only the kick of a donkey, but the lion is not dead. It was a little prince that I made big; it is a big prince that I will make small![295]

There was a large group in the room when this incident occurred, so Napoleon was partly speaking to his audience for effect as he so often did. Theatrics aside, his anger was clearly genuine and hardly astonishing. The question is why he trusted his Bavarian ally for as long as he did.

The reasons behind Napoleon's persistent confidence in Bavarian fealty were manifold and complex. In the first place, he had little intelligence to suggest that Bavaria was other than faithful. In no small degree, this lack of information was the result of problems with the French mission in Munich. Mercy d'Argenteau, though intelligent and loyal to the emperor, was inexperienced in diplomacy. His embassy was understaffed, he had no comprehensive network of informants, and he limited most of his interactions to the higher aristocratic circles, thereby depriving himself both of insights and influence. Furthermore, Wrede, Montgelas, and Montgelas's staff were deliberately attempting to deceive him. Some later French accounts pointedly accuse Mercy of being inept and exceedingly credulous of what his Bavarian interlocutors told him, especially in his extensive correspondence with Wrede whom he long saw as a devoted adherent of Napoleon.[296]

This is partly true but also partly unfair and inaccurate. Though he had nothing definitive, Mercy mentioned hints of Austrian approaches starting in mid-September and noted Wrede's clandestine meeting with Max Joseph and Montgelas even though he did not have any details on the substance of their discussions. Those reading Mercy's reports, however, may have underplayed his hazy worries until mid-September because Mercy himself dismissed these intimations and repeatedly mentioned Max Joseph's professions of loyalty.[297] If the king, an old friend of France and adversary of Austria, held to the alliance, the intrigues of others in his realm would surely come to naught. Moreover, Mercy was not the only Frenchman reporting approvingly on Bavarian attitudes. Berthier and Eugène both maintained regular correspondence with Max Joseph but neither detected any disloyalty. Eugène, for example, had called on the king while passing through Munich on his way to Italy in mid-May and reported favourably on his visit to his father-in-law. Similarly, one of Berthier's staff officers, Adjutant Commandant Pierre Auguste Fulbert de La Roche, Marquis de Fontenilles, carried dispatches to Munich in July and returned to report that 30,000 Bavarians were prepared to join the campaign entirely owing to 'the zeal of General von Wrede, his activity and his entire devotion to the emperor'. 'Generals, soldiers all seem very devoted to the emperor,' he concluded in a 1 August summary of his trip.[298]

Foreign Minister Maret on the other hand, became more sceptical as the autumn progressed, writing to Mercy with considerable alarm after his meeting with Raglovich in Dresden. Urgently querying the ambassador, he observed that it was difficult to believe that Mercy had not heard 'the rumours that are spreading everywhere' concerning Bavarian defection.[299] Maret's dubious view notwithstanding, no action was taken and, in the event, by the time his note to Mercy was written (1 October), opportunities for Napoleon to influence Bavaria were already fast evaporating.

An excess of credulity was exacerbated by interruptions in communications. Some, perhaps most, of Mercy's later reports were intercepted by Allied raiders or retained in Erfurt with a stack of other correspondence to preclude their capture. This was the case, for example, with the urgent messages Mercy sent reporting the Treaty of Ried and his efforts to warn of the threat to the French line of communications posed by the Austro-Bavarian army under Wrede.[300] It is likewise unknown whether two letters from King Friedrich of Württemberg ever reached Napoleon. Friedrich, always eager to highlight his neighbour's failings, wrote of his 'just concerns' that Austria and Bavaria had signed a convention on 3 October and provided more specifics in another letter eleven days later.[301] Of course, even if these messages had made their way to Napoleon's desk, they were far too late to affect Bavaria's policy shift.[302]

A second factor delaying Napoleon's appreciation of Bavarian disaffection was the emperor's own trust in Max Joseph and his faith in familial connections. He saw the Bavarian king as a model Rheinbund monarch and had once exclaimed to Narbonne, 'Voilà, this is how they all should be!' Considering his stepson Eugène's marriage to Max Joseph's daughter, Berthier's close ties to the royal family by marriage, and his own personal affection for the king, the emperor did not treat Bavaria as his top personal priority in 1813. The Danube front, after all, was a secondary theatre of operations. He believed Bavarian betrayal to be unlikely and could thus entrust management of communications with Munich to Berthier and Maret while focusing his own efforts on achieving a decisive result in the principal theatre of war along the Elbe. This may explain why there was almost no direct correspondence between Napoleon and Max Joseph during 1813 even though Montgelas and Wrede periodically communicated with imperial headquarters. As compared to the twenty-two letters he sent to King Friedrich of Württemberg that year, only three messages went to Max Joseph under Napoleon's signature (one each in January, March, and April). Instead, nearly all communication with the king was channelled through Berthier who sent twenty-seven letters to Max Joseph between April and September. Max Joseph likewise used Berthier as a conduit, dispatching only one known direct letter to Napoleon (3 March) during 1813.

These curious arrangements did not mean Bavaria was forgotten, nor would the outcome have been necessarily different had Napoleon and Max Joseph corresponded directly, but this preferred channel through Berthier did pose problems for Mercy. The staff officers delivering Berthier's messages seem to have gone direct to the king rather than through Mercy, so that he often found that the king had better, more current information than was available to him. Even more awkwardly, the updates he received from Maret (never enough instructions, he complained) sometimes contradicted what the king had learned from Berthier. These problems of correspondence – cross-communications, confusion, and interception – thus impeded both Napoleon's understanding of Bavaria's shift to the Allies and the chances of French policy prevailing over the threats and inducements offered by the Coalition. Again, it is by no means certain that better communications would have resulted in Bavaria staying in the Rheinbund, but earlier notification would have at least offered Napoleon an opportunity to counter the Coalition's diplomatic inroads in Munich and perhaps alter his military operations to adjust for Bavarian defection sooner than he did.

Two further aspects of Bavaria's defection need to be addressed before concluding this section. First is the role of Augereau's 'Observation Corps of Bavaria' in the Bavarian decision that autumn. A Bavarian manifesto issued on 14 October listed Napoleon's failure to protect his ally as a key reason for changing sides: *'The emperor did not deign to give a single thought to how to save or protect his most faithful ally. No word was received from him, no counsel, no encouraging promise to dissipate the government's alarms.'*[303] This assertion must be adjudged a considerable exaggeration. During the spring campaign, as discussed earlier, both Vienna and Munich saw the threat of Austrian attack as a convenient pretext for Bavaria to withhold its forces from the Grande Armée. The possibility of an Austrian invasion did become more real once Vienna declared for the Coalition. This, after all, was why Napoleon wanted Wrede's corps in the Danube valley as a deterrent in the first place (and, in his optimistic moments, as a potential offensive threat to Bohemia). Indeed, for a time during the late summer there was cause for concern as Reuß's command included 30,000 men under GdK Johann Graf Klenau around Pilsen (Plzeň) in western Bohemia as well as his own 30,000 in the Danube valley. Allied raiding parties were also a hazard, but Klenau's corps posed at least a theoretical threat to northern Bavaria that far exceeded the harmful potential of Cossacks or cavalry detachments. This threat from Bohemia receded when the armistice ended because Schwarzenberg called Klenau north into Saxony. Wrede and Reuß thus confronted each other on a more or less equal basis. Wrede on the frontier and many in Munich were doubtless aware of the diminution in danger, but the image of invasion remained a central theme in all Bavarian communications with the French. It even appeared in instructions Montgelas sent to Bavarian ambassadors in other Rheinbund capitals. As Max Joseph told Mercy one day in August: 'The emperor cannot demand that I defend myself alone against the Austrian army!'[304]

While the Bavarian government exaggerated its peril, however, some in Munich were stricken with true alarm. Max Joseph seems to have been one of these. Although it is possible that he consistently and cleverly dissembled in his interactions with Mercy and in his correspondence with Berthier, his fears seem to have been at least partly authentic, at least through mid-September when the border ceasefire and the waxing exchanges with the Allies lessened the danger. As summer waned into autumn, for instance, there was widespread talk of the court having to evacuate Munich for asylum elsewhere and Max Joseph specifically sent his heir from the Tyrol and Salzburg to Augsburg to be more distant from the scene of any possible Habsburg advance.[305] Max Joseph remonstrated with Mercy when much of Augereau's Corps of Observation departed for Saxony in early August (to form 14th Corps under Gouvion Saint-Cyr), especially as Augereau had unwisely told Wrede that he had no orders to march to the Danube valley.[306] Although these battalions were eventually replaced by fresh formations from France, Max Joseph was not convinced of their worth: 'The observation corps under Augereau's orders is nowhere to be seen ... the marshal is there by himself.'[307] His final letter to Berthier on 21 September echoed these overstated fears as he pleaded to have Raglovich returned: 'The Austrians make daily advances in the Tyrol ... Wrede can barely hold back Prince Reuß ... the northern borders of my kingdom are pressed by the enemy's light troops.'[308]

The arrival of Russian General Bennigsen's Army of Poland in Bohemia in early October excited another round of qualms as Max Joseph explained in a letter to Eugène.[309] The king's assessment of Augereau, his excessive apprehensions about Wrede's position, his nervousness concerning Bohemia, and his worries about his family's safety were consistent with his anxious character. Though extravagant, they were manifestations of genuine concern rather than solely designed as elements of some elaborate deception. Deception and evasiveness, of course, were also present (such as Wrede gulling Mercy with protestations of loyalty to Napoleon) and grew more dominant in the second half of September, but the authentic apprehensions of some Bavarian leaders, including Max Joseph, cannot be dismissed out of hand. In sum, then, Bavaria's incessant reference to fear of Austrian invasion during the summer and autumn was principally employed as a ruse to excuse its defection, but it was simultaneously a symptom of genuine worry on the part of the fretful king.

The second question is whether Bavaria, as the first core member to abandon the Confederation (not counting the Mecklenburg duchies as 'core members'), notified the French in advance. Max Joseph and Montgelas certainly tried to create an impression of Bavarian desperation in the context of recalling Raglovich and lamenting what they portrayed as an absence of French protection. Pulling Mercy aside during a shooting party in August, for example, the king told him, 'I will do all that depends on me to fulfil my commitments to the emperor; but if he does not come to my aid, I can answer for nothing.' Mercy passed these remarks and many similar ones to Maret uncritically, sometimes amplifying them from his own perspective. He thus reported on 13 September that, 'After the removal of the troops under the order of the Duke of Castiglione [Augereau] that people here had expected to see approaching the Danube, some have gone so far as to speak to him [the king] about negotiations with Austria at the price of some of his provinces, which he would be obliged to abandon.' Indeed, Mercy subsequently claimed that he warned Maret in a long note on 15 September of the pressure being placed on the king to change sides, pressure that was magnified by the recent French defeats. His post-war memoir relates his frustration at receiving no satisfactory answer from the foreign minister. There were thus hints aplenty, but Mercy detected no change in his interactions with Wrede or Montgelas or with the king, who continued to treat him with exceptional courtesy and seeming candour.[310] Moreover, he repeatedly reassured the emperor that the king remained firm and that 'there was no question of political changes in [French] relations with Bavaria, that all propositions in this regard on the part of Austria had been rejected and always will be'. Hints and apprehensions notwithstanding, therefore, there is no solid evidence that Bavaria provided its French ally with a clear warning of its impending defection and the clues that did appear were diluted by the affirmations of fealty Mercy received from his chief interlocutors.[311]

There is nowhere a specific statement reflecting Napoleon's thinking on Bavaria at this stage in the autumn campaign, but it is possible to speculate along the following lines. He did not have sufficient troops to conduct operations against a numerically superior enemy in Saxony, protect his lines of communication from the ubiquitous Allied raiders, and send enough men to the Danube to quell genuine Bavarian anxieties or to intimidate the kingdom into remaining loyal. The emperor likely had a good appreciation of the forces under Reuß and regarded Wrede's corps as adequate to contain them. Thus, like Oudinot at Bautzen, the Bavarians would simply have to hold the line until the issue was decided in the principal theatre of war. If this was Napoleon's approach, it suited very well those Bavarians (for example, Montgelas) who were demanding military assistance they knew Napoleon could not provide as a means of creating a pretext for defection. In the event, of course, thanks to Wrede and Montgelas, Bavaria's decision came before the grand battle at Leipzig, and had a direct effect on Napoleon's operations. Though he perhaps overstated the impact, the emperor was not far wrong when he wrote to his archchancellor on 25 October that, 'Bavaria's inconceivable and unexpected betrayal has upset all my plans and forces me to bring the war closer to our borders.'[312]

The Army, the Kingdom and the Nation

Leading his new Austro-Bavarian army, Wrede now headed for Hanau on the Main River where he would suffer a serious defeat and a serious wound on 30–31 October while he attempted to intercept Napoleon and the battered remains of the Grande Armée. Curiously, a small band of Bavarian Chevaulegers was on the other side of the field at Hanau because Oudinot had taken them with him as part of his escort when he was reassigned to the Young Guard after 12th Corps was disbanded in September. The marshal released them in the evening after granting them a large gratuity.[313] The Bavarians will reappear in this narrative in connection with Württemberg, Baden, Hesse-Darmstadt and Würzburg, but before they march off the stage, several points about the kingdom and its army in 1813 are worth highlighting.

First is combat performance. Rechberg's division was weak and suffered from poor security practices, but Zoller's brigade at Thorn acquitted itself admirably and, as shall be seen in Chapter 8, the same was true of Butler's lone regiment in Danzig. Owing to the manner in which Oudinot employed them, Raglovich's men had few chances to prove themselves in major battles, but they did well in those cases where they were engaged. Bautzen, Hoyerswerda, Luckenwalde, and Zahna were all instances of solid battlefield performance that earned sincere praise from Oudinot and other French commanders as well as Raglovich. The composite cavalry regiment was especially notable for its unanticipated competence. With the exception of the disconcerting surprise on the night of 16/17 August, the officers and men of the regiment earned for themselves a solid reputation even at Dennewitz after the loss of their much-admired colonel. Dennewitz showed the division at its best and worst. On the one hand, Raglovich demonstrated tactical skill and his soldiers displayed sturdy endurance as they retained their composure and held off enemy attacks through the dust and chaos of the initial retreat, one of the few formations to do so. On the other hand, the division nearly disintegrated during the confused withdrawal through the woods that night. This, however, was a fate it shared with every other nationality in Ney's Army of Berlin. French, Italian, Saxon and Württemberg units also crumbled and scattered in the dreadful disorder of the retreat. The Bavarians maintained sufficient discipline to capture Dahme late that night and gather in many of their stragglers, but Dennewitz and its aftermath were disasters from which the contingent never recovered. As with many other components of the Grande Armée that year, French and allied alike, the Bavarian units could be brittle, steady enough in battle, but difficult to reconstitute once knocked apart by a trial such as the retreat from Dennewitz.

The second point to consider is reliability. Like other elements of Oudinot's command and indeed the rest of the Grande Armée, the Bavarian contingent certainly suffered from desertion, but as best as can be determined its extent does not seem to have been much different from that experienced by the French regiments of the corps. Raglovich's worries notwithstanding, the laments that appear in subsequent Bavarian histories seem overstated if understandable. There were no cases of mass desertion and no unit defections as there were with other contingents. Major von Treuberg and his II/9th Infantry at Dennewitz stand out as a prime example: holding out against three Prussian attacks despite being surrounded and cut off from any hope of succour. The lack of desertions during the siege of Thorn is especially remarkable given the appalling impressions of the recent 1812 debacle, the hopeless outlook for the garrison, the incessant inducements from the enemy, and the innumerable opportunities the situation offered for individuals or groups to slip away. Similarly, conceptions of duty and honour – the nation's, the army's, the individual's – kept Maillot's brigade conscientiously performing its assigned tasks until the very end. Despite the ire aroused by the kingdom's defection, therefore, the officers and men of the Bavarian contingent departed with the respect of their French comrades-in-arms.

Finally, the Bavarian army's behaviour is another example of the largely particularist nature of military patriotism in 1813. Although generally located within a broad 'German' cultural context, officers and men clearly identified themselves as Bavarians at the time and objected first and foremost to the insults, burdens and restrictions they believed the French alliance had inflicted on their fatherland as narrowly defined. Popular attitudes – with the exception of the Tyrol and select social groupings in some other regions – were similar, compounded by widespread war weariness and hatred of conscription, another imposition specifically associated with France. The lengthy royal manifesto issued on 14 October stressed Napoleon's disregard for Bavaria as 'his most loyal ally', his refusal to make peace, and his failings as the protector of the Rheinbund with lengthy disquisitions on the 1812 disaster and the lack of support from Augereau's corps. There was only one reference to the new war as aimed at 'the independence of the German nation as well as the states of which it is composed'. Similarly, the king's 28 October proclamation 'To My People!' spoke of independence, peace, a European balance of power, economic wellbeing and 'the prestige of my crown'. It included vague reference to 'the sacred struggle' and 'the just cause', but no appeal to pan-German national sentiment.[314] As Julia Murken observes:

> This deep attachment of the Bavarian soldiers to their Bavarian homeland was also an expression of a specific 'Bavarian national consciousness'. Such a conception in the young kingdom was not fundamentally contradictory to the existence of a 'German nation', but categorically rejected a [unitary] nation-state.

As was seen with Völderndorff earlier, therefore, even in the highly Prusso-German nationalistic atmosphere of the later nineteenth century, Bavarian authors always emphasised their *Bavarian* identity in writing of the Rheinbund era.[315]

*

Bavaria's defection was a severe blow to Napoleon's hopes both militarily and politically. On the military side, the threat to his strategic rear forced him to contemplate equally unsavoury options: cut himself loose from his established line of communications and operate in northern Germany, or immediately retreat towards France via Erfurt and Würzburg with the Allies in pursuit, or face the increasingly united Allied armies in the hope of gaining a resounding victory. Often overlooked is the fact that Bavaria's defection also opened all the Tyrol to the Austrians and thus compromised Eugène's defence of the Kingdom of Italy as well.[316] Politically, the Bavaria action was a shock to the framework of the Rheinbund, already shaken by the disaster of 1812 and the reverses inflicted upon the Grande Armée thus far in 1813. The

Mecklenburg duchies, small, dubious latecomers, had not been a factor for their fellow monarchs, but Bavaria was an entirely different matter. As one contemporary observer wrote: 'Mecklenburg separated itself first, Bavaria tore apart the Rheinbund.'[317] Important as it was in itself, however, it was the combination of this political factor with the military dimension that proved decisive in the end. The concatenation of calamities suffered by Napoleon's subordinates, and, above all, the shattering defeat visited upon the emperor himself at Leipzig were most prominent, but the progress of Wrede's Austro-Bavarian army was also a determining consideration for the other states of southwestern Germany. The second volume of this study shall explore this aspect of the Rheinbund's collapse in greater detail.

By temporising through the spring and autumn campaigns and by switching sides when it did, Bavaria emerged from the Napoleonic Wars on the side of the victors. It was a triumph of realpolitik, what Montgelas later termed 'our wise restraint' (he contrasted Bavaria's policies with Saxony's).[318] Bavaria sought to demonstrate its new alignment and cement its position in the post-war order by Wrede's march to intercept Napoleon and by the army's not inconsiderable activity during the 1814 campaign in France (curiously, Bavarians were fighting on both sides for a time as the 13th Infantry continued to serve as a loyal element of the Danzig garrison until December). Even though it saw no combat, the kingdom also raised an unsustainably large army of 60,000 for 1815. Despite these costly exertions, it was not permitted to be a signatory to the 1814 Treaty of Paris and its representatives encountered enormous difficulties in achieving what they considered fair restitution at the Congress of Vienna. When the final territorial agreement was concluded in 1818, it left Bavaria with an overall increase in population but geographically divided because part of its compensation came from lands chopped away from France on the left bank of the Rhine. The kingdom, the Wittelsbach dynasty and the domestic reforms were thus preserved but hopes for a larger destiny seeped away and Bavaria would remain at best a middle power for the remainder of its semi-independent existence.

Intermission

I PAUSE HERE in the narrative of these unexplored aspects of the 1813 campaigns to avoid burdening the reader with an inconveniently weighty tome. Given the complexity of this sprawling conflict, the central role played by the Confederation contingents and the changing character of their contributions over time, splitting the account into two parts makes it possible to tell the complete story without either losing detail or producing an unmanageable volume.

After an introduction to set the context for the Rheinbund and its participation in the combats and sieges of 1813, this volume has examined two of the largest members of the Confederation, Saxony, which proved most loyal in the end, and Bavaria, the first to defect. Specifics and nuance, of course, matter. Though Saxony's Friedrich August later paid the price for his refusal to change sides, he and his court, as we have seen, vacillated for weeks during the spring and actually signed a convention with Austria that fundamentally contradicted the alliance with France. Bavaria's Max Joseph, on the other hand, was the first to repudiate the Rheinbund but only took this fateful step after months of agonising and temporising. Moreover, hesitant deliberations at the state level did not necessarily translate into troop performance. The Saxon contingent was only one of two instances where a major unit changed sides during a battle (the other being a Württemberg cavalry brigade), but the various components of the kingdom's army had demonstrated competence, courage and resolute loyalty for months prior to the final defection at Leipzig and the heavy cavalry served on through the final paroxysms of the *Völkerschlacht* debacle. The Bavarians had fewer opportunities to stand in the front line in combat but held to their duty despite the evident neglect from the government in Munich.

Falling between the two poles of Saxony and Bavaria, the remaining Rheinbund contingents are the subject of Volume II. These include the mid-sized forces of Württemberg, Baden and Hesse-Darmstadt as well as the much larger Westphalian army and small contingents from the host of central German microstates. Württemberg, Baden and Hesse-Darmstadt had provided the best Rheinbund troops in earlier wars and would largely uphold this tradition despite being wholly reconstructed after the 1812 catastrophe. Westphalia, on the other hand, was a bundle of contradictions, with turbulence and mismanagement inside the kingdom placing enormous demands on military leadership, demands that would mostly go unfulfilled with negative ramifications for combat performance. The tiny microstate contingents too would leave behind a dubious record of defeat and desertion in their last appearances as French allies. The second volume also describes the contributions from Berg, Würzburg and Frankfurt that ran the gamut from reliable to flighty. Variations between units within each of these contingents – and within the Westphalian army – highlight the importance of evaluating each formation on its own terms in addition to distinguishing among countries as they evolved over time.

Fortress warfare was a salient feature of the conflict and Volume II will also address Rheinbund involvement in the many sieges and blockades of 1813. This volume has discussed Thorn where the defence was almost entirely in the hands of Bavarians, but Rheinbund troops comprised a significant percentage of many garrisons from the Vistula to the Elbe. Their performances in fortress tasks spanned the spectrum from steadfastly dependable to desertion-prone. In Danzig, for instance, the Confederation contingents were exemplary, trusted by the fortress governor and inspiring to other elements of the garrison. In other situations, the Rheinbund troops were a potential threat to the defence, consuming resources and undermining morale while seeking opportunities to flee. The second volume thus examines each of the siege and blockade situations to assess the role and quality of the Confederation troops under these trying circumstances. Lastly, the volume concludes with a set of summary observations on the Rheinbund in 1813 and an appendix discussing the questions associated with draft evasion, desertion and defection.

I look forward to making this second half of the story available to the reading public within a few months.

Notes

Abbreviations Used in Notes

AHGA	Archiv für hessische Geschichte und Altertumskunde
AN	Archives Nationales, Paris
BayHStA	Bayerisches Hauptstaatsarchiv, Munich
BayHStA, GHA	″ ″ ″ Geheimes Haus Archiv
BayHStA, HS	″ ″ ″ Handschrift
CdN	Correspondance de Napoléon, 1858–70
CG	Napoleon's Correspondance Générale, 2004–18
CRE	Consortium on the Revolutionary Era (formerly Consortium on Revolutionary Europe)
DBKHG	Darstellungen aus der Bayerischen Kriegs- und Heeresgeschichte
Fabry, *Oudinot*	[Fabry, Gabriel]. *Étude sur les Opérations du Maréchal Oudinot du 15 Août au 4 Septembre 1813*, Paris: Chapelot, 1910
Fabry, *MacDonald*	[Fabry, Gabriel]. *Étude sur les Opérations du Maréchal MacDonald du 22 Août au 4 Septembre 1813*, Paris: Chapelot, 1910
Fabry, *Empereur I*	Fabry, Gabriel. *Étude sur les Opérations de l'Empereur du 28 Août au 4 Septembre 1813*, Paris: Chapelot, 1911
Fabry, *Empereur II*	Fabry, Gabriel. *Étude sur les Opérations de l'Empereur du 5 Septembre au 21 Septembre 1813*, Paris: Chapelot, 1913
Fabry, *Empereur III*	Fabry, Gabriel. *Étude sur les Opérations de l'Empereur du 22 Septembre au 3 Octobre 1813*, Paris: Chapelot, 1913
FBPG	Forschungen zur Brandenburgischen und Preußischen Geschichte
GLAK	Landesarchiv Baden-Württemberg, Generallandesarchiv, Karlsruhe
HStAD	Hessisches Staatsarchiv, Darmstadt
JdAM	Jahrbücher für die deutsche Armee und Marine
LABWHStA	Landesarchiv Baden-Württemberg, Hauptstaatsarchiv, Stuttgart
NASG	Neues Archiv für sächsische Geschichte
SHD	Service Historique de la Défense, Vincennes
SHSA	Sächsisches Hauptstaatsarchiv, Dresden

SIRIO	*Sbornik Imperatorskago Russkago Istoricheskago Obschestva*
ZfkWGK	*Zeitschrift für Kunst, Wissenschaft und Geschichte des Krieges*
ZHG	*Zeitschrift des Vereins für hessische Geschichte und Landeskunde*

A full Bibliography is included in Volume 2 of this work.

Preface

1. As Jean-François Brun has pointed out, the broader topic of the many types of foreign units in Napoleon's armies is deserving of much greater attention: 'Les Unités Étrangères dans les Armées Napoléoniennes: un Élement de la Strategie Globale du Grand Empire', *Revue Historique des Armées*, no. 255, 2009.
2. For thoughtful and concise introductions to the German nationalism question, see John Breuilly, 'The Response to Napoleon and German Nationalism', in Alan Forrest and Peter H. Wilson, eds, *The Bee and the Eagle: Napoleonic France and the End of the Holy Roman Empire, 1806*, London: Palgrave Macmillan, 2009, pp. 256–83; Helmut Walser Smith, *Germany: A Nation in Its Time*, New York: Liveright, 2020, Part II, as well as his 'Nation and Nationalism', in Jonathan Sperber, ed., *Germany: 1800–1870*, Oxford: Oxford University Press, 2004; and James J. Sheehan, *German History 1770–1866*, Oxford: Clarendon, 1989, especially pp. 371–88. The insightful essay by Robert D. Billinger, Jr. is especially useful as it focusses specifically on the Rheinbund: 'Good and True Germans: The "Nationalism" of the Rheinbund Princes, 1806–1814', in Heinz Durchhardt and Andreas Krug, *Reich oder Nation? Mitteleuropa 1780–1815*, Mainz: Zabern: 1998, pp. 105–40. Though centred on Prussia, Karen Hagemann's exhaustive study highlights many points applicable to Germany writ large, especially with respect to gender issues: *'Mannlicher Muth und Teutsche Ehre': Nation, Militär und Geschlecht zur Zeit der Antinapoleonischen Kriege Preußens*, Paderborn: Schöningh, 2002, pp. 374–93, 522–8.
3. This is the question of *Befreiungskrieg* (a princes' War of Liberation to oust Napoleonic France from its role in Germany) versus *Freiheitskrieg* (a people's Freedom War to open new channels of political representation and individual liberty). As Peter Brandt notes, the debate on the nature of these wars began as soon as the firing stopped: 'Die Befreiungskriege 1813 bis 1815 in der deutschen Geschichte', in Peter Brandt, ed., *An der Schwelle zur Moderne: Deutschland um 1800*, Bonn: Forschungsinstitut der Friedrich-Ebert-Stiftung, 1999, p. 83. Markus Junkelmann is worth citing here: 'One should rather speak of the War of the Sixth Coalition because the designation "Brefreiungskrieg" or even "Freiheitskrieg" brings an exclusively Prussian–German perspective to bear and marginalises the role of the Russians, Austrians, British and Swedes, furthermore, it is one-sidedly judgmental. Neither is the widely used plural "Befreiungskriege" justified as 1813–1814 deals with a single war and the war of 1815 can hardly be considered a "Befreiungskrieg"' (Marcus Junkelmann, *Napoleon und Bayern*, Regensburg: Pustet, 2014, p. 203, Note 117).

On this issue see works such as: Alexandra Bleyer, *Auf gegen Napoleon! Mythos Volkskriege*, Darmstadt: Primus, 2013; Walter Bruyère-Ostells, *Leipzig 16–19 Octobre 1813: La revanche de l'Europe des souverains sur Napoléon*, Paris: Tallandier, 2013; Mario Kandil, *Die deutsche Erhebung 1812–1815*, Stegen am Ammersee: Druffel & Vowinkel, 2011; Arnulf Krause, *Der Kampf um Freiheit: Die Napoleonischen Befreiungskriege in Deutschland*, Stuttgart: Theiss, 2013; Andreas Platthaus, *1813: Die Völkerschlacht und das Ende der alten Welt*, Berlin: Rowohlt, 2013; and Hans-Ulrich Thamer, *Die Völkerschlacht bei Leipzig: Europas Kampf gegen Napoleon*, Munich: Beck, 2013.

4. 'The so-called Wars of Liberation', notes historian Leighton S. James, 'became a leitmotif of German nationalist discourse in the nineteenth century' (*Witnessing the Revolutionary and Napoleonic Wars in German Central Europe*, New York: Palgrave Macmillan, 2013, p. 166).

5. H. W. Smith, *Germany*, p. xiii. William O. Shanahan observes that study of the Rheinbund was 'delayed by the patriotic disdain shown towards it by most German historians', see his 'A Neglected Source of German Nationalism: The Confederation of the Rhine', in Michael Palumbo and William O. Shanahan, eds, *Nationalism: Essays in Honor of Louis L. Snyder*, Westport, Greenwood, 1981, p. 111. Along similar lines: Bleyer, *Auf gegen Napoleon*, p. 238; Martin Kitchen, *A History of Modern Germany*, Chichester: Wiley-Blackwell, 2012, p. 6; Krause, *Kampf um Freiheit*, pp. 324–5.

6. First quote ('miserable impotence and servitude') from Ludwig Häuser, *Deutsche Geschichte vom Tode Friedrichs des Großen bis zur Gründung des deutschen Bundes*, Berlin: Weidmann, 1862, vol. I, pp. 695–700; second from the title of Wilhelm Koppen's *Deutsche gegen Deutschland: Geschichte des Rheinbundes*, Hamburg: Hanseatische Verlagsanstalt, 1936. Perhaps the best known propagator of such themes was Heinrich von Treitschke, *Deutsche Geschichte im Neunzehnten Jahrhundert*, Leipzig: Hirzel, 1879 (vol. I, pp. 353–9 for example). This denigration of the Rheinbund princes carried over into portrayals published in East Germany where Saxony's Friedrich August could be described as an 'enemy of German unity and an adherent to foreign domination' (Fritz Donath, Ernst Engelberg, Heinz Füßler, A. M. Uhlmann, *Leipzig 1813*, Leipzig: Veb, 1953, p. 123).

7. Karl Christian Kanis Gretschel and Friedrich Bülau, *Geschichte des Sächsischen Volkes und Staates*, Leipzig: Hinrichs, 1853, vol. III, pp. 451–2.

8. Eduard von Völderndorff und Waradein, *Kriegsgeschichte von Bayern unter König Maximilian Joseph I.*, Munich: n.p., 1826, vol. IV, p. 205.

9. There is an entire literature on 'ego-documents', but see in this connection Thomas Hippler, 'Problematischer Nationalismus: Kaiserkult und Volkssouveränität in Selbstzeugnissen deutscher Soldaten unter Napoleon', in Andreas Gestrich and Bernhard Schmitt, eds, *Militär und Gesellschaft in der Frühen Neuzeit, Themenheft Militär und Gesellschaft in Herrschaftswechseln*, Potsdam: Universitätsverlag, 2013, pp. 85–91; James, *Witnessing*, pp. 5–7. As an example of the transition from diary to published memoirs, see Christoph Ludwig von Yelin, '1812: Aus dem Tagebuch eines

württembergischen Offiziers', *Süddeutsche Monatshefte*, vol. II, 1908, as compared to his bitterly embellished recollections in book form: *Merkwürdige Tage meines Lebens*, Stuttgart: Sattler, 1817.

10. In addition to others, see Stephanie Poßelt, *Die Grande Armée in Deutschland 1805 bis 1814*, Frankfurt: Lang, 2013, pp. 289–93.
11. Ferdinand Sigmund von Praun, 'Tagebücher', BayHStA, HS 743. Christian von Martens, 'Tagebuch meines Feldzuges gegen Preußen 1813', LABWHStA, J 56 Bü 21, and his *Vor fünfzig Jahren: Tagebuch meines Feldzuges in Sachsen 1813*, two vols., Stuttgart: Schaber, 1862–63. This came to my attention thanks to Leighton James (*Witnessing*, p. 76).
12. Todd B. Berryman, 'Boundaries of Loyalty: Territorial Consolidation and Public Allegiance in Northwest Germany, 1797–1817', dissertation, University of North Carolina at Chapel Hill, 2004, p. 150/n. 40.
13. Dennis Showalter, *The Wars of German Unification*, London: Bloomsbury, 2015, p. 5. Karen Hagemann terms it a 'complex and often ambiguous identity' ('Francophobia and Patriotism: Anti-French Images and Sentiments in Prussia and Northern Germany during the Anti-Napoleonic Wars', *French History*, vol. 18, no. 4, 2004, p. 412). For an introduction to the much-debated concept of a German *Kulturnation* or 'cultural nation', see Georg Schmidt, 'Friedrich Meineckes Kulturnation: Zum historischen Kontext nationaler Ideen in Weimar-Jena um 1800', *Historische Zeitschrift*, vol. 284, no. 1, 2007.
14. In addition to the sources cited earlier on the dominance of the Borusssian narrative, see: Jörg Echternkamp, *Der Aufstieg des deutschen Nationalismus (1770–1840)*, Frankfurt: Campus, 1996, p. 175; Robert M. Citino, *The German Way of War*, Lawrence: University of Kansas, 2005, p. xiii; Katherine Aaslestad and Karen Hagemann, 'Collaboration, Resistance, and Reform: Experiences and Historiographies of the Napoleonic Wars in Central Europe', *Central European History*, no. 39, 2006, pp. 550–1, 569–79; and Uwe Puschner, 'Die Alldeutschen, die Völkischen und die Schlacht, 1913–1813', in Martin Hofbauer and Martin Rink, eds, *Die Völkerschlacht bei Leipzig*, Oldenburg: De Gruyter, 2017, pp. 347–60.
15. Ute Planert, *Der Mythos vom Befreiungskrieg*, Paderborn: Schöningh, 2007; Peter H. Wilson, *Iron and Blood: A Military History of the German-Speaking Peoples since 1500*, Cambridge: Belknap Press, 2023, (here pp. xlii–xlv, 279). For an early thrust in the direction of correcting the dominant Borussian cant, see J. R. Dieterich, 'Die Politik Landgraf Ludwig X. von Hessen-Darmstadt von 1790–1806', *AHGA*, vol. VII, 1910.
16. For an overview of the blockade and associated French customs/tariff practices as regards the German states, see Roger Dufraisse, 'Politique Douanière Française, Blocus et Système Continental en Allemagne', *Revue du Souvenir Napoléonien*, no. 389, June–July 1993.

Prologue

1. Napoleon to Jérôme and others, 18 January 1813, *CG*, no. 32332, vol. XIII, pp. 118–21.

2. The somewhat confusing taxonomy of wars against Napoleon describes seven Coalitions: 1792–7 (1st), 1798–1802 (2nd), 1803–5 (3rd), 1806–7 (4th), 1809 (5th), 1813–14 (6th), and 1815 (7th). Note that the 1812 campaign in Russia and the Peninsular War are not included in this categorisation.
3. Counting up the Rheinbund states is complicated by the fact that some were ruled cooperatively and met their troop commitments conjointly. The 27 whose troops participated in the 1813 campaigns included the four small principalities of the Reuß senior (Greiz) and junior (Ebersdorf, Lobenstein, Schliez) lines; their troop contingents are listed on one line in Chart 1. The *total* number of German states in the Rheinbund in April 1813 was 32: counting Nassau as two (Usingen and Weilburg), Reuß as four (one senior and three junior), and not including the two Mecklenburg duchies (which changed sides in March). The troops of Nassau and the five other principalities incorporated into its contingent, however, are not addressed in this work as they were committed to Spain and did not fight in Germany in 1813. Arenberg, the two Salm principalities and Oldenburg were annexed to France in 1810.
4. Tracking numbers of troops always leads to mares' nests and the data can only be approximate. Nonetheless, this range provides a sense of the scale of Rheinbund participation during 1813. The 70,000 represents my estimate of those 'present under arms' combined with those listed as 'detached' in late summer (August–September); this figure thus represents those available for combat. This present/detached figure includes approximately 42,400 with the field army, 19,139 in fortress garrisons (including Leipzig and Würzburg), and 8,500 Westphalian troops available inside the kingdom for home defence. The total comes to more than 88,000 if the 18,100 on the sick lists are added; these, of course, were part of the German contributions even if they could not take the field. For lack of data, those in hospitals in fortresses are *not* included in the 88,000, so the total figure is probably 2,000–3,000 higher (*c*. 91,000). The principal source is the mid-August 'Livret de Situation' prepared for Napoleon (2C708) combined with mid-September to mid-October data for fortresses (all SHD) and Specht for Westphalia; see Charts 45 and 50–56 in Vol. 2 of the present work for specific sources.
5. Approved by the Imperial Diet on 24 March 1803, this act (the *Reichsdeputationshauptschluss* or *Hauptschluss der außerordentlichen Reichsdeputation*) legitimised French conquests west of the Rhine and rearranged the remainder of old *Reich* through a vast and complex process that changed the status of nearly 70 formerly ecclesiastical estates and abolished 45 of the old imperial cities. Though most commonly known as the 'Imperial Recess', Christopher Clarke's rendering of the 'gargantuan' German term as a 'report' is more in line with the nature of the document; see his *Iron Kingdom: The Rise and Downfall of Prussia 1600–1947*, Cambridge: Harvard University Press, 2006, p. 295. As Shanahan points out, other stepping stones on this path included the Peace of Basel (1795), the Treaty of Campo Formio (1797) and

the Treaty of Lunéville (1801), followed by Napoleon's victory at Austerlitz (1805), 'Neglected Source', p. 112.

6. For a concise summary of the Rheinbund in the historical context of French policy and as an element of Napoleon's outlook, see Frederick C. Schneid, 'Kings, Clients and Satellites in the Napoleonic Imperium', *Journal of Strategic Studies*, vol. 31, no. 4, August 2008. As Schneid points out, the desire to counter or displace Austrian influence in Germany (and elsewhere) did not originate with Napoleon but had long been an element of French policy.

7. Reinhard Mußgnug, 'Der Rheinbund', *Der Staat*, vol. 46, no. 2, 2007, p. 250.

8. H. W. Smith notes that Poland was the 'feared prototype' for smaller German states who worried that the 'superstates' Austria and Prussia would start looking west (*Germany*, pp. 116–17).

9. Saxon kings had ruled Poland from 1697 to 1763, so there was a historical connection between the Saxon House of Wettin and the Polish throne.

10. Hans A. Schmitt's engaging phrase is from 'Germany without Prussia: A Closer Look at the Confederation of the Rhine', *German Studies Review*, vol. 6, no. 1, February 1983, p. 37; similarly, J. R. Dieterich in 1910 decried the superficial and tendentious practice of simply considering the Rheinbund princes 'Napoleon's satraps' or 'the Corsican's minions' ('Politik Landgraf Ludwig', pp. 450–3). See also Elisabeth Fehrenbach, 'Verfassungs- und Sozialpolitische Reformen und Reformprojekte in Deutschland unter dem Einfluss des Napoleonischen Frankreich', *Historische Zeitschrift*, vol. 228, 1979, pp. 292–3; and Ferdinand von Funck (GL Carl Wilhelm Ferdinand von Funck), *In Russland und in Sachsen 1812–1815*, Artur Brabant, ed., Dresden: Heinrich, 1930, p. 248. Some scholars argue that the Rheinbund was nothing more than a recruiting depot for Napoleon (Thomas Nipperdey, *Germany from Napoleon to Bismarck 1800–1866*, Daniel Nolan, trans., Princeton: Princeton University Press, 1996, p. 8; Jean Tulard, 'Napoléon et la Confédération du Rhin', in Eberhard Weis and Elisabeth Müller-Luckner, eds, *Reformen im rheinbündischen Deutschland*, Munich: Oldenbourg, 1984, p. 3), but others offer that this view is too simplistic and that its role altered over time (Georg Schmidt, 'Der napoleonische Rheinbund – ein erneutes Altes Reich?', in Volker Press and Dieter Stievermann, *Alternativen zur Reichsverfassung in der frühen Neuzeit?*, Munich: Oldenbourg, 1995, p. 232).

11. Of the many discussions on the introduction, modification and rejection of the Code Napoléon in Germany, a good starting point is Paul L. Weinacht, 'Les États de la Confédération du Rhin face au Code Napoléon', in Jean-Clément Martin, ed., *Napoléon et l'Europe*, Rennes: Rennes University Press, 2002; the classic study is Elisabeth Fehrenbach, *Traditionelle Gesellschaft und revolutionäres Recht: Die Einführung des Code Napoléon in den Rheinbundstaaten*, Göttingen: Vandenhoeck & Ruprecht, 1978; or from a modern academic-legalistic perspective, T. T. Arvind and Lindsay Stirton, 'Explaining the Reception of the Code Napoleon in Germany: A Fuzzy-Set Qualitative Comparative Analysis', *Legal Studies*, vol. 30, no. 1, 2010.

12. See: Eberhard Weis, 'Napoleon und der Rheinbundzeit', in *Deutschland und Frankreich um 1800: Aufklärung, Revolution, Reform*, Walther Demel and Bernd Roeck, eds, Munich: Beck, 1990, pp. 213–15; Karl Beck, 'Zur Vorgeschichte des Rheinbunds', dissertation, Universität Giessen, 1890; Schmitt, 'Germany without Prussia', p. 12; Helmut Berding, 'Le Royaume de Westphalie, État-Modèle', *Francia*, vol. 10, 1982, p. 348; and Boudon, 'L'Exportation du Modèle Français dans l'Allemagne'. For contemporaneous scholarly and public views, see Gerhard Schuck, *Rheinbund Patriotismus und politische Öffentlichkeit zwischen Aufklärung und Frühliberalismus*, Stuttgart: Steiner, 1994, especially Part III, pp. 215–300.
13. Axel Kellmann and Patricia Drewes, 'Die süddeutschen Reformstaaten (Bayern, Württemberg, Baden)', in Peter Brandt, Martin Kirsch and Arthur Schlegelmilch, eds, *Handbuch der europäischen Verfassungsgeschichte im 19. Jahrhundert. Institutionen und Rechtspraxis im gesellschaftlichen Wandel*, Bonn: Dietz, 2006, vol. I, p. 717.
14. Paul Sauer, *Napoleons Adler über Württemberg, Baden und Hohenzollern*, Stuttgart: Deutsche Verlags-Anstalt, 1987, p. 208.
15. Armin Owzar, 'Liberty in Times of Occupation: The Napoleonic Era in German Central Europe', in *Napoleon's Empire: European Politics in Global Perspective*, Ute Planert, ed., New York: Palgrave Macmillan, 2015, p. 71; Erwin Hölzle, 'Das Napoleonischen Staatssystem in Deutschland', *Historische Zeitschrift*, vol. 148, no. 2, 1933, p. 287; Schmidt, 'Der napoleonische Rheinbund', pp. 231–2; Nipperdey, *Germany*, p. 9.
16. Shanahan, 'Neglected Source', p. 116.
17. Among many who comment on this phenomenon, see Elisabeth Fehrenbach, *Vom Ancien Regime zum Wiener Kongress*, 4th edition, Munich: Oldenbourg, 2001, pp. 82–94.
18. Sheehan, *German History*, pp. 252–73.
19. Fehrenbach, 'Verfassungs- und Sozialpolitische Reformen', pp. 292–306; Eberhard Weis, 'Der Einfluss der französischen Revolution und des Empire auf die Reformen in den Süddeutschen Staaten', *Francia*, vol. 1, 1973, pp. 575–83.
20. Weis, 'Rheinbundzeit', p. 188; Echternkamp, *Aufstieg*, pp. 179–80. 'Conglomerate states' from H. W. Smith, *Germany*, p. 87. The Prussian king in 1806, for example, counted almost as many Poles as Germans among his subjects. Evidence of Westphalian efforts to promote the notion of the Confederation as representative of 'true' Germans is Ehrhardt Leth, *Annalen des Königreichs Westphalen*, Göttingen: Dieter, 1809.
21. Cited in Eberhard Weis, 'Napoleon und der Rheinbund', in *Deutschland und Italien im Zeitalter Napoleons*, Armgard von Reden-Dohna, ed., Wiesbaden: Steiner, 1979, p. 78.
22. Philipp Lintner, *Im Kampf an der Seite Napoleons: Erfahrungen bayerischer Soldaten in den Napoleonischen Kriegen*, Munich: Beck 2021, pp. 214–39.
23. Junkelmann, *Napoleon und Bayern*, pp. 134–5.
24. For overviews of these insurrections, see John H. Gill, *With Eagles to Glory*, 2nd edition, London: Greenhill, 2001, Chapters 7 and 9.

25. Although the word 'modernisation' is often interpreted now as overly prescriptive or even pejorative, the monarchs, statesmen and soldiers of the day saw themselves as modernising when they introduced wide-ranging reforms in all aspects of civil and military administration. For interesting discussion of some aspects of this term as applied to Germany, see John Breuilly, 'Modernisation as Social Evolution: The German Case, c. 1800-1880', *Transactions of the Royal Historical Society*, vol. 15, 2005.
26. Förster Fleck, *Erzählung Förster Flecks von seinen Schicksalen auf dem Zuge Napoleons nach Rußland und von seiner Gefangenschaft 1812–1814*, Cologne: Schaffstein, 1912, p. 7 (2008 reprint); Christian Faber du Faur and Franz G. F. Kausler, *Mit Napoleon in Russland*, Stuttgart: Steinkopf, 1987, p. 22.
27. Christian Schaller, *Fragmente aus dem Feldzuge gegen Oestreich im Jahr 1809*, Augsburg: Bürglen, 1810, pp. 26–7.
28. [Carl Heinrich Maximilian Freiherr von Czetteritz und Neuhaus] 'Erinnerungen eines Kavallerie-Offiziers', *ZfkWGK*, vol. VII, 1839.
29. Franz Ludwig August von Meerheim, *Erlebnisse eines Veterans der großen Armee während des Feldzugs in Russland 1812*, Dresden: Meinhold, 1860, p. 83.
30. John H. Gill, 'The Rheinbund in Russia 1812: The Württemberg Experience', CRE, *Selected Papers 2013*, Alexander Mikaberidze and Michael V. Leggiere, eds, Shreveport: Louisiana State University, 2016, pp. 195–211.
31. John H. Gill, '1809: Year of Emergence for the Rheinbund Armies', paper presented to the German Studies Association, 2005. The officers cited were Marshal Louis Nicolas Davout, GD Antoine Charles Louis Lasalle and GD Dominque Vandamme.
32. Porbeck to Großherzog Carl Friedrich, 14 April 1809, in Erich Blankenhorn, *1808–1814: Badische Truppen in Spanien*, Karlsruhe: Armeemusuem, 1939, pp. 21–2.
33. During 1809, for example, frictions between General Vandamme and the Württemberg contingent under his command or between Marshal Lefebvre and the Bavarian corps required Napoleon's personal attention. On the other hand, German complaints sometimes seemed overstated. A case of misinterpretation and 'protesting too much' occurred in Spain when French commanders sought to express their appreciation for the German victory at Meza de Ibor in March 1809: when a French officer arrived to tell Porbeck that the German troops had rivalled the French in courage, for instance, Porbeck took offence because he believed the Germans were superior to the French in every respect (he had recently witnessed a disgraceful case of French indiscipline); Nassau General-Major Conrad von Schäffer was likewise annoyed because he interpreted this phrase to mean that the French had also performed well, when they had not been involved in the engagement. See Karl Franz von Holzing, *Unter Napoleon in Spanien*, Berlin: Hugo, 1937, pp. 121–2; Conrad Rudolph von Schäffer, *Denkwürdigkeiten aus dem Leben des Freiherrn C. R. von Schäffer*, Georg Muhl, ed., Pforzheim: Dennig, 1840, p. 170. Note that Schäffer had transferred to Baden service by 1813 and became Karlsruhe's representative in imperial headquarters.

34. See for example: Sheehan, *German History*, pp. 385–6; Planert, *Mythos*, p. 643; Ute Planert, 'From Collaboration to Resistance: Politics, Experience, and Memory of the Revolutionary and Napoleonic Wars in Southern Germany', *Central European History*, no. 39, 2006, pp. 694–705; Bleyer, *Auf gegen Napoleon*, p. 209; Aaslestad/Hagemann, 'Collaboration, Resistance, and Reform', p. 558, Karl-Heinz Börner, 'Krise und Ende des Rheinbundes – hauptsächlich unter militärpolitischem Aspekt', *Jahrbuch der Geschichte*, vol. 38, 1989, p. 13.
35. Quote from Nipperday, *Germany*, pp. 54–7, but see especially Breuilly's chapter ('Response to Napoleon and German Nationalism') on the role of 'modernisation'. See also: Michael Hughes, *Nationalism and Society: Germany 1800–1945*, London: Edward Arnold, 1988, pp. 44–52; M. Mario Kandil, 'Der Befreiungskrieg in Westfalen und im Rheinland 1813/14 und die Wirksamkeit des neuen Konzeptes vom Nationalkrieg', in Veit Veltzke, ed., *Für die Freiheit – gegen Napoleon: Ferdinand von Schill, Preußen und die deutsche Nation*, Cologne: Böhlau Verlag, 2009, p. 203; Armin Owzar, 'L'Historiographie Allemande et le Mythe d'une "Guerre de Libération" en 1813. La Cas du Royaume de Westphalie', in *Revue d'Allemagne et des Pays de Langue Allemande*, vol. 47, no. 1, January–June 2015, pp. 131–2.
36. Planert, 'Collaboration to Resistance', p. 679; also Poßelt, *Grande Armée*, p. 36.
37. Laurent Gouvion Saint-Cyr, *Mémoires pour servir à l'Histoire Militaire sous le Directoire, le Consulat et l'Empire*, Paris: Anselin, 1831, vol. III, p. 24.
38. Oberst [then Major] Ludwig von Seiboltsdorf, quoted in Alfred Auvera, *Geschichte des Kgl. Bayer. 7. Infanterie-Regiments*, Bayreuth: Ellwanger, 1898, vol. I, p. 469.
39. Dr Christoph Heinrich Gross, in Paul Dorsch, *Kriegszüge der Württemberger im 19. Jahrhundert*, Stuttgart: Vereinsbuchhandlung, 1913, p. 59.
40. Johann Friedrich Gieße, *Kassel-Moskau-Küstrin 1812–1813: Tagebuch während des russischen Feldzuges geführt*, Leipzig: Dyk, 1912, pp. 17–18; Heinrich Friedrich von Meibom, *Aus napoleonischer Zeit*, Leipzig: Koehler & Amelang, 1943, p. 109; Johann Philip Bauer to his brother, 15 June 1812, in 'Aus dem Leben des Kurhessischen Generallieutenants Bauer', *Beihefte zum Militärwochenblatt*, Hefte 3–4, 1887, p. 110; Ludwig Wilhelm von Conrady, *Aus stürmischer Zeit: Ein Soldatenleben vor Hundert Jahren*, Wilhelm v. Conrady, ed., Berlin: Schwetschke, 1907, p. 196. For other disgruntled Westphalians, see [Johann Gottlieb Haars], *Ein Braunschweiger im Russischen Feldzuge von 1812*, Braunschweig: Scholz, 1897, p. 2; and Fleck, *Erzählung*, p. 5 (though it is difficult to know if some or all of their anti-French observations were added later). Sam Mustafa detects a difference between the attitudes of officers and men in the Westphalian army: see his *Napoleon's Paper Kingdom: The Life and Death of Westphalia, 1807–1813*, Lanham, Maryland: Rowman & Littlefield, 2017, pp. 248–53.
41. Heinrich U. L. von Roos, *Ein Jahr aus meinem Leben*, St Petersburg: Kray, 1832, p. 5. At the same time, Roos, a Württemberg army surgeon, also notes the high spirits prevalent among many of his regiment's (3rd Cavalry) officers. See also Gill, 'Rheinbund in Russia', CRE, 2016.

42. Wilhelm Meier, *Erinnerungen aus den Feldzügen 1806 bis 1815*, Karlsruhe: Müller, 1854, p. 80.
43. Karl von Suckow, *D'Iéna à Moscou: Fragments de ma Vie*, Paris: Plon, 1901, p. 66; and Faber du Faur/Kausler, *Mit Napoleon in Russland*, p. 107.
44. For Baden and Hessian losses, see Jean Camille Abel Fleuri Sauzey, *Le Contingent Badois*, vol. II of *Les Allemands sous les Aigles Françaises*, Paris: Terana, 1987; and *Les Soldats de Hesse et de Nassau*, vol. VI of *Les Allemands sous les Aigles Françaises*, Paris: Terana, 1988.
45. General von Scheler to König Friedrich, 12 December 1812, quoted in Carl Theodor Griesinger, *Geschichte des Ulanenregiments "König Karl" (1. Württembergischen) Nr. 19*, Stuttgart: Deutsche Verlags-Anstalt, 1883, pp. 88–9.
46. Strength from the 7th Corps' 1 February 1813 'Situation', in Frédéric Reboul, *Campagne de 1813: Les Préliminaires*, Paris: Chapelot, 1910, vol. II, pp. 549–54.
47. Lieutenant S. M. Sotta to his brother, in J. Thomas, *Un Régiment Rhénan sous Napoléon Premier*, Liége: Vaillant-Carmanie, 1928, p. 62.
48. Cynthia Joy Hausmann and John H. Gill (ed.), *A Soldier for Napoleon*, London: Greenhill, 1998, p. 112; Andreï Popov, 'Les Bavarois pendant la Campagne de Russie', *Tradition*, no. 253, January–February 2011, p. 46.
49. Christian von Martens, *Vor fünfzig Jahren: Tagebuch meines Feldzuges in Rußland 1812*, Stuttgart: Schaber, 1862, vol. I, p. 260.
50. For an overview of the Rheinbund in Russia, see Paul Holzhausen, *Die Deutschen in Russland 1812*, Berlin: Morawe & Scheffelt, 1912.
51. Report of GM von Schäffer, 7 August 1813, GLAK, 48/4346.
52. Although the view of the French as arrogant and pretentious was commonplace, I will often caveat German complaints with cautionary words such as 'perceived' and 'alleged' because many cases of German complaints seem to arise from misunderstandings or the routine frictions of military life in wartime.
53. While not revealing all, the bulletin outlined the army's woes with uncustomary candour: 29th Bulletin, 3 December 1812, in Pascal, *Bulletins de la Grande Armée*, vol. V, pp. 328–43.
54. Friedrich to Wintzingerode, 17 January 1813, in August von Schloßberger, 'Mutige und treffende Erwiderung des Königs Friedrich von Württemberg auf einen ungerechtfertigten Vorwurf des Kaisers Napoleon, d.d. 17. Januar 1813', *Besondere Beilage des Staats-Anzeigers für Württemberg*, 1889, p. 297.
55. 'Suffocating' from Breuilly, 'Response to Napoleon and German Nationalism', p. 263; 'newly awakened' from Owzar, 'Liberty in Times of Occupation', p. 77. As Rink and Hofbauer comment (*Völkerschlacht*, p. 42): the question was opposition to foreign rule, not *Wille zur Nation* ('drive to nationhood').
56. 'Impervious' from Sheehan, who describes the zealots as 'patriotic poets and quaintly clad gymnasts' in reference to Friedrich Ludwig Jahn, later a member of Lützow's band and known as the '*Turnvater*' (loosely 'Father of Gymnastics') for promoting physical exercise as preparation for patriotic endeavours (*German*

History, pp. 385–6). 'Zealots' from Breuilly, 'Response to Napoleon and German Nationalism', pp. 274–5. In a felicitous phrase, Christopher Arnold warns about the 'perils' of taking elite opinion as typifying an entire society ('Westphalian Soldiers and the Myth of the War of Liberation – Evolving Notions of Identity, Francophobia, and Soldier-Masculinity in Napoleonic Germany', masters thesis, Texas Tech University, 2014, p. 78)

57. Ute Planert, 'Dichtung und Wahrheit. Der Mythos vom Befreiungskrieg und die Erfahrungswelt der Zeitgenossen'; and Birgit Aschmann, 'Von der ständischen zur nationalen Ehre. Statuskonflikte im Umfeld des Krieges 1813', both in Hofbauer/Rink, *Völkerschlacht*, pp. 278, 299–302.
58. Helmut Walser Smith, 'Nation and Nationalism', in Jonathan Sperber, ed., *Germany: 1800–1870*, Oxford: Oxford University Press, 2004, p. 251.
59. Karl von Suckow, 'Mein Feldzug im Jahre 1813', *Hausblätter*, Stuttgart, 1863, vol. I, p. 226.

Chapter 1: A War to the Death

1. Napoleon to Jérôme and other Rheinbund monarchs, 18 January 1813, Napoleon I, *CG*, Paris: Fayard, 2016, no. 32332, vol. XIII, pp. 118–21.
2. Rector Schrader of Küstrin in Berg, 'Die Erfahrungen und Schicksale Cüstrins in den Jahren 1813–1814', *Schriften des Vereins für Geschichte der Neumark*, vol. XXVI, 1911, p. 34.
3. The Convention of Tauroggen has prompted a considerable literature, especially concerning the question of whether Yorck acted on his own or had secret instructions from King Friedrich Wilhelm III. Michael V. Leggiere provides a tidy summary and analysis in his *Napoleon and the Struggle for Germany*, Cambridge: Cambridge University Press, 2015, vol. I, pp. 75–9. See also the historiographical review by Michael Fröhlich, 'Die Konvention von Tauroggen und die Instrumentalisierung eines Mythos', in Portal Militärgeschichte, 13 August 2014, http://portal-militaergeschichte.de/froehlich_konvention [accessed December 2022]. For French historian Jean-Baptiste-Adolphe Charras, Yorck's action 'announced to the princes' of the Confederation that their own people might rise up 'without them, despite them, and perhaps against them', see his *Histoire de la Guerre de 1813 en Allemagne*, Leipzig: Brockhaus, 1866, p. 57. Carl von Clausewitz, who was personally involved in the affair, opined that it was 'next to certain that the Russian campaign would have found its limit on the Prussian frontier' had Yorck not defected (Carl von Clausewitz, *The Campaign of 1812 in Russia*, New York: Da Capo Press, 1995, p. 251).
4. MacDonald to Murat, 31 December 1812, in Reboul, *Campagne de 1813*, vol. I, pp. 192–3. See also Jean d'Ussel, *La Défection de la Prusse*, Paris: Plon, 1907.
5. MacDonald to Berthier, 2 January 1813, in Charles Auriol, 'Retraite du 10ᵉ Corps de la Grande-Armée de la Dwina sur Dantzig (1812)', *Spectateur Militaire*, no. 42, July–

August–September 1888, p. 300. See also MacDonald's 5 January 1813 observations on Prussian attitudes in Ussel, *Défection de la Prusse*, p. 131.

6. Napoleon to Jérôme and other Rheinbund monarchs, 18 January 1813, *CG*, no. 32332, vol. XIII, pp. 118–21. Though catalogued as 'Napoleon to Jérôme', the same letter was dispatched to the rulers of Bavaria, Württemberg, Hesse-Darmstadt, Frankfurt and Saxony. The one to Württemberg's king was unique in containing additional text – see Chapter 4.
7. Ibid.
8. In some French correspondence during early 1813, the Poles still carried the title of '5th Corps' from the invasion of Russia.
9. As for Prussia, Metternich told Friedrich Wilhelm's personal envoy in January that Prussian alignment with Russia would be welcome, but that the time was not right for Austria to involve itself. See Oskar Criste, *Österreichs Beitritt zur Koalition*, Vienna: Seidel & Sohn, 1913, pp. 18–29; and Wilhelm Oncken, *Oesterreich und Preußen im Befreiungskriege*, Berlin: Grote, 1876, vol. I, pp. 110–56. Many French then and since, of course, have eschewed the exculpatory and rather anodyne term 'hedging' to describe Austria's behaviour as a treacherous 'double game' (for example Édouard Driault, *La Chute de l'Empire: la Légende de Napoléon*, Paris: Alcan, 1927, pp. 66–109).
10. Julius Ottomar Hermann Freiherr von der Osten-Sacken und von Rhein, *Militärisch-politische Geschichte des Befreiungskrieges im Jahre 1813*, Berlin: Voss, 1906, vol. I, p. 217.
11. Journal entry for 1 February 1813 published in Jörg Titze, *Journale, Tagebücher, Befehle (II): Journale und Rapporte 01.01.1813–09.03.1813*, Norderstedt: Books on Demand, 2020, p. 25. For Austrians and Russians sharing the same village for billeting, see for example Funck, *In Russland und Sachsen*, p. 221.
12. Napoleon to Eugène, 22 and 24 January 1813, *CG*, nos. 32400 and 32448, vol. XIII, pp. 154–5, 178–9; Eugène to Schwarzenberg, 30 January 1813, in Jean d'Ussel, *La Intervention d'Autriche*, Paris: Plon, 1912, p. 165.
13. From the Austrian envoy's 3 February 1813 report in Oncken, *Oesterreich und Preußen*, vol. I, p. 105. French historian Édouard Driault considered the Austro-Russian arrangement more deleterious than Tauroggen, *Chute de l'Empire*, p. 52.
14. Principal sources for this section are Reboul, *Campagne de 1813*, vol. I, pp. 315–61, vol. II, pp. 223–86, 548–51; Friedrich Luckwaldt, *Oesterreich und die Anfänge des Befreiungskrieges von 1813*, Berlin: Ebering, 1898, pp. 56–8, 74–87; Ussel, *Intervention d'Autriche*, pp. 137–71; and Criste, *Österreichs Beitritt*, pp. 5–18. Also: Pierre Juhel, 'Kalisch: La Dernière Bataille de la Retraite de Russie', *Tradition*, no. 196, January 2004, p. 6. Austrian histories of their Auxiliary Corps vigorously insist that Schwarzenberg's behaviour was entirely 'loyal and correct', see Moritz Edlen von Angeli, 'Die Theilnahme des k. k. österreichischen Auxiliar-Corps unter Commando des G. d. C. (später Feldmarschalls) Fürsten Carl zu Schwarzenberg im Feldzuge Napoleon I. gegen Russland', *Mittheilungen des K. K. Kriegsarchivs*, Vienna, 1884; Wilhelm Edlen von Gebler, *Das k. k. Österreichische Auxiliar Corps im russischen*

Feldzuge 1812, Vienna: Braumüller, 1863; and Ludwig Freiherr von Welden, *Der Feldzug der Oesterreicher gegen Russland im Jahre 1812*, Vienna: Gerold, 1870.

15. Jarosław Czubaty, *The Duchy of Warsaw 1807–1815*, London: Bloomsbury, 2011, pp. 179–86.
16. On Murat's departure, see: Andrew Hilliard Atteridge, *Marshal Murat King of Naples*, Felling Tyne & Wear: Worley, 1992 (reprint of 1911 edition), pp. 243–5; Marcel Dupont, *Murat*, Paris: Hachette, 1934, pp. 272–5; Albert Espitalier, *Napoléon et le Roi Murat*, Paris, Perrin, 1910, pp. 191–99; and Maurice-Henri Weil, *Le Prince Eugène et Murat*, Paris: Fontemoing, 1902, vol. I, pp. 423–5.
17. Eugène to Auguste Amalie, 17 January 1813, in Albert Du Casse, *Mémoires et Correspondance Politique et Militarire du Prince Eugène*, Paris: Michel Lévy, 1859, vol. VIII, p. 134.
18. Napoleon to Eugène, 22 January 1813, *CG*, no. 32388, vol. XIII, p. 148.
19. On French command and leadership issues in early 1813, see Frederick C. Schneid, 'The Dynamics of Defeat: French Army Leadership, December 1812–March 1813', *Journal of Military History*, vol. 63, no. 1, January 1999.
20. Morand had commanded the 34th Division of 11th Corps during the summer of 1812, but his subordinate units were gradually detached and the number '34' was transferred to a new division formed at Königsberg in the autumn under GD Louis Henri Loison – *see* Chart 47 in Vol. 2 of the present work.
21. Strengths taken from the archival 'situations' published as annexes in Reboul, *Campagne de 1813*, vol. II. This is also a good point to introduce the superb tome on fortress warfare in 1813 upon which much of this work will rely: Thomas Hemmann and Martin Klöffler, *Der vergessene Befreihungskrieg*, Norderstedt: Books on Demand, 2018.
22. Eugène to Auguste Amalie, 17 February 1813, in du Casse, *Eugène*, vol. VIII, p. 363.
23. Rechberg would be promoted to *General-Leutnant* (GL) on 24 March 1813.
24. Eugène to Auguste Amalie, 8 March 1813, in du Casse, *Eugène*, vol. VIII, p. 411.
25. See, for example, Charras, *Guerre de 1813*, pp. 122–37; Rudolf Friederich, *Der Frühjahrsfeldzug 1813*, Berlin: Mittler und Sohn, 1913, pp. 148–50; Francis Loraine Petre, *Napoleon's Last Campaign in Germany – 1813*, London: John Lane, 1912, pp. 35–46; Frederic Natusch Maude, *The Leipzig Campaign*, London: Sonnenschein, 1908, p. 75. David Chandler, on the other hand, castigates Napoleon for issuing what he views as impossible and unrealistic orders, *The Campaigns of Napoleon*, New York: Macmillan, 1966, pp. 869–70.
26. The following draws heavily on Leggiere, *Napoleon and the Struggle for Germany*, vol. I, Chapter 2.
27. Text in Feodor Martens, *Recueil des Traités et Conventions conclus par la Russie avec les Puissances Étrangères*, St Petersburg: Ministry of Communication, 1885, vol. VII, pp. 74–9.

28. Oberst Knesebeck, report of 18 February 1813, in Oncken, *Oesterreich und Preußen*, vol. I, p. 245; partly provided in English in John Robert Seeley, *Life and Times of Stein*, Cambridge: Cambridge University Press, 1878, vol. III, p. 82.
29. Dominic Lieven, *Russia against Napoleon*, London: Allen Lane, 2009, p. 300.
30. The re-creation of the Prussian army is the subject of a large literature. As a starting point see the Prussian General Staff work, *Das Preußische Heer im Jahre 1813*, Berlin: Mittler & Sohn, 1914. On Prussia in general, see Clarke's magisterial *Iron Kingdom*, especially Chapter 11.
31. Martens, *Recueil des Traités*, vol. VII, pp. 81–6.
32. 'Aufruf an die Deutschen', in *Das neue Deutschland*, vol. I, no. 3, Berlin 1813, pp. 363–4; parts in English in Seeley, *Stein*, vol. III, pp. 107–8.
33. Herzog Wilhelm of Oldenburg was the titular head of this committee, but Stein was its driving engine (Seeley, *Stein*, vol. II, Chapter VI; Lieven, *Russia against Napoleon*, pp. 290–3). On Stein, see Paul Schroeder, *The Transformation of European Politics 1763–1848*, Oxford: Clarendon Press, 1994, pp. 452–6.
34. He is sometimes referred to as 'Osten-Sacken I' to distinguish him from two other Osten-Sackens who rose to senior ranks during the Napoleonic Wars.
35. Albert von Holleben, *Geschichte des Frühjahrsfeldzuges 1813 und seine Vorgeschichte*, Berlin: Mittler & Sohn, 1904, pp. 240–1; Leggiere, *Struggle for Germany*, vol. I, pp. 99–103.
36. Intentions for the Streifkorps are in Julius von Pflugk-Harttung, *Das Befreiungsjahr 1813*, Berlin: Union Deutsche Verlagsanstalt, 1913, pp. 72–3. On the high morale of the men in these detachments, see Lieven, *Russia against Napoleon*, p. 298.
37. There is no congenial English translation for *Streifkorps*, hence my use of the term 'raiding detachment' as this conveys the types of missions these groups undertook. At the time, they would have also been known as 'partisans' ('*Partisanen*' or '*Parteigänger*'), but that word was in the process of acquiring new connotations in the Napoleonic period, especially owing to the war in the Iberian Peninsula. Prior to the early nineteenth century, 'partisans' had been groups of either mercenaries (in the seventeenth century) or a mix of regular and irregular troops dispatched by an army commander to operate in the enemy's rear areas. They were directly subordinate to regular government forces and did not have the ideological component now commonly associated with 'people's war' and insurgency. Over time, they became more and more regular in composition, so that the *Streifkorps* of 1813, as indicated in the main text, were led by regular officers and generally included a mix of regular troops (predominantly cavalry) and Cossacks with perhaps two to six light cannons. Although their missions included fomenting unrest and rebellion in the Rheinbund states, very few were composed of romantic volunteers motivated by pure patriotism. Lützow's iconic band was thus unusual and not as successful as the more 'regular' detachments such as Thielmann's and Chernishev's.

    For excellent introductions to the topic of partisans in this era and the transition to a new definition, see the essays by Beatrice Heuser, 'Small Wars in the Age of

Clausewitz: The Watershed Between Partisan War and People's War', *Journal of Strategic Studies*, vol. XXXIII, no. 1, February 2010; and Martin Rink's many contributions, such as his 'The Partisan's Metamorphosis: From Freelance Military Entrepreneur to German Freedom Fighter, 1740 to 1815', *War in History*, vol. XVII, no. 1, January 2010; as well as their articles and others in 'La Petite Guerre', *Revue Historique des Armées*, no. 286, 2017. Further references are in the bibliography. My special thanks to Dr Martin Rink for his generous assistance.

38. Karl Klug, *Geschichte Lübecks während der Vereinigung mit dem französischen Kaiserreiche 1811–1813*, Lübeck: Rahtgens, 1856, vol. I, pp. 110–32.

39. Paul Steinmann, 'Zum 30. März 1813' and 'Chronik der Stadt Burg Stargard und ihrer Gemarkung im Rahmen der Landesgeschichte', *Das Carolinum*, vol. 29, no. 38, 1963, pp. 3–16. The first Cossacks had appeared on Mecklenburg's borders in late February and captured some horses bound for the French army before riding off to the south.

40. The late Queen Louisa of Prussia was a daughter of Herzog Carl II of Mecklenburg-Strelitz. Not only was he Friedrich Wilhelm's father-in-law, but his eldest son and heir (Georg) lived much of his life in the Prussian court, while his second son (Carl) was a brigade commander in the Prussian army.

41. Herzog Carl II to Friedrich Wilhelm III, 31 March 1813, in Julius von Pfulgk-Harttung, *Leipzig 1813*, Gotha: Perthes, 1913, p. 20. Werner Behm, *Die Mecklenburger 1813 bis 15 in den Befreiungskriegen*, Hamburg: Hermes, 1913, pp. 17–31; Klaus-Ulrike Keubke and Uwe Poblenz, *Die Mecklenburger in den Napoleonischen Kriegen 1806–1815*, Schwerin: Förderkries für Festung Dömitz, 2011, pp. 41–7, 115–17; Heinrich Francke, *Mecklenburgs Noth und Kampf vor und in dem Befreiungskriege*, Wismar: Schmidt & Cossel, 1835, pp. 129–66; Ernst Boll, *Geschichte Meklenburgs*, Neubrandenburg: author, 1856, vol. II, pp. 364–8.

42. Christian Ludwig Enoch Zander, *Geschichte des Kriegs an der Nieder-Elbe im Jahre 1813*, Lüneburg: Herold und Wahlstab, 1839, pp. 20–3; Georg Cardinal von Widdern, *Die Streifkorps im Deutschen Befreiungskriege 1813*, Berlin: Eisenschmidt, 1894, pp. 17–18. German accounts, without citing specific sources, routinely state that Morand had to leave behind six of his guns when he took his troops over the Elbe on boats and ferries on 17 March. These claims seem to have been exaggerations for propaganda purposes. Both the Saxon regimental diary and Morand's report are very detailed and neither mentions any such loss: entry for 17 March, in 'Auszug aus dem Tagebuch des mobilen Linien-Infanterie Regiments Prinz Maximilian', SHSA, Generalstab, 11339, Nr. 287; and Morand's report in Jean Jules André Marie Eutrope Cazalas, *De Stralsund à Lunebourg: Épisode de la Campagne de 1813*, Paris: Fournier: 1911, pp. 11–25.

43. Frédéric Reboul, 'Napoléon et les Places d'Allemagne en 1813', *Revue d'Histoire*, vol. 42, no. 125, May 1911, pp. 267–72 ; René Tournès, *Lützen: Étude d'une Manoeuvre Napoléonienne*, Paris: Charles-Lavauzelle, 1931, pp. 32–3. Napoleon was likely also concerned with the large remount depots near Hanover and Braunschweig (Börner, 'Krise und Ende des Rheinbundes', p. 17).

44. Vincent J. Esposito and John R. Elting, *A Military History and Atlas of the Napoleonic Wars*, New York: Praeger, 1964, Map 127.
45. Tournès, *Lützen*, pp. 36–44, 114–15.
46. For example, Friederich, *Frühjahrsfeldzug*, vol. II, pp. 211–14.
47. On Kutuzov and the tsar, see Alexander Mikaberidze, *Kutuzov: A Life in War and Peace*, Oxford: Oxford University Press, 2022, pp. 490–505.
48. In Osten-Sacken, *Geschichte des Befreiungskrieges*, vol. I, p. 457.
49. The 39th Division was also to include the Frankfurt contingent, but those troops had not yet arrived. As for Bavaria, Napoleon expected the kingdom to provide two full divisions as it had in 1812; numbered 28 and 29, these were to be formed, as in 1812, as their own separate corps, the 9th (decree of 12 March 1813, *CdN*, no. 19698, vol. XXV, pp. 63–5). In the event, only one Bavarian division, the 29th, joined the Grande Armée and the 28th Division was never formed – *see* Chapter 3.
50. Sweden's warrior king Gustavus Adolphus fought his last battle there, winning a victory on 16 November 1632, but being killed in the process.
51. Napoleon had expected and rather hoped that the Allies would attack on 2 May. He remained alert to the possibility of being attacked, but when the early morning hours passed with no news of an enemy advance (largely because Ney had failed to conduct the reconnaissance as ordered); he decided to proceed to Leipzig as previously planned. For a discussion of his thinking and the distinction between 'tactical' and 'strategic' or 'operational' surprise at Lützen, see Charles Louis Marie Lanrezac, *La Manoeuvre de Lützen 1813*, Paris: Berger-Levrault, 1904, p. 162 and pp. 130–6. A colonel when he wrote this work, Lanrezac would become embroiled in controversy as commander of the French 5th Army in 1914. See also Friederich, *Frühjahrsfeldzug*, vol. II, pp. 55–6; Osten-Sacken, *Geschichte des Befreiungskrieges*, vol. IIa, pp. 379–90; and Tournès, *Lützen*, pp. 302–7.
52. Crown Prince Friedrich Wilhelm to Charlotte, Dresden, 5 May 1813, in Herman Garnier, ed., *Hohenzollernbriefe aus den Freiheitskriegen 1813–1815*, Leipzig: Hirzel, 1913, pp. 45–7; Leggiere, *Struggle for Germany*, vol. I, p. 239.
53. The large discrepancy in casualties may result in part from the French counting lightly wounded who were not considered 'wounded' in Allied registries; see Lanrezac, *Lützen*, p. 168; and Osten-Sacken, *Geschichte des Befreiungskrieges*, vol. IIb, p. 546.
54. Carl von Clausewitz, *Hinterlassene Werke*, Berlin: Dümmler, 1862, vol. VII, p. 309, originally published anonymously in 1813 as *Der Feldzug von 1813 bis zum Waffenstillstand*.
55. Lützow, report of 8 June 1813, in Fritz von Jagwitz, *Geschichte des Lützowschen Freikorps*, Berlin: Mittler und Sohn, 1892, p. 104.
56. Sources for Bautzen include Modest Ivanovich Bogdanovich, *Geschichte des Krieges im Jahre 1813 für Deutschlands Unabhängigkeit*, St Petersburg: Hässel, 1865, vol. I/2, pp. 49–83; Paul Foucart, *Bautzen*, Paris: Berger-Levrault, 1897; James R. Arnold, *Napoleon 1813: The Battle of Bautzen*, Lexington, VA: Napoleon Books,

2015; Friederich, *Frühjahrsfeldzug*, vol. I, pp. 245–92; Osten-Sacken, *Geschichte des Befreiungskrieges*, vol. IIb, pp. 97–215.
57. For an analysis of the Prussian capital in Napoleon's thinking, see Michael V. Leggiere, *Napoleon and Berlin*, Norman: University of Oklahoma Press, 2002.
58. The 2nd Corps and 2nd Cavalry Corps (approximately 14,800) also came under Ney's orders, but these could not arrive near Bautzen until 22 May.
59. These figures are derived from Rudolf von Caemmerer, *Geschichte des Frühjahrsfeldzug und seine Vorgeschichte*, Berlin: Mittler und Sohn, 1909, vol. II, pp. 160, 182; and Osten-Sacken, *Geschichte des Befreiungskrieges*, vol. IIb, Annexes XI and XII. Foucart gives the French 115,000 with Napoleon and 87,500 under Ney (*Bautzen*, vol. I, pp. x–xi); Friederich presents 93,800 Allies against 158,500 French (*Befreiungskriege*, vol. I, p. 279). George Nafziger gives a slightly different organisation for the Allies, *Lützen & Bautzen*, Chicago: The Emperor's Press, 1992, pp. 333–7.
60. Some commentators divide the fighting into 'the Battle of Bautzen' (20 May) and 'the Battle of Wurschen' (21 May).
61. Bogdanovich, *Geschichte des Krieges im Jahre 1813*, vol. I/2, pp. 66–8.
62. Alexander Ivanovich Mikhailovsky-Danilevsky, *Denkwürdigkeiten aus dem Feldzuge vom Jahre 1813*, Dorpat: Kluge, 1837, p. 101.
63. Lauriston had four divisions, but only two (18th and 19th) and his cavalry were immediately available: Maison (16th) had been detached by Ney and the 17th was still approaching the battlefield.
64. As with Lützen, the difference in casualties is striking and may be in part explained by how each side counted 'wounded' and possible under-representation of Russian casualties. In addition to Lanrezac and Osten-Sacken, see Tournès, *Lützen*, p. 360.
65. See Chapters 9 and 10 in vol. I of Leggiere's *Napoleon and the Struggle for Germany* for a thorough discussion of the heated debates within Allied councils during this period.
66. Text of the armistice and the convention extending it are in Georg Feodor von Martens, *Nouveau Recueil de Traités*, Göttingen: Dietrich, 1817, vol. I, pp. 582–8. For the location see Hermann Garnier, 'Wo wurde der Waffenstillstand vom 4. Juni 1813 abgeschlossen?', *Zeitschrift des Vereins für Geschichte und Alterthum Schlesiens*, vol. 38, 1904, pp. 362–3; and Otto Koischwitz, 'Poischwitz oder Pläswitz?', *FBPG*, vol. 17, 1904, pp. 246–53.
67. A resident of Küstrin, however, complained that, 'The Prussian supply wagons seemed to be hitched to lame snails' (Schrader, in Berg, 'Erfahrungen und Schicksale', p. 41).
68. Osten-Sacken, *Geschichte des Befreiungskrieges*, vol. IIb, pp. 475–92. Osten-Sacken notes that news of Napoleon's drive east and the armistice may have prevented the premature surrender of Modlin.
69. Napoleon to Berthier, 24 May 1813, in Foucart, *Bautzen*, vol. II, pp. 40–1; Friederich, *Befreiungskriege*, vol. I, pp. 304–9; Osten-Sacken, *Geschichte des Befreiungskrieges*, vol. IIb, pp. 394–419; Karl Heinrich von Prittwitz, *Beiträge zur Geschichte des Jahres*

1813, Potsdam: Riegel, 1843, vol. II, pp. 201–97; Leggiere, *Napoleon and Berlin*, pp. 74–88. For Beaumont's ad hoc command: General Ange François Alexandre Blein, 'Campagne de 1813: 1er partie – Historique du 12e Corps, du 4 mai à la rupture de l'armistice le 17 août', SHD MR 688.

70. By the end of the armistice, Wallmoden's command included Russians, Prussians, Swedes, Hanseatic troops, Mecklenburgers, the Russo-German Legion (former prisoners of war), Hanoverians of the King's German Legion, several small Prusso-German volunteer units and a British rocket battery. A brigade of British regulars under Major-General Samuel Gibbs arrived in Stralsund during the summer but was not placed under Bernadotte's command. From Barthold Quistorp, *Geschichte der Nordarmee im Jahre 1813*, Berlin: Mittler und Sohn, 1894, vol. I, p. 131 and Anlage 3; John W. Fortescue, *A History of the British Army*, London: Macmillan, 1920, vol. IX, p. 237.

71. French casualties in this affair came to 18 officers and 550 men (Adolf Brecher, *Napoleon I. und der Überfall des Lützowschen Freikorps bei Kitzen am 17. Juni 1813*, Berlin: Gaertner, 1897, pp. 20–1). Alternatively, Fournier's biographer gives the losses as four officers and 586 men: Jean Delpech La Borie, *Le Général Fournier-Sarlovèze: Le Plus Mauvaise Sujet de Napoléon*, Paris: Publications de Paris, 1969, p. 158.

72. This overview of the raids in May and June is drawn from Osten-Sacken, *Geschichte des Befreiungskrieges*, vol. IIb, pp. 453–75.

73. The complex diplomatic situation is beyond the scope of this study, for insightful overviews, see Leggiere, *Napoleon and the Struggle for Germany*, vol. II, Chapter 1; and Lieven, *Russia against Napoleon*, pp. 317–28, 356–68. For the tempestuous exchange between Napoleon and Metternich in Dresden in June, see especially Munro Price, 'Napoleon and Metternich in 1813: Some New and Some Neglected Evidence', *French History*, vol. 26, no. 4, 2012; also Wolfram Siemann, *Metternich: Strategist and Visionary*, Cambridge, Massachusetts: Harvard University Press, 2019, pp. 352–6.

74. Dmitry Petrovich Buturlin, *Tableau de la Campagne d'Automne de 1813 en Allemagne*, Paris: Bertrand, 1818, pp. 1–2.

75. Karl Falkenstein, 'Karl Friedrich Wilhelm von Gersdorff', *Zeitgenossen. Ein biografisches Magazin für die Geschichte unserer Zeit*, Series 3, vol. 5, nos. XXXIII–XL, 1836, p. 37.

76. Denmark was prompted to this move largely because the Allies had promised Norway (under the Danish crown at the time) to Bernadotte as a guerdon for his joining the fight against Napoleon.

77. Friederich, *Herbstfeldzuges*, vol. I, p. 62; Leggiere, *Napoleon and the Struggle for Germany*, vol. II, p. 79.

78. Leggiere, *Napoleon and the Struggle for Germany*, vol. II, p. 79.

79. Figures for mid-September: Bogdanovich, *Geschichte des Krieges im Jahre 1813*, vol. II/1, pp. lxxiii–lxxix); see also *Feldzug der Kaiserlich Russischen Armee von Polen in den Jahren 1813 und 1814*, Friedrich Karl Ferdinand Müffling, ed., Hamburg: Hoffmann und Campe, 1843, pp. 7–9.

80. Leggiere provides an illuminating description of the tangled development of the Allied plan in *Napoleon and the Struggle for Germany*, vol. II, pp. 51–60.
81. From Carl von Clausewitz, *On War*, Peter Paret and Michael Howard, eds, Princeton: Princeton University Press, 1984, p. 583.
82. Friedrich Vollborn, *Erlebtes (III) vom 28.03.1813 bis mit 15.03.1814*, Jörg Titze, ed., Norderstedt: Books-on-Demand, 2013, p. 41. The 7th Corps' order of the day for the celebration was issued on 7 August: Jörg Titze, *1813: Die Sachsen im eigenen Land*, Norderstedt: Books-on-Demand, 2013, pp. 189–91.
83. Martin Carl Ignaz Kösterus, *Die Großherzoglich Hessischen Truppen in dem Feldzug von 1813 in Schlesien*, Darmstadt: Brill, 1840, pp. 38–9. The term 'iron dice of war' is derived from Schiller's poem 'Die Schlacht', one of several instances in this war when participants referred to his works (especially this phrase and the questions of loyalty addressed in his 'Wallenstein' plays).
84. See Leggiere, *Napoleon and the Struggle for Germany*, vol. II, pp. 111–27 for a detailed discussion of Blücher's actions at this point.
85. Hubert Camon, *La Guerre Napoléonienne: Les Systèmes d'Opérations, Théorie et Technique*, Paris: Chapelot, 1907, pp. 227–30. There was also an important political dimension as discussed in Chapter 8, see Pierre Juhel, 'Dresden 1813', in Gerhard Bauer, Gorch Pieken and Matthias Roggs, eds, *Blutige Romantik: 200 Jahre Befreiungskriege*, Dresden: Militärhistorisches Museum der Bundeswehr, 2014, pp. 99–100.
86. The entire Army of Bohemia numbered more than 250,000, of which an estimated 80,000 might have been available on the afternoon/evening of 25 August. For controversies on troop availability and Allied command problems, see Friederich, *Herbstfeldzuges*, vol. I, pp. 175–81; Edmund Glaise von Horstenau, *Feldzug von Dresden*, Vienna: Seidel & Sohn, 1913, pp. 148–73; Lieven, *Russia against Napoleon*, pp. 392–5.
87. David August Taggesell, *Tagebuch eines Dresdner Bürgers oder Niederschreibung der Ereignisse eines jeden Tages soweit solche vom Jahre 1806 bis 1851 für Dresden und dessen Bewohner von geschichtlichem, gewerblichem oder örtlichem Interesse waren*, Dresden: Kuntze, 1854, pp. 133–9.
88. Some units covered 120 kilometres in three days.
89. Saxon Hauptmann Karl Heinrich Aster was at his post near a French hospital on the east bank of the Elbe when the sick and wounded soldiers noticed Napoleon and his suite across the river: 'Between apprehending this and seeming to fall under the magic spell of Huon's Horn was but a moment. Crutches, canes, shakos, caps, everything flew up into the air. Most hopped about as well as they could, even on one leg, clapped their hands and shouted "*Vive l'Empereur!*" so loudly that the sound must have reached the emperor. We Germans looked at one another in astonishment and observed with amazement these men who seemed already at death's door as they danced about just as the healthy did and behaved like children around a Christmas tree.' ('Darstellung der am 26sten August 1813 stattgefundenen Angriffe der alliirten Armee auf die vor der Altstadt Dresden erbauten französischen Feldschanzen

Nr. III. und IV. und die dazwischen liegende Seevorstadt', *Archiv für die Officiere der Königlich Preußischen Artillerie- und Ingenieur-Korps*, vol. V, no. 10, 1840, p. 204).

90. Karl Heinrich Aster, *Schilderung der Kriegsereignisse in und vor Dresden vom 7. März bis 28. August 1813*, Dresden: Arnold, 1844, p. 189. Heinrich Aster was the younger brother of Thielmann's chief of staff, Oberstleutnant Ernst Ludwig von Aster. See similar observations by Westphalian Hauptmann Johann von Borcke, *Kriegerleben des Johann von Borcke 1806–1815*, Stanislaus von Leszczynski, ed., Berlin: Mittler und Sohn, 1888, pp. 256–63.
91. Gersdorff's diary in Falkenstein, 'Gersdorff', p. 49; also in Aster, *Dresden*, p. 192 (Gersdorff's name is sometimes spelt Gersdorf).
92. Schäffer's observations about Napoleon's actions at the bridge and his 'laconic speeches' to the passing troops were similar to Gersdorff's, see: Schäffer, *Denkwürdigkeiten*, pp. 246–8.
93. Phrase from Saxon General Anton Larraß, in 'Zur Beurteilung der Schlacht bei Dresden', *Dresdner Geschichtsblätter*, vol. XIV, no. 3, 1905.
94. Losses from Glaise von Horstenau, *Die Tage von Dresden*, p. 137; and Horstenau, *Feldzug von Dresden*, p. 299. See also Carl von Plotho, *Der Krieg in Deutschland und Frankreich in den Jahren 1813 und 1814*, Berlin: Amelang, 1817, vol. II, p. 69; and Johann Sporschil, *Der große Chronik*, Braunschweig: Westermann, 1841, vol. I, p. 444.
95. See, for example, Rudolf von Caemmerer, *Die Befreiungskriege 1813–1815: Ein strategischer Überblick*, Berlin: Mittler & Sohn, 1907, p. 56; Falkenstein, 'Gersdorff', p. 53.
96. Tauentzien's other divisions were employed on the army's left and right flanks.
97. Wietstock is spelt 'Wittstock' in many older sources.
98. Frictions between Bernadotte and Bülow at Großbeeren generated enduring controversies. The most pointed issue revolved around which of the two ordered the attack on Reynier, but in a broader sense, many Prussians at the time and later doubted Bernadotte's commitment to the Allied cause and contended that he intentionally allowed the Prussian corps to fight without support while withholding his Russian and especially his Swedish troops. Similar accusations are associated with Dennewitz. In addition to Friederich and Quistorp, see Ernst Wiehr, *Napoleon und Bernadotte*, Berlin: Cronbach, 1893, pp. 89–232; Friedrich Meinecke, 'Zur Beurteilung Bernadottes im Herbstfeldzuge 1813', *FBPG*, vol. VII, 1894; Julius von Pflugk-Harttung, 'Bernadotte im Herbstfeldzuge 1813', *JdAM*, January–June 1905; Julius von Pflugk-Harttung, 'Bülows Bericht über die Schlacht bei Groß-Beeren und die preußische Zensur', *FBPG*, vol. XXIII, 1910; Julius von Pflugk-Harttung, 'Zur Beurteilung Bernadottes 1813', *FBPG*, vol. XXV, 1913; and Bernhard Schmeidler, 'Bernadotte vor Großbeeren', *FBPG*, vol. XXIX, 1916.
99. Times given for the march out of the woods vary from 3:15 to 5:00 p.m.
100. [Fabry], *Étude sur les Opérations du Oudinot du 15 Août au 4 Septembre 1813*, Paris, Chapelot, 1910, p. 114. Fabry notes that Oudinot had allotted GD Jean Marie Antoine

Defrance's dragoon division to Reynier, but the division, for unknown reasons, did not march with 7th Corps.
101. Oberst Carl August von Bose's journal quoted in ibid., p. 111.
102. Durutte's often-maligned division had fought skillfully and courageously on 22 August (Friederich, *Herbstfeldzuges* vol. I, p. 409; and Clemens Franz Xaver von Cerrini de Monte Varchi, *Die Feldzüge der Sachsen in den Jahren 1812 und 1813*, Dresden: Arnold, 1821, p. 227).
103. Oudinot's after-action report, SHD, 2C154.
104. Karl August Unico von Lehsten, *Am Hofe König Jérômes*, Otto von Boltenstern, ed., Berlin: Mittler und Sohn, 1905, p. 127.
105. In addition to the contemporary reports from SHD and Fabry, *Oudinot*, chief sources used for this account of the Großbeeren operation were: Frank Bauer, *Großbeeren 1813*, Potsdam: Vowinckel, 1996; Jules Duval, 'Napoléon, Bülow et Bernadotte', *Spectateur Militaire*, vol. LXI, 1905; Friederich, *Herbstfeldzuges* vol. I, pp. 347–423; Friederich, *Befreiungskriege*, vol. II, pp. 139–67; Pierre Juhel, 'Août 1813: Napoléon Face à l'Europe Coalisée', *Tradition Hors Série*, no. 10, 1999; Leggiere, *Napoleon and Berlin*, pp. 149–76; Thierry Louchet, *1813 La Campagne d'Allemagne: Les Opérations de l'Armée de Berlin et la Bataille de Dennewitz*, Part 1, http://www.planete-napoleon.com/rubrique.php?id=3, 2014, p. 15 [accessed August 2020]; Quistorp, *Nordarmee*, vol. I, pp. 267–308; August Wagner, *Plane der Schlachten und Treffen welche von der preußischen Armee in den Feldzügen der Jahre 1813, 14 und 15 geliefert worden*, Berlin: 1821, vol. I, pp. 45–56.
106. See GB César Laville de Villa-Stellone's 'Mémoire sur le Siège et Défense de Hambourg', in Charles de Mazade, *Correspondance du Maréchal Davout*, Paris: Plon, 1885, vol. IV, pp. 290–5.
107. Le Marois to Berthier, 4 September 1813, in Gabriel Fabry, *Étude sur les Opérations de l'Empereur du 28 Août au 4 Septembre 1813*, Paris, Chapelot, 1911, Documents, p. 52. For Hagelberg in general see Friederich, *Herbstfeldzuges*, vol. I, pp. 424–37; Quistorp, *Nordarmee*, vol. I, pp. 398–437; and especially Gaston Gillot, *Le Général Le Marois: Un Aide de Camp de Napoléon*, Paris: Conquistador, 1957, pp. 192–200.
108. See reports to Napoleon from one of his aides-de-camp, GD Anne Charles Lebrun, in Fabry, *Oudinot*, pp. 167–9.
109. These important battles are treated in summary fashion in this work as very few Rheinbund troops were involved.
110. Berthier sent three letters to MacDonald on 23 August outlining his defensive role as Napoleon headed for Dresden, see *Registre d'Ordres du Maréchal Berthier pendant la Campagne de 1813*, Paris: Chapelot, 1909, vol. II, pp. 78–82. Napoleon did instruct MacDonald to push the enemy beyond Jauer, so the Army of the Bober's advance was not entirely outside his imperial intentions. MacDonald's strength calculated from Thierry Louchet, *1813 La Campagne d'Allemagne: Les Opérations de Napoléon du 30 Août au 8 Septembre*, http://www.planete-napoleon.com/rubrique.php?id=3, 2014, p. 15 [accessed August 2020].

111. The 31st Division of 11th Corps with its Westphalian brigade and the 39th Division of 3rd Corps (Badeners and Hessians) were not involved in the Battle of the Katzbach, nor was the all-French 17th Division of 5th Corps. The only German units present in the vicinity were the Baden Light Dragoons of 3rd Corps and the lone squadron of Würzburg Chevaulegers with the 11th Corps light cavalry brigade.
112. A number of works cover the Battle of the Katzbach and the related mini-campaign. The current study relies on Friederich, *Befreiungskriege*, vol. II, pp. 103–38; and Leggiere, *Napoleon and the Struggle for Germany*, vol. II, Chapter 6 (the most thorough account in English). See also: Friederich, *Herbstfeldzuges*, vol. I, pp. 223–346; Pierre Juhel, 'Août 1813'; and Hugo Freiherr von Freytag-Loringhoven, *Aufklärung und Armeeführung dargestellt an den Ereignissen bei der Schlesischen Armee im Herbst 1813*, Berlin: Mittler und Sohn, 1900.
113. Frédéric Koch, *Journal des Opérations du IIIe Corps en 1813*, Gabriel Fabry, ed., Paris: Teissedre, 1999, p. 61.
114. MacDonald to Berthier, 2 September 1813, in [Gabriel Fabry], *Étude sur les Opérations du Maréchal MacDonald du 22 Août au 4 Septembre 1813*, Paris, Chapelot, 1910, Documents, pp. 55–6.
115. The only German unit at Kulm was the newly formed Anhalt Jäger-zu-Pferde Regiment in the 1st Corps light cavalry brigade (*see* Chapter 7).
116. On Kulm, see Heinrich Aster, *Die Kriegsereignisse zwischen Peterswalde, Pirna, Königstein und Priesten im August 1813 und die Schlacht bei Kulm*, Dresden: Adler und Dietze, 1843; Maximilian Ehnl, *Schlacht bei Kulm*, vol. IV, Vienna: Seidel & Sohn, 1913; Pierre Juhel, 'Août 1813'; Friederich, *Befreiungskriege*, vol. II, pp. 85–102; Friederich, *Herbstfeldzuges*, vol. I, pp. 503–60. On the question of responsibility for Vandamme's isolation and the destruction of his corps, see especially Ehnl; Gabriel Fabry, ed., *Journal des Campagnes du Prince de Wurtemberg 1812–1814*, Paris: Chapelot, 1907 (300-page introduction and annexed documents); Albert Du Casse, *Le Général Vandamme et sa Correspondance*, Paris: Didier, 1870, vol. II; and John G. Gallaher, *Napoleon's Enfant Terrible: General Dominique Vandamme*, Norman, OK: University of Oklahoma Press, 2008, Chapter 10. Prussian and Austrian histories often term the fighting on 29 August 'the Engagement at Priesten' after a village several kilometres southwest of Kulm.
117. Napoleon to Berthier, 2 and 3 September 1813, *CG*, nos. 36180 and 36195, vol. XIV, pp. 518, 524; Berthier to Ney, 2 and 3 September 1813, *Ordres*, vol. II, pp. 143–4, 152.
118. Principal sources for Dennewitz include Friederich, *Befreiungskriege*, vol. II, pp. 173–98; Friederich, *Herbstfeldzuges*, vol. II, pp. 108–77; Pierre Juhel, 'Automne 1813: Napoléon et la Bataille des Nations', *Tradition Hors Série*, no. 15, 2000; Leggiere, *Napoleon and Berlin*, pp. 189–211; Louchet, *Bataille de Dennewitz*, Parts 1 and 2; Quistorp, *Nordarmee*, vol. I, pp. 446–552; Bogdanovich, *Geschichte des Krieges im Jahre 1813*, vol. I/2, pp. 293ff.; Wagner, *Plane der Schlachten und Treffen*, vol. I, pp. 67–90.
119. Many of these casualties were likely 'temporary', that is, men knocked loose from their units who later rejoined (Quistorp, *Nordarmee*, vol. I, pp. 466–7).

120. 'Die Schlachten von Großbeeren und Dennewitz', *Denkwürdigkeiten für Kriegskunst und Kriegsgeschichte*, vol. VI, 1820, p. 151.
121. According to the 4th Corps' campaign journal, SHD, 2C448bis.
122. This low knoll lies between Dennewitz and Neidergörsdorf north of the Ahe-Bach. It had no name at the time of the battle but is now the site of a Prussian monument ('*Denkmal*') erected in 1817.
123. Mellenthin's name is spelt 'Mellentin' in the Saxon *Rangliste* for 1813, but the more common 'Mellenthin' is used in this work.
124. Plotho, *Der Krieg in Deutschland*, vol. II, pp. 170–1.
125. Friederich, *Herbstfeldzuges*, vol. II, p. 154.
126. Oudinot's decision stirred lasting accusations that, despite the obvious negative consequences, he mulishly obeyed an ill-considered order out of spite for being superseded and then being poorly treated by Ney (Friederich, *Herbstfeldzuges*, vol. II, p. 154; Quistorp, *Nordarmee*, vol. I, pp. 482, 516). For a defence of Oudinot, see Kyle O. Eidahl, 'He "Deliberately Obeyed Ney's Order": Oudinot at Dennewitz', CRE, *Selected Papers 1999*, Owen Connelly, Charles Crouch, Donald D. Horward, William Olejniczak and Michael F. Pavković, eds, Tallahassee: Florida State University 1999, and his 'Napoleon's Faulty Strategy: Oudinot's Operations against Berlin, 1813', CRE, *Selected Papers 1995*, Bernard A. Cook, Kyle O. Eidahl, Donald D. Horward, and Karl Roider, eds, Tallahassee: Florida State University 1995. See also: Jules Nollet, *Histoire de Nicolas-Charles Oudinot*, Bar-le-Duc: Rolin, 1850, pp. 184–5.
127. The French 156^e Ligne, part of the brigade that had moved up on the left of Gölsdorf, became entangled in the fighting and lost heavily, its casualties for the entire day coming to some 1,582 killed, wounded, captured or missing (Regimental report, 16 October 1813, SHD, 2C167; also Quistorp, *Nordarmee*, vol. I, p. 519).
128. 12th Corps' campaign journal, SHD, 2C448bis.
129. Oudinot's after-action report quoted in Georges Duroisel, *93e Régiment d'Infanterie, Ancien Enghien & 18e Léger*, Roché-sur-Yon: Ivonnet, 1893, pp. 232–3. The square formations may explain how 12th Corps had more than 3,000 dead and wounded despite only one brigade (Gruyer's) being truly engaged.
130. Brun de Villeret who also supplies an account of his frustration at the orders and counterorders he received, see *Les Cahiers du Général Brun*, Paris: Plon, 1953, pp. 154–7; see also Louis-François Lejeune, *Memoirs of Baron Lejeune*, London: Longmans, Green and Co., 1897 (Worley reprint, 1987), vol. II, pp. 288–9. Those wishing to visit the battlefields of Großbeeren and Dennewitz today will benefit from two little booklets by Wolfram Peche in his 'Sachsen 1813: Der militärhistorische Lehrpfad' series: 'Schlacht bei Großbeeren 1813' and 'Schlacht bei Dennewitz 1813', published privately, Sebnitz, 2015 and 2014 respectively.
131. Martens, *Vor fünfzig Jahren*, vol. II, pp. 80–1; Lehsten, *Am Hofe König Jérômes*, p. 133.
132. Quistorp, *Nordarmee*, vol. I, pp. 541–2. Although two Prussian Landwehr squadrons were present, the majority of these horsemen were Russian regular cavalry and

Cossacks probably numbering between 5,000 and 6,000 with a battery of Russian guns.

133. Some Russian and Swedish troops, mostly cavalry and artillery, joined in the fight late in day, their contribution being especially important because the Prussians were tired and some batteries were running low on ammunition. Like Großbeeren, however, Dennewitz generated enduring controversies over credit for the success and deepened the bitter feelings between Bülow and Bernadotte. In addition to the Großbeeren sources cited above, see Hermann Granier, review of Ernst Wiehr's *Napoleon und Bernadotte* in *FBPG*, vol. VI, 1893; Richard Haedecke, *Die Schlacht bei Dennewitz – ein Sieg Bernadottes*, Berlin: Schall & Rentel, 1916; Felix Rachsal, 'Bernadotte und Bülow vor Wittenberg', *FBPG*, vols. XXV and XXVI, 1913; Leggiere, *Napoleon and Berlin*, pp. 212–28.

134. Ney to Berthier, 10 and 13 September 1813, Gabriel Fabry, *Étude sur les Opérations de l'Empereur du 5 Septembre au 21 Septembre 1813*, Paris, Chapelot, 1913, Documents, pp. 40–1, 75–6.

135. Ney to Napoleon, 7 and 14 September 1813; see also two reports of the same date from Napoleon's ADC GD Anne Charles Lebrun, Fabry, *Empereur II*, Documents, pp. 20–2, 93.

136. 'Rapport du Prince de la Moskowa', *Moniteur Universel*, no. 263, 20 September 1813; and *Leipziger Zeitung*, no. 187, 29 September 1813, in Heinrich von Aster, *Die Gefechte und Schlachten bei Leipzig im October 1813*, Dresden: Arnold, 1852, vol. I, pp. 50–1.

137. Berthier, *Ordres*, vol. II, pp. 207–8.

138. Gouvion Saint-Cyr, *Mémoires*, vol. IV, pp. 150–1.

139. Funck, *In Russland und in Sachsen*, p. 293, referring to *Macbeth*, V. vi.

140. Jean-Jacques Pelet, 'Des Principales Opérations de la Campagne de 1813', 6th Article, *Spectateur Militaire*, vol. II, 1826, p. 33.

141. August Marmont, *Mémoires du Maréchal Marmont, Duc de Raguse*, Paris: Perrotin, 1857, vol. V, p. 273.

142. This includes Lefebvre-Desnouettes's Young Guard division, the light cavalry brigades of Piré and Vallin, parts of the Leipzig garrison and GD Lorge's division from 3rd Cavalry Corps, even though Lorge was not under Lefebvre-Desnouettes's command (approximate strengths drawn from Paul-Jean Foucart, *Une Division de Cavalerie Légère en 1813*, Paris: Berger-Levrault, 1891). The 8,000 does not include the Poles of 8th Corps who were later tasked to assist in containing and defeating the Allied raiders. Given the discussion of the term 'partisan' in an earlier note (n. 37, *above*), it is interesting to read that Napoleon directed Lefebvre-Desnouettes to operate '*en partisan*' (Berthier to Lefebvre-Desnouettes, 11 September 1813, *Ordres*, vol. II, p. 179).

143. Friederich, *Herbstfeldzuges*, vol. II, pp. 49, 94–8; F. J. C. Rothauscher, 'Das Wirken des Streif-Corps unter dem k. k. Oberst Emanuel Grafen Mensdorff-Pouilly im Feldzuge 1813 in Deutschland', *Österreichische militärische Zeitschrift*, vol. XVII, no. 1, 1876; 'Tagebuch des Streifkorps unter Führung des k. k. Oberst Emanuel Grafen

Mensdorff-Pouilly', *Mitteilungen des K. und K. Kriegsarchivs*, vol. III, 1904; Josef Siebert, *Über den Streifzug Thielmanns im Feldzuge 1813*, Vienna: Seidel & Sohn, 1895.

144. Friederich, *Herbstfeldzuges*, vol. II, pp. 188–94; Quistorp, *Nordarmee*, vol. II, pp. 71–4. The tiny garrison of Bremen capitulated to Tettenborn (leading perhaps 2,000 men) on 15 October; the French retook the city on the 21st but evacuated it again on the 27th after learning of Leipzig. See Wilhelm von Bippen, *Geschichte der Stadt Bremen*, Halle: Müller, 1904, vol. III, pp. 379–88; K. J. von Zwehl, 'Die Befreiung Bremens von französischer Herrschaft durch Tettenborn im Jahre 1813', *Bremisches Jahrbuch*, vol. XX, 1902, pp. 163–87.

145. Unlike most, the detachment led by Russian Alexander Samoilevich Figner acquired a notorious reputation for murdering French prisoners and other infamous acts. 'This undisciplined group of freebooters resembled a robber band,' wrote Russian historian Bogdanovich (*Geschichte des Krieges im Jahre 1813*, vol. II/2, pp. 23–4). Trapped by the French near Dessau in October, Figner died while trying to escape by swimming the Elbe.

146. Wilhelm von Hochberg, *Denkwürdigkeiten des Markgrafen Wilhelm von Baden*, Karl Obser, ed., Heidelberg: Winter, 1906, p. 237.

147. Margaron to Lefebvre-Desnouettes, 16 September 1813, in Foucart, *Une Division de Cavalerie Légère*, p. 57.

148. Gersdorff to Durosnel, 6 September 1813, in ibid., p. 6.

149. Napoleon was sending Schäffer back to Baden to report the victory at Dresden. Schäffer had to travel by the east bank of the Elbe and was indeed briefly captured and held by Cossacks near Torgau until freed by French cavalry: Schäffer, *Denkwürdigkeiten*, pp. 251–2. Schäffer encountered Hochberg after leaving Torgau (Hochberg, *Denkwürdigkeiten*, p. 236).

150. Rothembourg to Curial, 23 September 1813, Gabriel Fabry, *Étude sur les Opérations de l'Empereur du 22 Septembre au 3 Octobre 1813*, Paris: Laval, 1913, Documents, pp. 32–3. Examples of such concerns are innumerable: see, for example, Augereau to Berthier, 31 May 1813 and a 1 June 1813 memorandum by a staff officer in the 32nd Division entitled 'Marauders and Subsistence', both in Foucart, *Bautzen*, vol. II, pp. 240–67.

151. Horstenau, *Feldzug von Dresden*, pp. 100–1, 116–17, 167, 265.

152. Müffling to Knesebeck, 20 September 1813, in Julius von Pflugk-Harttung, *Leipzig 1813*, Gotha: Perthes, 1913, pp. 154–6; quote from Friederich, *Befreiungskriege*, vol. II, p. 223. Friederich refers to these bands as 'a plague on the land'.

153. Friedrich Heller von Hellwald, *Der k. k. österreichische Feldmarschall Graf Radetzky*, Stuttgart: Cotta, 1858, pp. 200–1.

154. Aster, *Dresden*, p. 125–6. Although anecdotal, it is interesting to note Aster's reading of local sentiment about the soldiers who passed through Saxony in 1813: all were trouble, often terrifyingly so, but the French and Prussians ranked as better guests than either the Austrians or Russians. The Russians were undeniably the worst in local eyes, but the Austrians only slightly better as they were followed by 'a horde of Bohemians, men and women, who were only concerned with theft and plunder

... they belonged in no way to the combat troops rather to the *thieving personnel* of the invading enemy armies' (emphasis in the original). In another of his works, Aster states that 'the objective German' will never forget Russia's assistance against Napoleon, while also observing that Russia was acting in its own imperial interests (*Kriegsereignisse zwischen Peterswalde, Pirna, Königstein und Priesten*, p. 256).

155. The Battle of Leipzig has generated a considerable literature in German and French, but much less in English. For an introduction, see John H. Gill, 'Battle of Leipzig', Oxford bibliographies, March 2017, https://www.oxfordbibliographies.com/view/document/obo-9780199791279/obo-9780199791279-0126.xml. Principal sources: Bruno Colson, *Leipzig: La Bataille des Nations*, Paris: Perrin, 2013 (the best single-volume history of the battle); Friederich, *Befreiungskriege*, vol. II, pp. 284–364; Friederich, *Herbstfeldzuges*, vol. III, pp. 1–234; Maximilian Ritter von Hoen, *Feldzug von Leipzig*, vol. V, Vienna: Seidel & Sohn, 1913, pp. 367–669; Juhel, 'Automne 1813'; Frédéric Naulet, *Leipzig (16–19 Octobre 1813): La Fin du Rêve de Napoléon et de l'Empire Français*, Paris : Economica, 2014, pp. 187–254; and Petre, *Napoleon's Last Campaign*, pp. 324–85. Gilles Boué presents an interesting table comparing treatments of Leipzig in various languages as of 2012 in his *Leipzig 1813*, Paris: Histoire & Collections, 2012, p. 5.

156. Friederich, *Herbstfeldzuges*, vol. III, p. 5. This description follows the overview he provides at the opening of his volume.

157. There was a fifth gate (the Schloßtor) in the city walls, but this led only to the Schloß Pleißenburg, not outside the city. For a detailed description, see: Aster, *Leipzig*, vol. I, pp. 25–7.

158. Petre, *Napoleon's Last Campaign*, p. 325.

159. In another of the controversies associated with this war, Napoleon chose to leave 1st and 14th Corps to hold Dresden, thus depriving himself of some 34,000 men (not including the 3,600 of the Dresden garrison). Even Pelet remarks that 'It is difficult to know the true intentions of the emperor relative to Dresden and the troops that were left there,' ('Campagne de 1813', 7th Article, *Spectateur Militaire*, vol. II, 1827, p. 188).

160. The Austrian army used the term '*Armee-Abteilung*' ('army detachment' or 'army section') rather than 'corps' in 1813 because the word 'corps' had become oddly discredited after 1809 (Hoen, *Leipzig*, vol. V, pp. 2–3), but by this stage of the war *Armee-Abteilung* and corps were synonymous in practice. I have thus retained the more familiar term in this text. Gyulai's command would have had a strength of more than 27,000, but he had left a number of detachments along the Saale River, reducing his total available for his main mission. Figures from the tables in Hoen, *Leipzig*, vol. V; but note that the following article gives a considerably lower number (18,922 not including the raiding detachments and not subtracting the troops on the Saale): Friedrich von Seidel, 'Die Mitwirkung des k. k. dritten, von dem Feldzeugmeister Grafen Ignaz Gyulai befehligten Armeekorps während der Schlacht von Leipzig, bis zur Uebergang der Saale', *Österreichische militärische Zeitschrift*, vol. III, no. 8, 1836.

161. Jean Nicole Auguste Noël, *Souvenirs Militaires d'un Officier du Premier Empire*, Paris: Rolin, 1895, p. 157; and Colson, *Leipzig*, p. 226.
162. Frédéric Jacques Louis Rilliet, 'Journal d'un Sous-Lieutenant de Cuirassiers', *Soldats Suisses au Service Étranger*, Geneva: Jullien, 1908, p. 135. As Bruno Colson points out, some of Rilliet's memories may have been romanticised for posterity, but it is not difficult to imagine such sentiments in the mind of a junior officer between great battles (*Leipzig*, p. 233).
163. Bulletin of 15 October 1813, Adrien Pascal, *Les Bulletins de la Grande Armée*, Paris: Prieur/Dumaine, 1844, vol. VI, pp. 158–64.
164. On Merveldt and Bavaria, see Humboldt to Hardenberg, 19 October 1813, in Pflugk-Harttung, *Leipzig*, pp. 243–5; Hoen, *Leipzig*, vol. V, pp. 577–8; Colson, *Leipzig*, pp. 227–8; Pelet, 'Campagne de 1813', 10th Article, *Spectateur Militaire*, vol. III, 1827, pp. 110–11; John Fane (Lord Burghersh), *Memoir of the Allied Armies under Prince Schwarzenberg and Marshal Blucher*, London: John Murray, 1822, pp. 349–56; Theodor von Bernhardi, *Denkwürdigkeiten aus dem Leben des kaiserl. Russ. Generals der Infanterie Carl Friedrich Grafen von Toll*, Leipzig: Wigand, 1866, vol. III, pp., 498–501, 612–15; Agathon Jean François Fain, *Manuscrit de Mil Huit Cent Treize*, Paris: Delaunay, 1825, vol. II, pp. 376–8, 411–16. Fane and Bernhardi include Merveldt's account of the interview. Metternich did not find it convenient to reply to Napoleon's message via Merveldt until 9 November, sending the captive French diplomat Nicolas Auguste Marie Rousseau de Saint-Aignan back to the emperor with an answer, see Saint-Aignan's reports in Fain, *Manuscrit de Mil Huit Cent Quatorze* in *Mémoires des Contemporains*, Paris: Bossange, 1824, vol. II, pp. 49–56.
165. Losses from Friederich, *Befreiungskriege*, vol. II, p. 360. On the French side, these include an estimated 15,000 prisoners, 15,000 sick and wounded left behind in Leipzig and 5,000 deserters or defectors. Colson (*Leipzig*, pp. 361–81) offers a thorough analysis of casualties on both sides.
166. Locals found 114 corpses of men who had expired unattended in one barn alone (Robert Naumann, *Die Völkerschlacht bei Leipzig*, Leipzig: Weigel, 1863, p. 140). On civilian sufferings in general, see Karen Hagemann, '"Unimaginable Horror and Misery": The Battle of Leipzig in October 1813 in Civilian Experience and Perception', in Alan Forrest, Karen Hagemann and Jane Rendell, eds, *Soldiers, Citizens and Civilians: Experiences and Perceptions of the Revolutionary and Napoleonic Wars, 1790–1820*, London: Palgrave Macmillan, 2009.
167. Christoph Heinrich Ludwig Hussell, *Leipzig während der Schreckenstage der Schlacht im Monat October 1813 als Beytrag zur Geschichte dieser Stadt*, initially published in two editions in 1813. A third German edition appeared in 1814 and it has been republished in many languages since. See, for example, that edited by Gerhard Graf, Leipzig: Zentralantiquariat der DDR, 1987. Hussell's work, of course, also saw many printings because its 'particular one-sidedness' conformed nicely to Allied and British anti-French propaganda themes and this edition, published in the erstwhile East Germany, suited the regime's pro-Soviet submissiveness. See Roman Töppel,

'Zwischen Altem Reich und Deutschem Bund: Eine Epoche im Spiegel sächsischer Publizistik und Historiographie', in Guntram Martin, Jochen Vötsch and Peter Wiegand, eds, *200 Jahre Königreich Sachsen*, Beucha: Sax-Verlag, 2008, pp. 197–8.

Chapter 2: Saxony: The Price of Loyalty

1. Quoted in Dorit Petschel, 'Die Persönlichkeit Friedrich Augusts des Gerechten, Kurfürsten und König von Sachsen', in Uwe Schirmer, ed., *Sachsen 1763–1832: Zwischen Rétablissement und bürgerlichen Reform*, Beucha: Sax-Verlag, 2000, pp. 95–6.
2. See Dorit Petschel, *Sächsische Außenpolitik unter Friedrich August I.*, Cologne: Bühlau, 2000. This opening section draws heavily on her outstanding work. See also Reiner Marcowitz, 'Finis Saxoniae? Frankreich und die sächsische-polnische Frage auf dem Wiener Kongreß 1814/15', *Neues Archiv für sächsische Geschichte*, vol. 68, 1998, p. 158.
3. Petschel, *Sächsische Außenpolitik*, p. 14. See also her (as Dorit Körner), 'Sachsen und Preußen am Ende des Alten Reiches', in Martin/Vötsch/Wiegand, *200 Jahre Königreich Sachsen*, pp. 69–81; and Isabella Blank, 'Der bestrafte König? Die sächsische Frage 1813–1815', dissertation, Ruprecht-Karl University Heidelberg, 2013, pp. 1–29.
4. Friedrich August had not sought the Polish crown (Karl Heinrich Ludwig Pölitz, *Die Regierung Friedrich Augusts Königs von Sachsen*, Leipzig: Hinrich, 1830, vol. II, pp. 3–36). Indeed, as elector, he had turned down the opportunity to become Poland's king in 1791–2 when it became clear that he would have little authority and when the agreement of the neighbouring great powers could not be assured (Petschel, *Säschische Außenpolitik*, pp. 121–43).
5. Carl Wilhelm Böttinger and Theodor Flathe, *Geschichte des Kurstaates und Königreiches Sachsens*, Gotha: Perthes, 1870, vol. II, pp. 655–61; Theodor Flathe, *Neuere Geschichte Sachsens*, Gotha: Perthes, 1873, pp. 3–21.
6. Jacques Marquet de Montbreton de Norvins, *Portefueille de Mil Huit Cent Treize*, Paris: Mongie, 1825, vol. I, pp. 323–4; many others used this description for Friedrich August as well.
7. Petschel, *Sächsische Außenpolitik*, p. 226, from Talleyrand's instructions to Antoine Marie Chamans, comte de Lavalette, 22 January 1800, in Lavalette's *Mémoires et Souvenirs*, Paris: Fournier, 1831, vol. II, p. 400.
8. Petschel, *Sächsische Außenpolitik*, p. 310.
9. Ibid., pp. 16–28, 140–1, 305; Marcowitz, 'Finis Saxoniae?', p. 161.
10. Ibid., p. 302.
11. Johann Georg, Herzog zu Sachsen, 'König Friedrich August der Gerechte vom 14. Dezember 1812 bis 7. Juni 1815', *NASG*, vol. XL, 1919, pp. 55–6.
12. Emmanuel Augustin Dieudonné Joseph Las Cases, *Journal of the Private Life and Conversations of the Emperor Napoleon at Saint Helena*, London: Colburn, 1823, vol. III, pt. 6, p. 26.
13. This section draws on Oskar W. Schuster and Friedrich A. Francke, *Geschichte der Sächsischen Armee*, Leipzig: Duncker & Humblot, 1885, vol. II, pp. 293–314;

Wolfgang Gülich, *Die Sächsische Armee zur Zeit Napoleons: Die Reorganisation von 1810*, Beucha: Sax-Verlag, 2008; Peter Bunde, Markus Gärtner and Markus Stein, *Die Sächsische Armee 1810–1813*, Berlin: Zeughaus Verlag, 2009; and Jürg Nagel, *Sächsische Soldaten 1810 bis 1815*, Leipzig: Engelsdorfer, 2015, pp. 15–44. Jörg Titze provides a tidy summary in 'Die sächsische Armee nach der Heeresreform von 1810 und der Feldzug von 1812', in Uwe Niedersen, ed., *Sachsen, Preußen und Napoleon*, Dresden: Sächsische Landeszentrale für politische Bildung, 2013, pp. 195–205. Marcus von Salisch observes that the Saxon military reforms are perhaps better characterised as 'a reorganisation' as they did not touch on the 'the link between the military and society'; see his 'Die Napoleonischen Kriege als Auslöser von Reorganisationen: Das Militärwesen in Sachsen nach 1806', in Niedersen, ed., *Sachsen, Preußen und Napoleon*, pp. 85–92, and 'Das Beispiel Sachsens: Militärreform in deutschen Mittelstaaten', in Karl-Heinz Lutz, Martin Rink and Marcus von Salisch, eds, *Reform-Reorganisation-Transformation: Zum Wandel in deutschen Streitkräften von den preußischen Heeresreformen bis zu Transformation der Bundeswehr*, Munich: Oldenbourg, 2010, pp. 105–6.

14. For example: 'Die Erinnerungen des Generallieutenants von Funck', *Militärische Mittheilungen*, vol. IV, 1830, p. 29.
15. For the Saxons in 1809, see Gill, *Eagles*, Chapter 6.
16. Gülich (*Sächsische Armee*, pp. 101–3) points out that some officers had already begun submitting reform proposals in 1807.
17. See the age charts in Gülich, *Sächsische Armee*, appendices.
18. The light regiments could be employed in closed order like the line infantry, but they were also issued a distinct regulation for their particular light infantry functions, see Jörg Titze, ed., *Reglement für die Königlich Sächsische leichte Infanterie zu den Uebungen außer der geschlossenen Ordnung*, Norderstedt: Books on Demand, 2011.
19. Jörg Titze provides a thorough treatment of the artillery reforms in *Das Regiment Artillerie zu Fuß, die reitende Artillerie-Brigade und Handwerker-Kompanie 1810–1813*, Norderstedt: Books on Demand, 2012; excellent illustrations of the pieces are in Stephen Summerfield, *Saxon Artillery 1733–1827*, Nottingham: Partizan Press, 2009. For an overview of all Rheinbund artillery, see Paul Lindsay Dawson, *Napoleon's German Artillery*, Morrisville, NC: Lulu, 2010.
20. Contemporary Saxon sources sometimes referred to these regiments as 'dragoons' or 'light dragoons' even though no Saxon cavalry regiment had carried the dragoon designation since 1790 (see Anhang 16, in Schuster/Francke, *Geschichte der Sächsischen Armee*, vol. III).
21. Jörg Titze, *Das Sächsische Artilleriekorps: Die Regimentsartillerie 1806–1815*, Norderstedt: Books on Demand, 2017, pp. 14–16.
22. The Jägers supplied their own firearms and were the only rifle-armed element of the Saxon army. The line regiment *Schüzten* carried the same smoothbore muskets as their regiments; the light infantrymen were also issued smoothbores, albeit of a different model with some improvements that enhanced aim. See Jörg Titze,

Die königlich sächsische Infanterie (I): Die leichten Regimenter, die Regimentsschützen und das Jägerkorps 1810–1813, Norderstedt: Books on Demand, 2013.

23. Note that neither the *Polenz* Chevaulegers nor the *Niesemeuschel* Infantry had proprietors (*Inhaber*) in 1813. They were both thus technically 'vacant' but are referred to here by their previous designations both in line with contemporary practice and for convenience.

24. The Half-Invalid Companies ('*Halbinvalidenkompanien*') were garrisoned in Waldheim (1st, 176 officers/men), Liebenwerda (2nd, 122 officers/men) and Colditz (3rd, 118 officers/men). Each infantry regiment was to have a depot of 3 officers and 60 (line) or 52 (light) men, while the cavalry depots were to consist of 2 officers and 100 men (Saxon 1813 *Rangliste* and Jörg Titze, *1812: Die Sachsen in Rußland*, Norderstedt: Books on Demand, 2012, p. 11).

25. As in, for example, Alexander Querengässer, *LeCoq: Ein sächsisches Soldatenleben*, Berlin: Zeughaus Verlag, 2017, p. 108. I have chosen to expend a significant number of pages here as the Battle of Kalisch is (a) important for the Saxon contingent's history and (b) little known in the English-language literature.

26. Camille Rousset, *La Grande Armée de 1813*, Paris: Perrin, 1892, p. 10.

27. Principal sources for this section on Kalisch are Cerrini, *Feldzüge der Sachsen*, pp. 117–36; Reboul, *Campagne de 1813*, vol. II, pp. 270–344; Marcin Baranowski, *Bitwa pod Kaliszem 13 lutego 1813*, Zabrze: Inforteditions, 2006 (with my thanks to Dr Baranowski for his kind assistance); and Pierre Juhel, 'Kalisch: La Dernière Bataille de la Retraite de Russie', *Tradition*, nos. 196, 199 and 201, January, April and June 2004. Cerrini is an excellent source and many, perhaps most, subsequent descriptions simply follow his account, but Reboul and Juhel are especially important as they researched the reports written by French generals, the corps strength reports and the corps march journal, sources that are not considered in almost any other account of the battle. Similarly, Baranowksi drew on Wintzingerode's battle report and Polish memoirs for his account. Also important are: Bogdanovich, *Geschichte des Krieges im Jahre 1813*, vol. I/2, pp. 17–21; Moritz Exner, *Der Antheil der Königlich Sächsischen Armee am Feldzuge gegen Russland 1812*, Leipzig: Duncker & Humblot, 1896, pp. 77–86; *Geschichte des Königl. Sächs. Königs-Husaren-Regiments Nr. 18*, Leipzig: Baumert & Ronge, 1901, pp. 200–1; Albrecht Graf von Holtzendorff, *Geschichte des Königlich Sächsischen Leichten Infanterie*, Leipzig: Giesecke & Devrient, 1860, pp. 104–8; Osten-Sacken, *Geschichte des Befreiungskrieges*, vol. I, pp. 221–33; [Ernst Otto Innozenz von Odeleben], *Sachsen und seine Krieger in den Jahren 1812 und 1813*, Leipzig: Hinrich, 1829, pp. 77–87; Plotho, *Der Krieg in Deutschland*, vol. I, pp. 45–7; Georg von Schönberg, *Geschichte des Königl. Sächsischen 7. Infanterie-Regiments 'Prinz Georg' Nr. 106*, Leipzig: Brockhaus, 1890, pp. 54–6; Schuster/Francke, *Geschichte der Sächsischen Armee*, vol. II, pp. 332–4; Moritz von Süßmilch gen. Hörnig, *Geschichte des 2. Königl. Sächs. Husaren-Regiments Nr. 19*, Leipzig: Brockhaus, 1882, pp. 129–31; Wilhelm Clothar Ferdinand von Wintzingerode, *General der Kavallerie Ferdinand Freiherr von Wintzingerode*, Arolsen: Loewié, 1902, pp. 82–6. For Polish involvement: Zdzislaw Jan Malecki and

Pawel Golebiak, 'Bitwa pod Kaliszem 13 Lutego 1813 r.', *Zeszyty naukowe – inżynieria lądowa i wodna w kształtowaniu środowiska*, nr. 13, 2015, pp. 76–84; and Janusz Staszewski, *Kaliski Wysiłek Zbrojny 1806–1813*, Kalisch: Towarzystwo Przyjaciół Książki, 1931. See also Otto Wilhelm Karl Röder von Bomsburg, *Mittheilungen aus dem russischen Feldzuge an einen Offizier des Generalstabs*, Leipzig: Engelmann, 1818, vol. II, pp. 237–9.

28. Cerrini, *Feldzüge der Sachsen*, p. 117. The regiment's four artillery pieces, however, remained with the corps (Juhel, 'Kalisch', *Tradition*, no. 201, June 2004, p. 34).

29. Funck, *In Russland und Sachsen*, p. 229. Georg Schmeißer provides a harsh critique of Durutte's troops: 'Die Refraktärregimenter unter Napoleon I. und die aus ihnen hervorgegangene Division Durutte', *Beiheft zum Militär-Wochenblatt*, no. 23, 1890; while a rather over-heated defence of the division is in Adrien Paimblant du Rouil, *La Division Durutte*, Paris: Charles-Lavauzelle, 1896. See also M. de Maindreville, *Historique du 132ᵉ Régiment d'Infanterie*, Reims: Michaud, 1890; and Alain Pigeard's archivally-founded article: 'Les Régiments de Réfractaires 1810–1814', *Tradition*, no. 167, May 2001. On Durutte as an officer, see Emilien Bossuroy, 'Le général Durutte: parcours de la carrière d'un officier au service de la France 1792–1815', dissertation, University of Louvain, 2019; and V. E. Mouthon, *Précis de la Vie Militaire du Lieutenant-Général Comte François Durutte*, Douai: Contrejean-Campion, 1836.

30. Marc-Antoine de Reiset, *Souvenirs*, Paris: Calmann Lévy, 1904, vol. II, pp. 265–7; and Alain Pigeard, *Les Étoiles de Napoléon*, Paris: Quatuor, 1996, pp. 538–9.

31. An anonymous officer's recollections in 'Bewegungen und Gefechte des Königl. Sächsischen Corps, im Feldzuge von 1812', *Militärisches Taschenbuch*, 1819, vol. I, p. 188. I have used 'restrained' here for the original '*vornehm*' which could also be translated as 'refined'. See also Funck, *In Russland und Sachsen*, p. 17; 'Bruchstücke aus dem im Nachlasse eines königl. Sächs. Offiziers aufgefundenen Tagebuch, und einigen an seinen Freund in Sachsen in dem Feldzug 1812 geschriebenen Briefen vom Beginnen des Feldzuges bis zum Gefecht bei Kobryn', *Erinnerungs-Blätter für gebildete Leser aus allen Ständen*, 1819, pp. 411–13; and 'Skizze: Der französische Divisionsgeneral Graf Reynier, Oberbefehlshaber des königlich sächsischen Armee-Korps im Jahr 1812', *ZfkWGK*, vol. LXVIII, 1840, pp. 61–9.

32. Ernst Otto Innozenz Freiherr von Odeleben, *Réclamations du Colonel Baron d'Odeleben au Sujet 1° de la Traduction qu'on a Publiée de son Ouvrage sur la Campagne de 1813; 2° de quelques Passages contenus dans l'Ouvrage de M. le Baron Fain, Manuscrit de Mil Huit Cent Treize pour Servir à l'Histoire de Napoléon*, Paris: Delaunay, 1825, p. 31.

33. Those too ill or injured to move had to be left behind in Warsaw. For the experiences of one of these soldiers, see Johann Gotthelf Jacob, *Lebenslauf eines alten Soldaten*, Dresden: Jacob, 1844, pp. 34–44.

34. Reboul, *Campagne de 1813*, vol. II, pp. 282–3, 288–9.

35. Friedrich Maximilian von Mandelsloh, *Erinnerungen 1812–1814 (II)*, Jörg Titze, ed., Norderstedt: Books on Demand, 2021, p. 35.

36. Reynier to Eugène, 12 February 1813, in Duc Georges de Leuchtenberg, *Le Prince Eugène de Beauharnais à la Tête de la Grande Armée (16 janvier–15 avril 1813)*, Paris: Chapelot, 1915, pp. 229–30. The order of the day is in Exner, *Antheil der Königlich Sächsischen Armee*, pp. 80–1.
37. Friedrich Vollborn, *Erlebtes (I & II)*, Jörg Titze, ed., Norderstedt: Books on Demand, 2016, p. 176.
38. The 2nd Infantry, with a number of veteran officers and NCOs, was of considerable utility. The 7th Uhlans, on the other hand, had a poor reputation for discipline and combat effectiveness. See Baranowski, *Bitwa pod Kaliszem*, pp. 116–18. Żółtowski's command also included the 14th Infantry Regiment, but this was posted off to the south and only joined during the retreat.
39. Carl Buhle, *Erinnerungen aus den Feldzügen von 1809 bis 1816*, Bautzen: Schlüssel, 1844, p. 59.
40. Polish units around Kalisch included: 2nd and 14th Infantry Regiments, I/15th Infantry, 2nd Uhlans, a company of gendarmes, a company of veterans, and detachments/depots of 5th, 6th, 7th, 8th, 10th, 11th, 15th Uhlans and 14th Cuirassiers, along with a horse artillery battery and train troops. Mariusz Łukasiewicz, *Armia księcia Józefa 1813*, Warsaw: Mon, 1986, pp. 167–9; see also Staszewski, *Kaliski Wysiłek Zbrojny*, pp. 93–4; and Reboul, *Campagne de 1813*, vol. II, p. 445.
41. The frequency with which marches were conducted at night or during the early morning hours in this season of limited daylight and cold temperatures is surprising and worthy of further study. A possible explanation is that roads and tracks froze at night making them easier to traverse as compared to the impossibly muddy conditions often encountered during the day; watercourses might also be reduced in volume by overnight freezing allowing relatively easy passage (with thanks to Donald Sommerville for this insight).
42. Juhel, 'Kalisch', *Tradition*, no. 196, January 2004, p. 7.
43. Cerrini, *Feldzüge der Sachsen*, pp. 125–6; Reboul, *Campagne de 1813*, vol. II, pp. 291–4.
44. Süßmilch, *2. Königl. Sächs. Husaren-Regiments*, p. 130.
45. Bogdanovich, *Geschichte des Krieges im Jahre 1813*, vol. I/2, p. 18; Osten-Sacken, *Geschichte des Befreiungskrieges*, vol. I, pp. 217–18; Fabry, *Journal des Campagnes*, Gabriel Fabry, ed., Paris: Chapelot, 1907, p. 42.
46. Russian numbers from Osten-Sacken, *Geschichte des Befreiungskrieges*, vol. I, pp. 514–15. He estimates Reynier's strength as 12,000, plus some 3,000 Poles very few of whom were fit for combat. Reynier's official 'Situation' gave the corps 14,178 as of 1 February (including 89 Polish Uhlans) once the battalions assigned to Modlin are subtracted (printed in Reboul, *Campagne de 1813*, vol. II, pp. 548–51). Juhel estimates the Russians at 13,500 ('Kalisch', *Tradition*, no. 199, April 2004, p. 20). The number of Poles engaged is very difficult to assess, though some/all of the 2nd Infantry Regiment as well as the Krakus and possibly some line cavalry participated in the fighting in some fashion. Most of the Poles were green recruits, some had no uniforms and many of the depot cavalry had no horses.

47. Wintzingerode's after-action report, Russkij Gosudarstvennyj Voenno, Istoričeskij Arhiv (RGVIA), fond 846, no. 16; courteously provided by Dr Marcin Barandowski.
48. Mandelsloh, *Erinnerungen 1812–1814 (II)*, pp. 37–9. In his report, Liebenau refers to the companies as 'divisions': 'Einigen Nachrichten über das Gefecht bei Kalisch dem Grenadierbataillon Liebenau betreffend', SHSA, Generalstab, 11339, Nr. 289.
49. Buhle, *Erinnerungen*, pp. 60–2.
50. Nostitz's 16 February 1813 report in Jörg Titze, *Journale, Tagebücher, Befehle (II)*, pp. 77–9; [Christian Gottlob Herzog], *Sieben Jahre aus dem Leben eines sächsischen Artilleristen*, Dresden: Arnold, 1845, p. 19.
51. Wolffersdorff quoted in Artur Baumgarten-Crusius, *Die Sachsen 1812 in Rußland*, Leipzig: Wigand, 1912, p. 215–16. The sections on Wolffersdorff in Baumgarten-Crusius, supposedly from the lieutenant's diary, have to be used with extreme care – even more than usual in dealing with memoir literature. Much material was clearly added later, and major parts of the text appear to be Baumgarten-Crusius's own views and inventions as Jörg Titze found in comparing Vollborn's actual memoirs with Baumgarten-Crusius's rendition (see his introductory notes in his fine edition of Vollborn's memoirs cited above).
52. Vollborn, *Erlebtes (I & II)*, p. 181; 'Bewegungen und Gefechte des Königl. Sächsischen Corps', p. 186.
53. Christian Friedrich Frenzel, *Erinnerungen eines sächsischen Infanteristen an die napoleonischen Kriege*, Sebastian Schaar, ed., Dresden: Thelem, 2008, p. 144; Vollborn, *Erlebtes (I & II)*, p. 183.
54. Wolffersdorff, in Baumgarten-Crusius, *Die Sachsen 1812*, p. 218.
55. Vollborn, *Erlebtes (I & II)*, p. 182–3; Frenzel, *Erinnerungen*, p. 144.
56. Frenzel, *Erinnerungen*, p. 144. I have made no attempt to render Frenzel's naïve orthography into English. Note, however, that I have translated '*mit Tapferkeit und Muth*' as 'with brave hearts' to provide something closer to what a British or American officer of the day might have said.
57. Frenzel, *Erinnerungen*, p. 145.
58. Wolffersdorff, in Baumgarten-Crusius, *Die Sachsen 1812*, p. 220; Vollborn, *Erlebtes (I & II)*, p. 184–5. Cerrini avers that some number of soldiers drowned in crossing the Prosna; both Wolffersdorff and Vollborn state they remember no incidents of drowning. Having had some small personal experience with wading through an ice-covered stream, the author can attest to the degree of discomfort involved.
59. Baranowski, *Bitwa pod Kaliszem*, pp. 141–2; Łukasiewicz, *Armia księcia Józefa*, p. 168; Staszewski, *Kaliski Wysiłek Zbrojny*, p. 93.
60. Anger's report, SHSA, Generalstab, 11339, Nr. 289.
61. Fabry, *Journal des Campagnes*, p. 43.
62. Cerrini, *Feldzüge der Sachsen*, p. 136. Carl Friedrich Ferdinand Böhme provides a personal account of the brigade slipping past the Russians into Kalisch: *Tagebuch 2te Periode (II)*, Jörg Titze, ed., Norderstedt: Books on Demand, 2017, pp. 94–102.

63. F. W. Winkler, 'Bemerkungen über den Feldzug gegen Rußland in den Jahren 1812 und 1813 mit Hinsicht auf Cultur, Sitten, Landesart und Gebräuche', https://de.wikisource.org/wiki/Bemerkungen_über_den_Feldzug_gegen_Rußland_in_den_Jahren_1812_und_1813 [Accessed September 2016]. This is a case of Saxons referring to the light cavalry by their outdated title as 'dragoons'.
64. Reboul, citing Reynier's 'Journal de Marche', in *Campagne de 1813*, vol. II, p. 305. Russian officer Vladimir (or Woldemar) Löwenstern blamed Wintzingerode for not acting with enough energy and coordination (*Mémoires du Général-Major Russe Baron de Löwenstern*, Paris: Fontemoing, 1903, vol. II, p. 10).
65. Karl von Oppell, *Sammlung von Beiträgen zur Geschichte des Königl. Sächs. 1. Leichten Reiter-Regiments vacant Prinz Clemens*, Freiberg: Gerlach, 1857, p. 72.
66. Ferdinand Heinrich August von Larisch diary entry, in August von Larisch, *Oberst von Larisch: Ein Zeit- und Lebensbild*, Dresden: Baensch, 1888, pp. 73–4.
67. [LeCoq], *Beleuchtung des zweiten Theils der Schrift: Mittheilungen aus dem russischen Feldzuge an einen Offizier des Generalstabs*, Dresden: Walther, 1818, p. 56. In addition to chivalry, it is possible that the Russians may have hoped that such courtesies would entice the Saxons to change sides.
68. As usual, casualty figures are difficult to ascertain with accuracy. The figure in the text comes from Cerrini and seems reasonable, but Reboul adds an additional 500. Bogdanovich estimates Reynier's losses at 1,500 dead or wounded and another 1,500 taken prisoner, but this seems far too high, not to mention Plotho's claim of 3,500 total Saxon casualties. As for the Russians: Reynier thought they had lost 1,800, Bogdanovich gives the figure as 670 and Plotho estimates 'more than 1,600'. Polish losses, if any, are unknown.
69. Saxon contingent's march journal printed in Titze, *Journale, Tagebücher, Befelhe (II)*.
70. Cerrini, *Feldzüge der Sachsen*, p. 125–6; Reboul, *Campagne de 1813*, vol. II, pp. 291–4.
71. Wintzingerode's after-action report, RGVIA, courtesy of Dr Baranowski.
72. The Poles retreated via Ostrów Wielkopolski where they were apparently joined by their compatriots of the 4th Chasseurs Regiment (Staszewski, *Kaliski Wysiłek Zbrojny*, p. 93).
73. Saxon march journal in Titze, *Journale, Tagebücher, Befehle (II)*.
74. Vollborn, *Erlebtes (I & II)*, p. 185.
75. Mandelsloh, *Erinnerungen 1812–1814 (II)*, p. 40.
76. From Titze, *Die königlich sächsische Infanterie (I)*, p. 18; and his *Die königlich sächsische Kavallerie (II): Die Chevauxlegers-Regimenter 1810–1815*, Norderstedt: Books on Demand, 2020, p. 19. Additionally, the 6th Hussar Squadron, serving as corps headquarters escort, had 23 troopers and an officer in the saddle.
77. Aster, *Leipzig*, vol. I, p. 40.
78. Letters to Reynier from Langenau (26 February) and Thielmann (2 March), printed in Pierre Juhel, 'Die Truppen des Rheinbunds im Jahr 1813', in *Blutige Romantik*, pp. 58–9.

79. Quote from a copy of a letter Reynier forwarded to Eugène on 26 February with the observation that 'it will let Your Grace know what they are thinking in Dresden' (Leuchtenberg, *Prince Eugène*, pp. 237–40). The original letter was delivered by a Saxon officer along with a missive from the king and was almost certainly one of those sent by the king's adjutant GM Friedrich Carl Gustav von Langenau. See also: Reboul, *Campagne de 1813*, vol. II, pp. 446–7, citing letters to Reynier from Langenau (24 and 26 February) and from Thielmann (15 February).
80. Approximately 600 Leib-Cuirassiers, 400 *Zastrow* Cuirassiers, 350 light cavalry, 1,000 infantry plus the artillery and train troops.
81. The tale of these several months is very complicated, with depots, remnants and individual officers shifting to and fro with bewildering frequency in these urgent circumstances. Sources employed here are *Geschichte des Königl. Sächs. Königs-Husaren-Regiments Nr. 18*, pp. 202–4; Süßmilch, *2. Königl. Sächs. Husaren-Regiments*, pp. 133–41; Georg von Schimpff, *Geschichte des Kgl. Sächs. Garde-Reiter-Regiments*, Dresden: Baensch, 1880, pp. 320–4; and Titze's studies of the Saxon infantry, chevaulegers and artillery cited above.
82. Text of the convention in Jules de Clerq, *Recueil des Traités de la France*, Paris: Amyot, 1844, vol. II, pp. 356–9.
83. Gablenz's strengths as of 26 February: *Polenz* (186), Hussars (154), horse artillery (85, including 9 attached *Schützen*), 1st Light Infantry (428 combined into one battalion, including 13 attached from the 2nd Light Infantry and 6 from the *Liebenau* Grenadiers), French *voltigeurs* (217 under Major Cailhassou of the 132^e Ligne). Sources: Gablenz's 26 February 1813 report in Titze, *Journale, Tagebücher, Befelhe (II)*; Holtzendorff, *Leichten Infanterie*, pp. 110–11. Some men of the *Polenz* Chevaulegers and many of Cailhassou's *voltigeurs* seem to have escaped with Maury as well: the Saxon contingent journal (in Titze) states these were present at Kalisch at the end of the day without providing numbers. Juhel's careful research gives the five *voltigeur* companies a total of 627 men on 10 February (Juhel, 'Kalisch', *Tradition*, no. 201, June 2004, pp. 32–3). Although it is possible that more than 400 men fell ill or deserted between 10 and 13 February, assuming Holtzendorff's figure is correct, the more likely answer to this conundrum is that the majority of the five companies split off from Gablenz's column and joined Maury in the darkness and confusion.
84. Oncken, *Oesterreich und Preußen*, vol. II, p. 238.
85. In Pölitz, *Regierung*, vol. II, pp. 97–100.
86. This brief but complex period would benefit from deeper research, especially integrating French and Austrian as well as Saxon archives. This section relies heavily on the most comprehensive analysis, that of Isabella Blank, 'bestrafte König', pp. 44–118, supplemented by Oncken, *Oesterreich und Preußen*, vol. II, p. 229–95; the king's personal notes in Jenak, '*Mein Herr Bruder*', pp. 187–9; and Roman Töppel, *Die Sachsen und Napoleon*, Cologne: Böhlau, 2008, pp. 158–203. See also Peter Wiegand, 'Neue Interessen und neue Gesichtspunkte – Friedrich August I. von Sachsen als

Verbündeter Napoleons', in Martin/Vötsch/Wiegand, *200 Jahre Königreich Sachsen*, pp. 82–122.
87. Saxony maintained these ambitious territorial aspirations into the summer of 1813, see Rudolf Jenak, 'Sächsische Territorialwünsche im Sommer 1813', *Mitteilungen des Vereins für sächsische Landesgeschichte*, vol. I, 2004. With thanks to Dr Judith Matzke.
88. Böttinger, *Kurstaates und Königreiches Sachsens*, vol. II, p. 514; Petschel, *Sächsische Außenpolitik*, p. 312. Subsequent historians such as Oncken and Osten-Sacken were contemptuous of Saxony's attempts to hold itself on a par with Prussia, the latter terming the neutrality plan 'utterly ludicrous' (*Geschichte des Befreiungskrieges*, vol. IIa, p. 199).
89. Zezschwitz to Senfft (date uncertain, but during the king's stay in Plauen) in Joseph Woldemar von Zezschwitz, *Mittheilungen aus den Papieren eines sächsischen Staatsmannes*, Dresden: Zeh, 1864, p. 135.
90. See Töppel, *Sachsen und Napoleon*, for reactions to the Allies and the distinction between the court and the larger population, especially Chapter 2.8. The 25 April 1813 Saxon report on the arrival of the Allied monarchs is in Rudolf Jenak, *Sachsen, der Rheinbund und die Exekution der Sachsen betreffenden Entscheidungen der Wiener Kongresses (1803–1816)*, Neustadt an der Aisch: Schmidt, 2005, p. 149.
91. Stein to Russian Minister Nesselrode, 11 April 1813. It is worth noting that Stein saw little value in Saxony joining the Allied cause, scorned the population (insufficiently zealous in his eyes) and denigrated the 'proud, weak, stubborn king' (Georg Heinrich Pertz, *Das Leben des Ministers Freiherrn vom Stein*, Berlin: Reimer, 1851, vol. III, pp. 328–31); see also Seeley, *Stein*, vol. III, pp. 105–32. Württemberg agent's report in Albert Pfister, *Aus dem Lager des Rheinbundes 1812 und 1813*, Stuttgart: Deutsche Verlags-Anstalt, 1897, p. 220.
92. The pragmatic Russian partisan and advance guard commander, Colonel Denis Davydov, found these 'frequent, pompous announcements' rather tawdry, 'silly, ready-made phrases ... like a supply of sausages to feed to the Germans'. Nonetheless, they provided him with 'lofty, empty terms' to use in addressing the Dresden municipal officials when his small band of Cossacks appeared outside Dresden's walls in March (Denis Davydov, *In the Service of the Tsar against Napoleon*, ed. and trans. by Gregory Troubetzkoy, London: Greenhill, 1999, pp. 193–204).
93. Zezschwitz to Wintzingerode, 30 March 1813, in Zezschwitz, *Mittheilungen*, pp. 226–7; Senfft to Thielmann, in Herman von Petersdorff, *General Johann Adolph Freiherr von Thielmann ein Charakterbild aus napoleonischen Zeit*, Leipzig: Hirzel, 1894, p. 156. See also Senfft to Watzdorf, 4 April 1813, in Oncken, *Oesterreich und Preußen*, vol. II, p. 260: 'In particular the proclamations to the subjects must shake the foundations of every legitimate government and, through their example, disturb the peace of every state.'
94. See Senfft to Zezschwitz, 4 April 1813, in Zezschwitz, *Mittheilungen*, pp. 231–2; and the objections raised by Karl Christian von Kohlschütter (an official who accompanied the king to Prague) in *Akten- und thatmäßige Widerlegung einiger der*

gröbsten Unwahrheiten und Verläumdungen, welche in der Schrift Blicke auf Sachsen, seinen König und sein Volk, enthalten sind, originally published in 1815 (in response to a scurrilous pamphlet attacking Friedrich August) and reprinted in Ludwig Lüders and Karl Heinrich Ludwig Pölitz, *Diplomatisches Archiv für Europa*, Leipzig: Baumgarten, 1823, vol. III, pp. 441–2. For a citizen's disgust at the Allied statements, see Friedrich Laun, *Memoiren*, Bunzlau: Appun, 1837, vol. II, p. 220.

95. Töppel, *Sachsen und Napoleon*, p. 193. A Württemberg diplomat at the Saxon court would write that 'there was no sympathy for Russia and very little for Prussia ... One feared the German Jacobins' (Christoph Friedrich Karl Kölle, 'Erlebtes vom Jahr 1813', *Deutsche Pandora*, vol. I, Stuttgart: Literatur-Comptoir, 1840, p. 214).
96. Senfft to Thielmann, 8 April 1813, in Flathe, *Neuere Geschichte*, pp. 147–8.
97. Johann Georg, 'Friedrich August der Gerechte', p. 56.
98. Arthur Brabant, *In und Um Dresden 1813*, Dresden: Köhler, 1913, p. 114; and Langenau to Thielmann, 28 April 1813, Petersdorff, *Thielmann*, p. 113.
99. Durutte's campaign notes, 'Papiers Durutte', Archives of the Royal Army Museum, Brussels (RAMB), Boite 43 (with thanks to Bruno Colson). Wilhelm Adolf Lindau, *Darstellung der Ereignisse in Dresden im Jahr 1813*, Dresden: Arnold, 1816, p. 14; Larisch, *Zeit- und Lebensbild*, pp. 80–3. The Immediat-Commission's 12 March report on the disturbances is in Jenak, *'Mein Herr Bruder'*, pp. 182–3.
100. Unpublished portion from the diary of Leutnant Ferdinand Heinrich August von Larisch in Töppel, *Sachsen und Napoleon*, pp. 281–2.
101. As the marshal noted in Davout to Eugène, 9 March 1813, Mazade, *Correspondance du Maréchal Davout*, vol. III, pp. 526–30.
102. Ferdinand von Funck, *Erinnerungen aus dem Feldzuge des sächsischen Corps, unter dem General Grafen Reynier, im Jahr 1812*, Dresden: Arnold, 1829, pp. 211–12.
103. According to a Prussian patrol report, Liebenau's men had been ordered to avoid all hostile action if they encountered Russian or Prussian troops: Armand Freiherr von Ardenne, *Geschichte des Zieten'schen Husaren-Regiments*, Berlin: Mittler, 1874, p. 353.
104. Lindau, *Darstellung*, p. 7.
105. Carl August Weinhold, *Die Elbbrücke zu Dresden, historisch und malerisch dargestellt*, Dresden: Arnold, 1813, p. 26.
106. M. Eckhardt, 'Briefe aus den Märztagen 1813', *Leipziger Zeitung*, no. 41, 5 April 1904; Lindau, *Darstellung*, p. 19.
107. Senfft to Just, 20 March 1813, in Töppel, *Sachsen und Napoleon*, p. 167. Camillo Graf Marcolini, one of the king's closest advisors, worried about the how the destruction of the two bridges afflicted the king, see Friedrich August Freiherr Ô'Bÿrn, *Camillo Graf Marcolini*, Dresden: Schilling, 1877, p. 165. On the Meissen bridge, see Paul Markus, 'Die alte Elbbrücke zu Meißen', *Mitteilungen des Vereins für Geschichte der Stadt Meißen*, vol. II, 1891, pp. 483–5.
108. Kölle, 'Erlebtes', p. 211.
109. Napoleon to Eugène, 18, 24, 26 and 28 March 1813 and Napoleon to Friedrich August, 8 April 1813, *CG*, nos. 33294, 33421, 33448, 33500 and 33735, vol. XIII, pp. 608–9, 659,

670, 689, 790–1. For Davout's correspondence relating to the bridge, see Mazade, *Correspondance du Maréchal Davout*, vol. III, pp. 532–53.
110. The timing and motivation of the orders to LeCoq are unclear. LeCoq received his instructions on 21 March and some authors see this move as a royal reaction to the destruction of the bridge, but Davout was already reporting the possible Saxon shift to Torgau on 18 March, *before* the bridge was damaged (Davout to Eugène, 18 March 1813, no. 1233, *Correspondance du Maréchal Davout*, vol. III, p. 552). Blank ('bestrafte König', p. 72) describes the orders as a protective measure, prudent hedging rather than evidence of a decisive break. In a 14 April letter, Major Heinrich Carl Friedrich Ferdinand von Hausen, one of the officers in the garrison, told his brother that LeCoq had used reorganisation as a 'pretence' to slip out from under French orders (*Tagebuch und Briefe, 01.01.1812–02.02.1814*, Jörg Titze, ed., Norderstedt: Books on Demand, 2019, p. 45).
111. There are two points of confusion here. First is that some Saxon sources (e.g., Flathe, *Neuere Geschichte*, p. 123), state that the 100 Saxon troopers and four officers soon left on the initiative of the major commanding them – not as a result of any instructions – and that the major was later dismissed by the king. There is, however, no indication of any such insubordination in the 7th Corps report of events in late March, which simply states that the Saxon troopers departed for the cavalry depot in Plauen on 31 March; and Durutte merely notes that the commander was Major Friedrich von Fabrice of the Hussar Regiment (7th Corps 'Situation', 1 April 1813, SHD, 2C541; Durutte's campaign notes, RAMB, Boite 43). Second, Berthier told Napoleon that the lone squadron of Würzburg troopers in the field was attached to Durutte (Berthier to Napoleon, 16 April 1813, *Rapports*, vol. I, p. 37), but this small unit does not appear in any of the 7th Corps strength reports, but repeatedly appears in the 11th Corps 'Situations' for this time period and the rest of the war. Nor is there any reference to such an assignment in the quasi-history of the unit (Hermann Helmes, 'Die Würzburger Chevaulegers im Feldzuge 1812/13', *DBKHG*, vol. 11, 1902). It seems likely that Berthier confused the Wüzburg men with the Bavarian light horse.
112. Davout to Eugène, 23 March 1813, no. 1237, *Correspondance du Maréchal Davout*, vol. III, pp. 554–7.
113. Flathe, *Neuere Geschichte*, p. 124.
114. Langenau to Just (Saxon ambassador in Paris), 14 or 15 March 1813, in Petersdorff, *Thielmann*, p. 134.
115. 7th Corps 'Situation' for 1 April 1813, SHD, 2C541. This included 1,182 French, 109 Würzburgers, 1,449 Bavarians (still carried as the '19th Division' from 1812) and the 100 Saxon light cavalry (the latter not listed in the 'Situation').
116. Davydov was very pleased to have captured the Dresden Neustadt with his band of only 500 or so Cossack irregulars. His superior, however, General Wintzingerode, was furious, apparently because he wanted the prestige associated with capturing the Saxon capital for himself. He sent Davydov back to Kalisch to face examination and possible punishment for concluding a ceasefire without authorisation. Fortunately

for Davydov, the tsar and Kutuzov dismissed these charges; he was soon back at the battle front to end 1814 as a major general. See his *In the Service of the Tsar*, Chapter 8; and Vladimir Ivanovich von Löwenstern, *Mémoires*, Paris: Fontemoing, 1903, vol. II, p. 14.

117. This chronology of the events in Dresden between 7 and 27 March relies largely on Aster, *Dresden*, pp. 18–37; he addressed the technical aspects of the bridge mine and the subsequent rebuilding in 'Nachrichten über die Sprengung der Dresdener Elb-Brücke', *Archiv für die Officiere der Königlich Preußischen Artillerie- und Ingenier-Korps*, vol. IV, no. 7, 1838. Lindau, *Darstellung*, pp. 192–205 prints copies of the various municipal orders associated with this phase of the war. See also: Wilhelm Schäfer, *Chronik der Dresdner Elbbrücke*, Dresden: Adler und Dietze, 1848; Martin B. Lindau, *Geschichte der Haupt- und Residenzstadt Dresden*, Dresden: Kuntze, 1860.

118. Drawn from the 'Rapports' sections of the 7th Corps' 'Situations' for 1 and 15 April 1813, SHD, 2C541.

119. André Bonnefons, *Un Allié de Napoléon: Frédéric Auguste*, Paris: Perrin, 1902, pp. 404–5.

120. Friedrich Wilhelm's letter (9 April) and Friedrich August's reply (16 April) are in Johann Ludwig Klüber, *Acten des Wiener Congresses in den Jahren 1814 und 1815*, vol. VII, Erlangen: Palm und Enke, 1817, pp. 271–9. See also Johann Justus von Vieth, *Auszüge aus den Papieren eines Sachsen: Anekdoten und Ereignisse als Beiträge zur Geschichte des Königreichs Sachsen in den Jahren 1812 bis 1815*, Meißen: Klinkicht, 1843, p. 19. Prussia chose GM Levin Karl von Heister to deliver the king's message to Friedrich August in Regensburg; Napoleon, learning of his mission, directed Bertrand to 'Write to the Bavarians to attempt to arrest him' (Napoleon to Bertrand, 20 April 1813, *CG*, no. 33945, vol. XIII, p. 875).

121. Sources for the notion of a multilateral pact include: Flathe, *Neuere Geschichte*, pp. 127–9; Bonnefons, *Allié de Napoléon*, p. 401; Blank, 'bestrafte König', pp. 88–9, 101–5; Rudolf Jenak, 'Der königlich-sächsische Generalleutnant Johann Adolph von Thielmann als Kommandant der Landesfestung Torgau', *Mitteilungen des Vereins für sächsische Landesgeschichte*, vol. 10, 2012. The evaporation of this initiative was yet another example of the inability of the Rheinbund princes to collaborate, even in trying to escape the alliance.

122. Carl Wilhelm Böttinger, *Geschichte des Kurstaates und Königreiches Sachsens*, Hamburg: Perthes, 1831, vol. II, pp. 516–17; Schroeder, *Transformation*, pp. 464, 478–9.

123. Flathe, *Neuere Geschichte*, p. 152.

124. The convention is printed in Oncken, *Oesterreich und Preußen*, vol. II, pp. 636–7. Rudolf Jenak provides the Saxon drafts of the convention and describes the document as a result of the 'inner disunity, vacillation and characteristic imbalance' of the Saxon court: 'Die Realität der Österreichisch-sächsischen Konvention vom 20. April 1813', *Mitteilungen des Vereins für sächsische Landesgeschichte*, vol. V, 2007.

125. Austrian ambassador's report of a meeting with Senfft on 12 March in Oncken, *Oesterreich und Preußen*, vol. II, pp. 249–50.

126. Senfft to Zezschwitz, 30 April 1813, in Zezschwitz, *Mittheilungen*, p. 253.
127. Friedrich Christian Ludwig Graf Senfft von Pilsach, *Mémoires*, Leipzig: Veit, 1863, pp. 224–6; Hans Block, *Sachsen im Zeitalter der Völkerschlacht*, Leipzig: Leipziger Buchdruckerei, 1913, p. 73; Oncken, *Oesterreich und Preußen*, vol. II, pp. 282–93.
128. Napoleon to Friedrich August, 2 March, 6 March, 8 April, 15 April and 20 April 1813 (three letters), *CG*, nos. 32946, 33049, 33735, 33869, 33949, 33950, 33951, vol. XIII, pp. 441, 491, 790–1, 844, 877–8. Napoleon to Berthier, 19 April 1813, *CG*, no. 33916, vol. XIII, pp. 861–3. Napoleon to Maret, 1 April, 2 April, 4 April, 20 April 1813, *CG*, nos. 33565, 33590, 33631, 33955, vol. XIII, pp. 715, 730, 748–9, 879. Napoleon to Ney, 28 March 1813, *CG*, no. 33507, vol. XIII, p. 692.
129. Napoleon to Friedrich of Württemberg, 24 April 1813, *CG*, no. 34004, vol. XIII, pp. 901–2.
130. Blank, 'bestrafte König', pp. 61–6. The convention is printed in Martens, *Nouveau Recueil de Traités*, vol. I, pp. 591–5, albeit with the wrong date (8 *August* rather than April); this incorrect date was taken from the *Moniteur Universel* of 5 October 1813, no. 278 and carried forward in subsequent editions of Martens's work.
131. Napoleon to Maret, 28 April 1813, *CG*, no. 34041, vol. XIII, p. 919; Caulaincourt to GD Narbonne, 4 May 1813, in Norvins, *Portefeuille*, vol. I, pp. 293–6.
132. Friedrich August to Napoleon, 17, 19, and 24 April 1813, in Jenak, 'Mein Herr Bruder', pp. 150–6; Minister Hans August Fürchtegott von Globig's 9 May 1813 report in 'Miscellen', *Archiv für die Sächsische Geschichte*, vol. IV, 1878, pp. 360–3.
133. Napoleon had begun to suspect that something was afoot between his two nominal allies and that Friedrich August perhaps hoped 'to relieve his country by staying neutral' (Caulaincourt to Narbonne, 24 April 1813, in Norvins, *Portefeuille* vol. I, pp. 231–5); Tournès, *Lützen*, pp. 61–2.
134. Carl August to Friedrich August, 29 April 1813, in Flathe, *Neuere Geschichte*, pp. 348–9.
135. Gretschel/Bülau, *Sächsischen Volkes*, p. 475; and Petersdorff, *Thielmann*, pp. 201–2.
136. The letters to Friedrich Wilhelm III are in Klüber, *Acten des Wiener Congresses*, vol. VII, pp. 279–80. See also Otto Eduard Schmidt, 'Carl Adolf von Carlowitz und Ferdinand Funck', *NASG*, vol. LX, 1934.
137. Senfft to Watzdorf (enciphered), 7 May 1813, in Rudolf Jenak, 'Siegesmeldungen nach der Schlacht bei Lützen vom 2. Mai 1813', Dresden: n. p., 2018, p. 12 (with thanks to Martin Munke); Pölitz, *Regierung*, vol. II, p. 109.
138. Petersdorff, *Thielmann*, pp. 200, 219–20.
139. Senfft to Watzdorf, 7 May 1813, Jenak, 'Siegesmeldungen', p. 13; Rudolf Jenak, 'Die Note des Barons von Serra vom 8. Mai 1813 an den sächsischen König', *NASG*, vol. LXXXIII, 2012; Pflugk-Harttung, *Befreiungsjahr*, pp. 131–2.
140. Thielmann to Ney, 8 May 1813, in Albrecht Graf von Holtzendorff, *Beiträge zu der Biographie des Generals Freiherrn von Thielmann*, Leipzig: Nauck, 1830, p. 237; Ney to Napoleon, 2000, 8 May 1813, Foucart, *Bautzen*, vol. I, pp. 102–3.
141. Minister Johann Georg Friedrich von Friesen's report in Hermann Freiherr von Friesen, 'Napoleon in Dresden (8. Mai 1813)', *NASG*, vol. II, 1881, pp. 237–50.

142. Stadion's instructions, dated 7 May 1813, are in Oncken, *Oesterreich und Preußen*, vol. II, pp. 640–4. Watzdorf had discussed Stadion's mission with Metternich and relayed Saxony's concerns; Stadion would have heard similar points from the Saxons in Prague; he was then to call on the Allied leaders. In other words, Stadion was to meet the Allied powers first, *before* conducting any substantive negotiations with Saxony (Blank, 'bestrafte König', pp. 111–18).
143. Senfft to Watzdorf, 8 May 1813, Oncken, *Oesterreich und Preußen*, vol. II, pp. 288–9. Funck, criticising the move to Prague, ruefully observed that Napoleon would have forgiven Friedrich August had the king remained in Saxony or Bavaria and eschewed the approach to Austria, but having gone to Prague, he now had to return to the Napoleonic fold as a penitent (Funck, *Erinnerungen*, pp. 277–8).
144. Friedrich August to Napoleon, 8 and 10 May 1813, in Jenak, ed., *'Mein Herr Bruder'*, pp. 157–8. Friedrich August to Thielmann, 8 May 1813, in Holtzendorff, *Beiträge*, p. 238. Gersdorff was instructed to dissemble if asked about the convention with Austria, admitting that there had been discussions but denying any knowledge of the agreement (Friedrich August, instructions for Gersdorff, 8 May 1813, in Jenak, 'Thielmann', pp. 27–8).
145. In other words, the Saxon decision had already been taken *before* the arrival of Napoleon's latest and most threatening ultimatum: Böttinger, *Kurstaates und Königreiches Sachsens*, vol. II, p. 520; Blank, 'bestrafte König', p. 115; Falkenstein, 'Gersdorff', pp. 32–3. The Immediat-Commission reported Napoleon's words to Friedrich August on 8 May 1813, in Jenak, *Sachsen, der Rheinbund und die Exekution*, pp. 150–1.
146. Blank, 'bestrafte König', p. 119; Johann Georg, Herzog zu Sachsen, 'Karl von Watzdorf, 1759–1840', *NASG*, vol. XXXIX, 1918, pp. 16–21; and Roman Töppel, 'Watzdorf, Karl Friedrich Ludwig von', in *Sächsische Biografie*, herausgegeben vom Institut für Sächsische Geschichte und Volkskunde e.V., wissenschaftliche Leitung: Martina Schattkowsky, Online-Ausgabe: http://www.isgv.de/saebi [accessed December 2016]. Contrary to some descriptions, Napoleon did not demand their dismissal: Johann Georg, 'Friedrich August der Gerechte', p. 63. See also Georg von Schimpff who avers that the king and populace felt 'sad and oppressed': *1813. Napoleon in Sachsen*, Dresden: Baensch, 1894, pp. 43–9.
147. Roman Töppel, 'Die Stimmung in Sachsen während der Befreiungskriege 1813–1815', in *Helden nach Mass*, Leipzig: Stadtgeschichtliches Museum Leipzig, 2013, p. 31.
148. The following section draws primarily from Holtzendorff, *Beiträge*, pp. 88–134 (with published correspondence pp. 214–50), and Petersdorff, *Thielmann*, pp. 125–235; supplemented by Jenak, 'Thielmann als Kommandant'; and Zezschwitz, *Mittheilungen*, pp. 266–70. Other sources consulted include Thielmann's own exculpations in 'Ueber den General Thielmann und seinen Uebertritt in russische Dienste', *Deutsche Blätter*, no. 3, 19 October 1813; as well as K. von Hüttel, *Der General der Kavallerie Freiherr v. Thielmann*, Berlin: Laue, 1828; Hermann Oberreit, *Beitrag zur Biographie und Characteristik des Generals Freiherrn v. Thielmann*, Dresden: Hilscher,

1829; 'Notice historique sur la conduite du général saxon Thielmann en 1813', *Spectateur Militaire*, vol. VII, 15 April–15 September 1829; Friedrich Bülau, 'General Thielmann', in *Geheime Geschichten und Räthselhafte Menschen*, vol. X, Leipzig: Brockhaus, 1858, and 'Noch einmal über General Thielmann', in *Geheime Geschichten und Räthselhafte Menschen*, vol. XII, Leipzig: Brockhaus, 1860; Friedrich Heller von Hellwald, ed., *Erinnerungen aus den Freiheitskriegen*, Stuttgart: Cotta, 1864; K. Haebler, 'Neue Beiträge zur Characteristik des Generals von Thielmann', *NASG*, vol. XV, 1904; and Rudolf Jenak, 'Die politische Rolle der Festung Torgau im Frühjahr 1813: Die Errichtung der Landesfestung Torgau als Bestandteil der sächsischen Militärreform', *Sächsische Heimatsblätter*, vol. 57, no. 1, 2011.
149. Thielmann to Langenau, 18 February 1813, Heller, *Erinnerungen*, pp. 35–6.
150. Langenau to Thielmann, 18 March 1813 (in cypher), ibid., p. 45.
151. Thielmann to Langenau, 19 March 1813, ibid., pp. 47–8.
152. Holtzendorff, *Beiträge*, pp. 89–100; Petersdorff, *Thielmann*, pp. 133–43, especially Senfft to Thielmann, 8 and 27 March 1813 (pp. 133, 154). Many French believed he had also refused passage to Rechberg's Bavarians, but this situation is not clear (Frédéric Guillaume de Vaudoncourt, *Histoire politique et militaire du Prince Eugène Napoléon*, Paris: Mongie, 1828, vol. II, p. 144).
153. Holtzendorff, *Beiträge*, p. 113; Zezschwitz, *Mittheilungen*, pp. 266–70. The early idea came from GM Johann Justus Vieth von Golßenau, the Saxon commandant in Dresden. He urged Thielmann to turn the fortress over to the Coalition 'under the most advantageous conditions possible for the king and fatherland'. Vieth argued that this 'extraordinary, albeit unlawful and dishonourable step' was justified by the manifold dangers the kingdom and its ruler were facing. To keep 'the king clean in this matter', Thielmann could take the blame upon himself should Napoleon be victorious but in the more likely event of Coalition success, Thielmann could claim to have acted on secret orders from Friedrich August (Vieth, *Auszüge*, pp. 19–20).
154. Franciscus Xaver (Franz) von Dreßler und Scharffenstein, *Darstellung der Begebenheiten in Torgau, vor, während und nach dem Rückzuge der Franzosen aus Sachsen, in den Monaten Februar, März und April 1813*, Dresden: Arnold, n.d. [1813 or 1814]. Recently republished in Reinhard Münch, ed., *Des Königs Butterkrebse*, Leipzig: Pro Leipzig, 2011, pp. 15–24.
155. Holtzendorff, *Beiträge*, pp. 99–100.
156. Holtzendorff, *Beiträge*, pp. 110–19; Petersdorff, *Thielmann*, pp. 199–203; Pertz, *Stein*, vol. III, pp. 327–8; Flathe, *Neuere Geschichte*, pp. 144–5; Vieth, *Auszüge*, pp. 18–22; and Hermann von Boyen, *Denkwürdigkeiten und Erinnerungen*, Stuttgart: Lutz, 1899, vol. II, pp. 268–70. Petersdorff contends that the Yorck quote attributed to Thielmann in Pertz is unlikely. Vieth was convinced that Stein was driven by 'a sense of hatred and retribution' towards Saxony.
157. Boyen, *Denkwürdigkeiten*, vol. II, p. 268; Zezschwitz, *Mittheilungen*, pp. 266–9; intercepted letter from Dresden, 22 May 1813, in Foucart, *Bautzen*, vol. II, pp. 81–2.
158. Holtzendorff, *Beiträge*, p. 231; Petersdorff, *Thielmann*, pp. 187–9, 221–4.

159. Thielmann to an anonymous friend in Dresden, late April, Petersdorff, *Thielmann*, p. 184; Holtzendorff, *Beiträge*, pp. 110, 114, 249; Zezschwitz, *Mittheilungen*, p. 269. Major von Hausen wrote of the factions being created within the garrison's officer corps (Hausen, *Tagebuch und Briefe*, p. 49).
160. Friedrich August to Thielmann, 8 April, 19 April, 30 April and 5 May in Holtzendorff, *Beiträge*, pp. 245–8. Senfft and Langenau to Thielmann, 19 April 1813, in Petersdorff, *Thielmann*, pp. 193–4. Jenak shows that Senfft's warning was originally contained in the draft of the king's letter but someone (likely Senfft) decided to strike these lines from the royal missive and put them in Senfft's message instead (Jenak, 'Thielmann als Kommandant', pp. 9–10).
161. Hausen, *Tagebuch und Briefe*, pp. 46–7.
162. Holtzendorff, *Beiträge*, pp. 115–19, 228–30; emphasis in the original. Petersdorff disparages Sahr in his account (*Thielmann*, pp. 204–10). See also Julius Graf von Wartensleben, *Nachrichten von dem Geschlechte der Grafen von Wartensleben*, Berlin: Nauck, 1858, pp. 240–1.
163. Mandelsloh, *Erinnerungen 1812–1814 (II)*, pp. 44–8.
164. Contrary to contemporary practice, Thielmann did *not* request release from his king's service. Russian General Volkonsky snidely commented that 'the general's person, without Torgau and without the Saxon troops, is of little use to the Allies' (Holtzendorff, *Beiträge*, pp. 127, 135). Shortly after arriving at Russian headquarters, Thielmann told an acquaintance that he could not have stayed in Torgau under French command as Napoleon would have had him shot within 24 hours 'as he knew well that I had negotiated with Prussian generals' (Wilhelm Dorow, *Erlebtes aus den Jahren 1813–1820*, Leipzig: Hinrichs, 1843, p. 6). Thielmann's conduct in 1814 as commander of the Saxon contingent was controversial and disruptive, cementing in the minds of many Saxon officers his role as a traitor, see Querengässer, *LeCoq*, pp. 133–48.
165. Eduard von Aster, ed., *Kurzer Lebens-Abriss des weil. Königlich Preussischen General's Ernst Ludwig von Aster*, Berlin: Voss, 1878, pp. 40–3.
166. Hausen, *Tagebuch und Briefe*, pp. 50–1.
167. The battery was composed of four of the old Saxon light 8-pounders and two old 8-pound howitzers (Titze, *Das Regiment Artillerie*, p. 20).
168. Published sources for Lüneburg are Cazalas, *De Stralsund à Lunebourg*, pp. 28–57; Cerrini, *Feldzüge der Sachsen*, pp. 492–510; Johannes Anton Larraß, *Geschichte des Königlich Sächsischen 6. Infanterie-Regiments Nr. 105 und seine Vorgeschichte 1701 bis 1887*, Straßburg: Kayser, 1887, pp. 169–76; and Paul von Troschke, 'Das Gefecht in und bei Lüneburg am 2 April 1813', *Beiheft zum Militär-Wochenblatt*, 1903. These were supplemented by Bernhard Hülsemann, *Geschichte des Königlich-Hannoverschen vierten Infanterie-Regiments*, Hanover: Helwing, 1863, pp. 3–8; Bernhard von Jacobi, *Hannover's Theilnahme an der deutschen Erhebung im Frühjahre 1813*, Hanover: Helwing, 1863, pp. 44–52; Anton von Mach, *Geschichte des Königlich Preußischen Zweiten Infanterie- genannt Königs-Regiments*, Berlin: Mittler, 1843, pp. 217–21; Emile Simond,

Historique des Nouveaux Régiments Créés par la Loi du 25 Juillet 1887, Paris: Baudoin, 1889, pp. 172–6; and Hugo Freiherr von Dörnberg, *Wilhelm von Dörnberg: Ein Kämpfer für Deutschlands Freiheit*, Marburg: Elwert, 1936, pp. 106–14. For an almost street-by-street account of the fighting, see W. Görges, *Lüneburg vor hundert Jahren. Das Treffen am 2. April 1813, der erste Sieg in den Befreiungskriegen*, Lüneburg: Herold & Wahlstab, 1913; and a citizen's reactions are in Wilhelm Friedrich Volger, ed., *Die merkwürdigsten Begebenheiten in Lüneburg während der Jahre 1813 und 1814*, Lüneburg: Herold und Wahlstab, 1839.

169. Recorded in 'Auszug aus dem Tagebuch des mobilen Linien-Infanterie Regiments Prinz Maximilian', SHSA, Generalstab, 11339, Nr. 287.
170. According to Widdern (*Streifkorps*, vol. I, p. 43), an officer and 50 men of the Saxon regiment defected to Benckendorf on the way to Bremen. This claim is not mentioned in any other source.
171. Eugène to Napoleon, 21 and 23 March 1813, du Casse, *Eugène*, vol. IX, pp. 8–13.
172. Tettenborn to Dörnberg, 31 March and 2 April 1813, in Dörnberg, *Dörnberg*, pp. 103–5.
173. Ehrenstein's 'Relation des Gefechts in und beÿ Lüneburg, vorzüglich des Regiments Prinz Maximilian betreffend', 15 May 1813, SHSA, Generalstab, 11339, Nr. 287.
174. It was at this point in the fighting that a local woman named Johanna Stegman became an icon of the struggle against France by distributing cartridges to the Prussian fusiliers under fire.
175. Barthold von Quistorp, *Die Kaiserlich Russisch-Deutsche Legion*, Berlin: Heymann, 1860, pp. 34–6, 45–6, 257, 264; Venzky, *Russisch-Deutsche Legion*, pp. 81–7; Larraß, *6. Infanterie-Regiments*, p. 176; and Max Gottschalck, *Geschichte des 1. Thüringischen Infanterie-Regiments Nr. 31*, Berlin: Mittler und Sohn, 1894, pp. 1–15. Ehrenstein and several others too seriously wounded to move remained in the city and were thus freed when the French reoccupied it several days later (Ehrenstein to Gersdorff, 15 May 1813, SHSA, Generalstab, 11339, Nr. 287).
176. Leading Bavarian minister Montgelas complained in his memoirs that the haughty Saxon cavalry had committed unpunished excesses and generally behaved poorly during their sojourn in Bavaria (Maximilian Graf von Montgelas, *Denkwürdigkeiten*, Stuttgart: Cotta, 1887, p. 280).
177. Reynier to Berthier, 11 May 1813, Foucart, *Bautzen*, vol. I, pp. 137–8; and Titze, *Sachsen im eigenen Land*, pp. 12–17. Orders to Ney (5 May) and Reynier (two on 10 May) are in Berthier, *Ordres*, vol. I, pp. 79–80 and 92–6. In the second letter to Reynier, Berthier admonished him in the emperor's name for writing directly to the Saxon king; all communications were to go through imperial headquarters, he was told, or through GL von Gersdorff, the Saxon chief of staff, in extreme cases
178. Reynier to Napoleon, 19 May 1813, in Foucart, *Bautzen*, vol. I, pp. 274–5.
179. Schimpff, *Garde-Reiter-Regiments*, pp. 321–4; Süßmilch, *2. Königl. Sächs. Husaren-Regiments*, pp. 139–41; Thielmann to Langenau, 18 February 1813, in Heller, *Erinnerungen*, pp. 35–6; Titze, *Sachsen im eigenen Land*, p. 76. Strength figures from Nafziger, *Lützen & Bautzen*, p. 342; Jörg Titze, *Die Königlich sächsische Kavallerie (III):*

Das Husaren-Regiment 1810–1815, Norderstedt: Books on Demand, 2020, and *Die Königlich sächsische Kavallerie (II): Die Chevaulegers-Regimenter 1810–1815*, Norderstedt: Books on Demand, 2022.

180. Intercepted letter from Dresden, 22 May 1813, in Foucart, *Bautzen*, vol. II, pp. 81–2; Kurt Leonhardt, 'Denkschrift Dietrichs von Miltitz über seine Wirksamkeit in den Kriegsjahren 1806–1814', *Mitteilungen des Vereins für Geschichte der Stadt Meißen*, vol. IX, no. 1, 1913, pp. 16–17.
181. The relies primarily on Cerrini, *Feldzüge der Sachsen*, pp. 157–97, and Odeleben, *Sachsen und seine Krieger*, pp. 125–42, supplemented by regimental histories.
182. Ney to Napoleon, 2300, 21 May 1813, in Foucart, *Bautzen*, vol. I, pp. 328–30.
183. Eduard Rudolf Goebel, *Zwei Ritter der Ehrenlegion*, Radeberg: Pfeil, 1906, pp. 8–10; Ernst Otto Innozenz Freiherr von Odeleben, *Die Umgegend von Bautzen mit Beziehung auf die Schlacht vom 20. und 21. May 1813*, Dresden: Arnold, 1820, p. 57.
184. Charles Thoumas, *Les Grands Cavaliers du Premier Empire*, Paris: Levrault, 1890, vol. I, p. 216.
185. Süßmilch, *2. Königl. Sächs. Husaren-Regiments*, pp. 146–7; Oppel, *Sammlung von Beiträgen*, p. 77.
186. Cerrini, *Feldzüge der Sachsen*, p. 178; Mandelsloh, *Erinnerungen 1812–1814 (II)*, pp. 50–2. It was at this point that Napoleon's friend GD Gérard Christophe Michel Duroc, was mortally wounded. The Saxons in the low valley of the stream took few casualties as the Russian howitzers firing from the eastern bank were aiming too high, but a shell landed among Napoleon's staff instantly killing GD François Joseph Kirgener and leaving Duroc only a few hours to live.
187. Both quotations from Holtzendorff, *Leichten Infanterie*, pp. 124–5. See also Schönberg, *Königl. Sächsischen 7. Infanterie-Regiments*, vol. II, pp. 64–5.
188. The various Saxon losses for 7th Corps here are taken from 'Anzeige der in den Treffen am 21. und 22ten und 23ten May 1813 gehabten Verluste zu Todten, Blessierten und Vermissten', SHSA, Generalstab, 11339, Nr. 283 (printed in Titze with a date of 25 May, *Sachsen im eigenen Land*, p. 32). Cerrini (*Feldzüge der Sachsen*, p. 185) lists 40 dead, 500 wounded and 98 missing. The corps chief of staff reported 314 Saxon dead and wounded (no listing of missing) as of 23 May; the same report gave Durutte's losses as 152, thus roughly half of the Saxon figure. Cavalry casualties are from Latour-Maubourg's 24 May report (Foucart, *Bautzen*, vol. II, pp. 7–9).
189. Thümmel to Gersdorff, 23 May 1813, SHSA, Generalstab, 11339, Nr. 283.
190. See Larisch, *Zeit- und Lebensbild*, p. 99. Friedrich Wilhelm Hansch, *Geschichte des Königlich Sächsischen Ingenieur- und Pionier-Korps*, Dresden, 1898, pp. 196–7; Jörg Titze, *Das sächsische Ingenieur-Korps und die Pontonierkompanie 1810–1813*, Norderstedt: Books on Demand, 2012, pp. 26–8.
191. The 7th Corps 'Situation' for 1 June listed only ten Saxon deserters during 16–31 May (SHD, 2C541).
192. Quoted in Holtzendorff, *Leichten Infanterie*, p. 127.
193. Donath/Engelberg/Füßler/Uhlmann, *Leipzig 1813*, pp. 82–3.

194. Napoleon to Berthier, 19 and 21 June 1813, *CG*, nos. 34856 and 34800, vol. XIII, pp. 1272–3, 1282; *Journal de l'Empire*, 5 and 6 July 1813; Töppel, *Sachsen und Napoleon*, pp. 215–16; Johann Carl Gross, *Erinnerungen aus den Kriegsjahren*, Leipzig: Voß, 1850, pp. 73–6; Johann Carl Meissner, *Leipzig 1813: Tagebuch und Erinnerungen an die Völkerschlacht*, Kassel: Hamecher, 2001, pp. 36–56; Johann Christoph Leuschner, 'Bergung und Befreiung einer Abtheilung Lützow'scher Jäger', in Robert Naumann, ed., *Aus dem Jahre 1813*, Leipzig: Weigel, 1869; Ludwig Schlosser, *Erlebnisse eines sächsischen Landpredigers in den Kriegsjahren 1806–1815*, Wiesbaden: Staadt, 1914, pp. 65–76; Karl Große, *Geschichte der Stadt Leipzig*, Leipzig: Schmidt, 1898, vol. II, pp. 484–8. According to one source, Württemberg troops guarding the partisan captives looked the other way when citizens provided succour: Heinz Füßler, ed., *Leipzig 1813: Die Völkerschlacht im nationalen Befreiungskampf des deutschen Volkes*, Leipzig: Veb Bibliographisches Institut, 1953, p. 83.
195. The detachment left the Krakow area on 17 April and returned to Saxony on 6 June. For interesting observations from an Austrian officer who was detailed to oversee one of the Polish columns, see Karl Friedrich Ferdinand von Strantz, 'Marsch der Herzoglich Warschauischen Truppen (8. französische Armeekorps) unter dem Fürsten Poniatowsky, und einer Brigade Sachsen unter dem General von Gablenz, 1813 von Krakau durch die östreichischen Staaten nach Zittau in Sachsen', *ZfkWGK*, vol. 7, 1832, pp. 190–202. Curiously, Colomb and Lützow had learned of Gablenz's march and hoped to intercept him, only to be disappointed when they heard that the Saxons had already crossed out of Bohemia (Brecher, *Überfall*, p. 4).
196. Buhle, *Erinnerungen*, pp. 89–93.
197. Friedrich von Dreßler und Scharffenstein, *Bericht eines Augenzeugen von den Operationen des 4ten, 7ten und 12ten französischen Armeecorps unter Anführung der Generale Bertrand, Reynier und Oudinot, von Ankündigung des Pleischwitzer Waffenstillstandes, bis nach der Schlacht bei Jüterbock, vom 14 August bis 6 September 1813*, Dresden: Arnold, 1814, p. 8. The timing of his remarks is pertinent because his original diary notes did not include such gloomy perceptions, see Münch, *Butterkrebse*, pp. 33–69.
198. This section draws primarily on Aster, *Dresden*, pp. 301–22; and Schimpff, *Garde-Reiter-Regiments*, pp, 332–8. See also: Horstenau, *Feldzug von Dresden*, pp. 276–91, and his 'Die Division Mesko bei Dresden 1813', *Steffleurs Militärische Zeitschrift*, vol. I, no. 2, 1911. See also Attila Réfi, 'A Career with an Unfair Ending: The Life and Military Activity of the Austrian Lieutenant General Baron Joseph Meskó de Felsőkubin (1762–1815)', *Napoleonic Scholarship*, no. 9, December 2018.
199. Lunettes III and IV as well as one of the larger buildings on the perimeter each had a Saxon engineer officer and two sappers assigned to assist the French or Westphalian garrison (Aster, 'Darstellung', pp. 194–5); it is reasonable to assume that this distribution applied to the other defensive works as well.
200. Saxon accounts mistakenly refer to these as Austrians 'Jägers', but there were no Jägers on the northern side of the Weißeritz. These might have been *Grenzer* or simply skirmishers from a line regiment.

201. Wilhelm Bichmann, *Chronik des k. k. Infanterie-Regiments Nr. 62*, Vienna: Mayer, 1880, pp. 121–8.
202. Murat to Napoleon, 27 August 1813, Fabry, *Empereur I*, Documents, pp. 1–3.
203. Key sources for Großbeeren: Cerrini, *Feldzüge der Sachsen*, pp. 218–33; Odeleben, *Sachsen und sein Krieger*, pp. 151–60; Quistorp, *Nordarmee*, vol. I, pp. 267–308; Friederich, *Herbstfeldzuges*, vol. I, pp. 400–16; regimental histories; 7th Corps after-action summary, 26 August 1813, SHD, 2C154.
204. Napoleon sent an aide-de-camp to Friedrich August with an update on the battle and this praise for the Saxon regiments, Gersdorff, diary entry for 27 August 1813, in Marc le Bégue de Germiny, 'La Bataille de Dresde', *Revue des Questions Historiques*, vol. XXVI, 1901, p. 486.
205. Friedrich von Dreßler und Scharffenstein, *Bericht eines Augenzeugen*, p. 11.
206. Mandelsloh, *Erinnerungen 1812–1814 (II)*, pp. 56–9.
207. Friedrich Förster, *Geschichte der Befreiungs-Kriege 1813, 1814, 1815*, Berlin: Hempel, 1862, vol. I, pp. 768–9. Förster gives the regimental identity as *Niesemeuschel* but, assuming the anecdote is true, it is more likely that these cocky fellows were artillery officers.
208. Cerrini, *Feldzüge der Sachsen*, p. 223; Gersdorff to Berthier, 30 August 1813, SHD, 2C154; Durutte also tried to warn Reynier, 'Note sur la Bataille de Beeren', RAMP, Boite 43.
209. Prussian veteran and historian Friedrich Förster, evidently from talking with other veterans, highlighted the bitterness of the combat between Prussians and Saxons in his history of the war: Förster, *Befreiungs-Kriege*, vol. I, p. 772.
210. Bose's journal and the reports of Reynier and Blein, in Fabry, *Oudinot*, pp. 24, 104–6, 111. Durutte stated that the men were overcome by 'a transport of reckless courage', lost their formation and only found safety by 'throwing themselves hastily into the woods'. ('Note sur la Bataille de Beeren', RAMP, Boite 43; Mouthon, *Durutte*, p. 27).
211. Quotations from Quistorp, *Nordarmee*, vol. I, p. 294; and Gustav von Ziegler, *Erinnerungen aus den Jahren 1813/14*, Cologne: Greven, 1853, pp. 39–41. 'Wittstock' was a derogatory term for the Saxons referring to a battle in 1636 in which the Duke of Saxony had been defeated. See also Pohlmann, *Geschichte des Infanterie-Regiments Graf Barfuß (4. Westfälischen) Nr. 17*, Berlin: Mittler und Sohn, 1906, pp. 19–23.
212. Friedrich Gottlob Probsthayn, *Tagebuch vom 14.05.1813 bis 29.09.1814*, Konrad Probsthain and Jörg Titze, eds, Norderstedt: Books on Demand, 2016, pp. 20–4.
213. Oppell, *Sammlung von Beiträgen* p. 78.
214. Jörg Titze, ed., *Zur Geschichte der Sächsischen Leib-Grenadier-Garde (I)*, Norderstedt: Books on Demand, 2017, p. 22.
215. Hausen, *Tagebuch und Briefe*, p. 58.
216. Losses from Quistorp, *Nordarmee*, vol. III, pp. 185–6; Titze, *Artillerie-Korps*, pp. 234.
217. Seventh Corps, 'État des Pertes', 24 August 1813, SHD, 2C154.
218. Vollborn, *Erlebtes (III)*, p. 46.
219. Hausen, letter of 2 September 1813, *Tagebuch und Briefe*, pp. 54–9; Maximilian von Schreibershofen, *Maximilian von Schreibershofen: Erinnerungen 1805–1815*, Jörg Titze, ed., Norderstedt: Books on Demand, 2021, p. 101.

220. Friedrich von Dreßler und Scharffenstein, *Bericht eines Augenzeugen*, p. 23.
221. Cerrini, *Feldzüge der Sachsen*, pp. 250–3; Quistorp, *Nordarmee*, vol. I, pp. 372–3. See Chapters 3 and 4 for other Rheinbund troops.
222. Holtzendorff, *Leichten Infanterie*, pp. 136–7.
223. Larraß, *6. Infanterie-Regiments*, pp. 186–7; Quistorp, *Nordarmee*, vol. I, p. 339–43; Julius Vetter, *Chronik der Stadt Luckau*, Luckau: Meißner, 1904, pp. 236–43; Wobeser's report in Pflugk-Harttung, *Befreiungsjahr*, pp. 284–6. In total, the Prussians took 1,029 prisoners, 8 guns, 60 horses and a large magazine.
224. Accounts differ on the exact date and on the amount of money (Cerrini, *Feldzüge der Sachsen*, p. 217; Titze, *eigenen Land*, p. 131). LeCoq to Friedrich August, 26 and 30 August 1813, in Fabry, *Oudinot*, Documents, pp. 56, 78.
225. In addition to the sources cited below, this account of Dennewitz relies on Quistorp, *Nordarmee*, vol. I; Friederich, *Herbstfeldzuges*, vol. II; Juhel, 'Automne 1813'; and Louchet, *Bataille de Dennewitz*, Part 2. Note that the Saxon positions shown in Map 24 are slightly different from those in the excellent maps that accompany Quistorp in that Defrance and Bose are shifted somewhat northwest in accordance with the sketch map Reynier submitted as part of his after-action report (SHD, 2C154).
226. Cerrini, *Feldzüge der Sachsen*, p. 257.
227. Schreibershofen report to Gersdorff, 7 September 1813, SHSA, Generalstab, 11339, nr. 285; 'Relation d'un officier Saxon de la bataille de Niedergersdorff le 6 Septembre 1813 et des évènements qu'ils ont précédés', AN, AF/IV/1662B, Plaquette 3.
228. Frenzel, *Erinnerungen*, p. 167.
229. Seventh Corps after-action summary, AN, AF/IV/1662B, Plaquette 3.
230. In addition to Saxon sources, see Karl von Bagensky, *Geschichte des 9ten Infanterie-Regiments gennant Colbergsches*, Colberg: Post, 1842, p. 150.
231. 'Relation d'un officier Saxon', AN, AF/IV/1662B, Plaquette 3 (the drafter mistakenly wrote 'left wing' rather than 'right' in the original); Schreibershofen report to Gersdorff, 7 September 1813, SHSA, Generalstab, 11339, nr. 285. Given the similarity in wording, it is possible that Schreibershofen was the author of the 'Relation' as well.
232. Vollborn, *Erlebtes (III)*, pp. 46–50.
233. Reynier reported that Oudinot's move 'seemed like a retrograde movement' both to the Saxons and to the Prussians (Seventh Corps after-action summary, AN, AF/IV/1662B, Plaquette 3).
234. Reynier to Napoleon, 2 October 1813, AN, AF/IV/1662B, Plaquette 3; Holtzendorff, *leichten Infanterie*, p. 139. In his report, Borstell credited the Saxons with retiring in good order initially (Pflugk-Harttung, *Befreiungsjahr*, pp. 318–19).
235. Quoted in Duroisel, *93ᵉ Régiment d'Infanterie*, p. 232; Oudinot to Napoleon, 7 September 1813, Fabry, *Empereur II*, Documents, pp. 22–3. Morand also blamed the 'precipitous rout' of the Saxons (SHD, 2C448bis). The Westphalians apparently rode through the Saxon Jägers, prompting the Saxons to 'send a volley after them' (Holtzendorff, *leichten Infanterie*, p. 139).
236. Brun, *Cahiers*, p. 156.

237. 'Relation d'un officier Saxon', AN, AF/IV/1662B, Plaquette 3.
238. Seventh Corps after-action summary, AN, AF/IV/1662B, Plaquette 3.
239. Adolf Georg Wilhelm Leopold von Göphardt, 'Brigade Mellentin vom 14n August bis 7n September 1813', in Jörg Titze, ed., *Die Tagebücher von Johann Carl von Dallwitz (1812–1815) und Adolf Georg von Göphardt (1813)*, Norderstedt: Books on Demand, 2015, pp. 150–1. Mandelsloh recorded similar impressions of the fight for Gölsdorf and the retreat turning into a rout (*Erinnerungen 1812–1814 (II)*, pp. 61–4).
240. In a lively and intriguing polemic, the iconoclast Karl Bleibtreu noted the high number of missing among the Saxon casualties as compared to the battle losses (dead and wounded) suffered by the French. He makes some very good points about German hyper-nationalistic histories, but is imprecise with his statistics and does not take into account the large numbers of French stragglers and deserters as evident from Oudinot's report that he was only able to assemble 4,500 men from the combined 13th and 14th Divisions two days after the battle (Oudinot to Berthier, 8 September 1813, in Fabry, *Empereur II*, Documents, p. 23) – a manpower problem corroborated by the combining of the two divisions shortly thereafter. See Bleibtreu's three caustic essays in *Ein Lied von der deutschen Treue*, Leipzig: Deutscher Kampf-Verlag, 1906.
241. Holtzendorff, *leichten Infanterie*, p. 140. The subsequent praise of the Poles is also from this page.
242. Louchet, *Bataille de Dennewitz*, Part 2, pp. 25–9.
243. Larisch, *Zeit- und Lebensbild*, pp. 113–15. The subsequent quote about soldiers seeking to identify one another is also from this source.
244. 'Zur Schlacht von Dennewitz', *Militair-Wochenblatt*, no. 265, 21 July 1821.
245. Birnbaum to Gersdorff, 10 September 1813, SHSA, Generalstab, 11339, Nr. 285; Brun, *Cahiers*, p. 161.
246. Frenzel, *Erinnerungen*, p. 169; Vollborn, *Erlebtes (III)*, p. 50; Hausen, *Tagebuch und Briefe*, p. 64; Töppel, *Sachsen und Napoleon*, p. 305. Strength figures from Louchet, *Dennewitz*, pt. I, pp. 48–50 and pt. II, pp. 55–9. Order of the day for 8 September 1813 printed in Titze, *Sachsen im eigenen Land*, pp. 192–3. Some men were likely motivated to avoid capture by rumours that the Prussians had paraded prisoners through Berlin to be abused by the population.
247. 'Rapport de Monsieur le Général Brun de Villeret Baron de l'Empire sur la Défense de la Place Torgau', 11 January 1814; similar comments about Ney and the Saxons in Colonel Claude Pierre Ferdinand Girod de Novilars, 'Journal Historique', 9 January 1814; both SHD, 2C168.
248. Separate letters from Ney, Lebrun and Oudinot to Napoleon, 7 September 1813, and Ney to Berthier, 14 September 1813, in Fabry, *Empereur II*, Documents, pp. 20–3, 93. 'Rapport du Prince de la Moskowa', *Le Moniteur Universel*, no. 263, 20 September 1813; and *Leipziger Zeitung*, no. 187, 29 September 1813, in Heinrich von Aster, *Die Gefechte und Schlachten bei Leipzig im October 1813*, Dresden: Arnold, 1852, vol. I, pp. 50–1.

249. Birnbaum to Gersdorff, 10 September 1813, SHSA, Generalstab, 11339, Nr. 285; Reynier to Berthier, 10 September 1813, in Fabry, *Empereur II*, Documents, p. 42. Reynier to Napoleon, 2 October 1813, AN, AF/IV/1662B, Plaquette 3 (printed in Odeleben, *Réclamations*, pp. 36–40; the concluding sections also appear in Quistorp, *Nordarmee*, vol. I, p. 547 and Cerrini, *Feldzüge*, pp. 267–8, with slight variations). Reynier's 7 October letter to LeCoq is also in Odeleben (pp. 40–3) and Cerrini (pp. 268–70). Personal friction between Ney and Reynier exacerbated the situation, eventually leading Ney to demand Reynier's relief from command, while Reynier indirectly criticised Ney and asked to serve under a different superior.
250. Hausen, letter of 13 September 1813, *Tagebuch und Briefe*, pp. 60–5.
251. Larisch, *Zeit- und Lebensbild*, p. 118; similarly Mandelsloh, *Erinnerungen 1812–1814 (II)*, pp. 65–6.
252. See the insightful discussion in Töppel, *Sachsen und Napoleon*, pp. 283–4 from which this observation is drawn. The quotation is from Funck, *Erinnerungen*, pp. 214–15.
253. The concept for the reorganisation is in *Rapports du Maréchal Berthier à l'Empereur pendant la Campagne de 1813*, Paris: Chapelot, 1909, vol. II, pp. 142–6.
254. Eduard Franz von Wolffersdorff, 'Meine Erlebnisse in und nach der Schlacht bei Leipzig, während des 17., 18. und 19. Octobers 1813', in Robert Naumann, *Zum 19. October 1864*, Leipzig: Weigel, 1864, p. 9; Querengässer, *LeCoq*, pp. 125–6. LeCoq, of course, was not uniformly admired: Premierleutnant Friedrich Maximilian von Mandelsloh, for instance, recorded that he and Oberst von Mellenthin had strong differences with the general and Mandelsloh described his command style as 'a terroristic system' (*Erinnerungen 1803–1812 (I)*, Jörg Titze, ed., Norderstedt: Books on Demand, 2021, pp. 97–102).
255. Ney to Berthier, 8, 9, and 12 September 1813, and Reynier to Berthier, 10 September 1813, in Fabry, *Empereur II*, Documents, pp. 23, 33, 42, 63; Berthier to Ney, 11 September 1813, *Ordres*, vol. II, p. 175.
256. Quotes from correspondence in Fabry, *Empereur III*, Documents, pp. 17–22, 62, 214–16; Cerrini, *Feldzüge der Sachsen*, pp. 287–8; Wolffersdorff, 'Meine Erlebnisse', p. 9; similar disapproval in Mandelsloh, *Erinnerungen 1812–1814 (II)*, p. 67. Bernadotte, of course, highlighted the defection in his bulletin of 26 September (*Proclamations de S. A. R. le Prince-Royal de Suède et Bulletins publiés au Quartier-Général de l'Armée combiné du Nord de l'Allemagne*, Stockholm: Sohm, 1815, p. 73).
257. The proclamations are in Maximilian Poppe, *Chronologische Uebersicht der wichtigsten Begebenheiten aus den Kriegsjahren 1806–1815*, Dresden: Thomas, 1848, vol. II, pp. 158–60. For no longer wearing the uniform: Gretschel/Bülau, *Sächsischen Volkes*, vol. III, p. 517.
258. Ney to Berthier, 23 and 24 September 1813, in Fabry, *Empereur III*, Documents, pp. 17–18, 41–2.
259. Bernhard Lange, 'Die öffentliche Meinung in Sachsen von 1813 bis zur Rückkehr des Königs 1815', *Geschichtliche Studien*, Gotha: Perthes, 1912, vol. II, nr. 2, pp. 67–9. The Saxons were a special target for Allied appeals: see, for example, Poppe,

Chronologische Uebersicht, vol. II, pp. 150–2. The authors of *Leipzig 1813*, eager to stress an anti-West, 'workers and peasants' viewpoint, cite an unnamed sergeant from the 2nd Light Battalion as expressing delight at Bünau's defection and a desire to do the same; they provide, however, no source for this assertion (Donath/Engelberg/Füßler/Uhlmann, *Leipzig 1813*, p. 123).

260. Hans von Schimpff, *Geschichte der beiden Königlich Sächsischen Grenadier-Regimenter: Erstes (Leib-) Grenadier-Regiment Nr. 100 und Zweites Grenadier-Regiment Nr. 101*, Dresden: Höckner, 1877, pp. 162–3; Gottlob Freiherr von Hodenberg, *Das Königlich Sächsische 1. (Leib-) Grenadier-Regiment Nr. 100*, Dresden: Heinrich, 1883, p. 39.

261. An East German account claims that 'an unusual number' of Saxon officers feigned illness in order to take temporary leave of the army during this period; unfortunately, it cites no sources and provides no figures to support this claim (Donath/Engelberg/Füßler/Uhlmann, *Leipzig 1813*, p. 124; repeated in Platthaus, *1813*, p. 275.).

262. August Kummer, *Erinnerungen aus dem Leben eines Veteranen der Königlich Sächsischen Armee*, Dresden: Meinhold & Söhne, 1870, pp. 24–5; Vollborn, *Erlebtes*, pp. 55–6.

263. Gretschel/Bülau, *Sächsischen Volkes*, vol. III, p. 519; Kummer, *Erinnerungen*, p. 27.

264. See Thomas Hemmann's summary of this neglected operation: 'Napoleons letzte Manöver rechts der Elbe – der Vorstoß über Wittenberg und Dessau im Oktober 1813', in Niedersen, ed., *Sachsen, Preußen und Napoleon*, pp. 318–26.

265. Töppel, *Sachsen und Napoleon*, pp. 289–91; Hausen, *Tagebuch und Briefe*, p. 69; Holtzendorff, *leichten Infanterie*, pp. 145–7; Ernst Otto Innozenz von Odeleben, *Napoleons Feldzug in Sachsen, im Jahr 1813*, 2nd edition, Dresden: Arnold, 1816, pp. 321–4; August Redlich, *Clemens Franziscus Xavierus von Cerrini di Monte Varchi*, Dresden: Expedition der Freimüthigen Sachsen-Zeitung, 1852, pp. 32–3; Vollborn, *Erlebtes (III)*, pp. 59–63; Kummer, *Erinnerungen*, pp. 25–6. In his *Sachsen und sein Krieger*, p. 195, on the other hand, Odeleben says the Saxons did not cheer but were silent and angry. Holtzendorff gives the best transcript of Napoleon's remarks (*leichten Infanterie*, p. 347). Though the ceremony did not diminish their distaste for the French alliance, many Saxons were awed and moved by the power of the moment when Napoleon granted eagles to several nearby French regiments for the first time.

266. Unfortunately for the Saxon cavalry, Prussian Rittmeister von Colomb had been tasked to disperse or destroy their regimental depots. Through a combination of surprise and bluff, he and his men captured some 390 horses and 400 officers and men at Schleusingen on 13 October. Though released on parole, these men, their mounts and large amounts of equipment were thus lost to the Saxon army. Widdern, *Streifkorps*, vol. II, pp. 375–89; Titze, *Husaren-Regiment*, p. 30.

267. In a version of his diary published anonymously in the *Europäische Annalen* in 1817 ('Züge zur Geschichte Dresdens und des Krieges in Sachsen im Jahre 1813', vol. IV, p. 298), Wilhelm August Lindau (or his editor), wrote that some of the Saxons and Westphalians assigned to the Guard feared they would be compelled to follow Napoleon to the Rhine and might be incorporated into the French army. This

allegation does not appear anywhere else and is not included in the book version of his diary published in the previous year (Wilhelm Adolf Lindau, *Darstellung der Ereignisse in Dresden im Jahr 1813*, Dresden: Arnold, 1816).

268. Friedrich von Dreßler und Scharffenstein, 'Das sächsische Gardebataillon unter Commando des Capitains nachherigen Majors von Dreßler vom 14. August bis 5. November 1813', in Münch, ed., *Butterkrebse*, pp. 42–9; Jörg Titze, ed., *Zur Geschichte der Sächsischen Leib-Grenadier-Garde (I)*, Norderstedt: Books on Demand, 2017, pp. 56–61.
269. Falkenstein, 'Gersdorff', p. 58.
270. Charles Parquin, *Napoleon's Army: The Military Memoirs of Charles Parquin*, London: Greenhill, 1987, p. 161. Odeleben also observed this scene (*Napoleons Feldzug*, pp. 330–1).
271. Schimpff, *Garde-Reiter-Regiments*, pp. 338–41.
272. The preceding two paragraphs, including the quotations, are from Aster, *Leipzig*, vol. I, pp. 411–12, 422–7.
273. Aster, *Leipzig*, vol. I, pp. 363–4, 434–5, 500 (Eckardt's remarks); and Schimpff, *Garde-Reiter-Regiments*, pp. 343–7.
274. Titze, *Leib-Grenadier-Garde*, pp. 62–5.
275. 'Auszug aus dem Tagebuche Friedrich August Wilhelm Böhme's', in Naumann, *Völkerschlacht*, pp. 320–1.
276. The Bavarians remained behind temporarily at Eilenburg – *see* Chapter 3.
277. Böhme, 'Tagebuch', pp. 320–1.
278. Frenzel, *Erinnerungen*, p. 173; Böhme, 'Tagebuch', p. 321.
279. *Erinnerungen an Heinrich Wilhelm v. Zeschau*, Dresden: Ramming, 1866, pp. 52–3.
280. Reynier to Ney, 0030, 18 October 1813, SHD 2C158; in Colson, *Leipzig*, p. 229.
281. This is one of the most impenetrable aspects of this confusing day. In addition to Schreibershofen's memoirs (*Erinnerungen*, pp. 110–3), other reliable Saxon sources describe Schreibershofen's mission and Reynier's instructions to Zeschau for the supposed return to Torgau (e.g., Aster, *Leipzig*, vol. II, pp. 60–3). The French correspondence is in SHD, 2C158 (with thanks to Bruno Colson whose careful research is related in his *Leipzig*, pp. 229–30), but there is no hint of any such orders. Note that Heinrich Ulmann refers to alleged 'orders' from Ney to protect Durrieu's convoy but Ulmann seems to have completely misinterpreted the letters Colson cites (*Geschichte der Befreiungskriege 1813 u. 1814*, Munich: Oldenbourg, 1915, vol. II, pp. 254–5).
282. Mandelsloh, *Erinnerungen 1812–1814 (II)*, pp. 73–4 (his term is '*vaterländischen Festung*').
283. According to a note from the *Jena Allgemeine Literatur Zeitung* published in Gottfried Wilhelm Becker, *Der Krieg der Franzosen und ihrer Alliirten gegen Rußland, Preußen, und seine Verbündeten*, Leipzig: Engelmann, 1814, vol. III, pp. 80–1.
284. Some French Gardes d'Honneur, initially detailed to support the Saxons were fired upon when they rode up and may have skirmished with the Saxon horse for a

time: Jean Lamby, 'Itineraire d'un Brigadier du 2ᵉ Régiment des Gardes d'Honneur pendant la Campagne de 1813, en Saxe', Albert Dépréaux, ed., *Carnet de la Sabretache*, no. 287, January–February 1924, pp. 59–60.

285. François Dumonceau, *Mémoires,* Brussels: Brepols, 1958–1963, vol. II, pp. 377–8; in Colson, *Leipzig*, pp. 274–6. Dumonceau indicates that his regiment (5ᵉ Chasseurs-à-Cheval) was fired upon by two Saxon guns, but the Saxon pieces had already withdrawn towards Paunsdorf and defected with the rest of the division during the afternoon. Rilliet witnessed the Saxon cavalry defection as well but does not mention being fired upon at that time ('Journal', p. 140). Louis Alexander Andrault Langeron, *Mémoires de Langeron*, Gabriel Fabry, ed., Paris: Picard et Fils, 1902, pp. 326–7; Colson, *Leipzig*, pp. 275–6. Langeron leaves the reader with the erroneous impression that the Saxon cavalry joined in the fighting, but this was not the case.

286. An East German account cites 'an eyewitness' to assert that the soldiers were asked if they wanted to join the Allies and that the battalion defected once the men assented to the proposal (Donath/Engelberg/Füßler/Uhlmann, *Leipzig 1813*, p. 125). As usual with this particular book, the lack of sourcing and detail means the assertion requires further scrutiny.

287. Legation councillor Breuer, in Karl von Weber, 'Detlev Graf von Einsiedel, Königl. Sächsischer Cabinets-Minister', *Archiv für Sächsische Geschichte*, vol. I, 1863, p. 84.

288. *Zeschau*, pp. 52–4; Jörg Titze, 'Der Übergang der Sachsen am 18.10.1813', Sprotta: self-published, 2002, p. 13; Aster, *Leipzig*, vol. II, p. 121.

289. Breuer, in Weber, 'Detlev Graf von Einsiedel, pp. 84–5; and *Zeschau*, p. 54.

290. Böhme, 'Tagebuche', pp. 322–3.

291. Raabe's words are from a 26 November 1844 explanation published by his son in Alfred von Kretschmar, *Geschichte der kurfürstlich und königlich Sächsischen Artillerie*, Berlin: Mittler und Sohn, 1876, pp. 120–1.

292. Kummer, *Erinnerungen*, pp. 32–3.

293. Larisch, *Zeit- und Lebensbild*, pp. 124–5.

294. Titze, 'Übergang der Sachsen', p. 16. For the officer begging Reynier to leave, see notes by an anonymous French officer in the French edition of Odeleben's memoirs, *Relation Circonstanciée de la Campagne de 1813, en Saxe*, Paris: Plancer, 1817, vol. II, pp. 331–2. Pelet presents the warning being given to Reynier's chief of staff instead (Part 10 of 'Campagne de 1813', *Spectateur Militaire*, vol. III, 1827, p. 33). Reynier related his reaction in a conversation with Saxon GL von Funck while captive in Leipzig in early November, Funck, *In Russland und Sachsen*, pp. 331, 339.

295. Böhme, 'Tagebuch', pp. 323–4; Schreibershofen, *Erinnerungen*, pp. 110–13.

296. Frenzel, *Erinnerungen*, p. 178. On deceiving the troops, see Carsten Siegel and Thomas Janke, 'Sachsen und Napoleon 1806 bis 1813. Zusammen in die Niederlage', in Hofbauer/Rink, *Völkerschlacht*, p. 240.

297. Mandelsloh, *Erinnerungen 1812–1814 (II)*, pp. 75–7.

298. Saxon quotes from Probsthayn, *Tagebuch*, p. 37; and Böhme, 'Tagebuch', p. 324. For the Russians, see Karl von Wedel, *Lebenserinnerungen*, Curt Troeger, ed., Berlin:

Mittler und Sohn, 1913, vol. II, p. 106; and [Karl von Wedel], *Feldzug der Kaiserlich Russischen Armee von Polen in den Jahren 1813 und 1814*, Hamburg: Hoffmann und Campe, 1843, p. 44; and reports from Wedel, the Army of the North, and Bennigsen in Pflugk-Harttung, *Leipzig*, pp. 240, 289, 405–6.

299. Rilliet, 'Journal', p. 140.
300. 'Meldung von dem, was ich den 18. und 19. October 1813 über den Gang der Gefechte bey Leipzig weis', in Pflugk-Hartung, *Leipzig*, pp. 238–42.
301. Hoen, *Leipzig*, vol. V, p. 629. The number of Saxon guns cited here comes from the detailed studies by Titze and Larraß; Wedel and the Allied reports cited above mention as many as ten. MacDonald and other French writers claimed that the Saxons, presumably the infantry as well as artillery, fired on Durutte's men, but no Saxon sources, even those that celebrate the defection, make such a statement: Étienne Jacques MacDonald, *Recollections of Marshal MacDonald*, London: Bentley & Son, 1892, (reprinted Felling: Worley, 1987), vol. II, p. 72; Rilliet, 'Journal', p. 140.
302. Miltitz, who was present at this confabulation, claimed that Friedrich Wilhelm said the Saxons would be welcomed 'like brothers', but this seems likely a case where his effervescent passion for 'the good cause' prompted him to remember the scene in a pro-Prussian fashion (Leonhardt, 'Miltitz', pp. 23–4).
303. Zeschau to Reynier, SHD, 2C158, with thanks to Bruno Colson (see his *Leipzig*, p. 305); *Zeschau*, pp. 57–9. Note that Zeschau misdated this missive as 17 October and that he gave 600 as the number of men remaining.
304. Reynier to Berthier, 19 October 1813, SHD, 2C158, with thanks to Bruno Colson; see his *Leipzig*, p. 332.
305. Beroldingen's 22 September 1813 report from Gotha, in Pfister, *Lager des Rheinbundes*, p. 356.
306. Funck, *In Russland und Sachsen*, pp. 247–9.
307. Reynier to Eugène, 9 March 1813, quoted in Juhel, 'Truppen des Rheinbunds', in *Blutige Romantik*, p. 63, Note 15.
308. Albrecht Graf von Holtzendorff, *Berichtigung der Schrift: 'Erinnerungen aus dem Feldzuge des sächsischen Corps im Jahre 1812'*, Dresden: Walther, 1831, p. 117–18.
309. For a micro-level examination of the destruction wrought by French and Allied soldiers during the war, see Elke Schlenkrich and Ira Spieker, 'Ausgeplündert und abgebrannt. Alltag in der ländlichen Gesellschaft Sachsens im Kriegsjahr 1813', *NASG*, vol. 78, 2007 (with thanks to Dr Spieker). See also Kurt Krebs, *Sächsische Kriegsnot in den Jahren 1806 bis 1815*, Leipzig: Teutonia-Verlag, 1908. Tendentious as part of the anti-French propaganda campaign, but still interesting is *Sachsens Verwüstung durch die Franzosen 1813*, Leipzig: Engelmann, 1814.
310. Odeleben, *Réclamations*, pp. 13–14.
311. Hausen, *Tagebuch und Briefe*, p. 72; similarly, Kummer, *Erinnerungen*, p. 31.
312. 'Insulting bravado' is from a work of fiction: Jack Vance, *Throy*, Lancaster: Underwood-Miller, 1992, p. 160.
313. For example: Kummer, *Erinnerungen*, p. 31.

314. Raabe in Kretschmar, *Sächsischen Artillerie*, pp. 120–1; Schreibershofen in Aster, *Leipzig*, vol. II, p. 62. Moreover, as Töppel argues, for some of the men simple self-preservation in the face of likely defeat was a major factor in their decision to desert. He suggests that much of the stress on 'saving Saxony' was little more than an attempt to craft *ex post facto* excuses as participants such as Rysssel and Brause sought to justify what they knew to be a blatant violation of military duty. As he points out quite correctly, analysis of the defection must also take into consideration when the various accounts were written. See Töppel, *Sachsen und Napoleon*, pp. 291–302.
315. Modern historians Carsten Siegel and Thomas Janke thus refer to the defection as a 'reaction of war-weary soldiers in a hopeless battle', 'Sachsen und Napoleon 1806 bis 1813', in Hofbauer/Rink, *Völkerschlacht*, p. 245.
316. Frenzel, *Erinnerungen*, p. 178;
317. Buhle, *Erinnerungen*, pp. 100–3.
318. GM Vieth, who had fled to Bohemia on Napoleon's approach to Dresden after Lützen, wrote that the 'hard and difficult test of obedience' endured by the Saxon troops exhausted their 'moral strength' and led to the defection. Even he, who had urged Thielmann to deliver Torgau to the Allies in April, believed that this loss of 'moral strength' did not justify, but perhaps exonerated and excused the battlefield defection, 'a step that has been so harshly criticised and reprimanded, and not entirely without justification' (Vieth, *Auszüge*, pp. 25–6).
319. Schreibershofen, quoted in Aster, *Leipzig*, vol. II, p. 62.
320. Key for the Saxon defection are Aster, *Leipzig*, vol. II, pp. 55–63, 119–31, 144–60, 213–16, 273, 277–9; Johannes Anton Larraß, 'Zur Beurteilung der Überführung Königlich sächsischer Truppen zu den Verbündeten bei Leipzig am 18. Oktober 1813', *Beiheft zum Militär-Wochenblatt*, no. 10, 1906; Titze, 'Übergang der Sachsen', 2002, and his excellent 'Der 18. Oktober 1813. Die Kämpfe im Nordosten von Leipzig und der Übergang der Sachsen', in Niedersen, ed., *Sachsen, Preußen und Napoleon*, pp. 327–33. Supplemented here by Cerrini, *Feldzüge der Sachsen*, pp. 318–27; Colson, *Leipzig*, pp. 274–86; Holtzendorff, *leichte Infanterie*, pp. 147–52; Schönberg, *Königl. Sächsischen 7. Infanterie-Regiments*, vol. II, pp. 94–101 (correcting Cerrini's erroneous statement that the *Friedrich August* Battalion was captured in Taucha); 'Die sächsischen Truppen in der Schlacht bei Leipzig, den 18. Oktober 1813', *Der europäische Aufseher*, 2 and 6 November 1821; Töppel, *Sachsen und Napoleon*, pp. 291–302; and Ulmann, *Befreiungskriege*, vol. II, pp. 246–56.
321. Jean François Boulart, *Mémoires Militaires*, Paris: Librarie Illustrée, 1892 (reprinted Tallandier, 1992), p. 296.
322. Letter of 19 May 1814, in 'Un Revélois dans la Grande Armée 1804–1815', Maurice de Poitevin, ed., http://www.lauragais-patrimoine.fr/HISTOIRE/DE-GOUTTES/Jean-de-Gouttes.html [October 2015].
323. Jacques Alexandre François Allix de Vaux, 'Souvenirs Militaires et Politiques', *Journal des Sciences Militaires*, vol. 23, 1831, p. 67; Pelet, Part 10 of 'Campagne de 1813',

Spectateur Militaire, vol. III, 1827, pp. 31–6; Jean Baptiste Antoine Marcellin Marbot, *The Memoirs of Baron de Marbot*, New York: Longmans, Green and Co., 1905, vol. II, pp. 643–52. See also: Frédéric Naulet, 'La Trahison des Saxons', *Gloire & Empire*, no. 51, November–December 2013, p. 69. In addition to those already mentioned, prominent French memoirs on this incident include: Jean-Baptiste Barrès, *Memoirs of a French Napoleonic Officer*, London: Greenhill, 1988, pp. 183–4; Fain, *Manuscrit*, vol. II, pp. 422–5; Jean-Nicolas-Auguste Noël, *With Napoleon's Guns*, London: Greenhill, 2005, p. 18; and Jean Martin, *La Bataille et le Retraite de Leipzig*, Paris: Pichon-Lamy et Dewez, 1880, pp. 62–4.

324. Odeleben, *Napoleons Feldzug*, pp. 350–60; and his *Réclamations*, pp. 21–3.
325. The battle report on Leipzig containing this accusation appeared in *Le Moniteur Universel* and the *Journal de l'Empire* on 30 and 31 October 1813 respectively.
326. Napoleon's quotations are from Las Cases, *Napoleon at Saint Helena*, vol. III, pt. 6, pp. 55–66, 135–6.
327. Pelet's account includes harsh and partly mistaken comments about Bernadotte, see Part 10 of 'Campagne de 1813', *Spectateur Militaire*, vol. III, 1827, pp. 31–6; see also Marbot, *Memoirs*, vol. II, pp. 643–5. It is important to note that Pelet's disparagement of Bernadotte was founded in part on the post-battle bulletin issued by the Army of the North in which Bernadotte claimed credit for the Saxon artillery firing on the French; see that issued on 21 October 1813, in *Proclamations de S. A. R. le Prince-Royal de Suède*, pp. 90–101. Aster (*Leipzig*, vol. II, p. 146) dismisses the claim that the Saxon artillery commander gleefully took aim at the French as stated in Frédéric François Guillaume de Vaudoncourt, *Histoire de la Guerre soutenue par les Français en Allemagne en 1813*, Paris: Barrois, 1819, vol. I, p. 216.
328. Examples of exaggeration include Jean Camille Abel Fleuri Sauzey, *Les Saxons dans nos rangs*, vol. III of *Les Allemands sous les Aigles Françaises*, Paris: Terana, 1987; Stéphane Calvet, *Leipzig, 1813: La Guerre des Peuples*, Paris: Vendémiaire, 2013; Jean Thiry, *Leipzig*, Paris: Berger-Levrault, 1972. Walter Bruyère-Ostells links the defection to what he perceives as a shift towards 'total war' owing to the heavy reliance on artillery by both sides ('Les Troupes Allemandes de la Grande Armée à Leipzig (1813): Dépasser les Lectures Idéologiques d'une Défection', in Franck Mercier, Yann Lagadec and Ariane Boltanski, eds, *La Bataille: Du Fait d'Armes au Combat Idéologique, XIe–XIXe Siècle*, Rennes: Presses Universitaires Rennes, 2015, pp. 261–74), but I do not share this interpretation. See also his *Leipzig 16–19 octobre 1813*, Paris: Tallandier, 2013, Chapter 8.
329. Vaudoncourt, *Histoire de la Guerre*, vol. I, p. 218.
330. Las Cases, *Napoleon at Saint Helena*, vol. III, pt. 6, pp. 64–5.
331. Johann Carl Gross, *Erinnerungen aus den Kriegszeiten*, Leipzig: Voß, 1850, pp. 107–14; Flathe, *Neuere Geschichte*, pp. 224–5. Dufour was Jacques Ferdinand Dufour, a Leipzig businessman.
332. Cerrini, *Feldzüge der Sachsen*, pp. 326–7; Colson, *Leipzig*, p. 327. Prussian soldier-poet Friedrich de la Motte Fouqué states that a Saxon officer approached him and some

fellow Prussian officers on the evening of 18 October to announce the impending defection, but the timing and apparent location make this claim highly dubious (*Lebensgeschichte des Baron Friedrich de la Motte Fouqué*, Halle: Schwetschke, 1840, pp. 333–4).

333. Aster, *Leipzig*, vol. II, p. 170.
334. Auguste Jean Michel Isidore Thirion, *Souvenirs Militaires*, Paris: Berger-Levrault, 1892, pp. 298–99.
335. The Saxon officers' signatures are in SHD, 2C158 (with thanks to Bruno Colson); Caulaincourt's letter to the acting Saxon commander is in Fain, *Manuscrit*, vol. II, pp. 444–5; it was published in the *Moniteur*, no. 309, 5 November 1813.
336. Charles Pierre Lubin Griois, *Mémoires du Général Griois 1792–1822*, Paris: Plon, 1909, p. 249.
337. Johann Georg, 'Friedrich August der Gerechte', p. 71; Kölle, 'Erlebtes', pp. 226–7; and Naumann, *Völkerschlacht*, p. 366. See also Fain, *Manuscrit*, vol. II, pp. 437–40; Norvins, *Portefeuille*, vol. II, pp. 419–20.
338. Münch, *Butterkrebse*, p. 57; Titze, *Leib-Grenadier-Garde*, pp. 70–1.
339. Kölle, 'Erlebtes', p. 227. Wilhelm Meier, a doctor in the Baden brigade, likewise observed the emperor, recalling that, 'An indescribable calm lay upon his countenance as an expression of his inner greatness despite the dimming glory of his power' (Meier, *Erinnerungen*, p. 113).
340. Louis Victor Léon, comte de Rochechouart, *Souvenirs sur la Révolution, l'Empire et la Restauration*, Paris: Plon, 1892, p. 267.
341. Münch, *Butterkrebse*, pp. 58–61 (quotation); Titze, *Leib-Grenadier-Garde*, pp. 71–6; Weber, 'Einsiedel', pp. 87–8; Aster, *Leipzig*, vol. II, pp. 226–334. The prevailing confusion left details of these moments murky and contested. According to Bernhardi, Russian General Karl Wilhelm von Toll's biographer, Toll and Prussian Oberstleutnant Oldwig von Natzmer had been sent to the Saxon king with an ultimatum from the tsar and Natzmer led the *Anger* Grenadiers and some of the Leib-Grenadiers out to fire at the French. Other sources claim the Saxons were led by Rittmeister Carl Rudolph von der Schulenburg, a former Saxon officer now one of Schwarzenberg's adjutants. According to Schulenburg's account, he accepted a sword from the king in token of surrender and returned to Schwarzenberg; Bernhardi adamantly denies that Schulenburg was present at all. See: 'Die Gefangennahme König Friedrich Augusts am 19. Oktober 1813', *Leipziger Kalendar*, 1912, pp. 137–42; Bernhardi, *Toll*, vol. III, pp. 513–28; Hoen, *Leipzig*, vol. V, p. 655; Gneomar Ernst von Natzmer, *Aus dem Leben des Generals Oldwig von Natzmer*, Berlin: Mittler und Sohn, 1876, vol. I, pp. 164–8. Marmont claimed Saxons and Bavarians fired on his troops: the former, while unlikely, is at least possible; the latter is not ('Journal des opérations du 6e Corps', SHD, MR 686). French artillery Major Griois, who had admired the appearance and loyalty of the Saxon grenadiers on 18 October, hoped that the stories he heard about them were false: 'It would be painful to give credence to the rumour that the next day these same grenadiers fired from the

ramparts of Leipzig at the troops alongside whom they had been fighting the day before' (*Mémoires*, p. 249).
342. Baden's Graf Wilhelm von Hochberg, the sole person accompanying Bernadotte, noted that they barely had time to exchange courtesies before Bernadotte rushed out to welcome the arriving tsar (Hochberg, *Denkwürdigkeiten*, p. 257). There are various versions of exactly what transpired after Bernadotte left the king to greet Alexander and Friedrich Wilhelm III. Some of these suggest that Friedrich August hesitated too long or that the Allied monarchs did not see him or that he had no intention of meeting them. Whatever the specifics from the various accounts, what stands out is that neither the Russian tsar nor the Prussian king nor the Austrian Kaiser made any effort to seek out his Saxon counterpart. Rochechouart goes so far as to claim that Alexander intentionally snubbed the king to call on the queen (*Souvenirs*, pp. 267–8). See Blank, *bestrafte König*, pp. 134–6; Wedel, *Lebenserinnerungen*, vol. II, pp. 110–12. Metternich's typically haughty rendition of his call on the king is in Clemens von Metternich, *Aus Metternich's nachgelassenen Papieren*, Vienna: Braumüller, 1880, vol. I, pp. 174–5. Note that Bennigsen seems to have met the king before Bernadotte's arrival.
343. Rochechouart, *Souvenirs*, p. 268.
344. Quoted in Blank, *bestrafte König*, p. 136.
345. Principal sources for the king's situation after Leipzig: Blank, *bestrafte König*, pp. 132–44; the king's personal notes in Jenak, 'Mein Herr Bruder', pp. 189–91; Böttinger, *Kurstaates und Königreiches Sachsens*, vol. II, pp. 531–7; Gretschel/Bülau, *Sächsischen Volkes*, vol. III, pp. 520–32; Aster, *Leipzig*, vol. II, pp. 226–344; August Lebrecht Herrmann, *Friedrich August König von Sachsen*, Dresden: Walther, 1827, pp. 100–3; Johann Georg, 'Friedrich August der Gerechte', pp. 67–73, 91–3; Pölitz, *Regierung*, II/137–48; 'Sachsen heute vor fünfzig Jahren', *Die Grenzboten*, vol. XXIV, 1865; Weber, 'Einsiedel', pp. 86–93; Flathe, *Neuere Geschichte*, pp. 222–32. Note that Flathe portrayed Napoleon's meeting with the king in a very negative light (p. 226). The king's correspondence with the tsar and Kaiser is in Langeron, *Mémoires*, pp. 364–6. For correspondence with Napoleon between 14 and 19 October, see Jenak, 'Mein Herr Bruder', pp. 169–72.
346. The complexities of the 'Saxon question' and the associated 'Polish question' at the Congress of Vienna have been the subject of considerable scholarship. For introductions from the Saxon viewpoint with considerable published documentation and excellent maps, see Jochen Vötsch, 'Die "sächsische Frage" auf dem Wiener Kongress 1814/15', in Martin/Vötsch/Wiegand, *200 Jahre Königreich Sachsen*, pp. 169–84; essays by Reiner Groß, Rudolf Jenak, Peter Broucek and Winfried Müller, in Niedersen, ed., *Sachsen, Preußen und Napoleon*, pp. 458–66, 497–516; Rudolf Jenak, *Die Teilung Sachsens*, Dresden: Hellerau, 2007; and Jenak, *Sachsen, der Rheinbund und die Exekution*.
347. Cerrini, *Feldzüge der Sachsen*, pp. 334–5.
348. Saxon grenadiers writing in May 1815 after the riot in Liege (*see below*) in Steffen Poser, 'Zur Meuterei der sächsischen Truppen in Lüttich im Jahre 1815', 2004

Workshop in Leipzig, 'Armeen des Rheinbundes: Königreich Sachsen', with thanks to Thomas Hemmann.
349. Kummer, *Erinnerungen*, p. 22.
350. Raabe in Kretschmar, *Sächsischen Artillerie*, pp. 120–1; he expressed similar sentiments in a letter to the military journal *Minerva* in 1819 (SHSA, Generalstab, 11339, Nr. 281). The other quotes are from Hausen, *Tagebuch und Briefe*, p. 74; Probsthayn, *Tagebuch* p. 74; Wolffersdorff, 'Meine Erlebnisse', p. 27; Vollborn, *Erlebtes*, p. 71; and Holtzendorff, *Berichtigung*, p. 118.
351. Mandelsloh, *Erinnerungen 1812–1814 (II)*, p. 78.
352. Titze, *Husaren-Regiment*, p. 30.
353. Schuster/Franke, *Geschichte der Sächsischen Armee*, vol. II, pp. 368–70; Cerrini, *Feldzüge der Sachsen*, pp. 337–44; Johann Christian August Bürger, *Nachrichten über die Blokade und Belagerung der Elb- und Landesfestung Torgau im Jahre 1813*, Torgau: Wideburg, 1838, pp. 40–6. Cerrini mistakenly gives the date of the Saxon release from Torgau as 4 November.
354. Heinrich von Aster's diary quoted in Querengässer, *LeCoq*, p. 138; Mandelsloh, *Erinnerungen 1812–1814 (II)*, pp. 80–100; Schreibershofen, *Erinnerungen*, pp. 128–9.
355. Gülich, *Sächsische Armee*, pp. 242–9; Steffen Poser, 'Zur Meuterei der sächsischen Truppen in Lüttich im Jahre 1815', 2004 Workshop in Leipzig, 'Armeen des Rheinbundes: Königreich Sachsen'. Some accounts term the violence a 'mutiny', a term Stephan Freiherr von Welk disputes in his summary: 'Der Aufstand sächsischer Grenadiere gegen Feldmarschall Blücher im Mai 1815', *Sächsische Heimatsblätter*, no. 2, 2016.

Blücher and other Prussians at the time certainly considered the Saxons 'a horde of mutineers' ('Der Aufstand der Sachsen in Lüttich (2. Mai 1815), *Preußische Jahrbücher*, vol. 16, 1865, p. 165; Oscar von Lettow-Vorbeck, 'Die Meuterei des sächsischen Grenadier-Regiments Anfang Mai 1815 und die vorangegangenen Ereignisse, die hierzu Veranlassung gegeben haben', *Napoleons Untergang 1815*, Berlin: Mittler und Sohn, 1904, vol. I, pp. 491–509). Prussian General Johann Jakob Otto August Rühle von Lilienstern, who had been a key member of Blücher's staff in 1813, dismissed the Saxon soldier as having 'an easily excitable and extremely vulnerable temperament, especially when his ideas of national honour are touched'. For Rühle, the Saxons were no different from the soldiers of the former Grand Duchies of Frankfurt and Berg; being entirely rebuilt, they could not be considered as a body of troops who owed oaths and duties to the King of Saxony and thus were guilty of igniting a dangerous 'mutiny' ('Aufstand der Sächsischen Truppen in Lüttich', *Jahrbücher für wissenschaftliche Kritik*, nos. 211 and 212, November 1827).
356. My rough translation of '*Hat uns der Preuße das Land gestohlen/kann auch das Kreuz der Teufel holen*'. See Steffen Poser, *Hiob 38,11. Bis hierher sollst du kommen und nicht weiter; hier sollen sich legen deine stolzen Wellen: Denkmale erzählen über die Leipziger Völkerschlacht*, Beucha: Sax-Verlag, 1998, p. 11; and his 'Trotz Mangel an landschaftlicher Scenerie. Das Völkerschlachtdenkmal zu Leipzig', in Hofbauer/

Rink, *Völkerschlacht*, pp. 329–31 (which includes sardonic notes from contemporaries that Poser uncovered in his research). The raising of the cross was reported in the *Leipziger Tagesblatt*, 1–3 November 1814.
357. Larisch, *Zeit- und Lebensbild*, p. 118; Schreibershofen report to Gersdorff, 7 September 1813, SHSA, Generalstab, 11339, nr. 285. Similar sentiment is evident in Cerrini's history, *Feldzüge der Sachsen*, p. 262.
358. Jean Viennet, 'Souvenirs de la vie militaire', *Carnet de la Sabretache*, 1929, pp. 426–7.
359. Larisch, *Zeit- und Lebensbild*, p. 80; Mandelsloh, *Erinnerungen 1812–1814 (II)*, p. 78; Schreibershofen, *Erinnerungen*, pp. 113–15.
360. Wolffersdorff, 'Meine Erlebnisse', pp. 24–5. Schiller's *Wallenstein's Death*, with its themes of loyalty and hierarchy, was also the prism through which many Saxons viewed Thielmann in Torgau. This quote is taken from the F. J. Lamport translation, London: Penguin, 1979.
361. Querengässer, *LeCoq*, p. 135.
362. Querengässer, *LeCoq*, p. 126; Wolffersdorff, 'Meine Erlebnisse', p. 25; Redlich, *Cerrini*, p. 33–4.

Chapter 3: **Bavaria: The First to Fall**

1. Johann Georg, 'Friedrich August der Gerechte', p. 71.
2. Parts of this chapter are drawn from an unpublished paper presented at the annual conference of the Society for Military History in 1999: 'The Bavarian Army in 1813: Military Performance at the End of Alliance'.
3. Joseph was co-regent with his mother, Maria Theresa, from 1765 until her death in 1780.
4. Michael Doeberl, 'Bayern und Deutschland im Befreiungskriege', in *Bayern 1813*, Munich: Bayerland-Verlag, 1913, p. 18; Roger Dufraisse, *L'Allemagne à l'Époque Napoléonienne*, Bonn: Bouvier, 1992, pp. 245–66; Jacques-Olivier Boudon, 'Napoléon et la Bavière', 2006, at www.france-bayern.info (accessed April 2021); Weis, 'Einfluss der französischen Revolution', pp. 571–2. For a good recent overview of Bavaria's situation, see Martin Hofbauer, 'Die Sicht der Mittelmächte am Beispiel Bayerns', in Hofbauer/Rink, *Völkerschlacht*, pp. 219–29.
5. Michael Doeberl, *Entwickelungsgeschichte Bayerns*, Munich: Oldenbourg, 1912, p. 380; Eberhard Weis, 'Bayern und Frankreich in der Zeit des Konsulats und des ersten Empire (1799–1815)', in *Deutschland und Frankreich um 1800: Aufklärung, Revolution, Reform*, Walther Demel and Bernd Roeck, eds, Munich: C. H. Beck, 1990, p. 179; Junkelmann, *Napoleon und Bayern*, pp. 138–9.
6. Montgelas, *Denkwürdigkeiten*, pp. 299–300.
7. Marcus Junkelmann, *Montgelas*, Regensburg: Pustet, 2015, p. 98.
8. Eberhard Weis, *Montgelas: Eine Biographie*, Munich: C. H. Beck, 2008, vol. II, p. 656.
9. Ibid., vol. II, p. 661.
10. Quoted in ibid., vol. II, p. 660.

11. Quoted in Michael Doeberl, *Bayern und die deutsche Erhebung wider Napoleon I.*, Munich: Akademie der Wissenschaften, 1907, p. 356.
12. Gottfried von Boehm, 'Ein angeblicher Abdankungsantrag Napoleons an König Max Joseph von Bayern', *Forschungen zur Geschichte Bayerns*, vol. XI, 1903, p. 250.
13. Quote: Max Joseph to Ludwig, 12 September 1813, in Hans Wolf Schwarz, *Die Vorgeschichte des Vertrages von Ried*, Munich: C. H. Beck, 1933, p. 130. See also Doeberl, *Entwickelungsgeschichte*, p. 443; Junkelmann, *Napoleon und Bayern*, p. 154.
14. For summaries see Eugen Frauenholz, 'Die Eingliederung von Heer und Volk in den Staat in Bayern 1597–1815', *Münchener Historische Abhandlungen*, no. 14, 1940, pp. 28–32; and Gill, *Eagles*, Chapter 2.
15. On Max Joseph and Montgelas, see Weis, *Montgelas*, vol. I, pp. 439–44; Doeberl, *Bayern und die deutschen Erhebung*, pp. 375–6.
16. John H. Gill, 'Wrede in Russia: Alliance and Independence in 1812', CRE, *Selected Papers 1999*, Owen Connelly, Charles Crouch, Donald D. Horward, William Olejniczak and Michael F. Pavković, eds, Tallahassee: Florida State University, 1999. On Wrede in 1812: Johann Heilmann, *Feldmarschall Fürst Wrede*, Leipzig: Duncker & Humblot, 1881, Chapter 4; and his 'Das Ende des Bayerischen Heeres im Jahre 1812', *JdAM*, vol. XIII, 1874; also Doeberl, *Bayern und die deutsche Erhebung*, p. 364; and Heinrich Demmler, 'Die Neubildung der bayerischen Heeresabteilung nach dem Rückzuge aus Rußland 1812 und die Ereignisse bis zur Rückkehr in die Heimat 1813', *DBKHG*, no. 15, 1906.
17. Paraphrased from Gottfried von Böhm, 'König Max Joseph von Bayern 1813', in *Bayern 1813*, p. 7.
18. Pfister, *Lager des Rheinbundes*, p. 220.
19. Hruby to Metternich, 23 March 1813, in Schwarz, *Vorgeschichte*, pp. 113–14.
20. Alexander Winter, *Karl Philipp Fürst von Wrede als Berater des Königs Max Joseph und des Kronprinzen Ludwig von Bayern (1813–1825)*, Neue Schriftenreihe des Stadtarchivs München, Heft 7, Munich: Stadtarchiv, 1968, pp. 31–3. Doeberl credited Wrede for the speed of the decision (*Bayern und die deutschen Erhebung*, p. 400). Curiously, Wrede chose to send his neutrality memo under the pseudonym 'Hippolithus a Lapide' (used by the seventeenth century legalist and historian Bogislaw Philipp von Chemnitz), see note in Doeberl, *Bayern und die deutsche Erhebung*, p. 432.
21. Albrecht Liess, 'Kronprinz Ludwig von Bayern und Napoleon', 2006, at www.france-bayern.info (accessed April 2021). Joseph Hormayr zu Hortenburg, *Lebensbilder aus dem Befreiungskriege*, Jena: Frommann, 1841, vol. I, p. 106; Karl Theodor Heigel, 'Strasbourg, die Vaterstadt Ludwigs I. von Bayern', *Historische Vorträge und Studien*, vol. III, Munich: Rieger, 1887, p. 288. See also Theodor Bitterauf, 'Napoleon I. und Kronprinz Ludwig von Bayern', *Schriften des Vereins für Geschichte des Bodensees und seiner Umgebung*, vol. XXXIX, 1910.
22. Max Joseph to Ludwig, 12 September, 25 May and 9 April 1813, in Schwarz, *Vorgeschichte*, pp. 118, 123; for Montgelas, to whom Ludwig wrote four times in May, see Karl Theodor Heigel, 'Kronprinz Ludwig im Befreiungsjahr 1813', *Quellen und*

Abhandlungen zur neueren Geschichte Bayerns, Munich: Rieger, 1890, pp. 356–68. Ludwig's poem is printed in *Bayern 1813*, p. 1. Ludwig's modern biographer, Heinz Gollwitzer, describes the crown prince's behaviour as 'bordering on the panicked' (*Ludwig I. von Bayern*, Munich: Ludwig, 1997, pp. 153–5).

23. On Ludwig, see Roger Dufraisse, 'Napoleon und Bayern', in Hubert Glaser, ed., *Krone und Verfassung: König Max I. Joseph und der neue Staat*, Munich: Hirmer, 1980, pp. 225–7; Carl Theodor Heigel, *König Ludwig von Bayern*, Leipzig: Duncker & Humblot, 1872, pp. 33–7; Johann Nepomuk Sepp, *Ludwig Augustus, König von Bayern und das Zeitalter der Wiedergeburt der Künste*, Regensburg: Manz, 1903, pp. 12–38; and Gollwitzer, *Ludwig*, pp. 120–66. On Caroline, see Marcel Dunan, *Napoléon et l'Allemagne: la Système Continental et les Débuts du Royaume de Bavière*, Paris: Plon, 1942, pp. 53–4.

24. Johann Michael Antelsperger, 'Tagebuch', BayHStA, HS 442/2, entry for 11 January 1813.

25. Sources for the following include: Demmler's 'Neubildung' and his 'Anteil der Bayerischen Division Raglovich am Frühjahrsfeldzug 1813', *DBKHG*, no. 16, 1907; Georg Gilardone, 'Bayerns Anteil am Herbstfeldzuge 1813', *DBKHG*, no. 22, 1913; Peter Bunde, Markus Gärtner and Markus Stein, *Die bayerische Armee 1806–1813*, Berlin: Zeughaus Verlag, 2011 (uniforms).

26. Thomas Schuler, *'Wir sind auf einem Vulkan': Napoleon und Bayern*, Munich: Beck, 2015, p. 224.

27. Initial instructions specified that each have 121 men rather than the 150 that had been the authorised strength in 1812; this was increased to 137 later in March for the battalions assigned to the 'observation corps' on the kingdom's north-eastern border.

28. Quote from the edict announcing the new flags in Oskar Bezzel, *Das K. B. 4. Infanterie-Regiment König Wilhelm von Württemberg vom Jahre 1806–1906*, Munich: Lindau, 1906, p. 143.

29. As examples of this process, the 2nd Battalion of the 6th Infantry numbered 793 officers and men on 31 March, while its Reserve Battalion had been reduced to 221 (instead of more than 600). At approximately the same time, the II/5 Infantry marched for the border with 606 officers and men while its reserve battalion counted 344 on its rolls. See Friedrich von Fabrice, *Das Königlich Bayerische 6. Infanterie-Regiment*, Munich: Oldenbourg, 1896, vol. II, p. 459; and Hans Gerneth and Bernhard Kießling, *Die Geschichte des königlich Bayerischen 5. Infanterie-Regiments*, Berlin: Mittler und Sohn, 1893, vol. II, p. 463.

30. Each 1st Battalion contained the 1st Grenadier and 1st Schützen companies as well as the odd numbered fusilier companies. The 2nd Battalions with Raglovich's division thus had the 2nd Grenadier and 2nd Schützen companies along with the even numbered fusilier companies (2nd, 4th, 6th, 8th). The 13th Infantry's Reserve Battalion consisted of the companies numbered 9 through 12.

31. Friedrich Münich, *Geschichte der Entwickelung der bayerischen Armee seit zwei Jahrhunderten*, Munich: Lindau, 1864, pp. 245–50; Oskar Bezzel, *Geschichte des*

Königlich Bayerischen Heeres unter König Max I. Joseph von 1806 (1804) bis 1825, Munich: Schick, 1933, pp. 53–6. The fusilier companies in these 2nd Divisions were the 2nd and 4th.

32. Rudolf Ritter von Xylander, *Geschichte des 1. Feldartillerie-Regiments Prinz-Regent Luitpold*, Berlin: Mittler & Sohn, 1909, vol. II, p. 372.

33. A 'civil guard' ('*Bürgermiliz*') intended for basic policing within the kingdom was classified as the 'National Guard Third Class' (*National-Garde III. Klasse*).

34. This section is drawn from Erich Freiherr von Guttenberg, 'Die bayerische Nationalgarde II. Klasse in den Befreiungskriegen', *DBKHG*, no. 22, 1913; the quotation from the decree is on p. 177. The instructions for the mobile legions are contained in *Allegemeine Verordnungen über das Aufgebot der mobilen Legionen und die Errichtung eines National-Chevaulegers-Regiment*, Munich: Hubschmann, 1813. The 3 March 1813 letter to Napoleon is published in Doeberl, *Bayern und die deutschen Erhebung*, pp. 412–13.

35. First quote from Ludwig von Seiboltsdorf (a *Major* at the time), 'Das K. Bayr. Armeekorps in dem Feldzuge gegen Russland im Jahre 1812', BayHStA/HS 723, p. 199; second from Völderndorff und Waradein (a *Hauptmann* at the time), *Kriegsgeschichte von Bayern*, vol. III, p. 285.

36. Antelsperger, 'Tagebuch', BayHStA, HS 442/2, entries for 14 and 15 January 1813.

37. Seiboltsdorf, 'Armeekorps', BayHStA, HS 723, p. 271.

38. Author's estimate of strength from Wrede's 11 January 1813 report in Reboul, *Campagne de 1813*, vol. I, p. 137 and the replacement column figures provided in Demmler, 'Neubildung'. This figure is higher than Demmler's estimate of at most 6,300 for the entire force.

39. Vaudoncourt, *Prince Eugène*, vol. II, p. 128. I am forced to wonder if Napoleon's cause would have been served better by keeping the Bavarians together as a division instead of sending half of the force to garrison Thorn.

40. Demmler, 'Neubildung', p. 55.

41. Saint-Cyr, more or less recovered from the wound received at Second Polotsk in October 1812, was in Płock from approximately 13 to 20 January and attempted to resume command of 6th Corps, only to be rebuffed or at least staved off by Wrede according to one of Wrede's staff officers: August Prinz von Thurn und Taxis, 'Tagebuch eines Officiers im Generalstabe der bayerischen Armee im Feldzuge 1812', *Mittheilungen des K. und K. Kriegs-Archivs*, vol. VII, 1893, p. 264; Demmler, 'Neubildung', p. 59. Reboul, on the other hand, indicates that Berthier ordered Saint-Cyr to leave the 'corps' under Wrede (*Campagne de 1813*, vol. II, p. 14/N3). Saint-Cyr makes no mention of this in his memoirs.

42. Joseph Maillinger, 'Tagebuch des Hauptmanns Joseph Maillinger im Feldzuge nach Rußland 1812', Paul Holzhausen, ed., *DBKHG*, no. 21, 1912, pp. 148–55; Lintner, *Kampf*, pp. 285–6. Kurt Uebe, *Der Stimmungsumschwung in der Bayerischen Armee gegenüber den Franzosen 1806–1812*, Munich: Beck, 1939, p. 119; Uebe's little tome contains some useful insights, but its value is greatly diminished by its heavily

polemical nature. See the trenchant critiques in Julia Murken, *Bayerische Soldaten im Russlandfeldzug 1812*, Munich: Beck, 2006, pp. 178–9; and Junkelmann, *Napoleon und Bayern*, p. 203/n.111. The latter comments that Uebe's work, in keeping with the spirit of its time (*Zeitgeist*), 'strives to locate the alienation between the Bavarians and the French as early and as vehemently as possible, whereby he does not shy away from manipulation' of data and interpretations.

43. Wrede to Zoller, 28 January 1813, in 'Einschließung und Belagerung von Thorn im Jahre 1813', *Kriegs-Schriften herausgegeben von baierischen Offizieren*, vol. III, 1821, pp. 44–5. Most of this letter is also printed in R. von Hößlin and E. Hagen, 'Die Verteidigung von Thorn vom 20. Januar bis 16. April 1813', *DBKHG*, no. 3, 1894, pp. 31–2.

44. Demmler, 'Neubildung', pp. 59–61. Demmler states that Wrede confronted Davout near Posen when the latter was heading for the Oder and gave 'undisguised expression of his displeasure'. See also Lintner, *Kampf*, p. 188.

45. See Davout's letters to Napoleon, Eugène, Berthier, Duroc and Poniatowski, 7–21 January 1813, in Davout, *Correspondance*, vol. III, pp. 445–74 (quotes from letters to Berthier, 15 January, to Poniatowski, 21 January); and Leuchtenberg, *Prince Eugène*, pp. 182–93 (quote from letter to Eugène, 20 January). GB Maurellian, the future governor of Thorn, and his artillery chief, Capitaine Alphand, were both in Thorn while Davout was there and both reported that Davout did not think the fortress defensible (reports in SHD, 2C168).

46. The published materials on this confusing phase of operations contain no reference to such an order to Davout, nor is there any subsequent indication that he was chastised for intentional disobedience. For Wrede's accusation (apparently in a 29 January 1813 report), see Demmler, 'Neubildung', pp. 60–1; Fabrice, *Bayerische 6. Infanterie-Regiment*, vol. II, p. 423; Alfred Döderlein, *Geschichte des Königlich Bayerischen 8. Infanterie-Regiments*, Landshut: Rietsch, 1898, vol. II, pp. 327–8.

47. Seiboltsdorf, 'Armeekorps', BayHStA, HS 723, p. 278. Wrede's ire may have been heightened because he had received orders placing him – very temporarily as it turned out – under Davout's command.

48. I have dwelt on this incident at some length as it illuminates Bavarian attitudes in 1813, whether justified or not; it also tells us something about the historiography of Rheinbund attitudes towards the French and thus offers a suggestion on yet another small gap in our knowledge of the era. In addition to those already mentioned, sources consulted include: Gallaher, *Iron Marshal*; F. G. Hourtoulle, *Davout le Terrible*, Paris: Copernic, 1975; Frédéric Hulot, *Le Maréchal Davout*, Paris: Pygmalion, 2003; Alain Felkel, *Louis Nicolas Davout*, Hamburg: Osburg Verlag, 2013; Christiane d'Ainval, *Gouvion Saint-Cyr*, Paris: Copernic, 1981; Victor Bernhard Derrécagaix, *Maréchal Berthier*, Paris: Chapelot, 1905; S. J. Watson, *By Command of the Emperor: A Life of Marshal Berthier*, Cambridge: Ken Trotman, 1988 (reprint of 1957 edition); Franck Favier, *Berthier: L'Ombre de Napoléon*, Paris: Perrin, 2015; and Hasso Dormann, *Feldmarschall Fürst Wrede*, Munich: Süddeutscher Verlag, 1982.

49. Diary of Hauptmann Gustav Krafft paraphrased in Fabrice, *Bayerische 6. Infanterie-Regiment*, vol. II, pp. 408–9; Theodor Bitterauf, 'Zur Geschichte der Öffentlichen Meinung im Königreich Bayern im Jahre 1813 bis zum Abschluss des Vertrages von Ried', *Archiv für Kulturgeschichte*, vol. XI, 1910, pp. 59–60.
50. The following is drawn from Franz Schubert und Hans Vara, *Geschichte des K. B. 13. Infanterie-Regiments Kaiser Franz Joseph von Österreich*, Munich: Lindau, 1906, vol. I, pp. 264–80.
51. All quoted in Schubert/Vara, *K. B. 13. Infanterie-Regiments*, vol. I, p. 258. See also Max Leyh, *Die Feldzüge des Königlich Bayerischen Heeres unter Max I. Joseph von 1805 bis 1815*, Munich: Schick, 1935, p. 254. Note that 'Butler' is often spelt 'Buttler' as in the 1811 Bavarian Army *Rangliste*, but I have retained 'Butler' here as the more common version.
52. Modest Ivanovich Bogdanovich, *Geschichte des Feldzuges im Jahre 1812*, Leipzig: Schlicke, 1863, vol. III, pp. 388–9; Łukasiewicz, *Armia księcia Józefa*, pp. 24–5; Georges de Chambray, *Histoire de l'Expédition de Russie*, Paris: Chez Pillet Aîné, 1838, vol. III, p. 159; Reboul, *Campagne de 1813*, vol. I, pp. 279–83. The journal was published in Janusz Staszewski, *Dywizja Gdanska w Latach 1812–1813*, Gdansk: Society of Friends of Science and Art in Gdansk, 1937.
53. This account relies principally on Hößlin/Hagen, 'Verteidigung von Thorn'; Klöffler/Hemmann, *vergessene Befreiungskrieg*, pp. 198–207; 'Tagebuch', in Völderndorff, *Kriegsgeschichte von Bayern*, vol. III, pp. 393–462; Hausmann/Gill, *Soldier for Napoleon*, pp. 189–91; and French reports from SHD 2C168: Maurellian, 'Rapport sur les événements qui ont eu lieu devant Thorn', 18 April 1813; Chef de Bataillon de la Roche, 'Journal de Blocus & Siege de la Place de Thorn en 1813', 11 June 1813; Chef de Bataillon Jean-Baptiste Tholosé, 'Mémoire sur la place de Thorn', 18 April 1813; Capitaine Alphand, 'Journal du Siege du Thorn', 16 April 1813. Note that de la Roche's report was published in translation with extensive notes as 'Einschließung und Belagerung von Thorn im Jahre 1813', *Kriegs-Schriften herausgegeben von baierischen Offizieren*, vol. III, 1821 apparently from the copy in BayHStA, HS 728. These are supplemented by regimental histories and other sources as indicated. See also: F. von Kosen, *Journal der Kriegsoperationen der Kaiserlich-Russischen und der verbündeten Armeen von der Eroberung Thorns bis zur Einnahme von Paris*, Riga: Meinshausen, 1815, pp. 3–10; 'Gedanken über die Belagerung der Festung Thorn im Jahre 1813, und die Festung selbst', *Militairische Blätter*, vol. II, 1822; Russian siege journal in Plotho, *Krieg in Deutschland*, vol. I, Beilage XII; and K. Hoburg, *Die Belagerungen der Stadt und Festung Thorn seit dem 17. Jahrhundert*, Thorn: Lambeck, 1844. For those seeking a comprehensive modern study including the besiegers' views based on thorough research in French, Polish and Russian archives (if perhaps overly reliant on Deifl), see Andrzej Nieuważny, *Kampania 1813 r. na Północnym Zachodzie Księstwa Warszawskiego: Napoleońska Twierdza Toruń i jej Obrona*, Torun: Universytetu Mikołaja Kopernika, 2017.
54. Reboul, 'Napoléon et les Places d'Allemagne', p. 106.

55. Figures from official strength reports in Hößlin/Hagen, 'Verteidigung von Thorn', pp. 57–9.
56. Wrede to Zoller, 28 January 1813, in 'Einschließung und Belagerung', pp. 44–5.
57. Convoys of invalids were sent west during 27–31 January and again on 3 February (Völderndorff, *Kriegsgeschichte von Bayern*, vol. III, p. 401–3). If the anonymous editor of 'Einschließung und Belagerung' is correct (pp. 57–8), the fate of these men (mostly French and Italians) was often horrifying. The garrison provided an escort for some distance from the fortress, but then returned to Thorn, leaving these unfortunates to make their own way to Posen, 140 kilometres to the southwest. Abandoned by the civilian waggoners who had been hired to transport them and without medical care or other resources, many, perhaps most, perished in the most wretched circumstances. Note that these observations do not appear in de la Roche's original report.
58. Eugen Zoellner, *Geschichte des K. B. 11. Infanterie-Regiments 'von der Tann' 1805–1905*, Munich: Lindauer, 1905, pp. 127–30; Völderndorff, *Kriegsgeschichte von Bayern*, vol. III, p. 401.
59. This and the previous quotation from Antelsperger are from his 'Tagebuch', BayHStA, HS 442/2.
60. De la Roche, 'Journal de Blocus & Siege', SHD, 2C168.
61. Hauptmann Joseph Vögler, 'Tagebuch', BayHStA, HS 726. See Nieuważny, *Kampania 1813 r.*, pp. 214–19 for the Russian order of battle in early February.
62. Osten-Sacken, *Geschichte des Befreiungskrieges*, vol. I, pp. 170, 295.
63. 'Journal de Blocus & Siege de la Place de Thorn en 1813', BayHStA, HS 728.
64. In addition to putting up a brash front whenever Russian *parlementaires* approached, Savary and his men blew horns, beat drums and paraded about with uniform coats reversed to appear stronger than they were; they reportedly convinced the Russians that the castle was held in battalion strength.
65. Maurellian, 'Rapport', SHD 2C168.
66. Editor's comments in 'Einschließung und Belagerung', pp. 51–2; Völderndorff, *Kriegsgeschichte von Bayern*, vol. III, p. 417; Antelsperger diary entry for 14 February 1813, BayHStA, HS 442/2.
67. Osten-Sacken, *Geschichte des Befreiungskrieges*, vol. I, pp. 450, 552; Louis von Malinowsky I. and Robert von Bonin. *Geschichte der brandenburgisch-preußischen Artillerie*, Berlin: Duncker und Humblot, 1846, pp. 462–8. See Nieuważny, *Kampania 1813 r.*, pp. 276–8 for Barclay's order of battle at this stage.
68. Fleischmann was an unusual case: a soldier's son, he entered the army at the age of ten as a drummer, became an officer in 1799 and rose through the ranks to retire as a *General-Major*. Maximilian Ruith, *Königlich Bayerisches 3. Infanterie-Regiment Prinz Carl von Bayern 1698–1900*, Ingolstadt: Ganghofer, 1900, pp. 170–1.
69. On the city's citizens, see Karl Wilhelm Keferstein, *Die Belagerung und Einnahme der Stadt und Festung Thorn im Jahre 1813*, Thorn: Lehmann, 1826, pp. 58–9; and Klöffler/Hemmann, *vergessene Befreiungskrieg*, pp. 198–207.

70. Nieuważny gives slightly different figures (*Kampania 1813 r.*, pp. 293–5).
71. Josef Deifl, *Infanterist Deifl*, Eugen von Frauenholz, ed., Munich: Beck, 1939, p. 88. Deifl's popular 'Tagebuch' was completed in 1849 and has been reprinted several times, but, as Marcus Junkelmann wisely observes, it must be used with great caution: 'above all his anti-French and anti-Napoleon tirades ("boastful arrogance", "godless French", etc.) are to be seen as anachronistic as they find no equivalents in the documents of the time' (Junkelmann, *Napoleon und Bayern*, p. 203/n.111); see also Murken, *Bayerische Soldaten*, pp. 162–5.
72. Langeron, *Mémoires*, p. 166. He also stated that the French and Poles were drunk when they marched out, the Poles were dejected but calm, while the French were loudly maligning the emperor, their generals, their reverses and the retreat from Moscow.
73. Gerneth/Kießling, *Bayerischen 5. Infanterie-Regiments*, vol. II, p. 446; *Geschichte des Königl. Baÿer. 2ten Lin. Inf. Regiments Kronprinz von seiner Entstehung Anno 1682 bis 1826*, manuscript, n.p., n.d., p. 255.
74. Maurellian, 'Rapport', SHD 2C168.
75. Note that the copy of this report in the Bavarian archives includes the phase 'He was fully supported by the activity of Oberst von Hoffnaaß who had been named as the city commandant,' which is not in the copies de la Roche submitted (BayHStA, HS 728, translation in 'Einschließung und Belagerung', p. 107).
76. Hößlin/Hagen, 'Verteidigung von Thorn', p. 53.
77. Antelsperger diary entry for 15 April 1813, BayHStA, HS 442/2.
78. Bavarian strength for 7 June 1813 from SHD, 2C546; French strength from the situations of the French artillery and infantry, 9 and 11 June 1813, SHD, 2C168. The Bavarians had nothing but praise for Maureillan's performance, but Napoleon, angry at what he considered the hasty surrender of Thorn, subjected Maureillan to two commissions of inquiry, both of which exonerated him (see Bruno Colson, *Le Général Rogniat: Ingénieur et Critique de Napoléon*, Paris: Economica, 2006). Contrary to Wrede's fears, Napoleon did not blame the Bavarians. Bavarian casualties during the return march included 16 who died, 14 deserters, 236 left behind in field hospitals and 56 stragglers recovering at various halting points (Nieuważny, *Kampania 1813 r.*, p. 296).
79. Gerneth/Kießling, *Bayerischen 5. Infanterie-Regiments*, vol. II, pp. 452–5; Fabrice, *Bayerische 6. Infanterie-Regiment*, vol. II, pp. 447–52. These two excellent and well-sourced regimental histories both state that the disarmed brigade encountered Rittmeister von Colomb's Prussian raiding detachment south of Zwickau on 13 June and was thus delayed from proceeding until the Prussians were convinced that an armistice was in effect. Colomb's account and that of one of his officers, however, make no mention of the Bavarians: Friedrich August Peter von Colomb, *Aus dem Tagebuch des Rittmeisters v. Colomb*, Berlin: Mittler und Sohn, 1854; Gustav Callenius, 'Meine Erlebnisse bei dem Streifzuge der v. Colomb'schen Reiterschaar im Frühjahr 1813', *Der Beobachter an der Saale, Schwarza und Ilm*, nos. 27–29, 7, 14 and 21 July 1863;

see also Ardenne, *Zieten'schen Husaren-Regiments*, pp. 386–7. The manuscript history of the Bavarian 2nd Infantry (*Königl. Baÿer. 2ten Lin. Inf. Regiments*, pp. 272–3), on the other hand, states that the column was delayed by Lützow's raiders, but there is no mention of the Bavarians in the histories of that corps either and this seems simply erroneous.
80. Antelsperger diary entry for 16 June 1813, BayHStA, HS 442/2.
81. The principal source for this section is Demmler, 'Neubildung', pp. 61–96.
82. Wrede, passing through Görlitz on 10 February on his way back to Bavaria, unilaterally changed the orders to send the guns home. An officer had been sent to Thorn to seek ammunition, but the fortress, short itself, had none to spare. See Demmler, 'Neubildung', p. 61; and Xylander, *Geschichte des 1. Feldartillerie-Regiments*, vol. II, pp. 367.
83. Seiboltsdorff, 'Armeekorps', BayHStA, HS 723, p. 284.
84. Friedrich Winther, 'Tagebuch', BayHStA, HS 431, pp. 83–4.
85. Seiboltsdorff, 'Armeekorps', BayHStA, HS 723, pp. 287–8.
86. Quotations from Rechberg to Maximilian, 25 February 1813, in Demmler, 'Neubildung', pp. 67–9. Strength figures from same source; Döderlein (*Bayerischen 8. Infanterie-Regiments*, vol. II, p. 332) gives 2,132 officers and men fit for duty on 17 February and 1,470 on the sick list.
87. Rechberg report quoted in Döderlein, *Bayerischen 8. Infanterie-Regiments*, vol. II, p. 333.
88. Winther, 'Tagebuch', BayHStA, HS 431, p. 93.
89. Seiboltsdorff, 'Armeekorps', BayHStA, HS 723, pp. 295–6; Winther, 'Tagebuch', BayHStA, HS 431, pp. 94–6. Winther wrote that when he reported the division's strength to Durutte, the French general directed him to claim that it was three times stronger than it was.
90. According to a 17 March strength report; an additional 95 men were detached (Leyh, *Feldzüge des Königlich Bayerischen Heeres*, p. 474).
91. Seiboltsdorff, 'Armeekorps', BayHStA, HS 723, p. 274.
92. Details on these incidents are unclear. Demmler ('Neubildung', pp. 80–1) describes much skirmishing with the Russian horse, but an anonymous eyewitness (likely a Bavarian officer) portrays the Bavarians holding the Russian cavalry at bay with the firm countenance of their formations and a cannon shot or two: 'Berichtigung eine Stelle im 1ten Theile von Plothos Krieg in Deutschland und Frankreich', *Kriegs-Schriften herausgegeben von baierischen Officieren*, vol. IV, 1820, pp. 98–101.
93. Rechberg to Durutte, 30 March 1813, and Durutte's campaign notes, RAMP, Boite 43. Winther recorded that a Saxon major named von Berg (perhaps Carl August Maximillian von Berge of the Garde-du-Corps?) had been accompanying Durutte with a small detachment, but that these departed for Dessau on 1 April, but he provides no further detail ('Tagebuch', BayHStA, HS 431, p. 97).
94. Seiboltsdorff, 'Armeekorps', BayHStA, HS 723, p. 308. The only published sources on this incipient mutiny are Demmler, 'Neubildung', p. 86; and Döderlein, *Bayerischen 8. Infanterie-Regiments*, vol. II, p. 341.

95. Berthier to Napoleon, 21 April 1813, *Rapports*, vol. I, p. 61. Berthier told Napoleon that the division contained only 800–900 men, but Durutte's official report gave a total of 1,182 French and 109 Würzburg troops (1 April 1813, SHD, 2C541).
96. Seiboltsdorff, 'Armeekorps', BayHStA, HS 723, p. 312.
97. A court of inquiry initially assigned blame to the lieutenant responsible for guarding the guns, but he was later exonerated and reinstated. As a result, no one's career suffered from this embarrassment.
98. For Langensalza, see Demmler, 'Neubildung', pp. 88–95; Xylander, *Geschichte des 1. Feldartillerie-Regiments*, vol. II, pp. 370–1; 'Überfall bei Langensalza in der Nacht vom 12–13 April 1813', *Archiv für Offiziere aller Waffen*, vol. I, 1848, pp. 14–19; Hans Fabricius, 'Der Parteigänger Friedrich von Hellwig und seine Streifzüge', *JdAM*, vol. 94, 1895, pp. 269–76; Ernst Graf zur Lippe-Weißenfeld, *Geschichte des Königl. Preuss. 6. Husaren-Regiments*, Berlin: Königlichen Geheimen Ober-Hofbuchdruckerei, 1860, pp. 155–7; Widdern, *Streifkorps*, vol. I, pp. 70–6 (includes Hellwig's account).
99. Seiboltsdorff, 'Armeekorps', BayHStA, HS 723, p. 314.
100. Winther, 'Tagebuch', BayHStA, HS 431, p. 109.
101. This section draws principally from Doeberl, *Bayern und die deutsche Erhebung*; and Schwarz, *Vorgeschichte*; supplemented by Prinz Adalbert von Bayern, *Max I. Joseph von Bayern: Pfalzgraf, Kurfürst und König*, Munich: Bruckmann, 1957; vol. II of Weis, *Montgelas*; Junkelmann, *Napoleon und Bayern*; and other specific sources as noted below.
102. Montegelas, *Denkwürdigkeiten*, p. 300.
103. 'Process' from Weis, *Montgelas*, vol. II, p. 663.
104. Adalbert, *Max I. Joseph von Bayern*, p. 631; on the negotiations with Prussia, see especially Schwarz, *Vorgeschichte*, pp. 23–43.
105. Montegelas, *Denkwürdigkeiten*, p. 302.
106. Montgelas's memorandum, 25 April 1813, in Doeberl, *Bayern und die deutsche Erhebung*, pp. 417–22. See also Planert, *Mythos*, pp. 592–6.
107. Doeberl, *Bayern und die deutsche Erhebung*, p. 362.
108. Taken from Doeberl's term *Interessengemeinschaft* in ibid., p. 371.
109. Rechberg to Montgelas, 20 March 1813 and Montgelas's reply, 1 April 1813, both in Doeberl, *Bayern und die deutsche Erhebung*, p. 360. Max Joseph made similar comments to Ludwig in a 23 April letter, see Adalbert, *Max I. Joseph*, p. 637.
110. Montgelas, *Denkwürdigkeiten*, p. 264.
111. Daniel Klang, 'Bavaria and the War of Liberation, 1813–1814', *French Historical Studies*, vol. 4, no. 1, Spring 1965, pp. 28–30.
112. Montgelas, *Denkwürdigkeiten*, p. 266. In these memoirs, Montegelas repeatedly comments on the exaggerations of Coalition propaganda portraying Napoleon as the embodiment of evil.
113. On this complex topic, see Bitterauf, 'öffentlichen Meinung'; and Leonhard Rieger, 'Die Stimmung und Haltung der fränkischen Provinzen im Jahre 1813', dissertation, Ludwig-Maximilian University, Munich, 1921; and especially Planert, *Mythos*,

pp. 584–96. Also useful is Oskar Bezzel, *Studien zur Geschichte Bayerns in der Zeit der Befreiungskriege*, Munich: Bayerisches Kriegsarchiv, 1926, pp. 14–20, 26–45. Ludwig Scheibeck and Ulrich Thürauf also address public opinion with some useful citations from period sources, but, like Uebe, their works are densely infused with floridly tendentious anti-French nationalism: 'Die Deutschnationale Bewegung in Bayern 1806–1813', Munich: Hueber, 1914; and 'Die öffentliche Meinung im Fürstentum Ansbach-Bayreuth zur Zeit der französischen Revolution und der Freiheitskriege', Munich: Beck, 1918; similarly Sigmund Riezler, 'Ebbe und Fluth deutscher Gesinnung in Bayern', *Beilage zur Allgemeine Zeitung*, no. 57, 9 March 1901. What is evident from these studies, however, is the complex nature of dissatisfaction: it fluctuated with external events and varied considerably from region to region, between urban and rural populations and among social classes. In a broader context, see Gollwitzer, *Ludwig*, pp. 156–61.

114. Max Joseph to Berthier, 23 April 1813, Marcel Dunan, 'Nouveaux documents sur l'Allemagne Napoléonienne: Lettres du roi de Bavière au Maréchal Berthier (1806–1813)', *Revue Historique*, vol. CLXXXVI, July–December 1939, p. 139.
115. The conspirators in this peculiar plot, including Archduke Johann (one of the Kaiser's younger brothers), believed Metternich was too hesitant to initiate hostilities with France. Without Kaiser Franz's authorisation (or anyone else's), they aimed to force Austria into open war with Napoleon by igniting insurgencies in the Tyrol, the Vorarlberg and Illyria. Habsburg authorities, however, uncovered the plot and Metternich closely supervised its rapid suppression. Metternich may have come to suspect that Bavarian agents were behind the conspiracy as a means to compromise the archduke, a conclusion that seems far-fetched. For an exhaustive examination of this and an earlier incident in 1811, see Eduard Wertheimer, 'Die Revolutionierung Tirols im Jahre 1813', *Deutsche Rundschau*, vol. CXX, July–August–September 1904.
116. Report of the Senior Postmaster in Nuremberg, Ernst von Axthelm, 2 March 1813, in Doeberl, *Bayern und die deutsche Erhebung*, pp. 410–11.
117. Montgelas to Rechberg, 11 April 1813, in ibid., pp. 415–17; Deoberl also notes Max Joseph's ire about the Coalition proclamation from Kalisch in March (p. 367).
118. 'Erklärung' signed by sixteen junior officers to explain their decisions to join the Russo-German Legion, in *Berlinische Nachrichten von Staats- und gelehrten Sachen*, no. 35, 23 March 1813; Schwarz, *Vorgeschichte*, p. 39. At least four, possibly five, of the signatories were Bavarians.
119. Doeberl, *Bayern und die deutsche Erhebung*, pp. 362–3; Napoleon to Maret, 4 April 1813, *CG*, no. 33630, vol. XIII, pp. 747–8.
120. Schwarz, *Vorgeschichte*, pp. 19–30.
121. Max Joseph to Berthier, 23 April 1813 (emphasis in the original), Dunan, 'Nouveaux documents', p. 139.
122. Montgelas's comment to the Prussian envoy in early April, in Oncken, *Oesterreich und Preußen*, vol. I, p. 344; Doeberl, *Bayern und die deutsche Erhebung*, p. 367.
123. Ludwig to Max Joseph, 7 April 1813, in Schwarz, *Vorgeschichte*, p. 116.

124. Weis argues that Montegelas recognised that neutrality was unrealistic, but, keenly aware of the king's attachment to France, he used the neutrality option as a means to push Max Joseph towards eventual alignment with Napoleon's enemies (*Montgelas*, vol. II, p. 668).
125. Schwarz, *Vorgeschichte*, pp. 48, 59.
126. Ibid., pp. 62–5. Ludwig maintained covert contact with the Prussian envoy through an intermediary and, in his impassioned desperation, took the unauthorised step of writing a personal note to Austria's Kaiser Franz; this effort, however, came to nothing (Schwarz, *Vorgeschichte*, p. 54; Luckwaldt, *Befreiungskriege*, p. 205). Winter handily debunks the notion that Ludwig planned to depose his father in collaboration with Wrede (Winter, *Wrede*, p. 31).
127. Max Joseph to Ludwig, 14 May 1813, in Schwarz, *Vorgeschichte*, pp. 120–1.
128. Montgelas, *Denkwürdigkeiten*, p. 275.
129. Schwarz, *Vorgeschichte*, p. 8.
130. Mercy d'Argenteau to Maret, 3 and 24 May 1813, in Schwarz, *Vorgeschichte*, pp. 119, 122–3.
131. In Doeberl, *Bayern und die deutsche Erhebung*, p. 372.
132. Montgelas's memorandum, 25 April 1813, in ibid., p. 419.
133. Oncken, *Oesterreich und Preußen*, vol. II, p. 269.
134. Montgelas to Ludwig, 21 May 1813, in Schwarz, *Vorgeschichte*, p. 121.
135. Doeberl, *Bayern und die deutsche Erhebung*, p. 380; Montgelas to Ludwig, 25 May 1813, in Schwarz, *Vorgeschichte*, p. 124; and Caroline to Ludwig, 31 May 1813, in Adalbert, *Max I. Joseph*, pp. 645–6.
136. Strength table for 1 March 1813, in Johann Heilmann, *Feldzug von 1813: Antheil der Bayern seit dem Rieder Vertrag*, Munich: Deschler, 1857, p. 64. Most of the following relies heavily on Demmler, 'Raglovich'.
137. Joseph Dauer, *Das königlich Bayerische 10. Infanterie-Regiment*, Ingolstadt: Ganghofer, 1906, vol. V, p. 291.
138. Demmler, 'Raglovich', p. 172.
139. Napoleon to Max Joseph, 2 March 1813, *CG*, no. 32964, vol. XIII, p. 450; also Demmler, 'Raglovich', pp. 171–2. Although the overall French intention was clear, the numbers outlined in Napoleon's missive to the king were not consistent with those specified in great detail in a 6 March letter from the French ambassador to Montgelas; the latter listed 15 battalions, 40 guns and six cavalry squadrons that would be increased as circumstances permitted to 18 squadrons for 3,600 mounted men (printed in Heilmann, *Feldzug von 1813*, pp. 65–6).
140. Imperial decree of 12 March 1813, *Correspondance de Napoléon Ier publiée par Ordre de l'Empereur Napoléon III*, Paris: Plon, 1868, no. 19698, vol. XXV, pp. 63–5; Grande Armée, 'Livret de Situation', 15 March 1813, SHD, 2C708. The division was carried under Ney's 3rd Corps through April and, as late as mid-May, there were still official strength reports denoting Raglovich's as the 29th Division of the 9th Corps along with Beaumont's cavalry division consisting of the Bavarian regiment as its

140. (cont.) 1st Brigade and the Westphalian/Hessian 2nd Brigade under GB Wolff (SHD, 2C539 and 2C542).
141. The division reported an on-hand strength of 8,322 on 27 April as 25 officers and 1,365 men had not yet arrived (Demmler, 'Raglovich', p. 174).
142. Divisional strength report for 3 May 1813, BayHStA, 495a.
143. Raglovich to Wrede, 31 March 1813, in Schubert/Vara, *K. B. 13. Infanterie-Regiments*, vol. I, p. 355. The original of the first sentence is '*Der Zustand der Truppe ist nicht der glänzendste*'. See also Gerneth/Kießling, *Bayerischen 5. Infanterie-Regiments*, vol. II, pp. 466–7.
144. Comments about the state of troops from a 4 April 1813 report cited in Gerneth/Kiesling, vol. II, p. 466. Raglovich's comment on 'the spirit of earlier days' from Division Command to Max Joseph, 10 June 1813, BayHStA, 495a. Although Raglovich approved and signed all the division's correspondence with the king, I have used the designation 'Division Command' ('*vom Königlichen Divisions Commando*') to distinguish the official, and presumably more widely circulated, reports from the personal letters he sent to his monarch (cited as 'Raglovich to Max Joseph').
145. Max Joseph to Berthier, 23 April 1813, Dunan, 'Nouveaux documents', p. 139. Comprehensive statistics on the numbers of deserters are not available, but the supposedly unusual scale of desertion occurs repeatedly in regimental histories. Bavarian historian Oskar Bezzel described desertion as 'massive' in the units that recruited from the former Prussian districts of Ansbach and Bayreuth (Bezzel, *Das K. B. 4. Infanterie-Regiment*, p. 145); the units most afflicted were the 9th, 10th and 13th Infantry Regiments and the 6th Light Battalion (Demmler, 'Raglovich', pp. 179–80). The problem was doubtless exacerbated by the propinquity of these regions to the division's initial deployment zone.
146. Axthelm's 2 March 1813 report, in Doeberl, *Bayern und die deutsche Erhebung*, pp. 410–11; 13 March 1813 prohibition, in Tobias Friedrich Kroeger, *Zwischen eigenstaatlicher Souveränität und napoleonischem Imperialismus: Das bayerische Offizierskorps 1799–1815*, Munich: AVM, 2013, pp. 235–6. Dauer quotes a 9 March order that cites similar concerns about military attitudes being even more bitter towards the French than those of the populace (*Bayerische 10. Infanterie-Regiment*, vol. V, p. 292).
147. Raglovich to Max Joseph, 12 May and 17 June 1813; Division Command to Max Joseph, 28 May 1813, BayHStA, 495a.
148. Xylander, *Geschichte des 1. Feldartillerie-Regiments*, vol. II, pp. 398–400. As Xylander notes, however, 'we detect in the regiment little if any awakening of glowing hatred against foreign domination' (*Fremdherrschaft*, the common pejorative term for the Rheinbund period).
149. Raglovich to Max Joseph, 12 May, 22 May and 17 June 1813, BayHStA, 495a.
150. A seven-page letter from Raglovich to the king immediately after the Battle of Bautzen is a bitter indictment of Beckers: Raglovich to Max Joseph, 22 May 1813, BayHStA, 495a.

151. Quote from Raglovich to Max Joseph, 9 September 1813, other relevant letters are those of 12 May, 22 May and 10 June (all BayHStA, 495a). See also Demmler, 'Raglovich', p. 181. Raglovich's biographical information from M. J., 'Zur Erinnerung an den Königl. bayerischen General der Infanterie und General-Quartiermeister der Armee, Clemens von Raglovich', *JdAM*, vol. 36, 1887; and Friedrich von Furtenbach, 'Die Generale des Bayerischen Heeres im Feldzuge gegen Rußland 1812/13', *DBKHG*, no. 21, 1912, pp. 5–7.
152. Raglovich to Max Joseph, 12 May 1813, BayHStA, 495a.
153. The following is largely drawn from Demmler, 'Raglovich', pp. 186–91, supplemented by regimental histories.
154. Kroeger, *Souveränität und napoleonischem Imperialismus*, p. 243.
155. Napoleon to Clarke, 11 March 1813 and Napoleon to Ney, 13 and 20 March 1813, *CG*, nos. 33135, 33213 and 33358, vol. XIII, pp. 525–7, 565–8, 635–6; Leyh, *Feldzüge des Königlich Bayerischen Heeres*, pp. 298–9. As late as 10 April, Napoleon was still thinking of Wrede as commanding the Bavarian contingent as part of Ney's corps (Napoleon to Ney, 10 April 1813, *CG*, no. 33788, vol. XIII, pp. 810–11).
156. Max Joseph to Ludwig, 23 April 1813, in Adalbert, *Max I. Joseph*, p. 637; Demmler, 'Raglovich', p. 186; Gerneth/Kießling, *Bayerischen 5. Infanterie-Regiments*, vol. II, pp. 465–7. Tournès also writes that Bertrand expressed himself 'in violent terms', and these negative depictions left a deep imprint in Bavarian historiography (*Lützen*, pp. 38–40).
157. Napoleon to Bertrand, 14 April 1813, *CG*, no. 33843, vol. XIII, p. 836. See also Steven L. Delvaux, 'Witness to Glory: Lieutenant-Général Henri-Gatien Bertrand, 1791–1815', dissertation, Florida State University, 2005, pp. 212–17; this dispute receives only the briefest mention in Henri Chérot, 'Le Général Bertrand en 1813 et 1814', *Études de théologie, de philosophie et d'histoire*, vol. 90, 1902, pp. 189–90; and none at all in Jacques de Vasson, *Bertrand: Le Grande-Maréchal de Sainte-Hélène*, Issoudun: Laboureur, 1935.
158. Napoleon to Bertrand, 19 April 1813, *CG*, no. 33922, vol. XIII, pp. 865–6; Berthier to Raglovich and Berthier to Max Joseph, both 19 April 1813, Berthier, *Ordres*, vol. I, pp. 16–17, 20; Napoleon to Max Joseph, 20 April 1813, *CG*, no. 33958, vol. XIII, p. 880; Napoleon to Berthier, 21 and 24 April 1813, *CG*, nos. 33965 and 33997, vol. XIII, pp. 884, 898. Berthier's formal complaint to the king was accompanied by an optimistic personal letter outlining French strength (Berthier to Max Joseph, 19 April 1813, BayHStA, Geheimes Haus Archiv, Nachlass König Max I. Joseph 132; part in Adalbert, *Max I. Joseph*, pp. 635–6). For this episode, see also Döderlein, *Bayerischen 8. Infanterie-Regiments*, vol. II, pp. 344–7.
159. Demmler, 'Raglovich', p. 191. In his history, Völderndorff merely mentions his meeting with Napoleon and says nothing of the emperor's remarks about the Saxon king (*Kriegsgeschichte von Bayern*, vol. IV, p. 11).
160. Max Joseph to Berthier, 23 April 1813, Dunan, 'Nouveaux documents', p. 139.
161. Raglovich to Bertrand, 25 April 1813, SHD, 2C448bis; Napoleon to Ney, 26 April 1813, *CG*, no. 34019, vol. XIII, p. 909.

162. Printed in Franz Berg, *Geschichte des Königl. Bayer. 4. Jäger-Bataillons*, Landshut: Rietsch, 1887, vol. I, pp. 372–3.
163. Lintner, *Kampf*, pp. 179–80.
164. Dauer, *Bayerische 10. Infanterie-Regiment*, vol. V, p. 294. Some of Oudinot's complaints remind the author of instances in his own military experience.
165. Both quotations from Praun, 'Tagebücher', BayHStA, HS 743. It is useful to recall that Praun was a very junior officer on his first campaign. Moreover, such occurrences were by no means uncommon in the author's own military experience whether dealing with one's allies or one's own army. In this case, the Bavarians felt that they had been denied quarters in several towns along the way already.
166. Döderlein, *Bayerischen 8. Infanterie-Regiments*, vol. II, pp. 350–1.
167. Raglovich's impressions, in Division-Command to Max Joseph, 22 May 1813, BayHStA, 495a. Napoleon's quote from *Journal de l'Empire*, 23 June 1813.
168. Jean Camille Abel Fleuri Sauzey, *Nos Alliés les Bavarois*, vol. VI of *Les Allemands sous les Aigles Françaises*, Paris: Terana, 1988, p. 309; Emil Buxbaum, *Das Königliche Bayerische 3. Chevaulegers-Regiment*, Munich: Oldenbourg, 1884, p. 137.
169. Berg, *Königl. Bayer. 4. Jäger-Bataillons*, p. 374. As a linguistic curiosity, it is interesting to note that Germans often used the phrase 'make a hurrah' ('*ein Hurrrah machen*') in referring to Cossack attacks.
170. This section on Bautzen is drawn from Demmler, 'Raglovich', pp. 197–207; Raglovich's battle report (Division-Command to Max Joseph, 22 May 1813, BayHStA, 495a); and regimental histories.
171. Lintner, *Kampf*, pp. 180–3.
172. Demmler, 'Raglovich', p. 202; Osten-Sacken, *Geschichte des Befreiungskrieges*, vol. IIb, pp. 117, 141–9. Note that Lorencez's 14th Division only had one brigade at Bautzen as the other (Gruyer's) was still approaching from the southeast where it had skirmished on 18 May (the 156^e Ligne may have arrived towards the end of the fighting).
173. As Demmler notes, Oudinot likely felt quite isolated on the army's extreme right. Napoleon had understandably refused to send him any reinforcements and the marshal probably wanted to retain as much of the Bavarian division as possible intact as a final reserve.
174. Anecdotes regarding the 4th Light Battalion from an anonymous diary paraphrased in 'Die Bayern im Jahre 1813', *Neue Militär-Zeitung*, no. 31, 1 August 1857.
175. Friedrich Mändler, *Erinnerungen aus meinen Feldzügen*, Nürnberg: Lotzbeck, 1854, pp. 110–11.
176. Division-Command to Max Joseph, 22 May 1813, BayHStA, 495a.
177. 'Relation der Schlacht von Bautzen' (undated but immediately after the battle from context), and 'Schlacht bei Bautzen: Auszug aus den Erläuterungen über das was die Königl. Baierischen Truppen anbelangt' (undated but may have been compiled later), both in SHSA, Generalstab, 11339, Nr. 283. Why these accounts reside in the Saxon State Archives is unknown.

178. Mändler, *Erinnerungen*, pp. 111–12. Praun recalled that 'A *Vive l'Empereur* echoed through the ranks' on the announcement of victory ('Tagebücher', BayHStA, HS 743).
179. Division-Command to Max Joseph, 22 May 1813, BayHStA, 495a.
180. Demmler, 'Raglovich', p. 206; Buxbaum, *Königliche Bayerische 3. Chevaulegers-Regiment*, p. 138; Hermann Hutter, *Das Königlich Bayerische 1. Chevaulegers-Regiment*, Munich: Oldenbourg, 1885, pp. 223–4. Note that both Bavarian regimental histories mistakenly state that the French officer giving the order for the infelicitous attack was Beaumont rather than Reiset. Reiset makes no mention of the Bavarians in his memoirs (Reiset, *Souvenirs*, vol. II, pp. 437–40), but he evidently sparked a controversy by attempting to blame his Italian regiment for the lacklustre attacks at Bautzen (Arnold, *Napoleon 1813*, pp. 314–15).
181. Division-Command to Max Joseph, 22 May 1813, BayHStA, 495a; Bavarian Armee-Befehl, 25 June 1813; Oudinot to Berthier, 22 May 1813, Foucart, *Bautzen*, vol. I, p. 319; and *Journal de l'Empire*, 12 June 1813. Unterleutnant von Praun took great pride in recording the performance of the division at Bautzen ('Tagebücher', BayHStA, HS 743).
182. These figures come from the 12th Corps 'État des pertes' (as of 25 May) published in Foucart, *Bautzen*, vol. I, p. 319. The list of casualties Raglovich submitted on 22 May agrees as far as the number of killed is concerned but lists no wounded soldiers (only officers) and gives the missing as just 88. Demmler, who had full access to the Bavarian archives, does not consider the Bavarian reporting accurate in this case and relies on the report from Foucart (Demmler, 'Raglovich', note on pp. 206–7). Information on II/3 Infantry from Ruith, *Bayerisches 3. Infanterie-Regiment*, p. 176.
183. Berthier to Oudinot, 24 May 1813, *Ordres*, vol. I, pp. 133–5.
184. Division-Command to Max Joseph, 28 May 1813, BayHStA, 495a (note this is different from the message with the strength report).
185. The presence of both Beaumont and Wolff leads to confusion as to how to refer to this force of Rheinbund mounted troops (later designated the 29th Light Cavalry Brigade). Beaumont's ad hoc division had consisted of two French naval artillery battalions and four guns from 6th Corps as well as Wolff's Westphalian and Hessian cavalry, but he remained with Wolff even after the infantry and artillery had been returned to Marmont. Sources thus often refer to 'Beaumont's division' when the 'division' consisted of nothing more than Wolff's cavalry regiments; there were initially eight to ten squadrons (six to eight from Westphalia and two Hesse-Darmstadt), but the Bavarians were added when Wolff joined 12th Corps to raise the number to between fourteen and sixteen. In late May, the Bavarian regiment was considered the division's 1st Brigade under Seyssel, while the Westphalian and Hessian troopers constituted the 2nd Brigade under Wolff (SHD, 2C542). Another change took place during the armistice when the 1st and 2nd Westphalian Hussars (two squadrons each) were detached to 2nd Corps, leaving just three regiments: Bavarian Chevaulegers, Westphalian Chevaulegers-Garde, and Hessian Garde-

Chevaulegers. This text will generally use 'Wolff's brigade' or '29th Light Cavalry Brigade' even though Beaumont was present through most of the campaign.
186. Division-Command to Max Joseph, 6 June 1813, BayHStA, 495a; and Demmler ('Raglovich', p. 211); Völderndorff gives the total as 20–50 dead and wounded (*Kriegsgeschichte von Bayern*, vol. IV, p. 77).
187. Division-Command to Max Joseph, 28 May 1813, BayHStA, 495a.
188. The fate of these four pieces is unknown even to the diligent Xylander, *Geschichte des 1. Feldartillerie-Regiments*, vol. II, p. 379.
189. Demmler states that the term 'missing' sometimes served as a euphemism for men who had fallen behind on the march and made no effort to catch up with their units ('Raglovich', p. 180).
190. Praun, 'Tagebücher', BayHStA, HS 743.
191. This is an effort to reconcile the two commanders' reports: Raglovich to Max Joseph, 6 June 1813 (BayHStA, 495a); and Oudinot to Berthier, 7 June 1813 (Foucart, *Bautzen*, vol. II, pp. 363–6). Oudinot made no mention of the Bavarians rescuing the guns, instead, he condemned the 'misplaced audacity' of the Bavarian and Hessian horse and even claimed that they had sabred some of the French gunners (which seems highly unlikely). At the same time, Oudinot publicly praised the Bavarian regiment. Raglovich did indicate that the first two squadrons were disordered but said nothing about overrunning the battery in their flight. Nor did he report anything about the Hessian role. See also the Bavarian cavalry regimental histories, especially Maximilian Ulrich, *Die Königs-Chevaulagers*, Vienna: self-published, 1892, pp. 298–9.
192. Praun, 'Tagebücher', BayHStA, HS 743; Raglovich to Max Joseph, 18 June 1813, BayHStA, 495a.
193. As apposite as 'München' is for a Bavarian action, Demmler makes the entertaining error of giving the location of this final skirmish as Münchhausen.
194. This section relies heavily on Raglovich's reports from June to August 1813, BayHStA, 495a: 6 June (three letters), 10 June (two letters), 15 June, 18 June (two letters), 4, 12 and 13 August. There seems to have been only one report in July, this merely recording the presentation of the Max-Joseph awards to Oudinot and his staff (Döderlein, *Bayerischen 8. Infanterie-Regiments*, vol. II, p. 364). The most important of these is the lengthy missive from 18 June, almost all of which is reprinted in Auvera, *Kgl. Bayer. 7. Infanterie-Regiments*, pp. 526–8 (although Auvera delicately omitted the names of the officers Raglovich excoriated) and in Gerneth/Kiesling, *Bayerischen 5. Infanterie-Regiments*, vol. II, pp. 479–81.
195. Demmler, 'Raglovich', pp. 220–1.
196. Unless otherwise noted, quotations in the following paragraphs are from Raglovich to Max Joseph, 18 June 1813, BayHStA, 495a.
197. As there were no 'Italian' regiments per se in 12th Corps, Raglovich was evidently referring to French regiments that had spent many years stationed in the Italian peninsula.
198. Raglovich to Max Joseph, 18 June 1813, BayHStA, 495a.

199. Ibid.
200. Dauer, *Bayerische 10. Infanterie-Regiment*, vol. V, pp. 299–300.
201. Gerneth/Kiesling, *Bayerischen 5. Infanterie-Regiments*, vol. II, pp. 481–2.
202. Division-Command to Max Joseph, 10 June, and Raglovich to Max Joseph, 15 June 1813, BayHStA, 495a.
203. Division-Command to Max Joseph, 6 June, and Raglovich to Max Joseph, 18 June 1813, BayHStA, 495a. Max Joseph duly granted membership in his order to Oudinot and nine of his staff officers through the 25 June Armee-Befehl; Raglovich presented the awards on 10 July.
204. Kroeger, *Souveränität und napoleonischem Imperialismus*, p. 245.
205. Raglovich to Max Joseph, 4 August 1813, BayHStA, 495a.
206. Lintner, *Kampf*, pp. 180–3. Oudinot continued to use the Bavarians to guard the corps' baggage train during the second offensive towards Berlin, but this was likely because the threat of Allied Cossacks and cavalry made the rear areas so insecure. He did employ one of the brigades in the first line during the Engagement at Zahna when the threat to the rear was less.
207. Lejeune, *Memoirs*, vol. II, p. 279; Gerneth/Kiesling, *Bayerischen 5. Infanterie-Regiments*, vol. II, p. 478; Döderlein, *Bayerischen 8. Infanterie-Regiments*, vol. II, p. 363.
208. Mändler, *Erinnerungen*, p. 118; Döderlein, *Bayerischen 8. Infanterie-Regiments*, vol. II, p. 364.
209. This figure from the Grande Armée's 15 August 'Situation' (SHD, 2C708; also in Fabry, *Oudinot*, pp. 119–20) is approximately 300 men more than listed in the division's 31 July strength report, suggesting either routine vagaries in accounting or the return of some men from detached duty (or both). Note that this original French report is erroneous in several respects thus resulting in errors in the mid-August orders of battle in Nafziger and Bowden (such as including II/4 Infantry and a 'reserve' artillery battery). The strength figures for the individual battalions and squadrons, however, are very similar to the Bavarian 31 July report in most cases. Additionally, the French report does not reflect the change in Bavarian brigade commanders.
210. Schwarz, *Vorgeschichte*, pp. 76–8; and Montgelas to Ludwig, 24 July 1813, ibid., pp. 127–8; Doeberl, *Bayern und die deutsche Erhebung*, p. 380; Heigel, 'Ludwig im Befreiungsjahr 1813', p. 370.
211. Approximately 17,000 available on 1 June and 25,000 by mid-September: see Heilmann, *Feldzug von 1813*, p. 67; and Gilardone, 'Herbstfeldzuge 1813', p. 48.
212. Berthier to Max Joseph, 5 August 1813, BayHStA, GHA 132.
213. Napoleon to Berthier, 19 June 1813, *CG*, no. 35854, vol. XIII, p. 1272. Bavarian histories frequently cite this remark as proof of Napoleon's overbearing character and his unreasonable demands, but it is not clear if, when or how these comments were communicated to Munich. There is no such letter from Napoleon to Max Joseph and nothing along these lines appears in Berthier's extensive correspondence with the king (BayHStA, GHA 132). It thus seems unlikely that these remarks were

ever sent to Munich and subsequent historians have simply pulled them from the published versions of Napoleon's correspondence to other, non-Bavarian, recipients.
214. Berthier to Max Joseph, 17 June 1813, BayHStA, GHA 132. Printed in Oskar Bezzel, *Studien zur Geschichte Bayerns*, p. 21.
215. Napoleon to Berthier, 5 July 1813, *CG*, no. 35196, vol. XIV, p. 70; and Berthier to Montgelas, 18 July 1813, *Ordres*, vol. I, p. 299.
216. Max Joseph to Berthier, 15 June 1813, Dunan, 'Nouveaux documents', p. 142.
217. Berthier to Augereau, 18 August 1813, *Ordres*, vol. II, pp. 52–5.
218. Mercy d'Argenteau report, 16 August 1813, in Schwarz, *Vorgeschichte*, pp. 81–2.
219. A supposed draft letter from Napoleon discussing the replacement of Max Joseph with Ludwig occasionally appears in the literature (it originated from this article: Theodor Schiemann, 'Ein Brief Napoleons an König Maximilian Joseph von Bayern', *Historische Zeitschrift*, Neue Folge vol. 54, 1903). Boehm thoroughly debunks this specious claim; see Boehm, 'Ein angeblicher Abdankungsantrag Napoleons an König Max Joseph von Bayern', *Forschungen zur Geschichte Bayerns*, vol. XI, 1903.
220. These captives were militiamen from the Saxon Duchies and Reuß. Lützow claimed to have captured 200 in Roda and 100 in Schleitz (*see* Chapter 7). Jagwitz, *Lützowschen Freikorps*, pp. 70–1, 102–9.
221. Bezzel, *Das K. B. 4. Infanterie-Regiment*, pp. 145–7; Jagwitz, *Lützowschen Freikorps*, pp. 71–4; Rudolf Schwenk, *Die Lützower vor Hof*, Hof: Kleinschmidt, 1897, pp. 12–18.
222. The figures for 12th Corps in the French archives list an additional 104 men detached and 1,134 on the sick list yielding the total of 'effectives' as 5,868 infantry and artillery under Raglovich and 584 cavalry with Wolff. Curiously, the French records still include II/4 (547) even though this battalion never left Bavaria; adding these men brings the total as reflected in the Grande Armée's 15 August 'Situation' to 6,519 effectives (SHD, 2C708). Though still technically part of the 29th Division, it is not clear if II/4 was simply carried forward owing to lazy staff work or if the Bavarians intentionally included this battalion to appear stronger in the field than they were. Strength figures from Völderndorff (*Kriegsgeschichte von Bayern*, vol. IV, pp. 175–6) seem to include the sick and detached.
223. Division-Command to Max Joseph, 28 August 1813, BayHStA, 495a; Buxbaum, *Königliche Bayerische 3. Chevaulegers-Regiment*, p. 139; Hutter, *Königlich Bayerische 1. Chevaulegers-Regiment*, p. 225; Ulrich, *Königs-Chevaulegers*, pp. 300–1; Quistorp, *Nordarmee*, vol. I, pp. 205–7; Mach, *Königlich Preußischen Zweiten Infanterie*, pp. 251–2; Kurd Wolfgang von Schöning, *Geschichte des Königlich Preußischen Fünften Husaren-Regiments*, Berlin: Lüderitz, 1843, pp. 449–52. Seyssel recovered from his wounds, returned to service in time to fight against France and retired as a *General-Leutnant* to die in 1855.
224. Raglovich to Oudinot and Oudinot to Raglovich, both 17 August 1813, Fabry, *Oudinot*, Documents, pp. 20, 22.
225. Curiously, this brigade, under GB Auguste Jean Joseph Gilbert was from Defrance's division, not Lorge's.

226. Division-Command to Max Joseph, 28 August 1813, BayHStA, 495a; Quistorp, *Nordarmee*, vol. I, pp. 220–2.
227. These details from Division-Command to Max Joseph, 4 September 1813, BayHStA, 495a; Xylander, *Geschichte des 1. Feldartillerie-Regiments*, vol. II, p. 383; Gerneth/Kiesling, *Bayerischen 5. Infanterie-Regiments*, vol. II, pp. 485–8 (quotation); Döderlein, *Bayerischen 8. Infanterie-Regiments*, vol. II, pp. 373–4.
228. Division-Command to Max Joseph, 4 September 1813, BayHStA, 495a.
229. Völderndorff, *Kriegsgeschichte von Bayern*, vol. IV, p. 162; Louchet, *Bataille de Dennewitz*, pt. 1, p. 8; Fabry, *Oudinot*, p. 182; Mach, *Königlich Preußischen Zweiten Infanterie*, p. 258; Quistorp, *Nordarmee*, vol. I, pp. 375–6. Niedermeyer was called back to Bavaria on being promoted and turned over command to Weisse after Großbeeren (Emil Heinze, *Geschichte des Kgl. Bayer. 6. Chevaulegers-Regiments*, Leipzig: Klinkhardt, 1898, p. 419).
230. Rather than overburden the text with repetitive endnotes, readers are advised that all the Raglovich citations in this section are from the general's formal report (Division-Command to Max Joseph, 9 September 1813, BayHStA, 495a) and drafts of his private letters to the king (Raglovich to Max Joseph, 9 September 1813, BayHStA, 495a). The latter are printed in Fabry, *Empereur II*, Documents, p. 34 (in French); portions in Quistorp, *Nordarmee*, vol. I, p. 545. Other key sources are: Völderndorff, *Kriegsgeschichte von Bayern*, vol. IV, pp. 166–75; Louchet, *Bataille de Dennewitz*, pts. 1 and 2; Quistorp, *Nordarmee*, vol. I., pp. 375–6; and Bavarian regimental histories. See also: A. Erhard, 'Die Bayern in der Schlacht bei Dennewitz am 6. September 1813', *JdAM*, vol. XX, 1876.
231. Praun, 'Tagebücher', BayHStA, HS 743; Mändler, *Erinnerungen*, pp. 120–1.
232. Beaumont's after-action report, 5 September 1813, in Heinze, *Kgl. Bayer. 6. Chevaulegers-Regiments*, p. 420; Division-Command to Max Joseph, 9 September 1813, BayHStA, 495a. The Prussian detachment was commanded by Major Friederich Karl Heinrich von Clausewitz, a younger brother of the renowned Prussian military theorist (Rudolph Kopka von Lossow, *Geschichte des Grenadier-Regiments König Friedrich I. (4. Ostpreußischen) Nr. 5.*, Berlin: Mittler und Sohn, 1901, vol. II, Anlage 1.)
233. Praun, 'Tagebücher', BayHStA, HS 743.
234. Mändler, *Erinnerungen*, pp. 122–3. Similar scenes from Maillinger's diary are paraphrased in Döderlein, *Bayerischen 8. Infanterie-Regiments*, vol. II, p. 380.
235. Praun, 'Tagebücher', BayHStA, HS 743. Raglovich reported that the French and Bavarian artillery did not even have time to unlimber before being overwhelmed, but Praun's account is likely more accurate in this instance.
236. See Map 24: I have placed the destruction of II/9 southeast of Oehna based on Quistorp's detailed research (vol. I, pp. 527–8). Raglovich's report is not specific, but it is possible to infer that the battalion and battery were overrun slightly northwest of the village. It is also possible that the square and the guns started northwest of Oehna then moved to the southeast where they met their fate. See also Mach, *Königlich Preußischen Zweiten Infanterie*, pp. 269–70 (it is possible that the French

battery also fell into the hands of the Pomeranian Grenadiers); Schöning, *Königlich Preußischen Fünften Husaren-Regiments*, pp. 453–6; Pflugk-Harttung, *Befreiungsjahr*, pp. 318–19.

237. Mändler, *Erinnerungen*, p. 123.
238. Praun, 'Tagebücher', BayHStA, HS 743.
239. Mändler, *Erinnerungen*, p. 124.
240. Gerneth/Kiesling, *Bayerischen 5. Infanterie-Regiments*, vol. II, p. 494.
241. This description is largely taken from Heinze (*Kgl. Bayer. 6. Chevaulegers-Regiments*, p. 422) who seems to have relied on cavalry regimental records. He also recounts that the Bavarian chevaulegers, scouting towards Dahme, encountered Ney and one of his adjutants more or less alone in the dark and dank forest. The marshal spoke with them briefly before trotting off to join Raglovich and the division. For the Württemberg involvement, see Richard Starklof, *Geschichte des Königlich Württembergischen Zweiten Reiter-Regiments, ehemaligen Jäger-Regiments zu Pferde Herzog Louis*, Darmstadt: Zernin, 1862, pp. 371–2.
242. Mändler, *Erinnerungen*, p. 124.
243. Berg, *Königl. Bayer. 4. Jäger-Bataillons*, p. 382; Paul Kneußl, *Geschichte des k. bayer. 2. (vormals 3.) Jäger-Bataillons*, Würzburg: Stürz, 1899, p. 78.
244. Division-Command to Max Joseph, 9 September 1813, BayHStA, 495a.
245. Döderlein, *Bayerischen 8. Infanterie-Regiments*, vol. II, p. 380.
246. Heinze, *Kgl. Bayer. 6. Chevaulegers-Regiments*, p. 421.
247. Praun, 'Tagebücher', BayHStA, HS 743.
248. Divisional strength report for 14 September 1813, BayHStA, 495b. Völderndorff gives the cavalry a strength of 141 officers and men but is not clear about detachments (*Kriegsgeschichte von Bayern*, vol. IV, p. 178/note).
249. My rendering of '*jedoch bedarf es nur eine geringe Erschütterung mehr*' from Raglovich's personal letter to Max Joseph (draft), 9 September 1813, BayHStA, 495a. His worry about the effect of Dennewitz is from the formal report written the same day: Division-Command to Max Joseph, 9 September 1813, BayHStA, 495a.
250. 'The peasant's curse followed the steps of the French soldier,' wrote Völderndorff (*Kriegsgeschichte von Bayern*, vol. IV, p. 177).
251. Bavarian misbehaviour is implied in some of the memoirs, but see also Lintner, *Kampf*, p. 250.
252. Raglovich solicited the king's favour for 'every individual' in the division and made special mention of the 9th Infantry's worthiness.
253. Berthier to Ney, 17 September 1813, *Ordres*, vol. II, pp. 207–8; and Ney to Raglovich, 19 September 1813, Fabry, *Empereur II*, Documents, p. 186.
254. Raglovich to Oudinot, 17 September 1813, Fabry, *Empereur II*, Documents, p. 151. The Bavarians were especially grateful that Oudinot did not interfere with the internal administration of the division, Lintner, *Kampf*, pp. 182–4.
255. Praun, 'Tagebücher', BayHStA, HS 743; Sauzey, *Nos Alliés les Bavarois*, p. 336.
256. Praun, 'Tagebücher', BayHStA, HS 743.

257. Dauer, *Bayerische 10. Infanterie-Regiment*, vol. V, p. 307.
258. Raglovich to Max Joseph (draft), 16 September 1813, BayHStA, 495a; Lejeune to Raglovich, 10 September 1813, and Raglovich to Oudinot, 16 September 1813, Fabry, *Empereur II*, Documents, pp. 43, 136; Mändler, one of the selected officers, recounts the scene in his *Erinnerungen*, p. 125. One reason Raglovich cited for returning the officers was his desire to reduce the number of wagons that burdened the contingent. See also the extract of Oberst von Rummel's 26 October 1813 report, in Lintner, *Kampf*, p. 70/n. 206.
259. GM von Habermann (whose name the French seem to have heard as 'Ackermann'), Major von Hetzendorff and a number of others accompanied Raglovich. Oberstleutnant Anton Krauss took command of the cavalry regiment.
260. Völderndorff, *Kriegsgeschichte von Bayern*, vol. IV, p. 211/note.
261. Raglovich–Durosnel correspondence, 27 September, 1 and 3 October 1813, in Fabry, *Empereur III*, Documents, pp. 111–12, 230, 293–4; Bavarian ambassador's report, 29 September 1813, in Doeberl, *Bayern und die deutsche Erhebung*, p. 401; Berthier to Raglovich, 2 October 1813, *Ordres*, vol. II, p. 279 (the minute of this letter is dated 1 October in [Gabriel Fabry], *Lettres de l'Empereur Napoléon non Insérés dans la Correspondance*, Paris: Levrault, 1909, p. 219); Lintner, *Kampf*, pp. 69–70. Raglovich quotations are from a personal letter to Max Joseph (draft), 3 October 1813, BayHStA, 495a; Döderlein's portrayal (*Bayerischen 8. Infanterie-Regiments*, vol. II, p. 384) is useful but gives the misleading impression that some of the quotations are directly from Maret. Max Joseph did write a letter to Berthier on 21 September requesting Raglovich's recall (Adalbert, *Max I. Joseph von Bayern*, p. 656), but it is not clear that this missive ever reached its addressee – *see below*. The otherwise very useful Lefebvre de Béhaine errs in covering this period in that he takes Raglovich's *personal* departure for Bavaria to mean that the *entire division* (now just four battalions) was returning (François Armand Édouard Lefebvre de Béhaine, *Napoléon et les Alliés sur le Rhin*, Paris: Perrin, 1913, pp. 124–9).
262. GB Durrieu to Maillot and Maillot's reply, both 14 October 1813, in Völderndorff, *Kriegsgeschichte von Bayern*, vol. IV, pp. 350–1. The following draws heavily on Völderndorff's account as a participant (pp. 247–50) and the summary in Döderlein, *Bayerischen 8. Infanterie-Regiments*, vol. II, pp. 387–90. Divisional strength report for 5 October 1813, BayHStA, 495b.
263. Praun, 'Tagebücher', BayHStA, HS 743.
264. Maj. Peterson to the commander in Eilenburg, Völderndorff, *Kriegsgeschichte von Bayern*, vol. IV, p. 352. Raglovich's exact itinerary for his return to Bavaria is unclear, but according to Döderlein, his transit through Leipzig occurred at a point when he could meet the Allied sovereigns. He was well received by Tsar Alexander and Bernadotte, but Prussia's King Friedrich Wilhelm stiffly complained about Maillot's refusal to submit to Allied control. See Döderlein, *Bayerischen 8. Infanterie-Regiments*, vol. II, p. 384.
265. Quoted in Kroeger, *Souveränität und napoleonischem Imperialismus*, p. 261.

266. Maillot to Durrieu, 19 October 1813, Fernand Le Ploge, *La Défense de Torgau en 1813*, Paris: Berger-Levrault, 1896, p. 10 (this essay also appeared in the *Carnet de la Sabretache* the same year).
267. Völderndorff, *Kriegsgeschichte von Bayern*, vol. IV, pp. 247–54; Durrieu to Berthier, 24 October 1813 and the exchange between Narbonne and Durrieu are in Le Ploge, *Torgau*, pp. 6–13. Narbonne's interactions with Maillot are described in 'Journal du Siège de Torgau du 18 Octobre au 17 Nov, 1813', SHD, 2C168. *See also* Chapter 8.
268. Völderndorff, *Kriegsgeschichte von Bayern*, vol. IV, p. 254.
269. The Austrians claimed the capture of 80 Bavarians on 21 October at Kösen, see Hugo von Kerchnawe, 'Von Leipzig bis Erfurt', *Mitteilungen des k. und k. Kriegsarchivs*, vol. IV, 1906, pp. 412–23, 511.
270. Berthier to the *chef de bataillon* commanding the Bavarians, 24 October 1813, *Ordres*, vol. II, p. 383; Gerneth/Kiesling, *Bayerischen 5. Infanterie-Regiments*, vol. II, p. 502.
271. Auvera, *Kgl. Bayer. 7. Infanterie-Regiments*, pp. 532–5; Gerneth/Kiesling, *Bayerischen 5. Infanterie-Regiments*, vol. II, pp. 498–502.
272. In addition to specific citations, this section is founded on Doeberl, *Bayern und die deutsche Erhebung*; Schwarz, *Vorgeschichte*; Weis, *Montgelas*; and Adalbert, *Max I. Joseph*. See especially the extensive correspondence published in Doeberl and Schwarz.
273. Max Joseph to Berthier, 26 July 1813, in Gouvion Saint-Cyr, *Mémoires*, vol. IV, pp. 344–6.
274. Kroeger, *Souveränität und napoleonischem Imperialismus*, p. 252.
275. Ibid., p. 248; Lintner, *Kampf*, pp. 68, 90.
276. In Doeberl, *Bayern und die deutsche Erhebung*, p. 425.
277. For Hauptmann Prinz August von Thurn und Taxis, one of Wrede's key staff officers, it seemed that 'our cabinet was more inclined towards neutrality than an offensive alliance against France', August von Thurn und Taxis, *Aus drei Feldzügen 1812 bis 1815*, Leipzig: Insel-Verlag, 1912, p. 130.
278. Max Joseph to Crown Prince Ludwig, 12 September 1813, Schwarz, *Vorgeschichte*, p. 130.
279. Max Joseph to Mercy d'Argenteau, 14 September 1813, 'La Bavière en 1812 & 1813', *Revue Contemporaine*, vol. LXIX, 1869, p. 396.
280. The letter is published in full in Fane, *Operations of the Allied Armies*, pp. 345–6; parts in Schwarz, *Vorgeschichte*, p. 95. In an attempt to placate Allied impatience, the Bavarians backdated the royal signature to 10 September.
281. Max Joseph to Ludwig, 15 September 1813, Schwarz, *Vorgeschichte*, p. 130.
282. Thurn und Taxis, *Aus drei Feldzügen*, p. 124.
283. Napoleon to Maret, 5 August 1813, *CG*, no. 35742, vol. XIV, p. 303.
284. Reuß to Wrede, 16 September 1813, in Doeberl, *Bayern und die deutsche Erhebung*, p. 392.
285. Gilardone, 'Herbstfeldzuge', pp. 51–5; Edmund Glaise von Horstenau, *Die Heimkehr Tirols*, Vienna: Verlag für vaterländische Gesellschaft, 1914, pp. 71–110; Georg

Freiherr von Holtz, *Die innerösterreichische Armee 1813 und 1814*, Vienna: Edlinger's Verlag, 1912, pp. 1–7.
286. Max Joseph to Ludwig, 1 October 1813, Schwarz, *Vorgeschichte*, p. 135.
287. The Allied monarchs' letters are in Doeberl, *Bayern und die deutsche Erhebung*, pp. 425–7. Hruby threatened Bavaria with invasion by Bennigsen's army (Schwarz, *Vorgeschichte*, p. 98). The king relayed this news to Eugène in his 8 October 1813 exculpatory letter (Du Casse, *Eugène*, vol. IX, p. 284).
288. For example: Weis, *Montgelas*, p. 688.
289. Adalbert, Prinz von Bayern, *Eugen Beauharnais der Stiefsohn Napoleons*, Berlin: Propyläen Verlag, 1940, pp. 282–8. See pp. 293–8 for the attempt Metternich and Max Joseph made in November to separate Eugène from Napoleon by offering Eugène the Italian crown; an attempt that failed in the face of Eugène's sense of honour: 'I will gladly sacrifice my and my family's future fortune rather than break my oath [to Napoleon].' 'They want traitors, and that is all', he told his cabinet secretary (Antoine Darnay, *Notices Historiques sur Son Altesse Royale le Prince Eugène, Vice-Roi d'Italie*, Paris: David, 1830, pp. 216–31). Carola Oman also touches on this situation in her *Napoleon's Viceroy: Eugène de Beauharnais*, New York: Funk and Wagnalls, 1966, pp. 361–70.
290. Wrede's pressing too much was the king's phrase (Doeberl, *Bayern und die deutsche Erhebung*, p. 396). Wrede as 'true motor' is from Weis, *Montgelas*, p. 677.
291. This narrative follows Schwarz's conclusion (*Vorgeschichte*, pp. 104–5), but some historians argue that the king was persuaded when Wrede related a personal anecdote to suggest that Napoleon sought to become the 'universal monarch', a notion that terrified Max Joseph. The story originates with some comments by Wrede in 1830 as described in Joseph Weiß, 'Wredes und des Königs Abkehr von Napoleon', in *Bayern 1813*, pp. 43–4. See also Weis, *Montgelas*, pp. 683–4.
292. Max Joseph to Ludwig, 7 October 1813, in Schwarz, *Vorgeschichte*, p. 137. With the exception of the phrase 'my old father was right' (*'mein alter Vater hat Recht gehabt'*) the letter was in French as was usual with Max Joseph. Given his education and military service in France, the king was very comfortable with the French language; his use of such coarse phrases here was unusual and likely reflects his degree of despondency.
293. In addition to Doeberl, *Bayern und die deutsche Erhebung*, Mercy d'Argenteau, 'La Bavière en 1812 & 1813', and Schwarz, *Vorgeschichte*, principal sources for this section are Louis Pierre Édouard Bignon and Alfred Auguste Ernouf, *Histoire de France depuis le Commencement de la Guerre de Russie jusqu'à la Deuxième Restauration*, Brussels: Meline, Can et Cie, 1846, Chapter XIII; Driault, *Chute de l'Empire*, pp. 178–96; Guillaume de Garden, *Histoire Générale des Traités de Paix*, vol. XV, Paris: Amyot, 1848–87, Chapter XII; Lefebvre de Béhaine, *Napoléon et les Alliés*, pp. 26–142.
294. Beroldingen's 5 October 1813 report in Pfister, *Lager des Rheinbundes*, pp. 358–9. Beroldingen did report hearing of 'Bavaria's declaration of neutrality' from an officer of the Guard on 5 October, Beroldingen to Friedrich, report nr. 48, 5 October 1813,

LABWHStA, E 270a Bü 241, 'Berichte des württembergischen Generalmajors und Generaladjutanten Graf v. Beroldingen aus dem französischen Hauptquartier'. Napoleon to Murat, 9 October 1813, *CG*, no. 36711, vol. XIV, p. 751; similarly, Berthier had written to Ney and Kellermann on 3 October at Napoleon's direction to tell them that 'Bavaria has not changed its policy', *Ordres*, vol. II, pp. 189–90. The bulletin was no. 34, 15 October 1813, Pascal, *Bulletins*, vol. VI, p. 158–61: published in the *Moniteur*, 30 October and the *Journal de l'Empire*, 31 October 1813. Bruno Colson avers that Napoleon concentrated at Leipzig 'for purely military reasons' (*Leipzig*, p. 42). See also Pelet, 'Campagne de 1813', 7th article, *Spectateur Militaire*, vol. II, 1827, p. 182.

295. Mercy d'Argenteau, 'La Bavière en 1812 & 1813', pp. 403–4. At the time, the French believed Wrede had succumbed to his grievous wound.
296. Most notably Bignon/Ernouf, *Histoire de France*, Chapter XIII; more even-handed is Lefebvre de Béhaine, *Napoléon et les Alliés*, pp. 54, 96, 102–3, 129. Garden, on the other hand, proffers a defiant defence of Mercy.
297. Adalbert, *Max I. Joseph von Bayern*, p. 645.
298. Adalbert, *Eugen Beauharnais*, pp. 274–83; Lefebvre de Béhaine, *Napoléon et les Alliés*, pp. 94. For correspondence between the king and the viceroy, see du Casse, *Eugène*, vol. IX, pp. 282–98.
299. Maret to Mercy, 1 October 1813, in Schwarz, *Vorgeschichte*, pp. 108–10. Schwarz corrects Doeberl's misrepresentation concerning the number of reports Mercy sent during August and September; Doeberl, apparently relying on the editor of Mercy's memoir (note on p. 408 of Mercy, 'La Bavière en 1812 & 1813'), claimed the envoy sent only one report between 25 August and 25 September. In fact, he sent six during that period and a total of ten between 20 August and 2 October; several of these, however, were intercepted by the Allies, a point which Schwarz does not mention.
300. Mercy d'Argenteau, 'La Bavière en 1812 & 1813', pp. 398–9. Captured copies of his 28 and 29 September 1813 reports are in *Copies des Lettres Originalles et Dépêches des Généraux, Ministres, Grand Officiers d'État, etc., Écrites de Paris à Buonaparte pendant son séjour à Dresde, ainsi qu'une Correspondance de divers personnages de cette même famille entr'eux; Interceptées par les avant-postes des Alliés dans le Nord de l'Allemange*, Paris: Galignani, 1815, pp. 63–8. Similarly, the Austrians intercepted Eugène's reply to a letter Wrede sent him in mid-September (Adalbert, *Eugen Beauharnais*, pp. 279–80).
301. Friedrich to Napoleon, 3 October 1813. This missive is a candidate for the information that finally convinced the emperor that Bavaria had changed sides (when he was at Düben on 13 October), but it would have been too late to block the 8 October treaty even if it had made its way into Napoleon's hands in a timelier fashion. Friedrich's 14 October letter announced the Austro-Bavarian alliance and warned of the threat to Napoleon's line of communications; Friedrich had noted vague suspicions of Bavaria in a 24 August letter as well, but Napoleon did not respond to these remarks. All are in August von Schloßberger, *Politische und Militärische Correspondenz König Freidrichs von Württemberg mit Kaiser Napoleon I. 1805–1813*, Stuttgart: Kohlhammer, 1889, pp. 314–17, 321–4.

302. Likewise, Kellermann sent warnings on 15, 18 and 21 October (based on his communications with Jérôme and the French ambassador to Frankfurt), but these would have arrived too late to permit imperial intervention (AN, AF/IV/1662B, Plaquette 7).
303. Printed in Heilmann, *Feldzug von 1813*, pp. 138–45. Emphasis in the original.
304. Mercy d'Argenteau, 'La Bavière en 1812 & 1813', p. 389. Mercy reported the 'complaints ... ceaselessly repeated by the government concerning the hazardous position of the Bavarian corps', 25 August 1813, in Schwarz, *Vorgeschichte*, p. 83. The letter Montgelas signed out to the kingdom's ambassadors on 17 October 1813 is in Arthur Kleinschmidt, *Bayern und Hessen 1799–1815*, Berlin: Räde, 1902, pp. 246–7.
305. Adalbert, *Max I. Joseph von Bayern*, p. 651.
306. Berthier had informed the king of the change in the corps' composition and stated that Napoleon would attack into Bohemia should Bavaria be invaded. Berthier to Max Joseph, 5 August 1813, BayHStA, GHA, Nachlass König Max I. Joseph 132.
307. Mercy d'Argenteau, 'La Bavière en 1812 & 1813', pp. 390–1. The king was probably referring to the period between the departure of Saint-Cyr's troops and the arrival of their replacements, but reliance on shadow forces such as Augereau's command was standard Napoleonic practice (Gill, 'Conscripts and Deception: Napoleon's Rear Area Security Strategy: 1809 and 1813', paper presented to the Society for Military History, 2000). Berthier only issued orders for Augereau's reinforced corps to move east on 17 September (*Ordres*, vol. II, p. 207), so by the time the marshal left Würzburg some days later, Bavaria was already well on its way to joining the Coalition.
308. Max Joseph to Berthier, 21 September 1813, partly published in Adalbert, *Max I. Joseph von Bayern*, p. 656. However, it is not clear that the letter ever reached the marshal as there is no mention of it in French accounts of Raglovich's division and no evidence of a Berthier reply in the Bavarian archives (BayHStA, Geheimes Haus Archiv, Nachlass König Max I. Joseph 132). See similar statements by Max Joseph in his 8 and 15 October 1813 letters to Eugène (Du Casse, *Eugène*, vol. IX, p. 283–94).
309. Adalbert, *Eugen Beauharnais*, p. 284; Schwarz, *Vorgeschichte*, p. 98.
310. Mercy d'Argenteau, 'La Bavière en 1812 & 1813', pp. 391–7; Schwarz, *Vorgeschichte*, p. 109.
311. Napoleon's chronicler Las Cases wrote that the emperor received a confidential letter from Max Joseph towards the end of September in which the king stated he could only maintain the alliance for another six to eight weeks (Las Cases, *Napoleon at Saint Helena*, vol. III, Pt. 6, pp. 53–9, 64–5 134–5). Many subsequent writers seem to have accepted this statement uncritically (e.g., Heilmann in his biography of Wrede, p. 260), but there is good reason to be very sceptical of this claim. First, according to Lefebvre de Béhaine, there is no trace of such a letter in the French or Bavarian archives; second, it is difficult to imagine that one of the subsequent Bavarian historians would not have published the text if it existed; and third, there is no other external evidence to suggest that such a letter was sent. Max Joseph's 21 September

message *to Berthier* (not Napoleon) seems the best candidate for the alleged letter, but the published portions (Adalbert, *Max I. Joseph*, p. 651) neither provide this putative deadline nor does the text suggest such an ultimatum. Furthermore, no Bavarian historian has highlighted it in this connection, as would be expected. See the thorough analysis in Lefebvre de Béhaine, *Napoléon et les Alliés*, pp. 119–21.

312. Napoleon to Cambacérès, 25 October 1813, *CG*, no. 36850, vol. XIV, pp. 818–19.
313. Sauzey, *Nos Alliés les Bavarois*, p. 336.
314. Orders of the Day issued by Crown Prince Ludwig (16 October) and Wrede (15 October) also made some reference to 'Germany', but both emphasised the Bavarian king and Bavarian fatherland. All printed in Heilmann, *Feldzug von 1813*, pp. 75–6, 138–45.
315. Murken, *Bayerische Soldaten*, pp. 131–5. See also: Junkelmann, *Napoleon und Bayern*, pp. 157–9; Kroeger, *Souveränität und napoleonischem Imperialismus*, p. 302; and Lintner, *Kampf*, pp. 322–3.
316. Vaudoncourt, *Prince Eugène*, vol. II., pp. 278–82; Jacques Marquet de Montbreton de Norvins, 'Réponse à l'article anonyme, inséré dans la 11e Livraison du deuxième volume du Spectateur Militaire, sous ce Titre: Dispositions Relatives aux Opérations de l'Armée d'Italie, en 1814', *Journal des Sciences Militaires*, 1827, pp. 157–8.
317. Becker, *Krieg der Franzosen und ihrer Alliirten*, vol. III, p. 101.
318. Dufraisse, 'Napoleon und Bayern', p. 228. Montgelas: 'Saxony did not follow the example of our wise restraint but believed it should go a step further' (*Denkwürdigkeiten*, pp. 278–9).

Appendix
Synoptic Tables of Battles and Sieges/Blockades

(overleaf)

Rheinbund Participation in Major Battles of 1813

	Möckern 3–5 Apr.	Lützen 2 May	Bautzen 20–21 May	Großbeeren 23 Aug.	Dresden 25–26 Aug.	Katzbach 26 Aug.	Hagelberg 27 Aug.	Kulm 29–30 Aug.	Dennewitz 6 Sept.	Wartenburg 3 Oct.	Leipzig 16–19 Oct.
Saxony			•	•	•				•		•
Bavaria		•	•						•		•
Württemberg		•	•		•				•	•	•
Baden		•	•			•					•
Hesse	•	•	•								•
Westphalia		•	?		•		•		•	•	•
Frankfurt		•									
Würzburg	•	•	•				•		•		•
Saxon Duchies											
Anhalt								•			
Berg		•	•								•

Note: • simply indicates the presence of elements from the contingent on the battlefield. In some cases, the number of troops was very small, and those present were not always engaged in active combat (e.g., the tiny Hessian remnant with the Imperial Guard at Möckern in April or the lone Bavarian battalion in the rear at Leipzig). Some Westphalian artillery were likely present at Bautzen (with 6th Corps).

Rheinbund Participation in Sieges/Blockades (1813–14)

	Danzig Jan.1813–Jan.1814	Thorn Feb.–Apr.1813	Glogau 1 Feb.–May 1813	Glogau 2 Aug.1813–May 1814	Küstrin Mar.1813–Mar.1814	Torgau Nov.1813–Jan.1814	Magdeburg Nov.1813–May 1814	Dresden Oct.–Nov.1813	Modlin Feb.–Dec.1813
Saxony	•		•	•				•	•
Bavaria	•	•						•	
Württemberg	•				•				
Baden			•						
Hesse									
Westphalia	•				•	•		•	•
Würzburg						•			
Frankfurt	•			•		•			
Saxon Duchies	•								
Anhalt	•						•		
Lippe	•						•		
Reuß	•						•		
Schwarzburg	•						•		
Waldeck	•								

Note: end dates of the sieges/blockades indicate when the last French forces left each fortress. In some cases, the Rheinbund troops departed before the French (e.g., Magdeburg). Isolated individuals (*isolés* to the French) are not noted. See Chapter 8.

Index

'>' indicates a promotion during 1813

Alexander I, Tsar: 21, 30, 32, 33, 35, 40–3, 51, 60, 63, 65–8, 71, 95, 106, 109, 123, 151–2, 163, 169, 172, 182, 244, 249, 258, 279, 284, 293, 349, 352–7
Allied/Coalition military formations:
    Army of Bohemia (Main Army): 73, 74–7, 81, 86, 95, 104–10, 116–17, 151, 190
    Army of the North: 73, 74, 77, 81, 87, 89, 97–8, 105, 111, 117, 202, 244, 253, 331
    Army of Poland: 74, 105–6, 111, 117, 236, 355, 361
    Army of Silesia: 73, 74, 77, 81, 94, 105, 106, 109, 111, 116, 242
    raiding detachments (*Streifkorps*): 19, 27, 35–6, 39, 44–51, 55, 63, 68, 70–1, 74, 101, 106–9, 110, 116, 138, 172, 174–8, 210, 221, 291–2, 298, 313, 318, 321, 345, 361
Allix de Vaux, GD Jacques Alexandre François: 242
Altenburg, Engagement at (28 September): 106–7
Anhalt duchies and military units (*see also* Danzig): 150
Argenteau, François Joseph Charles Marie Mercy d' (French diplomat): 299, 328, 353, 357–62
Arrighi de Casanova, GD Jean Toussaint: 24, 75, 87, 105, 112, 120, 187, 224, 329, 336
Augereau, Marshal Pierre (Duke of Castiglione): 24, 36, 72, 73, 75, 112, 326–8, 360–2, 365

Austria: 4–13, 21–3, 28, 30–3, 35, 39–43, 50–2, 56, 59–60, 65, 67–8, 71–4, 80, 122, 123, 126, 128, 150–3, 156, 158–6, 169–71, 190, 241, 248–9, 255–9, 260–1, 284, 287, 293–301, 305, 325–8, 350–65, 367
Austrian military formations: 76, 83, 85–6, 105, 106, 109, 110–11, 116–20, 131–3, 149, 190–3, 222–3, 231–3, 236

Bachelu, GD Gilbert Désiré Joseph: 272–3
Baden, Grand Duchy of: 4–11, 13, 16–17, 24–5, 84, 108, 292, 363, 367–8
Baden military units:
    1st Brigade (39th Division): 52, 54, 58, 62, 75, 112, 114, 116
    2nd Brigade (Leipzig): 106, 112, 114, 117, 120, 244
    1st Light Dragoons: 52, 58
Barclay de Tolly, General of Infantry Mikhail Bogdanovich (Russia): 55, 61, 63–9, 115, 279, 281
Bautzen, Battle of (20–21 May): 27, 46, 59–69, 72, 122, 179–83, 186–7, 299, 300, 311–18, 319, 363
Bavaria, Kingdom of: 4–11, 21, 22, 43, 50, 72, 78, 79, 118, 121–2, 125, 151, 153, 156, 158–9, 246, 253, 255–61; politics & diplomacy: 292–301, 307–11, 325–9, 351–7; defection: 357–63, 365–6, 367
Bavarian military units (*see also* Thorn): 14, 17, 24, 25, 262–71, 364–5, 367–8
    Rechberg's division: 34–7, 48, 51, 153–8, 285–92, 363

29th Division: 24, 52, 54, 62, 65, 75, 87–9, 92, 96–7, 101–3, 105, 112, 292, 301–7, 363–4; spring campaign: 311–21; armistice period: 321–6; autumn campaign: 206, 209, 224, 228–9, 329–51

13th Infantry Regiment: 24, 28, 263–4, 265, 266, 270–3, 301, 303, 304, 315, 344–5, 363, 366

Chevaulegers: 157, 264, 265, 266, 289, 290, 292, 301, 304, 311, 312–14, 316–18, 320–1, 324, 329, 331, 333–4, 338, 340–1, 343–5, 363

Beaumont, GD Louis Chrétien Carrière de: 69, 96–7, 104, 318, 329, 334–6, 340

Benckendorff, Maj. Gen. (Russia): 46, 176

Berg, Grand Duchy of: 8, 17, 22, 24, 122, 368
  Lancers: 183
  unrest in: 38, 50

Bernadotte, Marshal Jean-Baptiste, Crown Prince of Sweden: 73, 74, 77, 81, 87, 89, 93, 96–7, 100, 104–7, 109, 111, 115, 116–18, 229–31, 243–4, 253, 331, 333, 347–9

Beroldingen, GM Joseph Ignaz von (Württemberg): 237, 357

Berthier, Marshal Alexander (Prince of Wagram): 95, 102–3, 161–2, 179, 211, 215–16, 217, 226, 229, 247, 255, 270, 296, 298, 300, 305, 308–10, 326–7, 348–50, 351, 358–61

Bertrand, GD Henri Gatien: 24, 54, 58, 61, 2, 64–6, 75, 87–93, 96, 98–103, 104, 112, 114, 117–18, 120, 200, 203–4, 218, 225, 308–11, 333–4, 343

Blücher, GdK Gebhard Leberecht (Prussia): 37, 45, 48–52, 53, 55, 57, 61, 63, 64, 66, 73, 74, 77, 80–4, 94–6, 103–6, 111, 115, 116–18, 153, 222, 224, 229, 244, 246, 251–2, 347

Blücher, Maj. Franz von (Prussia): 46

Bordessoulle, GD Étienne Tardif de: 181, 182–3, 188, 191, 193, 245–6

Brause, Oberst Friedrich Wilhelm August von (Saxony): 99–100, 188, 194, 199–200, 204, 205, 213, 217, 226, 231–6, 239, 241, 244, 251, 254

Bremen: 47, 49, 173–4, 176

Bruyère, GD Pierre Joseph: 181, 182–3, 186

Bülow, GL Friedrich Wilhelm von (Prussia): 37, 53, 55, 69–70, 77, 87–92, 97–102, 111, 115, 169–70, 195–7, 203–6, 232, 318–20

Carl August, Duke of Saxon-Weimar: 123, 152, 162–3, 251

Carra Saint-Cyr, GD Jean: 37, 38, 47, 173

Chernishev, Maj. Gen. Alexander Ivanovich (Russia): 46, 55, 71, 93, 107, 176

civilian experiences: 12–14, 18, 30, 45, 47, 82, 108–9, 121, 151–2, 154–6, 171, 173–4, 187, 202, 215, 239, 240–1, 243–4, 248, 252, 269–70, 273, 275, 281, 282, 288, 291, 322, 329, 331, 342

Colomb, Rittmeister Friedrich August Peter von (Prussia): 63, 70, 187

Cossacks: 19, 30, 33–9, 45–7, 63, 67, 77, 87, 92–4, 99, 101–2, 106–9, 111, 120, 134, 136, 138–40, 144, 146, 149, 157–8, 161, 168, 173–7, 194–6, 199–203, 215–16, 222, 229–30, 235, 239–40, 249, 267, 277–8, 284, 287–90, 312–14, 318, 323, 328, 331–3, 340–1, 348, 350, 361

Dąbrowski, GD Jan Henryk (Duchy of Warsaw): 54, 73, 75, 87, 93, 96, 103, 105, 112, 116, 120, 201, 203

Daendels, GD Herman Willem: 25, 54

Dalberg, Carl Theodor von, Grand Duke of Frankfurt and Prince-Primate of the Confederation: 6

Danzig, Siege of: 24–5, 30, 35, 51, 54–5, 69, 72, 75, 122, 264, 266, 271–5, 286, 301, 363, 366, 368

Davout, Marshal Louis Nicholas (Prince of Eggmühl): 12, 24, 36–7, 48–9, 53–4, 59, 70, 72–3, 75, 79, 81, 87, 93, 154–7, 168, 269–70, 275–79, 281, 288, 300

Denmark: 15, 71

Dennewitz, Battle of (6 September): 95–103, 189, 201, 203–14, 218, 220, 225, 238, 252–3, 334–43

Doering, GM Christoph Friedrich David von (Württemberg): 204

Dörnberg, Maj. Gen. Wilhelm Freiherr von (Coalition): 174–7

Dresden: 6, 25, 33, 36, 38, 44–51, 56, 59–60, 69, 72, 106, 108, 147–57, 159, 162–5, 168–72, 181–2, 189–90, 222, 238, 284, 300, 312–14, 318, 319, 321, 343–4, 346–7, 359; Battle of (25–26 August): 76–7, 80–7, 94–5, 109, 190–4, 246, 288–90, 297, 332–3, 352–3; Bridge: 48, 59, 83, 84, 153–7, 159, 170; political significance: 104, 220–1; siege of: 103–4, 112, 122

Duchy of Warsaw: *see* Poland

Durosnel, GD Antoine Jean Auguste Henri: 25, 343, 346–7

Durrieu, Adjutant-Commandant > GB Antoine-Simon: 105, 122, 224, 228–9, 348–9

Durutte, GD Pierre: 33, 37, 48, 54, 56, 62, 75, 88–92, 96, 99, 120, 131, 134, 136, 143, 153–8, 161, 179, 180–1, 186, 189, 194–200, 203–7, 211–12, 224–6, 229, 232–3, 237, 242–3, 288–91

Dutaillis, GD Adrien Jean-Baptiste: 25

Erfurt: 49, 50, 56, 106, 116, 150, 246, 350, 359, 365

Eugène de Beauharnais, Viceroy: 5, 15, 26–7, 32, 34–9, 44–9, 51–60, 72, 133, 147–8, 154–8, 238, 255, 258, 270–1, 279, 285–6, 290, 300, 327, 356, 358–61, 365

Euper/Thießen, Battle of (3–4 September): 96, 201, 334

Fornier d'Albe, GD Gaspard Hilarion: 25, 54

Fournier-Sarvlovèse, GD François: 91–2, 96, 101, 104, 205, 208, 212

Frankfurt military units: 24–5, 268

Franquemont, GL Friedrich von (Württemberg): 102

Franz I, Kaiser of Austria: 4, 43, 95, 150, 160, 164–5, 169–71, 241, 249, 354

French military formations:
 Army of Berlin: under Oudinot: 81, 87–94, 200–1; under Ney: 96–103, 203–6, 336, 339, 364
 Army of the Bober: 75, 81, 94–6
 Army of the Elbe: 37–8, 49, 52–5, 57, 59
 Army of the Main: 37, 52–6, 57
 Imperial Guard: 24, 34, 36, 52, 54, 56–8, 61–2, 65–8, 72, 75, 81, 82–5, 103, 105–6, 111, 116, 118, 128, 183, 214, 217, 220–4, 235, 242, 243 246, 247, 343, 347, 350, 363
 1st Corps/1813: 24, 75, 82, 85, 95, 104, 112; 1812: 269
 2nd Corps/1813: 24, 36, 54, 59, 62, 67, 75, 82, 85, 112, 115–16, 191–2; 1812: 266, 311
 3rd Corps/1813: 24, 52, 54, 56, 57, 59, 62, 65–7, 75, 78, 81, 94–5, 112, 115–16, 120, 185, 237, 308; 1812: 277
 4th Corps/1813: 24, 52, 54, 56–8, 62, 66, 67, 75, 81, 87, 96–103, 105, 112, 114, 117, 200–1, 204–5, 225, 308, 333–4, 336, 343; 1812: 34, 35
 5th Corps/1813: 24, 36, 52, 54, 56–7, 59, 61–2, 65–7, 75, 112, 115, 116, 183; 1812: 28, 131, 162
 6th Corps/1813: 24, 52, 54, 56, 57–62, 67, 75, 81–2, 85, 112, 115, 120, 181, 229; 1812: 262, 266–8, 271; 1812: 311, 324
 7th Corps/1812–13: 17, 24, 28, 31–7, 48, 54, 59, 62, 67, 75, 81, 87–93, 99–103, 104, 112, 116, 118, 126, 128–50, 153–8, 161, 179, 180–6, 188–90, 194–5, 200–5, 211–19,

220–6, 229–30, 240, 245, 288–9, 336, 348; 1809: 325; 1812: 129
  8th Corps/1813: 24, 54, 75, 112, 115, 116, 120; 1812: 269
  9th Corps/1813: 24, 72, 74, 75, 79, 112, 115, 116, 302; 1812: 129
  10th Corps/1813: 24–5, 35, 54, 72, 75; 1812: 28–30, 271–3
  11th Corps: 24, 36, 52, 54, 56–8, 62, 64–7, 75, 112, 115, 116, 120, 314
  12th Corps: 24, 52, 54, 56, 62–7, 75, 81, 87–98, 100, 102–3, 112, 185, 194, 200–14, 310–21, 329–63
  13th Corps: 24, 72, 75, 79
  14th Corps: 24, 72, 75, 81, 85, 89, 104, 112, 361
  1st Cavalry Corps: 24, 36, 52, 54, 56–8, 61–2, 75, 82, 105, 112, 129, 181, 182, 186, 188, 190–2, 222–3, 235, 244–5,
Friedrich, King of Württemberg: 7, 9, 19, 38, 143–4, 256, 359–60
Friedrich August, King of Saxony: 5–6, 48, 50, 59–60, 82, 119, 120–1, 123–6, 150–3, 155–66, 169–72, 179, 182, 194, 216, 220–1, 225, 227, 231, 236, 241–2, 246, 248–9, 367
Friedrich Wilhelm III, King of Prussia: 39–40, 47, 51, 55, 58, 63, 168, 236, 354

Gablenz, GM Heinrich Adolf von (Saxony): 132–8, 141, 144–5, 147–9, 162, 179, 189, 199, 203
Gersdorff, GL Karl Friedrich von (Saxony): 71, 82, 108, 165, 212, 221, 243
German nationalism and particularism: 9, 23, 172, 218, 219, 237, 282, 364–5
Girard, GD Jean-Baptiste: 73, 81, 87, 93–4,
Glogau, Blockade/Siege of: 25, 34–6, 47, 51, 53, 54–5, 67–9, 79, 136, 147, 190
Gouvion Saint-Cyr, Marshal Laurent: 14, 24, 75, 81–2, 84–5, 103–4, 262, 266, 361
Great Britain: 5, 21, 44, 72, 109, 175, 249, 257

Großbeeren, Battle of (23 August): 79, 86–94, 96, 97, 102, 108, 146, 194–203, 205, 215, 238, 253, 330–2

Hagelberg, Battle of (27 August): 87, 93–4
Halberstadt, Engagement at (29 May): 70
Hamburg: 38, 44, 47–8, 70, 72, 75, 81, 93, 122, 173, 301
Hammerstein, GD Hans Georg von (Westphalia): 54
Hanau, Battle of (30–31 October): 78, 79, 121–2, 357, 363
Hanseatic cities: 15, 47–8, 70–1
Haxo, GD Nicholas: 25, 54
Hellwig, Maj. Friedrich von (Prussia): 63, 291–2,
Hesse-Darmstadt: 8, 363
Hessian military units: 16, 22, 24–5, 105, 367–8
  39th Division: 52, 54, 58, 62, 75–6, 78, 91, 96, 112, 114, 116, 228–9, 260, 272
  Garde-Chevaulegers: 103, 114, 320, 330, 343
Hochberg, GL Graf Wilhelm von (Baden): 108, 112, 120
Hruby, Carl Eduard von Löwenberg-Hruby und Geleny (Austrian diplomat): 260, 352–5

Italian troops: 36, 54, 62, 64, 75, 88–91, 96, 99–102, 112, 181, 201–2, 322, 354, 364
Italy: 34–5, 40, 59–60, 72, 109, 294, 300, 308, 327, 354, 358, 365

'Jacobinism': 23, 42, 122, 152, 295, 297–8
Jérôme Bonaparte, King of Westphalia: 5, 7, 26, 107, 175, 291
Jett, GM Karl August Maximilian von (Württemberg): 204

Kalisch, Battle of (13 February): 32–7, 45–7, 52, 128, 130–47, 149, 190; Treaty of: 40

Kassel: Chernishev's attack on: 107, 291

Katzbach, Battle of the (26 August): 75, 94–5

Kitzen, Engagement at (17 June): 70–1, 73, 187

Königstein Fortress: 85, 130, 149, 154, 181, 221

Kulm, Battle of (29–30 August): 75, 79, 94–5, 109

Küstrin, Blockade/Siege of: 25, 27, 35–6, 51, 54–5, 79

Kutuzov, Marshal Mikhail Illarionovich (Russia): 27, 31, 41, 44–5, 47, 51

Langeron, General of Infantry Louis Alexander Andrault (Russia): 63, 77, 111, 115, 229–30, 235, 279, 281–2

Lanusse, GD Pierre: 87, 93

Laplane, GB > GD Jean Grégoire Barthélmy Rouger, comte de: 25, 54

Latour-Maubourg, GD Marie Victor Nicholas de Fay, marquis de: 24, 54, 58, 62, 75, 83, 112, 181–3, 186, 191–2, 222–3, 253

Lauriston, GD Jacques Alexander Bernard Law: 24, 36, 54, 57, 61–2, 64–8, 75, 112, 121, 182–3

LeCoq, GL Carl Christian Erdmann Edler von (Saxony): 88, 90–2, 96, 134–7, 140–1, 145–7, 153, 155, 157–8, 161, 188, 194–208, 211–14, 254, 288

Lefebvre, Marshal François (Duke of Danzig): 12, 325

Leipzig, Battle of (Battle of Nations): 77, 79, 103–6, 109–22, 166, 172, 190, 194, 214, 219, 220–37, 243–9, 252–3, 347–50, 363, 366, 367

Le Marois, GD Jean Léonor François: 25

Lübeck: 47, 70

Luckau, Capture of (28 August): 93, 101, 194, 202

Luckau, Engagement at (4 June): 69–70, 318–21

Lüneburg, Battle of (2 April): 173–8

Lützow, Major Ludwig Adolph Wilhelm von (Prussia): 60, 70–1, 73, 187, 328–9

MacDonald, GD Étienne Jacques (Duke of Taranto): 24, 28–30, 36, 54, 58, 61–7, 75, 81, 94–5, 102–3, 108, 112, 116, 118, 120–1, 271–3

Magdeburg: 25, 36, 48–51, 54–5, 70, 73, 79, 87, 93–4, 104, 107, 158, 290, 318, 357

Maillot de la Treille, Oberst > GM Nikolaus Hubert von (Bavaria): 304, 323, 332, 344–51, 364

Marchand, GD Jean Gabriel: 58

Maret, Hughes Bernard (Duke of Bassano): 161, 346–7, 359–60, 362

Margaron, GD Pierre: 105, 108, 112, 117, 120

Marmont, Marshal Auguste (Duke of Ragusa): 24, 54, 57, 58, 61, 62, 64–6, 75, 82, 83, 106, 112, 116–17, 120–1, 229, 243

Marwitz, Oberstleutnant Friedrich August Ludwig von der (Prussia): 107

Maureillan, GB Jean Poitevin Baron de: 25, 274–84, 286, 287

Maximilian I. Joseph, King of Bavaria: 246, 255–61, 266, 270–2, 293–301, 303, 308–10, 319, 321, 324–7, 331, 333, 341, 343, 346, 351–62, 367

Mecklenburg Duchies: 7–9, 14, 21, 22, 47, 70, 83, 159, 362, 366

Meissen bridge: 154–5, 288

Metternich, Clemens von (Austria): 31, 39, 60, 71, 153, 159–65, 249, 295, 298–300, 356

Möckern, Battle of (2–5 April): 47, 49, 51

Modlin, Blockade of: 25, 33, 35, 51, 54–5, 73–4, 79, 122, 131, 132

Montgelas, Maximilian Graf von (Bavaria): 7, 257–61, 266, 293–300, 325, 352–63, 366

Morand, GD Charles Antoine: 96, 98–9, 204

Morand, GD Joseph: 34, 36, 37, 47, 49, 129, 130, 173–8

Index

Murat, Marshal Joachim, King of Naples: 15, 16, 28, 30, 32–4, 72, 83, 85, 104–5, 115, 190–4, 223, 247, 270, 357

Napoleon: 37, 39–45, 47, 51, 89, 102–3, 149, 179, 186, 207, 217, 272, 305, 332, 348; birthday commemorations: 78–80, 325, 329; relations with Bavaria: 246, 255–62, 266, 271, 277, 293–303, 307–10, 326–8, 331, 341, 346–9, 351–63, 365–6; relations with Saxony: 38, 50, 123–7, 148, 150–53, 155–69, 172, 215, 221–2, 225–8, 232, 235, 237–43, 246–7, 250, 252–3; and the Rheinbund/ German troops: 3–14, 18, 20–5, 26, 178, 182–5, 187, 194–5, 200, 215, 219–20, 253, 308–9, 312, 349–50; and Russia/1812: 14–19, 284–5, 289; strategy, plans & operations: 19, 27–38, 48–9, 52–60, 62–77, 80–7, 94–6, 104–9, 112, 115–22, 190, 203, 211–14, 313–16, 318, 320

Narbonne-Lara, GD Louis Marie Jacques Amalric de: 25, 349, 359

Ney, Marshal Michel (Prince de la Moskowa): 24, 53, 54, 57–67, 75, 78, 80, 83, 96–104, 105, 115, 116, 161, 164, 172, 179, 182–3, 201, 203–6, 211–15, 217–18, 225, 229, 232, 235, 243, 253, 277, 308–10, 313, 334, 336–8, 342, 364

Normann, GM Karl Friedrich Leberecht Graf von (Württemberg): 114, 120, 229-30, 242

Oudinot, Marshal Nicholas Charles (Duke of Reggio): 24, 53, 54, 61, 62, 64–73, 75, 81, 87–97, 100–3, 108, 194–6, 200–4, 206–8, 211, 214, 253, 266, 310–25, 329–37, 342–5, 363–4

Pauline, Princess of Lippe-Detmold: 7, 23

Poland (Duchy of Warsaw) & Polish troops: 5–6, 16–17, 26–7, 33, 38, 40, 44, 51, 55, 71, 74, 109, 123, 125–6, 147, 149, 150, 179, 189, 262–3, 267–8, 274, 279, 284, 292

Poniatowski, GD > Marshal Prince Joseph: 24, 28, 33–4, 44, 51–2, 54, 75, 112, 120–1, 131, 133, 149, 162, 190, 223, 270

Prussia: 3–6, 9–12, 16, 21–3, 27–52, 56–60, 67–9, 72, 74, 81, 122, 219, 230, 255–6, 268, 271–3, 279; military units & operations: 45–7, 55, 62–6, 70–1, 76–7, 83–5, 87–102, 106–7, 109–17, 128, 174–8, 187, 194–202, 204–10, 232–4, 244, 248, 307, 312, 318, 320–1, 331, 334–40, 364; and Saxony: 123–6, 148, 150–3, 156, 158–60, 163–5, 168–71, 236–9, 241, 249–52, 254; and Bavaria: 258, 260–1, 281, 284, 291–2, 293–301, 305, 354–5

Raglovich zum Rosenhof, GL Clemens von (Bavaria): 96, 292, 301–47, 351, 353, 357, 359–364

Rapp, GD Jean: 24, 54, 73, 75, 79

Rechberg und Rothenlöwen, GM > GL Joseph Graf von (Bavaria): 36, 48, 51, 153, 155, 158, 271, 285–92, 295, 299, 303, 363

Reynier, GD Jean: 24, 28, 31–7, 48, 60, 62, 75, 83, 87–92, 96, 99–103, 104, 112, 121, 130–50, 153, 161, 165–67, 172, 179–80, 182–6, 188, 194–201, 203–12, 214, 218 220, 224–37, 238; defence of Saxons after Dennewitz: 212, 215–16; leadership qualities: 131–2, 154–5, 205, 241, 253–4, 288; tactical negligence: 132, 136–7, 140, 145–6, 196

Russia: 5–6, 9, 11–12, 21, 23, 29, 31–3, 35–6, 39–44, 106, 148–9, 190; military units & operations: 44–65, 67–74, 76–7, 83, 84–6, 89–91, 94, 97, 101–2, 107, 109–11, 116–18, 122, 130–46, 155, 173–8, 182–4, 201–2, 206, 223, 229–33, 278–84, 286, 290–1, 314–16, 318; and Saxony: 126–7, 130, 150–3, 156–8, 163–72, 236, 238, 246, 249, 250, 252–3; and

Bavaria: 261, 293–98, 300–1, 348–9, 354, 357, 361
Russian campaign (1812): 3, 11, 14–19, 27–8, 108, 126, 147, 154, 178, 214, 258–9, 262–71, 273, 275, 277, 285, 292, 301, 305, 311
Ryssel, Oberst > GM Xaver Gustav Reinhold von (Saxony): 180, 188, 198, 201, 213, 217, 228, 231–6, 239, 241, 244, 250–1, 254

Sahr, GM > GL Carl Ludwig Sahrer von (Saxony): 88, 90–1, 134, 136–7, 143–4, 147, 167, 169–72, 179–80, 184, 187–8, 194–200, 203
Saxon duchies and military units (*see also* Danzig): 123, 150, 328
Saxony, Kingdom of: 3, 6–8, 17, 21, 23, 27, 43, 45, 52, 56, 59–60, 70, 72, 80–1, 87, 104, 106, 108–9, 113, 187, 237–41, 249, 252, 253–4, 255, 258, 264, 284, 301, 308–9, 323–4, 328, 352, 361, 363; convention with Austria: 38–9, 50, 59–60, 158–65, 169, 346, 367; politics & diplomacy: 40–1, 123–6, 151–5, 166–72, 260, 292–5, 297–8, 300, 358, 366, 367
Saxon military units (*see also* Danzig, Glogau, Modlin): 126–30
  7th Corps: 17, 24, 28, 31–7, 48, 54, 59, 62, 67, 75, 81, 87–93, 99–103, 104, 112, 116, 118, 126, 128–50, 153–8, 161, 179, 180–6, 188–90, 194–5, 200–5, 211–19, 220–6, 229–30, 240, 245, 288–9, 336, 348
  Prinz Maximilian Infantry Regiment: 173–8, 194, 202
  Chevaulegers regiments: 128, 129–30, 134, 137–8, 140, 144, 149, 167, 180, 189
  Cuirassier regiments: 85, 114, 128–30, 148–50, 162, 166, 180–4, 190–4, 222–3, 244–6, 252–3, 367
Schwarzburg principalities: 150
Schwarzenberg, Feldmarschall Carl Phillip Fürst zu (Austria): 28, 32, 34, 73, 74, 76–7, 84, 104, 110, 115, 118, 131, 133, 149, 243–4, 252, 295, 361
Sébastiani de la Porta, GD Horace François Bastien: 24, 36
Senfft von Pilsach, Friedrich Christian Ludwig Graf (Saxony): 150–2, 156, 158, 160, 164–5, 170
Serra, Charles François Joseph: 161, 164
Seyssel d'Aix, Oberst Max Graf (Bavaria): 304, 312, 316–17, 320, 331
Spain: 12–13, 72, 109, 131, 240, 255
Stadion, Johann Philipp (Austria): 164–5
Stein, Baron Heinrich Friedrich Karl von und zum (Coalition): 23, 30, 43, 151–2, 163, 168–9, 249, 294–6, 300
Stettin, Blockade/Siege of: 25, 35, 37, 47, 51, 53, 54–5, 73, 79
Stockmayer, GM Ludwig Friedrich von (Württemberg): 204

Tauentzien, GL Bogislav Friedrich Emanuel Graf (Prussia): 77, 88–91, 96–9, 101–2, 104, 111, 202–4, 334
Tettenborn, Maj. Gen. Friedrich Carl Freiherr von (Russia): 46–9, 55
Thielmann, GL Johann Adolf Freiherr von (Saxony): 36–8, 51, 54, 60, 106–8, 110, 116–17, 120, 148, 150, 153, 157, 158, 163–72, 179, 211, 241, 250–1, 253, 260
Thorn, Blockade/Siege of: 269–70, 274–84, 363
Tilsit, Treaties of: 5, 124
Torgau, Blockade/Seige of (*see also* Thielmann): 25, 79, 104, 105, 122, 213, 221, 224–7, 241, 250–1, 348–50
Tyrol: 10, 256–7, 295–6, 302–3, 307, 328, 354, 356, 361, 365

Vandamme, GD Dominique René (Count of Unsebourg): 12, 24, 49, 53, 54, 70, 75, 82, 85–6, 95, 354

Victor, Marshal Claude (Duke of Belluno): 24, 36, 53, 54, 62, 67–8, 75, 83, 112, 191–2

Waldeck and military units: 107
Wallmoden-Gimborn, Lt. Gen. Ludwig Graf von (Coalition): 53, 55, 70, 73, 74, 77
Warsaw, Duchy of: *see* Poland
Wartenburg, Battle of (3 October): 79, 104
Westphalia: 7–8, 10–12, 14, 26, 38, 43, 97, 106–7, 122, 170, 175, 242, 257, 291, 346
Westphalian military units: 15–16, 24–5, 34, 36–7, 48–9, 52, 54, 70, 220, 260, 318, 330, 334–6, 367–8
    1st Infantry Regiment: 16, 28, 272–3
    31st Division (11th Corps): 75, 112
    Chevaulegers-Garde: 93, 101, 103, 114, 208, 343
Wintzingerode, Lt. Gen. Ferdinand Fedorovich (Russia): 45–6, 48, 55, 57, 77, 89, 91, 111, 132, 133, 138–40, 143–7, 152
Wittgenstein, General of Cavalry Peter Khristianovich (Russia): 37, 44–6, 49–51, 53, 55–8, 63–8, 76, 110, 152,
Wolff, GB Marc François Jérôme (Westphalia): 96–7, 103, 203, 324, 329–31, 334–6, 340, 343
Wrede, GL Carl Philipp Freiherr von (Bavaria): 79, 122, 258, 260–1, 266–71, 274–7, 283, 285, 292, 302–3, 307, 309–10, 324, 326–7, 351–63, 366
Württemberg: 5–9, 11, 14, 16–17, 19–20, 23, 151, 153, 156, 159, 187, 237, 247, 256, 260, 293, 326–7, 359–60, 363

Württemberg military units: 24–5, 71, 38th Division: 52, 54, 56, 61, 65–6, 75, 89, 93, 98–9, 101–2, 112, 114, 117, 201, 204, 209, 339, 364, 367–8
    Doering's Infantry Brigade: 204
    Normann's 25th Light Cavalry Brigade: 114, 120, 229–30, 242, 367
Würzburg military units (*see also* Modlin): 24–5, 33, 52, 118, 131, 134–6, 158, 180, 189, 200–1, 203, 205, 368

Yorck, GL Hans David Ludwig von (Prussia): 28, 30–1, 37, 39–40, 45–7, 55, 57, 61, 63, 64, 77, 104, 111, 116, 168, 230, 244

Zahna, Battle of (5 September): 97, 203, 334–6, 363
Zamosc, Blockade/Siege of: 35, 44, 51, 54–5, 73, 74, 79
Zeschau, GL v Heinrich Wilhelm on (Saxony): 213–17, 225–7, 229–37, 239, 241, 244, 247–8, 254
Zezschwitz, Joseph Woldemar von (Saxony): 151–2, 158, 160
Zoller, GM Friedrich von (Bavaria): 269–71, 274–87, 290, 292, 363
Żółtowski, GB Edward (Duchy of Warsaw): 135–6

Gazetteer

Numbers indicate maps

Modern/alternative names given in parentheses.

Ahe-Bach (Agarbach): 14, 24
Ahrensdorf: 12, 13
Aller River: 2, 3, 4, 5, 8, 9
Annaburg: 11

Bamberg: 28, 29
Baruth: 11, 12, 29, 31
Basankwitz: 7
Bautzen (Budyšin): 4, 5, 7, 9, 21, 29, 30
Bayreuth: 28, 29
Belgern/Bautzen: 7
Belgern/Elbe: 28
Bergedorf: 3, 4
Berlin: 3, 4, 5, 8, 9, 11, 12, 13, 14, 15, 24, 28, 29
Belzig: 11
Binnewitz: 7, 30
Blankenfelde: 11, 12, 13
Bober River: 4, 5, 9
Bohemia: 8
Borków: 19
Borna: 4
Brandenburg/Berlin: 11
Brandenburg/East Prussia (Ushakovo): 26
Braunsberg (Braniewo): 26
Braunschweig (Brunswick): 3, 9
Breitendorf: 21
Bremen: 3, 4, 5, 8, 9
Breslau (Wrocław): 3, 4, 5, 8, 9

Brzeziny: 18
Bülzig: 32
Bunzlau (Bolesławice): 3, 4, 5, 8, 9
Burgstädtel: 10, 22

Chlewo: 18, 19
Chemnitz: 3, 4, 5, 8, 15
Coburg: 3, 4, 5, 8, 9, 28, 29
Connewitz: 16, 17
Cottbus: 3, 4, 5, 8, 9, 28
Crossen (Krosno Odrzańskie): 3, 4, 5, 8, 9, 28
Crottendorf: 16
Częstochowa: 3, 18, 28

Dahme: 9, 11, 29
Danzig (Gdańsk): 1, 3, 4, 5, 8, 9, 26
Delitzsch: 15
Denkwitz: 7, 30
Dennewitz: 9, 11, 14, 24, 29 & Schematic 1
Dessau: 4, 5, 11, 15
Dölitz: 16
Dölzschen: 10, 22
Dornswalde: 31
Dösen: 16
Dresden: 3, 4, 5, 8, 9, 10, 15, 22, 28, 29
Drohmberg: 30
Düben: 11, 15, 16

Ebendörfel: 7, 30
Eilenburg: 11, 15, 16, 29

Gazetteer

Eisdorf: 6
Elbe River: 1, 2, 3, 4, 5, 8, 9, 10, 11, 15, 28, 29
Elbing: 26
Elster (Weiße) River: 15, 16, 17, 29
Engelsdorf: 16, 25
Erfurt: 3, 4, 5, 8, 9, 15, 28, 29
Euper: 32

Flossgraben: 6
Franconia: 3
Frankfurt-am-Main: 2
Frankfurt-an-der-Oder: 3, 4, 5, 8, 9, 28, 29
Freiberg: 15
Freyburg: 15
Friedrichstadt/Daugava (Jaunjelgava): 26
Friedrichstadt/Dresden: 10
Frisching River: 26

Gadegast: 11, 32
Galicia: 3
Galgenberg (near Leipzig/Wachau): 16
Galgenberg (near Leipzig/Schönfeld): 25
Gaußig: 29, 30
Garlstorf: 20
Gera: 15, 28
Glogau (Glogow): 3, 4, 5, 8, 9, 28, 29
Gnaschwitz: 30
Gnesen (Gniezno): 27, 28
Gohlis: 16
Goldberg (Złotoryja): 5
Gölsdorf: 14, 24
Gompitz (Compitz): 10, 22
Gorbitz: 10, 22
Görlitz: 3, 4, 8, 9, 21, 28
Gotha: 15, 28
Graudenz (Grudziądz): 3, 4, 5, 8, 9, 26, 27
Greiz: 15
Grimma: 15, 17
Großbeeren: 9, 11, 12, 13, 23
Großbeuthen: 12
Großer Garten (Dresden): 10
Großgörschen: 6

Grubditz: 7, 30
Guldengossa: 16
Gütergotz: 11, 12, 13

Hagelberg: 9, 11
Halbau (Iłowa): 4
Halberstadt: 3, 5, 8, 9
Halle: 4, 5, 8, 9, 11, 15, 16, 17
Hamburg: 1, 3, 4, 5, 8, 9
Hanover: 4, 5, 8, 9
Harz Mountains: 4, 5, 8, 9
Haynau (Chojnów): 5
Heinersdorf: 12, 13
Heiterer Blick farmstead: 16, 25
Herzberg: 11,
Hochkirch: 7, 21, 30
Hof: 28, 29
Holtendorf: 21
Holzhausen: 16
Hoyerswerda: 3, 4, 5, 8

Ilmenau River: 20

Jauer (Jawor): 5, 8, 9
Jena: 15, 28, 29
Jeßnitz: 30
Jühnsdorf: 13
Jüterbog: 11, 12, 14, 15, 24

Kaja (Caja): 6
Kalisch (Kalisz): 3, 4, 5, 8, 9, 18, 19, 28
Kaltenborn: 14, 24
Kassel: 3, 4, 5, 8, 9
Katzbach: 9
Kemlitz: 31
Kerzendorf: 12
Kitzen: 6, 8, 16
Kleinbeeren: 12, 13, 23
Kleingörschen: 6
Kleinzschocher: 16
Klix: 7
Kokanin: 19

Kolberg: 4, 5, 8, 9
Kolmberg: 16
Königsberg (Kaliningrad): 3, 26
Königstein: 4, 9, 28
Königswartha: 7
Köthen: 11
Krakow (Kraków): 1, 3, 18
Kreckwitz /Kreckwitz Heights: 7
Kropstädt: 11
Kulm: 9
Kulmsee (Chełmża): 27
Kurzlipsdorf: 11
Küstrin (Kostrzyn): 3, 4, 5, 8, 9, 28

Labiau (Polessk): 26
Langenau (Łęgowo): 26
Langensalza (Bad Langensalza): 4, 28
Lauban (Lubań): 5, 8, 9, 21
Leipzig: 3, 4, 5, 6, 8, 9, 11, 15, 16, 17, 25, 28, 29
Leopoldshain: 21
Leutewitz: 22
Licheterade: 13, 23
Liebertwolkwitz: 9, 16
Liegnitz (Legnica): 4, 5, 8, 9
Lilograben (stream): 13, 23
Lindenau: 16, 17
Linz: 1
Löbtau: 10, 22
Löwenberg (Lwówek Śląski): 5, 8
Löwenbruch: 12, 23
Lübben: 11, 31
Lübeck: 3, 4, 5, 8, 9
Luckau: 3, 4, 5, 8, 9, 11, 15, 29
Luckenwalde: 11, 29, 31
Lüneburg: 3, 4, 5, 8, 9, 20
Luppe River: 16
Lützen: 4, 5, 6, 15, 16, 17

Magdeburg: 3, 4, 5, 8, 9, 11, 15, 28, 29
Mainz (Mayence): 1
Maltershausen: 14
Marienberg fortress: *see* Würzburg

Markersdorf: 21
Markkleeberg: 16
Markranstädt: 16, 17
Marzahna: 11
Mehlteuer: 7, 30
Meissen: 4, 5, 8, 15, 28
Merseburg: 4, 5, 8, 9, 15
Meuchen: 6
Meuselwitz: 21
Mittenwalde: 12
Möckern/Elbe: 4, 11
Möckern/Leipzig: 16
Modlin: 3, 8, 9, 18
Montmédy: 1
Mückendorf: 31
Mulde River: 11, 15, 28, 29
Munich: 1

Narew River: 18
Naumburg: 15
Nauslitz: 10, 22
Nechern: 7, 21
Neisse River: 21
Neubeeren: 13, 23
Neu-Nimptsch/Dresden: 10, 22
Niedergörsdorf: 14, 24
Niemen River (Neman, Memel): 3, 26
Nimptsch (Niemcza): 5
Nossen: 28
Nunsdorf: 12
Nuremberg: 1
Nuthe-Graben: 12

Oder River: 1, 2, 3, 4, 5, 8, 9, 28, 29
Oderin: 31
Oehna: 11, 14, 24
Opatówek: 18, 19
Ortrand: 9

Parthe River: 16, 17
Paunsdorf: 16, 17
Pawłówek: 19

Gazetteer

Pegau: 15
Pesterwitz: 10, 22
Petrikau (Piotrków Trybunalksi): 18
Pielitz: 7, 30
Pilica River: 18
Pillau (Baltiysk): 3, 26
Pilsen (Plzeň): 1
Pirna: 9
Plagwitz: 16
Pläswitz (Pielaszkowice): 4, 5
Plauen: 3, 4, 5, 8, 9, 15, 28
Plauen/Dresden: 10
Pleiße River: 16, 17
Pleißkowitz: 7
Płock: 3, 18, 27, 28
Plösen: 25
Posen (Poznań): 3, 4, 5, 8, 9, 27, 28, 29
Prague (Praha): 1, 3, 4, 5, 8, 9, 28
Praust (Pruszcz Gdański): 26
Preititz: 7
Probstheida: 16, 17
Prosna River: 18, 19
Pruszków: 19
Purschwitz: 7

Quatitz: 7
Queis River (Kwisa): 4, 5, 8, 9

Rabenstein: 11
Radefeld: 16
Rahna: 6
Rahnsdorf: 32
Raudten (Rudna): 5
Regensburg: 1
Reichenbach: 5, 21
Ried: 1
Rieschen: 7, 30
Rochlitz: 28
Roda (Stadtroda): 5, 8, 15
Rohrbeck: 14, 24
Rosenberg: 26
Rosslau: 4, 5, 8, 11, 15

Rudolstadt: 15
Ruhlsdorf: 11, 12, 13, 23
Russów: 19
Rychwał: 18

Saale River: 4, 5, 8, 9, 11, 15, 28
Sagan: 3, 28, 29
Schleiz: 5, 8
Schleusingen: 28
Schlieben: 11, 29
Schloß Dybow (Zamek Dybów): 27
Schlungwitz: 30
Schönau: 16
Schönfeld: 16, 17, 25
Schöps: 21
Schmiedefeld: 5
Schwarze Elster River: 15, 28, 29
Schwarzer Schöps River: 21
Schwedt: 3, 4, 8, 9, 28, 29
Schweidnitz (Świdnica): 8
Schwerin: 3, 4, 5, 8, 9
Sellerhausen: 25
Silesia: 3, 4, 5, 8, 9
Skarszew: 19
Sohland am Rotstein: 21
Sommerau (Ząbrowo): 26
Spandau: 3, 4, 5, 8, 9, 11
Spree River: 7, 11, 21, 30
Sputendorf: 13, 23
Starsiedel: 6
Stawiszyn: 18, 19
Stendal: 3, 4
Stettin (Szczecin): 3, 4, 5, 8, 9, 28
Stötteritz: 16
Stralsund: 1, 3, 4, 5, 8, 9
Strehlen (Strzelin): 5
Striesen: 10
Stünz: 16, 25
Swędrnia stream: 19

Tangermünde: 3, 4, 5, 8, 9
Taucha: 16, 25

Tauroggen (Tauragė): 3, 26
Teplitz: 3, 8
Thorn (Toruń): 3, 4, 5, 8, 9, 27, 28
Thyrow: 12
Tilsit: 3, 26
Tłokinia: 19
Trebbin: 11, 12, 29
Troitschendorf: 21
Trunz (Milejewo): 26
Torgau: 3, 4, 5, 8, 9, 11, 15, 16, 28, 29
Turek: 18
Tykadłów: 19
Tyrol: 1

Unstrut River: 15

Vistula River: 1, 3, 4, 5, 8, 9, 18, 27
Volkmarsdorf: 16

Wachau: 16
Warsaw (Warszawa): 1, 3, 18
Warthe (Warta): 3, 4, 5, 8, 9, 28
Weimar: 3, 4, 5, 8, 9, 15, 28, 29
Weiße Elster River, *see* Elster
Weißenberg: 21
Weißenfels: 5, 8, 9, 15, 16, 17
Weißer Schöps River: 21
Weißeritz Stream: 10, 22
Weißig: 7

Werben: 12
Werben/Lützen: 6
Weser River: 2, 3, 4, 5, 8, 9
Wietstock (Wittstock): 12
Wilmersdorf: 12
Wilsdruff: 28
Wilthen: 30
Winiary: 19
Wittenberg: 3, 4, 5, 8, 9, 11, 15, 28, 29
Włocławek: 3, 18
Wohlaer Berg: 21
Wölfnitz: 10, 22
Woltersdorf: 12, 32
Wurschen: 7
Würzburg: 3, 8, 9
Wurzen/Leipzig: 16

Zahna: 11, 32
Zallmsdorf: 32
Zamosc: 1, 3, 8, 9
Zborów: 19
Zeitz: 15
Zelazków: 19
Zesch (Zesch am See): 31
Zittau: 28
Zuckelhausen: 16
Zwethau: 11
Zwickau: 15